D1357673

Habermas

For my wife Heidlind

Habermas

A Biography

Stefan Müller-Doohm

Translated by Daniel Steuer

polity

First published in German as *Jürgen Habermas: Eine Biographie*, © Suhrkamp Verlag, Berlin, 2014

This English edition © Polity Press, 2016

The translation of this work was supported by a grant from the Goethe Institut, which is funded by the German Ministry of Foreign Affairs.

Polity Press
65 Bridge Street
Cambridge CB2 1UR, UK

Polity Press
350 Main Street
Malden, MA 02148, USA

ISBN-13: 978-0-7456-8906-7

A catalogue record for this book is available from the British Library.

Library of Congress Cataloging-in-Publication Data

Names: Müller-Doohm, Stefan.
Title: Habermas : a biography / Stefan Müller-Doohm.
Other titles: J?urgen Habermas. English
Description: Malden, MA : Polity Press, 2016. | Includes bibliographical
  references and index.
Identifiers: LCCN 2015041865| ISBN 9780745689067 (hardback : alk. paper) |
  ISBN 9780745689081 (pbk. : alk. paper)
Subjects: LCSH: Habermas, J?urgen. | Philosophers--Germany--Biography. |
  Sociologists--Germany--Biography.
Classification: LCC B3258.H324 M8413 2016 | DDC 193 [B] --dc23 LC record available
at https://lccn.loc.gov/2015041865

Typeset in 10.5 on 11.5 pt Times New Roman MT
by Servis Filmsetting Ltd, Stockport, Cheshire
Printed and bound in Great Britain by Clays Ltd, St Ives plc

For further information on Polity, visit our website: politybooks.com

Contents

Contents

PART III SCIENCE AND COMMITMENT

PART IV COSMOPOLITAN SOCIETY AND JUSTICE

Preface

No one has the right to behave towards me as if he knew me.
                                                    Robert Walser[1]

Many labels have been attached to Jürgen Habermas over the
years: 'advocate of modernity' and 'master of communication', 'the
public conscience of political culture' and the 'Hegel of the Federal
Republic', the 'power at the Main',* the 'hothead of Frankfurt'
[*Frankfurter Feuerkopf*] and 'Praeceptor Germaniae' [teacher
of Germany], to name just a few.[2] That this list of references to
Habermas in the media – some of which are less than flattering –
could easily be extended demonstrates just how newsworthy he is
considered to be; his activities as an academic and as a commentator on contemporary developments certainly do not suffer from
a lack of public attention. Why then, in light of all this, write a
biography of this man, especially one that neither intends to place
Jürgen Habermas, the (somewhat unknown) private person, at its
centre nor aims to erect a monument to a 'master thinker' on the
occasion of his eighty-fifth birthday? After all, we live in times
which, according to Habermas himself, need neither heroes nor
anti-heroes. What has driven me, as a sociologist, into the arms
of biographical research, and has led me to try my hand at writing
a biography once again, is the conviction that the visible traces
of a life such as that of Jürgen Habermas are particularly suited
for a study of what was, in a certain sense, the central concern of
the sociological perspective from the very beginning: namely, the
dialectic between individual and society. How is it that someone in

---

* The River Main flows through Frankfurt, and the city is often referred to as the
'Mainmetropole', the metropolis on the Main. The German 'Macht am Main' plays on
the title of a patriotic song – 'Die Wacht am Rhein' [The guard at the Rhine] – associated
with French–German rivalry during the nineteenth century and up to the Great War. All
notes in the body of the text are the translator's, as are any additions in square brackets
in the Notes.

interaction with others becomes an individual, and that individuals thus become capable of forging their own unique and specific biographies, but only through a process of engagement with and within their times?

It is admittedly a great temptation to present *this* particular biography as a story of exceptional success. However, not only would that amount to a misleading attenuation of some of the darker strands in this life's biography (some of which are well known), it would also contradict its, at least on the face of it, conventional bourgeois trajectory. In conversations, Habermas has repeatedly emphasized that the more or less linear course his life has taken fitted into the parameters of the historical circumstances of his generation and fell within the possibilities offered to this generation's members in terms of realizing their personal ambitions under conditions of a regained freedom. If we were to take this self-characterization at face value, we might conclude that Habermas's *vita* proceeded from phase to phase in the even steps of a standard biography. And it is true that it was characterized by a continuity based on a great degree of outward security: childhood, schooling, student days, marriage, children, profession, etc. As in every life, there were of course ruptures, setbacks and turning points. What, then, makes this existence unique? Where lies the unusual within the usual?

Of course, it is obvious what a remarkable career Habermas has had. With his monographs and collected essays, which have been translated into more than forty languages, he has established a tremendous national and international reputation as a scholar, and as an author he has found a responsive audience even beyond the academic world. With this in mind, one might conclude that Habermas's biography is simply the story of his published work. However, his life is so fascinating precisely because it amounts to more than just a stack of learned books: here is someone who continually left the protective space of academia in order to assume the role of a participant in controversial debates and, in this way, sought to influence the development of the national mentality in his home country. And, we may add, he was successful in this. In that sense, the retracing of the events that formed Habermas's life provides only the *basso ostinato*, so to speak, for what is actually the main interest of this biography: namely, to present a portrait of the entanglement of his main profession with his second occupation, of the interrelations between the development of a philosopher's thought and the interventions of a public intellectual, as seen against the backdrop of contemporary events.

No matter where a biographer may place the emphases, he is always guilty of a certain presumption; this is simply to be acknowledged. Biographical research and writing always involve a certain indiscretion – one may even speak of biographical investigations as hostile acts. A biographer cannot but make a private life the object of his curious gaze. Even worse: he roams around in the life of his protagonist and assumes the authority to decide which events will be looked at in detail and which will only be touched upon, or which will be considered so insignificant as to be left out altogether. Thus, he has to decide which moments of a life will be omitted, which connections will be left out, and if and when gaps will be filled by means of applying the method of 'exact fantasy' (Theodor W. Adorno).

At such moments, a biographer is not that far removed from the novelist. He is as much in the dark as to the significance of the insights gained while reviewing the course of a life as the protagonist in Max Frisch's *Gantenbein* – 'What really happened?' In order to capture the ruptures and contradictions in a life's history, a biographer adopts the stance of Frisch's protagonist, who feigns blindness: 'I imagine.'[3] And then the search for the story of the story begins – a search in which, as compared to the novelist, the biographer may have the advantage that he can refer to a body of sources that guides his narration.

From all this follows that a biography may at best offer trustworthiness but never certainty. I believe that any attempt at representing the events that make up a life *as they really happened*, and be it on a miniature scale, is doomed to failure from the start. Thus, this biography does not claim to be true in that sense, and it must disappoint those readers who expect that the biographer will offer them a kind of intimate contact with the object of biographical curiosity, or that he may even include some sensational revelations about it.

This book shines the spotlight on Habermas's life and on significant movements in his thought and forgoes the chimera of an authentic representation of the person, as in a portrait. Instead, distinct types of texts are at the centre of this biographical study. To put it in simple terms: it is in the first instance about deeds and only in the second instance about the doer. I shall read first and foremost the traces left by Habermas as an author in the widest possible sense: as a philosopher *and* as an example of those intellectuals who, as doers, advance the political process.

The institutional spaces in which to find these traces are, of course, archives. Among them is my own Habermas Archive, which I compiled systematically over many years from sources I considered significant, such as available publications by Habermas, parts of his correspondence, interviews and autobiographical fragments, and the majority of the articles he published in daily and weekly newspapers and in cultural journals from 1953 onwards. In addition, there are photographs and other images, and also records of conversations with Habermas's acquaintances and contemporaries.[4] The principles employed in the selection, systematic compilation and then analysis of the sources from this and other archives were informed by the specific question asked by this biography: how did Habermas become the philosopher of communicative reason, on the one hand, and the influential public intellectual, on the other?

As far as the discursive practice of the intellectual is concerned, the centre of attention will be not Habermas's personality but his concrete interventions in the public sphere. In this context, an important aspect will be the question of how the various battles for attention and intellectual dominance in the interpretation of events, which Habermas continually engaged in (and some of which he also initiated), led to the development of polarizations within the public life of the Federal Republic. I also consider the question of which discursive means – or strategies in the politics of ideas [*ideenpolitische Strategien*] – he used as a protagonist in intellectual controversies. And, finally, I ask how Habermas, who is often assigned the function of an *opinion leader** of the left-liberal camp, if one wants to call it that, actually delineates his position through the process of his intellectual interventions.

This biography is structured by the interplay between philosophical reflections and intellectual interventions that characterizes Habermas's activities. For the most part it avoids focusing exclusively on the individual, and it eschews speculation about what Habermas might have 'thought' or 'felt' on this or that occasion. Rather, the aim is to present the interdependency of life and work within the historical context.

What role does the attitude of the biographer play in this? Without a doubt, the challenge of biographical writing is to succeed in walking the tightrope between intimacy and detachment, between the external perspective of neutral analysis and the internal perspective of hermeneutical exegesis and a sensitive understanding only possible on the basis of openness and empathy. This was no different for me; I also had to navigate my own path between intimacy and detachment. Along this path, I have tried to isolate certain threads from the tangled skein of Habermas's life history and thus to make visible how the trajectories of his life have developed. I proceed mostly in chronological fashion, though at times I go backwards or forwards in time in order to highlight connections that might otherwise be masked by the chronological surface. And there is another feature worth mentioning: those themes that have occupied Habermas throughout his life are focused on and magnified for the purpose of closer inspection. This is the case in particular where the continuities and discontinuities of Habermas's theoretical development are concerned. Here, too, I have held back with my own interpretations and mostly let Habermas speak for himself.

---

* 'Opinion leader' in English in the original.

Finally, I would like to mention that there are of course limits to what can be said in this biography. Everything purely private and intimate is excluded, unless it contributes something that is useful for understanding Habermas's philosophy and intellectual practice. And, naturally, this is an open-ended book – its subject is a *life and work in progress.**

---

* 'Life and work in progress' in English in the original.

Acknowledgements

After I had completed my Adorno biography, I told Jürgen Habermas that I intended to continue my activities in the field of biographical research and to make his life and work the next subject of my endeavours, with a view to reconstructing his role as a public intellectual as well as his intellectual path as a philosopher and social theorist. His reaction was altogether restrained. His concise response was that it felt strange to him that someone would want to 'rummage around' in his 'entrails'.

As my research progressed, Ute and Jürgen Habermas became more open towards the project, without ever giving up an appropriate restraint. I would like to thank them especially for retaining this balanced attitude between openness and distance. Without the opportunity of looking at drafts for Habermas's planned autobiography, of sifting through and making use of the more than 200 files of correspondence at the family home with my assistants, without the private conversations with Ute and Jürgen Habermas and their patience in answering my countless questions, this biography could never have been written.

Of course, the author is responsible in every sense for the content of his book. However, more people were involved in bringing it about than are mentioned on the cover. The authors in this wider sense are in the first place the academic staff of the German Research Foundation's projects on 'Jürgen Habermas als Sozialtheoretiker und öffentlicher Intellektueller' [Jürgen Habermas as social theorist and public intellectual] and on 'Ideenpolitik in der Öffentlichkeit' [The politics of ideas in the public sphere]. Christian Ziegler has built up an extensive press archive over the years and has documented and analysed Habermas's presence in the media. Franziska Charlotte Thiele, occasionally with support from Leiv Erik Voigtländer, carried out discourse analyses of the debates with great methodological skill, and Hartwig Germer concentrated on the investigation of the strategies used by left-liberal and liberal-conservative ideological groups in the battles over the politics of ideas from the late

1960s onwards. I owe all collaborators thanks not only for the time of our joint research but also for their help during the development and completion of the biography. I would also like to thank the German Research Foundation for the financial support, over five years, of the projects mentioned above.

Eva Gilmer's rigorous editing of the manuscript turned drafts into final versions, and ultimately into this book. The text profited from her feeling for language and her expertise to a degree which went far above and beyond the call of duty for an editor; for this, I would like to thank her. Thanks are also due to Christian Heilbronn for expert work on the print version.

Indispensable sources in writing this book were questions put in writing to individuals who played a role in Habermas's life, as well as conversations with them, which usually lasted several hours. I would like to mention Karl-Otto Apel, Günter Frankenberg, Ulrich Oevermann, Claus Offe and Spiros Simitis, and I thank all of them for their time and their recollections.

I am also indebted to all those individuals who provided me with important information, and various pieces of advice, during my work on this biography. Here I would like to mention Susanne Berghahn, Matthias Bormuth, Hauke Brunkhorst, Luca Corchia, Josef Dörr, Friedrich Wilhelm Fernau, René Görtzen, Adalbert Hepp, Friedhelm Herborth, Axel Honneth, Mathias Jehn, Thomas Jung, Oliver Kleppel, Ahlrich Meyer, William Outhwaite, Gerhard Pomykaj, Günter Rohrbach, Wolfgang Schopf, Bernd Stiegler, Albrecht Wellmer, Jürgen Woelke, Richard Wolin, Roman Yos, Raimar Zons and Dorothee Zucca. Finally, to those friends and partners in conversation who are not mentioned here by name, but who so reliably lent sympathetic ears to my ideas and questions, I offer my heartfelt thanks.

Oldenburg, March 2014

Illustration Acknowledgements

© juergen-bauer.com, Jürgen Bauer, Leidersbach: no. 31
Bpk-images/Foto Abisag Tüllmann, Berlin: nos. 17 and 25
Uwe Dettmar, Frankfurt am Main: nos. 32 and 33
© Frankfurter Allgemeine Zeitung GmbH, archive, Frankfurt am Main: no. 9
Private archive of Friedrich Wilhelm Fernau, Neuss: no. 3
Heimatbildarchiv des Oberbergischen Kreises, Nr. 5612: no. 7
Architekturbüro Hilmer & Sattler und Albrecht, Munich: no. 20
Barbara Klemm, Frankfurt am Main: no. 34
Ev Kriegel, Wiesbaden: p. 1
Cássio Loredano: Rio de Janeiro: p. 428
Franziska Messner-Rast, St Gallen, Switzerland: no. 27
Konrad R. Müller/Agentur Focus, Hamburg: no. 1
Rolf Oeser, Bad Vilbel: no. 30
Picture alliance/dpa: no. 29
Städtisches Gymnasium Moltkestraße Gummersbach: no. 5
Universitätsarchiv, Frankfurt am Main: no. 13
© Joachim Unseld, Frankfurt am Main, Nr. 242/29: no. 24

All other illustrations are from Jürgen Habermas's private archive or the archive of the Suhrkamp publishing house.

Prologue:
The Other among his Peers

It is true that I do not share the fundamental assumptions of 'Critical Theory' in the form in which they took shape at the beginning of the 1940s.[1]

Ironic birthday greetings from a cartoonist. Strictly speaking, Habermas does not belong in this well-known group portrait by the draughtsman, poet and jazz musician Volker Kriegel, who came into contact with the individuals it depicts during his time as a student in 1960s Frankfurt. What stands out when one looks at the image is the oversized figure of Max Horkheimer, a patriarchal figure towering over three important personalities, who are shrunk to dwarf-like size 'under him': Herbert Marcuse, Theodor W. Adorno and Jürgen Habermas. The message of the portrait – that this is the quadriga of Critical Theory – can only be taken ironically. It is true that Max Horkheimer, the *spiritus rector* of Frankfurt School Critical Theory and someone who, according to Adorno, had a 'flair for power relations',[2] wrote academic history during his lifetime. It was he who coined the term 'Critical Theory'. But he was anything but a selfless mentor to these three wholly different spirits, who were united under one roof in the Frankfurt Institute for Social Research but were certainly not always in agreement with one another. These three

did not form a tight-knit, like-minded community and certainly
not one that flocked around a charismatic 'leader', as for instance
the circle around the poet Stefan George or the Paris existentialists
around Jean-Paul Sartre. Rather, they were autonomous and independent representatives of different manners and styles of thinking.
Nevertheless, there was one common denominator, albeit a small
one, and that was an attitude which aimed at an enlightening critique of what they saw as social malformations.

It would certainly be an exaggeration simply to call Habermas
– who was, not only in this caricature but also in reality, much
taller than Marcuse or Adorno – the renegade within this group
of four philosophers. And yet he was the Other among his peers.
Habermas is about thirty years younger than Horkheimer, Marcuse
and Adorno, each of whom, in their own way, was an intellectual
role model for him. He therefore belongs to a different generation.
As opposed to the three older philosophers, he came not from a
Jewish family but from a Protestant environment. Habermas, whose
childhood and early youth fell in the time of National Socialism,
was spared the experience of racism and political persecution, as
well as the fate of exile. Further, it is another significant difference
between the Jewish left-wing intellectuals and Habermas that the
latter – despite his speech impediment, resulting from a cleft palate
– never saw himself as an outsider. Instead, it was largely his experience in the years immediately following the Second World War
that gave rise to his development as a *homo politicus*. The way the
political establishment of the young Federal Republic dealt with
the legacy of the criminal Nazi regime and the shortcomings that
became apparent regarding the creation of democratic forms of life
in Germany were both crucial to Habermas's political development.
But, despite all the critical distance that he maintained towards
the political situation around him – and still maintains today – he
always saw himself as an active participant in the social and political
process. Thus, in his case, there can be no talk of that fundamental
feeling of displacement and marginalization, that peculiar feeling
of not belonging, which accompanied Adorno or Marcuse all their
lives. In conversation, Habermas said that, all in all, his life took an
unspectacular course.[3] And, indeed, his biography does not contain
any deep fissures or discontinuities; it is above all a story of academic success, on the one hand, and of energetic interventions into
political affairs on the other.

While Adorno and Marcuse were occasionally in competition for
the approval of Horkheimer (who skilfully exploited this situation
to his strategic advantage), Habermas, as a temporary collaborator
of the restored Frankfurt Institute of Social Research, immediately
earned the explicit disapproval of its director. Horkheimer was irritated by the political commitments of the new assistant and by his

theoretical project, which aimed at an adaptation of Marxism as a philosophy of history for practical purposes. In the climate of restoration of post-war Germany, Horkheimer pursued a policy of pointed inconspicuousness, at least towards the outside world. This attitude was not shared by the majority of the institute's members and was difficult to reconcile with the non-conformism and the kind of progressive, Marxist social criticism that characterized the institute before its forced exile from Nazi Germany.

However, Habermas never saw the 'Frankfurt School' – as it became known to the world from the 1960s onwards – as a sharply defined programme. And this was possibly the most important reason why he was the Other among his peers at the time. 'For me', he admitted in an interview, 'there was no critical theory, no consistent doctrine.'[4] As points of orientation, he could take only those few scattered books and articles that were published up to the end of the 1960s. The institute's groundbreaking studies, its members from the Weimar years and from the time in American exile, 'these did not exist. Horkheimer had a great fear that we would get to the crate' in which the collected volumes of the *Zeitschrift für Sozialforschung* [Journal for Social Research] from the years 1932 to 1941 were stored away[5] – the journal that was programmatic for the original conception of Critical Theory. However, Habermas was not going to be deterred by this; for whoever wanted to do so could get hold of the legendary journal, 'this sunken continent' of the revolutionary legacy,[6] at the neighbouring Institut für Politische Wissenschaft [Institute for Political Science], where Carlo Schmid held a chair. Schmid's assistant, Wilhelm Hennis, had acquired the volumes from an antiquarian bookshop in Paris and made them part of the institute's library. Habermas's reading, in his own words, 'sharpen[ed] [his] sense of the precarious connection between democracy, state and the economy'.[7] However, in the early 1970s, partly under the influence of Anglo-American linguistic theory, Habermas began to develop his own paradigm of communicative reason and actions oriented towards reaching understanding; he thus departed from the course pursued by the representatives of the first generation of the Frankfurt School. From then on, his philosophy concentrated on 'clarifying the conditions under which moral as well as ethical questions can be answered in a rational fashion by those concerned.'[8]

Deviation and attribution. When Volker Kriegel's cartoon first appeared, Habermas was in his forties. He had already become aware of the deficiencies of classical Critical Theory at that point and had worked on the foundations of his own philosophical programme. The received wisdom that there is a strict continuity from the first through to the third generation of the Frankfurt School is therefore, upon closer inspection, incorrect. The trivial reason why Habermas is nevertheless perceived as one of the school's representatives is simply that, by the end of the 1960s, he had already taught for several terms at the Johann Wolfgang Goethe University in Frankfurt as an ordinary professor* of philosophy and sociology. And it must be seen as an irony of history that this was actually Max Horkheimer's old chair and that Habermas, of all people, had succeeded him. Habermas described his feeling about being identified with a theoretical school, in an interview with Wolfram Schütte and Thomas Assheuer in June 1993, as follows:

> [T]he labels attached to theories tend to say more about the history of misunderstandings than about the theories themselves. This also holds true for buzzwords such as 'discourse' or 'domination-free communication'. If you wish to concentrate, in the form of slogans, [on] conclusions drawn from a theory, you at least have to relate them to the problems from which the theory starts out. I started from the black-on-black of the older Critical Theory, which had worked through experiences of fascism and Stalinism. Although our situation after 1945 was different, it was this disillusioned outlook in the driving forces of a self-destructive social dynamics that first led me to seek the sources of an individual's solidarity with others, which have not yet totally evaporated.[9]

Instead of living off the legacy of Critical Theory, Jürgen Habermas carried out its transformation in terms of a communicative turn in social theory. Its point of departure is the rational potential in linguistic practice and its goal is the idea of a sound intersubjectivity as a 'glimmer of symmetrical relations marked by free, reciprocal recognition. . . . Connected with this', Habermas says, 'is the modern meaning of humanism, long expressed in the idea of a self-conscious life, of authentic self-realization, and of autonomy – a humanism that is not bent on self-assertion.'[10] While the still critical aspect of his social theory manifests itself in a *moral point of view*,† in holding on to the 'negative idea of abolishing discrimination and harm',[11] his postmetaphysical framework of thought keeps its distance from a philosophy of history which assumes the idea of an absolute negativity ruling over all of existence.

The intransigence Habermas displays in his public political interventions is a crucial reason why he is still counted as a member of the circle around Horkheimer and Adorno. It is these interventions that earned him the title of being a contrarian. He is connected with the radically critical thought that we identify with the Frankfurt

---

* 'Ordentlicher Professor', or 'Ordinarius', was the title of the highest rank of professor under the old German university system.
† 'Moral point of view' in English in the original.

School's readings of Hegel, Marx and Freud because he was present as someone raising crucial issues and as one of the dominant interpreters of transitional moments in the decades that witnessed the cultural and political liberalization of Germany. This role as a politically active public intellectual – as an active citizen of a democratically constituted polity who, as he once expressed it, rises to speak without having a political mandate – made him the main representative of the second generation of Critical Theory. Habermas, incidentally, would wish to see this activity as strictly separate from the function he performs as a scholar in teaching and research. 'What annoys me terribly', he once remarked disapprovingly, 'what gets to me, is the aggressiveness of people who do not see the role-differentiation in me.'[12] True to his word, Habermas has not only reasoned in theoretical terms about the 'peculiar non-coercive force of the better argument' but has personally made abundant public use of such reason.

PART I

Catastrophe and Emancipation

The moment of catastrophe is also the moment of emancipation.[1]

1

Disaster Years as Normality: Childhood and Youth in Gummersbach

> Our life-form is connected to the life-form of our parents and grand-parents through a mesh of familial, geographical, political, and also intellectual traditions which is difficult to disentangle – through an historical atmosphere, that is, which made us what and who we are today.[1]

Nineteen hundred and twenty-nine. Jürgen Habermas was born on 18 June 1929 in Düsseldorf, on the Rhine, the second of three children. It was a beautiful summer that year – the same year that Thomas Mann received the Nobel Prize for Literature and Erich Maria Remarque's anti-war novel *All Quiet on the Western Front* became a bestseller – but it was also a time shaken by economic crises and by attempts, from both the left and the right, to desta-bilize the Weimar Republic, whose imminent demise was slowly becoming apparent. Since the spring of that year, it had been clear that an economic depression could no longer be avoided. The year 1929 would go down in history as the beginning of the worldwide Great Depression. After the heroic times of the arts had long faded, the 'Golden Twenties' came to an end and real wages, which had up until that point been comparatively high, began to fall. People still danced the Charleston and the ladies' skirts still became shorter and shorter; from January, the picture houses showed *Ich küsse Ihre Hand, Madame* [I kiss your hand, Madame] – one of the last silent films, which, however, contained a single song. The film starred Marlene Dietrich in the female lead role, and the tango song, released the previous year and sung by Richard Tauber, became a hit, selling half a million copies.* In Munich, performances by Josephine Baker were banned because clerical circles feared for public decency, while in Berlin the newspapers reported acts of censorship by magistrates

---

* The interested reader may wish to dip into the atmosphere of the time by listening to the song at http://www.youtube.com/watch?v=q_guxRtoZB8 (accessed 23 October 2014).

aiming to prevent scandals at the Theater am Schiffbauerdamm. What could not be prevented were the gunfights between National Socialists and communists that broke out in the Reich's capital. These street battles were the tip of the iceberg, indicating growing political and ideological tensions.

> Thus, for instance, monarchists fought against republicans, conservatives against liberals and social democrats, *völkisch* nationalists against proponents of a state based on citizenship [*Staatsbürgergesellschaft*], anti-Semites against the advocates of a continuing social integration of Jewish Germans, those who glorified war against those who were sceptical towards war, mystagogues of the Reich against political realists, those who defended the thesis of a German 'Sonderweg'* against self-critical pragmatists, religious socialists against orthodox Lutherans, prophetic dreamers against supporters of routine politics, geopolitical dogmatists against clear-headed representatives of particular interests, those who sympathized with Italian fascism against the defenders of the republic, advocates of the total state against liberal democrats – it was a true witches' cauldron of political theories and phobias in which very categorical and often fundamentalist oppositions always set the tone.[2]

The death of the liberal-conservative politician Gustav Stresemann in October 1929 would lead to fatal consequences for sensible German foreign policy. In him, the country lost its most important representative – someone who had aimed to balance interests and to achieve understanding with other nations. He had, for instance, offered German support for Aristide Briand's extraordinary suggestion at the League of Nations to create a 'United Nations of Europe'.

The unemployment figures rose month on month during that year and passed the 8 million mark. On 24 October 1929, the New York Stock Exchange crashed, triggering a worldwide economic crisis: the Great Depression had begun. As a consequence, the National Socialists were able to raise their share of the vote in state elections significantly. Their propaganda was directed predominantly against the result of the negotiations in June over the conditions of Germany's payment of reparations following its defeat in the Great War, despite the fact that the so-called Young Plan actually meant a reduction of the annual burden and allowed Germany to pursue independent financial policies again.

A coalition cabinet of five major parties headed by the social demo-

---

* A term which denotes the idea that German history followed a 'special path' which differs from the development of other European countries, sometimes in association with the idea that the German people have a special historical mission.

crat Heinrich Brüning governed this republic that lacked republicans
and whose president was, in 1925, an aged Generalfeldmarschall
who was himself an opponent of republicanism. The government's
obvious weakness in leadership meant that the very party fundamentally opposed to the Weimar Republic succeeded in becoming
a mass movement. The 'Sturmabteilung' was expanded into an
effective terror organization and the Nazi Party set about creating its own media company from scratch. Gradually, the National
Socialists began to dominate public debate on all sorts of topics,
developed new initiatives for 'self-help' to combat unemployment,
and started aggressively propagating the almost messianic image of
the 'Führer'.[3]

This mixture of cultural sensations and politically explosive, economically catastrophic events would certainly have been observed
by the people of Gummersbach, a small town with a population of
18,000 in the Oberbergisches Land, set in the Prussian part of the
Rhine area. This was the home of the family of Grete and Ernst
Habermas. Perhaps later, when growing up, the boy would have
been told about the important events that took place in the year he
was born, a year in which there was certainly more shadow than
light. The Gummersbach Habermas would remember as an adult
was a place which, after the *Gründerzeit** and the turn of the century,
had been transformed into an 'urban community' and an 'industrial
city'.

> The route to the Gries butcher's shop passed the Gasthof Winter,
> the Café Garnefeld and the Wetzlars' house; and, on the way to my
> piano lessons in Winterbecke, I saw the Hotel Koester and the old
> Magistrate's Court once a week. ... From my youth I remember
> more strongly the electric tramway ..., the indoor swimming pool,
> the town hall, the Schützenburg, the community hall, and Schramm's
> toy shop.[4]

Worth mentioning too is the Vogteihaus[†] in the centre of the city,
known as 'Die Burg', as well as the Oberbergisches Land cathedral,
which was built in the eleventh century in Romanesque style as a
hall church, and the many dams in the densely wooded area of the
Oberbergischer Kreis.

In his childhood, the world of Karl May took a hold of the imagination of the adolescent boy, who confesses that for a long time he

---

* Literally 'time of the founders', sometimes referred to as the 'period of promoterism' –
a phase of rapid industrial development in Germany following the Franco-Prussian War
in 1870–1.
† The seat of a 'Vogt', a title in the Holy Roman Empire for a local or regional advocate
with legal and military power.

was egocentric and preoccupied with his own psychological problems.[5] As a pupil, he found plenty of books to read in the family
library, among them the novellas and novels of Gottfried Keller
and Conrad Ferdinand Meyer. Later, he would read Ernst Jünger's
Copse 125 and his diary *The Adventurous Heart*. The Björndal
trilogy by the Swedish author Trygve Gulbranssen and the novels
and plays by Selma Lagerlöf and Knut Hamsun also formed part of
Habermas's literary education.

The Protestant family in which Habermas grew up was the
product of petit bourgeois elements from his mother's side and a
lineage of civil servants from his father's, who had climbed up the
social ladder.

The name Habermas first appears in documents from Western
Thuringia in the second half of the century of the Reformation:
around 1570, Hanns Habermas was given the rights of a citizen
in Treffurt, a place north of Eisenach. From then on, there were
several generations of Habermases who lived in the residential city
as well-respected master cobblers.

The family. Ernst Habermas (1891–1972), the son of a parson,
who was later director of the teachers' seminary, and a large-scale
farmer's daughter, first entered the teaching profession at grammar
school level at the Oberrealschule[*] in Gummersbach.[6] He gave up
his first profession for financial reasons in 1923, shortly before his
wedding, in order to become the representative of the local branch
of the Bergische Industrie- und Handelskammer (IHK) [Chamber of
Industry and Commerce]. Already politically active in an association,
he studied, alongside his job, at Cologne University, where he was
awarded the title of Doktor der Wirtschaftlichen Staatswissenschaft
[Doctor of economic state science] for a thesis entitled 'Die
Entwicklung der oberbergischen Steinbruchindustrie' [The development of the stone quarry industry in the Oberbergische region].
After completing his time at the Oberrealschule in Gummersbach,
he at first enrolled in philosophy and philology at the universities in
Bonn and Göttingen, but he did not get beyond the state diploma
for secondary-school teaching in German, English and French. He
was an active member in Bonn of the Burschenschaft Alemannia,
a duelling fraternity whose motto was 'God, honour, freedom,
fatherland'. For thirty-five years Dr Ernst Habermas worked as a
managing director for the IHK. The family lived in a rented house at
Körnerstraße 33. When Ernst Habermas took up his post again after
the war, the family moved into a newly built house at Thalstraße 23,

---

* 'Realschulen' were originally schools providing a professionally orientated education.
From 1900 onwards they were formally given the same status as grammar schools.

which was also home to the office of the Chamber of Commerce. He held on to his post from 1956 until 1962, when his elder son, Hans-Joachim Habermas, a doctor of jurisprudence, took over his office. Both made a name for themselves as experts on the economic life of the region through their specialist publications.

It was convention at the time that Jürgen Friedrich Ernst, the second-born son, should be given the names of his grandfather and his godfather (his father's younger brother), both of whom were called Friedrich, as well as that of his father, Ernst. But perhaps it was also a hint at what the paternal line of the family expected from this descendant: the continuation of a tradition based on bour-geois education [bildungsbürgerliche Tradition] and of civil service [Beamtentum] in the spirit of a Protestant life.

In the recollections of the younger son, his paternal grandfather, Johann August Friedrich Habermas (1860–1911), figures as a kind of role model, as he was a particularly revered character within the family and its history.[7] He was a pastor who upheld the Prussian virtue of a strict work ethic. He was also a very headstrong man; several times he argued with the Church over his plans to found a free evangelical parish. As the acting director of the newly founded Prussian teachers' seminary, a position he held between 1904 and 1911, he was a respected citizen of Gummersbach who also earned plaudits as the author of a handbook on the Bible. Johann, the royal seminary director, is said to have had a German national mindset [eine deutschnationale Gesinnung]. He died of a heart con-dition in 1911, aged fifty-one, survived by his wife, Katharina, née Unterhössel (1872–1955), and six children. The 38-year-old widow received only a small pension, and the three girls and three boys had to grow up in austere conditions. Habermas's mother, Anna Amalie Margarete Habermas, née Köttgen (1894–1983), attended a secondary school and an all-girls school, finishing with the mit-tlere Reife.* She worked as a nurse during the Great War, and in the summer of 1923 she married Ernst Habermas, whom she had met two years earlier. Ernst took his time beginning a family. At the age of thirty-two he was finally in a secure position and able to provide for a wife and children. Like her husband, Margarete Habermas played the piano and had literary and artistic interests. However, as was customary at the time, she devoted herself entirely to the upbringing of her three children – two boys and a girl – and to being a housewife, first in Körnerstraße and then in Thalstraße. When visiting Düsseldorf, her two sons, Hans-Joachim and Jürgen, were fond of calling at the public house at the Gambrinus brewery

---

* The 'mittlere Reife' is gained after ten years of schooling and corresponds roughly to the British GCSEs and the US high-school diploma.

in Düsseltaler Straße, which was run by her parents, the master brewer and publican Julius Köttgen (1958–1936) and his second wife, Anna, *née* Theissen (1870–1947). Hans-Joachim was four years older than his brother. Their sister Anja was born in 1937, when Jürgen was already attending primary school. At the end of the 1950s, she started studying psychology, German, art history and education, and after qualifying as a teacher she worked in the teaching profession for some time. Following her marriage in 1964, the mother of three lived in Neuss.

In the year Habermas was born and the world economic crisis began, the economic decline and the rise in unemployment could also be felt in Gummersbach. Here, too, the Nazis made electoral gains: in April 1932, the party garnered a third of the votes in Gummersbach in the state elections for the Oberbergische. This was less than the national average – a fact explained by the greater sympathies that the nation's liberal bourgeoisie had for the DNVP, the German National People's Party. In the national elections on 31 July 1932, the Nazis won almost 13.8 million votes and became the largest party in the Reichstag. On 31 October 1932, Adolf Hitler visited Gummersbach, with all the concomitant ceremonies, torchlight processions and church services – it was the biggest political meeting ever to have taken place in the town up to that point. As a result of National Socialist propaganda – organized notably by Robert Ley, who came from the Oberbergisches Land and later became the head of the Deutsche Arbeitsfront [German Labour Front], and supported by the *Oberbergische Bote*, the leading regional newspaper, which was controlled by the Nazi Party – Adolf Hitler and the Nazis continued to gain ground.[8] On 5 March 1933, almost half of the electorate in Gummersbach voted for the National Socialists.[9] The year after the so-called seizure of power – after which Gummersbach became the seat of the regional headquarters of the Nazi Party – anti-Jewish activities and the arrest of political opponents took place in the Oberbergische municipality and the National Socialist terror that accompanied the political 'coordination' [*Gleichschaltung*]* began. The persecution of Jews in the city intensified after the pogroms of November 1938[10] and Jews were forced to sell their possessions at a loss, facts residents must surely have noticed. The National Socialist community of the people [*nationalsozialistische Volksgemeinschaft*] made itself visible in Gummersbach with parades, gatherings and celebrations for the summer solstice. Later, one of the outposts of the Gestapo would be located there.

---

* The term 'Gleichschaltung' denotes legal and other measures which brought state and civil society under National Socialist control and aimed at the Nazification of all aspects of life.

Jürgen Habermas was nine years old when local teachers organized an exhibition with the title 'Races, the people, family in the Oberbergische region' in the gymnasium of his hometown's secondary school.[11] As a young person growing up in this atmosphere in a small town, he probably experienced the totalitarian party state and its dictator Adolf Hitler simply as matters of fact to which one had to adapt. Ernst Habermas's national conservative orientation did not prevent him from becoming a member of the Nazi Party, which he joined as early as spring 1933. Like most of those belonging to the 'functional elite', he went along with the wave of self-coordination [Selbstgleichschaltung]. The new masters were greeted with a loyalty befitting the traditional ideas of an authoritarian state that already had wide currency, especially among civil servants. Ernst Habermas was the NSDAP's economic advisor for the county. In this role, he considered it,

> shortly before the outbreak of war in 1939, as one of the most important tasks for the future to alleviate the shortage of labour and to bind newly arrived workers to the region by intensifying house-building programmes . . . In addition, he called for a further rationalization of labour processes and an expansion of the use of machines in order to achieve the increase in productivity called for in Hermann Göring's Four Year Plan, despite the limited capacity in terms of labour power.[12]

Just as Ernst Habermas had joined the Great War in October 1914 as a volunteer, and had fought at the Western front near Verdun, the then 48-year-old volunteered for military service with the Wehrmacht at a time when Hitler's armies had begun to prepare for a war of annihilation. Previously, between 1933 and 1937, he had taken part in military exercises. In the Wehrmacht he initially held the rank of captain. In spring 1941, he was sent to the local garrison HQ at the French harbour town of Lorient, then to that at Brest, both on the Breton coast. The latter was developed into the largest German submarine base on the Atlantic and would later experience heavy bombardment from the Allies. Ernst Habermas was dispatched to the local garrison HQ with the rank of captain, and as the head of the civil administration his task was to requisition living quarters in the town for members of the Wehrmacht.[13] Later, when he had risen to the rank of major, he received the 'Kriegsverdienstkreuz I. Klasse' [Military cross of merit, 1st class]. Between June and August 1944, after the Allies had already landed in Normandy, he was involved in the defence of the city, which involved major losses on both sides.[14]

It was also in Brest that Ernst Habermas made the acquaintance of the literary scholar Benno Georg von Wiese und Kaiserswaldau, who was more than ten years his junior. Von Wiese had completed his doctorate under the supervision of Karl Jaspers in 1927, but according to Hannah Arendt's testimony he had no objections to the coordination* of the universities in 1933.[15] Ernst Habermas asked von Wiese whether he might give him his opinion on a comedy he had written, and this eventually led to an amicable relationship between the two. Later, von Wiese would write of Ernst Habermas that he had been a 'gentleman, even a grandseigneur', who

> sparkled with wit and human intensity. . . . His free *savoir vivre* of the Rhinelander, his calmness, his urbanity, his joyful and intellectually open temperament, his personal warmth and his brilliant *bon mots*, which always hit the nail on the head, I shall never forget. He did not follow conventions but nevertheless remained faithful to conservative traditions. . . . Ernst Habermas saw through the illusory world of the army, yet remained a committed soldier, if in harmonious combination with a flexible humanity.[16]

The days of childhood and youth. But let us return to the younger son of this committed soldier with a 'flexible humanity'. As a child, Jürgen received particular care and attention from his parents. He was born with a cleft palate, which required repeated surgical procedures from the very first years of his life. Despite these, he was still left with a nasal intonation. According to Habermas, the medical interventions he had to endure as a five-year-old and the lasting speech defect had a significant influence on the development of his thought. On the one hand, it made him realize that human beings depend existentially on each other; on the other hand, he personally experienced the significance 'of the medium of linguistic communication as a shared stratum without which individual existence would also be impossible'.[17] In an autobiographical retrospective in 2005, Habermas confesses that it was this specific experience that 'may have awakened . . . the sense of the relevance of our interactions *with others*' in him.[18]

From 1935, Habermas attended the Diesterweg primary school in Gummersbach. In 1939, he moved to the Oberrealschule (later to become the Städtisches Gymnasium) in Moltkestraße, a school with a focus on science and modern languages. His years at primary school were not without their dark side. Even as a septuagenarian, Habermas still recalled the difficulties 'I encountered when I had to make myself understood in class or during break while speaking with my nasal articulation and distorted pronunciation, of which I was completely unaware.'[19] It is easy to imagine how he was mocked

---

* See previous footnote.

and teased because of his speech defect. These early experiences of discrimination, Habermas would later say, made him morally sensitive to any kind of exclusion[20] and had an essential formative influence on his political thought.

Apart from the bullying on account of his speech impediment,[21] Habermas's childhood and youth differed little from that of his peers, who all saw themselves as parts of a large 'Volksgemeinschaft' [people's community], with all of its visible symbols: Volksempfänger [people's receivers],* Volkswagen and the Reichsautobahnen [Reich motorways], as well as other manifestations of the Führerstaat – for instance, the aestheticization and theatricalization of public power politics. In the years leading up to the outbreak of the war, the Habermas family went on summer holidays in Warnemünde, in Zinnowitz, and on Rügen island.

One of Habermas's friends from his early childhood days was Josef Dörr, a boy of similar age and of whom Habermas apparently was particularly fond. The first time the two boys met was in 1932, when Josef's family moved to Gummersbach. Shortly thereafter a still very young Habermas explored the surroundings of the town with the new arrival from the countryside. A black-and-white photograph shows the two of them dressed in their summer clothes, apparently in the garden of the Körnerstraße house, surrounded by a circle of playmates Habermas had invited for his sixth birthday. After April 1939, the two attended the Oberrealschule together. Whenever possible they would spend their free time playing outside in the densely wooded countryside surrounding the town. According to Josef, it was a carefree time, but one that came to an abrupt end with the outbreak of war in the summer of 1939. After the war, he says, they mostly discussed the future – what would become of them, but also what would become of the country. To Josef, Jürgen was a sociable character who exuded an impressive, though never arrogant, self-assurance.[22]

At the age of ten Habermas became a member of the Deutsches Jungvolk† and later of the Hitler Youth, in accordance with the law but perhaps also in accordance with his parents' opportunism.[23] In December 1936 these organizations had been given the status of Staatsjugend [state youth], and in March 1939 membership had been made compulsory. All ten- to fourteen-year-olds and all fourteen- to eighteen-year-olds had to be placed according to age and gender in the corresponding National Socialist youth organizations; the Hitler Youth, under the leadership of the 'Reichsjugendführer' [Reich youth leader] Baldur von Schirach, thereby became the

---

* A range of comparatively cheap medium- and long-wave radios introduced for propaganda purposes from 1933.

† Section of the Hitler Youth for boys aged ten to fourteen.

largest National Socialist organization. Membership entailed holding certain racial and ideological convictions.[24] In contrast to his friends, Habermas did not receive a notification that he was to join the Jungvolk, and he felt excluded as a result. His father rang the relevant office, whereupon his son was eventually admitted. But he did not feel comfortable in this environment, especially with the fights that formed part of the initiation rituals known as 'Pimpfenproben'.* In order to escape the obligatory paramilitary training and military exercises, which took place every Saturday, Habermas indicated that he wanted to become a medical doctor – which was indeed his intention at the time. Thus, he succeeded in being placed with the military doctors and being trained for medical service rather than with the boys who were trained for labour service [*Arbeitsdienst*] and the Wehrmacht. Soon it was his duty to hold courses on first aid in the rooms of the vocational school. He took over this task from a secondary-school boy three years his senior, Henner Luyken, who was drafted into the army and would practise as a doctor after the war. Luyken taught Habermas everything he needed to know as a first aider. More than half a century later, he could still remember his younger successor: 'He was an intelligent bloke, who enjoyed the job because he wanted to become a doctor.'[25]

Decades later, there would be attempts to criticize Habermas for his membership of the Hitler Youth. However, at least according to his own testimony, he was as little susceptible to the National Socialist ideology, with its ideas about a 'Herrenmenschentum' [master race], as he was the propaganda about the 'final victory'.[26] His experiences and attitudes apparently differed from those of Hans-Ulrich Wehler, who also grew up in Gummersbach, attended the same Oberrealschule as Habermas, and got to know him in the Hitler Youth. Like so many of his age, Wehler writes, he was determined to defend the 'Reich' in the face of the military supremacy of the Allies during the last months of the war. Habermas, who was two years older and had been confirmed in 1943, probably had a more distanced attitude towards this 'cult of the will'.[27] After all, his biology textbook at school listed three 'hereditary diseases', together with malicious pictures and comments: schizophrenia, clubfoot and cleft palate. But Habermas admits that, despite all this, it was difficult not to fall for the propaganda of the Nazis and their demagoguery and promises.

During the war years, Gummersbach also saw the introduction of food rationing cards. Later there were air raid alarms, burning

---

* 'Pimpf' referred to a boy who was a member of the 'Jungvolk'; 'Pimpfenprobe' = test of courage as an initiation ritual.

houses, destroyed tramways, damaged transport routes, and, of course, the dead and injured as a result of Allied bombing raids. The heavy bombardment of Cologne in May 1940, and in particular that of the night of 29 June 1943, could be seen from as far away as Gummersbach. And the situation would become even more dangerous: as late as March 1945, Hitler had personally ordered the commander of the army stationed at the Oberbergische to not retreat. Habermas had to be careful not to be senselessly sacrificed in the madness of the 'Endkampf' [final battle] during the last weeks of the war, as so many other young people were. He would surely not have failed to notice the 'Sondergerichte' [special courts] established in the region in March 1945, which passed numerous death sentences before the Nazis' capitulation. One of those sentenced was a young man from Gummersbach who had deserted his unit. He was given the death penalty and publicly hanged as a warning to others.[28]

In the autumn of 1944, the fifteen-year-old Habermas was at first meant to join the defence on the so-called Siegfried Line as frontline support ['Fronthelfer']. Then, in February 1945, he received a call-up letter for the Wehrmacht. 'It was sheer coincidence', says Habermas, 'that I was somewhere else [i.e. not at home, S. M.-D.] for one night, and on that night the military police came to look for me. Then, thank God, on 10 March the Americans came.'[29]

The conditions in Gummersbach at the end of the war were as nothing compared to the landscape of ruin found in the major cities of Germany. However, thousands of refugees and displaced persons meant that the town could not escape the consequences of the bombings and the havoc they wreaked.* And the measures taken by the American military administration to bring about the de-Nazification of political and economic life could be felt in Gummersbach as well.

After 1945. In Gummersbach, Habermas would see first his older brother and then, in January 1947, his father return from American captivity. Ernst Habermas had been taken as a prisoner of war by the Americans in September 1944 and had been sent to various camps, among them Ruston in Louisiana, and also Jerome and Dermott, both in Arkansas, before he was finally released at the beginning of January 1946, after a stopover in Boston. The POW camps in the USA followed the Geneva Conventions, and so the inmates were paid for their labour and treated relatively decently. In the case of Ernst Habermas, his excellent command of English also helped him get by. After his return home, he was

---

* 'Displaced persons' in English in the original.

categorized as a 'Mitläufer' [passive follower];* however, because
he had been a party member he was forced to wait for some time
before he could take up his post as the IHK's legal adviser, and
during this time the family lived on very little money. Some of the
rooms of the house in Körnerstraße were seized for refugees from
Silesia and bombed-out citizens from Cologne. In this precarious
situation, conflicts within the family could not be avoided, as the
daughter of the house, nine years old at the time, would later
remember. Ernst Habermas was also faced with the difficult task
of overcoming the emotional distance between himself and his by
now (almost) grown-up sons, which had opened up during his time
at the front and in captivity. In terms of his political orientation,
the erstwhile supporter of the national conservative DNVP now
leaned more towards the policies of the Christian Democrats than
towards the liberalism of the Free Democrats, and, quite in line
with the spirit of the time, he was actively committed to Franco-
German reconciliation.[30] Even before the Federal Republic was
founded, he was able to take up his post as syndic again, which he
held until his retirement.

Did Habermas ever discuss with his father the latter's Nazi
past? As a young man who felt ashamed and shocked by the Nazi
crimes, he very likely understood only too well what Thomas Mann
explained in his radio speech in spring 1945: 'We cannot possibly
demand of the violated people of Europe and all over the world
that they distinguish clearly and distinctly between "Nazi ideology"
[Nazitum] and the German people. If something like a people exists,
if something like Germany as a historical totality exists, then there is
also something like responsibility – quite independent of the highly
difficult problem of guilt.'[31] Did the pupil at secondary school, on
reading Karl Jaspers's The Question of German Guilt, ask himself
whether the denial of collective guilt made it easier to take refuge
in this lifelong self-deception – that never having acted wrongfully
as an individual means one is simply a victim of propaganda and
terror, and not a perpetrator? Whether or not Habermas saw his
father as a 'victim' in this sense must remain an open question. If we
take distance from the 'regime's policies of terror and annihilation
as the criterion',[32] then Ernst Habermas is, strictly speaking, not to
be counted as a member of the Nazi elite. There is no evidence to
suggest that he was a prototypical ardent follower of that 'greatest commander of all times'.[33] We should assume, then, that Ernst
Habermas was not a member of that 'generation of the unconditional'[34] born between 1900 and 1919 – that elite group of murderers

---

* The second lowest of five categories. The term suggests a passive compliance with the
political changes rather than active collaboration.

of the Third Reich who were totally committed to the idea of absolute leadership as well as to racial fanaticism and anti-Semitism, and who were prepared to take these ideas to the extremes.

Looking back on the political atmosphere in his parental home, Jürgen Habermas said that the religious attitude was Protestant and the political one was 'unremarkable for the time': 'namely, [it was one] characterized by a bourgeois adaptation to the political environment, while neither fully identifying with it, nor seriously criticizing it.'[35] However, in the Third Reich his father had been a respected representative of German industry and had reached the rank of major in the Wehrmacht. For the son, these facts do not appear to have been a reason for severing ties with his father or for otherwise distancing himself from him. According to his own testimony, it was clear to him that his father's past as a partisan of the Nazis was a heavy burden for the elder man to bear when trying to orient himself within a democratically constituted Germany, and one that weighed emotionally on him. In later years, Ernst Habermas indicated to his younger son that he wanted to talk about the subject.[36] Although the son would later become one of the most vehement critics of that 'communicative silence' [*kommunikatives Beschweigen*] and its pragmatic justification,[37] he shied away from confrontation with his father. He did not doubt that their political differences could not be bridged, but this did not touch upon their personal relationship. In an article in the *Frankfurter Allgemeine Zeitung*, Habermas wrote on 31 March 1999: 'Because we cannot know how we ourselves would have acted, a certain restraint in moral judgement when it comes to the mistakes of our own parents and grandparents is not to be explained as merely the result of our psychological inhibitions towards those closest to us.'[38]

Habermas has made no secret of his political differences with his father. In a letter of 1955 to Hans Paeschke, editor at the cultural magazine *Merkur*, he admits frankly 'that my father and I do not agree on political matters'.[39] Did Habermas not seek a confrontation with his father because he was about to leave the family context altogether? Maybe. The young Habermas's 'official' attitude during the post-war years on the question of the moral evaluation of behaviour during Nazi rule can be gleaned from an article which the 25-year-old wrote for the *Süddeutsche Zeitung* in October 1954:

> It seems to me that the officially maintained mental attitude [*Bewußtseinslage*] of rehabilitation will coincide with reality again only once the virtues of our fathers are perceived through the medium of those experiences we have made under conditions of historical exigency, and which therefore, more than any others, make it possible for us to find a contemporary and creative, in any case an appropriate answer. Thus, let us only note as the most valuable of these experiences

the reliable tact and sublime sensitivity of the younger generation
vis-à-vis the inhumane consequences of collective processes.[40]

Born in 1929

My generation got and took full advantage of all the opportunities
after the war. It dominated the intellectual scene for an abnormally
long time.[41]

Those born within a certain number of years may collectively be
addressed as a 'generation' because they share specific influences
belonging to their era. Despite the contingencies of personal difference and individual peculiarity, the members of Jürgen Habermas's
age group – and he himself is an outstanding example of this –
shared historically unique experiences during their childhood and
adolescent years in Nazi Germany. Such experiences give shape to a
certain mentality; they solidify into generational knowledge.

The sociologist Karl Mannheim compares these elements of a
knowledge that is determined by contemporary history and taken
up by a whole generation to language, which first forms behind the
backs, so to speak, of individual speakers, who then make their own
use of it. Thus, as Mannheim stresses, age itself does not make up
'the shared situation within the social space, but only the resulting
possibility of participating in the same events, life experiences etc.'[42]

What justifies designating the cohort of those born between 1927
and 1930 as the 'Flakhelfer'-generation,* or, with a different nuance
in meaning, as the 'generation of 1945'?[43] In the first place, the
fact that they spent practically their entire childhood and youth
growing up in National Socialist Germany and thus, in contrast to
their parents, could not imagine an alternative to this, their 'normal
world'. The fact that they experienced National Socialism at a
young age raises the question of whether the education as practised
by youth organizations and teachers under the dictatorship left a
lasting impression on the members of this generation, which, apart
from Habermas, included Ralf Dahrendorf, Günter Grass, Hans
Magnus Enzensberger, Martin Walser, Walter Kempowski, Heiner
Müller and Christa Wolf.[44] This remains a controversial question
on which Habermas has not explicitly commented. In one of the
rather rare references to his experiences as a member of the 1945
generation, he speaks of the 'non-heroic character . . . of my own

---

* 'Flak' is short for 'Flugabwehrkanone' = anti-aircraft gun. The 'Flakhelfer', anti-
aircraft gun assistants, were schoolboys born in 1926 and 1927, later 1928 and 1929, who
were drafted into anti-aircraft service instead of becoming soldiers during the last two
years of the war.

lifetime'.[45] This cautious formulation, referring to his biography as a whole, hints at the fact that the members of his generation did not accrue individual guilt by performing morally despicable actions, that they were too young to become perpetrators. This point was encapsulated by Helmut Kohl (born in 1930) and Günter Gauss (born in 1929) in the phrase 'the mercy of having been born [too] late'. Although the origins of the phrase are uncertain, Kohl in particular would invoke it frequently. Habermas describes his generation in similar terms and has in mind, 'strictly speaking, those who, without having done anything for it, simply because of the year group to which they belonged, could not discredit themselves by participating in or remaining silent about activities during the Nazi period, and yet were shaped by clear recollections of a fascism that bore consequences for the biography of every individual one of them.'[46]

For these cohorts, the impact of the dictatorship was limited to the time of their childhood and youth. For Habermas, probable formative influences, typical for someone of his generation, were the periodic absences of his father during the war years and during his time in American captivity. We may therefore assume with good reason that the age-specific father–son conflict would hardly have come into play.

Only once does Habermas allude to the fact that his father, quite apart from his role as the head of a family of five and as a citizen in his community, also performed the function of a mentor to his younger son. After the war, his father handed him literature on political economy by representatives of the school of ordoliberalism and recommended to him books by proponents of the free market, such as Wilhelm Röpke and Walter Eucken, authors who demonstrated 'the weaknesses of a "centrally administered planned economy" from the perspective of free market competition'. 'I was surprised at the time', Habermas says, 'by this neutral formulation of something which all the world called "socialism". In this way I came into contact with the ordoliberalism of the Mont Pelerin Society at a relatively early stage.'[47] As an adult, Habermas, who apparently felt no inclination towards symbolic patricide, would characterize his father in rather sober terms as someone with the ambitions typical of the educated bourgeois class, someone for whom the military was important in the first instance because it gave him the status associated with the title of a major.[48]

Besides the family (and here the part of the mothers is still usually ignored) and the youth organizations, it was of course the schools that shaped these generations in the time of National Socialism. The teachers in Gummersbach for the most part probably identified as closely with the National Socialist ideology as teachers anywhere else in the 'Großdeutsche Reich' [Greater German Reich] and in exceptional cases were as far from identifying with it as some elsewhere. According to Hans-Ulrich Wehler's recollections, the political spectrum reached from

> the firm Deutschnationalen, who would soon succumb to the extreme nationalism of the Nazis, to the upright freethinking liberal, who retained a cool and reserved, even ironic attitude towards the most recent history, even as late as 1944, as even we, as young Pimpfe, could sense. In general, a right-wing liberal conservatism was predominant, and in this the teaching body was in agreement with the majority of the pupils' parents, until the point at which some fanatic National Socialists – both teachers and parents – began to question this problematic consensus.[49]

For ten- to fifteen-year-old boys, it must have been difficult, maybe even impossible, to make sense of such a situation. Habermas at best probably possesses some vague memories of these pre-war years in which National Socialism enjoyed broad acceptance and its 'Führer' widespread admiration. In the end, however, it was mainly Habermas's disability, his congenital speech defect, that protected him, so to speak, against identification with the dominant ideology. He quite simply had 'no chance as an adolescent to identify with the dominant worldview'.[50]

'In the run-up to the real thing'. At the end of 1944, all men fit for military action aged between sixteen and sixty were called up for service in the 'Deutscher Volkssturm'. However, at fifteen, Habermas and those of his age were also at risk of being pulled into this criminal war of annihilation, when in February and March 1945 those born in 1928 and 1929 were drafted into replacement and training divisions.[51] Although in the end they were spared deployment to one of the war's fronts, which had by that time already disintegrated into chaos, they were nevertheless caught, in the words of Hans-Ulrich Wehler, 'in the run-up to the real thing'.[52]

Habermas was ensnared in this situation in August 1944, two months after the Allies' landing in Normandy. A family photograph shows him marching through his hometown in a procession with others of the same age, following an order of the local 'Gauleiter'. Their destination was a camp in which they were to be prepared for their deployment at the Siegfried Line, where they would dig anti-tank ditches. As a 'Fronthelfer' [front-line support], Habermas did not have combatant status, and thus he did not have to engage in armed military combat. Yet, he would certainly have looked ahead with trepidation at what was awaiting him and his peers – having senselessly to expose themselves to danger at the end of a lost war. In this unlucky situation, he was lucky: because he had been trained as a first aider, once he arrived at the front he was soon placed at the military district office [*Revierstube*] and did not have to take part in fighting.

Turning point: 1945

You become a new generation by creating something new.[53]

Democracy as the vanishing point. Habermas experienced the unconditional surrender of the Großdeutsche Reich not as a humiliation but, rather, as 'a liberation, historically and personally'. He spent the days of the first week in May – 'incidentally, the weather', he recalls, 'was very good'[54] – in his hometown with his mother and eight-year-old sister, the only members of his family still in Gummersbach at the time. Grete Habermas saw her family well through the years of her husband's military service and his captivity. Among the many stresses to which she was subjected, her daughter Anja recalls the nights of bombing spent in the cellar, food shortages, worries about her husband while he was in French and American captivity, and then later about her two sons. According to the testimony of her younger son, Grete hated the war. Her daughter speaks of her going through phases of depression which she tried to deal with through a certain strictness towards the children. Her younger son, too, emphasizes the unstable temper of his mother, who, he says, took over the role of the head of the family with courage during her husband's absence.

Relief over the fact that there was now peace and the dictator was dead was followed by the shock of learning about the incomprehensible destruction of European Jewry. In November 1945, Habermas heard on the radio about the Nuremberg Trials at the International Military Court involving twenty-four of the main war criminals, among them Göring, Ley, Keitel, Kaltenbrunner, Rosenberg, von Ribbentrop, Frank, Frick, Streicher, Jodl and Seyß-Inquart, and thus first learned of the true extent of the Nazi regime's atrocities. At the cinema, he watched the documentaries compiled for educational purposes by the American Counsel for the Prosecution of Axis Criminality, an institution which collected evidence for the prosecution of leading Nazi criminals; they showed the corpses and those who survived, as well as reconstructions of the methods of torture used by concentration camp personnel. 'Suddenly, our own history', Habermas says, 'was shown in a light that changed all essential aspects at one stroke. You suddenly realized that you had lived in a criminal political system.'[55]

How does a young individual react to such horrifying revelations? There is plenty of evidence to suggest that the Flakhelfer generation tried to accept the bleakness of the situation,[56] not least the question of guilt, as a challenge. Habermas was no exception, and he would soon follow two paths in order to meet that challenge. On the one hand, he would pursue a particular politics of the past and become a relentless critic of any kind of blindness towards what 'the Nazis have done to all that wears a human face'.[57] On the other, he would identify unreservedly with the idea of democracy. Although at the time he had finished his secondary-school education in Gummersbach, where, in 1949, the Christian Democratic Union (CDU) emerged as the strongest political force at local and regional elections in the Oberbergische, Habermas could not possibly have had very clear ideas of democracy as a political form of the state. He nevertheless placed his hopes in the possibility that the democratic constitution imported by the Western allies would endure and lead to a respectful and tolerant coexistence within the community. Thus the adolescent young man became gripped by the idea that Germany only had a future as a democracy – or, more precisely, as a democracy based on universalist values, modelled on the West.[58]

In retrospect, it seems obvious that the generation that entered adulthood at the time of Germany's liberation by the Allied powers would increasingly influence the development of post-war Germany from the mid-1950s onwards. Hans-Ulrich Wehler points out that it was not only the fact that they had experienced the effects of Hitler's dictatorship which shaped the ways of thinking and acting of a majority of young intellectuals at the time, but also the fact that they had witnessed its decline and the disbelief, shame and sorrow which followed when they learned about the monstrous crimes committed by their own people. All this marked a specific and, needless to say, severe *turning point* in the biographies of the members of that generation. But it also fostered their willingness to greet the 'new republic', founded four years after the Allies' victory, 'as an unexpected opportunity, and to accompany it with principled approval, but also with critical alertness'.[59] Wehler's explanation for the continuous political commitment of the 1945 generation, of which Habermas is an exemplar, is their wish to seize the opportunity to help create a democratic order. This meant that, in contrast to their parents' generation, silence was never an option for them: 'Among this younger German generation there was clearly a feeling of having to become involved . . . . As regards the circle of friends around Habermas, I do not even think that they were particularly aware of it, but they felt: We have survived, and now we have to get involved.'[60]

Habermas, indeed, is the embodiment of this attitude *par excellence*. He never wanted to be an 'acquiescent democrat'; he wanted to play an active part in the democratic process. He was intellectually curious, and from now on he would inform himself thoroughly about political developments. Regarding this curiosity, his uncle Peter Wingender, who ended up in Gummersbach towards the end of the war, may have played a role. He had a considerable library, which provided his nephew with philosophical literature. Habermas not only delved into the writings of Kant but also, in an old kitchen in the basement that he had made into his own private space, recited passages from Nietzsche's *Zarathustra* at the top of his voice. 'However', Habermas adds, 'in the end the associations with the decrepit slogans of the Nazis which the compiled version of the *Will to Power* evoked became too embarrassing.'[61]

In the course of the 1950s, Habermas would publicly speak out more and more frequently. His motif was that of contributing to the democratic stabilization of a new Germany (as it was for Ralf Dahrendorf, for instance). In the background was the fear of a possible relapse into the fascist mentality – a fear which would stay with Habermas right into the 1980s.[62]

For Habermas, the turning point of 1945 was not only an epochal rupture in the sense outlined above. It also, he says, triggered existential thought processes, 'without which I would hardly have ended up in philosophy and social theory'.[63] Indeed, the weeks around his sixteenth birthday coincided with some dramatic events. After the bloodiest war the world had ever seen, Germany ceased to be a sovereign state and lost its territorial integrity. On German soil, nationalism had turned out to be malevolent, to be a form of megalomania. German history had led to a 'return to barbarity'. And the Western notion of culture had 'become an alibi', as Max Frisch wrote at the turn of 1948–9 in the journal *Der Monat*.

The turning point also meant for Habermas an obligation to deal with what had happened, with a past which, according to his own later words, could not be discarded.[64] Understanding the 'Volksgemeinschaft' [people's community] as a totalitarian and murderous system of rule became, alongside an intense preoccupation with the legacy of the National Socialist past, a fundamental theme of Habermas's adult political life. Before starting university, he apparently began to reflect on this past, as well as on the question of his own guilt and that of the Germans as a nation. Towards the end of his time at secondary school, he gave up his wish to study medicine and became interested in contemporary history and philosophy. In his first *curriculum vitae*, which he had to present on 1 December 1948 for his Abitur,* he wrote:

My professional plan has always been to become a medical doctor. The lasting impressions which repeated operations of the mouth made

---

* The German equivalent of A-levels.

on me as a child must certainly be considered to be the reason for this. Later, training as a military first aider motivated me to occupy myself with human anatomy. A new horizon opened up for me when I began to think more independently. . . . My interest in understanding the nature of human beings has remained, only that the anatomical perspective, which in any case I had never adopted out of a predominantly scientific inclination, has broadened into a general biological, psychological and philosophical one.

In the same *curriculum vitae*, Habermas gives 'journalist' as his professional goal, and adds confidently that he 'wants to write in reaction to each day' [*aus dem Tag heraus*] – i.e., with a sense of the problems that are currently urgent – and not 'for the day'.[65] A few months before Habermas's Abitur, his father sent one of his essays to his friend the jurist August Dresbach, who at the time was the managing director of the Chamber of Industry and Commerce in Cologne and a member of the parliament of North Rhine-Westphalia for the CDU. Dresbach responded that the young author was a talented writer and recommended that he take a closer look at ordoliberalism.[66]

It was the personal experience of historical catastrophe that brought Habermas to philosophy and which determined the nature of his relationship with it.[67] In retrospect, he noted: 'The philosophical spirit of the time also contributed to my decision to study philosophy instead of medicine. I was captured by the enthusiasm for existentialist philosophy at the time.' And he acknowledges that he was 'captured by the opaque rustling of the vocabulary of an existentialism which I hardly understood'.[68]

For the unsettled adolescents, the teaching in the upper sixth form at the Oberrealschule between the end of 1945 and the examinations he took for his Abitur at Easter 1949 is unlikely to have provided sufficient orientation regarding the contemporary historical situation. According to Habermas, sensitive political topics such as National Socialism, the Second World War and Auschwitz were not covered.[69] Nevertheless, some of those who taught him at secondary school made a lasting impression. One of them was the art teacher Martin Jahn, who laid out for his pupils 'the differentiated network of a modernism that began with Courbet and Courot', encouraged them to think about Ernst Barlach's *Hiob*, and introduced them to architecture and industrial design. 'In the long term', Habermas says, 'the experimental approach and the constructivist streak, beginning with the early cubists, was what interested me more in painting than my initial enthusiasm for German expressionism would have suggested. Not a bad preparation for Adorno's posthumously published *Aesthetic Theory*.'[70]

Another teacher of whom Habermas has fond memories is Rudolf Klingholz, who taught Latin and, Habermas recalls, had an intellectual air about him. Habermas presented him with an unsolicited essay in which he undertook to refute Marxism. Klingholz not only taught Latin, he also talked passionately about avant-garde art, though he turned his nose up at Wolfgang Borchert, whom Habermas regarded highly. Borchert's drama *The Man Outside* was emblematic of the so-called Kahlschlagliteratur* of the immediate post-war years. The biology teacher Otto Bäcker, who – as Habermas was aware – had just returned from teaching for some time at a nearby elite National Socialist school, covered neo-Darwinism, ethology and hereditary genetics. He marked Habermas's paper in biology, on 'The animal fighting off its predators', as 'good'. Habermas would later say of his interest in the sciences at that time: 'They interested me not from a cosmological but from an anthropological point of view.'[71]

Habermas's philosophy classes held a particular significance for him, because in both the lower and upper sixth form they were taught by Peter Wingender, his father's brother-in-law, who had done his doctorate with the psychologist and linguistic theorist Karl Bühler in Vienna and who had moved from the destroyed Cologne to Gummersbach towards the end of the war. To this uncle, Habermas admits, he owed 'advice and orientation within the literature. He encouraged me to read Kant's *Prolegomena*, even if I did not get further in his *Critique of Pure Reason* than the transcendental aesthetic.'[72] A further philosophical influence was his Greek teacher, with whom he had private lessons and whom he also admired as a true philosopher: 'It was this teacher's ambition to acquaint me with the philosophy of his teacher Richard Semon, who in 1908 had published a work on *Die Mneme als erhaltendes Prinzip im Wechsel des organischen Geschehens* [Mneme as a principle of conservation within the organic process]. I learned everything I did not want to know about the dynamic of the "engrams".'

Habermas's marks and his teachers' evaluations show that he was a good pupil – if not an exceptional one, then at least one who was nevertheless remarkable in certain areas:

> Habermas is by far the most talented pupil in his class, and the one who pays the most attention to his intellectual development. He is

---

* Literally 'clear-cutting literature', also referred to as *Trümmerliteratur* [rubble literature]. Both terms have in mind not only the physical destruction but also a moral vacuum in the wake of 1945. Borchert's drama tells the story of a returning soldier who is turned away from every door and who finally commits suicide by drowning himself in the River Elbe. Devoid of any illusions regarding solidarity among those who survived, it paints the picture of a world in which the Other is 'no one at all' and self-interest and self-preservation are the only principles followed.

an independent thinker who feels both the need to gain clarity about
questions pertaining to one's view of the world and about literary
questions in independently designed texts which pursue their own
questions and the need to express his thoughts well. . . . His talent for
philosophical questions is altogether exceptional, and he formulates
them of his own accord without any external promptings. He had
already delved into philosophical works in his *Sekunda** years, and
did not rest until he was able take an independent stance towards
them.

The evaluation emphasizes the stylistic qualities of
Habermas's essays and points out his interest in the subject of
history 'for historical problems, especially in the area of constitutional law, and for theories of state law and of economic
development, all of which provided nourishment for his philosophical inclinations.'[73]

Of course, we should not attach too much significance to the
essays of a school leaver. But Habermas's exam piece of Easter
1949, 'Menschen in der Landschaft' [People in landscapes], written
in a kind of Sütterlin script, bears witness to the fact that the nine-
teen-year-old was fascinated by philosophical questions and was
already widely read in this area. He refers to topics such as the
subject–object relation, the relationship between man and nature,
the being-in-the-world of humans, the human being as deficient, its
character as a free being, etc. The first name to be mentioned is that
of Heidegger, then Darwin, Lamarck, Dilthey, the three great philosophers of antiquity – i.e., Socrates, Plato and Aristotle – and also
Marx. He makes mention too of Erich Rothacker, who would later
become his doctoral supervisor. It is worth noting that Habermas
also refers to a book by a physician and anthropologist published
in 1922: Paul Alsberg, *Das Menschheitsrätsel: Versuch einer prinzipiellen Lösung* [The riddle of mankind: attempt at a fundamental
answer][†] – a book which was obscure at the time Habermas wrote
the essays for his Abitur and which is completely forgotten today.
The sociologist Dieter Claessens later referred to Alsberg's bio-
sociological ideas in his work.[74]

Habermas would remain connected to this school in Moltkestraße,
where he passed his Abitur with good results. In December 2002, he
wrote an article for the school magazine, reminiscing about his time
there. His contacts with his fellow pupils fizzled out over the years,

---

* Years ten and eleven at secondary school.
† In 1970, Paul Alsberg published *In Quest of Man: A Biological Approach to the Problem
of Man's Place in Nature* (Oxford: Pergamon Press). In the introduction, he says: 'As no
English edition [of *Das Menschheitsrätsel*] has yet come out the author deemed it justifiable to rewrite his thesis in the English language' (p. 5).

as did his contact with Josef Dörr, with whom he had spent his early years in Gummersbach.

The womb is fertile still. In the short period between completing his Abitur at Easter and beginning his university studies in the autumn, Habermas mostly read. In addition to the books from his uncle's library he now had some texts from a communist bookshop in town – texts by Marx and Engels, Stalin and Plekhanov – which contain his studious pencilled underlining. He remembers having looked for literature that dealt specifically with questions concerning society: 'A text which again inspired me spontaneously to write an essay of my own was Herder's *Another Philosophy of History for the Formation of Humanity*. I must have read Kant's *Idea for a Universal History with a Cosmopolitan Aim* around the same time as well.'[75] Habermas also remembered discussions of Herder's essay that took place at courses he attended at a local adult education centre.

However, he also had other things to worry about. Given the severe supply shortages during these years of starvation, black markets and hoarding – the official food rations were below subsistence level[76] – Habermas, as a pupil, also had to do his bit to obtain food for the family, and to that end he worked on a farm near Mettmann in the Bergische Land. He was taunted several times by the other workers there because of his speech impediment: 'And then one of the other boys again made a remark. I had this pitchfork in my hand. I stuck it into the hay cart, turned around without saying a single word, went to my room, packed my stuff, without one further word, and went off. Emancipation, well, that word has different connotations for each of us depending on our life's history, but that was emancipation.'[77]

During these first years following the collapse of Hitler's dictatorship, 'when national pride migrated wordlessly into pride in the economy',[78] Habermas became firmly convinced that it was no less than a duty of his generation to confront the question of individual guilt and the collective responsibility of the Germans – especially since it was not at all clear that the spirit and authoritarian mentality of the regime had simply disappeared together with it. Habermas probably did not yet know Bertolt Brecht's phrase – 'The womb is fertile still, out of which this crawled'[79] – but its meaning corresponds precisely to what he, and many of his peers, are likely to have felt.

In retrospect, Habermas concluded that

> the intellectual vanguard of the old regime . . . – with a few exceptions
> – [had] survived de-Nazification unharmed. They felt immune to
> criticism from others and saw no reason to be critical of themselves.

The personal and intellectual continuities that persevered unimpeded beneath a layer of anti-communism which formed part of the repression of the past,* on the one hand, kept awake fears of a relapse into the authoritarian patterns of behaviour and elitist intellectual habits of pre-democratic Germany. And, in my case, these fears persisted even into the early 1980s. On the other hand, the anti-anti-communism with which we reacted to the unsettling character of the Adenauer era was accused of being totalitarian thinking.[80]

---

* 'anti-communism which formed part of the repression of the past' translates the compound noun 'Verdrängungsantikommunismus', which implies a psychoanalytic interpretation of post-war political attitudes as caused by the psychological mechanism of repression.

2

At University in Göttingen, Zurich and Bonn

'*I was highly politicized.*' The 'profile of the Adenauer era', with its political climate of restoration, in combination with the 'revelations concerning Auschwitz, [after which] nothing could be taken at face value', soon created the firm conviction in the young Habermas that a new start, in a democratic spirit, was needed.[1] 'For me', he would later recall,

> 'democracy', not Anglo-Saxon liberalism, was the magic word. The political constructions in the tradition of *Vernunftrecht*,* with which I was familiar from the popular accounts of them available at the time, combined with the pioneering spirit and the emancipatory promise of modernism. As students, we felt all the more isolated in the unchanged authoritarian setting of post-war society. The continuity of social elites and cultural prejudices through which Konrad Adenauer marshalled consent for his policies was stifling. There had been no break with the past, no new beginning in terms of personnel, no change in mentality – neither a moral renewal nor a reversal of the political mindset.[2]

His fundamental political attitude, in Habermas's own words, had been 'a product of "reeducation"':[3] in the years immediately after the war, he had had the chance both to learn the value of the democratic constitutional state introduced by the Western powers and to realize that it was of central importance to defend it and to be sensitive to any kind of uncontrolled power formation. Under the title 'Demokratie auf der Schlachtbank' [Democracy on the chopping block], the independent weekly newspaper *Der Fortschritt* in March 1954 published a long letter to the editor written by the then 23-year-old Habermas. In it, he pleads for the implementation of a

---

* Term for the Enlightenment conception of law as based on reason, which emerged throughout the seventeenth and eighteenth centuries through the secularization of the natural law tradition.

democratic practice in which 'citizens [act] as the ultimate and only selecting authority'. 'Who emerges as the best from the competition depends on their judgement. But if they are meant to judge, then it is necessary at least to present the competition in a comprehensible fashion.' For that, Habermas says, open and public debates are needed, as are parliamentary forms and political parties that guarantee that deviating views are heard. 'We need representatives again who have the stature and the will to take personal decisions.' Admittedly, the author of this letter is inclined towards an elitist conception of democracy, according to which the deeper meaning of democratic competition lies in identifying the best individuals. However, this kind of 'formation of an elite' is meant to be the result of an exchange of opinions that should take place in the absence of external influence and without pressure to toe the party line. Habermas bemoans the fact that in the realm of politics the influential party politician, the party official, wins out over the better argument. Democracy, he says, will end on the 'chopping block' unless there is success 'in sending independent individuals into the parliaments'.[4]

For the summer term of 1949, Habermas registered at the venerable 'Georgia-Augusta', the Georg August University in Göttingen, in order to major in philosophy, with history, psychology, literary studies and economics as minors. 'I was highly politicized. As I did not have any friends yet, and was also somewhat bored, I visited election campaign rallies and encountered practically all the figures who later entered Adenauer's cabinet or played some other important role.'[5]

During his time as a student in Göttingen, Habermas witnessed the ceremonies, radio speeches and debates that accompanied the founding of the two German states in May and October 1949. The conservative parties narrowly emerged as the strongest political force in the first election to the Bundestag, and Konrad Adenauer was elected as the first chancellor of the Federal Republic of Germany. The liberal politician Theodor Heuss became the first president of the Federal Republic and, in 1949, spoke publicly about the 'collective shame' of the Germans. In his inaugural speech, Paul Löbe, the 'Alterspräsident'* of the Federal Republic's first parliament, reminded his listeners of the burden of the National Socialist heritage, whereas Adenauer, in his first declaration of government policy, did not so much as mention German responsibility for the murder of more than 6 million Jews. And 'not a single German newspaper [demanded] a public declaration on the murder of the Jews, be it

---

* The title given to the oldest member of the parliament.

from the parliament or the federal government.'[6] The politically alert Habermas was outraged that the government employed individuals who had been active in the administration, in the judiciary or on the political scene at the time of the National Socialist regime, and that the young democracy did not take its renunciation of the old 'values' seriously enough.[7]

The young student, living as a lodger in Göttingen, took the obligatory entrance examination with the 68-year-old philosopher Nicolai Hartmann, though not on the latter's material ethics of value or ontology. Instead, Hartmann asked questions about Rilke and Kant. 'My studies', Habermas would later say,

> were characterized by a dichotomy between my philosophical and my political convictions. Only later did I realize that there was no real connection between the two. My interest in dramatic literature, in Georg Kaiser, Hasenclever, Wedekind and, of course, Sartre, served a mediating function. I could well imagine that the discussions about dramaturgy were the medium in which to discuss political questions at a higher level of generality.[8]

Apart from those with Hartmann, Habermas took other classes with Hermann Wein, who was working on a 'Realdialektik' [Dialectic of the Real],* as well as seminars with the historians Percy Ernst Schramm and Hermann Heimpel. There is conclusive evidence that the medieval historian Schramm held important positions during the Nazi period, for instance within the High Command of the Wehrmacht. Heimpel, the professor of medieval and modern history, who – as the director of the Max Planck Institute of History, founded in Göttingen in 1956 – was considered to be one of the most prominent representatives of his discipline after the war, was reputed at least to have sympathized with National Socialism. Habermas remembers living in relative isolation during his two terms in Göttingen. Apparently, he had enough time and leisure to write a play titled *Der Pazifist* [The pacifist] and to produce a draft for a dissertation on the theme of the 'Akt der Toleranz' [The act of tolerance], which he presented to Hermann Wein – and all this at a time in his studies when he had only just begun to familiarize himself with academic philosophy. There were plans for a production of the play at a small theatre, but the director, Hans Tietgens, had edited the text so substantially that Habermas withdrew his consent.

Alongside his studies, Habermas familiarized himself with those intellectual and cultural modernist movements that had been

---

* Hermann Wein, *Von hegelscher Dialektik zu dialektischer Anthropologie*, Munich, 1957.

prohibited as 'degenerate' in the Nazi era. In particular, he developed an interest in the fine arts. As early as 1946–7, he became acquainted with modernist painting, especially expressionism, through Josef Haubrich's collection of modernist art in Cologne, which Haubrich had been able to preserve throughout the Nazi period and the Second World War. As Habermas recalls: 'In museums in Düsseldorf I got to know contemporary painting – above all Baumeister and Nay, the two I appreciate most, but also Winter, Schumacher and Werner.'[9] In 1959, he visited the documenta II in Kassel,* where the expressionist works of pre-war modernism were exhibited alongside the most recent contemporary works of 'action painting' by Jackson Pollock, Franz Kline and Willem de Kooning. The predilection for abstract art of both Habermas and his wife is evident from their private collection, which contains works by, among others, Günter Fruhtrunk and Sean Scully. Habermas wrote in his homage to the latter, titled 'Traditionalist der Moderne' [The traditionalist of modernism]: 'Scully does not share the narcissistic doubts about modernism's capacity to continue.'[10]

Habermas recalls that during his time as a student he went to East Berlin a few times

> to the Schiffbauer Damm Theater,† as long as Brecht wasn't allowed to be performed where we were. . . . On the same occasion I also went to Humboldt University to visit the old seminar of my teacher Nicolai Hartmann. Those were the few contacts I had with the official world over in the East, which seemed as strange, as horrifying, and as authoritarian to me as the guards at the Friedrichstrasse subway station.[11]

While at university, Habermas read 'poems from Trakl to Benn', discussed the plays of Georg Büchner, Arthur Miller and Bertolt Brecht with his fellow students, and read Thomas Mann's novel *Doctor Faustus*, Hermann Hesse's *The Glass Bead Game* and Franz Kafka's *The Trial*. The contemporary films that were soon screened in post-war Germany played an important role for him – for instance, Carol Reed's *The Third Man*, starring Joseph Cotten and Orson Welles, and Marcel Carné's *Children of Paradise* [Les Enfants du paradis] (with Jean-Louis Barrault), as well as *Orpheus* and *Es war einmal* (also known as *Beauty and the Beast* [La Belle et la bête]) by Jean Cocteau, both of which had Jean Marais in the leading role.

---

* One of the world's most important exhibitions of contemporary art. First organized by Arnold Bode in 1955, it takes place every five years in Kassel.
† Brecht and Helene Weigel founded the theatre company Berliner Ensemble in 1949. In 1954, it moved from the Deutsches Theater to the Theater am Schiffbauerdamm, where it is still based today.

Habermas thus became familiar with avant-garde artists and saw them as preparing the way for the 'intellectual-moral renewal' he thought Germany urgently needed.[12]

Even back then, Habermas followed daily politics attentively. Because of his left-wing inclinations, he had his difficulties with the political parties standing for the elections in 1949. In the case of Kurt Schumacher's Social Democratic Party (SPD), he was concerned about the emphasis on the national question, which he considered anachronistic. In the newly founded CDU, there were too many individuals who represented continuity with the NSDAP for his liking. In 1949, Habermas attended an election campaign rally of the national conservative Deutsche Partei in Göttingen. This was a party that saw itself as, among other things, the mouthpiece for the expellees' associations. When those at the rally began to sing the first verse of the German national anthem alongside Hans-Christoph Seebohm – who, after the election, would be appointed to Adenauer's cabinet as transport minister – Habermas left the hall in disgust.[13] If he sympathized politically with anyone during these first years after the war, it was with Gustav Heinemann, who would later resign as minister of the interior in protest at the FRG's rearmament, pushed for by Adenauer.

> When I was eligible to vote for the first time, in the national elections of 1953, I cast my second ballot for the GVP*, Heinemann's party. With the first ballot I gritted my teeth and voted for the Schumacher SPD, which was far too nationalistic for my taste. Adenauer, the politics of normalization of an old man with a limited vocabulary, made my hair stand on end. Not only was he completely out of touch with the experiences and expectations of the younger generations, but he was also utterly insensitive to the kind of mental damage that was the cost of a restoration of attitudes, and not just attitudes, that throve under his wing.[14]

In 1950, with the outbreak of the Korean War, the Cold War suddenly heated up, a development presaged by the crisis in Iran that had been unfolding since 1945. That same year, Habermas went to study in Zurich for the summer term, something that was exceptional, even a privilege, for a German student at the time. Thanks to financial support from his father, who encouraged his son to go abroad, Habermas had the pleasure of studying for a term at the renowned University of Zurich. Zurich, which came through the war largely unscathed,† was an attractive place and was the first

---

* Gesamtdeutsche Volkspartei – the All-German People's Party.
† On 4 March 1945, Zurich was accidentally bombed by American planes, which dropped some 25 tonnes of explosives and incendiaries. There were five casualties.

major city outside Germany in which Habermas was able to spend an extended period of time – a gateway to the world for him. In the suburb of Oerlikon, he set himself up in a small room which he shared with Hans Herberg, a friend from his days in Gummersbach, with whom he used to play chess. At the university, he attended lecture courses and took seminars in philosophy, German literature and history. Among the professors who made a lasting impression on him were the philosophers Hans Barth (famous for his book *Wahrheit und Ideologie*, published in 1945),* who lectured on Marx and Nietzsche that summer term, and Wilhelm Keller, who offered a seminar on Kierkegaard. In his free time, he visited exhibitions at the Kunsthaus Zürich and frequently went to the theatre. There were productions of plays by, among others, Brecht and Hans Henny Jahnn at the Zurich Schauspielhaus. Habermas also went on extensive cycling tours through the Swiss countryside, with all its lakes and mountains. At the end of term, he and his friend cycled to the canton of Ticino, all the way to Chiasso, where they boarded a train to Rome – a journey that was free of charge to foreigners in the 'jubilee year for pilgrims'.

At Bonn University, where Habermas studied with great ambition from late autumn 1950, following his two terms in Göttingen and his intermezzo in Zurich, nothing resembling a renewal could be felt.[15] On the contrary, he encountered the 'world of the old German university'. The students, who were accorded the status of adults as a matter of course, typically addressed each other with the formal 'Sie', or with 'Herr' and 'Fräulein'. Only among friends was the informal 'du' commonly used. In philosophy seminars, the tone was set by the academic teachers. From them one could, to be sure, learn something about the pre-Socratics, about the thought of Wilhelm Dilthey or Humboldt, about Husserl, Martin Heidegger and neo-Kantianism; but the ability '[t]o pose radical questions and then answer them in a systematic way' was not being taught.[16] Despite the fact that the University of Bonn was seen as conservative in comparison to Göttingen, Habermas decided to go there, both for personal reasons and to pursue some promising opportunities. He had not felt comfortable in Göttingen, where he had failed with his project for a dissertation, and a friend from his youth, Manfred Hambitzer (who had been wounded in the war), had whetted his appetite for the city on the Rhine by mentioning an open-minded theatre group based there. Habermas had also heard through the grapevine that the seminars of the philosopher Rothacker, some of whose work he had read, were characterized by an atmosphere of open discussion.

---

* English edition: *Truth and Ideology*, trans. Frederic Lilge, Berkeley, CA, 1977.

In terms of his historical and political interests, Habermas felt most at home in the Department of History, headed by Richard Nürnberger, whose courses covered current issues such as the Yalta Conference, and who discussed the early writings of Marx in his colloquia. Habermas delved deeply into the new publications by Sartre, who – in part through his writings for the stage – opened the door to a new world for him. And he again occupied himself with Otto Friedrich Bollnow's volume on *Existenzphilosophie* [Existentialist philosophy], first published in 1940,* which he had already acquired as a schoolboy. Despite his 'brown' past,† Bollnow – a former member of Alfred Rosenberg's anti-Semitic Kampfbund für deutsche Kultur [Fighting League for German Culture] and of the NSDAP – had resumed teaching as a professor in Mainz as early as 1946. Wilhelm Jerusalem's *Der Pragmatismus* [Pragmatism], published by the Viennese philosopher and sociologist in 1907, also came to Habermas's attention during his schooldays; he had found it on his father's bookshelves.

During the years 1950–1, in his first terms at the Department of Philosophy in Bonn, where Wilhelm Perpeet was an assistant and Otto Pöggeler, Karl-Heinz Ilting and Hermann Schmitz were all working on their dissertations, Jürgen Habermas soon made an acquaintance who would be of the utmost importance during his later life. He got to know Karl-Otto Apel, seven years his senior and, with his doctorate already completed, assistant to Rothacker. As Habermas would recall decades later, Apel 'became philosophical mentor to a small group of students'. His character expressed 'the fundamental concerns of philosophy itself . . .: not to abandon the insights of hermeneutics, not to let go of any of the hermeneutic virtues, always to remain sensitive to historical context, always to seek out the strengths in the thoughts of an opponent.'[17] Apel, who harboured no illusions about the 'destruction of moral consciousness' experienced by his generation,[18] certainly noticed the talent in his young student. As Apel tells it, Habermas was not one of those who would set the tone in seminars or who stood out through his contributions to the discussions; rather, he had a reputation for being able to write remarkably quickly and well, and for putting down highly original ideas on paper. Apel was a talker, Habermas a writer.[19]

Habermas was so impressed by Apel's style of philosophizing that there developed a friendship between the two which has lasted to the

---

* The first edition of 'Existenzphilosophie' actually appeared in *Systematische Philosophie*, ed. N. Hartmann, Stuttgart, 1942.
† 'Trotz seiner "braunen" Vergangenheit': the expression 'brown past' is a colloquial term for someone who was involved in National Socialism, as brown was the colour of the NSDAP's uniforms.

present day. In particular, Apel's early reception of various strands of the philosophy of language would later have a decisive influence on the development of Habermas's own theories.

What about the influence on Habermas of the two full professors at Bonn, Erich Rothacker and Oskar Becker? Both had been very close to the 'National Socialist movement'.[20] The historian of science Gereon Wolters even called the sixty-year-old Becker – a former pupil of the phenomenologist Husserl and his assistant at the same time as his contemporary Heidegger – a 'Germanic-Nordic racist' who cultivated an 'anti-Semitism for aesthetes [*Schöngeister*]'.[21] Becker was banned from teaching after the war but was reinstated as a professor in 1951, thanks in no small part to Gadamer's support. He tried to formulate an alternative to Heidegger's *Being and Time*, an alternative which is forgotten today.[22] Because of his work on the foundations of mathematics, he is also considered to be one of the fathers of the school of methodological constructivism. According to his pupil Wolfram Hogrebe, 'his influence on the younger generation of philosophers at the University of Bonn after the Second World War is not to be underestimated', despite the fact that he 'was not an exciting lecturer'.[23] Hogrebe remembers Habermas, along with Paul Lorenzen and Karl-Otto Apel, as one of the conspicuous presences in Becker's lectures and seminars. One of Becker's classes, an 'Übung über die Philosophie Schellings' [Tutorial on the philosophy of Schelling], which he taught in the winter term 1950–1, gave Habermas the opportunity to become familiar with the works of the philosopher who would later become the subject of his doctoral dissertation.

Erich Rothacker, whose specialism was cultural anthropology, was also among the 'intellectual giants of the "Thousand Year Reich"'.[24] Early on, he had 'his finger on the pulse of the right'* and, even before 1933, signed an appeal by fifty-one university teachers to vote for Hitler. In 1933, he became a member of the Nazi Party and offered his services to Goebbels's Ministry for Propaganda with a proposed series of radio lectures to educate the people. With regard to university policies he fully adopted the aims of the party. There are no indications that Rothacker had any regrets after the war concerning his anti-Semitism and his blind accommodation to the dictatorship. On the contrary, at the first philosophy congress after 1945, he argued that one should turn one's back on the terror of the past and instead place one's hopes on a 'common denominator', one 'that must be adhered to under all circumstances' – and this, he suggested, was 'the heritage of antiquity and of Christianity'.[25]

---

* The German 'die Nase im rechten Wind' plays on the double meaning of 'right' – i.e., as referring to the 'political right' and as indicating the 'opportunistically right move'.

It is bizarre that Rothacker, in his *Heitere Erinnerungen* [Cheerful memories] of 1963, should treat his fatal involvement with National Socialism as an episode not even worth mentioning. Wolters states, not without bewilderment, that neither Becker nor Rothacker, nor many of their peers at German universities, took part in any serious attempt at 'philosophically reflecting on the horrors of war which they had directly or indirectly experienced'.[26]

It is hard to imagine that Habermas should have failed to notice the opportunism of his academic teachers. He may indeed have started to doubt that philosophy might save a person from political wrongdoing. But only shortly before completing his philosophy degree would he express his tremendous disappointment at the cowardice of a large number of philosophers, in a critique of Heidegger which was published in the *Frankfurter Allgemeine Zeitung* in 1953.

Influence of the doctoral supervisor? Decades after completing his studies, Habermas spoke of an uneasiness he felt with regard to Rothacker's politics. Nevertheless, Rothacker's project of a cultural philosophy had, he said, influenced him to some extent as a student, albeit not in a lasting way.[27] In any case, Habermas regularly attended all the lectures and seminars of his academic teacher from the winter term 1950–1 onwards, in part because he liked his interdisciplinary style of teaching. Without a doubt, he took up Rothacker's thesis that all human actions are embedded in a specific environment. He was also sympathetic towards the core claim of his cultural anthropology: that historically developed styles of living went hand in hand with particular outlooks on the world.[28] Rothacker was convinced that the types of knowledge belonging to the sciences and the humanities were guided by particular worldviews. Rothacker's influence on Habermas is demonstrated by the fact that he preferred the former's approach to cultural anthropology to Arnold Gehlen's naturalistic variant of it.[29]

Rothacker, for his part, seems to have thought highly of his doctoral student. He heavily annotated and preserved a paper Habermas had written for a seminar on Humboldt's philosophy of language, which Rothacker taught together with the linguist Leo Weisgerber in the winter term 1950–1 – a forty-page typescript, divided into fourteen sections, on the topic of 'Zeichen und Bedeutung' [Sign and meaning].[30] In it, the 21-year-old Habermas refers to texts by, among others, Husserl, Heidegger, von Humboldt, Cassirer and Bühler, as well as Weisgerber and Gehlen. The paper concentrates wholly on terminological clarification through a purely phenomenological analysis. In one of the central passages, Habermas provides a justification for the thesis that signs have their foundation in language and that beings without language therefore have no signs. Extensive parts of the paper are dedicated to the origin of signs and the significance of the primordial act of pointing which these origins show. Some points of this seminar paper can be read as anticipations, on a smaller scale, of the later theory of communication. For instance, Habermas talks about the 'circular structure of communication' and says: 'in all likelihood the desire for communication was the initial genetic trigger for the development of language.'[31] The following sentences from a section on 'Die Offenbarung' [Revelation] are characteristic of the writing style of the young student, which was still heavily influenced by the language of Heidegger: 'In the emergence of the sign out of the act of pointing the concealment of entities takes place. Words have stepped in front of the entities. Entities come towards us from out of the words. Thus, entities have entered into a new rupture. In the word, entities show themselves in that form in which they were received in the act of pointing.'[32] In an addendum, Habermas discusses what he calls the 'fundamental structure of speech' and reaches the conclusion that pointing is 'a limping substitute for speech itself'.[33] In an article written for the publisher S. Fischer's *Lexikon Philosophie* [Dictionary of philosophy], written four years after he had completed his studies and while he was at the Institute for Social Research, Habermas in a few short paragraphs refers explicitly to Rothacker's anthropology, more precisely to his concept of 'Lebensstil' [Style of life], in order to draw attention to the 'interconnectedness of attachment to the environment and openness to the world'. Historically acquired styles of living, he says, 'take the place of the "innate" forms of existence of animal species'. Paraphrasing motifs from Rothacker, Habermas writes: 'Humans live and act only within the concrete lifeworlds of their specific societies, never in "the" world.' Thus, he uses Rothacker to criticize forms of thought which assume anthropological constants and proceed 'ontologically, so to speak'.[34]

In the same year he completed this dictionary entry, 1958, Habermas also contributed to a large Festschrift for Rothacker. On the one hand this was an act of personal loyalty, while on the other it was an academic convention that Habermas apparently wanted to follow. Nowhere in his article, entitled 'Notizen zum Verhältnis von Arbeit und Freizeit' [Some notes on the relationship between work and leisure], is there any mention of the philosophy of his doctoral supervisor; instead Habermas repeatedly refers to Marx and the research findings in industrial sociology. The text, which contains some terminological vagueness in its sociological passages, pleads for an 'emancipatory' use of the increasing amount of free time in developed societies. Free time could be used to participate in political life, he says, because only through active commitment is it possible to contribute to the 'control of the execution of political power'.[35] These theses are a far cry from Rothacker's ideas, and the text reveals hardly any common ground between the two.

Apart from the seminars of these two full professors, who were both burdened by their past, Habermas attended the courses on Husserl offered by Johannes Thyssen and studied with the cultural philosopher and educationalist Theodor Litt, who presented a hermeneutical method informed by Dilthey in lectures delivered in a style ready for print. In Apel's estimation, the philosophy of the latter had to be ranked above that of his two colleagues. Litt had requested retirement in 1937 because of restrictions to his academic freedom. In 1947 he was appointed to a chair in Bonn, and in 1948 he published his *Mensch und Welt – Grundlinien einer Philosophie des Geistes* [Man and world – principles of a philosophy of spirit]. After the war, his work was focused predominantly on the renewal of educational science as well as on the nature of the relationship between the individual and society.

As a student in Bonn, Habermas studied Humboldt's philosophy of language in depth and, through Apel, came into contact with American pragmatism for the first time. He became acquainted with Fichte and Hegel by studying them on his own, as no seminars on them were offered. He would later comment, with at least a hint of irony, that 'from the academic stand-point, [he] grew up in a provincial German context, in the world of German philosophy, in the form of a declining neo-Kantianism, of the German Historical School, of phenomenology, and also of philosophical anthropology. The most powerful systematic impulse came from the early Heidegger.'[36] In addition, the writings of Max Scheler, Arnold Gehlen and Helmuth Plessner played a role in Habermas's philosophical development, as did those of Leo Weisgerber.

Doctorate on the philosophy of Schelling

Man's naturalness and historicity. Habermas's doctoral thesis, 'Das Absolute und die Geschichte: Von der Zwiespältigkeit in Schellings Denken' [The absolute and history: on the ambivalence in Schelling's thought], which he 'dedicated in gratitude' to his parents, testifies to the fact that Heidegger's fundamental ontology was a point of reference for him. The thesis was completed in February 1954, after only nine months. It presents an interpretation of the philosophy of the ages of the world on which Schelling had worked from 1810 onwards, at a time when his reputation as a child prodigy of his discipline was a distant memory. At the early age of sixteen Schelling had been given special permission to join the Tübinger Stift, where he studied with his older friends Hölderlin and Hegel and, in all likelihood, co-authored 'The oldest system programme of German

idealism' with them in 1795. At just twenty-three, Schelling became
a university teacher in Jena, where he joined the circle around the
two Schlegel brothers.

The doctoral thesis of the 24-year-old Habermas concentrates on
Schelling's writings from the years between 1809 and 1821, in which
the latter speculates on the Creation and on the relationship between
God, world and man. The thesis is 424 pages long and is divided into
thirty-four sections. Habermas planned and wrote it almost on his
own, with little advice or supervision from any of the three professors
Rothacker, Becker or Litt. It remained unpublished; only the typescript copies required by the faculty exist. At the end of the work, its
author felt obliged to remark: 'The difficulties of the exposition reflect
a lack of sovereignty over the material, which, in turn, is founded in
the genuine disproportion between the horizon of my own experience
and that of a philosophical genius of Schelling's stature. I considered it only appropriate not to veil this disproportion with editorial
measures.'[37] Some of the dissertation's central theses found their way
into an article that Habermas wrote eight years later. This article
was based on a lecture he gave in Heidelberg and was later (under
the title 'Dialektischer Idealismus im Übergang zum Materialismus
– Geschichtsphilosophische Folgerungen aus Schellings Idee einer
Contraction Gottes' [The transition from dialectical idealism to
materialism – some conclusions for the history of philosophy to be
drawn from Schelling's idea of a contraction of God']) incorporated
into *Theorie und Praxis* (1963), his second book.*

In his dissertation,[38] Habermas considers the following question:
How did this philosophical 'genius', who reflected on the historical existence of man as a unity of nature and spirit, conceive of the
relationship between the finite world and the absolute?[39] Habermas
analyses this relationship as a paradox, and in his interpretation of
the historicity of the absolute he examines the different phases in
the development of Schelling's philosophical system. Does Schelling
succeed in reconciling the philosophical reflection on the ultimate
foundations of all being with the historicity of the human world? Is
it just his diagnosis of a 'crisis of rational science' that is compelling,
or does he also coherently explain his claim about the priority of
being over thinking?

Habermas concludes that Schelling, who was as aware 'of man's
pre-historical naturalness as he was of man's historicity which alien-
ates him from nature',[40] failed with his speculations on the ages of
the world. Habermas thought it problematic that Schelling conceives of the historically unconditioned against the background of

---

* The article in question is not part of the English edition: *Theory and Practice*, trans.
John Viertel, London, 1974.

an ontological proof of God and anthropomorphism. Thus, he says, despite breaking with the priority of the I over nature, Schelling nevertheless is ensnared in the philosophy of the subject which he implicitly, as Heidegger, after him, explicitly, wants to overcome. Habermas criticizes Schelling for deriving the historical mode of being from a something, a primordial ground which, while itself without any grounding, is ahistorical.

Schelling understood creation as a two-sided act by God, an act that is interpreted as a negating withdrawal as well as an affirming opening up. One of the aims of Habermas's thesis is to investigate how this mystical history of creation influenced the wider thought of Schelling. With a touch of pathos, Habermas declares on one of the final pages: 'Thus, by bringing about the fall of God's perfect creation, man has started the process of the history of God anew. . . . The knowledge [of man, S. M-D] of himself as existing historically is the *lumen naturale* that he may use for lighting his dialectical endeavours to gain knowledge, and this is something he must do if he wants to fulfil his world-historical mission of bringing God's history to its end.'[41]

Only after he had completed the thesis did Habermas come across Karl Löwith's *From Hegel to Nietzsche*, in which the author reflects from the perspective of an increasing historicization on the dissolution of the Greco-Roman concept of the cosmos and of Christian-humanist thought, as well as on the way in which Marx and Kierkegaard appropriated the philosophy of absolute spirit. Habermas later said: 'It made such an impression on me that I subsequently added an introductory chapter on the Young Hegelians to my dissertation after I had completed the main part.'[42]

The later article on Schelling that formed part of *Theorie und Praxis* further elaborates on one of the ideas already touched upon in the thesis. Habermas tries to show that Schelling's idea of a sublation of political violence (as manifested in the form of the state) 'anticipates certain intentions of historical materialism'.[43] This includes, he argues, the ideas of a redemption of nature and the emancipation of man.[44]

Rothacker's report on the thesis emphasizes the rare talent of the doctoral student not only for dealing well with material from the history of philosophy but also for establishing its relevance for contemporary philosophical problems by applying a systematic approach. The thesis, he writes, 'unites both talents to a degree that has become rare today'. Rothacker concludes: 'It is altogether an outstanding piece of work. Its author may be counted, without hesitation, as on a par with junior lecturers. I cannot think of another mark doing more justice to the work but *egregia*.'[45]

The PhD examination caused Habermas some anxiety, as he had been left entirely to his own devices while writing the thesis and preparing for the *viva voce*. The latter took place on 24 February 1954 and included, apart from the major subject of philosophy, medieval and modern history (with Max Braubach as examiner) and psychology (with Vinzenz Rüfner as examiner) as minor subjects. The report on the examination, signed by the dean, Heinrich Lützeler, says: 'As an overall mark for the examinations we award: *magna cum laude.*' The graduation took place in the Baroque Hall of the Rheinische Friedrich-Wilhelms-Universität Bonn as part of the first formal doctoral awards ceremonies after 1945. The few letters exchanged between Rothacker and Habermas in the mid-1950s attest to the great appreciation that the professor had for his doctoral student, now turned doctor of philosophy, and vice versa. But Habermas, despite the age difference between them, did not see himself as a pupil of Rothacker in the sense of a faithful adherent, something he also expressed in his letters.[46]

In Bonn, Habermas concentrated wholly on the study of philosophy, in contrast to his time in Göttingen and Zurich. But he nevertheless continued to follow political events very closely, mostly by reading the newspapers, and he regularly visited the theatre in Bonn, Cologne and Düsseldorf. He watched plays by John Steinbeck, Eugene O'Neill, Paul Claudel, Sartre and François Mauriac. He also joined the student theatre group, directed by Hans Tietgens, and was involved in starting a university film club. Tietgens would later make a name for himself in adult education. Together with Habermas and Günter Rohrbach, he was a member of a discussion group which met regularly after joint visits to the cinema or theatre. There were passionate discussions and disputes at these meetings. Rohrbach, who went on to become one of the most important television and film producers in Germany, recalls that it was almost impossible to watch a film with Habermas without having to discuss it for two hours afterwards. According to Rohrbach, Habermas's main interest throughout these protracted exchanges was in discussing the socio-political effect of the films and plays, an interest inspired in him by Siegfried Kracauer's approach to film.[47]

With Tietgen's ensemble, Habermas travelled to the annual meeting of student theatre groups in Erlangen.[48] He also got involved in the Contra-Kreis-Theater, particularly well known in the university town Bonn. Apart from the classical authors, this theatre also produced contemporary plays such as *Les Mains sales* [Dirty hands] by Jean-Paul Sartre, *The Glass Menagerie* by Tennessee Williams, *The Living Room* by Graham Greene, and Arthur Miller's *All My Sons*. Günter Rohrbach and Wilfried Berghahn, who later founded the journal *Filmkritik*, also participated in the various student initiatives. Rohrbach mentions the fascination which the films of Italian neo-realism, in particular, exerted on the members of the group at the time: Luchino Visconti's *The Earth Trembles* [La terra trema];

Roberto Rossellini's *Rome, Open City* [Roma città aperta], starring Aldo Fabrizi and Anna Magnani; Vittorio de Sica's *Bicycle Thieves* [Ladri di biciclette]; and Michelangelo Antonioni's *Story of a Love Affair* [Cronica di un amore].

Another member of the inner circle of friends was Manfred Hambitzer, from Habermas's days in Gummersbach. An intense friendship developed over time between Habermas and Berghahn in particular. Berghahn, who studied in spite of the wishes of his family, had early on fathered a daughter and was thus forced to earn additional money by occasional journalistic work. He had met his wife Susanne, a seamstress, while still in his last year at school in Detmold and married her in 1952 in Bonn. This circle of friends shared a critical perspective on the daily politics of the young Federal Republic, as well as an interest in any novel development in the arts. At the beginning of the 1960s, Berghahn, then based in Munich, would visit the most famous European film directors and interview them for an exclusive series as part of the cultural programme of the Bayerischer Rundfunk.[49] Like Habermas, Berghahn did his doctorate in Bonn and, at the age of twenty-six, wrote his first study on Robert Musil, which was later turned into the well-known book *Robert Musil in Selbstzeugnissen und Bilddokumenten* [Robert Musil: a portrait in autobiographical notes and pictures]. He died of skin cancer in 1964, aged only thirty-four, but already a well-known literary and film critic. On his deathbed, Berghahn asked for his friend's promise to take care of his wife and two children. Four years later, Habermas would dedicate his *Knowledge and Human Interests* to him.

Speaking out as a freelance journalist

When the snake of philosophy narcissistically curls up for the eternal conversation of the soul with itself, the instructive objections of the world fade away unheard.[50]

The sound of Heidegger. Instead of attempting to pursue an academic career straight after his doctorate, the 24-year-old Habermas first chose to follow the professional path of a freelance journalist. In conversation, he said that he had been tired of intellectual work in general and of philosophy in particular.[51] The fact is that there was no position as an assistant for him in the Philosophy Department in Bonn, as he wrote to Hans Paeschke in May 1954.

Despite financial pressures – in a letter to the editor of *Merkur*, he remarked that he had to 'plan [his] journalistic activities according not only to inclination but also to economic need'[52] – Habermas turned down reviews and returned copies of books to newspaper editors if he considered them lacking in substance. Encouraged by its cultural editor, Adolf Frisé, he published articles in the *Handelsblatt*. He also published regularly in the large national newspaper *Frankfurter Allgemeine Zeitung* with the help of Karl Korn, who was both the cultural editor and one of the co-editors,[53] and in the renowned *Merkur* and the *Frankfurter Hefte*. Habermas often had to face objections from editors regarding the content and formal aspects of his texts. His correspondence with Hans Paeschke and Joachim Moras, the two editors in chief of *Merkur*, is one source of evidence for this. *Merkur*, the *Deutsche Zeitschrift für europäisches Denken* [German journal for European thought; *Merkur*'s subtitle], was founded in 1947 and for a long time remained in a precarious financial condition. For authors, it is an attractive place to publish, not only because of the high quality of its articles but also because it 'stands for the introspective search for the reasons underlying the moral and political catastrophe and for a widening in perspective which takes Western Europe as its point of reference.'[54] It is not surprising, then, that Habermas was very much attracted to it. Taking Christoph Martin Wieland's *Der Teutsche Merkur* as their model, the founders and editors of the journal excelled at soliciting contributions from across the political spectrum – from conservative authors such as Arnold Gehlen, Gottfried Benn, Ernst Jünger, Martin Heidegger, and even Carl Schmitt, to 'liberals' such as Theodor W. Adorno, Hannah Arendt, Jean Améry, Ralf Dahrendorf and, of course, Jürgen Habermas.[55]

Habermas's journalistic pieces cover a fairly broad range of themes. Apart from reviews of contemporary radio plays – a sophisticated literary genre in those days, which fascinated Habermas as providing a kind of 'acoustic stage' – he wrote film and theatre reviews, numerous book reviews (in which, from time to time, he referred to his academic teachers Becker and Rothacker) and critical essays on contemporary themes such as mechanization and the working world, the power of bureaucracy and the dangers of mass society, among others. He had already proven his journalistic skills while studying philosophy. The short-lived newspaper *Die Literatur*, for instance, published an article of his under the title 'Wider den moralpädagogischen Hochmut der Kulturkritik' [Against the arrogance of cultural criticism as moral education], which clearly demonstrates what was going through his head at the time. He draws on contemporary philosophical literature and asks, against the backdrop of anthropological research (Gordon W. Allport, Arnold Gehlen), about the relationship between man and technology, which he considers to be the key for an understanding of such social phenomena as the isolation of the individual, the eradication of differences between individuals and their increasing uniformity and mobility. 'As an instrument for the science-based domination of nature, its [technology's, S. M.-D.] character is that of a method that has become autonomous. . . . In analogy to logistics, technology develops out of the autocracy of the instrument.' Habermas considers the debate over technology's indifference towards purpose ['*Sinnindifferenz*'], as it is commonly practised in cultural criticism, to be just as inadequate as the attitude which moralizing educators take towards technology. Despite its considerable length, the article does not give a positive answer to the question of how we should deal with technology and suggests only that, instead of presenting premature answers, we should try to account for the significance of technology.

Habermas's review of a new edition of Gottfried Benn's *Die Stimme hinter dem Vorhang* in the *Frankfurter Allgemeine Zeitung* of 19 June 1952* shows that, on the one hand, he had some sympathies for the 'life-form of the artist', because it is 'totally self-sufficient', 'independence through inconspicuousness'. On the other hand, he registers some reservations not only against the 'anti-humanist catechism of absolute form' but also against the young Benn's credo that real life takes place in the ecstasy of the instantaneous. The second 'voice of the poet behind the screen', Habermas emphasizes, 'demands the justification of life, which is now experienced as historical existence.'

In a review of a run of puppet shows based on pieces by Pergolesi, Mozart and Offenbach and organized by the Bildungswerk [educational centre] and the student union, we read: 'We are well advised to take puppet plays seriously, so that we can have fun watching them.' The review, published in the *Frankfurter Allgemeine Zeitung* on 29 January 1953 under the title 'Die Ironie der Holz- und Gipsköpfe' [The irony of block and plaster heads], expresses the reviewer's fascination at the plays' capacity for parody, at the 'comic effects of the movements' and at the 'expressivity', in particular of the choreography.

A recurring theme of Habermas's journalistic work comes out clearly in his review of Ludwig Landgrebe's *Major Problems in Contemporary European Philosophy, from Dilthey to Heidegger.*† It was one of the first reviews he published, and it appeared in the culture section of the *Frankfurter Allgemeine Zeitung* on 12 July 1952. Here Habermas claims that all the 'glory and disaster' of Western thought 'found its conclusion in the technology of modern times'. Adopting a Heideggerian turn of phrase, he demands a change: 'Man must take on an attitude of listening to the things and learning to let them be, instead of dominating them.'[56] In this piece,

---

* Gottfried Benn, *The Voice behind the Screen*, trans. Simona Draghici, Washington, DC, 1996.

† New York, 1966. The original German title is *Philosophie der Gegenwart* (1952).

a still very young Habermas introduces a conception of progress
in which reason demands 'a kind of self-limitation' with regard to
what is technically possible, economically profitable and socially
effective.[57] He discussed the same theme in a lengthy report on the
meeting of the Association of German Engineers and an exhibition
on industrial design in Stuttgart, which was published on 30 May
1953 under the title 'Der Moloch und die Künste' [The Moloch and
the arts], again in the culture section of the *Frankfurter Allgemeine
Zeitung*. As a faithful Heideggerian, which he was at that point and
would continue to be for a considerable time, he denounces the domination of technical means over their practical purpose. Absolute
expediency, he writes, is a myth – as can be seen when looking at the
'carelessness' of technology 'towards things'. Technological products 'dictate to us what has to be considered as useful'. This, he says,
is 'the rule of the means', and this rule is the 'reason that the things
become separated from man and at the same time the reason for the
carelessness shown by man towards the things.'

In a sharply polemical film review spread over four columns
in the *Süddeutsche Zeitung* of 2–3 October 1954, Habermas criticized a film called *Morgengrauen* [Dawn]. The film, directed by
Viktor Tourjansky, was about the end of the war, and Habermas
was irritated in particular by the 'carefree attitude of a restoration
which ignores facts and experiences . . . when, for instance, presenting the defeat in 1945 as on a par with a lost tennis match.' In
the *Handelsblatt* of 6 January 1955, he published a glowing review
of a *Merkur* almanac, edited by Hans Paeschke and Wolfgang
von Einsiedel, under the title 'Deutscher Geist zwischen Gestern
und Morgen' [German spirit between yesterday and tomorrow].
Habermas wrote the piece at short notice, over a weekend, under
pressure from the cultural editor Adolf Frisé. In it, he examines
the question of how German intellectuals confront their own past.
The tone of the discussions, he writes, is set by 'the reign of grand
old men'. However, they face a youth that is without illusions and
that has a critical attitude towards pathos and any totalitarian
tendencies.

An article Habermas wrote for the fifth volume of the *Deutsche
Studentenzeitung* (published by the Association of German Student
Unions) just after the completion of his doctorate is worth men-
tioning because it reveals his political attitude at the time. Dieter
Wellershoff, who had written his PhD in Bonn on Gottfried
Benn, was in charge of the editorial work for the paper. Under
the heading '"Ohne mich" auf dem Index' ['Without me' on the
index],* Habermas analyses the reasons for the weariness about poli-

* The title suggests that certain political circles are trying to place the 'without me'

tics displayed by 'his' generation, particularly its younger members – a topic which was continually lamented during those years. The article begins with the thought that the way in which realpolitik is practised must be disappointing, especially for any citizen who is politically interested and enlightened. And such disappointment leads to indifference – i.e., a 'quietist inclination towards the private life, towards the personal and intimate'. Habermas further explains that citizens do not apathetically turn away from politics as such but, rather, from the political practices of the ruling parties: 'For there is a difference between someone not having any interest and someone being hindered from expressing their interest in a socially relevant way.' Therefore, he concludes, it is too simple to take the attitude of 'without me' as fundamentally expressing the disposition of today's youth. 'It is not the dates of birth but the responsiveness [*Resonanzen*] which separate the minds.' The explanation for the sceptical attitude, especially among the younger generation, towards any kind of accommodation to the status quo, Habermas says, can be found in the experiences both before and after 1945: in the haste with which de-Nazification had been carried out, the past had been laid aside, and Germany had claimed to play a role in world politics again. But he explicitly denies that his generation is generally uninterested in politics – and he apparently means this to apply to himself as well. However, it is true that a political and social order to which one could commit oneself still has to be found. There are plenty of concrete reasons for having reservations about politics, he writes. For instance, he sees German policies regarding Europe as unhelpful when it comes to the matter of ending the confrontation between East and West. He also criticizes the declared aim of almost all parties to restore the unity of Germany as nationalistic and the aspiration to rearm the Bundeswehr as ultimately undemocratic. In response to this article, the paper's editor received six lengthy letters, all of which agreed with the author.

An article on the occasion of the centenary of Søren Kierkegaard's death, which appeared on 12 November 1955 in the *Frankfurter Allgemeine Zeitung*, is remarkable for its length alone. Habermas interprets the work of Kierkegaard – who attended Schelling's lectures and whose thinking, according to Habermas, took the form of a 'dialogical refraction of the content of thought' – as a 'provocation of existence' [*Existenzprovokation*] and as a 'literary experiment' that makes use of the 'dialectical forms of pathos, of irony, and of humour'. Habermas refers mostly to some important letters of Kierkegaard's that had just appeared in German translation. They

---

attitude, which the article defends, on the index – i.e., to assume a position of authority and declare it impermissible.

show, he says, that 'his authenticity consists in showing others his inauthentic sides.' The aim of the 'father of existentialism' was 'to compensate' for the loss of meaning of religious teachings 'with a provocation of inwardness'.

In a review of the third edition of Karl Jaspers's *Philosophie* [Philosophy], in vol. 23–24 of the *Deutsche Universitätszeitung*, Habermas speaks positively about the 'impetus of a self-reflective philosophy' he finds in the existentialist philosopher's work. He agrees with an Enlightenment conception of philosophy which aspires to be more than an exact science, but which can also not simply ignore scientific thinking. 'Science guarantees the correctness, but philosophy in addition the significance of its findings.' It is noteworthy that Habermas expresses doubts over whether what Jaspers calls his liberal model of science based on competing authorities on knowledge and 'rational discussion' is sufficient in order to reach binding conclusions. Although discussion, he says, tends to turn into polemic, it can also 'be contained within the tolerant forms of rational communication . . ., because in principle all partners . . . can participate in a concrete truth.'

Writing on the occasion of Karl Jaspers's seventy-fifth birthday in the *Frankfurter Allgemeine Zeitung* of 23 February 1958, Habermas presents a portrait of him as a philosophical thinker who formulates the possibility of universal communication as a complement to the pluralism of traditions in world history. Habermas argues in terms of a philosophy of history by confronting Jaspers with the objective character of being as a power [*Herrschaftscharakter des Seins*]. Towards the end of the essay he talks about philosophy being saved by the distinction between belief (which is fundamental to it) and scientific insight. He writes: 'Jaspers's demand: in going beyond all doctrinal partisanship to hold on to one major partisanship, namely that in favour of reason . . . – this demand ends up undermining itself when it accepts the need to hold on not only to this partisanship but also to the impossibility of determining it in the form of rational propositions.'

Sociological and political themes. As a journalist Habermas wrote not only on philosophical topics but also on sociological and political questions. In the *Frankfurter Allgemeine Zeitung* of 23 July 1955, he proclaims no less than a 'comeback of German sociology', which he anticipated would take place in the wake of the publication of a *Lehr- und Handbuch zur modernen Gesellschaftskunde* [Text- and handbook on modern social theory], edited by Arnold Gehlen and Helmut Schelsky, as well as that of a dictionary of sociology. In his enthusiasm, the reviewer overlooks the fact that German sociology had by no means been forced 'into quarantine' during the Nazi period but that, on the contrary, there was continuity within the discipline – a fact attested to not least by the careers of the two editors of the handbook themselves. In this review, Habermas openly sympathizes with Gehlen's anthropology and speaks highly of the family as a 'binding element' and countervailing force in opposition to the anonymity of the big city. But he also expresses his appreciation for Otto Stammer's contribution to the handbook, titled 'Politische Soziologie' [Political sociology]. Stammer highlights the danger of democracy 'becoming a formal rule for the formation of a political will and its "idea" becoming frozen' as a result – a motif that would occupy Habermas throughout his entire career.

In 1955, at the ninth meeting of the society 'Der Bund' in Wuppertal, Habermas gave a talk on 'Kulturkonsum und Konsumkultur' [Consumption of culture, culture of consumption]. Helmut Schelsky had invited him to the meeting, and Arnold Gehlen, Günther Anders and Hans Freyer were also due to present papers.[58] In his comments on the theme of the meeting, which he would later elaborate further, Habermas refers to the 1950 book by David Riesman, *The Lonely Crowd* (German edition: *Die einsame Masse*, 1958), and defends the thesis that false consciousness 'takes on, so to speak, the nature of a factual power in the form of an externally controlled system of habits of consumption. That part of it which remains consciousness is the simple representation of the status quo on its surface and the prohibition to make visible the possibilities contained in actual reality.'[59]

In his review of Gehlen's *Urmensch und Spätkultur* [Primordial man and late culture] in the *Frankfurter Allgemeine Zeitung* of 7 April 1956, Habermas agrees with the diagnosis of contemporary society as suffering from a 'chronic ego-centeredness', but he strongly denies that this is a causal effect of the destabilization of institutions. In this review, Habermas not only talks of the 'burden of resentment' that Gehlen 'built up over a long time' but also accuses him of 'adopting the rationalist elements of enlightenment and . . . turning them against its humanist elements.'

An article in the *Frankfurter Allgemeine Zeitung* of 13 April 1957 reads as a sociological essay and critique of contemporary society. Here Habermas tackles a topic that clearly exercised him a lot at the time, namely the relationship between work and free time – or, rather, the thesis that the sphere of consumption reflects the compulsion to labour. Thus, he observes that people increasingly 'embark on a [strange] hunt for experiential riches' during their free time. The level of the productive forces 'would allow for the satisfaction of practically all needs', and yet the 'consumer, nevertheless, is kept in a state of neediness by a form of production which satisfies his actual needs only at the price of arousing new needs – new needs which are needs of production itself and no longer of human beings.'

Habermas's early journalistic work is often critical of culture and politics.[60] Although he would later classify these journalistic pieces as 'youthful sins',[61] they are more than just the immature productions of a young man trying in vain to gain a footing in the profession in which he initially wanted to make a living. Between 1952 and 1956, when he finally took up his post as an assistant in Frankfurt, he wrote more than seventy articles, most of which were published. He continued with journalistic work sporadically throughout his life, and he successfully used the print media as a forum for his critical commentaries and intellectual interventions. News journalism in the narrower sense, however, was never his cup of tea, even if he did occasionally take on assignments. His interests at the time were the conspicuous developments in intellectual and cultural life, and he had a particular interest in contemporary issues. In his early journalistic work, he was hesitant to draw political conclusions or to make political statements. There are no decisive expressions of opinion on Adenauer's policy of integrating Germany into the West, the uprising of 17 June 1953 in the GDR, or Germany's one-sided policies regarding military pacts, or on questions concerning German unity or European economic union.

It was only towards the end of the 1950s – with the 'turning of the tide' which led to a 'new political culture'[62] – that Habermas really began to show his true political colours. The triggers for this were the debate over the rearmament of the Federal Republic, which had once more become a sovereign state in 1955, and Adenauer's political path of restoration, which was becoming increasingly apparent. However, in the context of the domestic and foreign policy of the time it was impossible to push through the political alternatives Habermas had in mind, such as strengthening democracy in West Germany, confronting the crimes of the Nazi regime, turning away from the idea of a German 'Sonderweg',* and opposing the rearmament of the Bundeswehr. Remilitarization proved impossible to avoid. As the Cold War intensified, several of the member states of the North Atlantic Treaty, which had been signed in April 1949, had ended their opposition to West German rearmament, among them the USA and Canada. The Federal Republic of Germany joined NATO on 6 May 1955. On 14 May, eight Eastern European countries, including the GDR, under the leadership of the Soviet Union, reacted by signing the 'Treaty of Friendship, Cooperation and Mutual Assistance' (the Warsaw Pact). The widespread anti-communist atmosphere that dominated West German society meant that the CDU/CSU's political platform – freedom, security and sovereignty – was so successful that Adenauer was elected three times, in 1953, 1957 and 1961.

---

* See second footnote on p. 10.

The Bundeswehr was being built up from the time when the General Treaty of Paris finally took effect in 1955. In 1957, the year of the founding of the European Economic Community, the dispute in domestic politics over the Bundeswehr acquiring nuclear weapons capabilities intensified. Eighteen leading scientists, including the Nobel Prize winner Max Born, Otto Hahn, Werner Heisenberg, Max von Laue and Carl Friedrich von Weizsäcker, voiced their opposition in the so-called Declaration of Göttingen and announced that they would not 'participate in any way in the production, testing, or deployment of nuclear weapons'. A group of well-known intellectuals, among them Heinrich Böll, Erich Kästner, Axel Eggebrecht and Eugen Kogon, echoed the demands of the 'Göttingen Eighteen'.* Thus, the idea that remilitarization was the price to be paid for the Federal Republic's integration into the West was increasingly opposed by an ever more politicized public. In March 1958, the parliamentarian Walter Menzel, a member of the opposition SPD, started a campaign called the 'Kampf dem Atomtod' [Fight against nuclear death], which Habermas would join. In the spring there were mass rallies in several of West Germany's biggest cities, one of them in Frankfurt am Main, where Habermas was among the protesters. Under the title 'Unruhe erste Bürgerpflicht' [Unrest is the citizen's first duty],† he wrote in the Frankfurt student newspaper *Diskus* on 20 May 1958: 'Today it is no longer possible to prevent war by preparing for war'. He continues:

> It is therefore no coincidence if those politicians arguing for a policy of strength suffer from pangs of conscience. They do not even dare to call the thing by its name any longer. Some time ago the Nazis spoke of 'fresh milk without cream' when selling skimmed milk to the people. Today the politicians arguing for strength speak of the 'most advanced weapons' when selling A- and H-bombs to the people. It is magical practice – they turn events which lie outside the power of humans into a taboo. It is a magical picture of the world altogether – in each of their opponents they sense the powers of darkness and of 'remote control' at work.‡

---

* An allusion to the 'Göttinger Sieben', a group of seven professors in Göttingen who protested against the abolition of the comparatively liberal constitution of the Kingdom of Hanover in 1837. They were removed from their positions, and some had to leave the country.

† Inversion of a public notice in Berlin by Graf von der Schulenberg-Kehnert after the lost battle of Jena and Auerstedt in 1806: 'Jetzt ist Ruhe die erste Bürgerpflicht' [Now, keeping calm is the citizen's first duty]. It is still often used ironically in order to imply that someone is politically passive.

‡ 'Fernsteuerung', remote control, was an oft-used metaphor expressing the idea that the political actions of politicians and states were actually guided by Moscow as the communist centre of power.

Habermas criticizes the logic of a 'politics of strength' as well as a democracy that practises a 'politics of *faits accomplis*', in which the 'power' of the people is increasingly reduced to giving the nod to the decisions already taken by the government.[63] Habermas accuses the conservative government of having 'a picture of democracy' according to which 'it is desirable that the mass of citizens may be treated as a mass of immature individuals, so that, in the case of the crucial political questions, everything is decided for the people, but nothing together with the people.'

As a journalist Habermas wrote mostly for the print media, but from time to time he also took to the airwaves. His first more substantial contribution for radio caused a stir in intellectual circles. It formed part of a series created by the journalist Thilo Koch at Norddeutscher Rundfunk and was titled 'Der deutsche Idealismus der jüdischen Philosophen' [The German idealism of the Jewish philosophers]. Habermas concludes his contribution with a claim that was certainly intended to be provocative, namely that

> the Jewish heritage drawn from the German spirit has become indispensable for our own life and survival. . . . If there were not extant a German-Jewish tradition, we would have to discover one for our own sakes. Well, it does exist; but because we have murdered or broken its bodily carriers, and because, in a climate of an unbinding reconciliation, we are in a process of letting everything be forgiven and forgotten too . . ., we are now forced into the historical irony of taking up the Jewish question without the Jews.[64]

After completing his doctorate, Habermas was at first hesitant about pursuing an academic career. However, it became clear that he could not make a living on the basis of his journalistic activities alone. With support from Rothacker, he therefore applied to the German Research Foundation and received a two-year grant for a project on the concept of 'ideology'. The results from this period of study, in which Habermas deals extensively with the theories of Karl Marx and with Marxism, among other things, have never been published as a complete text, although elements found their way into a number of later articles.

Marriage. Habermas had already met his future wife during his first terms at Bonn University, where she studied history and German philology. Ute Wesselhoeft, born on 6 February 1930, was in her third term, and the two became acquainted through the courses given by the historian Richard Nürnberger. Female students were relatively few and far between in those days, and the male students courted Ute Wesselhoeft. Habermas invited her to the cinema. But it was only on a student excursion to a national meeting of university-based theatre groups that they became close friends. They shared an interest in modern art, film and literature, and both followed daily politics avidly.

Their wedding took place on 30 July 1955 in Bonn. A few weeks later, the couple went on holiday to the Dutch island of Schiermonnikoog, where they stayed in the Hotel Duinzicht. Of course, the newly-weds also visited the parents of the bride, Dr Werner Wesselhoeft, an economist, and Anna Margareta Wesselhoeft (née Watermann), who lived in Düsseldorf, at Golzheimer Straße 113, and had known their son-in-law for two years.

As an historian, Ute Wesselhoeft had of course told Habermas about the ancestry of the family he was marrying into. In 1798, one branch of the Wesselhoefts had settled in Jena, where Johanna Charlotte Wesselhoeft (1765–1830) married the well-known publisher Carl Friedrich Ernst Frommann (1765–1837). All the famous figures of the time, among them Goethe, Fichte, Hegel and Schelling, visited her salon in Jena. Two foster children grew up in the Frommann household, one of which was Hegel's illegitimate son, Ludwig, who later went missing while working for the East India Company. In the next generation, Robert Wesselhoeft (1796–1852), the son of the book printer Johann Carl Wesselhoeft, made waves in the world. As the head of the Jena Jünglingsbund,* i.e., the fraternity, he was one of those who made the invitation to the Wartburgfest.† After the prohibition of the student fraternities in the wake of the Carlsbad Decrees,‡ he was arrested in January 1824 and sentenced to fifteen years' imprisonment. He was pardoned after spending seven years in a prison in Magdeburg and shortly thereafter emigrated to the USA, where he worked as a medical doctor together with his brother Wilhelm Wesselhoeft. In Brattleboro (Vermont), the two of them founded an institution for hydrotherapy, and they are today considered to be among those who paved the way for homeopathy in the United States.

Ute Habermas-Wesselhoeft grew up in a Protestant family with a tradition of oppositional politics, in which political questions were discussed freely and openly. From the very beginning the family was antipathetic to the National Socialist ideology. Werner Wesselhoeft sympathized with the Tat circle, whose organ was *Die Tat*, a successful monthly journal edited between 1929 and 1933

---

* Literally 'Association of young men' – a secret organization which developed out of student fraternities.
† The Wartburgfest in 1817 was a meeting of students and some professors who were protesting against the reactionary politics that characterized many Germany states and calling for a German national state.
‡ A number of repressive measures agreed at a meeting called by Prince von Metternich after the assassination of the reactionary poet August von Kotzebue by Karl Ludwig Sand, a member of the radically democratic wing of the student fraternities.

by Hans Zehrer. Wesselhoeft had originally left the Church, but during the Nazi era he joined a brotherhood which belonged to the oppositional movement of evangelical Christians, the 'Confessing Church', which had formed around Martin Niemöller and Dietrich Bonhoeffer. Shortly after the war, in 1946–7, Werner Wesselhoeft contributed to a volume edited by Julius Ebbinghaus, a philosopher at Marburg University. The book was called *Die große Not* [The great destitution], and in his piece, 'Selbstbesinnung' [Self-reflection], Wesselhoeft demanded that those Germans who were incapable of a revolutionary coup towards the end of the war should ask themselves why they had been 'plunged into the deepest abyss of human misery'. He argued that a blind sense of duty, as well as the influence of propaganda, had made it easy for the Nazi faithful to commit the most cruel and abominable deeds without suffering any pangs of conscience. The ideology of the Volksgemeinschaft [people's community], he said, had grown in fertile soil during a time that saw the progressive 'mechanization of spirit and soul'. As an antidote to National Socialism, which he called the 'enemy of all', Wesselhoeft recommended democracy, understood as a political order that 'knows no duties decreed from above that would need to be carried out unthinkingly'.[65]

The daughter of this committed democrat attended an all-girls secondary school in Düsseldorf. After her state examination at Bonn University, for which she wrote a thesis on the itinerant priest Bockelson and the Anabaptists of Münster, Ute Habermas-Wesselhoeft did her teacher training and then worked for some time as a Studienassessorin.* Jürgen and Ute's marriage produced three children: Tilmann (born in 1956), Rebekka (born in 1959) and Judith (born in 1967). The two older children decided to embark on academic careers, while Judith pursued a career in publishing.

It is difficult to overestimate the significance of the role Habermas's wife played in his political commitment; it was and continues to be an intellectually lively marriage. The majority of the texts later collected in the series *Kleine Politische Schriften* [Short political writings] did not leave Habermas's desk without Ute giving them the nod. And in questions concerning history, politics or the arts, Ute, with her wide-ranging education, was the children's first port of call.

What role did Habermas play in this family? Well, it could be said that it was the role of a traditional father. His academic ambitions as a university teacher took priority and he increasingly intervened publicly as an intellectual. When he worked at home – and that was almost always – his family respected his need for quiet. In short, the Habermas family exhibited the classical distribution of gender roles.

---

* Title of a teacher who has not yet been approved as a civil servant.

As he later put it: 'I only fully realized the joy of having children, and of being with them, after I had become a grandfather. The father was too involved in the events of the day, and lacked distance from them, when he should have been there for his children more often.'[66]

The beginnings of a career as a public intellectual

It is this capacity to get irritated which turns scholars into intellectuals.[67]

The public sphere is a stage. Whoever steps onto it must be prepared for the possibility of evoking the disapproval of the audience. This was precisely the experience Jürgen Habermas, as a 24-year-old student, had when he first walked out onto that stage.

At some point towards the end of July 1953, with the weekend approaching, Karl-Otto Apel gave Habermas a copy of Martin Heidegger's recently republished *Introduction to Metaphysics*, a publication without any commentary of the latter's 1935 Freiburg lecture course on the topic. Apel drew Habermas's attention to a passage towards the end of the course in which the author speaks of the 'inner truth and greatness of this movement'.* Habermas, who had held Heidegger in high regard up to that point, could not believe what he had read: '[H]ow can one of our greatest philosophers do such a thing?'[68] His outrage at 'this lecture, which is suffused with fascism down to the level of stylistic detail', led him to write an article within a matter of days.[69] The form of this article shows that there was more at stake here than an admirer of Heidegger suddenly realizing how opportunistically the revered thinker had actually behaved and continued to behave.

> Thus, today protection [*Hut*], recollection [*Andenken*], guardianship [*Wächterschaft*], graciousness [*Huld*], love, apprehension [*Vernehmen*], surrender [*Ergeben*] are spoken of wherever, in 1935, the violent deed was called for . . .. The appeal changed colours at least twice, according to the political situation, while the conceptual pattern of the summons to authenticity and of the polemic against fallenness remained stable. The lecture of 1935 mercilessly unmasks the fascist colouring of that time.[70]

Above all, Habermas's article is an expression of his disappointment with, and anger at, the 'communicative silence' [*kommunikatives*

---

* Martin Heidegger, *Introduction to Metaphysics*, trans. Gregory Fried and Richard Polt, New Haven, CT, 2014, p. 222.

Beschweigen] concerning the recent past. Habermas saw this 'silence' as closely connected with the anti-communist attitude that became mainstream after the bloody suppression of the workers' revolt in the GDR by Russian tanks on 17 June 1953.[71]

For Habermas, '[t]he only way to come to terms with [his] incredulous outrage was to put it in writing.'[72] The only person to whom he showed the finished manuscript was Ute Wesselhoeft. Neither of them will have harboured any illusions about the extent of the possible damage to Habermas's reputation, and most likely they also talked about the possible consequences publication might have for his chances in securing an academic career. At the time, it was simply considered indecent to remind anyone of the fact that not so long ago they had practised the Hitler salute as one of the Führer's faithful Volksgenossen [national comrades]. The scandal was unavoidable. Habermas sent his text to Karl Korn,[73] who printed it, under the heading 'Mit Heidegger gegen Heidegger denken' [Thinking with Heidegger against Heidegger], on almost a whole page of the *Frankfurter Allgemeine*'s supplement 'Bilder und Zeiten' on 25 July 1953.

Apart from Heidegger's jargon, the elitism of his intellectual style, and his natural aversion to the democratic egalitarianism of the Western tradition, Habermas was particularly taken aback by the comment about the 'inner truth and greatness' of the National Socialist movement. Heidegger had openly sympathized with the 'völkisch *revolution*' even before 1933, and as a member of the NSDAP he was evidently fascinated by Hitler. As Jaspers suspected, Heidegger apparently had the idea of 'wanting to lead the leader'.[74] Habermas did not so much reproach the Freiburg philosopher of fundamental ontology for these sympathies and delusions and the political error on which they are based; nor did he want to denounce his philosophy. What infuriated him was the fact that Heidegger was prepared to publish these lectures almost eighteen years after they had been given, and just eight years after the end of the war, without commentary and with only minor amendments to the text. In other words, Heidegger had made no reference at all to the incomprehensibility of the events that had taken place or to his own calamitous political misjudgements. Heidegger had at no point broken his silence on the Shoah. Habermas, as a student of philosophy, grew up within the Heideggerian intellectual cosmos,[75] and he was now confronted with the question of whether this seemingly heroic refusal of critical self-reflection was not, after all, connected with the substance of Heidegger's philosophy. His article poses the question:

> Can the planned murder of millions of human beings, which we all know about today, also be made understandable as fateful errancy

in terms of the history of being as fateful? . . . Is it not the foremost duty of thoughtful people to clarify the accountable deeds of the past and to keep the knowledge of them alive? Instead, the majority of the population, and most of all those responsible then and now, practise continued rehabilitation. Instead, Heidegger publishes his eighteen-year-old words about the greatness and inner truth of National Socialism. . . . It appears to be time to think with Heidegger against Heidegger.[76]

However, Habermas apparently did not want to say farewell to Heidegger's *prima philosophia* altogether. He seriously asks the question of whether it can be saved in the course of its own critique.[77] Can the truthful substance of Heidegger's thinking of fundamental ontology, which makes him 'the most influential philosopher since Hegel', be distinguished from the ideological errors and political misinterpretations of his analysis of Dasein, an analysis of Dasein which 'seeks to ground human Dasein from itself both in its historicality and in its totality'?[78] According to Habermas, the deficiencies in Heidegger's thought consist, on the one hand, in the fact that the diagnosis of the forgetfulness of being [*Seinsvergessenheit*] ignores its own prehistory, part of which is an idea of God, which culminates in the Christian ideas of equality and freedom. On the other hand, in Heidegger,

the dialectical plasticity of modern developments does not emerge clearly; it is this dialectic that gives creative legitimacy to that form of thinking which aims at mastery through objectification . . . . Added to this, however, is an elementary self-deception on Heidegger's part. He presented his insights, which were supposed to lead to the encounter between planetary technology and modern man; he lectured on these insights in 1935, under conditions that were established by this technologically determined situation and that were still very much in effect. It was thereby virtually inevitable that he would initiate that automatism of misunderstanding that falsified his intention of overcoming technologized life when this intention was actually carried out.[79]

Habermas's new critical perspective on Heidegger constituted a revision of his hitherto thoroughly positive view of the latter's philosophy. Heidegger's thought had informed Habermas's doctoral thesis on Schelling – which was incomplete at that point – as well as his review, published on 12 July 1952 in the *Frankfurter Allgemeine Zeitung*, of a new publication by the phenomenologist Ludwig Landgrebe. At the end of his highly favourable review of Landgrebe's book *Major Problems in Contemporary European Philosophy, from Dilthey to Heidegger*, Habermas wrote that the post-war philosophy of 'the older professors' first had to reach the required standard before it could then 'enter into a fruitful discussion with Heidegger'.[80] But now he did not see Heidegger exclusively as an exceptional thinker. He certainly was that, Habermas thought – but now he had also been exposed as a representative of a generation that had failed twice within a short period of time. The two full professors at Bonn, Becker and Rothacker, also belonged to this generation, and Habermas knew about their involvement with the Nazi regime. It was also his father's generation, and with his father Habermas shied away from private discussions about these matters. Instead, he focused on the 'godfather' of German philosophy and, for the first time, referred to what he called the 'guard kept by public critique'. From that point on, he would fulfil this function of intellectual guardianship with increasing vehemence.

Habermas's article elicited various responses. Christian E. Lewalter from Hamburg, the conservative cultural editor of *Die Zeit* (which, under the chief editorship of Richard Tüngel, was far from liberal at the time), in the edition of 13 August 1953, situated Habermas in proximity to Adorno, who was described as a phobic character given to hasty denunciations of others: '[a]s a neo-Marxist', Lewalter writes, Adorno 'practises the journalistic persecution of all alleged "fascists", from Richard Wagner to Ernst Jünger.' Lewalter further accuses Habermas of 'hatefulness' and of suffering from a 'compulsion to persecute', arguing that the sentence about the 'inner truth and greatness of this movement', which Habermas cited as evidence, actually relates to the 'encounter between technology and man' and was, in truth, a critical remark about the Nazi movement.

Habermas published a letter to the editor in the *Frankfurter Allgemeine Zeitung* of 29 August as a direct response not just to Lewalter, but also to the journalist Rudolf Krämer-Badoni and the essayist and critic Egon Vietta, among others. *Die Zeit* had refused to print the letter. Habermas writes: 'Does Heidegger today limit himself to rendering the Nazi movement intelligible within the context of the history of Being, and does he, as a consequence, become a "symptom" himself, namely a "symptom" of our general tendency towards rehabilitation . . .?' And he further explains:

> My highly revered teacher, Prof. Rothacker, once said in a stimulating seminar that Heidegger always must ask the question: Which way will you roll, little apple? This is an amusing expression for the fundamental dependency [*Ausgeliefertheit*] of a thinker belonging to Being for whom everything new, simply because of its newness, acquires the rank and honour of being the authoritative measure as a temporal particularity [*das Jeweilige*].

Thus, the question needs to be asked 'whether those mistakes [*Fehlleistungen*] which were made on certain occasions, and not because of certain historical and destined conditions, are also to be accepted *en bloc* as destiny, or if what occurs in such instances is not, rather, a call for truth that one is either able to answer or not able to answer.' The same edition of the paper featured a sharply worded letter to the editor by Wilfried Berghahn, who said it was a catastrophe 'that eight post-war years have passed without the most basic intellectual conditions for coming to terms with fascism being established.' Berghahn took the side of his friend Habermas, as did Karl Korn, who presented him as the 'philosophically well-trained representative of a student generation' and as possessing a new intellectual attitude.[81] Two weeks later, Korn went on the offensive again, summarizing the development of the controversy for the paper and quoting passages on the theme of guilt from *Being and Time*.

How did Heidegger himself react? The philosopher – who usually considered 'the publicness of the "they"' an abomination – finally, on 24 September 1953, spoke out by way of a letter to the editor of *Die Zeit*. He confirmed Lewalter's interpretation with respect not just to the incriminating sentence but also to the lectures in general: 'his [Lewalter's] interpretation of other sentences identifies my political position since 1934 correctly.' In conclusion, he remarks: 'There are today only very few who can gauge what, at most, it was possible to say in such a lecture at the time. But I know that those listening among the listeners did understand very well what was being said.' Three weeks later, Martin Heidegger would deliver his acclaimed lecture on 'The Question Concerning Technology' to a packed audience at the Bayerische Akademische der Schönen Künste, followed by a discussion with Werner Heisenberg which attracted public attention.* Hans Carossa, Ernst Jünger and José Ortega y Gasset were also present at Heidegger's lecture, which ended with the ominous words 'For questioning is the piety of thought.'[82] These words were certainly not aimed at Habermas.

No matter how divided the public was at the time, and no matter how unequal the opponents – in one corner the established master thinker, in the other an unknown student of philosophy – the controversy Habermas sparked off marked the beginning of a long process which would gather momentum from '1968' onwards. Sons and daughters began publicly to put questions to their parents and teachers; the young democracy began to grow up.

---

* Heisenberg spoke on 'Das Naturbild der modernen Physik' [The image of nature in modern physics] as part of the lecture series in which Heidegger's 'The Question Concerning Technology' was delivered.

Three decades later, following the publication of books by Víctor Farías and Hugo Ott, Heidegger's involvement with National Socialism was again being publicly discussed.[83] Habermas repeated his accusation that Heidegger had evaded the topic of the singularity of the destruction of European Jewry by consciously making use of an 'abstraction through essentialization';[84] and he continued to criticize his *transformation* of theory *into world views*' [*Verweltanschaulichung der Theorie*].[85] But at this point the mood with regard to 'Heidegger-bashing'* had long since shifted, and Habermas also made clear that '[t]he clarification of Martin Heidegger's political behaviour must not serve the purpose of a wholesale debasement. . . . [As] we belong to those born later who cannot know how *they* would have behaved under the conditions of a political dictatorship, we are well advised to refrain from moral evaluations of actions and omissions during the Nazi era.'[86] This warning against cheap inferences from the person to his work, something Habermas would stress repeatedly, has a concrete biographical background. For he at no point made a secret of the fact that Heidegger's philosophy, before the 'turn', had left a strong impression on him, and had left traces in his own thinking as well as the thinking of intellectual figures close to him. Herbert Marcuse, for instance, a disciple of Heidegger, attempted a Marxist transformation of existentialist philosophy. And Habermas, in his own way, continued Heidegger's project of overcoming the philosophy of consciousness. In his lectures *The Philosophical Discourse of Modernity*, published in 1985, he returns once more to the question of the connection between Heidegger's life and work. Here he interprets the later Heidegger's theme of the abandonment of being – the loss of the meaning of being – less as an expression of regret at his involvement in the German catastrophe and more as an attempt to find an explanation of it, an arrangement with it, and a justification for it, for himself. The later philosophy, Habermas says, is 'the result of the experience of National Socialism, of the experiences of an historical event, experiences which *befell* Heidegger, so to speak'.[87] In short, Habermas blames Heidegger not so much for his attitude during the years of Nazi rule as for his refusal to admit his wrongdoings after 1945.

Without a role model? Of course, Jürgen Habermas was not the first 'thinker', and certainly not the first philosopher, to assume the role of public intellectual in order to criticize the manner in which the Germans deal with their history. Thomas Mann is particularly noteworthy in this regard,[88] as is Karl Jaspers, who was banned

---

* 'Heidegger-bashing' in English in the original.

from publishing and had been forced into retirement by the Nazis in 1937. Jaspers was involved in re-establishing the University of Heidelberg after the war and accepted an invitation to take up a full professorship in Basle in 1948. Early on he had condemned the Germans' indifference to their historical responsibility.[89] As mentioned before, Habermas had by all accounts been impressed and inspired by Jaspers's *The Question of German Guilt*, published in 1946, in which he writes that 'all citizens of a state are collectively responsible for the political guilt of a criminal state.' Jaspers saw at the time, Habermas writes, 'without a sense of political liability, the continuity with a state which established concentration camps, and with a society in which the murder of arbitrarily defined minorities had become possible, would not end.'[90]

Dolf Sternberger's statements on political attitudes towards the past also influenced Habermas. Sternberger was responsible for the journal *Die Wandlung*, in which he published a number of his own articles. Habermas was also influenced by the discussions of National Socialism and the genocide in the *Frankfurter Hefte*, which Eugen Kogon, Walter Dirks and Clemens Münster edited from 1946 onwards.[91] And regarding the blindness of many Germans to the destruction of European Jewry, the publications of Theodor W. Adorno, who returned to Germany only at the end of 1949, were of particular importance for Habermas. Just a few weeks after his return from the USA to the University of Frankfurt, Adorno had put his finger on the open wound of German guilt through his critical pieces on contemporary issues. Habermas did not yet know Adorno personally, but nevertheless he could not have missed the latter's dictum from his 1951 essay 'Cultural Criticism and Society': '[t]o write poetry after Auschwitz is barbaric.'[92] He might also have listened to Adorno's radio talk 'Die auferstandene Kultur' [The resurrected culture], broadcast on 18 April 1950 as part of the *Abendstudio* [Night studio] programme of the Hessische Rundfunk and published in the *Frankfurter Hefte* in May 1950. Here Adorno argues – much as Hannah Arendt was arguing around the same time in her article 'The Aftermath of Nazi-Rule: Report from Germany' in the journal *Commentary* – that the Germans are evading the question of what has happened. Instead of reflecting on the causes of totalitarianism, Adorno says, there is a flight into the safety of tradition and the past. His thoughts culminate in the thesis that, in post-war Germany, education has the function of 'letting the past horror and one's own responsibility be forgotten and repressed'. 'Culture [is a suitable means] for covering up the return to barbarism.'[93] Hannah Arendt also reaches the conclusion that all the Germans' bustle serves only to fend off the reality of the past. There is, she says, a general indifference; totalitarianism continues to have an effect even under democratic conditions. The

Allies' de-Nazification programme blurs the differences between the various reasons for joining the party: membership could sometimes be explained by need and fear, but it had sometimes been a voluntary decision made out of conviction. In addition, those who were not de-Nazified, and thus compromised, constitute a politically dangerous interest group.[94] However, it was Adorno who explicitly referred to the critical function of intellectuals in his increasingly frequent public statements, and who created a new role through his specific kind of public use of reason – a role that clearly appealed to the young Habermas. Indeed, his talk of the 'guard kept by public critique' in the article on Heidegger may even be a first reference to this new role model, whose closeness he would soon seek.

PART II
Politics and Critique

Historical experiences are only candidates for the conscious appropriation without which they cannot exercise an identity-constituting force.[1]

3

Education intellectuelle
in Café Marx

Adorno's assistant. In the short period between 1954 and 1955, when Habermas had earned his living mostly by writing articles for newspapers and journals, he had already been supported by Adolf Frisé, an editor at the Hessische Rundfunk. Frisé, who lived in Bad Godesberg, was not only an acknowledged expert on Robert Musil but also produced the legendary *Abendstudio*, a programme which ran between 1956 and 1962 and which featured, among others, Theodor W. Adorno, Max Horkheimer, Hans-Georg Gadamer, Siegfried Lenz and Hans Magnus Enzensberger. Frisé offered to arrange for Habermas to meet Adorno, who was a distant acquaintance of his, in Frankfurt. At that time, the philosopher and sociologist was not yet as famous as he was to become in the 1960s. The conversation took place at the Café Marx – the nickname given to the Institute for Social Research shortly after it was founded in 1923; later, Georg Lukács would polemically rename it the 'Grand Hotel Abyss',[1] a label which caught on as it fitted the spirit of the time.*

Adorno, who had been delivering lectures on 'Heidegger und die sprachliche Verwirrung' [Heidegger and linguistic confusion] during the winter term 1951–2,[2] was probably interested to meet the author of the much discussed critique of Heidegger in the *Frankfurter Allgemeine Zeitung*. Habermas had also just published his first

---

* In his preface to the reissue of *The Theory of the Novel* (Cambridge, MA, 1971 [1920], p. 22), Lukács wrote: 'A considerable part of the leading German intelligentsia, including Adorno, have taken up residence in the "Grand Hotel Abyss", which I described in connection with my critique of Schopenhauer as "a beautiful hotel, equipped with every comfort, on the edge of an abyss, of nothingness, of absurdity. And the daily contemplation of the abyss between excellent meals or artistic entertainments can only heighten the enjoyment of the subtle comforts offered" (*Die Zerstörung der Vernunft*, Neuwied 1962, p. 219).' Needless to say, seen from the terraces of that hotel, Georg Lukács cut the figure of a henchman who provided an ideological justification for the totalitarian regimes of the Eastern bloc during the Cold War. The expression 'Café Marx' – an allusion to Horkheimer – gained some currency in the post-war years, when the institute's Marxist credentials became a matter of some dispute.

major article, in the August 1954 edition of *Merkur*: 'Die Dialektik der Rationalisierung' [The dialectic of rationalization]. He would later say that this article – in which he wrote of the 'pauperism in the sphere of production and consumption' – already contained the essential motifs of his mature philosophy.[3] Adorno had indeed noticed this essay on 'compulsive- and pseudo-consumption', as we know from a letter he wrote to Habermas dated 14 December 1955.[4] He invited Habermas to Frankfurt knowing that, initially, he could offer him only a kind of 'vocational placement'. Beside the fact that there were no positions available at the time, Adorno had little say in relation to appointments so long as Horkheimer was the director of the institute (which he was until 1964). He could not really make any decisions on these matters without Horkheimer.

The title of Habermas's *Merkur* article suggests some overlap with the *Dialectic of Enlightenment*, which Horkheimer and Adorno had written during their time in the USA and which was published in 1947. But, despite some clear commonalities, Habermas denied that he had had the book in mind when writing his article.[5] However, he did draw on Marx, Heidegger, Gehlen, Rothacker and the French sociologist Georges Friedmann. In a letter to Adorno, dated 20 December 1955, he confirms the date for the meeting and writes that he had studied the *Dialectic of Enlightenment* so long ago that it 'only tacitly . . . directed and enriched his approach'.[6] Nevertheless, the text contains sentences such as this: 'The occident has elevated one particular attitude to the status of exclusive authority, namely that of making available, and thus it has created a high culture whose virulence . . . constitutes a world historical novelty.'[7]

Adorno and Horkheimer's chief topics in the *Dialectic of Enlightenment* are the causes and consequences of the reduction of reason to instrumentality and the failure of the Enlightenment in the history of civilization. Habermas, by contrast, adopts a perspective that is informed in part by a critique of technology, as well as by the sociology of industry and labour, from which he investigates the phenomena of alienation in the areas of standardized production and compensatory consumption. His diagnosis, reminiscent of Heidegger's analysis of technology, is that the 'machine culture' increasingly penetrates everyday life in order to dominate it more and more:[8]

> In a machine culture, this kind of alienation becomes universal. Our world is filled with the rhythm of the machines and, the more this is the case, the less we are aware of it: machines for research fill the experimental sites, the institutes, laboratories and observatories; the machines of production fill factories and offices with their noise, with their buzzing and clicking; the machines for transport, first of all the aeroplanes and cars, move along the straits in the sky

and on the earth; the technical means of communication, such as the telephone and telegraph, the camera and microphone, connect the most distant places; the entertainment machines, from film to amuse-ment machines, make sure the nerves remain in hypertension; and the machines of civilization, from the multi-mixer to the micro-camera, produce the artificial excess in our craving for comfort. .... In addi-tion, and this is what matters in this context, those machines with the maximum reach are at the same time the ones that remove the human being the furthest from nature, from fellow human beings, and finally even from himself. Is there a chance at all that, in a manner of speaking, we may cleanse technological progress of pauperism?[9]

Despite drawing on very different sources, Habermas's cri-tique of technological rationality bears a striking resemblance to Horkheimer and Adorno's philosophical and historical interpre-tations, at least in terms of the general diagnosis. Habermas also views technological rationality as a form of domination; however, regarding the question of what to do in the face of these develop-ments, their positions differ widely: while Horkheimer and Adorno trust in the work of the concept [*Anstrengung des Begriffs*] and hope for a kind of *salto mortale* leading to an enlightened enlightenment, Habermas somewhat vaguely expresses the opinion that, in times in which 'civilization itself has become a threat', a new attitude is needed.

An article Habermas published soon after, in the *Frankfurter Allgemeine Zeitung* of 27 November 1954, adopts a similarly critical tone with regard to contemporary culture and is typical of his think-ing at the time. The title is 'Autofahren: Der Mensch am Lenkrad' [Driving: man behind the wheel], and it uses traffic as an example of the switch from technical perfection to control.[10] 'The perfect car', he writes, 'turns the ground into a track and the landscape into an area; the function of steering is "overdetermined" by centralized agencies and driving increasingly becomes an externally regulated activity.' Although the car, he says, degenerates into a 'single purpose instru-ment', driving is 'something like a hermeneutic science' in which the driver must 'permanently translate foreign texts, foreign worlds, styles, manners and quirks'.

Habermas had just passed his driving test, and so had recently become one of those 'men behind the wheel'. And he enjoyed it. He had cycled as far as the South of France (Aigues-Mortes and Le Grau-du-Roi) as a student. Now, in the autumn of 1953, together with his brother Hans-Joachim and his friend Manfred Hambitzer, he borrowed a grey 1936 Opel (nicknamed 'Little Greyling') from his parents and embarked on a journey that lasted several months. They drove to France, explored Spain, and got as far as Portugal. For the travellers, the comfort of a car was a new experience, but for Habermas it was also an ambiguous one, as he made clear in his article:

> In which way the perfection of the driver binds him, and which tendency the 'alienation' takes on in this case, becomes quite obvious when we make an overall comparison between a bicycle tour, say through the Rhône Valley down to the Mediterranean coast, and a car journey that takes the travellers all the way to Portugal and Andalusia within the same space of time. Under the tread of the car tyres the earth turns into asphalt. A transformation brought about by progress which makes man free, or however else one wants to express this process. But what is going to happen when our semi-automatons of the road become more and more automated, when the drivers are tracked and planned, and when their subordination to the instructions given by the machines, the network of roads and the norms regulating the traffic becomes ever more complete, when the energies deciding on directions are shifted more and more towards centralized agencies? Then, the car will lose not just the earth underneath but also its grip on the surface; what remains will be the 'driving lane'.

Habermas describes the narrow backstreets of Murcia, 'which the tourist guides claim is the ugliest city in Spain'; he speaks of the 'countless potholes' on 'the coastal road towards Cartagena', of the salt marshes and the donkey carts.

Following the short correspondence in December 1955 and the conversation with Adorno on 6 January 1956, Habermas became an official member of the Institute for Social Research, and Adorno's first personal assistant, in mid-February of the same year. For the first few months he received no remuneration, but from 1 August he was paid a monthly salary of 751 Deutschmarks, 1 Mark above the threshold for obligatory social insurance. 'My concern', Habermas wrote to Adorno, 'is to establish a connection with empirical social research (which, of course, does not therefore need to exhaust itself in the empirical).'[11]

Habermas's salary as an assistant was particularly welcome because his wife Ute had just given birth to their first child, Tilmann, on 17 May 1956, after having passed her first state examination in February. Although Habermas also still received the temporary grant from the German Research Foundation, this was not enough to support a family. Hence his journalistic activities, which were meant to generate additional income. Habermas had no real alternative at the time but to move from Bonn, Weberstraße 29, to the city on the Main, first into a modest room at Eschenbachstraße 36, then into a loft at Feldbergstraße 9, and finally to Wolfsgangstraße 121. An application for a teaching post as a lecturer in sociology at the University of Würzburg had failed, as had his attempts to use his contacts with the industrial sociologists Hans Paul Bahrdt and Heinrich Popitz in order to secure a post at the Sozialforschungsstelle Dortmund [Centre for Social Research, Dortmund], which was directed by Gunther Ipsen and Hans Linde, and later by Helmut Schelsky.[12]

Before all this, in the summer of 1955, Habermas had attended a meeting of German post-war sociologists, organized by Schelsky and attended by, among others, Helmuth Plessner, Heinrich Popitz, Hans Paul Bahrdt, Karl Martin Bolte and Ralf Dahrendorf, on which he wanted to write a report for the *Frankfurter Allgemeine Zeitung*. He later developed closer relationships with some of the sociologists he met there, for instance Schelsky; even with Plessner, a personal relationship would develop. But he was particularly impressed by Dahrendorf, who was the same age as him and, despite being the youngest participant, attracted attention 'with his forceful eloquence as well as his uncompromising and authoritative demeanour and his somewhat crude presentational style. What made him stand out from the rest even more was his avant-garde confidence in brushing aside old ideas.'[13] Dahrendorf's intellectual style and attitude – not wholly unlike his own – particularly impressed Habermas, and the two would go on to develop a lifelong friendship, despite the fact that Habermas was sceptical about the liberal free market ideas which began to shape Dahrendorf's views at the time.

Habermas's conclusions about the meeting were mixed. All of the papers, he wrote, had ignored the important question of whether class antagonisms and social conflicts were frozen within contemporary society, despite the fact that most workers viewed society as divided. Thus, he said, there was a danger that post-war society was on the way towards 'a kind of positive restoration', which was beginning to take shape in the form of 'a conformist attitude towards the compulsions and attainments of technological progress'.[14] One might think that this way of looking at things was also helpful in working with Adorno, the diagnostician of 'damaged life', at the Institute for Social Research.

Mutual trust between Habermas and the Adornos

During his first months at the institute, Habermas had increasingly more contact with Adorno, who made sure that he had enough work to do. He would compile literature for Adorno's papers or write introductions for empirical studies in which he had not even been involved. And, as early as the winter term 1956–7, he was meant to teach a tutorial on 'Soziologische Begriffe' [Sociological concepts] together with Helge Pross, who was two years his senior and Horkheimer's assistant. At the same time, Adorno charged him with designing an empirical 'study of the problem of leisure time'. Soon, in May 1957, Habermas would present a memorandum that would provide the theoretical basis for the intended study. Hellmut Becker had had an advisory role in drafting the memo. Habermas's point of departure is the thesis that the 'arbitrary nature of leisure activities' is a 'fiction' because leisure time is still 'to a large extent determined by the concrete shape of industrial labour'. And he develops a typology of attitudes informing the way leisure time is spent which is meant to guide the empirical investigations.[15]

Throughout those months, Habermas became a witness to Adorno's manner of thinking; this was also a new experience, and one that impressed him deeply. In retrospect, he described how Adorno's attempt at 'creating a theory of the dialectical development of contemporary society, setting out from the Marxist tradition', had affected him: 'That was unheard of for me . . . Suddenly and for the first time philosophical and political matters were being brought together.'[16] Despite 'the intrepidness' of Adorno's 'fearless thinking', Habermas also sensed that he was dealing with a personality that 'was defenceless . . . among proper adults – i.e., in situations in which routinized types exploited his weaknesses because they either did not realize or did not want to accept that Adorno's specific weaknesses were profoundly connected with his eminent qualities.'[17] He experienced his superior – who seldom acted as a superior towards him, because he was altogether incapable of dealing with institutional power – as someone who would prefer to dedicate himself entirely to his writing. Habermas developed an understanding of the peculiar role Adorno played: an anti-bourgeois bourgeois citizen who was a professor at a state university and the director of an institute that was financially dependent on research contracts,[18] and at the same time a 'freelance' intellectual who made statements on controversial contemporary issues in the media (preferably via the culturally progressive radio stations of the time) and a subversive thinker and author with literary ambitions.

Habermas had mixed impressions as a collaborator at the institute. He admired Adorno's multifaceted and unique style of thought, as well as the tradition of the Institute for Social Research. However, the predominant group spirit, which could be quite elitist, irritated him. 'I felt like a figure from a novel by Balzac – the awkward and uneducated boy from the country whose eyes are opened by the city. I became aware of the conventionality in my thinking and feeling.'[19] He did not fail to notice that 'time had two dimensions' at the institute. On the one hand, the aim was to establish sociology as a modern academic discipline in post-war Germany and to gain a reputation for the institute by carrying out relevant research projects. On the other hand, the intellectual movements that had been decisive in Germany up until 1933, including the German-Jewish intellectual tradition, were ubiquitous there. Habermas let himself be swept up in the 'lava of thought in flow'.[20] 'Never before', he would later recall, 'had I come across such a differentiated intellectual complexity in the state of its emergence – in the mode of movement before it actually solidifies into written form.'[21]

Adorno was the person closest to him at the institute, and Habermas looked to him for 'support', which Adorno provided. He 'was the first one that I really liked, loved in a certain sense, and in whom I encountered this complete incongruence between the openness, the freedom of artistic radicalness at the writing desk, and the way of life.'[22] Those were the years in which Adorno published a series of important books: *Minima Moralia* was followed by *Dissonanzen* [Dissonances] and *Metakritik der Erkenntnistheorie*;* then followed *Aspekte der Hegelschen Philosophie* [Aspects of Hegel's philosophy] and the first volume of *Noten zu Literatur*.† It was obvious to Habermas that he would read these books. But Adorno not only fascinated him as an author who 'actually lived in the world of the objective spirit at his writing desk, for whom everything else was more or less a dependent variable';[23] he was also fascinated by him as one of the few intellectuals who would speak out in public in order to make critical statements on political, social and cultural issues. For Adorno, these were issues such as the absence of a working through of Germany's past, the stalled democratization of the universities, the tendencies towards pseudo-culture [*Halbbildung*] or the manipulative effects of television, which was becoming ever more pervasive in Germany at the time.[24]

While, at the Institute for Social Research, Habermas was busy interpreting the empirical data from a survey on the political awareness of students (which, incidentally, showed that, compared to other groups in society, they had little interest in political matters), Adorno provoked the public of the Federal Republic with his claim that the people of the country did not 'truly experience it [democracy] as their own'.[25] He warned against the afterlife of National Socialism within democracy and considered this hidden afterlife to be more of a threat compared with openly fascist tendencies against democracy. Apart from his notable and continual presence as a critic of anti-democratic attitudes, Adorno, as one of the institute's directors, inspired various research projects. Habermas became familiar not only with Adorno's specific conception of sociology as a science in the service of enlightenment and with some of the professional practitioners of this discipline, such as

---

* T. W. Adorno, *Against Epistemology: A Metacritique*, Oxford, 1982.
† T. W. Adorno, *Notes to Literature*, vol. 1, New York, 1991.

Ludwig von Friedeburg and Egon Becker, but also with unconventional minds such as Alexander Kluge and Karl Markus Michel. Friedrich Weltz, born in 1927, and also an assistant at the institute, became a good friend to both Habermas and his wife. Weltz introduced the philosopher to the methods of empirical social research. Apart from Ivo Frenzel, Ulrich Gembardt, Joachim Kaiser and Thilo Koch, all of whom worked as journalists for newspapers or radio stations, Habermas developed a friendly relationship with Spiros Simitis, whom he met at one of Adorno's seminars. Simitis, who came from Greece, had studied law in Marburg and after his doctorate became the assistant of Wolfram Müller-Freienfels in Frankfurt, where, in 1963, he submitted his Habilitation to the faculty of law. The title was 'Der Sozialstaatsgrundsatz in seiner Bedeutung für das Recht von Familie und Unternehmen' [The significance of the welfare state principle in family and corporate law]. At Ute and Jürgen's home he met the psychoanalyst and Freud scholar Ilse Grubrich, whom he would later marry. The Habermases acted as witnesses at the wedding – a traditional Greek Orthodox ceremony which included dancing around the bride and groom with floral wreaths.[26]

Despite all his affinities with Adorno, and with the Marxist-influenced Frankfurt circle more generally, Habermas also sensed the self-referential and dogmatic atmosphere of a sworn community, a 'spirit of the house', which had to be accepted:

> When I came to Frankfurt, it struck me that Horkheimer and Adorno did not pay much attention to contemporary philosophy. . . . I also never got the impression from Adorno that he had read Heidegger intensely. . . . This selectivity was somehow exotic. . . . Subjectively, I saw myself as someone who, compared to a very narrow, almost dogmatic selection of 'acceptable' texts, was a little less prejudiced in his reception of philosophical and scientific traditions.[27]

This 'lack of prejudice' was certainly one of the reasons why Habermas was at first not at all convinced that he had found the right place to build a career. He wrote to Hans Paeschke: 'Without being able to blame anyone for it, except maybe myself for my insufficient willingness to adapt in certain respects, it has become clear to me that I can hardly stay here for very much longer.'[28]

Considering the uncertainty around the initial arrangements between Adorno and Habermas, this sceptical attitude was justified. Moreover, at that point Habermas had already received an offer from Hans-Georg Gadamer to take up an assistant's post at the Department of Philosophy in Heidelberg, but he declined. Adorno was clearly the greater intellectual challenge. Only later would Habermas make his way to the Ruprecht-Karls-Universität.

A unique learning process. Despite some reservations and uncertainties, Habermas liked the fact that his new position at the Institute for Social Research allowed him to widen his academic horizons. As a trained philosopher he had the opportunity, and indeed was compelled, to turn more towards the still comparatively young discipline of sociology, in relation not only to its philosophical foundations and theoretical concepts but also to the methods of empirical social research, which were entirely new to him. Thus, Habermas has described his collaboration with Adorno between 1956 and 1959 at the Institute for Social Research as a learning process.

Adorno took the time to read and annotate the draft manuscripts of his assistant in detail.[29] He also made a habit of dropping in on him in his office on the first floor of the institute and presenting him with the thoughts that were going through his head, usually about what he was writing at the time. Habermas was thus in the extraordinary situation of being able to watch his teacher philosophizing and immediately experiencing his 'presence of consciousness, spontaneity of thought and force of formulation'. He recalled, 'Adorno's thoughts did not show the process through which they had emerged; they left him, so to speak, in a finished state . . .; he could not reduce the tension of thinking for one single moment. As long as you were in Adorno's presence, you were in the movement of his thought.'[30]

Beyond their working relationship, a certain personal closeness also developed between Habermas and Adorno, and from time to time they would meet outside of work. When Ute and Jürgen Habermas were at the Adornos around Christmas 1957, Gretel Adorno told them that she had given her husband a silver food pusher, a utensil for children, which the visitors were to admire. As is well known, Adorno's idealization of his childhood experiences knew no limits, and, Gretel said, he had beamed with joy over his present.

Habermas maintained a friendly relationship with Gretel Adorno, who was also working at the institute at that time. She took a shine to the young Habermas because he reminded her of Walter Benjamin, who was a friend from her days in Berlin and someone she corresponded with for many years. Benjamin had taken his own life while fleeing from the Nazis in 1940.[31] It was Gretel who tried to explain the intricate connections between Jewish-Messianic and Marxist thought in Benjamin. She encouraged him to write a review of Benjamin's *Schriften* [Writings], which she edited with her husband in 1955. Although Habermas's wife collected the two 'light-brown clothbound volumes' from the publisher for her husband, and he let himself be drawn into the 'mixture of lucid sentences and cryptic allusions, which did not seem to match any genre',[32] he was unable to comply with Gretel's request. Benjamin's thought was still too alien to him at that time. And, in the final analysis, it probably remained alien to a certain extent, even though, in 1972, he contributed to a worldwide Benjamin renaissance with his essay 'Bewußtmachende oder rettende Kritik – die Aktualität Walter Benjamins' [Consciousness-raising or rescuing critique – the actuality of Walter Benjamin].[33] We will return to this essay later. Habermas reports that he saw Paul Klee's *Angelus Novus* – which Benjamin interprets as an expression of the catastrophic nature of progress in his 'Theses on the Philosophy of History'* – in Gretel Adorno's office at the institute, which was opposite his own. As much as all this fascinated him, the review remained stored away in a drawer.[34]

None of this diminished Gretel Adorno's trust in Habermas. For instance, she shared with him the secret – still well kept at the time – of which author wrote which parts of the *Dialectic of Enlightenment*: 'that the title essay and the chapter on de Sade were mostly by Horkheimer, and the chapters on Odysseus and the culture industry mostly by Adorno'.[35] Most importantly, though, she encouraged him to attend her husband's philosophy lectures with her. At that time, these were still being held in small lecture halls. In the summer term of 1956, Adorno lectured on 'Darstellung und Kritik der reinen Phänomenologie' [Representation and critique of pure phenomenology] and on 'Probleme der neueren Industriesoziologie' [Problems in recent industrial sociology]. These were followed by lecture courses on 'Probleme der Moralphilosophie' [Problems of moral philosophy][†] and 'Einführung in die Philosophie' [Introduction to philosophy], as well as seminars on 'Dialektik der Aufklärung' [Dialectic of Enlightenment] and on the 'Begriff der Ideologie' [The concept of ideology] in the winter term 1956–7. Later, there were lectures on, among other things, 'Einleitung in die Geschichtsphilosophie' [Introduction to the philosophy of history] and 'Erkenntnistheorie' [Epistemology].[36] The first time, Habermas says,

> I found it difficult to follow the lecture – blinded by the brilliance of the expression and delivery, I floundered behind the sequence of thoughts. Only later did I notice that this dialectic frequently solidified into a mannerism too. The dominant impression was the claim of enlightenment which sparkled from out of the darkness of the not yet understood – the promise that connections *kept secret* would be made transparent.[37]

---

* 'Geschichtsphilosophische Thesen'. The German title of Benjamin's theses is actually 'Über den Begriff der Geschichte' [On the concept of history]. However, it is rendered in English as *Theses on the Philosophy of History*.
† These have been edited and translated into English: *Problems of Moral Philosophy*, Cambridge, 2000.

Freud lectures. Habermas was just getting his bearings in Frankfurt and was busy learning 'sociology on the job'[38] when the institute organized a lecture series, in cooperation with Alexander Mitscherlich, that garnered a great deal of attention. Mitscherlich was professor of psychosomatic medicine in Heidelberg and later became the first director of the Sigmund Freud Institute (originally founded in 1960 under a different name). The reason for the lectures was the centenary of Sigmund Freud's birthday. The presentations all dealt with the scientific status of psychoanalysis, and in the spring and summer of 1959 Habermas attended all of them, including those by René Spitz, Michael Balint, Franz Alexander, Gustav Bally and Ludwig Binswanger. He was deeply impressed: 'Scarcely more than a decade after the end of the war, this elite group of scientists appeared in front of a German audience in order to report on the progress of their discipline, which had been expelled so shamefully in 1933.' 'I cannot say', Habermas continues, 'what I, who had encountered Freud only in connection with pejorative remarks during my study of psychology, found more fascinating: the impressive personalities or the brilliant lectures.'[39] 'These presentations', Habermas wrote recently, 'swept through Germany like an intellectual flash flood arriving from another world.'[40] Both in his conference report, which appeared in the *Frankfurter Allgemeine Zeitung*, and in his recollections from 2011, Habermas, as well as highlighting Alexander Mitscherlich's and Erik H. Erikson's remarks on psychoanalysis as a therapeutic method and as a theory of the unconscious, draws particular attention to the two lectures by Herbert Marcuse, who spoke about some of the ideas from his *Eros and Civilization*, which was just about to be published. For Habermas, Marcuse was altogether 'a revelation', he remembered in a radio interview. 'When I read the young Marcuse, the articles from 1930, that was exactly what I had been looking for, namely Marx and Heidegger.'[41]

Marcuse, who had studied with Husserl and Heidegger, and who had become a member of the Institute for Social Research while in exile, now came to Germany as professor of philosophy and politics at Brandeis University in Massachusetts. In both Frankfurt and Heidelberg in July, he spoke about 'Trieblehre und Freiheit' [Theory of the drives and freedom] and 'Die Idee des Fortschritts im Lichte der Psychoanalyse' [The idea of progress seen from a psychoanalytic perspective]. In his article for the *Frankfurter Allgemeine Zeitung* – which, incidentally, shows how quickly he had adapted to the Frankfurt *façon de parler* – Habermas attests to Marcuse's

> courage in releasing utopian energies as free of inhibitions as if we were in the eighteenth century and not our own times. He . . . caused even the most hard-boiled characters to enter into reflection: reflection

on the extent to which we all unconsciously share in the conventional resignation and affirm the *status quo* in thought without examining the appropriateness of a 'concept' or the objective possibilities of its historical unfolding.[42]

In short, Habermas was plainly quite enthusiastic about Marcuse. For him, the first meeting with this unconventional thinker was 'the moment when we first faced an embodiment and vivid expression of the political spirit of the old Frankfurt School'.[43] Apart from this, the lecture cycle was of considerable importance for the development of Habermas's own theoretical thinking. For the first time it became clear to him 'that Freud had created a serious scientific theory and laid the foundation for a momentous psychoanalytic research tradition.'[44]

For Horkheimer, Habermas's report on the lecture series for the *Frankfurter Allgemeine Zeitung* and the Swiss *Nationalzeitung* was reason enough to ask to speak with his co-director's assistant. It was, in fact, the first conversation they had. Horkheimer was unhappy and criticized Habermas for not having placed due emphasis on the role of the Institute for Social Research as the main organizer of the event. Habermas, for his part, was surprised – on the one hand, by the 'us and them' pattern underlying this criticism but also, on the other, by the fact that Horkheimer, whose thought and published work expressed a critique of traditional authoritarian structures, seemed to think that he could tell his collaborators what they were to say in their own publications.[45]

Horkheimer's animosity towards the 'dialectical Mr H.'

The eventful relationship between Habermas and Horkheimer is a story in itself, whose unfathomable aspects are open only to speculation. In any case, from the very beginning it was not a very good relationship. Habermas noticed that Adorno's dependence on Horkheimer took extreme forms, sometimes bordering on obsequiousness, and felt that he had to defend the sensitive Adorno against the demonstrations of superiority coming from the older director of the institute. He also disliked Horkheimer's tendency towards political opportunism, and as a young assistant he was astonished how much the latter would try to arrange himself with the existing form of society and the political situation. Back then, he may not have realized that Horkheimer was guided by a positive attitude towards Western democracy, which he wanted to defend against those from the left as well as the right who held it in contempt – an attitude Habermas himself would later adopt in his own way.

Habermas certainly took note of the differences between Adorno's and Horkheimer's thinking, which they themselves probably considered to be of only superficial importance. He would explicitly thematize them and observed that, since his return from exile, Horkheimer had hardly developed any new approach in social theory, and 'much less [had shown] an identification with the old'.[46] Compared to Adorno's, it seemed that Horkheimer's thinking had come to a standstill. Adorno's personal commitment, in particular to academic teaching, stood in stark contrast to this. Here, according to Habermas, he became entirely absorbed by his role as an enlightenment thinker, and

> he accomplished the feat of squaring the negativism of his philosophical teachings with the reformism of an intellectual who had trust in the independent spirit of public discourse. . . . In this, we see the educator of the people at work who . . . unearthed everything that was musty and authoritarian in order to expose it to the subverting dialectic of public speech. Notwithstanding the critique of the enlightenment at the level of theory, what Adorno practised in public was a Kantian education towards maturity.[47]

Horkheimer was probably relieved that the necessary financial means were now available and a new collaborator had begun his work at the institute. In those days, the individuals in charge were permanently looking for qualified personnel, and the promising young sociologist Ralf Dahrendorf had just left the institute at short notice.[48] Having only recently taken up the post, rather than conducting empirical research projects under the auspices of Horkheimer, he now accepted the offer of an appointment to a chair at the University of Saarbrücken.

Horkheimer must at least have been familiar with Habermas's name, because in February 1955, in response to a query from him, he had provided Habermas with information on the subject of 'ideology'. This, as mentioned previously, was the topic of a project Habermas pursued with the support of the German Research Foundation following the completion of his doctorate and before joining the institute. However, to begin with, Horkheimer, who was frequently absent during that period on account of a visiting professorship at the University of Chicago and other external commitments, took little notice of Adorno's new assistant from Bonn. That would soon change through the intervention of someone with whom Horkheimer maintained collegial relations but whom he rather distrusted, as he was a former pupil of Heidegger. Horkheimer most likely knew that Gadamer, along with his teacher, had signed the 'Vow of Allegiance of the Professors of the German Universities and High Schools to Adolf Hitler and the National Socialist State' in November 1933.[49]

Hans-Georg Gadamer, the leading figure in the renewal of philosophical hermeneutics, taught in Heidelberg and in 1953, together with the philosopher Helmut Kuhn from Munich, had founded the journal *Philosophische Rundschau*. In a letter of 18 January 1956, he asked Habermas for a review essay on contemporary movements in Western Marxism. This was not an easy task; indeed – at a time when the Cold War was already firmly established and the demonization of communism very much in vogue – it was a delicate one. Even in academic circles there was widespread consensus that Marx was simply old hat and could be treated as irrelevant. Gadamer knew that the young philosopher was working on the concept of ideology, that he was a good writer, and that only a little while ago, in 1955, he had published a review in *Merkur* with the title 'Perspectives on Marx'. In this review, he had discussed the publications of, among others, Auguste Cornu, Ludwig Landgrebe, Heinrich Popitz and Ralf Dahrendorf, whose works he used as a point of departure for his own critique of Marx.[50] Habermas's own reading of Marx at the time focused mainly on two points: on the one hand, the theory of revolution, which Marx develops within the framework of a philosophy of history, and, on the other, the theory of reification,* as it is presented in particular in the *Economic and Philosophical Manuscripts*. Habermas seized the opportunity to publish an article in a respected specialist journal with a philosophically learned audience, and accepted Gadamer's offer.

Literature review on Marx and Marxism. When Gadamer finally saw Habermas's extensive literature review in December 1957, he did not hesitate to publish it in his journal. For 'here was someone', as he later recalled, 'who was obviously positively inclined towards fundamental Marxist ideas, but who avoided all political judgement and limited himself to the conceptual analysis of the Marx literature in question. I was impressed by the way he was able to distinguish between the two and to adapt to the scientific standards of the journal.'[51]

In volumes 3 and 4 of 1957, Habermas, indeed, provides an instructive overview of the relevant contemporary publications on the topic, guided by the following question: How can historical materialism be used for an analysis of the present without treating Marx as a classical canonized author? First, Habermas, like Marcuse – and with similar clarity – rejects all varieties of dogmatic

---

* Marx does not use the term 'reification' [Verdinglichung], but his discussion of alienation, estrangement, and commodity fetishism provides the grounds on which the term came to prominence in twentieth-century Marxist theory. See Gillian Rose, *The Melancholy Science: An Introduction to the Thought of Theodor W. Adorno*, London, 1978, and Axel Honneth, *Reification. A New Look at an Old Idea*, Oxford, 2008.

Soviet Marxism.[52] Then, he pursues the question of how to reflect on alienation in a way that is appropriate to the present. Not, he answers, by treating it, like Heidegger, as a 'cipher of a metaphysical accident' but, rather, by regarding it as 'the name for a factually given situation of pauperism'.[53] However, the pivotal point of his review is the question of how significant a role the unity between the philosophy of history and the theory of revolution, as inherited from Marx, can play today. In more concrete terms: How does the relevant literature treat the young Marx's conception of the self-sublation of philosophy into revolutionary practice?

With the phrase 'empirically verifiable philosophy of history with a practical purpose', Habermas hints at his own programme, which he would develop in the following years.[54] Its object would be the history of the species [*Gattungsgeschichte*] as a self-reflexive formative process. His main interest in the concept of revolution derives from an epistemological perspective – i.e., as part of a 'doctrine of the categories of critique' [*Kategorienlehre der Kritik*].[55] Against Heidegger, but also against Marx, he points out that under only one specific historical condition could we expect that, parallel to the revolutionary transformation of society, the critique of that society is turned into practice, and that is if the historical and the revolutionary processes intertwine. Habermas writes that 'society . . . [is] always already such that it has to change.'[56] Knowledge of the when and how of this change is dependent on precise social scientific insights about the aspects of crisis within a society, based on empirical research, on the one hand, and on the type of social critique developed by Marx and, following him, Marxists such as Marcuse, Merleau-Ponty and Sartre, on the other. The aim of such social critique, which takes the place of philosophy as the teaching of the moral good, is not to provide yet another interpretation of a world gone wrong but, rather, to unveil the contradictions within an existing society in order to find starting points for changing it. Habermas refers to the practical impulses of historical materialism, which in 'its original form . . . must be understood as a philosophy at once of history and of revolution, as a revolutionary humanism which departs from the analysis of alienation and takes as its destination the practical transformation [*Revolutionierung*] of the existing social conditions'.[57] The fact that Habermas concludes his article with a long quotation from Marcuse's *Trieblehre und Freiheit* [Theory of the drives and freedom], which says that, despite the progressive development of the productive forces, the realization of historically possible forms of freedom is prevented by repressive techniques of domination, is revealing of Habermas's own philosophical position at the time.

However, Habermas not only pays tribute to Marcuse and to Adorno's materialist critique of foundational philosophy

[*Ursprungsphilosophie*],* at the very beginning he also mentions Horkheimer's early interpretation of historical materialism as an example of an unorthodox appropriation of Marxist theory. But all these precautionary measures did not protect the author of this 'philosophical discussion' from falling out of favour with the institute's director, who – several years before his official retirement as professor of philosophy and sociology – already spent most of his time with his wife in the Swiss town of Montagnola at Lake Lugano, and yet continued to claim the right to determine the politics at the institute.

Horkheimer expressed his deep reservations about Habermas in a long letter to Adorno, which he wrote, he says, despite 'arthritis and stupidity'. He altogether disliked not only Habermas's political activities, especially his active stance against the rearmament of the Bundeswehr, but also his publications. Horkheimer brushed aside the political activities against nuclear armament as a mass movement orchestrated by the Eastern bloc. In his diary notes from that time, we find the following entry, dated 'mid-May 1958': those united in opposition to nuclear arms 'repeat the French Revolution in the age of technology, in an impoverished and vulgarized form with their protests and silent marches. The "people" as the supreme category of the rushed and fixated thinking of students, functionaries, all kinds of interested parties. . . . But the young people agree only in the sense that they want to be active.'[58]

Horkheimer thought he had also detected such blind political activism in Habermas, but his polemic against him centred on the review essay for Gadamer's journal. For Habermas, who is called 'the dialectical Mr H.' by Horkheimer in his letter to Adorno, revolution means 'a kind of affirmative idea, a finite absolute, an idol, which thoroughly falsifies what we mean by critique and critical theory.'[59] This manifests itself, he continues, in the way that Habermas '[does] philosophy as much violence as sociology. Marx, in his hands, becomes a bogeyman . . . [w]ho writes like H., is blinkered, despite all cleverness, and lacks *bon sens*.'[60] It is to be feared that this 'H.' 'destroys the attitude [*Gesinnung*] and social understanding of our students with conceptual fetishes . . . . But we may not allow the truly careless attitude of this assistant to ruin the institute.'[61] Horkheimer emphasizes that they had always been aware 'of the futility of the thought of salvation [*Rettung*] through revolution'.[62] The appeal to revolution, which he imputes to Habermas, would help 'the gentlemen in the East' or would play 'into the hands of the potential fascists within'. Horkheimer reaches the conclusion

---

* Adorno's term for any philosophy that presents itself as *prima philosophia*; see his *Against Epistemology*.

that Habermas is 'an exceptionally lively and active character' who has learned all sorts of things at the institute, but 'hardly anything to do with the experience of social affairs'.[63] He asks Adorno in no uncertain terms to request that the 29-year-old leave the institute.

In this instance, Adorno, who was almost devoted to Horkheimer, did not accede to his demands; he stood by his assistant. The original letter contains numerous annotations which make clear how little Adorno agreed with Horkheimer's objections.[64] In later letters to Horkheimer, Adorno would openly express his appreciation for Habermas.[65] After all, he knew his assistant well, while Horkheimer had spoken to him in person only once – a fact Horkheimer readily admitted, namely when he read him the riot act over his report on the Freud lectures. Adorno tried to explain his own take on these matters to Horkheimer.

Looking back at this phase in the relationship, or rather non-existent relationship, between Horkheimer and Habermas, one wonders whether there was, after all, something to Horkheimer's accusations – leaving aside all the insults that clearly stemmed just from his bias against the young and politically committed assistant. Adorno was certainly the first to sense how similar Habermas's interpretation of the materialist understanding of history and philosophy was to the position Horkheimer had suggested in the first programmatic volumes of the *Zeitschrift für Sozialforschung*. And Adorno said so in his reply to Horkheimer.[66] Both Horkheimer and Habermas shared a conviction inspired by socialism, infused with a scepticism regarding the philosophy of history, that it is possible to transcend the antagonistic condition of bourgeois-capitalist society. Habermas no doubt centred his review of Marxist literature round the crucial question of how the truth content of the theory of revolution was to be judged. But this evaluative attitude was by no means the same as a 'continuously repeated commitment to revolution . . . as the innate purpose of philosophy', as Horkheimer assumed.[67] There is much to be said for the suspicion Adorno obviously had, namely that a large part of Horkheimer's anger was fuelled by the fact that Habermas reminded him of his own past as a social revolutionary, which he did not want to think about after the war. In addition, he had deep-seated fears of being associated with the politically motivated activities of an intellectual who was always prepared to offer opposition. Habermas came very close to a view which Horkheimer was always persuaded by: that the idea of revolutionary practice cannot be understood in a timeless fashion. Decades later, Habermas described his political attitude during the period of the Cold War as anti-anti-communist.[68] As we shall see, there were several shifts in the way he understood Marx. We have to leave open the question of whether Horkheimer misunderstood Habermas, or whether he understood him all too well.

Habermas had heard rumours about Horkheimer's threatening letter to Adorno, but in any case it is hardly surprising that he was stunned when, following Horkheimer's death in July 1973, he first actually set eyes on it among Horkheimer's posthumous papers.[69] Although he had a vague idea about Horkheimer's animosity towards him during his time as an assistant at the institute, he could not possibly have expected such a defamatory complaint. A letter to Marcuse, written in February 1977, expresses his astonishment: 'This literature review can have looked like a revolutionary pamphlet only to someone who was plagued by Wilhelminian anxieties at the time.'[70] Later, Habermas would be able to muster considerable understanding regarding Horkheimer's behaviour. Horkheimer, he said, retained 'his radically pessimistic fundamental convictions behind an armour of fear and tactical adaptation – a private solution which deserves our respect in light of the diary entries which have only been published posthumously.'[71] In retrospect, he even considered Horkheimer's request to have him dismissed 'psychologically quite plausible', and added that Horkheimer's suspicion towards him had 'not been entirely wrong. At the time, I did not understand the intellectual stature that Horkheimer must have had during the 1930s.'[72]

As far as Adorno's role in all this is concerned, the 'Hippopotamus' stood firm against the 'Mammoth', to use the nicknames the two friends had for each other from their years in Californian exile. Adorno again defended Habermas when Horkheimer, in another letter, decided not to publish the empirical study on the political consciousness of students that Habermas had undertaken with Ludwig von Friedeburg, Christoph Oehler and Friedrich Weltz, and for which Habermas had written an extensive introduction on the theory of democracy used as the framework for the study. This was a research project centred on the question of the students' attitude towards Germany's young democracy and the question of whether, and to what extent, they were prepared to participate in the political process. In his introduction, to which Horkheimer took exception, Habermas reflects on the 'concept of political participation' and begins to explain the changing function of the universities in terms of the increasing scientification of society, which leads to the economy encroaching upon academic institutions. This rise in power on the side of private economic interests, he argues, has to be opposed with general 'political control of the functions of private capital ownership'.[73] Habermas also raises the question of how the threat of a de-politicization of the masses could be avoided and the participatory element of democracy strengthened. He refers to the model of social democracy developed by the political scientist

Wolfgang Abendroth (partly in lectures he was invited to deliver at the Institute for Social Research by Adorno) in order to give the concept of political participation a foundation in the theory of democracy. Habermas defines democracy as a form of life which goes hand in hand with a free society and the maturity of its members. This understanding of democracy corresponds wholly with the analyses of politics and educational sociology which Adorno developed at the end of the 1950s.

Horkheimer, however, sensed a resurrection of the concept of revolution behind the postulate of a social democracy in which the state would guarantee the material conditions for the political participation of all citizens. Thus, he wrote to Adorno: 'The word revolution, probably due to your influence, has been replaced with the "development from a formal to a material, from a liberal to a social democracy".'[74] Horkheimer also took offence because, as he saw it, Habermas was exaggerating the seriousness of the present political situation in Germany – in which the conservative parties had begun to prepare legislation for emergency laws – by dramatizing it as part of a development that could lead to an authoritarian state.

Adorno remained more or less unperturbed by all this. In a letter to Horkheimer, he even called the introduction to *Student und Politik* [Students and politics], which was to be the title of the published version of the study, a 'showpiece' and 'masterpiece', insisting that it should 'under all circumstances remain part of the book': 'Habermas really rolled up his sleeves.'[75] Habermas even reported on the outcomes of the study at a meeting of German sociologists in the autumn of 1959 in Berlin, in a presentation titled 'Einfluß von Schule und Hochschulbildung auf das politische Bewußtsein der Studenten' [The influence of school and higher education on the political consciousness of students]. But it was all to no avail: Horkheimer's wholesale criticisms, with which his best friend Friedrich 'Fritz' Pollock agreed, meant that the publication of the findings was significantly delayed. And in the end it appeared not in the Institute for Social Research's book series but in the series 'Soziologische Texte' [Texts in sociology] issued by the Hermann Luchterhand publishing house, in 1961. On 3 June 1960, Habermas wrote to the director of the institute:

> The negotiations with the Luchterhand publishing house, about which Herr von Friedeburg kept you informed, have progressed quite far by now. The publisher shows such great interest in the study that he wants to publish it in time for the book fair in September at the latest. Contrary to our initial assumption, the investigation, understandably, is not meant to be part of the series on political science but part of the parallel series of sociological texts.[76]

Habermas would soon publish his first two books with this publishing house.

Thus, life at the institute remained uncomfortable for Habermas. And so in July 1959 when, with the help of Hans-Georg Gadamer, he again received a scholarship from the German Research Foundation, this time for his Habilitation, he decided without further ado to give up his post there in favour of an 'existence as a scholarship holder', as he expressed it, with a mixture of irony and embitterment, in a letter to Joachim Moras of *Merkur*.[77] This was a risky decision. Ute could not believe her ears when her husband announced that he had handed in his notice;[78] after all, their daughter Rebekka had been born that July, and so they were now a family of four. But Habermas had good reasons for his decision, and he was not exactly lacking in self-confidence regarding his talents. He knew that the support of Adorno, who had only just been made a full professor and who had not yet really cemented his position within the faculty,[79] would probably not be enough to secure his Habilitation. And Horkheimer, who only a short while ago had wanted to get rid of Habermas as quickly as possible, made his support for his Habilitation dependent on his participation in another empirical study at the institute regarding German judges. For this project, Horkheimer had found some money. But it was out of the question for Habermas to postpone writing his Habilitation for several years. Hellmut Becker, a legal adviser at the institute, interpreted Horkheimer's condition with the necessary clarity: Habermas should not harbour any illusions. He had already invested plenty of time in the project, and a first draft of it, which he had shown to Adorno, was practically finished. In addition, there were economic reasons which suggested that he should obtain a fixed academic position with the goal of gaining a professorship as soon as possible.

The 'most promising intellectual'

This reorientation, and his departure from the institute, forced Habermas to change his business model, as it were. In retrospect, we might say that the process of planning his life and career and, at the same time, gaining intellectual self-assurance took place in four stages. Neither this nor his thinking as a social theorist generally developed in a linear fashion, as a brief look ahead may illustrate.

To begin with, Habermas sounded out his chances for a Habilitation elsewhere. This brought him to Wolfgang Abendroth, the 'partisan professor'[80] in the country of the 'Mitläufer',* and

---

* See footnote on p. 20.

thus to Marburg, where his Habilitation was passed following an examination which went anything but smoothly. Even before the completion of this process, he had been appointed as an extraordinary professor of philosophy at the University of Heidelberg and thus had become a civil servant for life. This was a fairly respectable and secure position. In Heidelberg, the second stage in his career, he began to establish himself as a scholar with a broad area of expertise, part of which was critical Marxism as well as the hermeneutic tradition, the theory of the social sciences and psychoanalysis.

The third stage was Habermas's high-profile involvement in a debate that would go down in history as the 'positivist dispute', a controversy that was started in 1961 at a workshop of the German Society for Sociology in Tübingen by Adorno and the philosopher Karl R. Popper, who taught at the London School of Economics. In his two contributions to this controversy, Habermas defended the position of Critical Theory against 'Critical Rationalism' and helped to foster a perception of the 'Frankfurt School' as an independent paradigm within the social sciences.

In the fourth stage, Habermas was finally offered full professorships of philosophy and sociology at the Freie Universität Berlin, as well as at the Johann Wolfgang Goethe-Universität in Frankfurt am Main, at the beginning of 1964. Habermas accepted the Frankfurt post and thus became the direct successor to Max Horkheimer, of all people, who in the intervening years had, however, changed his opinion of him. Maybe he had been impressed by the way the young assistant had withdrawn from the institute; maybe he had been impressed by the many positive reactions to the study on *Student und Politik* [Students and politics], which he had so harshly criticized.[81]

In any case, when Habermas applied for a grant from the Studienbüro für politische Bildung [Academic office for political education],[82] which organized and gave financial support for study visits to the USA, and asked Horkheimer whether he would act as his main referee, he received his full support. Even more than that: by the time the trip to the USA finally materialized, which was not until 1965, Horkheimer seemed to have completely forgotten his old prejudices. In a letter to the American Jewish Committee, he waxed lyrical about Habermas, declaring him to be one of the 'most promising intellectuals in Western Germany'. There are worse *billets d'entrée* to the Anglo-American academic world.[83]

Habermas played his part in improving the atmosphere between the two. On the occasion of Horkheimer's seventieth birthday, he congratulated him in a cordial letter, and, at the annual meeting of sociologists that commemorated Max Weber's hundredth birthday in April 1964 in Heidelberg, he spoke alongside the famous American sociologist Talcott Parsons in a plenary session chaired by Horkheimer. In his paper titled 'Wertfreiheit und Objektivität'

[Value freedom and objectivity],[84] Habermas offers a critical discussion of the American structural functionalists and of Max Weber's decisionism and political authoritarianism. And he continued to try to maintain a good relationship with Horkheimer, encouraging him to publish a collection of early texts. When the two volumes appeared under the title *Kritische Theorie* [Critical Theory] with S. Fischer in 1972, Habermas wrote to him, saying: 'As I now realize, not without a certain degree of astonishment, our interests coincide even down to the level of details.'[85]

At the meeting of sociologists in Heidelberg, Habermas also met Herbert Marcuse again. Marcuse was one of the keynote speakers and presented a powerful critique of Weber's theory of domination and bureaucracy. He also gave Habermas a copy of his *One-Dimensional Man* as a gift. The work, published in the USA in 1964, contained a handwritten dedication quoting Walter Benjamin: 'To the hope of those without hope.'[86] These are also the words with which *One-Dimensional Man* closes. The congress was one of the last occasions on which Habermas saw the three protagonists of the first generation of critical theorists together. And, again, he witnessed the differences not only in their temperaments but also in their ways of thinking, which by then had split up into Adorno's dialectical negativism, Horkheimer's pessimistic philosophy of history, and Marcuse's revolutionary utopianism.

Inaugural lecture in Frankfurt. The historic assembly hall of the university was filled to capacity when Habermas gave his inaugural lecture on 28 June 1965, despite the fine summer weather outside. Habermas had chosen 'Erkenntnis und Interesse' [Knowledge and interest] as his title, and he immediately announced to his audience that his intention – 'after almost a lifetime had passed' – was to return to a question originally posed by Horkheimer, namely that of the relationship between traditional and critical theory, in order to clarify the foundations of a type of science which claims to pursue emancipatory interests in its search for knowledge.[87] He had sent the manuscript of this inaugural lecture to Horkheimer, who could not be present on the day but expressed in his reply to Habermas 'how pleased' he was 'about the content'; Habermas, he wrote, had 'taken up questions which are truly crucial, and had formulated them in the most advanced way possible for us today'.[88] It is hard to tell whether Horkheimer actually read the text with any great care; the original manuscript in the archive looks almost untouched and bears no annotations.

One passage, however, he most certainly would have liked, because it bears striking parallels to some ideas that had occupied Horkheimer in the 1940s. In a series of letters to Adorno dating from 1941, he reflected on the relationship between reason and language and asked whether language possessed a transcendental status, and thus was more than just a medium for the description of the world. Back then, he managed to express his intuition about the philosophy of language clearly: 'To address someone in language fundamentally means to acknowledge him as a potential member of a future association of free human beings. Speech presumes a shared relationship towards truth, hence at heart an affirmation of the existence of the other who is addressed, actually of all existing others according to their possibilities.'[89] And now, almost twenty-five years later, Habermas stated something in his inaugural lecture that not only contained his future research programme *in nuce* but – unbeknown to him (he did not yet know of the Horkheimer–Adorno correspondence) – also picked up the thread started by Horkheimer two-and-half decades earlier: 'That which elevates us above nature is the only fact which we can know according to its own nature: *language*. Its structure is what posits maturity* *for us*.'[90] As it would turn out, Habermas's inaugural lecture in Frankfurt was the beginning of an international academic career, but one that was nevertheless not free of obstacles and discontinuities.

---

* The German term is 'Mündigkeit'. As in the case of the translation of the famous opening sentence from Kant's 'An Answer to the Question: What is Enlightenment?': 'Aufklärung ist der Ausgang des Menschen aus seiner selbstverschuldeten Unmündigkeit' = 'Enlightenment is man's emergence from his self-incurred immaturity', the association of Unmündigkeit/Mündigkeit with 'Mund', and hence the capacity of speech, is lost in translation. In the purely technical sense, to be 'mündig' means to have come of age and hence to be legally entitled to speak and act for oneself, and also to be responsible for one's acts (of speech or otherwise). In the present context, it obviously acquires an additional moral dimension. See Kant (1970), 'An Answer to the Question: "What is Enlightenment?"', p. 54 ['Beantwortung der Frage: Was ist Aufklärung?', in *Werke in sechs Bänden*, ed. Wilhelm Weischedel, vol. 6, Darmstadt, 1983, pp. 53–61; here: p. 53].

4

Under the Aegis of Conflicting Personalities: Abendroth and Gadamer

Habilitation. As has already been suggested, Habermas had difficulties finding adequate support for his Habilitation after leaving the Institute for Social Research. He turned first to Helmut Schelsky and Helmuth Plessner, both of whom reluctantly turned down his request, explaining that they wanted to give preference to the promotion of young scholars from their own institutions. Habermas had a similar experience when he made initial enquiries with the conservative political scientist Arnold Bergstraesser in Freiburg and with the Heidelberg ethnologist Ernst Mühlmann, who had adapted to the ideology of the Third Reich after the Nazis seized power.[1]

With the encouragement of his friend Spiros Simitis, Habermas in the end turned to a complete outsider, the political scientist and state theorist Wolfgang Abendroth, who taught in Marburg and was the 'only Marxist scholar at a German university' at the time.[2] After an initial enquiry by phone, Abendroth expressed interest both in the topic of the Habiliation and in Habermas himself.

> When Wolfgang Abendroth answered the telephone, he declared his name like a fanfare, a kind of wake-up call – the evening light audibly turning into dawn.* Abendroth met any caller with a cheerful voice without any suspicion or reservation, exposed himself to the caller unprotected, even before he knew who it was. Wolfgang Abendroth granted the world his trust in advance, and the world often disappointed him.[3]

The political scientist invited Habermas to his Oberseminar [advanced seminar], which took place every Thursday, and after he had made his personal acquaintance and had read Habermas's 'Strukturwandel der Öffentlichkeit' [Structural transformation of

---

* Habermas plays with the literal meaning of Abendroth's name, 'Abendrot', 'evening red' – i.e., the red sky at night.

the public sphere]* very closely, he accepted the text, which was essentially complete, for the Habilitation.

A friendly relationship quickly developed. In Habermas's view, Abendroth was 'unpretentious and peculiarly unaffected by professional vanity, the striving for prestige and private ambition'.[4] His open solidarity with the labour movement distinguished him not only from almost all the other full professors with civil servant status but also from the dogmatic Stalinist factions in parties such as the KPD or DKP.† 'As an anti-anti-communist light amid the murky atmosphere of the Cold War era', he was an exceptional figure.[5] In Marburg, Habermas saw that 'for very few individuals . . . had the principle of domination-free discussion become a central issue [*Lebensfrage*] to a similar degree as for Wolfgang Abendroth',[6] who was one of the rare few who confronted the still influential right-wing conservative school of thought of Carl Schmitt and his disciple Ernst Forsthoff, by opposing it with his understanding of a social democratic state, informed by Hermann Heller's theory of state law. If today 'it is accepted that the welfare state is a condition for the legitimacy of the democratic state based on the rule of law',[7] then this is also due to Abendroth, Habermas said in a speech on the centenary of his birth.

Despite Abendroth's support, the success of Habermas's Habilitation was not a forgone conclusion. Apart from Abendroth, the sociologist Heinz Maus, the historians Peter Scheibert and Fritz Wagner, and the educationalist Leonard Froese produced written reports on the work. But Abendroth was the only one who reconstructed it step by step and commented on the individual findings of the study. He criticized the fact that the historical emergence of a public sphere is exclusively analysed using the model of the bourgeois public. But he approved of the sociological analysis of the decay of the public sphere and the solution to this problem proposed by the thesis: the threat of a progressive de-politicization should be countered with the introduction of democratic mechanisms within the political parties and institutions. The other examiners all referred to Abendroth's comments. While Maus praised the interdisciplinary orientation, Scheibert complained about the critical perspective on capitalism and Wagner about the tendency to explain historical and social developments in terms of the influence of economic factors. Froese limited himself to the remark that the author had been pressed for time. Nevertheless, the examiners were unanimously in favour of passing the Habilitation.[8]

---

* Later published under the same title: see bibliography of Habermas's works under 1962.

† Kommunistische Partei Deutschlands and Deutsche Kommunistische Partei, two West German communist parties. The DKP, founded in 1968, is the successor to the KPD.

After Habermas's oral presentation on the theme of 'Elitetheorie und Demokratie' [Theory of elites and democracy] and the ensuing discussion, the members of faculty in attendance voted overwhelmingly in favour of passing the candidate, and the dean of the Philosophy Faculty shook his hand and awarded Habermas the *venia legendi* *for political science. Some rather more observant colleagues, however, noted that the examination rules required the presence of a majority of faculty members – a requirement that had not been met. On a technicality, then, the Habilitation was at first not recognized and the degree not formally ratified, and for a while the whole process faltered. But Abendroth, a jurist, threatened to go to the administrative court and, in the end, successfully argued that the oral act of awarding the *venia* was legally binding. And so, in December 1961, Habermas gave the first inaugural lecture of his academic career. Before he spoke, the dean handed him the official document but then immediately left the auditorium – an affront which contributed to the already tense atmosphere. In a letter of 7 June to 'dear Herr Paeschke', Habermas complained that the 'irrationality of German universities . . . shows up with all clarity in connection with the procedures of the Habilitation: it certainly preoccupies the candidate to such a degree that he does not have the peace of mind necessary for any reasonable activities.'[9]

In his inaugural lecture of December 1961 Habermas spoke about 'The Classical Doctrine of Politics in Relation to Social Philosophy'.[10] The lecture first presents a synopsis of important positions in political philosophy, those of Machiavelli, Thomas More, Hobbes, Locke and Vico, and Habermas then marks the transition from the classical concept of politics in the tradition of Aristotle to the modern understanding of politics. In doing so, he intends to reawaken a concept of politics that has been forgotten. While for Aristotle politics consists of instruction in right practice and serves the purpose of the good and just life, the aim of modern 'scientific' political philosophy is to gain knowledge in a methodical fashion, a knowledge that exclusively serves the purpose of production, domination and application. Thus, it is fundamentally a matter of technically applicable knowledge, and Habermas draws the conclusion that such a discipline, which takes the natural sciences as its ideal, must equate practice with technology. In turn, however, this raises the question of how

the promise of practical politics – namely of providing practical orientation about what is right and just in a given situation – [can] be

---

* Within the German university system, the *venia legendi*, literally 'permission to read', is awarded after a successful Habilitation and gives the candidate the right to represent a particular subject in teaching and research.

redeemed without relinquishing, at the same time, the rigor of scientific knowledge, which modern social philosophy demands in contrast to the practical philosophy of classicism. And, conversely, how can the promise of social philosophy – to furnish a theoretical analysis of social life as a whole – be redeemed without relinquishing the practical orientation of classical politics?[11]

At the end of his lecture, Habermas alludes to the topic of his Habilitation by mentioning the 'mediating function of public opinion' and emphasizing the enlightening and emancipatory function of the historical unfolding of a political public.[12]

The extended text of this lecture opens the collection of essays published in 1963 under the title *Theorie und Praxis* [Theory and practice], and Habermas often made use of the material in his later lectures on the history of sociology. The lecture's reconstructions of stretches from the history of ideas also found their way into the entry on sociology which Habermas wrote for the *Evangelisches Staatslexikon* [Evangelical dictionary of state theory], edited by Hermann Kunst and Siegfried Grundmann in 1966.[13] Habermas's parents, incidentally, arrived in Marburg from Gummersbach in order to be present at their son's inaugural lecture, which was, after all, an important event in his life. After the quarrels within the faculty, Habermas was probably quite relieved that he was able immediately to turn his back on Marburg. But he maintained his relationship with Abendroth and his family until Abendroth's death in September 1985.

Professorship in Heidelberg. Habermas's reputation as a Marxist predated his decision to undertake the Habilitation in Marburg. When a friend from his days in Bonn, Karl-Otto Apel, called him 'a neo-Marxist in public for the first time', he shuddered.[14] However, the label apparently did no great harm to his fledgling academic career. Even before Habermas had completed his Habilitation, Hans-Georg Gadamer became very active in securing an extraordinary professorship for him at the University of Heidelberg.

News that he could expect an appointment in Heidelberg reached Habermas while he was on holiday in Gummersbach in August 1961. He reacted to this exciting piece of information, and the new task ahead of him, by developing a case of pneumonia and was bedridden for some time. In the autumn of 1962, Habermas's family of four moved from Frankfurt to the city on the Neckar, where they lived in a flat at St-Stephans-Weg 2 in the Handschuhsheim district. His office was in a seminar building at Augustinergasse 15. This happy development was also a kind of fresh start for him: 'In Heidelberg, from 1961 on, Gadamer's *Truth and Method* helped me to find my way back into academic philosophy.'[15]

Gadamer, the successor to Karl Jaspers's chair in Heidelberg, was still little known at the time. From the very beginning, he was a strong advocate for Habermas and succeeded in convincing the faculty of his merits, even though another candidate, Karl-Otto Apel, was closer to him in philosophical terms.

> It was very difficult to push this through . . . Löwith was determined to have Apel, and I said no, I'd rather have someone who covers what we cannot do. Apel was already well known and a very serious character. Like Habermas, he was a pupil of Rothacker, and he would have been the obvious choice. But I resisted this at the time and fought for Habermas.[16]

Thus, it was not Habermas's dissertation on Schelling, with its Heideggerian orientation, that was decisive for Gadamer; rather, it was precisely the fact that Habermas was not a member of the hermeneutic school of thought, and was actually considered somewhat of an outsider in academic philosophy due to the sociological and political-scientific approach of his Habilitation on 'The Structural Transformation of the Public Sphere'. Gadamer respected Habermas as a partner in conversation who did 'not see the other person primarily as an opponent, even in confrontation',[17] and he valued him as one of the few philosophers in West Germany who was familiar with the tradition of Hegel and Marx. And, indeed, in the first lecture he gave at the Department of Philosophy in July 1961 – thus still before his appointment (arguably the most important appointment of his life) – Habermas talked about 'Dialektischer Idealismus im Übergang zum Materialismus' [The transition from dialectical idealism to materialism].* The lecture makes a connection between Schelling's political philosophy and his philosophy of history and Marx's materialism, interpreting the latter as a theory which traces the conditions of domination over inner and outer nature and demonstrates that the 'naturalization of man' and the 'humanization of nature' both failed.[18]

Habermas had tried to clarify his position with respect to scientific Marxism even earlier in a lecture he had given in Zurich in 1960 upon the invitation of the Philosophische Gesellschaft [Philosophical Society]. In this text, titled 'Between Philosophy and Science: Marxism as Critique', Habermas rejects orthodox interpretations of Marxism and criticizes strictly economic readings of the famous but easily misunderstood concepts of 'base and superstructure'. He also begins to doubt the explanatory value of the

---

* The lecture was later turned into an article which, however, has not been translated into English. See footnote on p. 44.

categories of 'alienation' and 'pauperization', which he had still referred to approvingly in his literature review article of 1957. The idea of class antagonism as a motor of revolutionary change in society now also seemed questionable to him, particularly in the context of the Federal Republic at the time: 'And any class consciousness, especially a revolutionary class consciousness, is not to be found in the main strata of the working class today. Every revolutionary theory, under these circumstances, lacks those to whom it is addressed . . .'[19] Marx, Habermas argues, simply did not anticipate that, in times of an expanding welfare state in which real wages rise along with productivity, class consciousness might just disappear and the self-sublation of the capitalist economy through its crisis might not occur, as he assumed it would. Marx further underestimated the ability of the state to stabilize capitalism, as well as the economic system's capacity for self-correction. Habermas also considered the theory of surplus value untenable. The only aspect he still thought relevant was Marx's critique of the uneven distribution of the private ownership of the means of production, which was the cause not only of income inequality but also of the anarchic character of the capitalist process of accumulation.

At the end of his lecture, Habermas asks whether critique, as a form of reflection situated between philosophy and the positive sciences, '[m]ust . . . not open itself to the historically variable horizon of experience provided by the socially concrete lifeworld, . . . in order to legitimize the critical initiative as such?'[20] In other words, instead of focusing on the proletarian revolution, which in today's lifeworld is a dim prospect, the critical mind should focus on 'a progressive democratization of society', which 'is not excluded from the outset, even within the economic order of capitalism'.[21] From this point on, Habermas would maintain this vision of a capitalism that can be tamed by a social democracy guaranteed by the rule of law. At the same time, this vision marks the juncture where Marx's and Habermas's theoretical endeavours diverge, even if the latter's may have grown out of his engagement with the former's. In a conversation, Habermas stressed: 'I am not a Marxist in the sense of believing in Marxism as a readily available explanation for everything. But it was Marxism that provided me with the impetus and the analytical tools to investigate how the relationship between democracy and capitalism developed.'[22]

Habermas and Gadamer. During the three years that they were colleagues in Heidelberg, Gadamer and Habermas grew to appreciate one another. According to Habermas, Gadamer made Heidelberg 'the philosophical centre of the Republic [for] two, three decades', and in philosophers 'such as [Dieter] Henrich, [Robert] Spaemann, [Wolfgang] Theunissen and [Ernst] Tugendhat assembled the best of the next generation around himself'.[23] In Habermas's view, Gadamer had begun 'Urbanizing the Heideggerian Province',[24] which was true inasmuch as Gadamer had long since been moving away from Heidegger's fundamental ontology and had been developing his own philosophy of language and understanding.[25] *Truth and Method*, the sixty-year-old Gadamer's *magnum opus* on the *Grundzüge einer philosophischen Hermeneutik* [Principles of a philosophical hermeneutics],* appeared in 1960, one year before Habermas took up his post in Heidelberg. When Gadamer was awarded the Hegel Prize by the city of Stuttgart on 13 June 1979, Habermas in his laudation acknowledged his philosophy as a form of hermeneutics that was unique in highlighting the 'linguistic inter-subjectivity that unites all communicatively socialized individuals from the outset'.[26]

But his preoccupation with Gadamer's hermeneutics from 1961 onwards was also important for the development of Habermas's own theory. At one point, he described it as 'a bridge . . . . From here, I could look back at the shore on the Bonn side of the river, which I had left behind while in Frankfurt, despite continuous contact with my friend Karl-Otto Apel. At the same time, *this* bridge allowed me a view of another shore, the one I was striving to reach.'[27]

Despite all this, Habermas questioned 'hermeneutics' claim to universality', especially after his detailed studies on the logic of the social sciences.[28] As he pointed out in his contribution to the Festschrift for Gadamer's seventieth birthday, he considered Gadamer's hermeneutics to be a way out of the 'truncated rational-ism' of the positivist model. Nevertheless, in Habermas's view, the hermeneutic understanding of meaning must be complemented by ideology critique if it is to avoid becoming the mere semblance of understanding. He sensed a certain conservatism among practition-ers of hermeneutics because they did not allow enough space for the force of reflection in the process of understanding, and thus gave this process a tendency towards the affirmative. In an interview with Jean-Marc Ferry, Habermas said: 'We cannot choose our tradi-tions, but we can know that it is up to us *how* we continue them. . . . Any continuation of a tradition is, after all, selective, and it is precisely this selectivity that must today pass through the filter of cri-tique.'[29] These differences in opinion were also revealed in a remark Gadamer made in conversation with the *Kölner Stadtanzeiger* in 1980: 'I do not understand why Habermas still expects everything from "emancipation". People have long since been looking for iden-tifications, for relief, for a new order. They understand that only he who has also acquired discipline can free himself from blindly

---

* This subtitle is not adopted in the English translation of the work.

accepted authorities. Among many radicals who invoke Habermas a spirit of blind obedience rules – not the dialogue without coercion.'[30] And yet, at no time was the relationship between Habermas and Gadamer seriously harmed. In that sense, too, the years in Heidelberg were altogether good for Habermas.

Habermas's encounters in Heidelberg. At thirty-two, Habermas was by far the youngest of the professors at the Department of Philosophy in Heidelberg. He offered courses in social philosophy and the philosophy of science, on the logic of the social sciences [*Gesellschaftswissenschaften*], on positivism and pragmatism, and even on aspects of cybernetics, which was beginning to find its way into the social sciences. Gunter Hofmann, who later became an editor with *Die Zeit*, remembered the impression Habermas made on his students in his first seminars:

> Even the smallest of the lecture halls is far too big for the few students who follow the lectures of the young university teacher. Nevertheless, as a backbencher, as the political term would be, one after all wants to listen to this Jürgen Habermas, who has now joined the hermeneutician Hans-Georg Gadamer after taking such peculiar detours via Frankfurt and the leading lights of Critical Theory, Adorno and Horkheimer, and the 'partisan professor' Wolfgang Abendroth in Marburg. From the very beginning one gets the impression that, notwithstanding how dark, strange, and highly complicated all this may sound, this is not just abstract social philosophy – it aims right at the centre of the frozen conditions of the times.[31]

At the end of the summer term 1962, the 'young university teacher' gave his inaugural lecture on 'Hegel's Critique of the French Revolution', in which he presents the thesis that Hegel's philosophy of revolution is, in truth, a critique of revolution that has the purpose of saving philosophy: 'Hegel makes revolution the heart of his philosophy in order to preserve philosophy from becoming the procurer of revolution.'[32]

Habermas appointed Oskar Negt, whom he knew from Frankfurt, as his assistant. Negt was born in 1934 on an estate in Eastern Prussia to a family of smallholder farmers and labourers and was only marginally younger than his superior. He had studied philosophy and sociology with Horkheimer and Adorno in Frankfurt and had completed his doctoral thesis on Hegel and Auguste Comte under Adorno's supervision in 1962. Since 1956, he had been a member of the Sozialistischer Deutscher Studentenbund [Socialist German Students' Union] (SDS) and sympathized openly with both the trade union movement and democratic socialism. It was, apparently, just these 'left' leanings that led Habermas to offer him the position in the first place. He guessed, Negt would later say, that he 'was a particularly dyed-in-the-wool orthodox Marxist. But, of course, such "orthodoxy" should be equipped with arguments.'[33] For

> Habermas needed a lively counterpoint. He picked his assistants on the basis of their capacity to contradict. In those days, I had to have discussions for whole days and nights with him. He demanded an enormous justificatory effort from an opposing position. That helped him to grow. Habermas needs unruly resistance, even today.* That characterizes the style of his intellectual life.[34]

Habermas was invited to participate in a private seminar which Gadamer held in his house. At one of these meetings, his first and only personal encounter with Heidegger took place:

> The seminar given by Heidegger was held in the large living room, separated off by double-doors, in Bergstraße 148; I was not impressed. It was my only encounter (from my side, a silent one) with the old man, who had a somewhat authoritarian demeanour – Gadamer said to me the next morning, clearly saddened: 'It is a shame that you did not get to know Heidegger when he was still great.'[35]

Another colleague at the university and interlocutor was Karl Löwith. Born in Munich in 1897, Löwith held the second chair of philosophy in Heidelberg from 1952 and had been friendly with Gadamer since the 1920s. He was also the only one of Heidegger's students to pass his Habilitation during his time in Marburg.[†] Later, he would become one of the fiercest critics of his teacher's political stance. Löwith was also among those who were forced to emigrate; he worked at the New School for Social Research in New York for three years. While still in Heidelberg, Habermas wrote a review article of his best-known works for *Merkur*, which was critical of Löwith. In particular, he held that Löwith, the 'superior mind',[36] had, like Heidegger, 'literally explained the doomed history of two thousand years of Western development through the background history of a philosophically and theologically decisive understanding of the world.'[37] Despite this criticism, a warm and friendly relationship developed between the Löwith and Habermas families, who spent many evenings together.

However, it was his encounter with the medical doctor and psy-

---

* 'Habermas braucht den Widerhaken, immer noch.' 'Widerhaken', literally the barbed hook on a fishing rod, is an unusual metaphor, indicating not only an antagonism, but also a connection between two discussants.
† Heidegger held an extraordinary professorship in Marburg between 1923 and 1927.

choanalyst Alexander Mitscherlich and his third wife, Margarete Mitscherlich-Nielsen, that was of outstanding importance for Habermas's intellectual development. Alexander Mitscherlich was born in 1908 in Munich and after the war became a member of the Heidelberger Aktionsgruppe zur Demokratie und zum freien Sozialismus [Heidelberg Initiative for Democracy and Free Socialism], which formed around Alfred Weber and Karl Geiler.[38] Mitscherlich was also in contact with Dolf Sternberger, Eugen Kogon and Walter Dirks.[39] He was an extraordinary professor for psychosomatic medicine at Heidelberg University and the first director of the Institut und Ausbildungszentrum für Psychoanalyse und Psychosomatik [Institute and Training Centre for Psychoanalysis and Psychosomatics] in Frankfurt, which was founded in 1960 and later, in 1964, renamed the Sigmund Freud Institute.

With the support of Adorno, Horkheimer and Habermas, Mitscherlich was appointed to a chair for psychoanalysis and psychosomatic medicine at the Johann Wolfgang Goethe University in 1973.[40] After a first private meeting in Heidelberg, a lifelong friendship developed between the Mitscherlich and Habermas families. Ute and Jürgen Habermas would later remember 'a social, open, intellectual household with an *haute bourgeois* lifestyle'.[41] His conversations with the Mitscherlichs intensified Habermas's interest in psychoanalysis as a cultural theory and method, and Freud's theory played an important role in his writings in the years following his arrival in Heidelberg.[42] Not only would Alexander Mitscherlich's 1963 *Society without the Father* make a lasting impression on him;[*] in the obituary, Habermas later wrote for him, he said that *The Inability to Mourn*,[†] a book written and published by the psychoanalyst together with his wife, was 'published at a time when the political culture of this country could not have been stimulated in a clearer and more beneficial way by any other book.'[43] Apparently, Habermas saw more in Mitscherlich, twenty years his senior, than just a teacher in psychoanalytic matters. He was a kind of intellectual role model[‡] for him, someone who combined 'sociability and culture' in his person. Habermas was impressed by the fact that he was a knowledgeable collector of modern paintings, but even more by the 'everyday humanism of his relaxed, and yet considered manners in social interactions'.[44]

Marianne and Gerd Kalow formed another hub of Habermas's

---

* Alexander Mitscherlich ([1963] 2003), *Auf dem Weg zur vaterlosen Gesellschaft: Ideen zur Sozialpsychologie*, Weinheim; English edn: *Society without the Father: A Contribution to Social Psychology*, London, 1992.

† Alexander and Margarete Mitscherlich ([1967] 2007), *Die Unfähigkeit zu trauern: Grundlagen kollektiven Verhaltens*, Munich; English edn: *The Inability to Mourn: Principles of Collective Behaviour*, New York, 1975.

‡ 'Role model' in English in the original.

social life in Heidelberg. Marianne worked as a translator and later became an editor at the Suhrkamp Verlag. Gerd was a writer and journalist and, from 1964, the editor of the *Abendstudio* at the Hessischer Rundfunk. The couple resided in one of the most desirable flats in the city.

In the early summer months of 1963, on the occasion of the opening night of Brecht's *A Respectable Wedding* at the Stadttheater, Siegfried Unseld and his first wife, Hilde, travelled to Heidelberg and visited Ute and Jürgen Habermas. There had been some sporadic contact between them before, in Frankfurt, when Habermas was Adorno's assistant. But in the meantime Habermas had gained a certain reputation as a philosopher and social theorist, which made him a figure of interest for Unseld, who was constantly looking for new opportunities. Habermas's books so far – *Student und Politik* [Students and politics], *The Structural Transformation of the Public Sphere* and *Theory and Practice* – had all been published by Luchterhand Verlag, and at that point Habermas still had a good relationship with the editor of its academic series, Frank Benseler. But this did not keep Unseld from courting Habermas, not least because his plans for the expansion of Suhrkamp included a widening of the academic division. Unseld and Habermas got on well with each other. Habermas was fascinated by this man, only five years his senior, whose presence filled the room; and he was, moreover, convinced by his ideas as a publisher. Unseld, for his part, was not deterred by Habermas's inclination towards escalating their sometimes aggressive debates. Their relationship soon became a friendship, despite the fact that they were not always of the same opinion.

The real purpose of Unseld's visit to Heidelberg was to convince Habermas to be one of the editors for a series of theoretical texts for which he so far only had vague ideas. When Habermas and his family moved back to Frankfurt two years later, this project was actually realized, and, as it turned out, at exactly the right moment in time, for the younger reading public in particular would develop a keen interest in philosophy and social theory in the following years. Looking back, Habermas remembered:

> The trigger for the development of an academic programme fell . . . in the year 1963. Number 12 of the *edition suhrkamp* was the reprint of a text by Ludwig Wittgenstein, which had already been published in 1960 as part of volume 1 of the *Gesammelte Werke* [Collected works]. The unexpected success of the small book with a red cover, containing the apparently almost incomprehensible *Tractatus Logico-Philosophicus*, made the publisher think. The times seemed ripe for scientific titles, even in the narrower sense of the word. . . . After Benjamin and Adorno, Unseld had tied Bloch and Wittgenstein to his

publishing house. He now wanted to continue this successful train of events into the next generation, his own.[45]

The Theory series. On 21 June 1963, Siegfried Unseld and his editor Walter Boehlich had had an initial meeting in Frankfurt with the four philosophers Theodor W. Adorno, Jürgen Habermas, Hans Heinz Holz and Wilhelm Weischedel in order to discuss the publisher's plans for a philosophy series with the working title Logos: Philosophische Texte [Logos: philosophical texts].[46] Apart from the classic texts studied as part of a philosophy degree, the series was to incorporate the writings of neglected Enlightenment authors who were rarely, if ever, considered a part of mainstream academic philosophy.[47] The series was later realized in a modified form as 'sammlung insel' [Insel collection].*

A few days after the meeting, Habermas voiced his reservations over the composition of the advisory editorial group. While he spoke of Weischedel, who was born in 1905, as an 'eminently sympathetic and superior intellect', he criticized Holz, a contemporary of his and a pupil of Bloch, for being unable to integrate his left-wing political interests with 'his philosophical knowledge'. 'Holz behaves like Lenin and then mentions Nicolai Hartmann – I find him astonishing', Habermas wrote in a letter to Unseld,

> while, to be honest, I am no less astonished by you when you expect fundamentally different decisions (regarding your series) than you could expect from, for instance, Mr Gadamer – that is, a very intelligent, humanistically inclined, knowledgeable selection from the texts of a worthy tradition, a principle of selection which I would advise you to adopt because it guarantees a decent quality.[48]

In the same letter, Habermas makes numerous initial suggestions for a selection of philosophers, among them,

> of course, the sophists . . . In a different category, there should be the neo-Pythagorean and neo-Platonic traditions of Hellenism, against whose gnostic claims the Church Fathers and school philosophy alike had to defend themselves. Here, we already find almost all of the motifs which could never be worked through by Christianized medieval philosophy without leaving the scars of hereticism. What Bloch calls the Aristotelian left developed not along this mystic lineage, but along the more naturalist and enlightenment lineage – i.e., the Jewish-Arabic traditions of the High Middle Ages. In more recent times,

---

* The Insel Verlag was originally founded in 1899 and was taken over by Suhrkamp in 1963.

both deviating lineages could again be followed: on the one hand, the pre-history of modern science in late Renaissance from Ludovico Vives's text on the soul to Bacon and Galileo; later, with a main focus on the eighteenth century in England and France, social and political philosophy (including Mandeville, Ferguson, John Millar, Bentham, Helvetius, Holbach, a number of articles from the *Encyclopédie*, Morelly, Meslier, Condorcet, de Sade) – and, on the other hand, the literature of the older German mystics and representatives specifically from Jewish and Protestant mysticism (Luria and the younger Kabbala, Böhme) up to Swabian pietism (why not bring something by Oetinger, who already reads more or less like Schelling), and then conclude with Baader, Steffens and one of the more abstruse pieces by Schelling: say Clara, for instance. This would bring us up to the official philosophers. Here, I would not reproduce the standard texts but, rather, those that are not included in traditional teaching as primary texts, be it because they are too mystical or too political, such as, for instance, Fichte's *Der geschlossene Handelsstaat* [The closed commercial state], Hegel's Jena *Realphilosophie*, or Schelling's first *Weltalterfragment*.* Finally, there is an urgent need for a reception of pragmatism, which is so far entirely repressed and only admitted in the form of Heidegger's ready-to-hand: Peirce, James, Dewey, Mead, Morris. Also a few texts from Vienna positivism . . . And, I might add, also a few linguistic analyses, although the conservatism of the old Wittgenstein[†] causes enough harm as it is (in Germany): apart from some nice essays by prominent Oxford scholars like Urmson and Winch, there are also some quite progressive [*aufklärerische*] texts: ethical writings by Stevenson or Hare.[49]

Despite these many and varied concrete suggestions, Habermas concludes his extensive letter, no doubt to Unseld's surprise, by saying that he wanted to end his involvement with the project with these hints.[50] He refers to a number of time-consuming commitments; he was, he said, among other things, an author for the Luchterhand Verlag and also editor at Kiepenheuer & Witsch. But, in conversation by telegram, letter and telephone, Unseld quickly managed to get Habermas back on board, and Habermas, in turn, spoke in a letter of a moment of 'inner reflection' which had brought about a 'change of mind'. He added that, provided there was sufficient remuneration, he could scale back other activities and thereby increase his involvement with Suhrkamp. Such an involvement was all the more desirable for Unseld and Karl Markus Michel, the

---

* Translated into English as *The Ages of the World*, trans. Frederick de Wolfe Bolman, Jr., New York, 1942.
† Presumably, this refers to the later Wittgenstein of the *Philosophical Investigations* rather than the early Wittgenstein of the *Tractatus*.

editor in charge of the new programme, as other publishing houses were working on similar projects: the Europäische Verlagsanstalt was preparing a series entitled Politische Texte [Political texts], edited by Wolfgang Abendroth, Ossip K. Flechtheim and Iring Fetscher, and the Luchterhand Verlag also planned to strengthen its theory programme, with the sociologists Heinz Maus and Friedrich Fürstenberg acting as editors. To begin with, Habermas and his colleague in Heidelberg, Dieter Henrich, were meant to be responsible as editors for the new theory programme, after Adorno and Weischedel had withdrawn from the project early on due to work commitments, and Unseld had decided to do without the collaboration of Hans Heinz Holz. However, in consultation with the publisher, it was then decided that two more philosophers, Hans Blumenberg and Jacob Taubes, would be included as editors.[51] The series 'Theorie 1' was meant to offer classical philosophical texts which had not received much attention in Germany. The editions were to have either an introduction or an afterword by an expert, commissioned by one of the editors. The series 'Theorie 2' was meant to have a more contemporary orientation and contain texts by living authors from the humanities and social sciences.

At the same time, a second project was launched by Suhrkamp. Apparently against Habermas's advice, the first *Kursbuch*, edited by Hans Magnus Enzensberger and Karl Markus Michel, was published in June 1965. Between 1965 and 1970, four editions would appear each year without Habermas publishing even a single item in this influential and widely read journal, despite repeated invitations from Enzensberger.[52]

Planning for the Theory series dragged on for over two years, as can be seen from extensive correspondence. During that time, the editors, who made a plethora of suggestions at their meetings, increasingly competed for originality. On 4 February 1966, Habermas wrote to Karl Markus Michel: 'I contemplate the mutual efforts of Mr Blumenberg and Mr Henrich from the necessary distance.'[53] Dieter Henrich, in turn, in a letter of 7 February 1966, expressed his doubts over the cooperation with Blumenberg, who tended to step out of line and go his own way.

These concise remarks indicate that from the very beginning there was continual friction between the editors, who watched each other suspiciously in their efforts at influencing Unseld. Unseld, for his part, apparently had varying degrees of sympathy for the editors. Thus Blumenberg, who complained about the lack of solidarity within the group, left the editorial team after about two years and would later criticize the hasty start of the 'Theorie' series as not very impressive.[54] On Habermas's suggestion, he was replaced by the sociologist Niklas Luhmann. Habermas and Henrich respected each other; Taubes's actions, however, were difficult to fathom.

His attitude towards Habermas is evident in letters he would later write to Carl Schmitt, in which he says that Habermas would 'shout his "mighty" word *ad* fascist intelligence into the meeting room of the advisors'. In another passage, he mocks the 'braying of the Habermasse'.*[55] It is true, though, that Habermas already enjoyed a privileged position at the Suhrkamp Verlag at that time. In a four-page memorandum in which Unseld and Karl Markus Michel summarized the state of affairs, the arrangements and agreements that had been made, they say:

> The most important person is Mr Habermas. . . . He will end his cooperation with the Becker Institute in Berlin in order to use his energies fruitfully and more usefully for the 'Theorie' project. He received a monthly salary of 500 Deutschmarks from the Becker Institute.† Obviously, the Suhrkamp Verlag must not offer him less. . . . The contract with Habermas and Henrich for Theorie 1 stipulates the following payments: 1. A one-off payment of 2,000 Deutschmarks for the planning phase. (This honorarium has already been paid and was well deserved.) 2. An honorarium as editors of 200 Deutschmarks for each published title – i.e., roughly 2,000 Deutschmarks each year, as we anticipate publishing ca. ten titles per year. 3. A fee dependent on sales of 2.5% of the retail price in the case of new editions (from 5,000 sold copies onwards). The contract with the editors should cover the following points. 1. The Suhrkamp Verlag publishes a Theorie section which will be edited as a whole by Blumenberg, Habermas, Henrich and Taubes. 2. The Theorie section is comprised of the series Theorie 1, Theorie 2 and a *Jahrbuch Theorie* [Theory yearbook]. Theorie 1 consists of philosophical texts with introductions, Theorie 2 of more recent studies from the areas of philosophy, sociology, psychology, ethnology, linguistics, history of science, etc. ('Humanities').‡ . . . Should any differences in opinion arise between Mr Habermas and Mr Henrich on the one hand, and Mr Blumenberg or Mr Taubes on the other, the editors concerned will work to reach a consensus.

For the editors, the prospect of being involved in ensuring that affordable, properly edited study texts for university courses became available was as attractive as the financial aspect, which would in the end be limited to a monthly advisory fee of 500 Deutschmarks. During the initial planning phase for the scientific programme,

---

* This is a pun on the fact that the plural form of Habermas's name yields the term 'Masse', hence can also be read as the 'Haber mass' – i.e., (blind) followers of Habermas.
† The Max-Planck-Institut für Bildungsforschung, Berlin [Max Planck Institute for Educational Research]. See the last paragraph of this section.
‡ 'Humanities' in English in the original.

Habermas went to the publishing house roughly once a week in order to discuss the state of play with Michel.

The two series were finally launched in the autumn of 1966. The first volume of Theorie 1 was an edition of Hegel's *Politische Schriften* [Political writings], with an afterword by Habermas, on the first page of which he stated boldly: 'The history of the world is the medium of experience in which philosophy must prove itself and may fail. . . . And it has to prove itself with regard to a theory of the present age: by offering an understanding of the contemporary situation within the context of world history.'[56]

The plans for the *Jahrbuch Theorie*, a kind of successor project to Horkheimer's *Zeitschrift für Sozialforschung* [Journal for Social Research], were apparently also far advanced at that point. We may deduce this from a letter of 22 December 1966 in which Jacob Taubes invited Hannah Arendt to contribute to the first volume of the yearbook with an essay on Sartre's *Critique de la raison dialectique** (the German translation with the title *Kritik der dialektischen Vernunft* appeared in 1967).[57]

Habermas was opposed to this project on the basis that they could not currently hope to match the quality of the old journal. From another memorandum of 14 July 1965 we learn that he suggested to Unseld that Suhrkamp should instead take over the Berlin journal *Das Argument*, which, he adds, appealed primarily to young left-wing intellectuals. In the end, this takeover never happened, and the plan for a journal or yearbook for the social sciences was never realized. Instead a decision was taken in favour of a discussion forum in book form, the series 'Theorie-Diskussion', to which Habermas contributed two volumes: *Hermeneutik und Ideologiekritik* [Hermeneutics and ideology critique] and *Theorie der Gesellschaft oder Sozialtechnologie: Was leistet die Systemforschung?* [Theory of society or social technology: what can systems theory do?] Of the latter, co-authored with Niklas Luhmann, 14,000 copies had to be printed in 1971, the year of its publication. Unseld was right: 'Scientific interest, theoretical curiosity, grow and grow.'[58]

After a quarrel with Unseld over the relaunch of the edition suhrkamp in which he accused the publisher of a political change of direction, Habermas left the editorial group of the Theorie series in 1979.[59] A little later, Unseld decided to discontinue the three separate series, or rather to integrate them into the Wissenschaftliches Hauptprogramm [main programme for academic titles], for which Friedhelm Herborth was meant to be the responsible editor.

This period of increasing activity as an advisor to Suhrkamp, which took up more and more of his time, was one of the main

---

* Jean-Paul Sartre, *Critique of Dialectical Reason*, London, 2004.

reasons why Habermas substantially reduced his advisory work for the Max-Planck-Institut für Bildungsforschung in Berlin [Max Planck Institute for Educational Research]. The institute had been founded in 1961 and was headed by its first director, Hellmut Becker. Habermas, who had become an advisor immediately after the multidisciplinary research institute's inception, ended his involvement with it altogether in 1971 when he became the director of his own Max Planck Institute. However, he continued his cooperation with the social and educational scientist Wolfgang Edelstein, who took up the directorship of the institute in Berlin in 1973. Edelstein was born the same year as Habermas, and he had undertaken his first study trip to the USA with him. As late as 1983, Habermas published a volume with him entitled *Soziale Interaktion und soziales Verstehen: Beiträge zur Entwicklung der Interaktionskompetenz* [Social interactions and social understanding: essays on the development of interactive competence]. Later, between 1982 and 1994, Habermas again served two terms as a member of the institute's academic advisory board. From 1969 onwards, his former assistant in Frankfurt, Ulrich Oevermann, carried out his important research at the institute on class-specific conditions of socialization and their influence on linguistic behaviour. Oevermann had given up his post as Habermas's assistant in order to pursue full time his research at the institute in Berlin, while holding a visiting professorship at the university in Frankfurt.

A man of the democratic left

Thinking the public sphere. In 1960, the year the first Easter March against nuclear armament took place, Habermas dealt with the difficult relationship between politics and morality, using Kant's essay on *Perpetual Peace*, Hegel's *Elements of the Philosophy of Right* and Jaspers's *The Atom Bomb and the Future of Man*. He also spoke on the topic at the VI. Deutscher Kongress für Philosophie [Sixth German Philosophy Congress] in Munich:

> Kant's design for a cosmopolitan condition is no longer the concrete shape of postulates for the improvement of the world deduced from moral philosophy; in the present situation it rather defines the limits of the chances for survival of the world as a whole as recognized by theory. . . . After all, we have for the first time a situation in which the question of the legal norms for international conflicts . . . of the elimination of war the fate of the world as a whole has become thematic.[60]

Where the 'whole' is at stake, philosophy as a critique of the state of the world can be no more than another player alongside human beings who act responsibly and determine their situation 'in forms of rational discussion'.[61] The lecture shows how Habermas's interest in politics guided his philosophical analyses from early on and how he took pains not to overestimate the potential of purely academic philosophy for a diagnostic understanding of the present.

On 17 September 1961, the elections for the fourth German Bundestag took place. They were dominated by the Berlin crisis, after the government of the German Democratic Republic had decided a month earlier to seal off East Berlin by erecting a wall in order to stem the tide of refugees, who were fleeing daily from East to West. From the Western Allies' point of view, this measure was in clear contravention of the four-power status of Berlin, and they responded by demanding that the Soviet Union remove roadblocks and put a stop to the building of the wall. British and American troops took up positions at the remaining border crossings. Despite all this, the GDR intensified its measures. A few days after the building of the wall had begun, Chancellor Adenauer visited West Berlin. His hopes that the Berlin crisis might give a boost to his party in the forthcoming national elections were not quite met. The coalition of CDU and CSU lost their absolute majority and received only 45.3 per cent of the vote, down from 50.2 per cent four years earlier. The Social Democrats, with Willy Brandt standing for the chancellorship for the first time, made substantial gains (+ 4.4 per cent), as did the FDP (+ 5.1 per cent), which achieved one of its best ever results in national elections, with 12.8 per cent of the second vote.[62] And so in November a coalition of CDU/CSU and FDP [Free Democratic Party] was formed, and Adenauer was elected chancellor once again. Support among the electorate for Adenauer's politics of 'Keine Experimente!' [No experiments!] slowly began to diminish,[63] but at the beginning of the 1960s a majority of the West German population was still concerned mostly with securing or improving their material standard of living. 'Fear of the past, flight from politics, indifference towards democracy' still characterized the political atmosphere at the end of the Adenauer era.[64]

In January 1961, Habermas published his article 'Die Bundesrepublik – eine Wahlmonarchie?' [The Federal Republic – an elective monarchy?] in a special issue of the prestigious cultural journal *Magnum*[65] titled *Woher wohin – Bilanz der Bundesrepublik* [Whence, whither – taking stock of the Federal Republic]. In his contribution, he discusses the lack of party-political alternatives, a theme which had yet to gain prominence at that time, as well as the causes of what is nowadays referred to as political apathy. Habermas worries that there can be no real alternative, on account of the pressures to conform within the political system. Election campaigns, he writes, are conducted on the model of consumer-oriented advertising, which promotes the de-politicization of the electorate. 'Far-reaching decisions are not publicly discussed by citizens, and then, by casting their vote, the fundamental principles are fixed. In reality they are launched according to criteria of public relations even before the election,* in order to . . . increase the "popularity" of the great men, who . . . today replace the immediate relationship of the individual with politics.'[66]

This critique of the *Kanzlerdemokratie* [Chancellor democracy], which is still (or again) relevant today, as well as of the manipulative public relations work of the political parties and personality-driven reporting of the media, drew on the findings of Habermas's Habilitation on *The Structural Transformation of the Public Sphere*. It had been published by Luchterhand Verlag in 1962 and was dedicated 'To Wolfgang Abendroth in gratitude'.[67] The book was a great success, seeing several editions within just a few years, and it quickly became a standard text in various disciplines and a steady seller which, over the decades, has been translated into more than thirty languages.[68] Even today, the study hits a nerve, since a continuously transforming public sphere produces ever changing effects on political practice. With a few caveats, Habermas's claims about the problems resulting from the commercialization accompanying the organization of the mass media in the private sector, and in West Germany from the tendency towards the formation of monopolies in the media sector, remain valid today. At the end of the 1960s, the leading voices of the *Außerparlamentarische Opposition*† [extraparliamentary opposition] would make use of his diagnosis of emerging power formations within the public sphere in their fight against the Springer press.

Apart from that, Habermas's prediction for the 'fate' of the public sphere – by which he means, to be precise, the bourgeois public sphere – is gloomy. Fundamentally, his book tells the story of its decline beginning at the end of the nineteenth century, which led to an overlapping of the once separate public and private spheres. The cause, he argues, was 'this dialectic of a progressive "societalization" of the state simultaneously with an increasing "stateification" [*Verstaatlichung*] of society'. This dynamic 'gradually destroyed the basis of the bourgeois public sphere – the separation of state and society.'[69] A transformation of the public sphere's political function also took place, in parallel with the transformation of its social structure. To the extent that the public spheres of mass democracies are produced by media of mass communication, which, in turn, act primarily with the aim of selling their goods, a progressive

---

* 'Public relations' in English in the original.
† The Außerparlamentarische Opposition, APO for short, formed in 1966 in reaction to the Great Coalition between CDU/CSU and SPD, with no relevant party-political opposition left in parliament.

de-politicization of the public sphere takes place. The commodities produced by the media industry, which are intended both to stimulate and to satisfy consumer needs, are 'more likely to give rise to an impersonal indulgence in stimulating relaxation than to a public use of reason'.[70] A critical publishing culture is replaced with a demonstrative and manipulative one that serves the purpose of propagating the positions of influential interest groups.

Habermas draws the conclusion that the media of mass communication do not constitute a neutral medium for the articulation of a public sphere, regardless of whether they are private-sector organizations, like most of the press, or public bodies, like some of the radio and television stations in the Federal Republic. Rather, they represent elements of power within the public sphere which are used for the purpose of legitimizing state policies as well as being instrumentalized by economic and political interest groups. A public sphere deformed by power formations, Habermas says, is a contradiction in itself; it even turns into the very opposite of what it used to be, or at least what it was meant to be, because the establishment of powerful mass media goes hand in hand with the exertion of external influence on the public sphere. Thus, as Habermas puts it in a preface to the 1990 edition of the book, there emerges a new 'category of influence, namely the power of the media', which employs the public sphere for its own ends.[71] The appropriation of the public sphere by the particular interests of media groups, Habermas says, constitutes the end point of a 'refeudalization' of the public sphere. This tendency is clearly evident in the various forms of political propaganda, advertising, marketing and public relations.* And the fusion of entertainment and information is ultimately one of the reasons why citizens increasingly retreat into the private realm and why political apathy spreads.

Democratization from within. In the concluding part of his study, Habermas bootstraps his way out of his pessimistic historical analysis and sketches some possible solutions. The principle of publicity, he suggests, has to be reinterpreted and understood as a principle of the welfare state. In other words, within a democracy which, as a welfare state, preserves a continuity with the liberal constitutional state, the effectiveness of discursive, democratic political opinion- and will-formation must be guaranteed by making the requirements of publicity binding on all institutions involved in this process. Thus, the mass media in their institutional organization and 'inner structure must first be organized in accordance with the principle of publicity'[72] – hence they must correspond to democratic principles in

---

* 'Marketing' and 'public relations' in English in the original.

their internal workings. Democracy within organizations, Habermas hopes, would not only provide institutionally guaranteed spaces of critical publicity but also, in particular, increase the opportunities for political participation – the 'participation of private people in a process of formal communication conducted through intraorganizational public spheres'.[73]

In the preface to the 1990 edition, Habermas retrospectively criticizes the logic of decline informing his study, as expressed in particular by the normative hierarchy between an 'idealistically elevated past and a cultural-critical distortion of the present'.[74] He understands the public sphere no longer in terms of an assembled public but, rather, as a process through which a society reaches an understanding of itself and enlightens itself about its own political will.

After *Structural Transformation* had been published by Luchterhand as volume 4 of 'Politica', the two editors of this series, Wilhelm Hennis and Roman Schnur – the former a pupil of the theorist of state law Rudolf Smend, the latter of Carl Schmitt – disagreed over whether Habermas's volume of collected essays *Theory and Practice* should also be included in it. Hennis insisted on making the title part of the series and, in 1963, the two fell out over the matter. The work finally appeared as volume 11.[75]

Positions in the dispute over the right form of critique and good politics

The positivist dispute. In 1961, a workshop of the Deutsche Gesellschaft für Soziologie [German Society for Sociology] took place in Tübingen. The meeting has since become legendary as the opening round in the so-called positivist dispute (in German sociology). Ralf Dahrendorf, who had just been appointed to a chair in Tübingen, was the initiator of the conference, and Karl R. Popper and Theodor W. Adorno were the main speakers on the topic of 'Die Logik der Sozialwissenschaften' [The logic of the social sciences]. Popper opened the discussion with a paper in which he presented his philosophy of science, which he labelled 'Critical Rationalism', in the form of twenty-seven theses. In the second paper of the session, Adorno used Popper's theses to demonstrate the position of Critical Theory as an independent paradigm. To the surprise of many of those present, the discussion of the two papers, in which Habermas participated, was hardly contentious. Rather than explicitly setting their positions in opposition to each other, Popper and Adorno did no more than present the fundamental assumptions of their respective positions regarding the theory of science. Maybe Habermas thought the discussion too cautious, but in any case he found Adorno's arguments weak, which led him, according to his own testimony, to initiate a second round in the positivist dispute not quite two years later. This time, the tone was more heated. In his contribution to a Festschrift on the occasion of Adorno's sixtieth birthday, Habermas launched a full-frontal attack against Critical Rationalism's understanding of science and provoked an equally sharp response from Hans Albert, which the philosopher published in the *Kölner Zeitschrift für Soziologie* in 1964.[76]

Habermas's contributions to the positivist debate removed any doubts as to whether he should be considered a member of the Frankfurt circle, as he fully supported Adorno's position. And yet he was guided by a thought which went beyond Adorno's mode of thinking – that is, 'the idea of a rationality with unconstrained validity in a "domination-free discussion"'.[77] Popper and Albert, by contrast, were committed to a 'bisected rationalism', because their scientific analyses were limited to the treatment of technically resolvable tasks, which had to be distinguished from practical-normative questions.[78] For Habermas, one of the advantages of Adorno's type of dialectical thinking was that it 'takes the social context of life as a totality which determines even the research itself'.[79] In other words, any research, no matter how objective it tried to be, and how methodologically well grounded it was, still remained embedded in the lifeworld, and this social context needed to be accounted for in a self-reflexive manner. Therefore, 'the hermeneutic explication of meaning . . . [has to replace] the hypothetical-deductive connection of propositions.'[80] With hindsight, it is clear that the contributions to the positivist debate, which Habermas published in 1963 and 1964, were exploratory investigations in the theory of science, and that in this sense they were 'products' on a path that would turn out to be a dead end for him. At the beginning of the 1970s, Habermas would abandon his attempt at grounding a critical science on the basis of epistemology and the theory of science.[81]

It seems that the debate over the logic of the social sciences led to some resentment on both sides. Albert, in a letter he wrote to his great idol Popper in November 1963, still expressed himself in comparatively favourable terms about his opponent. Habermas, he said, was 'infected with "dialectics", but very tolerant and eager to learn', having made quite some effort at understanding Critical Rationalism. Further letters followed which were less polite. In November 1969, Popper wrote to Albert: 'I have now received the "Positivist Dispute"' – i.e., the book edited by Adorno which contained the most important contributions to the debate. 'Well, poor Adorno is dead – but, alas, he did not know what intellectual responsibility (or righteousness) means. And Habermas is a blockhead. It is simply impossible to tell what kind of damage he is still going to cause in the future.' A little later, Albert admitted that Habermas

was 'a star in intellectual circles, a much admired man'. Popper con-
soled his correspondent by assuring him that the pieces of wisdom
uttered by these dialectical minds were nothing but 'trivialities . . .
expressed in the language of magic formulas'.[82] However, Habermas
also knew how to lash out, and he did so in several texts, among
which 'Gegen einen positivistisch halbierten Rationalismus' [Against
a positivistically bisected rationalism],* explicitly titled 'Eine Polemik'
[A polemic], stands out. It appeared in 1964 in the *Kölner Zeitung
für Soziologie*. In *Knowledge and Human Interests* he would again
express his criticisms of positivism. Popper, for his part, throughout
his life defended himself against being characterized as a 'positivist'.
To a certain extent, he may be right; his position has little to do with
the positivism of, for instance, the Vienna Circle. And the idea of a
unitary science was also alien to him.

In October 1962, Habermas attended the Deutscher Kongress
für Philosophie [German Philosophy Congress] in Münster. The
theme was 'Philosophie und Fortschritt' [Philosophy and progress].
Habermas gave a paper on 'Naturrecht und Revolution' [Natural
law and revolution] and also listened to a paper by Adorno in which
he developed 'the dialectic of progress itself':

> Progress means: to step out of the magic spell, even out of the spell of
> progress that is itself nature, in that humanity becomes aware of its
> own inbred nature and brings to a halt the domination it exacts upon
> nature and through which domination by nature continues. In this
> way it could be said that progress occurs where it ends.[83]

Habermas later remarked that here one heard an 'author' speak
amid the 'civil servants' of academically approved philosophy.[84]

Might it have been the theses advanced by Habermas in a lecture
he gave in January 1962 in Berlin on 'Kritische und konservative
Aufgaben der Soziologie' [Critical and conservative tasks of sociol-
ogy][85] that led to an invitation by the SDS just a few months later?†
In any case, on 4 October 1962 Habermas gave the main lecture at
the SDS conference in Frankfurt am Main. He had been in contact
with the SDS for some time and maintained these contacts even
after the SPD severed all links with its student organization over
political differences. The SDS found it hard to reconcile itself with its
'mother party's' Godesberg programme‡ and stood up for a social-

---

* The existing English translation of the title omits the 'against': 'A positivistically
bisected rationalism', in *The Positivist Dispute in German Sociology*, trans. Glyn Adey
and David Frisby, London, 1976, pp. 199–225.
† Sozialistischer Deutscher Studentenbund [Socialist German Student Association].
‡ The Godesberg programme of the SPD, adopted on 15 November 1959 at a party
convention in Bad Godesberg, marked a move away from Marxist ideas and towards the
political centre.

ist alternative both to the latter and to the dogmatic party-centred communism of the East German SED.* When in October 1961 a support organization for the SDS was created upon the initiative of the social scientists Wolfgang Abendroth and Ossip Flechtheim, Habermas joined immediately. He wrote a short preface sympathizing with the aims of the students for the SDS's Hochschuldenkschrift [university communiqué] *Hochschule und Demokratie* [University and democracy], written by Wolfgang Nitsch, Uta Gerhardt, Claus Offe and Ulrich Karl Preuß.[86]

However, Habermas's lecture at the delegates' conference, and the ensuing discussion, also marked the beginning of what would become an increasingly tense relationship with the 'intellectual wing' of the student body's political left, as the SDS styled itself. At that early point, Habermas had already warned against two possible 'temptations': to act as the intellectual cadre of a new party or to become professional revolutionaries and concentrate exclusively on the political underground.[87]

The Spiegel *affair*. October 1962 was a 'torrid month'. On 14 October, the Cuban Missile Crisis began in earnest, and at the end of the month the young democracy in West Germany faced its first real test. On 26 October 1962 the main editor of the magazine *Der Spiegel*, Rudolf Augstein, and the magazine's editors-in-chief were arrested in a cloak-and-dagger operation on the vague suspicion that leading journalists working for the magazine were guilty of revealing state secrets in a critical article on a NATO manoeuvre. Immediately after the arrest, a flood of public protests took place to express doubts over the legality of the operation, ordered by the defence minister, Franz Josef Strauß. What outraged left-wing intellectuals and liberal spirits such as the publicist Sebastian Haffner or the political scientist Karl Dietrich Bracher was the sheer audacity of a political class that openly asserted a right to act above the law. In September 1963, Hermann Höcherl (CSU), the minister of the interior at the time, expressed this view with cynical clarity. Höcherl said that, after all, the staff of the Verfassungsschutz [Office for the Protection of the Constitution] could 'not run around with the Basic Law under their arm at all times'.[88]

Among the many protests was a petition submitted to the president of the Bundestag, Eugen Gerstenmaier, who had been a member of the Kreisauer Kreis and thus active in the resistance against Hitler.† In the petition, initiated by members of the

---

* Sozialistische Einheitspartei Deutschlands = Socialist Unity Party of Germany.

† The circle around Helmuth James Graf von Moltke and Peter Graf Yorck von Wartenburg, which formed in 1940. The name of Moltke's manorial estate in Silesia was Gut Kreisau.

University of Heidelberg and signed by, among others, Alexander Mitscherlich, Dolf Sternberger, Karl Löwith, Alexander Rüstow and Peter Wapnewski, as well as by Habermas, it said:

> The absence of democratic continuity in Germany, the memory of the decline of the Weimar Republic, and the ensuing rupture in our tradition of the rule of law during the Hitler era obliges all of us to safeguard the constitutional order and political decency. The monitoring of governmental activities is the task of the parliament as a whole.[89]

And, this time, the parliament fulfilled its duty. There were tumultuous discussions, and within a short period of time the *Spiegel* affair turned into a veritable political crisis. On 19 November 1962, the ministers from the FDP resigned in protest at Strauß, who finally resigned on 30 November. In mid-December, the coalition government collapsed and Adenauer had to form a new cabinet.

Almost three decades later, Habermas would write that, as a result of the Spiegel affair, the intellectuals who intervened were now taken seriously, because they had clearly been able to mobilize the public in a way the political class could no longer ignore. And the intellectuals, for their part, felt they could trust 'the force of social integration that lay in a public that wanted to change attitudes through argument.'[90]

During the first half of the 1960s, Habermas was again very active in journalism. He wrote an article for *Die Zeit*, published on 12 June 1964, in which he refers to Peter Weiss's play *Marat/ Sade*,* which premiered on 29 April at the Schillertheater in Berlin, directed by Konrad Swinarsky. He defended the play against Rolf Hochhuth's 'Christian tragic drama' *The Deputy*, which premiered at the Theater am Kurfürstendamm (Freie Volksbühne), directed by Erwin Piscator. Habermas had seen both plays in Berlin. In contrast to Hochhuth, who used the means of documentary theatre in order to present the attitude of the Vatican towards the Holocaust on the stage, Weiss did not, according to Habermas, make use of contemporary history and also did not, like Brecht, work on the basis of a 'pre-determined truth'.

In July 1963, Habermas published a polemic against the initiative for 'Moralische Aufrüstung' [Moral Re-Armament] in the 'Marginalia' section of *Merkur*. He wrote of this group, which claimed to represent 'Western' values, that its aggressive campaign

---

* Thus the rather short English title for *Die Verfolgung und Ermordung Jean Paul Marats dargestellt durch die Schauspieltgruppe des Hospizes zu Charenton unter Anleitung des Herrn de Sade* [The hunting down and murder of Jean Paul Marat, represented by the theatre group of the asylum at Charenton under the direction of Mr de Sade].

against minorities, such as homosexuals, pacifists and intellectuals, was constructed exactly 'on the model of anti-Semitism' in order to 'help prepare future pogroms – that is, the persecution of groups that have previously been exposed to the explosive mixture of political fear and moral contempt.'[91]

In April 1964, a group of left-leaning citizens, among them Wolfgang Abendroth, Max Born, Helmut Gollwitzer, Erich Kästner, Alfred von Martin, Hans Erich Nossack and Renate Riemeck, as well as a large number of pastors and priests, wrote an open letter to Ludwig Erhard, who was chancellor following Adenauer's resignation in October 1963. Werner Wesselhoeft, Habermas's father-in-law, was one of the signatories. Habermas knew about the letter, which argued against policies of increasing armaments and of acquiring nuclear weapons. He wrote an accompanying article in the *Blätter für deutsche und internationale Politik* [Newssheet for German and International Politics], in which he called for an 'abstention from military calculations, which, in the light of the nuclear stalemate now reached between East and West, can neither produce the correct result nor correspond to political requirements in a time of easing tensions.'[92] When Erhard invited him to a discussion on the topic of 'Deutschland aus innerer und äußerer Sicht' [Germany as seen from the inside and outside] at the end of July 1964, he declined, citing health reasons.

It is obvious that Habermas was still committed to a strict pacifism at the time. On 18 September 1964, he published a scathing critique of some ideas of the right-wing conservative publicist Armin Mohler in *Die Zeit*. Mohler had written his doctorate on *Die Konservative Revolution in Deutschland, 1918–1932* [The conservative revolution in Germany 1918–1932] with Herman Schmalenbach and Jaspers, before working for some time as Ernst Jünger's private secretary. He was the head of the Carl Friedrich von Siemens Stiftung until 1985 and is generally considered to be one of the pioneering thinkers of the new right. In *Die Fünfte Republik: Was steht hinter de Gaulle?* [The Fifth Republic: what does de Gaulle stand for?], published in 1964, he uses the patriotic foreign policies of Gaullism as his example in promoting a concept of statist power politics that bases the self-assertion of sovereign states on a balance of terror in the face of the destructive potential of nuclear weapons. Following a discussion between Mohler and Marion Gräfin Dönhoff, in *Die Zeit* of 28 August 1964,* Habermas responded with an article in the same paper on 18 September: '[t]he violent substance of a potentially unrestrained self-assertion of sovereign states against each other has lost its barbarian innocence.' The absurdity, he says, is that, while

---

* Marion Gräfin Dönhoff was deputy-editor-in-chief of the paper at the time.

the major nuclear powers possess an effective potential threat in the form of their thermonuclear weapons, the use of these means of violence was simply forbidden on the grounds of self-preservation. The idea of a 'Weltinnenpolitik' [global domestic politics], favoured by President Kennedy – this is the first time that Habermas uses this concept, as well as that of a 'Weltöffentlichkeit' [global public sphere] – takes account of this 'peculiar dialectic of threats'. 'The policies of arms limitation and of diminishing the gap between rich and poor peoples that are needed today result from the imperatives of power politics and yet imply their self-sublation.'[93]

Habermas used his review of Karl Jaspers's latest book, *The Future of Germany* (published in early 1965 by Piper Verlag),* in *Die Zeit* (13 May 1966) to comment on the 'Verjährungsdebatte', the parliamentary debate about the statute of limitation for Nazi crimes that had taken place on 10 March. Like Jaspers, he criticized the fact that the parliament had 'fundamentally accepted the principle of limitation because of the desire finally to "draw a line under" the crimes.' And he also shared Jaspers's concerns over the possibility that the German Rechtsstaat [constitutional state] could become a mere façade, pointing to the *Spiegel* affair and the prohibition of the KPD as examples of basic rights being disregarded. However, Habermas took issue with Jaspers's armchair defeatism, against which he said that a democracy depends on the fact that citizens take the organization of their social life into their own hands.

Around the same time, Hans Paeschke suggested to Habermas that he write a regular international press review as a column in *Merkur*. He declined the offer, saying that, while he was attracted to the idea, it was too much for a single person. And he added:

> Finally, as far as my regular collaboration is concerned, my wife, who knows well enough how I work, has by now convinced me that this is only going to happen if fixed routines are agreed. Thus, I might for instance agree to provide at the beginning of every quarter (or even just at the beginning of every university term) a critical report on new publications or on topical themes from my area, which chiefly involves sociological-political-philosophical interests.[94]

The high value Habermas attached to politics as a form of acting within civil society is illustrated by his review of Enzensberger's collection of essays *Politics and Crime*, in the *Frankfurter Allgemeine Zeitung* of 17 October 1964.† Under the heading 'Vom Ende der Politik – oder die unterhaltsamen Kolportagen des Kriminalberichterstatters

---

* The German title – *Wohin treibt die Bundesrepublik?* [Whither drifts the Federal Republic?] – is less neutral than the one chosen for the English translation.
† Hans Magnus Enzensberger, *Politics and Crime*, New York, 1974.

Hans Magnus Enzensberger' [On the end of politics – or, the enter-taining pieces of Hans Magnus Enzensberger, the crime reporter], he criticizes Enzensberger's generalizing perspective, which attempts to subsume any form of politics under the concept of crime. However, with the establishment of democratic constitutional states, politics no longer operates in a legal vacuum, nor does the law simply mirror domination. For this reason, the seemingly radical formula of 'the presence of Auschwitz', which Enzensberger tries to use to 'recognize the dark connection between morality and politics', is highly problematic. Like Hannah Arendt, Habermas observes the 'banality of evil',[95] although he does not feel entirely comfortable with this formulation, because – as the end of the review has it – 'there are de-mythologizations which are insufficient to break the power of myth, or the myth of power. If no dread remains, the monsters return.' Habermas's resistance to the thesis of an 'identity in substance between politics and crime',[96] which became increasingly popular from the mid-1960s onwards and which, from his perspective, probably appeared to be cheap and simplistic, shows what exercised him at the time, and, we may assume, still exercises him today: that politics is not a special sphere of society from which a scientist should keep a distance in order to avoid getting their hands dirty. Instead of treating it with scorn, contempt or disgust, a scientist should take politics and its democratically legitimized organizational spaces seriously, should use these spaces for 'interventions' in order to influence attitudes and bring about change. This is not the attitude of a revolutionary; it is that of a reformer. Habermas's journalistic pieces from that period provide good evidence of what kind of reforms he had in mind at the time. On the one hand, he began to promote a strictly democratic interpretation of the constitution, coming close in this to the slogan later used by Willy Brandt: 'Mehr Demokratie wagen' [Let's risk more democracy]. With this attitude, Habermas opposed the concept of a 'formed society', which the advisor to the chancellor Rüdiger Altmann, also a pupil of Abendroth,[97] had developed.* On the other hand, Habermas supported demands for a reform and democratization of the universities, which had been intensifying since the mid-1960s, and he occupied himself with the aims and political activities of the student movement, which was growing in size and public importance.

Educational and university policies. The study on *Student und Politik* [Students and politics], whose radically democratic introduction so infuriated Horkheimer, was not the first time Habermas dealt with

---

* This concept aimed at the formation of strong and stable common interests within society and the avoidance of conflicting particular interests, which would allow for a strong state representing the interest of the commonwealth.

the topic of the 'universities and politics'. In the spring of 1957, he had tackled the 'Chronische Leiden der Hochschulreform' [The chronic illness of the university reforms] in *Merkur*, using results from the study *Universität und Gesellschaft* [University and society], which had been carried out at the Institute for Social Research under the direction of Adorno and in cooperation with, among others, the sociologists Hans Anger and Friedrich Tenbruck.[98] Habermas argued that university reform as an automatic process of continuing rationalization is limited to short-term measures and amounts to no more than an affirmative reformism which ignores the core elements of a university, namely the unity of science, the unity of research and teaching, and academic freedom in teaching and learning. Even at that early point, Habermas was already criticizing the specialization of individual disciplines, which was leading to an increasing distance between subject areas, as well as to the bureaucratization of the institution and the increasing formalization of the teaching curriculum. According to Habermas, if a progressive spirit was to dominate the universities, it could do so only if they opposed the technocratic tendencies of the age, maintained their independence from state influences, and did not exclusively reward efficiency and utility: 'The university can no more escape the new forms of interconnection than any other institution. It adapts to advances from two sides: both the state and the economy approach it as major clients, so to speak.'[99] Thus, the researcher is in danger of falling into a double-bind: on the one hand, he tries to legitimize the results of his research in terms of their technical utility and, on the other, he must insist on their being value-free. The outcome of this, Habermas writes, is that the results lose their orientation towards practical life; they are no longer 'a catalyst for life'. The aim of any future university reform worthy of the name therefore has to be to create the space in which the actual purpose of a university can be pursued: the self-reflection of science, which entails first and foremost reflection on the practical consequences of science for life, on their social-practical effects and on the relationship between science and society.

Six years later, Habermas published another article in *Merkur*. 'Vom sozialen Wandel akademischer Bildung' [On social changes in academic education] diagnoses the failure of academic education, which, it claims, has been reduced to little more than a preparation for professional life. Referring to the situation at the beginning of the 1960s, Habermas says that university degree courses in general teach useful skills, 'but the capacity to utilize [*Verfügenkönnen*] in which the sciences specialize is not the same as the capacity to live and act' that one could previously have expected of those who were academically educated.[100] He asks what an adequate contemporary concept of education might look like. His solution consists not in a return to the institutions of the nineteenth century, which aimed at forming the character of the bourgeois educational classes, but in the inculcation of capacities that he defines in rather abstract terms as making possible the 'return of the power of technical control to the realm of consensus between acting and negotiating citizens'.[101] Habermas means to say that not everything that is technically possible should therefore also be automatically carried out; rather, this should happen only when what is technically possible also earns universal approval. Against Helmut Schelsky, who held that technologically advanced sciences and even political decision-making allowed only for the application of fact-based regularities, Habermas avers that technological progress loses that 'seeming appearance of being automatic, once there is reflection on the social context of interests which determine the precise direction it takes . . . However, the task of translating the scientifically reified relationships back into the net of lived relations falls in the first instance to the sciences themselves.'[102] Hence, the system of university education had to be adapted to this new challenge.

During those years, Habermas and Schelsky corresponded extensively, in particular on questions of educational policy. Their correspondence was quite insistently maintained by Schelsky, who had a reputation not only for having an anti-Marxist attitude but also for having a good sense for public relations.[103] In 1963, his book *Einsamkeit und Freiheit: Die Idee und Gestalt der deutschen Universität und ihrer Reformen* [Solitude and freedom: the idea and form of the German university and its reforms] was published, and Habermas discussed it on a radio programme. After that, Schelsky was invited to participate in projects for university reforms in Bielefeld, where he established the Zentrum für interdisziplinäre Forschung [Centre for Interdisciplinary Research], which became the nucleus for the University of Bielefeld founded in 1969. After 1970, he distanced himself slightly from his former intellectual companion Arnold Gehlen and began to reflect more critically on the latter's book *Moral und Hypermoral* [Morality and hypermorality]. At the same time, he seems to have developed a certain sympathy for Habermas's ideas on 'education as moral sovereignty' and 'reflection as self-awareness of the sciences', which he discussed over several pages in his letters to Habermas. He also agreed with Habermas that science has a political dimension.[104]

In 1961, Habermas had reviewed Schelsky's earlier *Anpassung oder Widerstand: Soziologische Bedenken zur Schulreform* [Adaptation or resistance: sociological reservations regarding the reform of the schools]. The review was critical of how Schelsky conceives of education, namely as a private process transcending the sciences. Habermas distances himself from Schelsky's objections to a 'Schonraumpädagogik' [pedagogy of sheltered spaces] – i.e., to an education of pupils 'at the expense of those competencies'

which 'would turn . . . schools into "leadership institutions". When
Schelsky declares that an educational society would be "a serious
threat to human freedom", his argument must rest on a tacit anthropological premise which says that human nature would not be able
to learn cultural patterns of experience and social patterns of behaviour without the threat of sanctions.'[105] Habermas did not share this
premise. Despite their many openly discussed differences, Schelsky
did not end his correspondence with Habermas – on the contrary,
in the following years, he deluged Habermas with letters in which
he mostly focuses on their common ground. Even when Habermas
published a biting critique of Arnold Gehlen in *Merkur*, in which he
accused Gehlen of denouncing 'humanitarianism' and defending the
'substantiality of institutional power', Schelsky agreed with him in
principle, despite raising some objections.[106]

Habermas's numerous publications on educational and university policies in the late 1960s and throughout the 1970s express more
than just his special interest in the future shape of an institution
of which he himself is a part. They always at the same time reflect
the themes which occupy him as a philosopher and sociologist: the
relationship between theory and practice, between the public sphere
and democracy, between hermeneutics and empirical work. But
the main questions which crystallized in the mid-1960s, and which
would exercise him for some years to come, were the following:
What is the status of a self-reflective epistemology in a social science
guided by the distinction between 'is' and 'ought'? From which processes does this 'ought' result? How can it convincingly be argued
for? The core of Habermas's interest was 'to name the normative
ground [*Rechtsgründe*]* of critique'.[107]

---

* The technical term 'Rechtsgrund' [legal ground] is obviously used metaphorically in
this context. In *Philosophical-Political Profiles*, the translation of 'Rechtsgründe der
Kritik' is 'reasons for the right of criticism' (p. 106). However, the point is not the right to
practise criticism but the normative ground of that practice.

5

Back in Frankfurt:
Torn between Academic
Work and Political Practice

Successor to Max Horkheimer. After Horkheimer had signed his retirement document, a university commission was created to appoint a chair of sociology and philosophy at the University of Frankfurt. According to a letter from the minister for culture and education dated 30 August 1961, Horkheimer was released from his duties as a professor with effect from 1 April 1962. However, he continued to teach, at least occasionally, and to participate in faculty business. And what's more, together with Adorno, the philosopher Bruno Liebrucks, the theologian Johannes Hirschberg, the educationalist Martin Rang and the philologist Alfred Rammelmeyer, Horkheimer was a member of the committee to appoint his successor.[1] The commission's members were at cross-purposes and found it difficult to identify candidates with the required qualifications in both sociology and philosophy. And so, at the behest of the dean, two lists were initially drawn up, one of pure philosophers and one of individuals with qualifications in sociology and philosophy. Apparently, Adorno called Habermas and asked him to suggest suitable candidates, alongside Habermas himself. On 8 May 1963, Habermas wrote to Adorno:

> After pondering over this for a long time, the only names that remain are really the ones which, as far as I know, have been discussed at your faculty on previous occasions, namely first of all Mr von Kempski, then also Mr Lübbe, who, compared to all the others, philosophizes with a certain quality, although in the interest of the university one should add that he is politically influenced by Gehlen and Carl Schmitt to a certain degree. .... Of course, I would have first mentioned my friend Karl-Otto Apel had he not taken up a chair in Kiel just last summer.[2]

There were only two names on the list of candidates with the double qualification: Hermann Lübbe and Jürgen Habermas. On the list of philosophers there were three candidates, none of whom had a particularly outstanding profile: Eugen Fink, Gerhart Schmidt and Joachim Kopper. A preamble to the list also mentions Horkheimer's former assistant Karl Heinz Haag. At various meetings of the commission, and later at the decisive faculty meeting, Adorno and Horkheimer expressed their unambiguous support for appointing Habermas, against the vote of Liebrucks.[3] According to Adorno, Habermas was best suited 'to combine theoretical sociology and philosophy', and for Horkheimer he was the only 'individual of distinction' among the philosophers. Adorno and Horkheimer used all of their tactical skills in order to push through their candidate, who, as they pointed out, was an established philosopher and sociologist. The fact that Habermas did not want to take over the directorship of the Institute for Social Research did not, according to Horkheimer, create a problem, because the request for another chair in sociology had already been made. That chair would be created imminently, so that arrangements for appointing his successor as director were in place. When, in a vote with three abstentions, Habermas was indeed nominated as the first candidate on the list, Rammelmeyer suggested he be named *unico loco* – i.e., the only candidate for the job – a suggestion that was approved in a vote with two abstentions. Thus, in July 1963 the faculty presented the minister with a list that consisted of only one candidate .[4]

In their letter of 26 July to the Hessian minister for culture and education, the Faculty of Philosophy called the appointment urgent, and the dean pushed for permission to do without the usual list of three candidates. The faculty, he wrote, selected Habermas as the sole candidate because 'no other comparable candidate is available'. The appointment, the letter says, is 'a matter of great urgency . . ., because the Freie Universität Berlin is . . . also extremely interested in Mr Habermas.'[5] On 26 February 1963, Horkheimer had already written to Habermas, saying he should decide in favour of Berlin only 'if Adorno's and my wish, which you know, will not be fulfilled'.[6] In the negotiations between Habermas and the Hessian Ministry of Culture, an agreement was eventually reached regarding a special salary, guaranteed teaching fees and generous staffing of the chair, and Habermas officially accepted the appointment in January, taking up his post at the Faculty of Philosophy for the summer term 1964. Later, he would tell his predecessor 'how much [he] experienced succeeding [him] in [his] teaching post as an honour, and as an even stronger motivation to work here, as far as [he] could, in [his] spirit.'[7]

In a letter of 29 September 1964 to the Ministerialrätin [ministerial undersecretary] Helene von Bila, Habermas listed with absolute clarity the conditions which needed to be fulfilled if he were actually to take up the appointment at Frankfurt: 'Since the return of Mr Horkheimer and Mr Adorno, sociology in Frankfurt has developed into a prestigious and internationally respected part of German post-war sociology. In contravention of common academic practice, this school of thought does not find the adequate conditions for replenishment at its own university. Additional staffing is more urgently required today than ever before.' Habermas made use of his position as a newcomer, demanding nothing less than the creation of a further chair in the Faculty of Philosophy. 'After all', the letter to von Bila says, 'this matter could be considered a test case for finding out whether organizational decisions regarding the question of who represents sociology at the University of Frankfurt are taken in a purely objective fashion, or whether they aim to discriminate against certain schools of thought.'[8] From another letter, we may conclude how Habermas saw his position at his new workplace. On 18 November 1965, he wrote to Ludwig von Friedeburg, who at that time still occupied the chair of sociology at the Freie Universität Berlin but had been offered a full professorship in sociology in the Faculty of Philosophy at Frankfurt University; he was also supposed to become the third director of the Institute for Social Research alongside Adorno and Rudolf Gunzert. During the negotiations over his appointment, and with Habermas's blessing, von Friedeburg was able to secure the promise that a new, separate sociological faculty would be created in Myliusstraße. Habermas wanted to be on good terms with his future colleague early on and wrote to him:

1) I only came to Frankfurt because the chair here allows me to pursue my philosophical and sociological interests at the same time. I practise philosophy and sociology to the same extent here. 2) I have no institutional interests at all. That does not mean that I am uninterested in empirical research. . . . My ambitions certainly include the organization of theoretically well-prepared and intelligently designed investigations. . . . 3) For these purposes it is sufficient for me to give lectures and seminars in sociology and, in rather old-fashioned and contented style, to live in the outbuildings of institutionalized research, pursuing individual and cooperative scholarship with two assistants. Prior to my appointment I asked for a reward in return for my forgoing this institutional influence, namely that I should not be involved in the examinations in sociology. . . . 4) I came to Frankfurt assuming that Horkheimer and Adorno's explicit assurance over the legal title for a Department of Sociology at our faculty would be honoured. . . . I attach importance to this legal title because I do not, under any circumstances, wish to see an amalgamation of philosophy and sociology at the level of departments or assistants.[9]

The new post meant that the family had to move from Heidelberg to Frankfurt, and they did so in 1965. This time, they did not live in the city. Following all-day excursions that Habermas took with his assistant Ulrich Oevermann, they decided in favour of Steinbach, a small town on the edge of the Taunus Mountains. They moved into an end-of-terrace house, Hohenwaldstraße 48, a relatively narrow place with rooms over two floors. Habermas's study was in the loft. It took little more than thirty minutes to travel from home to his office at the Department of Philosophy in the main building of the university; later, his office would be located in the Department of Sociology at Myliusstraße 30.

During those years, Sabine Berghahn, the daughter of Habermas's deceased friend,[10] was living in Steinbach. She was struggling with various problems and, in particular, had severe difficulties at school. For around two years from Easter 1966 onwards, she lived with the Habermas family and attended the Goethe Gymnasium in Frankfurt. The routine of family life soon led to better results for her at school. Sabine Berghahn, who is today a Privatdozentin in legal and political science, remembers that the man of the house in Steinbach enjoyed the privilege of being allowed to withdraw from the family in order to pursue his academic work; not infrequently, she recalls, he returned home in the evenings ranting and raving about the behaviour of colleagues and the endless faculty meetings and other events.[11] Berghahn remembers a particularly unpleasant experience for Habermas, when the appointment of Peter Szondi, who was considered for a chair of German philology in 1964 and was emphatically supported by Adorno and Habermas, the two non-disciplinary members in attendance at the appointment committee, fell through due to the opposition from certain colleagues, in particular the German scholar Heinz Otto Burger.[12] Many years later, in the summer of 2005, the abortive appointment would cause ripples once more, following comments on the 'Szondi affair' made in a journal article by the medievalist Klaus von See and then by Lorenz Jäger in the *Frankfurter Allgemeine Zeitung* of 6 July. The tenor of these comments was that Adorno, with his 'elitist and missionary self-understanding', had tried to exert undue influence on the appointment proceedings in order to expand the power base of the Frankfurt School at the university. In his response to Jäger's comments, published on 13 July, Habermas spoke in detail about the presentation of the events by the, in his words, 'right winger of the features section':

Even before I had taken up my post at Frankfurt, and as a result of a decision taken at a faculty meeting at which I had not been present in person, I had become a member of an appointment committee for a chair in philology. Immediately after the formal opening of the first meeting by Dean Kraft, Otto Burger, whom I did not know personally at that time, took his chance to speak. Wholly unexpectedly, and aggressively, he turned towards me, a young colleague who only a few weeks earlier had been visited by the dean in Heidelberg with a request to accept the appointment at Frankfurt. Of course, I do not remember the exact words, but because of the atypical breach of protocol I remember their meaning very well: they, the German philologists, knew, of course, that Mr Adorno had placed me on the committee in order to push for the appointment of Peter Szondi. He wanted to warn me up front that, in Frankfurt, German scholars appointed a German scholar. I looked at the dean, who was obviously irritated but did not react at first. I said to him that I assumed that with this display the meeting was over, and left the room. . . . The incident sticks in my memory because, when I told Gadamer and Löwith how shocked I had been, they sensed an opportunity to keep me in Heidelberg. Indeed, Arthur Henkel, the then dean of the Faculty of Philosophy in Heidelberg, discussed the matter with the ministry in Stuttgart and invited me for negotiations about possibly remaining in Heidelberg.[13]

1965 was an eventful year. Habermas worked on his inaugural lecture, which, as he knew well, was eagerly anticipated. The Czech philosopher Karel Kosík invited him to give lectures in Prague, and there were also preparations for a period of research in the USA, which had been in the pipeline for some time. In March, a month before flying out to New York, Habermas travelled with his wife to Yugoslavia. It was his first stay in the 'Eastern bloc', albeit in a country in which debates on the 'idea of a "Third Way" inspired discussions'.[14] Habermas was there as the guest of a Zagreb-based 'philosophy of practice' group. The group, which was later banned, had been started up by Gajo Petrović and from 1963 organized an international summer school with lectures and discussions on the island of Korčula, attended mainly by philosophers and social scientists who were sympathetic towards an undogmatic Marxism. The lectures were printed in the multilingual edition of the important journal *Praxis*, published in Zagreb. 'The very first evening', Habermas later reminisced, 'being served delicious Dalmatian ham and a heavy Croatian red wine, Ute and I were so passionately embraced by the enthusiastic circle that any resistance to these wizards of hospitality would have been in vain.'[15] Habermas used the opportunity to try out a draft of his inaugural lecture in front of an audience of trained philosophers, among them Milan Kangrga, Predrag Vranicki and Rudi Supek.

The students of philosophy and sociology were very interested in the lectures and seminars Habermas was offering at Frankfurt from the summer term 1964 onwards. Students taking the seminars were expected to deal with a high volume of reading and to take an active part in discussions. In addition, their presentations had to be submitted in written form in order to be hectographed and distributed

to all participants ahead of the seminars. The courses had an international character that was not unusual for Frankfurt. Habermas
assumed, for instance, that publications from the Anglo-American
tradition were read in the original. Early on, he had started to
acquaint himself with the pragmatism of John Dewey, George
Herbert Mead and – urged on by his assistant Ulrich Oevermann
– Talcott Parsons. Throughout his life, he would comment on
American politics and culture, and from the time of his professorship at Frankfurt he took ever more frequent trips to the USA.

Habermas's teaching at Frankfurt gradually attracted more and
more students from all over the world. Part of the reason for this
was certainly the pull of the name the 'Frankfurt School'. Outside
of Germany, Habermas was seen as its youngest and most productive mind, although his teaching practice did not aim to uphold any
particular tradition in the orthodox sense. His lectures and seminars
were characterized by an atmosphere of both discipline and openness. Participation in the discussions was explicitly invited, even if
the more advanced students and his assistants during his time in
Frankfurt – Oskar Negt and Albrecht Wellmer in the philosophical courses, Ulrich Oevermann and Claus Offe in the sociological
courses – were naturally the main contributors. For the most part,
Habermas would write down his lectures and read them out. His
lecture scripts often run to 250 typewritten pages, all littered with
handwritten corrections and additions, sometimes continuing onto
separate sheets and notes. At the beginning of the first lecture, he
told his students directly: 'You will have to prepare yourself for a
specialist lecture containing rather complicated individual ideas.'
Gunter Hofmann, who had also attended some of the lectures during
Habermas's time in Heidelberg, and who would later become one of
the editors-in-chief at the weekly newspaper *Die Zeit*, remembers
the following scene:

> I recall how one of my fellow students interrupted Jürgen Habermas's
> lecture in the university's largest auditorium to ask him whether he
> could express himself a little less complicatedly, for it was so difficult
> to understand him. One half of the audience applauded. He promised
> to do his best in order to be intelligible, Habermas replied, whereupon
> the other half of the audience started booing. To those who were now
> booing, Habermas continued, he could promise that his good inten-
> tions were bound to fail.[16]

In personal conversations, both Oevermann and Offe emphasized
the close collaboration that characterized their time as Habermas's
assistants. There were regular exchanges about their work, and
everyone was eager to learn from one another, even when research

areas differed. The dealings they had with Habermas were profit-able not only because of his intelligence. He also had a sense of humour, was an interesting character, and, beyond purely profes-sional matters, there were invitations to dinner and discussions at the family home in Steinbach, where one might happen to meet Alexander Mitscherlich or Karl Heinz Bohrer. Offe stressed the fact that the assistants were given great freedom in the arrange-ment of their working times. Their tasks included the preparation of reading lists for seminars, giving advice to students on their presentations and seminar protocols, and participating in research colloquia. There was a good 'horizontal osmosis', says Offe, who even back then was won over by the combination of communication and rationality with a simultaneous abstention from any philosophy of values [*Wertphilosophie*]. Habermas, however, did not shy away from drawing his attention to substantial gaps in his knowledge of philosophy and psychology. Oevermann, by contrast, stressed the fact that, during his time as his assistant, he was already criticizing Habermas's programme for a social theory. Habermas tolerated this critical attitude, but it did lead to many heated debates. 'In hindsight', Oevermann reminisced,

> it is almost impossible to imagine, during this time of great theoret-ical-analytical transformation in the social sciences, what wealth of material Habermas covered, soaked up, communicated in systematic fashion in his teaching, and offered to be tested. And, in addition, he established all sorts of general orientations in the field with great far-sightedness. . . . And we should not forget the great effort to confront a '68 movement – particularly active in Frankfurt as the home of Critical Theory – with the reality principle. . . . Habermas confronted the often arrogant distancing from the Anglo-American literature and research, which was denounced as being positivistic – how often stu-dents in Frankfurt moaned about the perfectly natural, but to them novel, demand that in some seminars they had to read exclusively English or French texts – with relentless insistence, sometimes also with a caustic sarcasm: 'You think that in your reading of Hegel you hold the key for an understanding of the innermost core of this world in your hand, but you never present the key, let alone that you would unlock anything with it.'[17]

'Geschichte der Soziologie' [History of sociology], 'Analysen ges-amtgesellschaftlicher Systeme' [Analyses of society-wide systems], 'Interfamiliäre Sozialisationsprozesse' [Interfamilial processes of socialization], 'Probleme der politischen Soziologie' [Problems in political sociology], 'Durkheim, Pareto, Freud', 'Theoretische Ansätze in der neueren Soziologie' [Theoretical approaches in recent sociology], 'Ursprünge moderner Erfahrungswissenschaft' [Origins of modern empirical science], 'Probleme des Naturrechts' [Problems in natural law], 'Materialistische Dialektik' [Materialist dialectics], 'Probleme einer materialistischen Erkenntnistheorie' [Problems of a materialist epistemology], 'Geschichtsphilosophie' [Philosophy of history] – these are some of the courses Habermas taught in those years. As he covered a comparatively broad range of themes, it is all the more striking that there is something missing from the list: a lecture or seminar on the problem of 'fascism'. After all, the wish to understand this rupture in civilization had been one of the young Habermas's essential reasons for turning to philosophy in the first place. It is therefore remarkable that, as a professor of philosophy and sociology, he was apparently not particularly interested in the work that was discussed under the rubric of 'theories of fascism'.

In the spring of 1965, Jürgen Habermas had a period of study in the United States for the first time. He was invited by the Studienbüro für politische Bildung [Study Council for Political Education], and the trip itself was organized by the Institute for International Education in Washington, DC. In his application letter to the Studienbüro für politische Bildung, Habermas wrote that he was interested in psychological and sociological studies relating to the teacher training for *Social Studies*.* In his letter to the dean asking for two months' leave, he mentions that he intended 'to make contact with, among others, his colleagues Kirchheimer in New York, Bendix and Lipset in Berkeley, and Janowitz in Chicago'.[18]

Habermas's first stop was New York, where he was staying with Rolf Meyersohn. Meyersohn, whose topics of research were leisure time and the media, was only a little older than Habermas. The two had met before in Frankfurt, where Meyersohn spent the academic year 1960–1 as a visiting professor, and where he would again hold a visiting professorship at the Institute for Social Research in 1966. A friendly relationship developed between the two families, whose children were of a similar age. After New York, Habermas travelled to Michigan and spent a few weeks at the University in Ann Arbor. From there, he travelled on to Boston and then to the psychoanalyst Bruno Bettelheim's Institute in Chicago. Near Santa Barbara, in California, where Habermas had to undergo surgery to have his appendix removed, he met up with Leo Löwenthal, who at once told Siegfried Kracauer about this 'enjoyable visit'.[19] During his journey, Habermas also got to know Mike Rossmann, who would later make a name for himself as one of the leaders of the student movement in Berkeley: 'That was a few months after the "free-speech movement" had begun. He was the first who confronted me with these "crazy new ideas" – as I called them back then.'[20]

---

* 'Social studies' in English in the original.

After his return, Habermas wrote a seven-page report for the Studienbüro. 'During my study trip', he writes,

> I had the opportunity to visit schools (in Ann Arbor, Chicago, Palo Alto) and observe lessons (social studies).* We received information about the school system and the way teacher training is organized. For me personally, it was also important to get to know American universities. In the two weeks that we lived on the campus of the University of Michigan, in particular, I was able to study the teaching of philosophy and sociology very well. Finally, we had the opportunity to study the political behaviour of professors and students at a critical moment. The criticism levelled against the government's foreign policy decisions regarding Vietnam and Santo Domingo led to new forms of academic protest (teach-in),† which emerged precisely during the weeks of our visit. The student unrest at Berkeley, by contrast, appears to reflect more fundamental changes in the political attitude of young people‡ in a highly industrialized welfare society.[21]

Research interests. Habermas did all his teaching on a few consecutive days, as a rule Thursdays and Fridays, with his advanced seminar in philosophy taking place on Saturdays between 10 and 12. This gave him enough free time 'at a stretch' to work intensively on articles and books. He was enormously productive during those years: in 1967 the extensive literature review *On the Logic of the Social Sciences* was published as a special volume of the *Philosophische Rundschau*. After several pirate editions had appeared, it was supplemented with four further chapters and published as a book under the same title, first in 1970, and then again with a further four chapters in 1982.

In this literature review, Habermas summarized the state of play in the methodology of the social sciences. He took up themes again from his two previous contributions to the positivist debate from the beginning of the 1960s and combined arguments that he had put forward against the claim to universality made by the empirical-analytical sciences. His criticism of positivism is motivated essentially by the intention to claim a historical-hermeneutical perspective for research in the social sciences, although he also warned against taking this too far, using sociology as an example:

> The linguistic infrastructure of society is one aspect of a context which is also constituted by real constraints [*Realitätszwänge*], however symbolically mediated they might be: by the constraints imposed by

---

* 'Social studies' in English in the original.
† 'Teach-in' in English in the original.
‡ Habermas uses the term 'Jugendliche', which typically refers to teenagers but, strictly speaking, would not have applied to many of the students he has in mind.

outer nature which enter into the procedures of technological domination, and by the constraints of inner nature which are reflected in
the repression exerted by social conditions of power. . . . Sociology,
therefore, must not let itself be reduced to a hermeneutical sociology.
It requires a frame of reference which, on the one hand, does not . . .
naturalistically ignore the symbolic mediation of social action but,
on the other, does not lapse into a linguistic idealism that completely
sublimates social processes into cultural tradition.[22]

The text contains a motif that Habermas would emphasize more
and more over the coming years: the critique of what he calls the
paradigm of the philosophy of consciousness. 'Today', he writes
in *On the Logic of the Social Sciences*, 'the problem of language
has taken the place of the traditional problems of consciousness:
the transcendental critique of language replaces that of consciousness.'[23] The occupation with the phenomenology of Alfred Schütz,
with the ethno-methodology of Harold Garfinkel and with George
Herbert Mead's concept of reciprocal role expectations was of
crucial importance in the advancement of what Habermas would
later call the 'turn towards linguistic pragmatics in sociology'. The
objects to be investigated were no longer subjective mental acts,
but speech acts. The intersubjectivity of linguistic communication
between several actors took the place of the subjective intentionality of individuals. And the concept of the lifeworld also gradually
began to move to the centre of his social theory, which took on an
increasingly complex shape.

Upon the first publication of the text, Habermas received numerous positive responses in the form of letters from, among others,
Lucien Goldmann, Aaron Cicourel, Jacob Taubes, Leo Löwenthal,
Helmuth Plessner and Helmut Schelsky. Claus Grossner's joint
review of Habermas's articles and Albrecht Wellmer's *Methodologie
als Erkenntnistheorie* [Methodology as epistemology], titled
'Philosophie deutscher Revolutionäre' [Philosophy of German rev-
olutionaries] and published in *Die Zeit* of 1 October 1967, called
these texts the most profound contributions to the positivist debate
available so far.

In 1968, a volume of collected essays on *Technik und Wissenschaft
als 'Ideologie'* [Technology and science as 'ideology'] appeared in
the edition suhrkamp series. In the title essay, which he dedicated
to Herbert Marcuse on his seventieth birthday, Habermas criticizes
Max Weber's famous analysis of the process of rationalization in
advanced industrial societies, which he complains is one-sided due
to its limitation to the systems of 'technology' and 'economy'. At
the same time, he contrasts his own position with Marcuse's utopian
idea of an altogether different form of technology and science and
calls for a differentiation between two fundamental concepts (which,

however, he would later come to revise): that between purposive-rational work and communicative interaction – or, in other words, between system and lifeworld. As a consequence of the increasing interdependence between research and technology, Habermas says, science becomes the primary productive force. He criticizes the technocratic form of political-administrative decision processes and the decisionism of factual constraints that goes along with it, both of which are brought about by the increasing scientization [*Verwissenschaftlichung*] of politics. These tendencies pose a serious threat to democratic self-determination.[24] Dietrich Deininger summarized it accurately in the *Frankfurter Allgemeine Zeitung*: 'Today, humanity is . . . threatened not by technological development as such but by the orientation of practical life in accordance with technology, by the technological politics of a state-ruled capitalism that does not discuss and resolve conflicts but avoids them, and which strives not for maturity among the population but towards its de-politicization.'[25]

In search of an epistemological foundation for critique

Knowledge-guiding interests. In addition to the collection of essays for the edition suhrkamp, Habermas published another, weightier book in 1968, namely his *Knowledge and Human Interests*. It appeared in the newly founded Suhrkamp series 'Theorie' (mentioned in the previous chapter) and, if we include the dissertation on Schelling, was his third monograph. *Knowledge and Human Interests*, which, incidentally, is dedicated to his friend Wilfried Berghahn, was also his first major attempt at developing his idea of a theory of society in systematic fashion, an attempt that drew on epistemology. The book explicates a theory of reason as reflective knowledge – i.e., as critique through the medium of self-reflection – starting out from the premise that any form of knowledge is tied up with interests that are deeply rooted in human nature. Critique 'releases the subject from dependence on hypostasized powers.'[26] Habermas wants to show that self-reflection is more than just metaphysical speculation and can accomplish more than introspection. For him it is a peculiar form of rationality which has the same status as the two scientific forms of rationality – i.e., causal explanation and hermeneutic understanding.

Setting out from the thesis that the history of humanity is characterized by labour, language and domination, Habermas carves out three fundamental interests guiding knowledge, each of which has its corresponding scientific model: the model of the natural sciences corresponds to the interest of taking purposive influence on objects, the model of the humanities [*Geisteswissenschaften*] corresponds to the interest in understanding – i.e., in the decoding of symbolic forms of expression – and the social science or ideology critique and psychoanalytic model corresponds to the interest in critique (of domination). From this, he derives the distinction between positivist, hermeneutic and critical types of science: 'The approach of the empirical-analytic sciences incorporates a *technical* cognitive interest; that of the historical-hermeneutic sciences incorporates a *practical* one; and the approach of critically oriented sciences incorporates the emancipatory cognitive interest.'[27] Habermas defines cognitive interests as general cognitive strategies, as 'the specific viewpoints from which we can apprehend reality as such in the first place'.[28] As in the work of Karl-Otto Apel,[29] they have a quasi-transcendental status – that is, their validity is *a priori*. Habermas is convinced that, by gaining insight into cognitive interests, the ultimate frame of reference of any knowledge can be uncovered. Because the '*emancipatory interest in knowledge*' is not anchored in the fundamental modes of action, labour and interaction, it has only a 'derivative status', but is no less important for it.[30] For '[i]t guarantees the connection between theoretical knowledge and an "object domain" of practical life which comes into existence as a result of *systematically distorted* communication and thinly legitimated repression.'[31] In other words, critique guided by emancipatory cognitive interests raises a state of affairs to the level of consciousness, and its concrete content depends on the forms in which domination manifests itself historically; it thus changes with the circumstances. This emancipatory cognitive interest, which Habermas first touched on in his inaugural lecture at the University of Frankfurt, resides in language.

Marx and Freud. Habermas refers to Sigmund Freud's psychoanalysis and Karl Marx's critique of ideology as paradigmatic examples of the critical, and hence emancipatory, model of science, even though they both suffer from what he calls a 'scientistic self-misunderstanding' because they see themselves as belonging to the wrong kind of scientific model, namely that of the natural sciences. Thus, in order to rescue their critical potential, they have to be given a novel reinterpretation.

To Marx, Habermas stresses, we owe the insight that the fundamental category for gaining knowledge of history is not thinking (as with Hegel) but, rather, man's interactions with nature – i.e., that the self-constitution of the species is based on social labour. However, against his better knowledge, Marx operates with a limited instrumental concept of labour under which 'the materialist concept of the synthesis of man and nature is restricted to the categorial framework of production.'[32] Habermas, who certainly appropriates the materialist perspective, expresses the essence of his critique of Marx as follows: 'If Marx had not thrown together interaction and labour under the label of social practice [Praxis], and had he instead related the materialist concept of synthesis likewise to the accomplishments of instrumental action and the nexuses of communicative action, then the idea of a science of man would not have been obscured by identification with natural sciences.'[33]

Habermas tries to compensate for the deficits in Marx's theory by making Freud's theory of individual psychology useful for a model of critical science and by transferring the psychoanalytic model to the level of a critical analysis of society. First, he clarifies that social critique refers to objectively unnecessary domination. The extent of the latter, he concludes, is given by the difference between the degree of repression that is actually institutionally exercised and the degree that is necessary according to the historical stage of material development. It is necessary, he says, to bring this difference to consciousness within society, with the aim 'that the validity of every norm of political consequence be made dependent on a consensus arrived at in communication free from domination.'[34]

For Habermas, psychoanalysis is a prime example of a critical and emancipatory science – or, more precisely, of a critical and emancipatory procedure – because domination-free communication is at the core of its practical method: 'The analytic situation makes real the unity of intuition and emancipation, of insight and liberation from dogmatic dependence, the unity of reason and the interested employment of reason.'[35] Psychoanalysis comes so close to the ideal type of a critical-emancipatory science because the interpretations of the analyst are valid only insofar as the analysand appropriates them as valid insights. And, by analogy with this, a critical analysis of society proves to be correct only to the extent that its interpretations of social ills and conditions of suffering impact on the process of society enlightening itself, and thus have a practical effect.

Shortly after the book appeared, Karl-Otto Apel and Niklas Luhmann both wrote to Habermas. In his letter, Apel thanks him for sending the work and also for the friendly words of dedication added by the author, before – over eight pages – discussing Habermas's theses on the identity of reflection and emancipation and of theory and historical practice. He identifies a tension within the emancipatory cognitive interest between critique as philosophical reflection and critique as practical commitment. Luhmann, in his letter of 2 January 1969, writes that the publication had fascinated him and that he admires the interpretations as well as the language. However, he cannot agree with the opposition between labour and interaction, or between domination and communication, because labour without interaction and communication without domination are inconceivable for him. He also raises objections to the privileged position given to language; according to him, language does not achieve a sufficient reduction of complexity.[36]

The letters from Apel and Luhmann were far from being the only commentaries on the book. In 1974, Winfried Dallmayr edited a volume called *Materialien zu Jürgen Habermas' 'Erkenntnis und Interesse'* [Materials on Jürgen Habermas's 'Knowledge and Human Interests'], which contains discussions on epistemology by, among others, Gian Enrico Rusconi, Günter Rohrmoser, Nikolaus Lobkowicz and Lorenz Krüger. Habermas tried to take these criticisms on board.

Revisions. Of all his books, *Knowledge and Human Interests* is probably the one Habermas felt most ambivalent about. As early as 1973, when it was republished with a new afterword as the first title in the series 'suhrkamp taschenbuch wissenschaft' [suhrkamp science paperbacks], he already considered it to be 'in need of revision'. In that afterword, he writes: 'the unexpectedly intensive and far-reaching discussion about it has raised so many questions that I would have to write a new (and *different*) book if I wanted to deal with all of them in a systematic way.'[37] Nevertheless, he addresses 'five problem areas' and, in particular, revises his concept of critical self-reflection.

> It occurred to me only after completing the book that the traditional use of the term 'reflection', which goes back to German idealism, covers (and confuses) two things: on the one hand, it denotes the reflection upon the conditions of potential abilities of a knowing, speaking and acting subject as such; on the other hand, it denotes the reflection upon unconsciously produced constraints to which a determinate subject . . . succumbs in its process of self-formation.[38]

The former he now calls 'rational reconstruction', the latter 'critique'. Only through the mode of critique can the causes of systematically distorted communication be detected.

The republication of *Knowledge and Human Interests* was another welcome opportunity for *Der Spiegel* to discuss Habermas. Under the title 'Immer reden' [Keep talking], an anonymous reviewer commented on the idea of a 'communicative community of mature individuals', calling it a definitive turn away from Marxist orthodoxy. Habermas responded with a letter to the editor: 'You can "distance" yourself from individuals or from utterances, but not from scientific traditions, which, after all, exist in order to be tested and revised. One does not qualify as a Marxist by virtue of a confession of faith in an author whose main work is about a hundred years old by now. By suggesting that this is the case, you repeat the customary stereotypes and those familiar from the DKP.'[39]

Thirty years after the first publication of *Knowledge and Human Interests*, Habermas again commented on his early book. He observes how attached he was at the time to figures of thought and conceptual schemata from the philosophy of history. 'What back then I analysed from an epistemological perspective as the constitution of object domains, I today describe from the perspective of linguistic theory as pragmatic "presuppositions about the world".'[40]

Habermas had been working on linguistic theory long before 1968. And in the winter term 1969–70, he presented a paper as the basis for a seminar discussion at Frankfurt University titled: 'Vorbereitende Bemerkungen zu einer Theorie der kommunikativen Kompetenz' [Preliminary remarks on a theory of communicative competence]. In the few years between 1968 and this paper, something else took centre stage, namely the debate over the question 'revolution or reform?'

Thinking with the protest movement against the protest movement

Without the opposition of the left liberals – and occasionally even of the left intelligentsia . . . a deep identification with a social order whose universalistic principles anchor a potential for self-criticism and self-transformation [would never have emerged].[41]

During his second period in Frankfurt, at the Johann Wolfgang Goethe-Universität between 1964 and 1971, Habermas was exceptionally productive in academic terms. But the time was also characterized by the fight for reform in higher education and – of course – by his perpetual engagement with the anti-authoritarian student movement. For Habermas, the reform of higher education ultimately meant one thing: democratization. In concrete terms, this meant that membership in committees taking academic decisions should be open to everyone carrying responsibility in teaching and research. In addition, all decisions of relevance to political and practical life that were taken within the space of the university should be the outcome of public discussion and a process of democratic will-formation.

In January 1966, Habermas gave a talk at the Universitätstage [Conference of universities] in Berlin, in which he emphasized the role of critique. Politically, critique was especially important now, he said, 'because we can no longer afford an unreflective implementation of scientific information into the context of the social practice of life.' The practical consequences of scientific-technological progress could only be controlled, he said, if we 'continue with this progress through the lens of reflection'.[42] He aimed for an 'organization of social relations according to the principle that the validity of every norm of political consequence be made dependent on a consensus arrived at in communication free from domination.'[43]

Of course, such ideas fell on fertile ground at a time when sociology was expanding and, as the key science of the twentieth century, was seen as synonymous with the critique of society and of the contemporary state of affairs. As a reaction to the missed, or blocked, chances for reform during the post-war period, which was increasingly seen as a regressive and brittle time, a new, politically aware and predominantly critical intelligence emerged, which turned out to be an ideal sounding board for Habermas's scientific activities and journalistic interventions.[44]

There were, to be sure, many developments that may have triggered the social and political turbulence of those years, among them the escalation of the Vietnam War, which was diplomatically supported by the government of the Federal Republic as one of the USA's allies; the activities of the US secret service, the CIA, in South America; the increasingly radical civil rights movement in the United States; the worldwide emergence of anti-colonial movements; the Six Day War in the Middle East; and the military coup in Greece. In terms of the Federal Republic's domestic politics, we must add the debates about the emergency laws whose introduction was planned from the mid-1960s onwards; the monopoly of power enjoyed by the Grand Coalition formed by the Christian and Social Democrats, led by the former member of the NSDAP and strict anti-communist – 'I say only: China, China, China!' – Kurt Georg Kiesinger, which governed from December 1966 onwards; and, finally, the success of a radical right-wing party, which made it into a number of regional parliaments, for instance in Hesse and Bavaria. In the wake of these global and national political events, youth and student protest movements continued to grow and become increasingly radicalized. They also attracted greater media attention, in part because their 'direct actions', happenings, sit-ins and the like made for such exciting press and television coverage. The media therefore happily reported on them, and they had a considerable and broad impact on the public.

Many of the large-scale events organized by opposition forces took place in Frankfurt – and Habermas was right in the thick of it. He signed a declaration addressed to Chancellor Ludwig Erhard and handed it to him in November 1965. It demanded an end to the air attacks on Vietnam, a peaceful resolution to the conflict, and the political neutrality of all of Vietnam. Speaking at a congress organized by Rudi Dutschke and the SDS with the title 'Vietnam – Analyse eines Exempels' [Vietnam – analysis of an example], Habermas called the Vietnam War illegitimate and an expression of aggressive anti-communism.[45] The main speaker at the conference was Herbert Marcuse, while others included Wolfgang Abendroth, Norman Birnbaum and Oskar Negt.

Even before the formation of the Great Coalition, Habermas – together with Iring Fetscher, Ludwig von Friedeburg and Alexander Mitscherlich – was one of the signatories of an open letter to the leader of the SPD, Willy Brandt, which issued a warning about the emergence of a monopoly of power. Speaking at a panel discussion, Habermas said that, under the influence of Herbert Wehner and Helmut Schmidt, the Social Democrats were prepared to enter into 'government with a run-down CDU/CSU' for strategic reasons, but in doing so they provided 'an alibi for the veiling of the bankruptcy . . . We have reason to fear the new government more than the old one.'[46] The fact that Habermas sympathized with the idea of a small coalition of SPD and FDP (which had never existed up to that point), led by Willy Brandt as chancellor, did not keep him from openly criticizing the opportunistic behaviour of the SPD. The SPD, he said, had nipped the emergence of internal party democracy in the bud. Even worse, he feared that the principle of parliamentarianism as such was threatened, because, 'if nine tenths of all parliamentarians belong to the governing parties, conflicts are resolved to the exclusion of the public.'[47]

How the political elite dealt with serious social conflicts would soon become apparent. When the student protest movement, as part of the New Left, began to grow nationally in the summer of 1967, the majority of the elite reacted repressively, making the fateful error of bowing to the pressure of the Springer press,[48] which was stirring up public opinion against the protesting students, among others. The situation escalated when the shah of Persia, Mohammad Reza Pahlavi, and his entourage paid a state visit to Germany and travelled to Berlin on 2 June 1967. Their itinerary included a gala performance of *The Magic Flute* at the German Opera that evening. But the performance also attracted a demonstration, planned by students and members of the Iranian opposition organized by the AStA* of the Freie Universität Berlin, in protest against the leader who – to say the least – ruled his country with an iron fist. The Berlin police – who, on the instruction of the senator of the interior Wilhelm Büsch, had been taking a hard line on student unrest for some time – violently broke up the protest. In the course of their actions, 26-year-old student Benno Ohnesorg was shot in the head by a plain-clothed officer, who was later revealed to be a Stasi informant.

The death of Benno Ohnesorg marked the turning point in the history of the student protest movement. Feelings were running

---

* Allgemeiner Studentenausschuss – i.e., the Students Union.

high over the circumstances of the shooting. While the majority of
those in positions of political responsibility defended the actions of
the police, supported in their stance by the popular press – 'Students
threaten: we will shoot back' was *Bild*'s headline on 5 June 1967
– the students, and others, spoke of political murder. Sebastian
Haffner, for instance, wrote in *Der Stern*: 'This was a systematic
pogrom, planned in cold blood, executed by the police of Berlin on
the students of Berlin.'[49] Other intellectuals also raised their voices
and strongly condemned the actions of the police. And what happened in Frankfurt? Jürgen Habermas was deeply shocked by the
events and phoned acquaintances in Berlin to get a clearer picture
of the situation. He was particularly concerned that the gradual
dismantling of democratic principles, which had already begun
with the preparation of constitutionally embedded emergency laws,
would now gather pace. And, indeed, the emergency laws would be
passed by the Grand Coalition with the necessary two-thirds majority in the parliament on 30 May 1968, almost exactly a year after the
death of Benno Ohnesorg. This much is clear: during the years of
the student protests, Habermas's sympathies and his commitments
lay with those left-wing socialist forces arguing for a transformation of the capitalist structure of the economy along the lines of a
welfare state, rather than with the anti-authoritarian and anarchist
leftist groups who wanted to bring about an increasing awareness
of repressive social conditions through acts of direct provocation.[50]

Between 3 and 9 June 1967, demonstrations against the actions
of the police in Berlin took place all across the Federal Republic.
Hundreds of thousands took to the streets. On 9 June, Ohnesorg's
funeral took place in Hanover amid outpourings of public sympathy. Following the funeral, a conference took place in his honour.
The title was 'Hochschule und Demokratie – Bedingungen und
Organisation des Widerstandes' [The university and democracy –
the conditions for and the organization of resistance]. Only four
professors had been invited: Wolfgang Abendroth, Margherita von
Brentano, Hartmut von Hentig and Jürgen Habermas. In his 'Rede
über die politische Rolle der Studentenschaft in der Bundesrepublik'
[Speech on the political role played by the study body in the Federal
Republic], Habermas characterized the state-sanctioned police
operations against the students in Berlin as terror in the sense of
intentional intimidation. In his eyes, the student protest was a legitimate and urgently necessary expression of democratic consciousness
and political commitment:

> It was and still is the task of the student opposition in the Federal
> Republic to compensate for the lack of theoretical perspective, the lack
> of critical awareness of cover-ups and of the branding of others as her-
> etics, the lack of radicalness in the interpretation and implementation

of our social and democratic constitution, the lack of foresight and imagination – to compensate for these deficiencies.[51]

Habermas called for public protests against the looming emergence of an 'authoritarian performance society', but at the same time he also warned against an activism at any cost and against the danger of 'provoking a transformation of the indirect violence of institutions into manifest violence'. That, he said, would be 'masochistic – i.e., not satisfaction but submission to precisely that violence'.[52] Hans-Jürgen Krahl of the SDS in Frankfurt opposed Habermas, saying the claim that the provocation of violence is itself fascist was no longer valid. The 'bloody and brutal lashing out' of the violent machinery of the state, which had been unleashed and could be mobilized against the students at any time, was only possible, he said, because the students were not organized and reacted in a chaotic fashion. As such it was necessary for the students, devoid as they were of actual weapons, 'to find ritualized forms of provocation and to publicly represent . . . a . . . physically manifested attitude of non-violence in the street'.[53] Rudi Dutschke, by that time the leading figure of the student movement, accused Habermas of '[killing] the subject to be emancipated with his senseless objectivism'. When Dutschke spoke out against the ruling 'irrational' democracy and its established rules and in favour of alternative forms of action, not excluding the possible use of violence, Habermas was alarmed but did not immediately react. Only later, long past midnight, when he was about to leave the congress, did he change his mind; he returned from the car park ('I was already in my car') to the hall, where the discussion continued. In his 'Question to Rudi Dutschke' (the name given to Habermas's intervention by the documentary film-makers Hans Dieter Müller and Günther Hörmann in their *Ruhestörung*), Habermas suggested that Dutschke, who was no longer present at that point, supported a voluntaristic ideology 'which was called utopian socialism in 1848, but which under present conditions – I believe I have reason for using this terminology – must be called "left-wing fascism".'[54] The audience was split down the middle and reacted with both booing and applause.

This phrase was just what the media had been waiting for. Many of them reported, with gleeful undertones, that the mentor of the student opposition – the title they themselves had previously bestowed on Habermas – had disowned its increasing radicalism. In an article for the *Kursbuch* titled 'Die Studenten und die Macht' [Students and power], Habermas's assistant Oskar Negt accused him of being the victim of his own ambivalent attitudes – he was a member of the liberal left without a specific party-political affiliation who, on the one hand, believed he could 'recognize the substantial elements of a humanitarian liberalism in the pathos of reason, autonomy, enlightenment and public discussion' but, on the other hand, was repelled by militant forms of protest. Negt pushed the point further:

> The accusation of a 'left fascism' is the expression of a stage in the disintegration of liberal-bourgeois consciousness, which is shocked by the palpable fragility of the democratic institutions and rules of Germany and yet cannot detect the end of all security and freedom in the socialist alternatives . . . 'Left fascism' is the projection of the fascist tendencies immanent to the system onto marginal groups that are easy to discriminate against.[55]

Claus Offe, who was also active within the SDS, expressed a different opinion, albeit many years later:

> I think that Habermas did not say anything wrong on 9 June 1967 in Hanover. Misled by their interpretation of the situation, what the emotionally agitated students brought forward in terms of violent confrontational fantasies was simply unreasonable. There was a perverse preparedness to use violence in the name of determination, the seriousness of the situation, and the competitive demonstration of authenticity of a kind with which we are otherwise familiar only from fascists – but this time it came from the left. Habermas was deeply repulsed by this. He considered this interpretation of the situation off the mark. And rightly so.[56]

A decade later, Habermas admitted that he had 'reacted a tad too much as a bourgeois intellectual' with his remark about left-wing fascism, that it was 'a bit out of place', even if it was meant to be nothing but 'an *internal* critique of the method of the protest movement'.[57] Back in 1967, however, the tide began to turn for him. While so far the student protest groups had sought a close relationship with him, they now distanced themselves or even opposed him.

As far as his academic career was concerned, Habermas was in an excellent position during those turbulent years, in spite of all his 'non-academic' activities. In 1967, he received not just one but two attractive offers: a chair at the University of Constance, founded in 1966 as a newly reformed institution, and a chair in Hamburg. As he was already in negotiations with Constance, he had to withdraw his application to Hamburg, where Carl Friedrich von Weizsäcker would have welcomed him as a colleague. And, in the end, he also declined the offer to join the university at Lake Constance, which had been initiated by Dahrendorf – Frankfurt had 'improved' his working conditions both financially and in terms of personnel. His request for sabbatical leave in the winter term 1967–8 had also been granted. In his letter to the dean, dated 14 April 1967, he cites as the reason for his request that he wanted to accept an invitation to the New School for Social Research in New York. He had been offered the Theodor-Heuss Chair for the period 1 September 1967 to 1 February 1968, a position sponsored by the Federal Republic and appointed by the New School. The letter from the New School to the relevant ministry of Hesse, expressing the hope that Habermas's application for leave would be granted, states that the teaching programme for the coming term was based on the assumption that they would 'have a prominent representative of German sociology visiting New York'.[58]

Visiting professor in New York. In the summer of 1967, Habermas and his whole family flew to New York. In his luggage, he had several manuscripts. Together with Ute, Tilmann and Rebekka – now both of school age – and the six-year-old Judith, he moved into Rolf Meyersohn's apartment near Central Park. It had become temporarily available because the Meyersohns had decided to stay in London during the months of Habermas's visiting professorship. In mid-August, the two families holidayed together in Maine.

On 10 October, Habermas wrote to Margarete and Alexander Mitscherlich in Heidelberg,[59] saying how comfortable he felt in New York. He enjoyed his seminars and lectures, and any initial fears had turned out to be unfounded. His two older children attended the Rudolf Steiner School in the smart Upper East Side. He praised the American students, who he claimed were far less dogmatic than the German ones with regard to their political attitudes. But he also observed the destructive side of American society, the most powerful country in the world, whose cities showed a great degree of 'deterioration and violence'. While in New York, Habermas kept in close contact with his secretary Heide Schneider in Frankfurt. He wrote to her: 'we receive many invitations, and I also study hippies and radicals* of all kinds.'[60]

Habermas made many acquaintances, among them the sociologist Daniel Bell, who had just begun work on a study that would cause a stir when it appeared in 1973 under the title *The Coming of Post-Industrial Society* (the German translation *Die nachindustrielle Gesellschaft* followed two years later). Hannah Arendt invited him to her flat on Riverside Drive for coffee on a Sunday afternoon, where he met Wystan Hugh (W. H.) Auden and Uwe Johnson.[61] Johnson and his family lived in New York between 1966 and 1968, partly financed by a grant from the Rockefeller Foundation.[62] Six months before their meeting in New York, Habermas had written a review for *Merkur* of Arendt's *On Revolution* (*Über die Revolution*),

---

* 'Hippies' and 'radicals' capitalized and in English in the original.

which appeared in German translation in 1965. On 9 March 1966 he wrote to Hans Paeschke that Arendt was 'a terribly reactionary but at least as impressive a character. I find it not only logical but also something to be respected that, in the end, she has the courage to rehabilitate the soviet republic [*Räterepublik*] as the only type of republic that is conceivable today.' In another letter, he says: 'I hope I did not tread on Mrs Arendt's toes too much. That was not at all my intention, because Mrs Arendt is a shining and very lively counter-example to the very deep-seated prejudice which says that women cannot philosophize.'[63]

The New York branch of the Goethe Institute invited Habermas to give a talk. Hannah Arendt introduced him and chaired the discussion. His topic was the differences between the student protests in Berlin and those in Berkeley and Paris. In his opinion, the political activities of the students in Berlin, Frankfurt and other places had an aim beyond the long overdue reforms of the universities – a transformation of social structures. He interpreted the contemporary processes of politicization in West Germany as, in general, a reaction to the rigid authoritarian structures of post-war society, of which a young generation that had grown up in affluence and took seriously the constitutional principle of democratic participation had to be critical. This generation, he said, refused to accept that, 'despite the high level of technological development, the life of the individual was still determined by an ethos of competitiveness, by the pressure to fight for social status, by the values of possessive reification [*possessive Verdinglichung*] and of the substitute gratifications being offered.'[64] The report on the event in the *Frankfurter Allgemeine Zeitung* mentioned a 'very long and lively discussion' in which 'many of those who spoke [pointed out] similarities as well as differences between the radical student movement in the Federal Republic and in the United States.' According to the reports, in the course of the discussion, Habermas described the student activities in opposition to the Vietnam War as justified and having international significance.[65]

Habermas apparently considered his stay in New York and at the New School an important step in his career. In his report of 8 March 1968 for the Volkswagen Foundation, which had supported his six months in the USA financially with 12,000 Deutschmarks, he wrote:

Working at the New School was highly satisfying. Colleagues were exceptionally accommodating. It was possible to enjoy the advantages of being a visiting professor without having to put up with the usual disadvantages associated with that status. I was integrated into the life of the faculty and the department as much as I so wished. The students treated me as a professor like any other. In short, a visiting professor in no way occupies a marginal position at that place. . . . On the basis of my personal experiences, a Theodor Heuss professorship is an almost ideal opportunity for a German scholar who has not yet lived in the USA to get to know the American system (even if it is a German version of it) and to establish personal academic contacts.[66]

A few weeks after the Habermas family had moved back to Germany, he wrote to Meyersohn: 'We are Steinbach peasants again. Though even Frankfurt has somehow taken on the character of a village.' What had once been a fast-paced city now turned out to be a place of 'provincial sleepiness'.[67]

Back in Germany, throughout the eventful year of 1968, Habermas became a harsher critic of the activism of the militant student groups and their leaders. He had plenty of opportunities to do so, one of them being a few days after his return at a panel discussion on 8 February 1968 in Frankfurt, which formed part of a series of events organized by the Berlin SDS under the title 'The Critical University'. There, he spoke about 'The Role of Students within the Extraparliamentary Opposition' and once again went on the attack. In a direct confrontation with Hans-Jürgen Krahl, he referred to mistakes the protest movement had made and advised the SDS to look for allies in the progressive parts of the trade unions and the publishing media. In the *Frankfurter Allgemeine Zeitung*, which at that time still had a good relationship with Habermas, Karl Heinz Bohrer reported that there were two irreconcilable positions faced off against each other: on the one side the leaders of the SDS, who pushed for a revolutionary, and if necessary violent, transformation of the 'fascistoid' system; on the other Habermas, who wanted to use the constitutional possibilities and spaces offered by parliamentary democracy. 'Therefore, enlightening rather than usurping forms of protest were needed', Bohrer wrote.

On 17 and 18 February 1968, immediately following the beginning of the Vietcong's Tet offensive, the International Vietnam Congress took place in Berlin. Only a few weeks later, events rapidly escalated: on 4 April, Martin Luther King, Jr., the Nobel Peace Prize laureate and preacher of non-violence, was shot dead in Memphis, Tennessee, by James Earl Ray. On 11 April – Maundy Thursday – Josef Bachmann, a young man from a right-wing radical background, attempted to assassinate Rudi Dutschke in broad daylight. Dutschke was seriously wounded but survived.[68] In the USA as well as in West Berlin these two events led to severe unrest.

In mid-May, Habermas travelled to the 'frontline city' for a discussion about the dangers of radicalism in the student opposition, appearing alongside Herbert Marcuse and other left-wing intellectuals, among them Klaus Meschkat, Bahman Nirumand and Jacob Taubes. The discussion took place following a large-scale event organized by the Freie Universität, where Marcuse had presented a talk to 4,000 students on alternatives to the existing social system and on the revolutionary subject.

Habermas was also one of the organizers of the congress on 'Notstand der Demokratie' [Democracy in a state of emergency], which was to take place in Frankfurt on 28 May 1968. Numerous writers, scientists, artists, publicists and publishers accepted the invitation, and in the end there were about 1,000 participants. The event took place in the main studio of the Hessischer Rundfunk and was broadcast live on television. There was something of a storm when Hans-Jürgen Krahl of the SDS stepped up to the podium and accused those present of a 'betrayal of the extraparliamentary opposition'. The *Frankfurter Allgemeine Zeitung* (30 September 1968), however, called the congress the 'first comprehensive attempt by German intellectuals at collectively addressing a political question'. Habermas himself did not speak, maybe on account of his general aversion to public occasions broadcast on television. But he did join the demonstration directly following the event, and in the hopelessly overcrowded meeting hall of the Bettinaschule, situated in Frankfurt's Westend, which had been occupied by the pupils for several days, he discussed the political consequences of the emergency laws, and how they could be resisted, with Heinrich Böll, Hans Magnus Enzensberger, Rolf Hochhuth and Martin Walser.[69] Hans Magnus Enzensberger, in particular, distinguished himself at the time as a spokesperson for revolution, an idea many left-wing intellectuals had in mind in those years around 1968. Not only were the means of production to be nationalized, he thought, but the repressive power of the state was also to be crushed, 'in order thus to establish . . . a genuine autonomy of the masses'. In particular, there was to be a 'revolution of the base' in order to counter the manipulative effects of the 'consciousness industry'.[70]

In the line of fire from his own side

Plea for non-violence. On 2 June 1968, more than 2,000 participants attended a meeting of the nationwide Schüler- und Studentenkongress [Association of Pupils and Students] at the University of Frankfurt. It was the Saturday before Whitsun, and the university had just been renamed 'Karl Marx University' after an intervention by the students. The meeting took place within the atmosphere of the Easter unrest over the attempted murder of Rudi Dutschke. The tabloid press of the Springer corporation had made a habit of smearing the leading thinker of the student movement as a communist provocateur. A few weeks before the attack, *Bild*, for instance, told its readers: 'One must not leave all of the dirty work to the police.'[71] Following the attack, there were mass demonstrations

in many West German cities, and in some places these now escalated into openly violent attacks against buildings belonging to the
Springer press, which were protected by the police. The intention
was to stop the corporation from delivering its newspapers.

The blockades by the students were in part the consequence
of a hearing involving Springer which took place on 9 February.
Habermas had been explicitly invited to the hearing but did not
want to attend. When in October he was asked to make a statement
as an expert witness in support of a group of students who had to
defend themselves in court for having taken part in the blockade of
Springer buildings, he refused to do so, writing to the lawyer Klaus
Croissant: 'I am not in a position, as an expert witness, to establish
an empirically demonstrable connection between the activities of
the Springer press and the assassination attempt at Dutschke.'[72]

Apart from the power of privately owned media companies with
a monopoly on opinion formation, which was a recurrent topic
at the time, two further questions were addressed at the Whitsun
conference: What risks does the extraparliamentary opposition run
with its partly violent activities (which were an immediate response
to the passing of the emergency laws three days earlier)? and How
can we create conditions which allow us to replace the traditional
authoritarian structures of the educational system with institutionally guaranteed free spaces, in which clarifying processes aiming at
self-understanding within and between scientific cultures can take
place?

At the heart of the 'battle zone of student protests', as Alexander
Kluge called it, Habermas again forcefully argued his point, as he
had done in Berlin, that there was no alternative to constitutionally embedded parliamentary democracy, even if the gap between
the constitutional norms and constitutional reality was obvious.
It was the task of social critique to uncover the causes of this discrepancy. Taking the critical diagnosis of a technocratic politics
defined in terms of factual necessities as his given point of departure,
Habermas noted something that would exercise him more and more
in the years to come, namely the insufficient clarification of normative questions concerning the practical aspects of communal life.
According to Habermas, the new means of demonstration developed
by pupils and students, which included the intentional violation of
rules, were not only appropriate but, as non-violent resistance, also
legitimate in order to counter the process of de-politicization. As the
social situation in Western Europe could by no means be considered
revolutionary, violent actions against reactionary counter-forces
were not only dangerous but also ineffective.[73] By contrast, the
protest movement, as he saw it, would be capable of dismantling,
over time and piece by piece, the ideology of performance within
affluent societies, which was in any case beginning to crumble. It

was, however, doomed to fail if it tried to justify its approach with
a critique of capitalism and imperialism taken from Marx's revolutionary theory: 'Whoever thinks revolutionary transformation is the
tactic to be adopted under the present circumstances, and practises
revolutionary agitation, is simply falling prey to a delusion.'[74] For
this reason, the protest movement had to forgo any kind of violence
and should limit itself to the use of symbolic means of provocation.

Abisag Tüllmann's photographs of Habermas during the heated
debates at the congress show him in the lion's den, presenting his
social-psychological interpretation of the 'pseudo-revolutionaries'
and responding to objections to the six theses he had presented. He
tore into the individual who assumed the 'role of the agitator' and
practised activism as an end in itself (Hans-Jürgen Krahl), the one
who assumed the 'role of the mentor' and carelessly used formulas
such as 'the great refusal' in order to justify violent action (Oskar
Negt), and also the one who delighted in the 'role of the visiting harlequin at the court of the pseudo-revolutionaries' and went
into raptures about the spectacle of permanent provocation (Hans
Magnus Enzensberger).[75] The pictures were taken as Habermas
implored the audience to adopt a realistic view of the political
situation, which – to his mind – was not at all latently fascistic.
He stands close to the microphone; in his left hand he holds a
few pages of notes for the presentation he had just given – 'Über
Taktik, Ziele und Situationsanalysen der oppositionellen Jugend'
[On the tactics, aims and the situational analysis of the oppositional
youth]. Another picture shows him speaking freely, gesturing with
his right hand. He does not wear a suit but is casually dressed. Here
is someone who obviously tries to present himself not as a professor pontificating 'from above' but as someone who is one among
many committed participants and wants to convince the others in
a battle of arguments. 'Discourse free from domination' might be
a good title for this series of photographs – with or without a question mark.

Habermas's criticism of the students' activism and his accusation of 'left-wing fascism' was not without its consequences. Heavy
counter-criticism can be found in a volume of pieces by authors close
to the SDS, *Die Linke antwortet Jürgen Habermas* [The left responds
to Jürgen Habermas], which contains fifteen responses to the 'six
theses on the tactics, aims, and situational analyses of the oppositional youth'.[76] In his introductory contribution, Oskar Negt writes:
'What unites the individual articles is . . . neither an unconditional
solidarity with the protest movement nor the affirmation and explanation of a coherent theory of which it could be said that the tactics
of indirect actions would be based on the long-term strategy of a
politicization of the public and of changing society along socialist
lines.'[77] In political terms, he says, Habermas represents a 'residual

liberalism' which, in social-theoretical terms, he has overcome. It is 'fear of the still institutionally bound-up potential for violence shown by historically obsolete systems of domination, whose actualization, however, can be triggered on the slightest occasion, which determines Habermas's beseeching appeals not to provoke latent violence and not to undermine liberal positions, even if their emancipatory function has long since been shown to be deceptive'.[78]

In Wolfgang Abendroth's contribution, one senses a wish to win Habermas back for the revolutionary socialist camp. However, not only does he think the slogan 'left-wing fascism' wrong-headed, he also claims that Habermas has given up his socialist position in favour of an internal liberal critique. Social and political changes, Abendroth says, cannot be brought about by 'convincing the holders of power', as Habermas believes, but only through revolutionary changes in the economic base of society.[79]

In an open letter, Furio Cerutti – Habermas's first Humboldt fellow, who had moved from Heidelberg to Frankfurt with him in 1964 and later became professor of political philosophy in Florence – accuses his teacher of grounding his critique of the pseudo-revolution in 'an objectivist *conception of revolution*', which took revolution not as a process but as a state. 'You seem to forget', he writes, 'that the revolution first has to make a journey through purgatory!'[80] Klaus Dörner's critique sets out from the 'use of clinically pure concepts in political discussion'. Such 'sanitized political discussion', he claims, takes place outside the very political public that Habermas himself promotes. 'It is . . . a weakness of the Habermas paper that it looks at the new techniques (and their infantilism) in isolation and does not analyse them sufficiently in the overall context of the political movement.'[81]

The article by Reimut Reiche defends the 'new sensibility', which, he says, is incompatible with the 'anti-emotional rationality' demanded by Habermas.[82] Claus Offe, like Habermas, considers the techniques of a limited violation of rules as the novel aspect of the opposition. But what determines their actions, he says, is

> the shared realization that a regressive process is taking place which captures all domains of social life and possibilities of freedom . . . The threats posed by a new fascism . . . affect . . . the social system in its totality. It is not a plan for a new society (a category that has become suspect) but the collective experience of an old social structure, and the repression which congeals within it, that mobilizes the new oppositional movements.[83]

According to Klaus Meschkat, Habermas has a false idea of the motivations of the student movement, which was precisely not interested in exerting political power. Habermas's mistake, he writes, is to derive the criteria for judging which actions are right or wrong directly from a general theory of the times, which is situated at a high level of abstraction. . . . Jürgen Habermas's ambition to play a unique part as an independent critic slowly makes him . . . look so similar to those urbane journalists from Hamburg whose political principles do not exceed a vain display of impartiality that you can hardly notice a difference.[84]

In the mind of the editor, the volume was 'not an anti-Habermas publication' but 'a public controversy within the New Left, whose purpose first and foremost is to reach clarity about its political self-understanding'.[85] However, Habermas abstained from this controversy; he turned down an invitation to contribute a response to the volume.

A revolutionary situation? Whether there was a revolutionary situation in capitalistically organized societies was a question exercising progressive minds very much at the time. When Habermas was again invited to the summer school on the Adriatic island of Korčula by Gajo Petrović in August 1968, he addressed this question in detail, this time from a strictly theoretical perspective. He gave a presentation on the topic 'Bedingungen für eine Revolutionierung spätkapitalistischer Gesellschaftssysteme' [Conditions for revolutionizing late capitalist social systems]. On the basis of his recent research on science as the primary productive force, he tried to demonstrate that Marx's theory of crisis was no longer valid for modern societies characterized by progress, growth and economic stability. He considered illusory a revolutionary theory that derives the overthrow of capitalist systems from the mass experience of exploitation and pauperization. For the system of actually existing socialism to become an attractive alternative model, it would, in his mind, first have to undergo a process of democratic reform. But that such reforms were unrealistic had been proven by the military invasion of Prague under the leadership of the Soviet Union – an event which was unfolding just as the Marxist theoreticians met, and which had taken them by surprise.

The question of revolution or reform was also the topic of a discussion organized by the Luchterhand publishing house at the end of the Frankfurt Book Fair in the last week of September 1968 under the title 'Autorität und Revolution' [Authority and revolution]. Theodor W. Adorno and the Frankfurt authority on protest Hans-Jürgen Krahl were on the panel. When the latter called for a 'propaganda of action' within the framework of a global revolutionary strategy and at the same time accused Habermas (who was in the audience, along with Günter Grass) of distancing himself from the student movement for tactical reasons, Habermas spontaneously responded: 'Whoever has listened to what Mr Krahl has just said must have got the impression of a party leader calling insubordinate intellectuals to order.'[86] Habermas said that it was fatal that the political movement immunized itself against critical objections and thus especially against those intellectuals who sympathized with it and wanted to enter into discussion with it. This conflict between certain groups within the student movement, on the one hand, and the theoretician of society and other intellectuals, on the other, intensified over the coming months.

Even at the dignified Suhrkamp publishing house, a protest movement emerged. It was directed against a figure of authority, namely the publisher himself. A number of editors became less and less willing to accept the leadership style of Siegfried Unseld, which they saw as patriarchal. Following the death of Peter Suhrkamp in 1959, Unseld had succeeded him as the sole publisher; 50 per cent of the shares in the publishing house remained in the possession of the Swiss Reinhart family, which had provided the designated successor with the capital he needed to acquire the remaining 50 per cent from Klaus Suhrkamp, the son of Peter Suhrkamp from his first marriage and, after the death of the latter's wife 'Mirl' (also in 1959), his sole heir. In order to strengthen their position, the editors Walter Boehlich, Anneliese Botond, Karlheinz Braun, Günther Busch, Karl Markus Michel, Klaus Reichert, Hans-Dieter Teichmann, Peter Urban and Urs Widmer formed an alliance and presented their boss with an 'editorial charter' setting out the authority of the editorial team. The charter stipulated that an assembly of all editors had the power to make decisions not only about the shape of the programme but also about distribution, marketing, payments, policies regarding personnel issues, and so on. Martin Walser used the term 'socialization', which quickly caught on. According to the 'editorial charter', Unseld, who was after all a personally liable partner of the publishing company, would have had just one vote among many. He felt not only pushed aside but also deeply hurt, and he used all the means at his disposal to defend himself against what he considered an attempt effectively to remove him from power. He was hoping for support from his most prominent authors, such as Max Frisch, Martin Walser, Theodor W. Adorno and Jürgen Habermas, and decided to rally his troops around him. In his *Chronik eines Konflikts* [Chronicle of a conflict], Unseld summarizes his conversation with Habermas on 11 October as follows: 'Habermas considered the editorial charter an unacceptable demand, a transgression of negotiable boundaries, a limitation of authority in decision-making, which, in turn, affected the foundations of investment, and hence of the existence, of the publishing house. ... Habermas declared his willingness to take part in the conversation on Monday evening.'[87]

In mid-October 1968, shortly after the end of the Frankfurt Book Fair, a solution was sought at a meeting in the conference room of the publishing house, then still situated at Grüneburgweg 69. Apart from the editors and the two authorized signatories of the company, those present were the authors Jürgen Becker, Günter Eich, Uwe Johnson, Hans Magnus Enzensberger, Max Frisch, Hans Erich Nossack and Jürgen Habermas. In the course of the negotiations, which lasted into the early hours of 15 October, it became clear that Habermas, like some of the others, supported the position of the publisher. The day before, he had asked to be shown the company accounts and had made himself familiar with the situation regarding ownership. It was clear to him that the Reinhart family, who had lent Unseld the funds necessary for him to take over the publishing house, and with whom Unseld had a trusting, personal relationship, would never agree to a socialization of the company. And he reached the conclusion that, given the economic situation, the collective management of a publisher like Suhrkamp was not feasible. As the sole managing partner of the company, Unseld would also need to be vested with the corresponding decision-making authority. In the *Chronicle of a Conflict*, Unseld wrote that Habermas,

> using all his theoretical armour, presented the thesis that it would be nonsensical if a publishing house that brought out the right kind of progressive literature, which all in all worked well, and with which the authors as the forces of production, as a group as well as individually, were happy, was exposed to an experiment that would put the publisher's present impact at risk. In his opinion, the editorial charter would jeopardize the capacity to make the right decisions as well as the basis for investment.[88]

Peter Urban, one of the rebellious editors, has his own perspective on the evening:

> It was long past midnight when, finally, Jürgen Habermas embarked on a comprehensive lecture regarding the structures of the system that, take it or leave it, was in place in the FRG, and within which 'socialist' structures or structures of basic democracy of the kind the Suhrkamp editors apparently had in mind were purely illusory, for legal reasons of corporate law, and also for other reasons – that was the final word. And we, the editors, understood: our 'just cause' was not just: our attempt to risk more democracy within the publishing house was obviously incommensurable with the free capitalist constitutional order (at least this is how the majority understood him), and it had – not even with aplomb – failed. Silently, we went our separate ways. I can distinctly remember how I felt at the time: get out of here, up and away, go home. My colleagues must have felt similarly,

because there was no one even outside the building with whom to share a cigarette.[89]

The conflict finally ended with Unseld agreeing to hold a weekly meeting of editors in order to improve the 'structure of communication'. The editors and Unseld still argued over which concrete decisions had actually been made during the night of 14 October and how far these reached. Again, the publisher asked for help from Habermas, who called the attitude of the editors 'pure madness'.[90] At the end of this dispute, which was exhausting for all sides, some of the editors, among them Walter Boehlich, Karlheinz Braun, Peter Urban and Urs Widmer, as well as some authors, decided to leave Suhrkamp, and in 1969 they founded their own publishing house based on the model of participation – the Verlag der Autoren.

Habermas showed solidarity with Unseld, and, as the latter was exceptionally appreciative of loyalty, Habermas's standing with Suhrkamp after the 'editors' revolt' was even stronger than before. He used his influence on the publisher in order to make sure that Karl Markus Michel and Günther Busch, competent programme planners, would stay and remain in charge of the edition suhrkamp. As Michel was not satisfied simply to implement the suggestions of the external editors of the 'Theorie' series, his relationship with Habermas was not always free of tensions.

Another recurrent conflict during these months was sparked off by the question of the structures of participation at university institutes. In endless debates, Habermas argued again and again against external advisory boards or boards of trustees, which would allow allegedly independent representatives of society to intervene in the governance of the university from outside. He opted for a model of academic self-government based on parity – i.e., a university of groups – though – partly with the Basisgruppe Soziologie [Sociology grassroots group] in mind, which was holding an active strike – he insisted on a qualified majority of professors being involved in matters to do with research and appointments.

Habermas's suggestions for reform of the university were collected together and published in his book *Protestbewegung und Hochschulreform* [Protest movement and university reform] in 1969. The slim volume, bound in bright orange, had a price of 5 Deutschmarks and soon become essential reading for any student with political interests. *Der Spiegel* called it a last effort not to let the protest movement 'end in the dead-end street of pseudo-revolution'.[91] Although in some of the published material Habermas scaled back his earlier criticisms of the students' activism, Sebastian Haffner wrote in the journal *Konkret*: 'The introduction which opens this volume is one of the sharpest and most unsparing critiques the APO has had to endure so far. And, to be honest, it is also the most apt critique.'[92] And Karl Korn, whose review for the literary supplement of the *Frankfurter Allgemeine Zeitung* is generally sympathetic towards the book, maintains that its author has found the 'remedy against the reification of life': critique. 'From this perspective, we may assume, liberalism is meant to be understood as militant again.'[93]

Habermas's principles of democratization, which he developed with Ludwig von Friedeburg, Erhard Denninger and Rudolf Wiethölter at the end of October 1968 as a draft for a new Higher Education Law for Hesse, and which he published in the press, did not go far enough in the eyes of the student groups around the SDS. The authors said that decisions regarding higher education policy should be taken according to the rules of political will-formation, with the exception that this should not apply to decisions requiring expert academic knowledge. For this reason, Habermas rejected the demand of the Basisgruppe Soziologie that the autonomous organization of study degrees should be guaranteed by a decision-making body in which professors would not have a majority. The students' rallying cry that the 'bourgeois' academic institutions needed to be destroyed caused an almost allergic reaction in Habermas, for in it he saw the foundation of enlightenment and critique threatened. 'Habermas was exceptionally courageous at the time', Ulrich Oevermann once said in an interview. 'He stuck his neck out for everyone else. At teach-ins he . . . stood up and spoke his mind. I have enormous respect for that; it was not easy, and it was very brave at the time.'[94]

In a philosophical seminar on 'Probleme einer materialistischen Erkenntnistheorie' [Problems of a materialist epistemology], which he taught in the winter term 1968–9, Habermas put forward his viewpoint in the form of a position paper to be discussed.[95] The seminar took place on Saturday mornings in the overcrowded rooms of the Philosophical Institute in Dantestraße, which were used partly as library space. In the eyes of the very popular magazine *Der Stern*, the event was sensational enough for it to send a photojournalist to cover it for a leading story that would appear under the title 'Die Revolution frißt ihre Väter' [The revolution devours its fathers]. The photos that have been preserved evoke the emotionally charged atmosphere that accompanied debates in those days.[96]

The position paper was written specially for the seminar and argued that science must not be made subservient to political action:

The only measure of success for the preparation of action is the effectiveness of the acts to which it gives rise. The success of scientific procedures is measured against standards which, if they are being adhered to, guarantee the progress of knowledge. Among these are general rules for argumentation and for reaching consensus, the requirement of explication, the requirement of legitimacy for the validity of claims, methodological clarification and the probing of research tools.[97]

Of course, it would be naïve to assume that the relationship between the professor and his students in Habermas's seminars was always egalitarian. After he had criticized one of his students for giving a rather slapdash presentation, the student expressed his personal disappointment in a letter to the professor, which was later published by a student grassroots group. The letter said that he had only tried to 'create an atmosphere for communication free from fear', but now he was forced to recognize that it had been naïve of him to assume 'that you [i.e., Habermas] would be prepared to agree to a diminution in your authority.'[98]

That Habermas was, indeed, not prepared to accept such a diminution was evident when, in December 1968, students first occupied the Department of Sociology, of which he and von Friedeburg were the heads, and later the Institute for Social Research in Senckenberganlage, of which Adorno was director. Adorno called the police and had the occupiers removed, partly out of fear that the contents of the institute might be destroyed, partly out of fear of legal consequences. When Marcuse expressed his outrage over this in a letter from distant America, Habermas wholeheartedly sided with Adorno, who had been completely overwhelmed by the situation. On 5 May, Habermas wrote to Marcuse:

> For two and a half months (while also tolerating a ten-day occupation of the department in December) we have taken every opportunity to discuss with the activist students why their demands are not acceptable. These demands are part of an illusory transfer of a partisan strategy into our situation. They explicitly amount to a transformation of departmental activities, materially and functionally, into an organizational centre for a direct battle to be fought inside and outside the university. I closed the department here at a point when the agitators were threatening to enter the engine room and destroy the machines and, at any moment, to enter the library and bring the books out onto the street. The students then turned around in front of the closed doors and instead went to the institute in order to continue the commotion there. It is necessary to be aware of these contexts. And commonplaces do not change anything about them: here the students, there the police. You will have the necessary imagination and honesty to imagine an exactly analogous situation at your own department.[99]

In the time that followed, Habermas shared the fate of Adorno and many other professors. Again and again, there were disruptions

of various sorts to which, unlike many of his colleagues, he almost
always reacted with an initial preparedness to enter into a discussion. His tolerance, however, also had its limits, as an incident on 14
November 1968 illustrates. On this day, Hans Imhoff, well known
in Frankfurt as an activist, disrupted Habermas's lecture in the large
Lecture Hall VI in order, as he announced, to give a new kind of
'inaugural lecture' himself. At first, Habermas left the lectern with
the microphone in order to have a discussion with Imhoff; Imhoff
refused, remarking that this would be too ritualistic. Habermas then
insisted on a vote on Imhoff staying or leaving – and lost. After
Imhoff imitated Habermas's nasalization, Habermas adjourned his
lecture to reconvene the following day and left the lecture hall in no
hurry.[100] When he was attacked on a less personal level, however, in
most cases he tended to go on the offensive and to draw his opponent into a debate.

In political terms, these years saw the beginning of a new era for
the Federal Republic. In October 1969, Willy Brandt became the
first social democratic chancellor, a chancellor who wanted 'to risk
more democracy' and was making visible efforts at reconciliation
and dialogue with countries within the Soviet sphere of influence.
In particular, the chancellor's visit to Poland on the occasion of the
signing of the German–Polish Treaty of Warsaw became a historical landmark. His 'Warsaw Genuflection' on 7 October 1970 was
noted all over the world.* A year later, Brandt received the Nobel
Peace Prize for his policy towards the East. With regard to domestic
politics, he also emphasized dialogue and sought links with intellectuals, whom he invited to Bonn for roundtable discussions. In
November 1970, Habermas took part in one of them. When, a week
later, he sent a thank-you letter for the invitation, he praised Brandt
for the general direction he had taken in his domestic and foreign
policies. It was a kind of politics that deserved trust, he said. But
he also dared to express criticism. Thus, he felt that the problem
of ownership structures was being avoided, primarily for strategic
reasons to do with elections. This threatened a further intensification of the 'tendencies towards the concentration of uncontrolled
economic power based on capital ownership'. 'My worry', his letter
to the chancellor said,

> is that social democracy may have a blinkered perception due to a
> fear of its own tradition. In the medium term, the control of economic
> power – and today that means the extension of global governance
> into a structural planning (which does not, from the very beginning,

---

* Brandt spontaneously went down on his knees in front of the monument commemorating the Warsaw Ghetto Uprising during the Second World War.

discriminate against interventions in private investment decisions)
– will become unavoidable if the government does not want to be passively driven along in questions of policy but, rather, wants to develop
alternative priorities to be decided upon politically. This, today, is the
topic of the most advanced academic discussions and has nothing to
do with Marxist orthodoxy.[101]

In the same period, Habermas, not yet forty years old, celebrated one successful publication after another, much to the joy
of Unseld, with whom he had been on first-name terms for some
time now. Apart from the titles already mentioned, another success
was a Festschrift for Herbert Marcuse, which Habermas edited on
the occasion of the latter's seventieth birthday. Several reprints
appeared within a short period of time. In his preface, Habermas,
who very much admired the theoretician of the New Left, took a
critical stance and claimed that Marcuse's postulate of a 'natural
right to resistance' was a source of continual misunderstanding.
According to Habermas, violence can have 'emancipatory effects'
only if 'it is *compelled* by the crushing power of a situation that is
generally recognized as unbearable'[102]

Death of Adorno. Habermas and his family spent the summer holidays
in 1969 in Switzerland, where the news of Adorno's death reached
them. He had died on 6 August during his holidays in the canton
of Wallis, also in Switzerland. Habermas broke off his holiday and
attended the funeral, which took place on 13 August in Frankfurt
in the presence of some 2,000 mourners. At the graveside he said his
farewell, and on the occasion of Adorno's birthday in September he
wrote a moving obituary published in *Die Zeit*. 'Adorno', it says,
'never accepted the alternatives of remaining child-like or growing
up . . . In him there remained a vivid stratum of early experiences
and attitudes. This ground of resonance reacted hypersensitively to
a resistant reality, revealing the harsh, cutting, wounding dimensions of reality itself . . . The vulnerability of the senses and the
intrepidness of his fearless thinking belonged together.'[103]
Although there was a reluctance to recognize it, with Adorno's
death the University of Frankfurt had lost a crucial focal point
of its intellectual life. He also left a large gap in the cultural life of
Frankfurt, as would soon become clear. Habermas was aware of the
expectations that now came to rest on him, especially regarding the
continuation of the tradition of Critical Theory, even if Horkheimer,
Marcuse and Löwenthal were all still alive. He made no secret of the
fact that he was not one for 'business as usual': 'The traditions that
survive are only those which change in order to fit new situations.'[104]
And in his obituary for Adorno he affirmed that no successor would
ever match his 'incomparably brilliant ingeniousness'.[105] Thus, after

Adorno's death, Habermas held on to the idea of a theory of society that would present 'starting points for the overcoming of suffering and unhappiness that result from the structures of the social context of life', but he reduced the demands placed on such a theory and emphasized that it could not be responsible 'for coping with the fundamental risks of human existence – such as guilt, loneliness, illness and death'. 'One might say', he said in a conversation with Gad Freudenthal in the city of Jerusalem's Guesthouse, 'that the theory of society has no comfort to offer in the face of the individual's need for salvation.'[106]

It became increasingly clear to Habermas that a social theory had to take the form of a theory of modernity capable of explaining modernity's accomplishments as well as its potential for generating crises and pathologies. That was the major theoretical project he would pursue in the years to come. And one of the first demands of such a project was a change of theoretical approach, moving away from epistemology and towards a theory of language – or, more precisely, a theory of linguistic communication.

A new track in philosophical thought

Being human is the fearlessness ultimately left to us once we have had the insight that only the perilous means of an ever-so-fragile communication can resist the dangers of a universal fragility. *Contra Deum nisi Deus ipse.*[107]

Habermas's linguistic turn has its roots not only in his study of the classical philosophy of language but also, unsurprisingly, in his preoccupation with social scientific and psychological schools of thought. He appropriated the analyses of language of John L. Austin, Noam Chomsky and John R. Searle but also received important influences from the developmental theories of Jean Piaget and Lawrence Kohlberg. What he calls, in the afterword to the new edition of *Knowledge and Human Interests*,* 'rational reconstruction' now takes centre stage, and it is the aim of this reproductive procedure to render visible a system of rules which is responsible for the production of meaning and sense.

At this point, Habermas still had in mind a theory of the competencies involved in linguistic communication, and what he called 'universal pragmatics' was the domain to which this exceptionally abstract theoretical programme was to be applied. Later, after many a discussion with Karl-Otto Apel, he introduced the name 'formal

---

* The new German edition of *Erkenntnis und Interesse*, 2008.

pragmatics' for the attempt to reconstruct the practical, pre-theo-
retical knowledge – the conditions for communication – that would
establish the general preconditions for action aimed at reaching
understanding. His hope was that, by establishing the rules governing the everyday practice of communication, it would become
possible to uncover the indispensible conditions of critique – where
critique is now understood as the reason-governed ability to reach
a transparent decision in favour of the better argument – in order
to promote what is in the equal interest of all. If it is possible to
demonstrate that rational standards are part of the communicative
actions of everyday practices, then, so the idea runs, the standards
for critique that social theory employs when criticizing social ills can
be derived from them.

This is not the place to present this stage in the development
of Habermas's theory in all its complexity. But, in brief, the most
important steps and elements are the following: speech act theory,
the concept of validity claims, the combination of actions aimed
at reaching understanding with validity claims, and the resulting
schema of the 'three worlds'. The analysis of speech acts ultimately
leads him to the thesis that a normative commitment between actors
can only be produced by speech aimed at reaching understanding
and leading to agreement.[108] Whether or not a speech act is acceptable is based on its implicit rationality claims. The listener assumes
that the speaker is prepared to vouch for the claims if necessary.

Habermas first linked the concepts of action aimed at reaching
understanding and of validity claims in his essay 'Vorbereitende
Bemerkungen zu einer Theorie der kommunikativen Kompetenz'
[Preliminary remarks on a theory of communicative competence] of
1970. While in the case of constative speech acts the claim to truth
is emphasized, in the case of regulative speech acts it is the claim of
normative correctness, and in the case of representative speech acts
that of subjective truth or authenticity. The validity claim to comprehensibility, which in earlier versions of the theory Habermas had
distinguished from the other three, he later dropped, on the grounds
that comprehensibility is not a validity claim in the proper sense but
a rule immanent to language that has to be complied with.

Just as there are three types of validity claims effective in linguistically mediated actions, so too are three corresponding worlds
constituted: the objective world of existing states of affairs, the social
world of legitimate rules of interpersonal relations, and the subjective world of experiences and sensations available to the acting
subject. In the first place, these rather formal ways of relating to the
world have a heuristic function. More is needed in order to explain
the actual success of communication, namely a shared background
of everyday convictions and certainties on which the actors draw.
It is the lifeworld shared by all actors which provides this common

background. And it is impossible to escape the knowledge encapsulated in it, just as it is impossible to escape the horizon of the lifeworld. The actors cannot step outside of that horizon.

While 'normal' communicative action is a form of interaction that takes place spontaneously against the backdrop of the lifeworld, a duty to provide justifications determines the processes of clarification which Habermas calls 'discourse'. In addition, these processes must conform to certain conditions in order to be successful. Among these principles of discourse, as Habermas would point out repeatedly throughout the following years, are, first, the full inclusion of all those affected; second, the equal distribution of rights and duties to participate in debates; third, a communication situation that is free from coercion; and, fourth, participants who are oriented towards reaching understanding.

It was always clear to Habermas that no communication situation in real life can fully conform to these exacting requirements of discourse. The assumption that validity claims, which are implicitly raised in everyday actions, could become the explicit topic in an ideal discourse is hypothetical. According to Habermas, discourse is 'not an institution, it is a counter-institution *par excellence*.'[109] Discourses differ according to their function. Thus, the function of theoretical discourse is to examine validity claims to truth. In practical discourses, validity claims to normative rightness are investigated. And the task of aesthetic critique is to open up the realm of the expressive for evaluation without, however, being able to establish intersubjectively binding standards in this area. The same holds for the interpretation of wishes and inclinations that are sensuously perceived as feelings and moods. The clarification of emotions and affects as elements of the inner nature of subjects can be achieved within the framework of a therapeutic critique.[110] The consensus which marks the end of discourse is only rational if it conforms to the criteria for intersubjective approval. Thus, Habermas links the criteria for truth and correctness to intersubjectivity.

At this early point in his work, Habermas already had a pragmatic view of truth and correctness which focused on the capacity to act and the practical consequences of actions. The background to this view is his conviction (which he still holds, in a more or less unaltered form, today) that there is no access to reality that is not linguistically mediated. Reality only exists as dependent on language. Subjects think and act within the web of language. They are socialized and become individuated through the medium of language. The world is not all that is the case, but the totality of propositions about it. In a certain sense it may be given as such, but for us it is given only in language. We can disclose it only through language's forms of rationality.

Habermas is not the kind of philosopher who sits in a lonely room and broods over their ideas before facing the public with a fully developed theory. Quite the opposite: he publicly tests his ideas even at the early stages in the development of a theory. In this case, he used a review of Arnold Gehlen's polemical late work *Moral und Hypermoral* [Morality and hyper-morality] for *Merkur* as an opportunity to present his emerging concept of the ideal speech situation for public discussion. With the provocative title 'Imitation Substantiality', Habermas's essay led the editor of *Merkur*, Hans Paeschke, to add the following introductory note:

> For more than fifteen years, *Merkur* has benefited from contributions made by Arnold Gehlen and Jürgen Habermas, which were markers put down at opposite ends of the ideological as well as the moral fields of contemporary tensions . . . Both thinkers tolerate it to encounter each other as antagonists in this journal, and so far – mindful of the stature of the other – they have not raised their hands against each other. Now that one of them has done so, with a personal commitment which *ex negativo* shows the importance he attaches to the opponent, we consider it all the more appropriate that the confrontation should happen in the same place.[111]

If Paeschke's hope had been that Gehlen would be interested in joining a debate in *Merkur* over ethics, he was wrong. As an author he stayed well clear of the journal from then on. But Rüdiger Altmann raised his voice in the following edition of *Merkur*, under the title 'Brüder im Nichts?' [Brothers in nothingness?], and presented his position on Habermas's critical discussion of Gehlen's ethics.[112]

In contradistinction to Gehlen, whose anthropology is based on the assumption that human beings are in many respects 'deficient beings' and therefore, as a matter of principle, require solid institutional limits of some kind or other for their stability, Habermas provides a justification for the idea that the basic norms of rational speech create a sufficient foundation for an autonomous moral commitment. His critique does not aim in the first instance at the potentially anti-humanist and anti-democratic implications of Gehlen's ideas.[113] Rather, it aims at the very idea of providing an anthropological foundation for an ethics that is meant to counteract a rampant subjectivity of the kind that Gehlen invokes as a terrifying spectre in his work. Habermas asks Gehlen why he eschews the option, available to us in modern societies, of a universalistic morality, according to which 'the system of norms is . . . based exclusively on the "legislation of reason".'[114] For Habermas, the solution to the problem of how individual autonomy and universal morality can be reconciled is to be found in the principle of discourse as a 'public process of will-formation that is bound to the principle

of unrestricted communication.'[115] He turns against the emphasis
on institutions in Gehlen's thought and considers it a mistake to
derive morality from anthropology. Rather, as he explains, morality
results from the basic norms of speech, which can be used to justify
the standpoint of freedom. Accordingly,

> [t]he determinations of the intelligible ego thus recur as idealizations
> of the speech situation in which practical questions are argued about.
> These idealizations are of course already implied in all speech, no
> matter how distorted, for with each communication (even in attempts
> to deceive) we are claiming to be able to discriminate true from false
> assertions. However, in the final analysis the idea of truth requires
> recourse to an agreement that, if it is to be capable of holding as an
> *index veri et falsi*, has to be conceived as if it were achieved under the
> ideal conditions of an unrestricted discussion free from coercion.[116]

Writing books. At the end of the 1960s, a generational change was
also due at the Institute of Social Research. But when Habermas
was made the offer of succeeding Max Horkheimer as the director of
the house at the Senckenberganlage, he demurred. He feared that he
would become absorbed in administrative tasks and would not have
enough time left for his research and, most importantly, for writing
books. And he was convinced that 'one can change the shape of
debates with books': 'it is possible, if necessary by writing articles
for the daily press, to become involved in the process of changing
attitudes; of course, no one can intentionally change attitudes, but
for such change to take place interpretations are nevertheless important.'[117] At the beginning of 1969, Habermas declined an invitation
from the permanent delegate of the Federal Republic at UNESCO,
the educational, scientific and cultural organization of the UN based
in Paris, to become director of their philosophy division. He would
have been the successor to the Swiss philosopher Jeanne Hersch.

However ambitiously Habermas may have pursued his theoretical projects, and however important the practice of writing may
have been to him as such, he did not completely subordinate his
private life to his career. He maintained numerous friendships and
led a more or less normal family life, including summer holidays in
the foothills of the Bavarian Alps, in Switzerland, Greece, France
and Italy. He also did not want to become entirely co-opted by
Siegfried Unseld and his publishing house, and so he acted as editor
of the programme in sociology at Kiepenheuer & Witsch. This had
been arranged by Dieter Wellershof, a friend of Habermas's from
their student days at the university in Bonn. Wellershof had been an
editor at the Cologne-based publishing house since 1959, and today
is a highly acclaimed novelist, essayist, lyricist and author of radio
plays. One of his poems is dedicated to his friend:

Truth is not
the correspondence of consciousness
with its object because
consciousness cannot verify
this correspondence
which presumably is only the correspondence
of question and answer
thus a collusion.
Once we have grasped this
then
we must think of
another theory
in order to make our madness
more agreeable
to our reason.[118]

6

In the Ivory Tower of Social Scientific Research

From Frankfurt to Starnberg. For six weeks in February and March 1971, in addition to his normal teaching commitments at Frankfurt University, Habermas was visiting professor at Princeton University. In the Christian Gauss Lectures, which he delivered at Princeton, he further developed his 'theory of communicative competence' and developed the outline of a linguistic foundation for social theory. The lectures cover the 'philosophical motivation of the turn from a philosophy of consciousness to a pragmatics of language which Karl-Otto Apel, with a different emphasis, endeavours to carry out under the title of a "transformation of philosophy".'[1] This was the beginning of what is now referred to as the 'linguistic turn' in Critical Theory.

It is obvious that this research agenda was difficult to reconcile with what a number of philosophers and sociologists in Frankfurt had in mind, especially those who remained committed to the Marxist tradition of Critical Theory – one thinks, for instance, of Oskar Negt, Alfred Schmidt, Hermann Schweppenhäuser, or those working at the Institute for Social Research. When the directorship of the institute was to be decided, Habermas politely declined, but in truth he never thought (or at least, at this point, had long since stopped thinking) of himself as a member of the inner circle* of the Frankfurt School, a view of himself that many individuals felt resentful about (and maybe still do today). In 1970, a very public conflict broke out during discussions about who should succeed Adorno. Habermas suggested appointing the Polish philosopher Leszek Kołakowski, who was known for a series of philosophical essays that were critical of Marxism and discussed possible reforms of communism. Since 1968 he had taught outside of Poland, in Montreal and Berkeley, among other places. When at the beginning of March 1970 the philosophical faculty at Frankfurt published an

---

* 'Inner circle' in English and italicized in the original.

open letter in the *Frankfurter Rundschau*, which set out objections to this suggestion and attacked Habermas, he fought back. He also sent an open letter to the daily newspaper, in which he warned against misunderstanding Critical Theory as a kind of institution 'that must be maintained by recruiting orthodox believers'.[2] Soon afterwards, the faculty nominated Kołakowski *primo et unico loco** as the successor to the chair,[3] but he declined – in light of the open dispute over his appointment, he did not want to come to Frankfurt. And so the conflict between Habermas and certain sections of the student body – and the assistants who sympathized with them – deepened. Accompanying this controversy were more disruptions to his seminars and lectures.

The gruelling and perpetual conflicts at Frankfurt certainly formed one of the reasons why Habermas decided to leave at the end of 1971. The year before, he had already been made the attractive offer of becoming one of the directors in Bavaria at the newly founded Max Planck Institute for the Study of Living Conditions in the Scientific and Technical World, and, after carefully considering the offer, he finally accepted it. He did not take this step lightly; to begin with, he hesitated about the prospect of becoming co-director (with von Weizsäcker)† of an institute that was to provide a framework for carrying out very different kinds of research – a set-up that had never been tried before. Habermas's vacillation is evident in the draft of a letter to von Weizsäcker, which was never sent. The letter, dated 12 February 1971, says that Habermas had tried to put himself in the position of his co-director and had reached the conclusion, as he puts it, 'that you [i.e., von Weizsäcker] cannot possibly see a social scientific research institute with an empirical research agenda, with all the implications this has for the selection of staff, the interests of the collaborators, the style of working, the daily discussions, and (at least in the present times) also the political orientation, as the fulfilment of your actual intentions.'[4] In the same draft letter, Habermas also indicates that he wanted to take his group of collaborators in Frankfurt with him, and that he was not prepared to settle for the staff already at the Max Planck Institute. This, too, he writes, could potentially lead to conflicts. At the same time, Habermas harboured doubts as to whether 'the directorship of an empirically orientated institute' was actually something he would be good at. However, the directorship of such an institute was 'the only conceivable legitimation for the decision to go to Starnberg'. At the end the letter, he says: 'Everything still speaks in favour of not staying here in Frankfurt. But because this is unambiguously the case, I should not

---

* As the only suggested candidate.
† Carl Friedrich von Weizsäcker (1912–2007).

deceive myself or you over the fact that the motivations to leave would outweigh those to come to Starnberg to a worrying extent.' Despite all his scruples and ambivalences, Habermas ultimately saw himself as capable of taking part in shaping an institute that had set itself the task of investigating the various aspects of the 'scientific and technical world' on a large scale. In any case, this is how Carl Friedrich von Weizsäcker sketched the task in his proposal for setting up the institute. The prominent scientist, natural philosopher and pacifist was clearly of the opinion that Habermas was the right man for the job:

> I approached him, to his surprise, solely on my own initiative; for me, it was a lucky coincidence that he was prepared to come. My initiative had to do with the fact that in the discipline of sociology, in particular, I felt I had a deficiency that needed to be rectified. . . . Even more important to me was that he was naturally even closer than me to the socially critical attitude which motivated a part of the younger generation of scientists with whom I had to work; at the same time, he was never prepared to compromise on the principles of the rule of law, non-violence and tolerance, as well as strictly insisting on scholarly rigour. I needed a partnership with such a man, and he granted that to me.[5]

Habermas's imminent departure from Frankfurt caused a stir in the media. Without even having spoken to him, *Der Spiegel* reported on 30 November that Habermas no longer wanted

> to be hindered by the duties of a teaching post from developing his critical theory of knowledge, which he considers to be a precondition for any future form of humanism. . . . In future, Habermas will be able to dedicate himself to theory without distraction in his retreat, the Starnberg Mühlberg-Schlößl, the seat of the Institute [of the Max Planck Society], a kind of German art nouveau version of Oxford.

In a letter to the editor, Habermas replied on 14 December 1970: 'In order, as you write, to develop a "critical theory of knowledge", I would not need to join an institute. The only actual motivation for taking this step would be to get empirical investigations underway for which I do not have the necessary leeway in Frankfurt.'

The media, in general, spoke of the beginning of the end of Critical Theory. Karl Heinz Bohrer (in the *Frankfurter Allgemeine Zeitung*, 4 December 1970) remarked that 'crocodile tears . . . were shed over the alleged passing of the so-called Frankfurt School.' But Bohrer added that it was wrong to subsume Habermas under a Frankfurt School that had been inflated into mythic proportions. Habermas, Bohrer said, did recognize 'the function of class', like Adorno and

Horkheimer, but he was prepared 'to acknowledge the results of the bourgeois battles for freedom to a much larger extent than seemed appropriate to a Marxist faced with the situation of the 1930s.' Like Bohrer, Habermas himself tried to undercut the dramatization of his departure from Frankfurt by explaining what had motivated his decision. He informed Max Horkheimer and Herbert Marcuse of his decision, and he told Horkheimer that the situation in Frankfurt had changed significantly after Adorno's death. Apart from that, he listed two reasons for moving to Starnberg, near Munich: 'I have excellent conditions for research there. I can fill fifteen academic posts, and I have broad financial scope to decide freely on the projects to be developed.'[6] In his letter to Marcuse, Habermas explained:

> I have more motives for leaving Frankfurt than I have for going to Munich. My future here in Frankfurt would mean that I would have to use all my labour power for teaching, more precisely for teaching introductory courses in sociology. Within the context of a reorganization of the university, for which I myself am partly responsible, the new Department of Sociology will have the task of introducing to sociology and politics not only all future teachers but also, as part of their *Grundstudium*,* all law students and students of economics. This means that more than half of all students will have to be taught by our department. If you add to this the fact that we do not enjoy the privilege of American professors of having to teach only two or four hours per week, but rather have to teach six to eight, then my wish to extract myself from the (altogether sensible) imperatives of mass education† is, I hope, at least understandable. . . . To begin with, there was resistance to the foundation of Weizsäcker's institute from representatives of industry. I feel much more comfortable with the fact that the institute was founded in opposition to these resistances. Contrary to what *Der Spiegel* had to report, there are, of course, no conditions whatsoever attached – otherwise I could not go there.[7]

In his reply, Marcuse showed understanding for Habermas's decision to go to Starnberg, but added that he regretted Habermas's departure from Frankfurt: 'somehow it is a "symbolic act" which is part of the end of the Frankfurt School.'[8]

A six-page letter to Claus Offe, written in May 1970, provides some insights into Habermas's ideas from the very beginning regarding the work to be done at the Max Planck Institute. He wanted to persuade Offe, who was on a research visit to the USA at the time,

---

* The first two years of study, followed by the *Hauptstudium*, the third and fourth year.
† 'Mass education' in English in the original.

to join him at Starnberg and, to this end, offered him a permanent position – the only one available. He begins his letter by saying that he did not expect the Max Planck Society to place any restrictions on the orientation of the research and then gives reasons why the new position was preferable to a professorship in Frankfurt: the situation at the Institute for Social Research was desperate, in terms of both personnel and innovative perspectives in research, and Habermas was 'tired of continuing to play the burdensome social psychological role of a substitute father'.[9] Apart from that, increasing teaching duties left him hardly any time for his own theoretical work. And, for the latter, the Max Planck Institute offered the necessary space, which during the first year of its existence was to be used by the staff for seminar-type discussions in preparation for future projects.

> The seminars should serve the purpose of creating a certain shared fundamental knowledge for all social scientific collaborators, and first of all establish certain standards for work and discussion which, after this initial phase, should no longer be questioned in this institute. . . . Once this seminar phase is completed, the decisions regarding the projects and the composition of the project teams should be taken.

With great optimism, Habermas expresses his conviction that under these new working conditions the continuity of research could be guaranteed to an extent that would be impossible to achieve at a university, certainly at present, and most likely also in the future. Then he informs Offe about the envisaged research clusters and about possible candidates to fill the fifteen positions available, and asks him to comment on these. In this context, he mentions a number of names as candidates for PhD scholarships, among them Tilman Allert, Klaus Eder, Hartmut Neuendorff, Edith Kirsch, Wolfgang Streeck, Ekkehart Krippendorff and Hans-Joachim Giegel.[10]

Offe replied immediately, but not at all emphatically. He missed neither the tone of authority in his boss's words nor the gentle pressure being exerted on him. Habermas wanted to push his assistant into making a quick decision so that he could pursue his research plans. Offe, according to his own testimony, knew 'that Jürgen Habermas was *the* intellectual force for people like me'.[11] And so, despite a few reservations over whether it was justifiable, in terms of higher education policy, to take university research elsewhere, and whether the research aims under discussion might not be overly ambitious, Offe responded to Habermas with a 'qualified yes'.

Habermas also wanted to bring Albrecht Wellmer to Starnberg, but, in his case, things proved to be more difficult. Wellmer was a temporary professor at the University of Toronto at the time, and Habermas wanted him to become a third director at the Starnberg institute. In December 1971, he wrote to him full of optimism: 'We may in the end after all succeed in creating a proper social theory.'[12] That this would not be without difficulties – and not only because of Wellmer – would become increasingly apparent in the years to come.[13]

Without a scapegoat. On 18 February 1971, an article by Winfried Heidemann appeared in the *Diskus*, a newspaper edited by students in Frankfurt, under the title 'The Persecution and Assassination of Theory, Performed by Jürgen Habermas'.* Heidemann feared that Habermas was no longer committed to the unity of research and teaching, and that he was trying to save his neck by withdrawing into a pure research institution and thus escaping a situation that he himself, with his efforts at reforming and restructuring the university, had helped to create. On 4 June, Habermas responded with a letter to the editor of the paper, in which he refers to the unique opportunity of conducting broad-based social research on questions such as the emergence of potentials for conflict or the factors determining state policies on science. His concluding remarks betray some bitterness: 'Apart from that, it would probably be helpful for a number of students and colleagues (and for me a relief) if an ambivalently cathected object of projection should disappear from the Frankfurt scene.'[14]

The decision to move to Starnberg was at the same time a decision against the secure position of an employee of the state of Hesse with full civil servant status. The time-frame for the planned projects at the Max Planck Institute also suggests that the position of co-director, which Habermas finally took up on 1 October 1971, was a very long-term commitment.[15] Starnberg is a small, semi-rural town about 25 kilometres southwest of Munich, at the northern end of Lake Starnberg, and a popular destination for day trips. In terms of per capita income, it is one of the richest places in Germany. There, the Habermas family realized a long-held dream of building a larger house more suited to their personal needs and their own architectural tastes. Siegfried Unseld provided a five-year loan for the purchase of a building plot just outside the centre of town in May 1971. Habermas soon paid off the loan with the help of a building loan agreement with a bank.[16]

The house was designed in the Bauhaus style by the Munich architects Christoph Sattler and Heinz Hilmer and set on a sloping

---

* The title is an allusion to Peter Weiss's play *The Persecution and Assassination of Jean Paul Marat Performed by the Inmates of the Asylum of Charenton under the Direction of the Marquis de Sade*, better known in English as simply *Marat/Sade*.

hillside. Building it took one and half years, during which time the Habermas family stayed in Steinbach. In a jointly edited volume, the two architects later published an article, along with photographs, in which they describe the architectural planning and design of the house:

> Conversations with the client about the Wittgenstein house in Vienna were important points of departure for the design. The layout develops along a stretched-out cube which, due to the sloping position, is one and a half storeys high on the southern entrance side and three storeys high on the northern side. The living area, being situated on the first floor, is removed from the damp forest soil. The garden can be reached from a terrace that extends from the house. The different parts of the house are lined up along the length of the axis. From within the axis, the mutual positioning of the rooms and the dimensions of the house along its length can be surveyed. The library is also situated to the side of this axis. Winding stairs connect the different floors and lead to a roof terrace hidden from view.[17]

While the house was being built, Habermas had a small, furnished, two-bedroom flat in the nearby village of Pullach at his disposal. Every other weekend, he drove from Munich to Steinbach. In October 1972, the family finally moved into their new home.

In 1971, Suhrkamp published *Philosophical-Political Profiles*, a collection of portraits of famous philosophers and social theorists, such as Adorno, Bloch, Benjamin, Gehlen, Jaspers, Plessner and Wittgenstein. The book carried the dedication 'In memory of Theodor W. Adorno'.* A little later, the volume on *Theorie der Gesellschaft oder Sozialtheorie: Was leistet die Systemforschung?* [Theory of society or social theory: what can systems theory accomplish?], mentioned previously, appeared in the 'Theorie' series. It immediately became the topic of intense discussion and marked the beginning of the debate between Habermas and Niklas Luhmann, the leading figure of systems theory.

The success of his publications did not prevent the occurrence of a short-lived but bitter episode between Habermas and Suhrkamp. In December 1971, Ute Habermas rang Siegfried Unseld to tell him that she and her husband were annoyed about defamatory statements made about Habermas in a book of poems by the Cuban poet and intellectual Heberto Padilla, which had been published in the edition suhrkamp. Under the heading 'Theodor W. Adorno returns from the dead', the book, which had been recommended by

---

* The dedication is absent from both the extended German edition of 1981 and the English translation.

Hans-Magnus Enzensberger and translated by Günter Maschke, contained the following lines:

> Those who knew him, do not find it surprising
> that Theodor Adorno returns from the dead.
> In both parts of Germany
> everyone is waiting for him,
> except, of course,
> Habermas and Ulbricht.[18]

In a letter of 22 December 1971, Unseld apologized for the 'unacceptable' publication of the poem. In a letter to Günther Busch, Habermas had earlier declared that he would withdraw his own titles from the programme (which was, after all, important for him), and would no longer publish in the series. Unseld at once took the decision not to print any more copies of the volume of poetry in question and to pulp the print sheets. This seems to have appeased Habermas; books by him continued to appear in the edition suhrkamp.[19]

Benjamin conference. For a symposium in honour of Walter Benjamin, who would have turned eighty in July 1972, Habermas produced a programmatically titled lecture on 'Consciousness-Raising or Rescuing Critique – the Actuality of Walter Benjamin', which he presented in Lecture Hall VI of Frankfurt University.[20] He was standing in at the event, organized by Suhrkamp Verlag, for the literary scholar Peter Szondi, who should have delivered the keynote address but committed suicide six months earlier, probably on 18 October 1971. There were further presentations from Werner Kraft, Adrienne Monnier, Hans Sahl, Gershom Scholem, Hermann Schweppenhäuser and Rolf Tiedemann. Ernst Bloch, Max Frisch and George Steiner also made their way to Frankfurt. Siegfried Unseld was in hospital following a car accident, and Uwe Johnson, who was there in his stead, said a few words of welcome.[21] Decades later, Habermas recalled the

> programme of the small conference: in the evening, Gershom Scholem gave a paper at the Palmengarten* on 'Benjamin and his Angel', in which he clarified the mysterious title of remarks from the early thirties – *Agesilaus Santander*. The following day, lectures were given at the university in Lecture Theatre VI, where, at that point in time, one could almost still sense Adorno's spirit. In the afternoon Ernst Bloch – philosophizing in narrative style while smoking a pipe, as was

---

* Palm houses, situated a stone's throw from the main university buildings.

his wont – opened a discussion chaired by Alfred Schmidt, in which
Max Frisch and George Steiner participated, among others. This was
the same Steiner who six months later would coin the term 'Suhrkamp
culture' in the *Times Literary Supplement*.[22]

In his lecture, Habermas points out that the motif of rescuing plays
a fundamental role in Benjamin's thought, and in particular in his conception of critique, before contrasting it to his own understanding of
critique. While 'rescuing critique' is based on the Messianic intention
of wresting a vision of liberated life from the catastrophic unfolding
of history, consciousness-raising critique relies on the possibility that
historically unnecessary, and to that extent illegitimate, domination
is compelled to justify itself because of processes of enlightenment.*
Habermas clearly states that only a kind of consciousness-raising
critique, which focuses on social institutions and renders visible the
extent to which they are amalgamated with power,† is appropriate
at the present time.[23] To that extent, critique has nothing to do with
an arcane intellectual knowledge, but derives its motivation and
substance from concrete social and political events. This, he argues,
results in a new determination of the goal of emancipatory philosophy: 'In complex societies, emancipation means the participatory
transformation of administrative decision structures.'[24] But even
consciousness-raising critique comes at a price:

> Is it possible that one day an emancipated human race could encoun-
> ter itself within an expanded space of discursive will-formation and
> yet be robbed of the light in which it is capable of interpreting its life
> as something good? The revenge of a culture exploited over millennia
> for the legitimation of domination would then take this form: right
> at the moment of overcoming age-old repressions, it would harbour
> no violence, but it would have no content either. Without the influx
> of those semantic energies with which Benjamin's rescuing criticism
> was concerned, the structures of practical discourse – finally well
> established – would necessarily become desolate.[25]

The remaining months of 1972 were wholly taken up by the initial
phase of research at the Max Planck Institute, where two research

---

* It is worth pointing out that the German 'Aufklärung', as a single word or in compound nouns, has a semantic penumbra that differs slightly from that of 'enlightenment'.
'Aufklären' can also mean 'to solve a crime' or 'to clear up an error'. Sexual education
is 'Sexualaufklärung', usually shortened to 'Aufklärung'. Thus, the German is arguably
closer to the idea of progress through knowledge, the discovery of new facts, rather than
referring just to a historical period and its social and political agenda. 'Eine aufgeklärte
Gesellschaft' is not so much an 'enlightened society' as a society of independently minded
citizens, where power is exercised in a transparent and accountable fashion.
† The German 'Gewalt' can mean 'power' but also 'violence'.

clusters were created shortly after Habermas had taken up his post. While the focus of the group around von Weizsäcker was on quantum theory, questions regarding the prevention of war, the economy and the history of science, the group around Habermas concentrated on an analysis of the symptoms of crises in late capitalist societies.

During his first fourteen months in Starnberg, Habermas had to commute between Munich and Frankfurt, and so he used his stays in the latter city for conversations with Siegfried Unseld, during which he made suggestions for publications in the 'Theorie' series. By letter, he also asked the publisher for a further short-term loan.[26] The impetus for this request was the snowballing costs of completing the new house in Starnberg. Habermas was even toying with the idea of selling it. But another change of place, he wrote, would be almost too much, not least because of the children and Ute, who had just taken up a part-time post as a teacher of German, history and social studies at the nearby rural boarding school in Kempfenhausen. The attachment to Starnberg was not particularly strong at the time – and would never compare to that to Frankfurt. And Munich, as Habermas recently said, also 'retained an alien element' for him, and did not alter his 'sentimental attachment to Frankfurt'.[27]

Between academic management and research

At the Max Planck Institute Habermas's area of competence and responsibility, as co-director alongside von Weizsäcker, far exceeded that of a normal chair.[28] This was apparently not obvious when one entered the institute as a visitor:

> At the end of Starnberg, behind an imposing villa, there is a small bungalow whose freshly painted external walls serve only to highlight the provisional nature of the house. I walk towards the bungalow and stop in front of a garden gate. Is there no entrance? Then, suddenly, the gate opens, I am kindly asked to step inside the Max Planck Institute for the Study of Living Conditions in the Scientific and Technical World – or, more precisely, into one of the four 'quarters' in Starnberg which make up the institute. We go into the entrance hall; light-painted walls and a narrow corridor, doors with little nameplates on them. One of them says 'Jürgen Habermas', a small room that is overflowing with just a desk and a seating area.[29]

The direction and goals of the various research groups and projects were discussed in endless meetings. They were all meant to be oriented by the guiding question of the Max Planck Institute, which was, in Habermas's words: 'How can the power of technological control be recaptured by the consensus of acting and negotiating citizens?'[30]

> Roughly speaking, this is the question of how the effects of capitalist growth, which needs to be systematically analysed, rebound . . . on the structures of the lifeworld. . . . Our problems are still [to explain] how this capitalist economic system, with its quite healthy rate of growth, destroys those conditions of life that are structured in such a way that they have to be described in categories of a theory of action.[31]

For the execution of the various interdisciplinary research projects, Habermas had fifteen research posts for social scientists at his disposal; in fact, he would never fill all of them. When he began to work at the institute in October 1971, together with Claus Offe, Ulrich Rödel, Rainer Döbert, Klaus Eder, Rainer Funke, Brigitte Bub, Sigrid Meuschel, Hartmut Neuendorff and others, the researchers working directly with him were divided into three work areas. One group was meant to investigate the potential for crises in capitalist societies from a primarily economic perspective. A second group looked at the potential and the limits of state intervention in the case of global social crises. And a third group focused on the problem of how to explain the potential for protest, but also apathy, in young people. All three projects were meant to undertake social-theoretical as well as empirical work. In order to deal with this broad range of research, it was necessary to recruit further collaborators. Claus Offe, who was given free rein by Habermas in the choice of his colleagues, soon appointed Rainer Funke, Günter Schmieg and two of Sontheimer's assistants, Volker Ronge and Manfred Glagow. Later, the sociologists Gertrud Nunner-Winkler, Edith Kirsch and Manfred Auwärter and the philosopher Ernst Tugendhat joined the staff. Habermas provided the theoretical framework in the form of his book *Legitimation Crisis*, which appeared in 1973 in the edition suhrkamp. He described it as a hypothetical 'sketch of an argument'.[32]

Legitimation Crisis. The basic hypothesis of the book is that symptoms of crises in fully developed capitalist societies result from an imbalance between, on the one hand, a state pursuing generalizable interests and, on the other, a capitalist economic system that ignores the criteria of public welfare – an imbalance that becomes increasingly salient. This leads to attempts by the economic sector, which is dominated by the imperative of maximizing profits, to influence the processes of political decision-making, which results in the alteration of other areas of society 'in accordance with priorities that take shape as a function, not of generalizable interests of the population, but of private goals of profit maximization'.[33] Furthermore, if decisions are not taken on the basis of a 'justified consensus', a legitimation deficit builds up, which indicates

> that it is not possible by administrative means to maintain or establish effective normative structures to the extent required. During the course of capitalist development, the political system shifts its boundaries not only into the economic system but also into the socio-cultural system. While organizational rationality spreads, cultural traditions are undermined and weakened. The residue of tradition must, however, escape the administrative grasp, for traditions important for legitimation cannot be regenerated administratively.[34]

If legitimation deficits become ubiquitous, they grow into full-blown crises. These have partly economic causes; their symptoms, however, occur predominantly in the political and socio-cultural spheres.[35] At the time, Habermas did not exclude the possibility that, if legitimation crises escalated sufficiently, societies might cease to be democratic in order to escape the need for justification which is normatively embedded in the constitutional rule of law. Legitimation crises have negative effects on social cohesion, because the latter is dependent on the existence of justified and, in that sense, trustworthy norms. In addition, motivational crises may also occur when old traditional forms lose their motivational force and, as a consequence, for instance, the performance ideology is no longer credible. In spite of all the efforts by state institutions to keep legitimation deficits at bay, Habermas is sceptical about the effectiveness of such strategies: '*There is no administrative production of meaning.*'[36]

The political scientist Wilhelm Hennis levelled one of the sharpest criticisms against the theory of late capitalism as well as against the concept of legitimation crises.[37] According to Hennis, to deny the legitimacy of the democratically constituted Rechtsstaat undermined the level of democratization that had been achieved and endangered rather than protected democratic achievements.[38] Furthermore, the policy problems faced by states at the time – the first oil crisis of 1973 had just triggered a worldwide economic recession – were hardly substantial enough to warrant the use of a category such as 'legitimation crisis'. But most of all, Hennis said, it was important to avoid Habermas's mistake of playing off the concept of a substantial democracy against that of a formal democracy.[39] Rather, legitimate rule rests on three factors, which had to be scrutinized: the standing of the members of the political leadership, the capacity of public services for coping with tasks at hand, and the stability of institutions which guarantee freedom. Hennis acknowledged that there were legitimation deficits in all three of these areas, but he disputed the claim that they were caused by the class structure of late capitalism.

'The class structure of developed industrial societies is a barrier that is far too fluid, too easy to overcome and dissimulate, for it . . . ever to have produced legitimation crises by itself.'[40] Instead, Hennis argued, it was the beginning of a 'new era of large-scale imperial spaces [*imperiale Großräume*], for which it had at no point in history so far been possible to develop a legitimate form of rule' that gave new urgency to the question of legitimacy.[41]

In his reply to Hennis at the Congress of Political Scientists in Duisburg in the autumn of 1975,[42] Habermas explained the causes of legitimation crises: there is the potential threat from class conflicts, a concept Habermas retains. Then, in democratically organized societies, 'the level of justification [of a political order] has become reflexive'[43] because, in their case, fundamental political decisions require the uncoerced consent of all concerned parties. For this, in turn, it is necessary that everyone involved takes part in discursive processes of will-formation as free and equal citizens. The state, for its part, has to provide the legal requirements for such participation. And it is also the task of the state to guarantee the functioning of economic processes, for instance through indirect steering measures such as stimulus packages, without acting as a market player itself. Habermas thus answered his opponent: 'If under these restrictive conditions the state does not succeed in keeping the dysfunctional side effects of capitalist economic processes within bounds acceptable to the voting public, if it is also unsuccessful in lowering the threshold of acceptability itself, then manifestations of delegitimation are unavoidable.'[44]

The daily routine of a researcher. The programmatic text on legitimation crises was also a sign of how important it was to Habermas that the research in Starnberg would produce demonstrable results. He put his collaborators as well as himself under significant pressure, a pressure that was further increased by the enormous problems in coordinating the interdisciplinary work at the institute. The two directors treated each other with great respect, despite the substantial discrepancy between them in terms of age and intellectual style. But, as their theoretical temperaments were so very different, there were inevitably differences of opinion concerning questions of staffing and organization. Playing table tennis together in the lecture hall of the institute – something Habermas, in any case, thought a waste of time – did little to change that. Weizsäcker saw Habermas as an ambitious colleague who set much store by strict academic standards, as 'a member of the scientific age who took Marx seriously'. At the same time, according to von Weizsäcker's judgement, Kant's categorical imperative was 'close to [Habermas's] heart. In order to be legitimate, a moral norm must be rational, and, in order to be rational, it must be possible to universalize it. That is the only valid justification for the egalitarianism of the enlightenment.'[45]

It soon became more and more obvious that Starnberg was not exactly the research paradise that would offer Habermas the freedom he needed in order to dedicate himself to his real passion, the development of his own theory of society. While he had quoted the threatening burden of teaching duties as a reason for leaving Frankfurt, he was now obliged to fulfil the duties of a director of the institute, the scale of which he had probably misjudged. Claus Offe, who accepted an appointment to a chair in Bielefeld as early as 1974, described the working atmosphere at the institute in Starnberg as catastrophic and beset by persistent rivalries. Everyone secretly thought that everyone else was an idiot, and very few were able to cooperate, which affected not only the relationships between the research groups but also those within the groups. In Offe's own group, which consisted of Rainer Döbert, Ulrich Rödel, Günter Schmieg and Volker Ronge, quarrels were an everyday occurrence. And, apart from all that, the privileged but isolated working conditions encouraged tendencies towards self-neglect and alcoholism, at least in some cases. According to Offe, Habermas performed his duties as a director, but only after a fashion. He tried to avoid the conflicts within the institute as much as he could. Leading a large institute was simply not his cup of tea. The jurist Günter Frankenberg, who was the head of the institutional board for some time, remembers that the atmosphere was extremely intellectualist and tense. There was a permanent competition to be the most brilliant and original; even the informal morning tea sessions in the rooms of the secretariat were verbose demonstrations of spontaneous ingenuity, with Habermas, who was concerned with other matters, as the unattainable standard. On the one hand, in order to set people at ease, Habermas declared that *normal science* was the goal;* but, on the other, he was ruthlessly critical of the presentations at the regular colloquia, especially those by his own collaborators. According to Offe, descriptions such as 'a potpourri of half-digested material' were among the more innocuous. On the basis of a 'robust self-confidence', Habermas believed that he was 'entitled to pass judgement', and he did not shy away from making 'downright unjust negative judgements about people'. Frankenberg, by contrast, emphasizes that, as a rule, the director of the institute fulfilled his duty of care even in cases where there were reservations regarding the qualification of collaborators. He always acknowledged original ideas and references to literature that was new to him. And he absorbed what was useful for his

---

* 'Normal science' in English in the original.

theoretical interests and was always on the lookout for new ideas, inspirations and critique. That was one of the reasons why he initiated debates within the institute and invited external scientists and lecturers from all over the world – for instance, the philosophers Herbert Marcuse, Thomas McCarthy and Charles Taylor and the sociologists Aaron Cicourel, Lawrence Kohlberg, Alain Touraine and Niklas Luhmann.[46]

In August 1973, Habermas again visited Korčula and presented a paper on 'Die Rolle der Philosophie im Marxismus' [The role of philosophy within Marxism].[47] The starting point for his deliberations was the thesis that bourgeois consciousness had become cynical. The absolute self-belief of science had prevailed. Against this scientism, the radical self-reflection of philosophy had to be rallied. The conference, on the theme of 'The Bourgeois World and Socialism', was overshadowed by the death of Max Horkheimer, who had unexpectedly died of heart failure a few weeks earlier, on 7 July, in Nuremberg. Habermas acknowledged him in his paper as a representative of a non-dogmatic Marxism but did not write an obituary. Fifteen years later, he would give a lecture at a conference on the occasion of Horkheimer's ninetieth birthday: 'Remarks on the Development of Max Horkheimer's Work'.[48]

Resistance from Munich. In the spring of 1972, during a time of political liberalization, the Red Army Faction (RAF) carried out a series of bomb attacks on US military installations. A little later, the police arrested leading figures of the terrorist group, among them Andreas Baader, Gudrun Ensslin and Ulrike Meinhof. In the public debate on the causes of terrorism that followed, conservative politicians and intellectuals in favour of a 'militant democracy', but also 'the man in the street', accused the representatives of Critical Theory, even left-wing intellectuals in general, of intellectual complicity. This mood persisted even after the SPD, for the first time in the history of the Federal Republic, emerged from the national elections in November of that year as the strongest political force. The ensuing short period of reform was accompanied by the increasing fragmentation of the anti-authoritarian protest movement, a movement which, according to Habermas, had 'lost its way, be it on the way towards party-based communism and neo-Stalinism, be it on the way towards becoming an alternative culture – both have equally led into isolation.'[49]

Habermas experienced for himself just how heated the atmosphere had already become in this early phase of terrorism – and this was only the beginning – when the philosophical faculty of the Ludwig Maximilian University in Munich rejected his application for an honorary professorship, something that would have been a mere formality under normal circumstances. In the official letter from the university, written in December 1973, the vice-chancellor, Nikolaus Lobkowicz, expressed his regret over the vote against Habermas. Evidently, the faculty did not shy away from the scandal that ensued. Many saw it as a political move by the conservative Bavarian minister for culture and education Hans Maier, who saw the higher education law in Hesse, which Habermas had helped to shape, as a thorn in his side. In Bavaria, where Franz Josef Strauß's party called the shots, Habermas's unequivocal stance on everyday political matters – for instance, the anti-radicals decree and the professional prohibitions associated with it[50] – was met with suspicion, to say the least.

In a detailed letter of Whitsun 1973, Hans Maier clarified that he had in no way intervened against a possible appointment of Habermas as honorary professor. However, he said, Habermas had to be prepared to accept the consequences of having chosen a state which, in matters of higher education policy, followed a different path from the one Habermas had supported in Hesse. The minister accused Habermas of, on the one hand, wanting to pursue his own research interests in privileged conditions while, on the other, seeking to exert influence on higher education policy by taking up a teaching post in Munich, as his assistant Claus Offe was already in the process of doing. In his response of 15 June 1973, Habermas explained that the connection with the university was important for a director of a Max Planck Institute because it gave him the opportunity of promoting the next generation of academics. He took exception to the moralistic tone of Maier's letter: Maier was asking him to foot the bill, so to speak, for the Hessian higher education law and, at the same time, complaining that he was withdrawing to focus on pure research.

> If I had been looking for a comfortable solution for myself in 1968, I would have gone either to Constance or to UNESCO in Paris. On the other hand, I am surprised by your moralistic tone when you suggest that my (after all only natural) commitment to matters of higher education policy during the time of the revision of the law for higher education in Hesse should disqualify me from being able to choose more intense research work over the joys and sorrows of administration, of teaching, and of higher education policy for the future years of my life, in which I still hope to have some productivity. That the opportunity to do so arose was accidental; that I took it was a well-grounded decision. In my opinion, the latter does not require justification,[*] and certainly not to the resentful members

---

[*] '... war Zufall; dass ich diese Möglichkeit ergriffen habe, ein gut begründeter Wille. Er bedarf in meinen Augen einer Rechtfertigung nicht.' It may appear contradictory that a 'well-grounded' decision does not require justification. The difficulty arises from the

of a Bund Freiheit der Wissenschaft [Association for Freedom in Science].[51]

The latter was an association of conservative university teachers founded in 1970 in reaction to the student movement. Hans Maier was a member, as were Hermann Lübbe, Robert Spaemann, Odo Marquard and Wilhelm Hennis.

Habermas was still smarting from the Munich rejection when, at the beginning of 1974, he learned that the city of Stuttgart was going to award him the Hegel Prize. Dieter Henrich, as the president of the International Hegel Association,* gave a speech paying tribute to Habermas. After the Lord Mayor, Arnulf Klett, had handed the certificate to Habermas in the Mozart Room of Stuttgart's City Hall, he gave his acceptance speech. Habermas asked the question: 'Können komplexe Gesellschaften eine vernünftige Identität ausbilden?' [Can complex societies develop a rational identity?].† His answer was: the identity-building self-images of national and cultural societies must be subject to the principle of mutual recognition. Collective identities are constructions, which are only persuasive if their formation is a commonly shared and open process. Habermas used the prize money of 15,000 Deutschmarks to pay off part of the debt on the newly built house.

Habermas and his family spent the summer holidays 1974 in Capoliveri on the island of Elba. The same year, Habermas made the acquaintance of Richard Rorty at a conference on Heidegger in San Diego. Years later, he still remembered the occasion vividly:

> At the opening of the conference, a video of an interview with the absent Herbert Marcuse was screened, in which he described his relationship with Heidegger in the early 1930s in milder terms than the sharp post-war correspondence between them would have led one to expect. Much to my annoyance, this set the tone for the unpolitical veneration of Heidegger that prevailed throughout the entire conference.

In his talk, Rorty tried to combine the voices of Dewey, the Wittgenstein of the *Philosophical Investigations* and Heidegger in order to get 'the world-disclosing function of language' into view. 'At that time', Habermas writes,

---

German phrase 'begründeter Wille', literally 'justified will'. Presumably, Habermas wants to say that he took a reasoned decision that does not require *further* justification.

* The 'Internationale Hegel-Vereinigung', founded in 1962, should not be confused with the 'Internationale Hegel-Gesellschaft, founded in 1953. See below.

† The speech was a shortened version of the text, which may be found in Habermas and Dieter Henrich, *Zwei Reden*, Frankfurt am Main, 1974, and again in: Habermas (1976), *Zur Rekonstruktion des Historischen Materialismus*, pp. 92–126.

I found the juxtaposition so obscene that I lost my composure in the discussion. Surprisingly enough, the distinguished colleague from Princeton was not in the least irritated by the robust protest from the German backwoods; he was instead so kind as to invite me to his seminar. For me, that visit to Princeton marked the beginning of a friendship as happy and rewarding as it was instructive.[52]

For September 1974, Habermas planned to attend the conference of the International Hegel Association on the theme of 'Dialectics', which was to take place at Lomonosov University in Moscow. However, the organizers, under the leadership of their head Wilhelm Raimund Beyer, the founder of the society and editor of the *Hegel Jahrbücher* [Hegel yearbooks], made it absolutely clear that he was not welcome there. *Die Zeit* published the correspondence between Beyer and Habermas under the title 'Ein Satyrspiel um Philosophen, Politik und Vereinsmeierei' [A satyr play about philosophers, politics, and small-minded club culture]. Beyer complains about the fact that Habermas did not register personally for the conference but had his secretary do it for him. And, apart from that, Habermas had been known not to turn up despite having registered, and there were also problems with accommodation. In his reply of 10 June, Habermas confirmed his registration, to which Beyer flatly replied: 'I regret to have to inform you that we – unanimously – feel that we have to uphold our negative reply.' In his response to this letter, Habermas countered:

> I consider any fears that you have regarding the potential role I may play, quite frankly, ridiculous, and – should they be genuine – unworthy of a scientist. I repeat my wish to participate in the Moscow congress. . . . You also mention yet again my refusal to meet up with you to discuss some kind of preliminary agreement: my dear Mr Beyer, in what kind of country do you think we actually live? I have a simply motivated aversion against having to deal with a colleague more than necessary if that colleague is incapable of perceiving me under any category other than that of class enemy.

Beyer finally concluded this ludicrous exchange of letters, saying: 'The International Hegel Society does not want a "Hegel Prize laureate" in its midst; it remains a philosophical society.'[53]

Habermas was one of the speakers and discussants on a panel at the 17th Congress of German Sociologists, which took place in October 1974 in Kassel. The theme of the congress was 'Theories in Comparison', and Habermas presented results from research undertaken at the Max Planck Institute on questions of moral development within society. This was an area in which his group at the institute had something quite substantial to offer, in particular

the 'social psychology group' around Rainer Döbert and Gertrud
Nunner-Winkler, which was investigating the potential for conflict
and apathy among adolescents, with particular attention to the formation of ego identity and social identity in contemporary society.
This project, too, clearly bore the stamp of Habermas, not least
because it started out from his theses on the emergence of interactive
competence, which he had laid out in two articles, the 'Notizen zum
Begriff der Rollenkompetenz' [Some notes on the concept of role
competencies] of 1972 and 'Moralentwicklung und Ich-Identität'*
of 1974.[54]

A theory about the impossibility of not learning

Developmental processes of humankind and of human beings. The
'Starnberger Studien' [Starnberg studies], which were published in
various places, demonstrate that the research at the institute did
indeed lead to presentable results.[55] And Habermas was also publishing at a tremendous rate. Only three years after the *Legitimation
Crisis*, a collection of essays appeared entitled *Zur Rekonstruktion
des Historischen Materialismus* [On the reconstruction of historical
materialism]. The introduction explains what is to be understood
by 'reconstruction' in this context: it is an attempt at dismantling a theory of social development, such as that of Marx, and
at reassembling it in such a way that it can be linked up with contemporary theoretical approaches. The aim of Habermas's research
at Starnberg, pursued together with the sociologists Klaus Eder
and Rainer Döbert, was to demonstrate 'some of the structural
homologies between the history of the species and ontogenesis'.[56]
This required the preliminary clarification of two questions: Which
evolutionary logic did the development from neolithic societies to
modern societies follow? and How can we explain the logic of the
ontogenetic development from a subject that acts on the basis of
conventions to one that acts on the basis of principles? Habermas
was guided by the assumption that there is not only a parallel
between cognitive and moral development; further, he was trying
to demonstrate analogous patterns in social development, while
warning against a confusion of concrete historical events (which
are the objects of a narrative historiography) with what he calls an
evolutionary theory of the historical succession of learning levels:
'Evolutionary theory is concerned neither with the totality of history
nor with individual historical events . . .. The subjects of evolution

---

* Also in Habermas (1976), *Zur Rekonstruktion des Historischen Materialismus*, pp.
63–91. English translation: 'Moral Development and Ego Identity', *Telos*, no. 24 (June
1975), pp. 41–55.

are societies and the acting subjects integrated into them. Evolution can be read off a hierarchical pattern of increasingly comprehensive structures which needs to be rationally *reconstructed*.'[57]

Habermas shows that the distinction between labour and interaction must also be drawn from the perspective of an evolutionary theory of development, because the learning processes in the area of production followed an entirely different course compared to those concerning the developing worldview: 'The species learns not only in the dimension of technologically useful knowledge decisive for the development of the productive forces but also in the dimension of moral-practical consciousness decisive for structures of interaction.'[58]

The human species, which, for Habermas, is characterized by the fact that it 'cannot but learn', not only acquires better and better technological knowledge but also learns in the moral and practical domains that are decisive for forms of communal life. Individuals learn by growing into the symbolic structures of their lifeworlds. The learning processes they undergo in the spheres of 'language', 'cognition' and 'interaction' result in a continuously increasing autonomy from external nature, the social world and inner nature: 'The learning process in which structures form is also a process of ego-production [*Selbsterzeugungsprozess*] insofar as it is only in the course of this process that the subject transforms itself into a subject with the capacity for knowledge, language and action.'[59] Language is of central importance in this process, because ego development takes place in the medium of everyday communication: 'For a living being that maintains itself in the structures of ordinary language communication, the validity basis of speech has the binding force of universal and unavoidable – in this sense transcendental – presuppositions.'[60]

Now, what about the ability of societies to learn? Despite a clear turn towards a theory of social actors, at this stage in the development of his theory Habermas designs a model of social learning which, according to him, can be analysed just as well in terms of socio-cultural developmental stages. Or at least this can be said of the *logic* of development, which, he insists, differs from its *dynamic*. What drives this logic are real systemic problems: 'A society is able to learn in a constructivist sense by taking on the evolutionary challenges in the face of which the available steering capacities fail, and by meeting them through syphoning off and *institutionalizing* the excess of individual innovative potential (which is already latently available in worldviews).'[61] Thus, social systems can form new structures if they make use of the given level of learning in socialized subjects in order to improve their steering capacity. Ontogenetic learning processes, however, run ahead of shifts in social evolution. Insofar as the learning of societies is dependent on the learning of its members, societies learn only in a metaphorical sense. Social learning processes are themselves subject to a dialectic of progress: new capacities for solving problems are always accompanied by the recognition of new problematic situations.

At this point in time, Habermas already held the thesis that the development of normative structures 'is the pacemaker of social evolution, for new principles of social organization mean new forms of social integration.'[62] He suggests making a distinction between worldviews, identity formation, and the legal and moral system when analysing normative structures. On this basis, he goes on to formulate provisional stages in the development of social formations: neolithic societies, early high cultures, developed high cultures, the societies of early modernity.

Responses. The book, consisting in part of previously published articles, did not meet with universal approval. At the Salzburger Humanismusgespräche [symposium on humanism],* an elderly Leo Kofler launched a full-frontal attack on Habermas, calling him an 'anti-Marxist' who 'couldn't tell Marx's insights from Frankfurter sausages'.[63] Martin Meyer's review in the *Neue Züricher Zeitung* (17 September 1976) also reached the conclusion that, from the perspective of Marxist orthodoxy, Habermas had become a heretic because his 'rejection of the idea that the direction of history can be discerned marks the "turning point" in the thought of a sociologist who for a long time had a friendly relationship with the Marxist philosophy of history.' Wolf Lepenies's review in the *Frankfurter Allgemeine Zeitung* (16 August 1976) focused on the distinction between historical research and historiography, on the one hand, and evolutionary theory, on the other – something of a marginal point. Habermas, Lepenies argued, 'provided sociology with a developmental logic as theoretical backbone, so to speak'. The reviewer of *Der Spiegel* liked the fact that a neo-Marxist such as Habermas put the category of language (as a necessary condition of self-consciousness and of acting in solidarity), rather than that of labour, at the heart of his social theory. Willy Hochkeppel, in *Die Zeit* (18 March 1977), by contrast, doubted that Habermas's dismantling of historical materialism was successful in the intended constructive sense, as he ultimately had Stalin's dogmatic version of Marxism in mind. Eva Hesse, in turn, pursued the traces of structuralist thought in Habermas over a whole page of the *Frankfurter Rundschau* (26 March 1977):

In his reconstruction, Habermas unfolds a kind of 'structuralist historicism' which applies the structuralist principle of homology in the

---

* An annual event organized the Austrian broadcasting station ORF.

widest possible sense. This enables him to see every element at a particular temporal point, be it of an economic, technological, moral, legal, cognitive or political nature, as analogous to every other element. On the one hand, the evolutionary stages are treated as 'synchronic' and perfectly meaningful within themselves while, on the other hand, they appear as transient points within a diachronic movement – i.e., they are relativized as genetic and historical phases and thus appear as in need of supplementation with regard to their meaning. It is world history represented as the road 'paved by the devil with destroyed values' (M. Weber) – a fascinating project.

Habermas's daily life during that time was very much structured by his commitments at the institute and by work on the development of his own theory. Nevertheless, he did not lead a withdrawn life in Starnberg. At weekends, there were outings to the delightful surrounding countryside; he would go swimming in Lake Starnberg in the summer or skiing in the mountains in the winter. Max Frisch, Martin Walser and Reinhard Baumgart visited the house in Ringstraße. Habermas had a friendly relationship with Hilde Domin. Ute and Jürgen Habermas met other Suhrkamp authors, some of whom they knew, some of whom they had not previously encountered, at the publisher's soirées in the Klettenbergstraße in Frankfurt – among them Peter Weiss, Uwe Johnson, Hans Magnus Enzensberger, Peter Handke, Thomas Bernhard and Ingeborg Bachmann. At one of these gatherings, Habermas recalls, Peter Handke asked him what he thought about the music of the Beatles. Habermas answered that he did not know the Beatles, to which Handke reacted by slapping him – a sort of dust-up that, according to Habermas, was not unusual at the time.[64] When Habermas expressed his enthusiasm over the text of Peter Weiss's stage biography of Hölderlin, which premiered at the Württembergisches Staatstheater in Stuttgart in 1971, Unseld mentioned this to the author. On 17 January, Weiss sent Habermas a friendly letter from Stockholm, in which he set out the changes to the text he intended to make before its performance and said that he was open to suggestions from Habermas. In June 1976, Max Frisch asked Habermas for advice regarding a speech he had to deliver in the autumn of that year at the Peace Prize ceremony in the Paulskirche in Frankfurt. There is an entry on an earlier visit by the Habermas family in Switzerland in Frisch's *Dienstbüchlein* [Military service booklet], containing the description of a scene from a hiking tour they took together: 'Picnic, I build a proper fireplace and light a fire in order to grill some sausages. THE SWISS SOLDIER! The dear visitor [i.e. Habermas, S. M.-D.] smiles unsuspectingly, and at once I get peeved again, silently peeved.'[65]

In October 1976, Habermas was awarded the Sigmund Freud

Prize for Scientific Prose by the Deutsche Akademie für Sprache und Dichtung. He was, we can assume, particularly pleased about receiving this honour; he had originally wanted to become a journalist, and he continued to take writing very seriously as a scientist and intellectual. In a short statement, the academy explained that the work of Jürgen Habermas, the thinker, was 'the work of his language. The identity of subtle insights and subtle style means that his language "represents its own disappearance with the appearance of thought"'. In his acceptance speech, Habermas talked about the infiltration of social scientific terminology into everyday language.[66]

The minefield of political interpretations in the 'German autumn'

Apparently in this country you have to be a socialist if you want to fight for liberal principles.[67]

Keeping your nerve. 1977 would go down in history as the year of the 'German autumn'. Within only a few months, the confrontation between the terrorist members of the Red Army Faction and the state came to a dramatic head. And the intellectual debates between the left-liberal and the liberal-conservative camps became even more trenchant. After a two-year trial, the leading RAF terrorists in Stammheim prison on the outskirts of Stuttgart, who had repeatedly gone on hunger strike in protest at the conditions of their imprisonment, were due to be sentenced the following spring. After having visited the high-security complex, Jean-Paul Sartre spoke publicly of human rights violations. On 7 April, Germany's chief public prosecutor, Siegfried Buback, his driver, Franz Goebel, and a policeman, Georg Wurster, were murdered in broad daylight in Karlsruhe by the 'Ulrike Meinhof Command', a group belonging to the second-generation RAF. On 30 July, Jürgen Ponto, the chairman of the Dresdner Bank's board of directors, was shot dead in his house in Oberursel. On 5 September, Hanns Martin Schleyer, the president of the Confederation of German Employers' Associations as well as of the Federation of German Industries, was kidnapped in Cologne and later (probably on 18 or 19 October) murdered by the 'Siegfried Hausner' Command. On 13 October, the Lufthansa plane *Landshut* was hijacked on its way from Palma de Mallorca to Frankfurt by four members of the Palestinian terror group PFLP (Popular Front for the Liberation of Palestine). One of the aims of the hijackers was the release of the RAF terrorists in Stammheim. Helmut Schmidt's government acted on *raison d'état*, hastily passing the 'Kontaktsperregesetz' – a law that allowed for the isolation of the prisoners from one another, from their lawyers, and from the outside world – and a gagging order for the media which, for its part, mostly abstained from any critical reporting. At the same time, the state's security organizations made use of illegal methods in order to obtain information in the so-called Lauschangriff [bugging attack].

After the storming of the *Landshut* by the GSG 9* in the early hours of 18 October 1977, which ended in the liberation of all the hostages and the death of three of the four hostage-takers, the leading figures of the first-generation terrorists, Andreas Baader, Gudrun Ensslin and Jan-Carl Raspe, were found dead in their cells in the high-security wing of Stammheim prison, where they were all serving life sentences. Irmgard Möller survived stab wounds to her chest. Ulrike Meinhof had already hanged herself from the bars of her prison cell a year earlier. The attacks caused 'the most severe crisis in Germany's domestic politics yet, because the Federal Republic had felt committed to the maxim of a "militant democracy", and so ready to defend itself, but had not reckoned with the murderous militancy of the RAF. The ad hoc legislation against the new form of terrorism intensified the level of legal regulation.'[68] In the face of rigorous new policing measures, such as the introduction of dragnet searches, as well as the passing of a package of special anti-terror laws in 1977, *Der Spiegel* warned against the threat of the rule of law being dismantled in the midst of a collective hysteria.

It suddenly seemed obvious 'where the Federal Republic stood in the case of doubt: with one foot in the authoritarian camp.'[69] There was an undeclared state of emergency, which was nevertheless very real.[70] In Habermas, this brought up old fears of a relapse into 'old times': 'The domestic situation, which had intensified into a pogrom-like state of tension after the kidnapping of Hanns Martin Schleyer in 1977, pushed me into leaving the theoretical ivory tower and, let's say, taking sides in the battles of daily politics.'[71] He was of the opinion that such murderous left-wing terrorism strengthened the repressive potential within society – 'as if the right which had been discredited in the shadow of National Socialism had only waited for an opportunity to rise again against the "ideas of 1789".'[72] The public debate about the politically unstable situation in Germany became even more charged when left-wing intellectuals were openly referred to as dogs, rats and flies at party-political events of the conservative wing.[73] The 1978 film *Germany in Autumn* bears impressive witness to those 'leaden years'. It was an attempt by a number of film-makers, among them Rainer Werner Fassbinder, Alexander

---

* Grenzschutzgruppe 9 der Bundespolizei = Border Protection Group 9 of the Federal Police – a counter-terrorism and special operations unit.

Kluge, Edgar Reitz and Volker Schlöndorff, to document the tangle of contemporary events.[74] Habermas watched the film, and in a letter to Alexander Kluge he expressed his admiration, in particular regarding the 'documentary scenes' filmed by the latter: 'without your insistently interviewing and commenting voice, without the Klugean fixation on history and the military, on fictional quotation, on the circumstantial, the film's heterogeneous elements would probably have fallen apart and would not have become something that triggers such an immensely ambivalent, memorable and complex reaction.'[75]

Dispute with Sontheimer; attack by Golo Mann. At the height of the dramatic events of the German autumn – there were even debates about the reintroduction of the death penalty prompted by calls from the right[76] – Habermas published an open letter to the political scientist Kurt Sontheimer. Habermas had had a collegial relationship with Sontheimer from the early 1960s onwards. His letter of 1977, which he published in the journal *Merkur* and which was later reprinted in a book, *Briefe zur Verteidigung der Republik* [Letters in defence of the republic], co-edited with Freimut Duve, Heinrich Böll and Klaus Staeck, discussed the causal relationship that his Munich colleague had been claiming, both on TV and in print, existed between terrorism and what he took to be 'left-wing theory' – the sort of claim many national conservative characters of the Christian democratic parties were making at that time. Talk about an advancing 'civil war' was rife within these circles, and there was a growing tendency towards criminalizing any critique of society as such. This culminated in the suggestion that such critics should be deprived of their basic rights as citizens. This alarmed Habermas, and he pointed out the absurdity of 'blam[ing] those who tried to understand the problems of legitimation and motivation for causing them'.[77] He feared that he and his fellow citizens were, in the face of terrorism, sliding 'into a fascistic disintegration of our political culture'[78] and 'into a militarization of our attitudes [*Gesinnung*] and a para-militarization of our society. . . . If we do not succeed in dedramatizing the terror, if we do not succeed in living with the terror *as if* it were an ordinary crime, then the fight against terrorism will itself contribute to building the very stage on which terrorism first unfolds and maintains itself.'[79]

This open letter led to a debate between Habermas and Sontheimer in the *Süddeutsche Zeitung* of 26 and 27 September 1977. Sontheimer assumed, despite all the differences in their interpretations of the situation, that they shared the intention of wishing to defend democracy as such. Apart from that, however, it was incontrovertible for him that 'no *sufficient* explanation for the political terrorism . . . was possible without taking into account the radical politicization in the student movement, the actors' intellectual background,* which was furnished by left-wing theory, [and] the discontent over our political situation, which was fed to the point of satiety by the new critical consciousness.'[80] Using the words of the journalist Dieter E. Zimmer, Sontheimer said it would be 'deception to deny the left-wing roots of terrorism'.[81] Habermas belonged, he said, to the circle of individuals that had encouraged 'the radical opposition to the bourgeois-democratic system'.[82]

That the murderous terrorism from the left was to be condemned, Habermas responded, was as cheap and self-evident a point as the insinuation that there was an identity between the ways of thinking of the RAF and the exponents of critical Marxist theory was absurd or malicious. The RAF had, indeed, declared on several occasions that there were no commonalities with the left, insofar as the latter rejected violence and armed struggle. And the SDS had already distanced itself from those who wanted to express their opposition through militancy and terrorism after the RAF had carried out arson attacks on department stores in Frankfurt on 2 April 1968.[83] He was not obliged, Habermas said, to distance himself from positions that justified terrorism because he had not ever taken such a position. And he warned: 'If this time around the left-wing intellectuals are declared to be the internal enemy, and if they are morally neutralized through public defamation, would that not amount to a serious weakening of the alliance of those individuals who, when necessary, confront the erosion of the republican identity of our polity?'[84]

In a contribution to *Der Spiegel*, published under the title 'Probe für Volksjustiz – Zu den Anklagen gegen die Intellektuellen' [Rehearsing popular justice – on the accusations against the intellectuals] on 10 October 1977, Habermas again made it clear that Adorno, as the most important representative of the Frankfurt School, had openly spoken out, along with others, against the use of any kind of violence as early as 1968. It was pogrom-like propaganda to declare Critical Theory the intellectual origin of terrorism, Habermas continued, and he now took the opportunity to describe his previous use of the term 'left-wing fascism' as an 'overreaction'. But he also insisted, referring to the examples of Heidegger and Carl Schmitt, that scientists had to weigh up the political effects of what they said and had to take responsibility for them, without 'extending it in moralizing fashion to the point where one freezes for fear of the vagueness and uncertainty [of the effects]. All that would remain would be silence', a silence unworthy of the intellectual. For

* '... ohne den von linken Theorien ausstaffierten geistigen Hintergrund der Akteure': the meaning of the term 'actors' is ambiguous – it may refer either to the 'terrorists' or to those active in the student movement.

this reason, he was under no circumstances prepared to be intimidated, and if necessary he would report on the German situation in the international press – a slightly odd threat from someone who could have a platform in virtually any of the leading media outlets in Germany. Following the dispute with Sontheimer, Habermas turned to his former assistant Oskar Negt in a letter of 29 October:

> I consider the political situation to be of so much concern that some of us feel that we want to find a slightly more systematic orientation. In this context, here is my question: Would it be both possible and agreeable for you to pay an informal visit to Starnberg some time and speak to a few of us here about the situation of the left in the Federal Republic?

Negt wrote back that he was pleased to receive the invitation and accepted.[85]

Golo Mann's reaction to Habermas echoed that of many right-wing conservative politicians, for instance Franz Josef Strauß and Alfred Dregger.[86] His article in the *Neue Rundschau* in January 1978 bore the title 'On Professor Jürgen Habermas's Art of Thinking' and accused him of having downplayed the symptoms of terrorism from the very beginning. His explanations would do nothing to help understand terrorism, he said, and it would not be of any help either if, in response to acts of terror, he were simply to say 'I did not mean it that way. – How, then, did you mean it?'[87]

Habermas did not respond to this directly, but he wrote a letter to the editor of *Die Zeit*, in which he praised an article by Fritz J. Raddatz, then the editor-in-chief of the weekly's cultural pages.[88] Under the title 'Bruder Baader?' [Brother Baader], an allusion to Thomas Mann's 'Bruder Hitler', Raddatz had asked: What are the causes of terrorism in a society that does not hold itself to account over its own moral failure? 'It is the fathers of this state which begin to undermine it. They cannot bear any doubts about themselves, or about the society they have created – and they do not understand that repressed doubts congeal into despair.'[89]

In the autumn, at a point when even the serious media were demanding an end to the closed season on critical intellectuals, Peter Brückner, professor of social psychology at the University of Hanover, was removed from office. Disciplinary proceedings against him were opened and he was banned from university premises. This was the second time this had happened: he had been accused of supporting the RAF in 1972 and suspended for two terms. Brückner's removal the second time had been preceded in September 1977 by a call from the CDU-led government of Lower Saxony for thirteen university teachers to sign a pledge of allegiance because they had contravened the requirement of political moderation in civil service law. These men had caught the attention of the politicians as the editors, together with another thirty-five colleagues from other parts of the Federal Republic, of *Buback – an Obituary*, in which the pamphlet of the so-called Göttingen Mescalero was documented.[90] This somewhat confused and in many ways problematic text had first been published in the newspaper of the student union at the University of Göttingen and had become the subject of contemporary debates because only excerpts had been quoted in a distorting fashion by the media. The main difficulty was that it acknowledged a 'secret delight' at the murder of the chief federal prosecutor, despite all its criticism of the assassination.* Habermas claimed that the 'case of Brückner' was an exemplar of the kind of rabble-rousing that was being directed at intellectuals in Germany.[91]

At the end of 1977, Max Frisch gave a speech in front of the delegates of the SPD party convention, in which he referred to the Habermas–Sontheimer–Mann controversy:

> Time to have a go at the intellectuals once again . . . Certainly, this does not refer to Professor Kurt Sontheimer, who exempts himself from the distress of the intellectuals by means of an about-face, or Professor Golo Mann, who declared a civil war this autumn – which is more than just disproportionate nonsense; 'After all, you know', Habermas replies, 'the resolution of the paradox of a situation akin to civil war without parties engaging in a civil war is fascism.'[92]

In a letter to Habermas, the British historian Eric Hobsbawm praised the firm position he took against Sontheimer: 'I am afraid I think we are about to enter an era in which we have yet again to fight "for the position of enlightenment" – and not only in your country; and that means against the renegades of the middle ground and the "new right".'[93]

The more the interpretation of the fundamental values of the democratic constitution became the subject of a controversy over political ideas, the more forthright Habermas became in the public defence of his position. This battle over interpretive authority and over the scarce resource of public attention led not only to sometimes exaggerated polarizations but also to the consequence (at least at that point in time) that the strategies for gaining dominance in the battle of political ideas became ends in themselves; the real issues increasingly moved out of sight. This opened the floodgates for a loss of differentiation and for schematic generalizations. While

---

* The opening of the pamphlet containing the remark about the author's 'klammheimliche Freude' was published widely, but not later passages which are critical of the use of violence. For the full text, see www.n-tv.de/politik/Der-anonyme-Mescalero-Brief-article146962.html.

conservative forces saw themselves as the guardians of state authority and threatened by terrorists, the other side painted a gloomy
picture of the dangers emanating from a law-and-order state.[*]
Decades later, Habermas acknowledged that these conflicts spi-
ralled out of control and that they led to personal insults that had
long-lasting effects within a particular intellectual generation.[94]

Theoretical work and the diagnosis of the contemporary situation.
Shortly after the kidnapping of Hanns Martin Schleyer, Herbert
Marcuse (along with Heinrich Böll and Rudi Dutschke) was
prompted by Fritz J. Raddatz to publish an article in *Die Zeit*
(23 September 1977) under the unambiguous headline 'Murder
Must Not be a Weapon of Politics'. In complete agreement with
Habermas, Marcuse saw the terror of the RAF as a clear break with
the aims of the student movement.

At Habermas's invitation, Marcuse visited the Starnberg Institute
in July 1977. They were still friends – even a minor motor accident,
resulting from Habermas and Marcuse trying to fend off a wasp
inside the car, did not seriously dampen their spirits. Their discussions, however, were nevertheless contentious. Both agreed that the
student movement, which had once stood for a 'new sensibility', had
disintegrated – under the pressure of increasing repression, Marcuse
stressed. But with regard to social theory their positions were unmistakably opposed. Several times, Habermas criticized Marcuse's
notion of reason, which the latter, Habermas said, situated at the
level of individual erotic needs, simply following Freud's theory
of the drives. According to Marcuse, 'we can form the picture of
a general savage only on the basis of reason, and never the other
way around. And reason, or being rational, lies indeed within the
drives, namely in the urge of erotic energies to stop destruction.
This is exactly how I would define reason.'[95] Habermas, by contrast, claimed that reason was something given exclusively through
language. '[T]hen rationality resides in the organization of an uncoerced general will-formation – i.e., in the telos of the non-violent
intersubjectivity of communication.'[96] These divergent views ultimately also led to significant differences in the two men's evaluation
of democratic constitutional systems. While Habermas saw a quali-
tative difference between the latter and fascism, Marcuse assumed
that bourgeois democracy was undermined by the power of high
finance and was thus latently fascist.

The tension between economic power and democracy had also
been the subject of a critique of the SPD's long-term programme
('Framework 85') that Offe and Habermas published with the

---

[*] 'Law-and-order' in English in the original.

economists Sigrid Skarpelis-Sperk and Peter Kalmbach in *Der Spiegel* on 24 February 1975. Under the title 'A Biedermeier Path towards Socialism?', the authors began by identifying a problematic change in the political climate resulting from the most recent media campaign by liberal-conservative forces, and then went on to accuse the SPD of the post-Brandt era of representing an opportunistic realism and 'quietism'. If the SPD wanted to hold on to a 'democratic path towards socialism', the party would need to be prepared to question the capitalist economic system. In the first instance, this would require the willingness to opt for a direct steering of the economy by the state in order to set limits to 'the monopolist pricing behaviour' which, within global capitalism, had long since taken the place of the supply and demand mechanism. While interventions on the side of production structures had, in effect, meant the provision of funds to enterprises, projects for infrastructure improvements had failed due to the financial crisis of the state. Political reforms limited to these very modest steering instruments would lead only to electoral defeat, which would necessarily 'damage the cause of democratic socialism'.

In a riposte to the article, Wilhelm Hennis classified the suggestion of testing the use of legal means for directly steering the economy as 'a kind of leveé en masse plus enabling act'.[97] Habermas responded to this formulation in a letter to the editor, saying: 'This, in the vocabulary that Hennis knows so well how to use, is what you call a denunciation.' He also said of Hennis that he 'always half believed in his well-played role of the paragon of virtue.'[98]

In December 1977, Gajo Petrović complained that the journal *Praxis*, a forum for non-dogmatic Marxism and democratic socialism, and the summer school on Korčula were threatened by interventions from the Yugoslavian regime under Tito. Habermas supported Petrović with an article in which he stressed the importance of the group around *Praxis* 'for the aims of a socialist self-administration and the relentless critique of all forms of bureaucratically distorted socialism'.[99] Three years earlier, he had already signed an open letter to Marshall Tito which criticized repressive measures against intellectuals and the repression of academic freedom.[100]

At the end of this difficult year, in December 1977 Habermas and his wife travelled to Israel for the first time. The occasion for this was the eightieth birthday of the Jewish philosopher Gershom Scholem, originally from Berlin, who had dedicated himself, more fully than any other scholar, to the exploration of Jewish mysticism.

How magnanimous he was when, upon our first visit to Israel, he put his city, Jerusalem, at our feet. As a generous and thoughtful host he had made sure that we would have the privilege of staying in the Mishkenot Sha'ananim, the old hospital of the Montefiore

opposite the Mount of Olives, which the city has turned into a luxuri-
ous guesthouse. He had organized a car and driver from the Academy
of Science and first drove to Mount Scopus with us, where the university is situated, and to another place from which the view encompasses
two opposite sides, down to the Old City and far out to the hilly desert
landscape. He showed us the city and tirelessly commented on every
corner of it. He led us, past the odd camel herder, to Jericho, this
miracle of a flowering and flourishing oasis in the middle of the desert,
and just outside the city gates of Jerusalem, along the road to Tel
Aviv, introduced us to the inhabitants of a kibbutz.[101]

At the Israeli Academy of Science, Habermas presented a paper to
a handpicked audience on the concept of rationality in Max Weber's
work. In the evening, he visited Gershom Scholem's house, together
with Siegfried Unseld and Hellmut Becker. Scholem showed them
around his famous library of more than 10,000 books. The following day, the official ceremony in honour of Scholem took place at
the Cultural Centre of the German Embassy in Tel Aviv. After a
short address by Unseld, Habermas praised Scholem's philosophical
achievements, which, he said, stood in the best traditions of German
intellectual history. Habermas's speech, 'The Torah in Disguise', as
he himself formulated it, was a 'speech of gratitude' for the fact that
in Scholem's writings the treasures of the world of Jewish mysticism
are 'spread out before the eyes of all'.[102] Especially after the catastrophe of the twentieth century, intellectual life in Germany was in
need of the German-Jewish traditions and acquired

> the right [to them] – even and precisely after Auschwitz – in the
> measure that we can, in carrying them forward productively, make
> use of them so as to direct upon ourselves the gaze of those exiles who
> were schooled in Marx, Freud and Kafka, in order to identify the
> estranged, the repressed, the rigidified parts in ourselves as something
> split off from life.[103]

On 5 May 1978, in an article for *Die Zeit*, Habermas asked:
'Where are the liberals . . ., why are the liberals not brave enough
to protect the principles for which they have stood?' 'By now', he
continued, 'the word "liberal" has become a pseudonym for the
new militancy of the old right-wing intellectuals.' According to
Habermas, the expanding practices of 'institutions for ideological
protection', such as the so-called anti-radicals decree, intended to
keep critics of the system away from civil service, 'trigger fear in a
whole generation, produce despair, and keep people from identifying with the things for which our by now mostly cynical Republic
was once meant to stand.'[104] As an example of the 'ban from civil
service', he mentioned the case of a relative of his: his sister-in-law,

Mrs W., as a teacher had applied to become a civil servant but was rejected explicitly on grounds of her membership of the German Communist Party (DKP). In response, Marion Gräfin Dönhoff, the editor of *Die Zeit*, sent a long personal letter to Habermas, in which she defended the political achievements of West Germany and lashed out against a left that staged 'masquerades' such as the Russell Tribunal.*[105]

In August 1978, Habermas and his family went to Brittany for their summer holiday. During that time, Habermas read the draft of an essay written by Axel Honneth in 1976 titled 'Von Adorno zu Habermas: Zum Gestaltenwandel kritischer Gesellschaftstheorie' [From Adorno to Habermas: on the transformation of critical social theory], which Honneth would later publish in *Merkur*.[106] The essay's main thesis is that Habermas had bid farewell to Adorno's concept of rationality, one based on the philosophy of consciousness, in order to develop a concept of reason anchored in linguistically mediated intersubjectivity. On 13 September 1978, Habermas wrote to Honneth saying the essay had 'touched [him] in an unusual way': 'I had never made my relationship to Adorno clear to myself, and now someone comes along who not only writes about it, but actually understands it better than I do myself. I think that you are right in almost every respect.'[107]

In November 1978, Habermas travelled to Warsaw for a guest lecture at the Institute for Sociology, accompanied by his son Tilmann.

Edition suhrkamp, Volume 1000. Amid all his lectures and travels, political debates and public interventions, his organizational duties and the quarrels at the Starnberg Institute, from the beginning of his time in Starnberg Habermas tried to get down on paper the major work that had been planned for some time. He assured his publisher again and again that he would withdraw from all his commitments in order to complete the *Theory of Communicative Action*, for which the rough outline had already been established. But first he had to take care of a publication project which Siegfried Unseld had persuaded him to undertake a while previously. The thousandth volume of the edition suhrkamp was coming up, and Habermas was to edit it. The idea was to present a kind of interim survey of developments and trends in contemporary politics and culture. The title, in an allusion to Karl Jaspers, was 'Stichworte zur "Geistigen Situation der Zeit"' [Notes on the intellectual situation of the times]. It was certainly high time for drawing some interim conclusions.

---

* Organized by Bertrand Russell, Jean-Paul Sartre and others in 1966, the tribunal investigated American foreign policy and military intervention in Vietnam.

In 1979, the Federal Republic celebrated the thirtieth anniversary of the founding of the state. For ten years a socialist-liberal coalition had formed the government, during which time Gustav W. Heinemann was the president. And there was a debate over whether the crimes committed during the Nazi era were subject to a statute of limitation. What Unseld had in mind was a two-volume publication with contributions from the leading left-wing intellectuals in Germany that would mark a kind of caesura – also with respect to the future direction of the edition suhrkamp. Habermas harboured a growing suspicion that the publisher planned to redirect the series, in which many of his own titles were published, away from social criticism. He had grown particularly fond of it because over the course of its existence it had produced a 'lure towards theorizing'.[108] In a letter to Unseld, he sharply criticized the recent tendencies in the policies of the publishing house.[109] Unseld had expressed his intention to reduce the number of sociological titles and increase the number of new literary texts. There were rumours about differences between Unseld and his editor Günther Busch over the political orientation of the programme. Evidence for this was the fact that Raimund Fellinger and Bernhard Landau joined as lectors in 1979, and Günther Busch was expected to cooperate with them, particularly regarding the future programme of the edition suhrkamp.[110]All these were reasons why Habermas accused Unseld of surrounding 'the profile of the publishing house with a "fog of liberal conservatism"'.[111] Habermas distanced himself from Suhrkamp's policies: 'You move in a world of Rotary Club members that has nothing in common with me.' And he insisted on being kept 'at a visible distance from all' of its plans.[112] In another letter to Unseld, written six months later, he went even further and threatened to leave the publisher and take all his titles with him should a change in political direction be implemented.[113] Habermas's wife Ute had encouraged him to take this hard line and also to get in touch with Hans Altenhein, the managing director of Luchterhand, in order to discover whether it would be possibile, as a former author of theirs, to move back to them. He openly told Unseld about this: Altenhein, he said, had reacted 'extremely fairly'. Regarding his rights as an author, Habermas added that he did not have the intention 'of turning this into a "formal case"* should you insist on your oppositional stance.'[114]

Unseld responded at once and wrote to Habermas to reject the initial accusations.[115] He explained to his author that the remarks regarding a political reorientation of the publishing house rested

---

* 'Case' in English in the original. Habermas uses the informal 'Du', as he and Unseld were on first name terms.

exclusively on conjecture, and that Suhrkamp looked after Habermas's rights with his best interests in mind and would continue to do so even if he moved to another publisher. Unseld even made the generous offer of republishing all of his titles in the main programme, as Habermas himself had demanded, thus succeeding in placating his agitated author. The first result of this agreement was the volume *Kleine Politische Schriften I–IV* [Short political writings I–IV], which came out in hardcover in the main academic series [Suhrkamp Wissenschaft].

Under the shadow of these disputes, Habermas celebrated his fiftieth birthday in June 1979 in his home in the Ringstraße in Starnberg. In addition to his family, several of his friends were present, such as Reinhard Baumgart, Gershom Scholem, Herbert Marcuse, Martin Walser, Alexander Mitscherlich, Ernst Tugendhat, Albrecht Wellmer and Spiros Simitis. Unseld was also there and gave him a first edition of Fichte's *The Vocation of the Scholar* (1794) as a present, as well as arranging an official reception at the Hotel Bayerischer Hof in Munich the following day. Gershom Scholem, who had come from Jerusalem, was again the centre of attention 'with his lively stories'. 'He was also the one', Habermas remembers, 'who knew exactly what befits a bourgeois environment and rose to speak at midnight in a friendly and celebratory tone "because it cannot be that there is no speech".'[116] At this evening of birthday celebrations, Habermas also observed that Herbert Marcuse 'remained unusually shy in the background'.

> From similar encounters I was familiar with the strange phenomenon of friends and others of the same generation, who were otherwise anything but restrained, withdrawing from Scholem's presence as if they suffered from a guilty conscience. . . . It was an advantage not to be Jewish when meeting Scholem. Thus, one did not fall into the category of intellectuals who had made the great mistake of opting for an all too trusting assimilation.[117]

Volume 1000 of the edition suhrkamp finally appeared in late autumn 1979. It was made up of thirty-two contributions, including pieces by Klaus von Beyme, Ralf Dahrendorf, Iring Fetscher, Oskar Negt and Alexander Kluge, Hans and Wolfgang Mommsen, Claus Offe, Martin Walser, Albrecht Wellmer, and Hans-Ulrich Wehler. In his introduction, Habermas speaks ironically about the type of author who bundles together 'the many-folded robe of topicalities'. Karl Jaspers's 'great gesture of being the teacher of a nation', he says, is also outdated.[118] Nevertheless, his remarks contain points of reference for a comprehensive analysis of the contemporary situation: in the 'other Republic', which had been evoked by regressive political forces, a danger existed that political differences would be resolved on the model of a 'paramilitary campaign at the frontline of a semantic civil war'.[119] The only alternative to this regressive tendency, which is accompanied by a hunt for 'subversive intellectuals' fuelled by the opinions disseminated in the media, is 'to bring back to memory once again the concept and dignity of modernity – that is, of the dimensions of an *unreduced* rationality.'[120]

The circumstances around the emergence of the two volumes may have been characterized by a certain turmoil – Günther Busch, who had been responsible for the edition suhrkamp ever since its inception, left the publishing house after sixteen years at the beginning of 1980 and joined the Europäische Verlagsanstalt and later S. Fischer – but the reaction to their publication, just in time for the Frankfurt Book Fair, was unspectacular. The thirty-three authors were united in their hope for a liberal democracy, the idea of which was associated with the constitutionally guaranteed possibility of practical-rational discourse in the public sphere, and their common enemy was a 'conservative militancy' which placed social critique in proximity to terrorism, wrote Detlef Horster in the *Frankfurter Rundschau* (27 September 1979). In the *Frankfurter Allgemeine Zeitung* (3 November 1979), Hermann Rudolph, by contrast, gave short shrift to the publication, looking at it from the perspective of political ideology. The collection, he wrote, discussed almost exclusively the situation of a left that found itself on the defensive and tended to stylize itself as 'this Republic's keeper of the Holy Grail', while at the same time 'demonizing its critics'. Another purely polemical review appeared in the *Frankfurter Allgemeine Zeitung* (12 December 1979), this time by Jürgen Busche: Habermas, it said, had acted as a collector of essays to which he had added an introduction

> in which he explains what they meant to say. According to this introduction, what the essays meant to say was that he and his friends had encountered a lot of adversity recently, and that for quite some time he had been looking for a chopping block in order to reduce anything distasteful to little splinters. . . . The *Stichworte* turned out to be an inventory of fragments from a lost illusion.

A similar tone was adopted by Kurt Sontheimer's review of the anthology for the *Deutsche Zeitung* (21 December 1979). He complained of a maudlin left with a tendency towards 'interpreting democratic debates, of which intellectual confrontation is an essential part, as a kind of paramilitary scene where the citadel of truth was attacked by its enemies.' However, Sontheimer welcomed the fact that, within the left-wing critique of the present, the concept of the lifeworld had taken centre stage, a concept that made it possible to identify the threats emanating from excessive administration and dysfunctional markets. Robert Leicht attributed a great degree of self-reflection to the left-wing intellectual community around Habermas (*Süddeutsche Zeitung*, 10 November); four days later, Dieter Lattmann emphasized that the authors' collected snapshots of their analyses of the present took the wind out of the sails of those right-wing intellectuals who claimed interpretive authority on similar matters. In *Der Spiegel* (8 October 1979), Reinhard Baumgart published a scathing review under the title 'Trübe Beleuchtung' [Dim illumination]: 'The only thing that holds the two volumes together is the covers.'

Resignation

Crisis management. From a distance, the Max Planck Institute in Starnberg, with its thirty-five academics, looked like home to a great deal of productive research. The lengthy reports and impressive publications lists in the Max Planck Society yearbooks bore witness to that. But in 1975 there was trouble, and it came from outside. Habermas had to defend himself against accusations from colleagues, led by the vice-chancellor of the Maximilian University in Munich, Nikolaus Lobkowicz. Following a conference on 'Gefährdete Wissenschaft' [Science under threat], they claimed, with great publicity, that Wolfgang van den Daele's research group on the 'Finalisierung der Wissenschaft' [Finalization of science] at the Starnberg Institute was working on a project that aimed to advocate the external control of research on the basis of ends and goals set by the state. Habermas countered this claim by saying that he felt it was 'a threat to science when scientific criticism was practised for the purpose of political discrimination'.[121] The research group further explained the concept of finalization* and referred to the fact that there were, indeed, no reliable criteria for the control of research, and also that 'finalization' simply tried to capture the way in which research referred to social ends, without therefore violating the principle of objectivity.

But, even within the Max Planck Institute, conflicts between the individual project groups, the two major sections and individuals became more and more frequent. Structures for participation had been developed and were practised in a way akin to those at university institutes. One of the implications was that the members

---

* 'Finalization'/'Finalisierung' is used in a specific sense in this context: 'The perspective of the finalization of science embodies a growing coincidence of theoretical aims and social norms.' Gernot Böhme, Wolfgang van den Daele and Wolfgang Krohn, 'Die Finalisierung der Wissenschaft', *Zeitschrift für Soziologie*, 2(2) (1973), pp. 128–44; here: p. 128; online at www.zfs-online.org/index.php/zfs/article/viewFile/2202/1739. The quotation is taken from the English abstract given at the beginning of the article.

of the institute often decided autonomously about when they would be present. While the interdisciplinary group headed by von Weizsäcker preferred relaxed and more experimental work patterns, Habermas's group very much emphasized that working hours had to be observed and the professionalism of academic discipliness maintained. Both cooperation and communication between the groups would become more and more difficult over time, and they increasingly shut themselves off from one another. This was particularly apparent during the joint meetings attended by researchers of both sections. In this context, the different theoretical languages of natural and social scientists also played an important role.[122]

Von Weizsäcker was due to retire in 1980 because of his age. Towards the end of the 1970s, then, both directors intensified their efforts at persuading the Max Planck Institute to create a third section led by an established economist.[123] Although Habermas had concrete plans for the research at the institute to take on an exclusively social scientific orientation, for a long time he continued to respect the interests of von Weizsäcker and the members of his research division, who wanted to carry on with their own projects. Finally, in the spring of 1980, during consultations between Habermas, the senate of the Max Planck Society, its president, Reimar Lüst, the general secretary, Dietrich Ranft, and the advisory board, a final decision was taken to focus the institute entirely on the social sciences in the future; it was anticipated that the area headed by von Weizsäcker would be dissolved at some point, as there seemed to be no other obvious candidate for the directorship.[124] At the same time, negotiations were underway with Ralf Dahrendorf, director of the London School of Economics. Habermas could well imagine cooperating with Dahrendorf within the framework of a reconfigured Max Planck Institute for Social Sciences, despite some differences between them regarding the status of empirical social research, and despite the fact that Dahrendorf had in mind the model of an Institute for Advanced Studies* in the style of Princeton's; Dahrendorf was interested in leaving behind the model of an institute focused on one individual. The two of them were in agreement that two further directors should be appointed in order to divide the institute into four sections in the future. To this end, initial discussions were had with the psychologist Franz Weinert and the political scientist Klaus von Beyme.

The press, from *Der Spiegel* to the *Bayern Kurier*, happily reported these developments and internal political wrangling, mostly commenting with derision, even *schadenfreude*. The *Bayern Kurier* (11 November 1978) wrote that von Weizsäcker had early on made the

---

* 'Institute for Advanced Studies' in English in the original.

inexcusable mistake of bringing 'the influential neo-Marxist and chief inspiration for the New Left, Jürgen Habermas, to Starnberg. Habermas at once developed his [area] into a stronghold and hotbed of historical materialism whose anti-capitalism also affected the area of his colleague von Weizsäcker.' Dahrendorf's surprise withdrawal in May 1979, in particular, was the source of much sensationalist coverage in the papers. Jost Herbig wrote in *Der Spiegel* (3 May 1980) that the 'surprise appearance and exit' of Dahrendorf was symptomatic of the conceptual deficit in the planning procedures and an embarrassing episode.[125] Despite all this, Habermas continued to organize the restructuring of the institute into four social science sections. As a new name for the cluster on 'Comparative Analysis of Institutionalization and Internalization of Value Systems', he suggested the sociologist Wolfgang Schluchter from Heidelberg, who had gained a reputation as a Max Weber scholar. A number of staff from the economy group (Volker Fröbel, Jürgen Heinrich, Otto Kreye, Utz Peter Reich) exploited the prolonged period during which directorial posts needed to be filled in order to exert pressure once again via the works council with the aim of being taken over into the planned purely social scientific institute.

Again denied an honorary professorship in Munich. In this year of the institute's restructuring, the senate of the Ludwig Maximilian University again rejected an honorary professorship for Habermas – a clear sign of the hardening of the political stand-offs within the academic world and elsewhere. In Frankfurt, he had already held such a professorship for five years. Bavaria's prime minister, Franz Josef Strauß, did not shy away from calling Habermas a 'fighting force of the cultural revolution' [*Sturmvogel der Kulturrevolution*].* Nikolaus Lobkowicz, by then president of Munich University, and the Bavarian minister for culture Hans Maier also openly expressed again their dislike of the left-wing intellectual. At a congress titled 'Enlightenment Today: Conditions of our Freedom', the philosopher of science Gerhard Radnitzky, alluding to Habermas, demanded a 'decontamination of the pollution of our science'.[126] Habermas would soon draw his conclusions from this renewed affront.

Was the senate of the university in Munich influenced by Strauß's bizarre propagandistic formula? Seven years after the philosophy faculty had declined an honorary professorship for Habermas, the social science faculty, on the initiative of Karl Martin Bolte, who represented an empirically grounded approach to the analysis of

---

* The literal translation of 'Sturmvogel' is 'storm bird'. It is the name of a family of birds (petrels), as well as the bomber version of the Second World War jet-powered ME 262 plane. Strauß's expression mixes more than two semantic, as well as historical and political, categories.

social structures, promoted close cooperation with Habermas and
the Max Planck Institute. This was the reason why the faculty, or
rather the Institute for Sociology, quite understandably pursued the
goal of an honorary professorship in theoretical sociology being
awarded to Habermas. Habermas was clearly very interested in
working more closely with the sociologists in Munich, as he was
about to develop new perspectives in the social sciences for the
Max Planck Institute. In addition, there were offers on the table
from Frankfurt and Berkeley. Thus, it was time to make a decision
regarding his professional future.

In the summer of 1980, Habermas received a letter from Nikolaus
Lobkowicz telling him that there would be no majority for an honorary professorship, even if it were formally applied for by the faculty.
Put plainly: the president had brought the matter before the senate
even before the faculty had handed in the application, knowing that
the result of the vote would be a 'no'. There were again rumours
that the Ministry of Culture had exerted some influence. Bolte felt
personally obliged to tell Habermas in a telephone conversation
that the decision by the senate had nothing to do with his academic
qualifications. Rather, three reasons had been decisive: first, the
fear that the students might be politically influenced; second, the
impression that Habermas was generally considered to be a difficult
person; and, third, the generally complicated relationship between
the university and the Max Planck Society. In the end, only twelve
of the professors at the large Munich University were prepared to
express their solidarity with Habermas in a declaration.

The end of a major project. Habermas spent several weeks in Berkeley
giving guest lectures and holidayed in Mexico with his wife. After his
return from America, the humiliation at the hands of the University
of Munich and the time-consuming negotiations and quarrels over
staffing policies moved him to resign as director of the Max Planck
Institute. He explained his motivation for doing so in a letter to von
Weizsäcker and in an article in *Die Zeit*. He told von Weizsäcker
that he was resigning in the face of a mentality which abused the
privileges of academic work for private ends. The letter continues:

> I am myself a member of a union and consider labour law to be
> an historical achievement. However, I cannot comprehend ruthlessly
> instrumental behaviour. ... The protection against redundancy of
> members of the works council does not serve the purpose of circum-
> venting the normal observation of notice periods in the course of the
> closure of a unit and in compliance with the redundancy plan. ...
> Further, I am worried that the behaviour I just described will set a
> negative precedent. I could not continue practising my kind of person-
> nel policies, as opposed to yours, if the behaviour of your staff serves

as an example among the scientists of the new institute. . . . In my present situation I would therefore not wish to take responsibility for scientists I have not selected and of whose professional qualifications and proficiency I am, as you know, not able to assure myself.[127]

In his letter to the president of the Max Planck Society he then complained in even plainer terms about the 'destructive behaviour' of the staff members, who pursued their own interests 'without showing any consideration for the overall conditions a research institute needs for its existence'. This would lead to 'an asymmetry between duties and rights, with which' he, Habermas, '[could not] live in the long run'.[128] It is likely that Habermas's decision to step down as director was motivated not only by the fact that von Weizsäcker's collaborators intended to take legal action in order to retain their posts but also by the intention of the senate and the executive board of the Max Planck Society to go through with the trial before the labour courts, and to have Habermas representing them in court. He was in no doubt about the political implications of all this and the possible effects it might have on public opinion – and he drew appropriate conclusions. These went so far as to announce that he would also withdraw from the Max Planck Society as an academic member, a role that was separate from his function as a director, as soon as he had found a professional alternative.

In his article in *Die Zeit*, Habermas wrote that he had wanted to avoid the legal quarrels over employment instigated by the claimants, but that, leaving this aside, he also had a sceptical attitude in general towards the research focus of the economists who remained after von Weizsäcker's departure. And he was afraid of ossification in the personnel set-up and did not want to be forced into employing scientists whose qualifications did not match his research projects.

> Had the four economists sued their way into my area of work, I fear that this would have set a negative precedent, and I expect that aspects of social security would become ends in themselves. In the long term, research institutes cannot function if they do not make sure there is a certain mobility among the younger scientists and that, in this way, they preserve their capacity for innovation.[129]

The reactions in the press came in short order. Hans Heigert in the *Süddeutsche Zeitung* (14 April 1981) put it concisely: 'The result will now be lunacy. The Max Planck Society will dissolve a whole institute because of four academics it does not want, but also cannot make redundant.' Wolfram Schütte, in the culture section of the *Frankfurter Rundschau*, reached the following conclusion: 'Habermas's understandable capitulation does not conform to the tendencies of the times; the events it brings to an end, however, do.

The end of this major project suits these tendencies in a disastrous way.' Other comments, for instance in the *Rheinischer Merkur* or in *Christ und Welt*, used his resignation in order to settle their accounts with Habermas as a representative of a 'German ideology' and of the Frankfurt School as such. The polemical tone of these reactions is typical of the intellectual climate of the time and of the years to follow. Directly next to Habermas's own article in *Die Zeit* appeared a vicious polemic by the editor of the paper's culture section, Ulrich Greiner, which culminated in his reproaching Habermas for failing as a director and describing him as invoking 'the mechanisms of the market like a mad Rank-Xerox salesman'.

The affair also led to a serious dispute between Reinhard Baumgart and Habermas at the private birthday celebration of the music critic Joachim Kaiser in Munich. The two had been friends for a long time, spending holidays together at Lake Garda, in Aiguebelle on the Riviera, in the Engadin and in Brittany. Now Baumgart accused him in the heat of the moment of defending himself with 'the arrogance of the mounted SS against the plebeian rank and file'.[130] Habermas was outraged and taken aback. 'It was', according to Baumgart,

> the end, not surprisingly. A telephone conversation between our two wives, initiated by mine as an attempt to reconcile the two silly wranglers, only made the catastrophe complete, and it ended in anger and tears. Three years later the two wranglers took to a podium in Regensburg, one after the other, and stood before a microphone in order to introduce themselves as newly elected members of the Darmstadt Academy for Language and Poetry, presenting their careers, their work and their aims, and ending with the usual expression of modesty – that they did not really deserve this honour, etc. The next day, they bumped into each other on the platform, exchanged civilities and then each looked for a separate compartment in the express train to Munich.[131]

Taking stock. One might be tempted to interpret the end of this old friendship as symptomatic of all the farewells and divisions that characterized Habermas's life in the 1970s – that is, in the time between his departure from Frankfurt and his resignation from Starnberg. He was able to further consolidate his academic reputation, especially in the international context, and within the public discourse his voice was as important as ever. His level of academic productivity was undiminished. His *magnum opus*, *The Theory of Communicative Action*, was written during the Starnberg years and appeared in 1981. It is remarkable that, in retrospect, von Weizsäcker spoke fondly of their cooperation. In July 1987, Habermas had wished him a happy seventy-fifth birthday and, in his letter thanking Habermas, von Weizsäcker wrote:

If I was asked to express my own feelings in retrospect, I would say that the weakness of our institute in the 1970s was – apart from many other points one may also make – that we were too far ahead of the general mindset, and that we did not quite possess the intellectual means to express what we wanted to say, in contrast to the existing public consciousness in politics as well as in the sciences. In this context, I must say that in my memory of these years the conversations with you in particular, or even sometimes the written or non-verbal debates, were almost the most fruitful aspect. I think I did know what I did when I tempted you to come to Starnberg. Whether it was a good move for you is another question. Of course, there was also a small tactical aspect involved on my part: I wanted to serve up to the militant leftists I had brought to the institute a well-established left-wing director who would at last impose law and order* on them. And you did that to perfection. But what was really of interest to me was always the intellectual exchange with you, because – if I may put it like this – we were and are so different that again and again I was confronted with thoughts from you that would never have occurred spontaneously to me. And this, after all, is the greatest enrichment one can receive from a conversation.[132]

This generous perspective on the time they worked with each other does not alter the fact that this period ended in disaster. It also changes nothing about the fact that, in contrast to the previous decade, in which it seemed Habermas's star could only ever rise, discord and failure now also entered the picture. In spring 1971, Habermas left the highly regarded, well-financed and well-staffed chair of philosophy and sociology at the Johann-Wolfgang-Goethe University in Frankfurt under circumstances that were unpleasant for all concerned. There were tense conflicts with the students over questions of study reform and the political role of academic disciplines, as well the ongoing disputes with colleagues over the successor to take Adorno's chair. The accusation that he had betrayed Critical Theory and the Marxist left probably also affected him. In addition, there were the defamatory claims from the conservative end of the spectrum that he had slipped from the noose of the higher education reforms in Hesse that he himself had initiated. Despite his strong affiliation with Frankfurt, with the city's urban culture and its German-Jewish intellectual tradition, he went to rural Bavaria, ignoring the opportunities that would have opened up for him through closer integration into the Institute for Social Research.

The high expectations Habermas had for a Max Planck Institute, directed by him and informed by his interests, were in the end

---

* 'Law and order' in English in the original.

disappointed. Today, he freely admits that it was a mistake to take on the co-directorship of an institute of such dimensions. The idea that it would allow him to carry out innovative interdisciplinary research without any disturbances turned out to be an illusion. In addition to this 'inner-institutional' failure, Habermas says, 'there were, of course, the two politically motivated rejections by the University of Munich (to accept me, as is common practice, as an honorary professor).'[133]

When the end of the institute was finalized in spring 1981, Habermas was, of course, not facing ruin. And defeatism, it seems, is in any case something alien to him. But he did need to adapt himself to new circumstances, and he considered upping sticks and leaving the Federal Republic in order to take up an offer from the University of California in Berkeley. Habermas once said that he would 'take the blame for anything that's left-wing on his own head'. After this decade, he was certainly under no illusions about the price he would have to pay for this in Germany. He had a lingering impression that there were far fewer misunderstandings about him in the USA than in Germany, and that he was more accepted there.[134] This view is confirmed by Claus Offe, who points out that Habermas's reputation is stronger in the English-speaking world, and also in Latin American and East Asian countries, than it is in his native country. Although there are some in Germany who might call themselves Habermasians, Offe doubts that one can speak of a 'Habermas School' in the proper sense.[135]

PART III
Science and Commitment

Public commitment is the . . . more important, task of philosophy.[1]

7

Genius Loci:
In Frankfurt for
the Third Time

Frankfurt is not a city whose beauty captivates the *flâneur*. One has to live there. But then it gains the affection of its citizens through the openness, transitoriness and directness of the conflicts that are carried out in it, the connections it establishes and the ideas that collide in it. Frankfurt owes its sharp and instantly recognizable profile . . . to a rough and unvarnished intellectuality which opens itself up to the attractions and the dissonances of a modernity rich in tensions.[1]

Continuing the project of modernity. After the quarrels in Starnberg and the double affront from the University of Munich, it was again Frankfurt, his old 'home', which attracted Habermas. After his resignation from the Max Planck Institute, he had applied to both Bielefeld and Frankfurt. Günther Patzig from the Department of Philosophy at the University of Göttingen enquired as to whether he might want to join them there, and Gerhard Brandt, the director of the Institute for Social Research between 1972 and 1984, wanted to bring him to the department in Frankfurt. Habermas did not pursue these offers further, as it was already clear at that time that he would accept a more suitable appointment to a chair in philosophy at the Johann Wolfgang Goethe University. The city of Frankfurt had already expressed its appreciation for Habermas in September 1980, when a board of trustees established by the magistrate decided to award him the Theodor W. Adorno Prize. (The first recipient of the prize, which came with an award of 50,000 Deutschmarks, had been Norbert Elias, three years earlier.) At the award ceremony in the Paulskirche, the lord mayor of Frankfurt, Walter Wallmann (CDU), honoured him for a philosophical oeuvre that invites controversy. Wallmann explicitly defended the Frankfurt School against the common accusation that it prepared the intellectual ground for the terrorism of the 1970s, and the laureate acknowledged this with visible satisfaction. The philosopher Michael Theunissen, from Berlin, gave a speech paying tribute to Habermas in which he distinguished between Adorno's conception of a negative dialectics and Habermas's normative dialectics. Looking back at Habermas's work, he discerned Adorno's presence in it – both, he said, are 'intellectuals who are open towards everything lively, within science and philosophy as well as outside it' – but Habermas's 'normativism' soon emancipated itself from the 'negativism' of the dialectician and his philosophy of history. 'The different language games the teacher and his former pupil acquired indicate a difference in their styles of thinking, and this, in turn, indicates the difference between the traditions that are central for them.' Theunissen stressed in particular Habermas's important realization 'that the progress of technical-instrumental knowledge does not automatically represent an advance in practical consciousness.'[2] Habermas's acceptance speech, with the programmatic title 'Modernity: An Unfinished Project', contains in embryo the harsh criticisms of 'tendencies highly critical of modernity' – that is, the rise of postmodern thinking – that he would further elaborate in *The Philosophical Discourse of Modernity*. But it is not just the postmoderns – whom he labels 'New Conservatives' – who come off badly in the speech. The pre-modern, old-style conservatism does not fare much better, nor does – perhaps surprisingly from today's perspective – 'young conservatism', with which he associates the Green Party and the growing number of its supporters, and which he considers to be anti-modern.[3] According to his typology, '[l]ike every other typology . . . a simplification', the 'Young Conservatives' cultivate an 'anti-modernism' and 'locate the spontaneous forces of imagination and self-experience, of affective life in general, in what is most distant and archaic . . . In France, this tradition leads from Georges Bataille through Foucault to Derrida. Over all these figures hovers, of course, the spirit of Nietzsche, newly resurrected in the 1970s.'[4] While the 'Old Conservatives' recommend a 'return to positions *prior* to modernity', the 'New Conservatives', like the early Wittgenstein, Carl Schmitt or the later Gottfried Benn, hold that science should not be expected to provide orientation in the lifeworld, that politics 'should be immunized as much as possible from the demands of moral-practical justification', and, finally, that the purpose of art should be limited to that of private edification. 'With the definitive segregation of science, morality and art into autonomous spheres split off from the lifeworld and administered by specialists, all that remains of cultural modernity is what is left after renouncing the project of modernity itself.'[5] Following Adorno, Habermas pleads for a continuation of a modernity that is enlightened about itself. It would only be possible to complete this project through gaining a self-reflective awareness [*Besinnung*] of modernity's 'aporias' and the reasons for its failure.

Habermas also had in mind the political developments in the Federal Republic in the early 1980s when he gave his speech in the Paulskirche. Helmut Schmidt, who had recommended to his fellow party members that they should read not only Marx but also Popper, was confirmed as chancellor of the SPD–FDP coalition after the national elections in October 1980 but managed to stay in office only for another two years. The technocratic turn in politics that his government inaugurated contributed to the fact that alternative left-wing movements began to spring up everywhere and became increasingly important. There were mass demonstrations against the NATO double-track decision, against property speculation in the cities, against nuclear power, and against large infrastructure projects such as the expansion of Frankfurt airport.

Although Habermas sympathized with these political aims, at the end of his speech in the Paulskirche he nevertheless formulated a clear critique of the fixation of the new social movements on self-experience, affectivity and the archaic. This was reason enough for the left-wing alternative *Tageszeitung*, founded in 1978, to conduct an interview with Habermas, the 'manager of the modernity project', in which he again distinguished his left-wing positions from the politics of the Greens. He granted that the alternative movement could 'represent a substantial capacity for resistance if that part of it with the capacity to act practises a clever form of politics and also makes sure that it remains publicly present and visible in the media.'[6] *Die Tageszeitung*, he said, played a major role in achieving this second point. The paper was

> firstly a project on which I look kindly because it is an initiative that grew out of the alternative movement. It can serve the purpose of keeping a particular way of thinking and living present in the general public or establishing it there in the first place. . . . In that sense, I always had sympathies for this project. . . . I also feel a bit cut off from your spheres in a small ivory tower such as this [i.e., the Max Planck Institute, S. M.-D.]. And I cannot just rely on my son and elder daughter to make sure that I do not lose touch altogether. Maybe this interview will help me make an impression on them for once.

One of the questions towards the end of the interview was what a left-wing politics might mean in the present moment. According to Habermas, such a politics had two major aims: (1) to maximize political participation; and (2) to minimize exploitation and disenfranchisement. More for systematic than for political reasons, he rejects socialism as the form society should take: 'Socialism is not a form of life but a particular infrastructure of forms of life, which . . . can only come about as something unpredictable, and even then only in the plural form. I believe that it is a contradiction to speak of *the* socialist society.'[7]

This judgement, however, did not prevent him from honouring a 'genuine socialist', namely Rudi Dutschke, who died in Denmark on 24 December 1979 as the result, ultimately, of the attempt on his life in 1968.* In his obituary in *Die Zeit*, Habermas wrote that Dutschke's life reminded him of biographies of a bygone era, those of professional revolutionaries, of German emigrants in the nineteenth century. Dutschke, he said, combined power of vision with a sense for the concrete. His 'political-tactical sense never tempted him to behave in a purely instrumental fashion, not even in the most difficult political conflicts.' Habermas made out a certain resemblance between Dutschke's work and Hannah Arendt's idea of a 'radically democratic, non-instrumental politics, one that requires communicatively flexible forms of organization.'[8]

Between January and April 1980, Habermas held a three-month visiting professorship at Berkeley. This gave him the opportunity to take part in a symposium in San Diego in mid-March which was held in memory of his friend Herbert Marcuse, who had been close to Rudi Dutschke and who had also died in 1979. In his paper, which opened the event, he emphasized the fact that Marcuse, as 'the first Heideggerian Marxist', had trusted in the 'rebirth of rebellious subjectivity'.[9] Having returned to Berkeley, he presented at a conference on 'Morality and the Social Sciences'. The aim of his paper was to persuade his American audience of the advantages of a hermeneutic sociology as opposed to a sociology that he saw as reducing itself to the empirical dimension. The latter was strongly represented in the USA, for instance among those influenced by the sociologist Robert K. Merton. According to Habermas, if hermeneutic procedures are to satisfy the methodological standards of objective science, the interpreters must make themselves familiar with the (historical, social) context within which symbolic utterances can be established as objects of interpretation, because '[i]nterpreters cannot understand the semantic content of a text if they do not make themselves aware of the reasons the author could have brought forth in his own time and place if required to do so.'[10]

In the early 1980s, once the quarrels over the edition suhrkamp's change of direction had ended and he had returned to Frankfurt, Habermas's relationship with Suhrkamp and Siegfried Unseld improved again. The publisher voluntarily increased his monthly honorarium as an advisor and helped foster the friendly relations between Frisch and Habermas that had existed since the 1960s. Unseld, for instance, invited Habermas to Zurich to join Frisch's seventieth birthday celebrations in mid-May 1980, together with Gershom Scholem, Otto F. Walter, Alice Miller and Peter Bichsel.

---

* See chapter 5, note 68.

A monster of a book. 1981 was an important year in Jürgen Habermas's academic career. He was offered chairs at two famous American universities, Berkeley and Yale, even before he resigned from the Max Planck Institute and took up his attractive new position at Frankfurt University. There was also the publication of his major two-volume work *The Theory of Communicative Action* in November of that year. Habermas, by now fifty-two years old, dedicated the book to his wife, Ute Habermas-Wesselhoeft. The publisher, Siegfried Unseld, decided on a print run of 10,000 copies of the work, which was clearly aimed at a specialist audience, and travelled to Munich to hand over the two volumes, fresh off the press, to the author (while he was on his way from the Bayerischer Hof to the Siegestor, according to his travel diary).

The thousand pages of Habermas's *magnum opus* completed a process of reflection and research that had stretched over a period of ten years. In an interview conducted with younger philosophers and sociologists – among them Eberhard Knödler-Bunte, Axel Honneth and Arno Widmann – just before its publication, Habermas described the highs and lows he experienced while working on the book. He also spoke about the intuition that was central for the conception of the 'monster', a book which, he said, had 'become hopelessly academic':[11] 'This is the intuition that a *telos* of mutual understanding is built into linguistic communication. Along this path one comes to a concept of communicative rationality which . . . is also at the basis of Adorno's few utterances concerning the unspoilt [*nicht-verfehltes*] life.'[12]

In the course of this very open exchange of ideas, Habermas acknowledged that he got to his theory of communicative rationality only after a few dead ends, after he had 'thrown away several first versions' and it had become clear to him in the course of the working process how he had to construct a social theory that developed 'the focusing power of a burning glass, and throw[s] a bright spotlight on the present'.[13] The book, he said, was an attempt to defend the cultural and political achievements of modernity, even if he still retained the impression 'that something is deeply amiss in the rational society in which [he] grew up and in which [he] now live[s].'[14] Towards the end of the interview, he provided a small glimpse into his 'workshop':

> I experience the problems that occupy me at any given moment in an almost physical way, so I am happy when something seems to be working out for me. I am very seldom euphoric . . . I must have paper in front of me, blank paper, written on paper, books around me . . ..
> One needs to invest oneself in the work, and then the problems begin to move with the writing.[15]

The magnum opus

> Rather, the idea of reason . . . is built into the way in which the species
> of talking animals reproduces itself. Insofar as we perform any speech
> acts at all, we are also subject to the peculiar imperatives of that power
> which, under the honourable title of 'reason', I would like to derive
> from the structure of all possible speech. This is the sense in which I
> take it to be meaningful to talk of the social life process as having an
> immanent relationship to truth.[16]

The Theory of Communicative Action is a large-scale synthesis of
various philosophical and social-theoretical research areas that had
occupied Habermas at various points from the mid-1970s onwards.
Obviously, there was a price to pay for embarking on such a project
over a comparatively long period of time, not least with regard to
his social life. In a very personal letter to Hans-Ulrich Wehler, he
hinted that he suffered under the strain of writing, year after year,
and that he had shown a 'narcissistic side of his character' to those
near him.[17]

Habermas understands his theory 'as a framework within which
interdisciplinary research on the selective pattern of capitalist modernization can be taken up once again'.[18] Taken together, his remarks
on the concepts of language and reason, on the concepts of action
and system, as well as that of the dialectic of social rationalization
and its pathologies, provide a conceptual foundation on which a
theory of modernity can be erected: 'In good Hegelian terms, the
formation of basic concepts and the treatment of substantive issues
belong inseparably together.'[19] The cornerstone of his project was
the specific version of linguistic pragmatics that he had developed
during the 1970s. This pragmatics 'helped me to develop a theory
of communicative action and of rationality. It was the foundation
of a critical theory of society and it paved the way for a discursive-
theoretic conception of morality, law, and democracy.'[20]

According to Habermas, in modernity, science, morality and
art have separated into independent spheres, setting individuals
into a reflective relationship towards their traditional convictions
and towards their ways of thinking and acting in general. It is this
essential trait of modernity and its institutions, such as the democratic state under the rule of law, which, Habermas argues, must
be defended against the threat of one-sided developments that may
result from, in particular, the dominance of capitalist as well as
administrative principles of exploitation and organization. The
forces of communication in interaction must be mobilized as the
opposite pole to the power formations within the economy and
state: in relating to each other, human beings communicate about
the ends they want to invoke in justifying their individual and

collective actions. 'Communication' here means 'a process of mutually convincing one another in which the actions of participants are coordinated on the basis of motivation by reasons.'[21]

Habermas's focus on communication as the originary mode of action introduces the central motif of his social theory: a paradigm shift from strategically orientated and instrumental action to communicative action oriented towards reaching understanding. He elevates understanding to the status of the genuine communicative form of reason, which aims at the intersubjective recognition of what he calls 'criticizable validity claims'. He had begun to develop the concept of validity claims during the 1970s.[22] Following on from the speech act theory of John L. Austin and John R. Searle, Habermas introduces a number of conceptual distinctions in his *Theory of Communication Action* in order to modify Austin's and Searle's ideas for his own purposes. He uses this modification to mark out the essence of the formal pragmatics he had laid out at the beginning of 1971 in his Christian Gauss Lectures at Princeton University: 'the three acts that Austin distinguishes can be characterized in the following key phrases: to say *something*, to act *in* saying something, to bring about something *through* acting in saying something.'[23] Regarding the relationship between an actor and the world, Habermas makes use of the formal concept of the 'three worlds', which he had also already sketched in the Gauss lectures. For each of the three worlds – the objective world of states of affairs, the social world of valid norms and the subjective world of intentional experiences – there are corresponding realms of knowledge which follow their own individual logic: the cognitive-instrumental, the moral-practical and the aesthetic-expressive.

The theory of action

Reason in communicative action. The theory of speech acts, the formal concept of the three worlds, and the theory of validity claims are the elements of a model of rationality, and in the eight main chapters of his work Habermas attempts to demonstrate its superiority over, for instance, utilitarian or functionalist models. To this end, he uses 'his' model of rationality for the development of a theory of social action by deriving three types of action from the forms of rationality and their associated validity claims. Habermas's first step is to survey the concepts introduced by traditional sociological theory, in particular that of Max Weber, Talcott Parsons and Erving Goffman, in order to describe in detail instrumental (or strategic) action, normatively regulated action and dramaturgical action. In the course of doing so, he jettisons the dualism between labour and interaction that he had retained up until the 1960s (as late as, for example, an article published in 1967, 'Arbeit und Interaktion' [Labour and interaction]). He now calls instrumental action a behaviour towards material objects which treats these objects as means for the realization of human purposes. If such instrumental action relates to (human) subjects – i.e., if the other actors come into play only as means towards ends under the perspective of maximizing benefits – then this is 'strategic action'. In the case of normatively regulated action, the actors follow socially recognized rules. Dramaturgical action describes a form of self-stylization in which the intentional experiences of subjects (experiences of consciousness, intentions, wishes and suchlike) are expressed. All three (or four)* types of action are ideal types – i.e., in reality they (almost) never occur in their pure form. And they all presuppose an ability to think and speak that is bound up with specific systems of rules.

The three types of action establish relationships with the objective, social and subjective worlds, and they allow for the corresponding validity claims of truth, (normative) rightness and sincerity (truthfulness): only the communicative model of action relates to all three worlds and aspects of validity. It 'presupposes language as a medium of uncurtailed communication whereby speakers and hearers, out of the context of their preinterpreted lifeworld, refer simultaneously to things in the objective, social, and subjective worlds in order to negotiate common definitions of the situation.'[24]

Habermas sees communicative action as reasonable because here the coordination of actions takes place as an intersubjective achievement on the basis of a mutual understanding [*Verständigung*] regarding states of affairs, norms and experiences. The communicative consensus [*Einverständnis*] is fed by the soundness of reasons. The aim of understanding [*Verständigung*] is consensus [*Einverständnis*] in the sense of a rationally motivated recognition of the implicitly offered actions. Such a consensus is achieved on three levels. First, an actor intends to make a true statement so that the interlocutor can share his knowledge. Second, he wants to carry out actions which are correct with regard to a given normative context, so that an interpersonal relationship can be established in which both participants mutually recognize each other. And, finally, an actor strives to express his feelings and wishes truthfully, so that what he says is believed by others.

This focus on understanding and consensus replaces the monological approach of the philosophy of consciousness, centred on the subjective orientation of a rational actor, with an intersubjective concept of action coordination. This aspect of action coordination

---

* There are three or four types, depending on whether instrumental actions that have human beings as their object (strategic actions) are counted separately.

through the obligation-generating force of speech acts is as central to Habermas's interactionist approach as the assumption of a goal-oriented or 'teleological structure is fundamental to *all* concepts of action.'[25]

System and lifeworld

Culture, society, personality. As a complement to the category of communicative action, Habermas introduces the concept of the lifeworld. With this concept, the resources of meaning that communicative actors draw upon (i.e., the 'material' they employ in processes of reaching understanding) is also meant to be removed from the realm of monological subjectivity and intentionality. Habermas develops it by critically distancing himself from the phenomenological reflections of Edmund Husserl and Alfred Schütz, as well as from Thomas Luckmann. He agrees with these three that the 'lifeworld' refers to a horizon within which socialized individuals encounter each other: 'The lifeworld is, so to speak, the transcendental site where speaker and hearer meet.'[26] Habermas describes this horizon as a pool of intuitive knowledge about the objective, social and intersubjective worlds which actors involuntarily employ when they establish their interactions on the basis of shared interpretations of certain situations. Communicative acts always relate to specific situational segments of a lifeworld, which provides the necessary background for the required understanding and the concrete context of action. 'A *situation* is a segment of *lifeworld contexts of relevance* [*Verweisungszusammenhänge*] that is thrown into relief by themes and articulated through goals and plans of action; these contexts of relevance are concentrically ordered and become increasingly anonymous and diffused as the spatiotemporal and social distance grows.'[27] Habermas considers the knowledge stored in the lifeworld as deeply embedded, holistic and unproblematic. The structures of the lifeworld are a kind of background, and they have the character of certainty. They find expression in socially established practices and manifest themselves in reliable solidarity.

Habermas distinguishes between three components in order conceptually to articulate the structures of the lifeworld. First, he defines 'culture' as the traditional knowledge that actors need to have at their disposal in order to reach understanding with others. Second, 'society' refers to a legitimate order which is valid for actors and which they use in order to regulate their membership of certain groups. And, third, 'personality' is taken to be the sum of competencies which the partners in an interaction must possess and which, at the same time, express their identities. In contrast to the phenomenological tradition, these structural components of the lifeworld

– culture, society, personality – are not based on creations of an experiencing subject but, rather, are reproduced intersubjectively in the course of the understanding-oriented actions that take place within the context of the very same lifeworld.

From the perspective of understanding, interactions within the horizon of the lifeworld lead to the renewal of cultural knowledge; from the perspective of action coordination they lead to social integration; and from the perspective of socialization they lead to the formation of personal identity. By making use of the knowledge embedded in the lifeworld, actors at once change and reproduce it. As soon as an element of the lifeworld becomes problematic, it loses its character as a background certainty and becomes an object of discursive examination.

Habermas is convinced that, 'the further the structural components of the lifeworld and the processes that contribute to maintaining them get differentiated, the more interaction contexts come under conditions of rationally motivated mutual understanding.'[28] Through this process of progressive rationalization, the lifeworld loses its quasi-dogmatic character. What endures is whatever earns recognition as a result of the practice of discursive argumentation. Habermas sees the increasingly important role played by science within the lifeworld as an indication of this development. The growing pressure to provide reasoned justifications in the form of arguments, the establishment of democratic forms of opinion and will-formation in politics, and professional standards in the area of education are all evidence for this growing importance of science within the lifeworld.* Political decisions taken by party functionaries or associations, for instance, have to be justified to their members and to the public. In raising children, parents rely less and less on their own experiences and routines when faced with difficulties and, instead, consult the wide array of self-help literature available, or avail themselves of the opinions of recommended experts such that, when it comes time to make a decision, they can act in a way that is backed up by reasons.

The state and the economy Another feature of the process of rationalization which is typical of modernity has to do with the material reproduction of society on the basis of organizational forms of cooperation required by the division of labour. According to Habermas, the progressive division of labour within modern societies can only work in 'action systems that make provision for *institutionalizing organizational power and exchange relations*'.[29] On the one hand,

---

* The reference is unambiguously to 'Verwissenschaftlichung der Lebenswelt'. There is, of course, an interesting tension between this 'positive' process and the colonization of the lifeworld.

the lifeworld is institutionally differentiated into the two spheres of private and public and, on the other, there is increasing systemic complexity, and so the need for social steering grows.

Habermas therefore conceives of social order not only as a communicatively structured lifeworld but also as system. He postulates two corresponding central mechanisms of integration that produce this order: the mechanism of social integration and the mechanism of system integration. While the reproduction of the symbolic structures of the lifeworld requires action with an orientation towards reaching understanding, the material basis of society must be secured by purposive activities. Accordingly, Habermas suggests a definition of societies as '*systematically stabilized* complexes of action and *socially integrated* groups' – that is, he recommends we consider society as 'an entity that, in the course of social evolution, gets differentiated both as system and as a lifeworld'.[30]

The material reproduction of pre-modern societies (tribal societies, class-based societies) is by and large integrated into the symbolic reproduction of the lifeworld. Certain processes of differentiation occur only with modernity and the separation of symbolic and material reproduction: 'system and lifeworld are differentiated in the sense that the complexity of the one and the rationality of the other grow. But it is not only qua system and qua lifeworld that they are differentiated; they get differentiated from one another at the same time.'[31]

The system structures which evolve because of the necessity of material reproduction in increasingly complex societies differentiate, in turn, into the specialized sub-systems of state and economy. Each of these has its own steering medium: power and money. These allow for purely functional coordination. This type of action coordination (through monetary transactions or administrative control) requires relatively little communicative effort, and thus vast numbers of actions can be efficiently coordinated in these ways. Within the rationalized lifeworld various media emerge which take account of the increasing need for reaching understanding. These communicative media, such as expert reputation and the accepted value of moral leadership, produce rationally motivated trust and thus allow for the shortening of processes leading to understanding.

Lifeworld and system become increasingly uncoupled as present societies are steered more and more systemically through the media of power and money. This uncoupling creates the danger that systemic mechanisms of integration, because of their superior efficiency, might win out over social mechanisms of integration, which coordinate action on the basis of understanding. The result is a mediatization of the lifeworld.

Habermas assumes, however, that in principle the steering media influence the lifeworld in a regulated and institutionally safeguarded fashion. This task is fulfilled by the fundamental institution of law. On the one hand, law contains the normative self-understanding of the members of a lifeworld. On the other, as an independent steering medium it regulates the systemic influence that the economy and administration have on the private and the public spheres. But, despite attempts at legal regulation, imbalances within material reproduction can arise. If the crises that result from the autonomous dynamic of the economy and the administration can be avoided only at the cost of disturbing the process of symbolic reproduction, as Habermas assumes, then there is an increasing danger of a 'colonization of the lifeworld'.[32] It is not that this colonization is caused by the rationalization of the lifeworld or increasing systemic complexity as such. Rather, Habermas explains, when expert cultures decouple themselves from the communicative contexts of everyday action, a 'cultural impoverishment of everyday communicative practice' occurs. The reification of everyday communicative practice is not the result of the uncoupling of the money-mediated and power-mediated sub-systems from the lifeworld. Reification arises only once mechanisms of economic and administrative rationality enter into areas of action that resist a transition to the steering media of power and money due to the fact that they are fundamentally reliant on understanding for the purpose of action coordination. In this regard, Habermas speaks of an 'irony of the world-historical process of enlightenment . . .: the rationalization of the lifeworld makes possible a heightening of systemic complexity, which becomes so hypertrophied that it unleashes system imperatives that burst the capacity of the lifeworld they instrumentalize.'[33]

The public response to the *magnum opus* came swiftly, but the first reactions were not exactly euphoric. Some reviewers simply claimed that they did not understand what the book was about. Others complained about what they thought was missing, while still others asked where 'Habermas as a person' could be found in the two volumes. The reviews had titles such as 'Ein Wahn wird wahr' [A mania becomes reality] or 'Nouvelle Cuisine der Theorie' [The nouvelle cuisine of theory]. Jürgen Busche's early review on 27 February 1982 in the *Frankfurter Allgemeine Zeitung* exceeded a whole page and, using original quotations, sketched the theoretical history forming the basis of Habermas's concept of communicative reason. Busche correctly commented on Habermas's political attitude: 'If there was and is such a thing as the experiment of the Federal Republic, then Habermas's thought takes an affirmative stance towards it.' What he blamed the theory of communicative action for was not its 'trust in a will towards consensus formation that will make the strongest argument victorious', but rather that

Habermas ignored the influence 'which death, in all societies, has on the acting and thinking of the individuals. . . . You cannot escape metaphysics by not speaking about it.'

In *Der Spiegel* (22 March 1982), under the title 'Nun sprecht mal schön' [Now go and speak nicely], Karl Markus Michel, once an editor at Suhrkamp, remarked that the author's concept of rationality was not only guilty of 'Eurocentrism' but also degraded 'the reader to the status of an apprentice' and tried to teach him 'how he must communicate in order to be blessed with the higher evolutionary consecrations. Because that is the aim of the master.' And, towards the end of his article, Michel addressed the author directly: 'Dear Jürgen Habermas, was this really necessary? I reproach you not for having written an academic book but, rather, for conceiving of the gateway to the academic world as being as narrow as the eye of a needle. The camel you ride through it comes out the other end as an infinite tapeworm.'*

Hauke Brunkhorst's review in the *Frankfurter Rundschau* (13 March 1982) was generally positive. The sociologist stressed the fact that the author succeeded in providing the foundations for a solid notion of reason through a more precise concept of intersubjectivity within communicative speech. In a letter, Habermas formally thanked Brunkhorst for the essay, 'which is the most instructive reaction to my book I have received so far.'[34] A short while later, the editor of the culture section of the *Süddeutsche Zeitung*, Klaus Podak, commented in the paper's weekend edition on the 'assessments' in the press so far. Under the title 'Verteidigung unverkürzter Vernunft' [A defence of unrestricted reason], he attested to their 'stupidity, infamy, opportunism', and went on to offer his own comments on the new publication:

> Jürgen Habermas's *Theory of Communicative Action* is taking the side of unrestricted reason, a . . . reminder of how vitally necessary it is to reach self-understanding. . . . And when one comes to the realization that without this . . . understanding a society becomes worthless, then communicative action turns out to be the indispensable building block for a society worthy of human beings.

With a few exceptions, Habermas can hardly have been satisfied with the reactions in the media. Strangely, *Die Zeit* of 30 April printed an anonymous letter to the editor whose author called Podak's very positive review in the *Süddeutsche Zeitung* merely

---

* The imagery being played with in this passage is not fully translatable. There is, of course, the biblical 'It is easier for a camel to go through the eye of a needle than for a rich man to enter the kingdom of God', but also the German idiomatic expression for long and convoluted sentences, 'Bandwurmsätze' – literally, 'tapeworm sentences'.

'poetry written by a philosopher'. In a letter to Albrecht Wellmer (3 August 1982), Habermas understandably lamented the fact that the reviews were more about his personality and his political attitude than they were about the book. And he again expressed his misgivings over this fact in a letter to the Berlin sociologist Urs Jaeggi (3 August 1982), who had reviewed the two volumes over half a page in *Die Zeit* (2 April 1982). Jaeggi had criticized Habermas's theory for its academic jargon and distance from reality. 'What use is it to a twenty-year-old student to be confronted with a language and with problems which he does not understand, or at best understands only at an abstract level – and, to make matters worse, which have because of their abstractness lost their edge?' Habermas did not accept Jaeggi's excuse that the editor had substantially truncated his review, and blamed him for allowing himself to be manipulated by Fritz J. Raddatz and Ulrich Greiner, both editors at *Die Zeit*. Habermas concluded: 'in any case, for eighteen months now the *Zeit* features section . . . shows maliciousness in ever new variations.'[35]

Habermas spent the time around the publication of the *Theory of Communicative Action*, before officially taking up his new post in Frankfurt, travelling to give lectures and fulfilling obligations to the publisher. In June 1981, he presented a paper on 'Die Philosophie als Platzhalter und Interpret' [Philosophy as stand-in and interpreter] at the congress of the International Hegel Association in Stuttgart. Among other participants at the congress were Donald Davidson, Hilary Putnam, Willard Van Orman Quine and Richard Rorty. In his lecture, Habermas continued his discussion of the philosophical currents of postmodernism that he had begun in his acceptance speech for the Adorno Prize and put forward the thesis that the figure of the philosopher as master thinker has had its day. At least since science, law, ethics and art have emerged as independent spheres, philosophy has become a scientific discipline among others, and it cooperates with them instead of assigning them their place within the disciplinary canon. Thus, the role of philosophy has to be defined in defensive terms. It is that of a stand-in for comprehensive analyses that make universal claims. The interpretative diagnoses of the times by Sigmund Freud, Émile Durkheim and Max Weber are exemplars of this: 'Each inserted a genuinely philosophical idea like a detonator into a particular context of research.'[36] In addition, philosophy operates as a mediator between the highly specialized knowledge of experts and everyday practices.

In Marburg, Habermas struck up a debate with Wolfgang Abendroth on 'The Antagonistic Society and Democracy'; in Munich, he spoke at the opening of an exhibition about modern and postmodern architecture; in Berlin, he was a speaker at an international conference where he explained the concept of communicative action; and in Hamburg, he gave a lecture on 'Moralität und

Sittlichkeit' [Morality and ethical life]. Further afield, he engaged in public debates with the Greek-French philosopher Cornelius Castoriadis in Yugoslavia and presented lectures upon the invitation of the Goethe Institute in Spain and Italy.

Before his return to Frankfurt, an important part of Habermas's extensive travel itinerary was a five-week visit to Japan in the autumn of 1981. He happily accepted a generous invitation from the Japanese National Science Foundation – his first opportunity to visit a country whose culture would come to make a deep impression on him. A group of Japanese translators had the ambition of making all of Habermas's works – including the 'monster' – available to the Japanese readership as soon as they appeared. On his visit, Habermas got to know and appreciate the social philosopher Kenichi Mishima of Tokyo's Keizai University – 'That man speaks better German than we do . . ., a literarily sophisticated, measured German à la Thomas Mann.'[37] Three decades later – during which time Habermas would repeatedly return to Japan – he would give the speech honouring Mishima on the occasion of his receiving an honorary doctorate from the Free University in Berlin. For him, he said, Mishima had always been a stimulating partner in conversation because his social-theoretical way of thinking is 'sensitive to the cultural plurality within the processes of modernization; at the same time, it is cautious not to exaggerate cultural traditions into closed totalities.'[38]

On 21 February 1982, upon hearing of Gershom Scholem's death, Habermas went to Jerusalem as quickly as possible. Overnight, he drafted a memorial address – in vain, as it turned out. In a funeral service that took place in the presence of Shimon Peres, later to become the eighth president of Israel, the mayor of Jerusalem, Teddy Kollek, and the state president Yitzhak Navon, a speech by a German professor would not have been suitable. 'I stood', Habermas later remembered, 'in front of the cloth-wrapped corpse lying on the stretcher, without a coffin, listened to the speeches in Hebrew, which were incomprehensible to me, followed the funeral procession all the way up to the cemetery, and also put my stone on the freshly dug grave. It was an unsentimental event.'[39] In May of the same year, Habermas was again in Israel upon an invitation from Yehuda Elkana and gave lectures at the universities of Tel Aviv and Jerusalem.

In the summer of 1982, his friend Alexander Mitscherlich died; the two had known each other since Habermas's days in Heidelberg. At the funeral at Frankfurt's main cemetery, Habermas paid tribute to the physician and psychoanalyst. With books such as *Society without the Father* and *The Inability to Mourn* in mind, he stressed the fact that Mitscherlich, 'as an example of a scientific-literary intellectual', had

had 'a decisive influence' on the mentality of the Federal Republic.[40] Among the speakers at the academic commemoration, which took place at the university on 22 October, were Hermann Argelander, Iring Fetscher, Siegfried Unseld, Helmut Thomä and Paul Parin. Habermas spoke about the way in which Mitscherlich had unfolded the 'emancipatory meaning' of Freud's theory through the medium of clinical experience by understanding psychoanalytic therapy 'as an intersubjectively practised form of self-reflection'.[41]

Habermas's first lecture course in Frankfurt in the summer term 1983 and in the winter term 1983–4 was titled 'Theorie der Modernität' [Theory of modernity] and discussed the central problem with which he was preoccupied at the time, namely that of giving an account of the Janus-faced nature of modernity. He presented parts of this work in the famous 'salle 8' at the Collège de France in Paris, where he had been invited by Paul Veyne. On the first evening, he met Michel Foucault for dinner, and throughout the six weeks of Habermas's stay there were many friendly meetings between the two. But in Paris, the centre of postmodernity, Habermas's statements also tended to meet with incomprehension.[42] Nevertheless, he continued his attempts to defend modernity against its detractors within the context of various lectures at American universities, among them Cornell and Boston College.

Frankfurt again In April 1983, Habermas moved out of his office at the Max Planck Institute in Leopoldstraße 24 and, with his new job in Frankfurt starting, moved into his office in the Institute of Philosophy in Dantestraße 4-6, at the border between the Westend and Bockenheim parts of the city and in the immediate vicinity of the Institute for Social Research. In his office, he put up a photograph of Adorno. According to the civil service contract between him and the minister for culture for Hesse, Habermas was 'employed as a salaried professor at the Department of Philosophy for an open-ended period of time. His responsibility is to represent the discipline of philosophy, in particular social philosophy and philosophy of history, in teaching and research.'[43] His income was set at the highest professorial grade, in accordance with the civil service regulations of Hesse and his previous salary at the Max Planck Society, although his contract did not 'establish a right to be taken over into the civil service'.[44] For the winter term 1982–3, Habermas asked to be released from his teaching duties.

Expectations were high at the university, and so the atmosphere was tense when Habermas gave his first lecture in the summer term 1983, in the biggest lecture theatre in the university in front of a conspicuously large audience. His preliminary remarks might have surprised some listeners. First, he announced that he would be organizing an international conference in the autumn in order to mark Adorno's eightieth birthday. Second, he declared that in his interdisciplinary research he had no intention of carrying on the tradition of a particular school. His central focus would be neither ideology critique nor determinate negation but, rather, the question of 'whether modernity must today be considered a finished programme – or rather still an incomplete project'.[45]

Some two years later, the revised lectures from this first term at Frankfurt were published as a book, *The Philosophical Discourse of Modernity*. It was dedicated to his daughter Rebekka, 'who brought neo-structuralism closer to home'. In the form of such diverse theories as those of Jacques Derrida, Michel Foucault, Georges Bataille and Cornelius Castoriadis, this neo-structuralism exercises Habermas in the book, as does the pessimistic attitude towards reason that pervades Adorno and Horkheimer's *Dialectic of Enlightenment*.[46] And Habermas is equally critical in his engagement with Niklas Luhmann's systems theory, which, he says, takes an affirmative stance towards the increasing complexity within functionally differentiated societies.

The Philosophical Discourse of Modernity is primarily a book on philosophy, and in it Habermas really lays his cards on the table. He plays his concept of communicative reason off against certain currents in modern and contemporary philosophy in order to strengthen it against possible objections. The book received considerable international attention, and reactions were more heated than in the case of most of his earlier publications. While the responses in Germany were mixed, critical voices dominated in both France and America.[47] The book was meant to be available quickly in the English-speaking world. Ute Habermas-Wesselhoeft was involved in its translation for an American publisher, and she deserves credit for many linguistic improvements and the sharpening of its content.

Philosophical writing Habermas sees himself as an author who operates at a high level of abstraction and who works in a synthetic fashion when researching and writing. 'As a result', he says,

> my satisfactions lie more in a synthesis of argumentation. Earlier, I used to enjoy fabricating texts. This aspect of the 'pretty tongue', as Grass once said about Adorno, has retreated more and more. More recently, I have put up with rougher discourse in order to develop something even when a text is not the result. Of course, there is still the ambition that there should be a text with introduction, exposition, interpolations, and so on, but the setting up of perspectives on problems is now more important.[48]

The Philosophical Discourse of Modernity contains an 'Excursus on levelling the genre distinction between philosophy and literature', in which Habermas reflects on the role played by the literary in philosophical language, at least where the latter has not become scientistic.[49] Even a philosophy that has become modest and binds itself to the principles of scientific verifiability, he declares, still claims to provide an understanding of the complex totality of the world through the interpretations it offers: to transform its own time into thought through 'universalist problematics and strong theoretical strategies'.[50] The conceptual work of a world-disclosing philosophy 'maintains this relationship to totality with a reflectiveness lacking in the intuitively present background proper to the lifeworld.'[51] The reason why it is permissible for philosophical language (and literary criticism) to draw not only on logical forms of representation but also on the resources of rhetoric has to do with the fundamental character of a philosophical spirit that aims at interpreting the world. Habermas distinguishes sharply between the genre of literature and the genre of philosophy, yet he considers it unproblematic if the prose of the philosopher (like occasionally that of the expert) makes use of the 'illuminating power of metaphorical tropes', not least in order 'to link up indirect communications with the manifest contents of statements'.[52] Habermas reaches the conclusion that the great philosophers have also been literary authors of distinction. We might ask, then, whether this verdict also applies to Habermas himself, who, as previously mentioned, in 1976 was awarded the Sigmund Freud Prize for Scientific Prose by the German Academy for Language and Literature.[53]

Aesthetic elements can also be found, in varying degrees, in Habermas's philosophical and social-theoretical writings, in particular in the form of metaphorical expressions – one of the means of poetic speech.[54] However, the metaphorical elements present in the texts – the 'avenging force' of communicative reason, for instance – are not constitutive of the process of reasoning within the development of the theoretical thought. Habermas uses linguistic imagery to illustrate the decisive points in his abstract argumentations when, for instance, inspired by Hegel's *Phenomenology of Spirit*, he speaks of an 'ossuary' [*Schädelstätte*] to which the historical process is reduced; or when he calls a philosophical thought an 'explosive device' that is built into an interpretation; or when, alluding to Wittgenstein's *Tractatus*, he says of Nietzsche that he uses 'the ladder of historical reason in order to cast it away in the end'.[55] In that sense, as illustrations of abstract points, the metaphors have a primarily cognitive function.[56]

When engaging in philosophical or sociological explication, Habermas limits himself to the method of argumentative proof; here, the aesthetic composition of words is not decisive. Expressive verbal and linguistic constructions, which also occur in his scientific prose, serve the purpose of explanatory argumentation. Where he makes use of rhetorical stylistic elements in his scientific texts, he does so in order to push a thesis to its limits and/or to simplify it into a model.[57]

There can be no doubt that Habermas employs a characteristic linguistic style which, as he himself says, changed over the course of decades of writing. His style draws on both broad erudition and a wide vocabulary, but it does not pursue the artistic manner of Nietzsche, Benjamin or Adorno.[58] When discussing these philosophers (mentioned here as examples) in, for instance, *The Philosophical Discourse of Modernity*, Habermas draws on their linguistic repertoires and traces the grooves of their characteristic styles without, however, simply imitating their idioms.

As a result of their logical exposition, the textual structure of Habermas's scientific books is transparent. And he avoids any esoteric or priestly tone in his linguistic style. Hints at profundity and invocations of ultimate origins [*Beschwörung eines Ursprünglichen*] are alien to him. In his critical 'interventionist' texts in daily and weekly newspapers, in particular, he uses the professional language of the philosopher and social scientist only to a limited extent,[59] while erudite language prevails.[60] In this context, he coins neologisms such as 'executive federalism', 'species ethics' or 'an awareness of what is missing',[61] which capture strikingly the essence of the state of affairs to be depicted. Some of the titles of his books have even entered everyday language – for example, 'structural transformation', 'new obscurity' and 'nachholende Revolution' [a belated revolution].*

Everyday life in Frankfurt

Teaching. Despite Habermas's move to Frankfurt, the family kept the house in Starnberg as their main place of residence. For a transitional period, Habermas lived in the guest apartment of the Unseld family in Klettenbergstraße, but soon he rented a flat in the Westend. He tried to concentrate all his teaching duties into two weekdays. Under the title 'Suhrkamp Lectures',† he agreed with Siegfried Unseld a prestigious series of talks by internationally renowned speakers such as Michel Foucault, John Rawls, Ronald Dworkin, Charles Taylor, Pierre Bourdieu and Alain Touraine. The publisher paid for the speakers' travel expenses and put them up in the guest apartment. This was something of an attempt to re-create the financially comfortable situation Habermas enjoyed during his time at

---

* See Habermas (1990), *Die nachholende Revolution*.
† 'Suhrkamp Lectures' in English in the original.

the Max Planck Institute, when he was able to invite academics from all over the world to Starnberg. In conversation with his publisher, he suggested the idea of collecting the posthumous papers of Walter Benjamin, Theodor W. Adorno and Herbert Marcuse in a central archive and making them available for research. He also suggested a thematic focus on the 'self-understanding of modernity' within the so-called Weißes Programm;* and indeed, in addition to literary titles, the series included Richard Rorty's *Philosophy and the Mirror of Nature*, Barrington Moore's *Injustice*, Benjamin Nelson's *On the Roads to Modernity*, and George Devereux's *Ethnopsychoanalysis*.

During this third period in Frankfurt, Habermas was more engaged in academic teaching than in his previous years there, not to mention the 'teaching-free time' in Starnberg. While his assistant and his academic staff, according to their own testimony, were relatively free to pursue their own interests,[62] Habermas tried to provoke the students' interest in 'his themes'. He taught seminars on 'Neo-structuralism' and on 'Individuality, Subject, Identity' over several terms with Axel Honneth, an academic member of staff who had just passed his doctorate. And he persuaded Karl-Otto Apel, who succeeded him at the Johann Wolfgang Goethe University in 1971, to offer joint courses on 'Problems in the Philosophy of Language' and 'Problems in Discourse Theory'. Together with Charles Taylor and John R. Searle, who were invited as visiting professors, he worked on 'Problems of Speech Act Theory' in the summer terms of 1984 and 1985.

Habermas proved himself to be a challenging teacher and a strict examiner. As the main supervisor of dissertations, he suggested the predicate *summa cum laude* only a few times over his thirty years of teaching: the first time for Albrecht Wellmer in 1966, then for Bernhard Peters and Klaus Günther, and finally for Cristina Lafont, Rainer Forst and Lutz Wingert. Throughout his entire academic career, only two individuals passed their Habilitation with him, namely Albrecht Wellmer and Axel Honneth. After Habermas's retirement, he was involved in the Habilitations of Rainer Forst, Cristina Lafont and Peter Nielsen.[63] Little wonder, then, that something of an elitist atmosphere began to develop around Habermas's professorship.

The Adorno conference, which had been planned for some time, finally took place in September 1983. It attracted a huge number of participants but faced criticism for its schematic division into four separate colloquia on the themes of 'dialectics', 'methodology', 'aesthetics' and 'social theory'. In *Der Pflasterstrand*, a newspaper edited by Daniel Cohn-Bendit and popular in Frankfurt's alternative

---

* 'White programme': the books had all-white covers.

scene, the ethnologist Ulf Matthiesen complained that Habermas was a 'festival director' whose 'controlling hand' was responsible for the fact that the conference had been far too academic and that Adorno's 'explosive force' could not be felt.[64] At a small gathering in the evening in the Feuerbachklause, near the university, Habermas defended himself against the criticisms. During the discussion, he accused Matthiesen, in particular, of having malicious intentions 'that serve only to confirm the opinions of those who in any case already bear malice towards us', as he is quoted in the article in *Der Pflasterstrand*. According to the article, Habermas also pleaded for understanding regarding the decision of the last living representative of Critical Theory, the 83-year-old Leo Löwenthal, not to present his 'Reminiscences of Adorno' publicly at the conference but instead to give it at an exclusive event organized by Suhrkamp. It had been more of an occasion, he said, for the nostalgically minded.

The 'Wende'[*]   In the first constructive vote of no confidence[†] in the German parliament, the leader of the CDU, Helmut Kohl, became chancellor of the Federal Republic on 1 October 1982. In the run-up to his election, the coalition between the Social Democrats and the Liberals had broken down, in part because of the 'Lambsdorff paper', in which the minister of the economy, Otto Graf Lambsdorff, had suggested setting economic policy on a decidedly neo-liberal course. After early national elections in March 1983 confirmed the new coalition between the Christian Democrats and the Liberals, there began the long era of the CDU chancellor Helmut Kohl. Kohl had already been demanding an 'intellectual-moral turn' while he was fighting the 1980 election campaign; now, in setting out his government's policies, he spoke of an 'intellectual-moral challenge' that politics had to face. When interviewed in Starnberg by Hans Ulrich Reck for the *Basler Magazin*, a supplement of the *Basler Zeitung*, Habermas remarked that the 'intellectual-moral renewal' promoted by the CDU was a matter of calling a 'halt to reflection' and propagating 'fixed values'. It meant nothing but a return to pre-modern times, he said, 'which, it is hoped, will miraculously regenerate certainties – a cushion of tradition, that is, which buffers the blows wherever monetary and bureaucratic steering and control fail.'[65] He juxtaposed this attitude with a radical concept of freedom, a freedom which can only be conceived 'as being internally connected with a network of interpersonal relations' – that is, 'as

---

* 'Wende', or 'turn', here refers to the end, with the election of the CDU–Liberal coalition, of a thirteen-year period of dominance for the SPD that had begun with the election of Willy Brandt as chancellor in 1969.

† A constructive vote of no confidence requires that a new candidate is elected at the same time as the old one is dismissed, thus avoiding a power vacuum.

being connected with the communicative structures of a community which guarantees that the freedom of some is not established at the expense of the freedom of others. . . . The individual cannot be free unless all are free, and it is impossible for all to be free unless all are free communally.'[66]

The change in government in Bonn took place within the context of the NATO double-track decision, which was a major issue in German foreign and domestic politics from the early 1980s onwards. In 1981, the hardliner* Ronald Reagan was elected the fortieth president of the United States. After talks with the Soviet Union failed, he pushed for the implementation of the double-track decision, part of which was to involve the stationing of 'Pershing II' middle-range rockets and of twenty-four multiple rocket launchers for ninety-six 'Tomahawk' nuclear cruise missiles in Western Europe, including Germany. Helmut Schmidt, while still chancellor, and the right wing of the SPD were in favour of these plans, which led to a head-on confrontation within the party. This was one of the reasons why the Green Party entered parliament for the first time in 1983. In the autumn of that year, the stationing of the missiles, which was already under way, was signed off by parliament, voted through with the CDU, CSU and FDP as the new parties of government. Meanwhile, a broad-based peace movement had formed outside the political establishment, and the country now saw its biggest demonstrations to date: 120,000 demonstrated on 20 June 1981 at the Congress of the Protestant Church; 300,000 took part in the demonstration for peace in the Hofgarten in Bonn on 10 October 1981, with the number rising to 400,000 exactly a year later in the same place; 200,000 demonstrated on 11 September 1982 at a concert organized by the 'Artists for Peace' initiative, which had been founded by Eva Mattes and others. Finally, on 22 October 1983, a date shortly before the parliamentary vote, a national day of protest was declared: 1.3 million people participated, of whom 200,000 formed a human chain reaching from Stuttgart to Neu-Ulm;† 500,000 met in the Hofgarten in Bonn alone. Numerous well-known politicians, scientists, artists and intellectuals joined the protests. The so-called celebrity blockade at the rocket-launch site in Mutlangen, in which the Literary Nobel Prize laureate Heinrich Böll as well as Walter Jens, Oskar Lafontaine and Petra Kelly took part, attracted worldwide attention.

Habermas sympathized with the increasing resistance to the armament policies. But compared with previous years, when he had taken an active part in demonstrating against, for instance,

---

* 'Hardliner' in English in the original.
† A distance of about 100 kilometres (60 miles).

the 'nuclear policies' of Konrad Adenauer or Franz Josef Strauß, he was clearly more restrained. In September 1983, shortly after the Adorno conference, he was, however, one of the speakers at an event organized by the forum of the SPD, partly in response to the mass demonstrations. It took place in the 'Redoute' of the Prince Elector in Bad Godesberg,* and Habermas spoke alongside Heinrich Böll, the constitutional judge Helmut Simon and Ronald Dworkin. On this occasion, he once again attempted to persuade the Social Democrats that civil disobedience – for instance, the blockade of military installations or human chains – as well as other forms of calculated violations of rules were part of the political culture of a democratic state under the rule of law. Habermas admitted that the breaking of rules implies the morally motivated intentional viola- tion of certain legal norms. But this violation, he argued, was of an exclusively symbolic character and could be seen as a 'test for the maturity of the first democratic republic on German soil'.[67] And he repeated his defence of morally motivated resistance, including the practice of civil disobedience, in an article in *Die Zeit*. Here, as in his presentation at the cultural forum of the SPD, and later at a panel discussion in Frankfurt on 23 November and at a confer- ence at the University of Constance shortly thereafter, he explained that the

> possibility of justified civil disobedience ... [results] from the fact that, even within a democratic state under the rule of law, legal regula- tions can be illegitimate. Of course, they are not illegitimate according to some arbitrary private moral sense, or some special rights, or a privileged access to the truth. The only relevant criteria are moral principles that are understood by all; on these, the modern consti- tutional state bases the expectation that it will be accepted by the citizens of their own free accord.[69]

Foucault At the end of 1983, the prominent French daily newspaper *Le Monde* carried out a survey on the theme 'Reason Today'. In this context, it asked Habermas to provide a statement based on the discussions he had had with his French colleague Michel Foucault. In the course of several private meetings between the two in Paris in March of the same year, the reservations they had towards each other were dispelled. In his reflections on 'Reason Today', which were also published in *Die Zeit*, Habermas emphasized that, despite all the differences there were between philosophical thought in France and Germany, commonalities existed: an interest in the

---

* A part of Bonn where most of the foreign embassies were located while Bonn was still the capital.

dignity of the particular and marginal, the turning away from the philosophy of consciousness, and the critique of the one-dimensional instrumental rationality of subject-centred notions of reason. He once again advocated the force of a reason that encompasses self-reflection, because only such a reason is in a position 'to set in motion again the interplay between the cognitive-instrumental dimension, on the one hand, and the practical-moral and aesthetic-expressive dimension, on the other. Under conditions of alienated everyday practice, this motion has been arrested like a mobile whose parts have become stubbornly interlocked.'[69]

In June 1984, the international press reported the death of Michel Foucault at the early age of fifty-seven. Habermas, in *Die Tageszeitung*, wrote an obituary of the archaeologist of modernity and theoretician of power, whom he had only recently got to know and appreciate. He began with a portrait of a 'vulnerable, personally irritable, morally sensitive' intellectual, and then focused on a theme that would have been the topic of a conference on enlightenment that they had planned together: 'The period of Enlightenment . . . marks the entrance into a modernity that sees itself condemned to draw on itself for its consciousness of self and its norm.'[70] He pointed out that, in one of Foucault's last lectures on enlightenment, he did not interpret the processes of the production of knowledge simply as processes of the production of power. Rather, the will to knowledge is also based on impulses that come from the critique and self-critique of an enlightenment that is enlightened about itself. At the time there were quite a few readers who could not help but think that Habermas was trying to claim Foucault, whose aporias Habermas had repeatedly tried to come to terms with, for his own project.[71]

In November 1984, after he had completed the Messenger Lectures at Cornell University and seminars at Boston College, Habermas gave a speech at the invitation of the president of the Spanish parliament. The international press reported on the speech – 'The Crisis of the Welfare State and the Exhaustion of Utopian Energies' – in detail. In it, Habermas pleaded for a world to come, in which all energies were not exclusively directed at optimizing those parts of society that are organized along lines of purposive rationality through increasing legalization, bureaucratization and monetarization, but which would be able to appreciate and make use of the emancipatory potential of communication free from domination to be found in everyday practice. Because such communication is the source of solidarity within society, 'the utopian emphasis shifts from the concept of labor to that of communication.'[72]

A secret Schmittian? Shortly after Habermas's return from Spain, a major conference, on the theme of 'The Frankfurt School and its Consequences', took place in Ludwigsburg between 10 and 15 December 1984. It was organized by the Humboldt Foundation, and the speakers included Iring Fetscher, Albrecht Wellmer, Gajo Petrović and Thomas McCarthy.[73] Habermas formulated and presented 'Drei Thesen zur Wirkungsgeschichte der Frankfurter Schule' [Three theses on the reception of the Frankfurt School], in which he maintained that there could be no question of a school with a clearly defined identity, despite the manifold impulses which various disciplines had received from the Critical Theory of Horkheimer, Adorno and Marcuse. Not surprisingly, he mentioned his own theory of communicative action as a contemporary version of Critical Theory, albeit one which partly breaks with the tradition.

An American political scientist teaching in England, Ellen Kennedy, ensured that this event would not be just any old academic conference. In her presentation, she traced the effects of Carl Schmitt's thought on Walter Benjamin, Otto Kirchheimer, Franz Neumann, Herbert Marcuse and Jürgen Habermas – i.e., those individuals she considered representative of the Frankfurt School. With regard to Habermas, she claimed that his early critique of certain phenomena of mass democracy and of the loss of power of the parliament and the public sphere, and the corresponding increase in the power of administrations, parties and political associations, exhibited parallels with the views held by the 'crown jurist of the totalitarian state'[74] on the crises of liberalism and the principle of the Rechtsstaat and of representation. Despite all the differences in their political values – which Kennedy explicitly emphasized – Habermas, she said, was 'secretly' influenced by Schmitt's idea of democracy by plebiscite and his contrasting of liberalism and democracy.[75] As evidence, she referred to Habermas's work between 1961 and 1973, as well as to his concept of civil disobedience, which he had presented for the first time in 1983 at the cultural forum of the SPD mentioned above.[76] The way he played off the ideal of a substantial democracy against the existing liberal state, she argued, was a repetition of Schmitt's analysis of popular sovereignty.[77] In conclusion, she proposed that Habermas's critique was associated with 'a rejection of the legitimacy of representational institutions' and of 'the legitimacy of majority rule'.[78]

It is easy to imagine Habermas's response to these interpretations. Of course, at the conference he vehemently defended himself against the accusation that his political theory had borrowed elements from Schmitt's anti-liberalism or his concept of sovereignty. 'There is nothing more absurd for Carl Schmitt', a visibly agitated Habermas said, 'than to insist on the fact that, within a democratic state under the rule of law, political power requires and is capable of acquiring legitimacy – more precisely, legitimacy by way of argument.'[79] However, this and other objections did not deter Kennedy (who at the time was in contact with Wilhelm Hennis in Freiburg, one of Habermas's 'favourite opponents') from publishing her theses in a more developed form two years later in the journal *Geschichte und Gesellschaft* [History and society]. The journal, edited by Hans-Ulrich Wehler, printed a piece in the same volume, along-side Kennedy's, by the political scientist Alfons Söllner, in which he unpicked Kennedy's theses one by one.[80] Soon afterwards, the American historian of science Martin Jay and the state theorist Ulrich K. Preuß also published articles which sought to demonstrate the vast gulf between Schmitt and Habermas.[81]

When Carl Schmitt's 1923 treatise *The Crisis of Parliamentary Democracy* was published in the USA, translated and with an introduction by Kennedy, Habermas seized the opportunity to write a review for the *Times Literary Supplement*. Under the title 'Sovereignty and the "Führerdemokratie"', he offered a critique, in the strongest possible terms, of the polarization of liberalism and democracy in Schmitt's theory. In a subsequent letter to the editor, Kennedy complained that Habermas was trying to prevent an unprejudiced reception of Schmitt's thought within the Anglo-American academic world.[82]

In November 1985, shortly after his return from a lecture tour in Japan, where he met with his publisher Siegfried Unseld in Tokyo, Habermas received two honours at once. The city of Munich awarded him the Geschwister Scholl Prize and, on the Day of the Constitution in Hesse, the minister of the state, Holger Börner, presented him with the Wilhelm Leuschner medal in Biebrich Castle. In the City Hall in Munich, Alexander Kluge gave a speech honouring his friend. In his acceptance speech, Habermas reminded the audience of the morally motivated civil courage of the White Rose and expressed his delight at being honoured for his 'role as a part-time intellectual'.[83] In his acceptance speech for the other prize – the highest honour to be bestowed by the state of Hesse, named in memory of the social democrat and trade unionist Wilhelm Leuschner – the laureate admitted his surprise at receiving a 'medal awarded by the state'. As in Munich, he spoke about the function of the public intellectual: to measure society according to its own norms and criticize violations of those norms. Civil disobedience, he said, was one expression of such criticism.

In a lecture at the Heinrich Heine Institute in Düsseldorf in February, Habermas explained how the social situation of the intellectual in Germany was difficult. The case of Heine, in particular, he said, shows how completely the practice of the 'part-time' intellectual, who raises his voice on political matters but whose 'main professional' activities are not devoted to politics, depends on a responsive public sphere. For many reasons, in Germany such a sphere had constituted itself only belatedly. Thus the man of letters, the educated man, who either shies away from any contact with politics or pushes for a place within the political apparatus, is still held in much higher esteem. What was alarming, however, Habermas added, was the more recent and ever more popular figure of the 'counter-intellectual': someone who considered those intellectuals (who maintained a critical attitude and insisted on reasons) to be a kind of social pathology, and who acted 'using the means of the intellectual in order to show that, actually, intellectuals should not exist.'[84]

In the context of the lasting discussions between left-wing liberals and liberal conservatives during the years of the 'Tendenzwende' [turn in political orientation], with the so-called Historians' Debate marking the climax, Habermas would soon have plenty of occasions to engage with those he considered typical 'counter-intellectuals'.

8

New Projects

Reaping the fruits. Despite the partly negative reaction to its publication, *The Theory of Communicative Action* quickly became
established as an important text and was much discussed in professional circles. Within four years (1985), the book was in its third
edition, a paperback version, revised and with a new preface by the
author, bringing the total number of printed copies up from 20,500 to
24,500. Further editions followed, first in the edition suhrkamp and
finally, in 1995, in the suhrkamp taschenbuch wissenschaft series.[1]
In June 1986, the first conference dedicated exclusively to the work
took place at the Centre for Interdisciplinary Research in Bielefeld.
The organizers were Otfried Höffe and Herbert Schnädelbach. In
a public lecture in the main hall of Bielefeld University, Habermas
addressed the question 'Treffen Hegels Einwände gegen Kant auch
auf die Diskursethik zu?' [Do Hegel's objections to Kant also apply
to discourse ethics?].[2] During the two-day conference, Habermas
discussed with Karl-Otto Apel the latter's favourite topic – 'ultimate
justification' – defended his theory of validity claims against the
charge that it does not distinguish sufficiently between true knowledge and morally correct actions (levelled against the theory by
Martin Seel, among others), and admitted that there were deficiencies in his treatment of the expressive dimension. In discussion with
Hans Joas and Axel Honneth, Habermas insisted on a two-stage
model which connects the theory of action with the theory of the
system in such a way as to make plausible the *a priori* of a lifeworld.[3]

In spring 1987, a conference took place at the Goethe Institute
in Madrid on the theme of 'Philosophy of Action and of
Communication'. Among the participants were Donald Davidson,
Richard Rorty, John R. Searle and Thomas McCarthy and, on the
German side, Karl-Otto Apel, Friedrich Kambartel and Herbert
Schnädelbach. One of the highlights of the event was a debate
between Searle and Habermas.[4] At this summit of philosophers,
despite their differences, both argued against the thesis suggested
by Niklas Luhmann that it is not language, but consciousness itself,

that thinks.[5] At the fourteenth German Philosophy Congress in Gießen, Habermas gave an evening lecture entitled 'The Unity of Reason in the Diversity of its Voices', in which he pleaded for a 'modest' conception of reason which would provide space for manifold individual ways of life in peaceful coexistence. He summed up this form of existence in the concept of an 'intact intersubjectivity', which must be seen as 'a glimmer of symmetrical relations marked by free, reciprocal recognition. . . . Connected with this is the modern meaning of humanism, long expressed in the ideas of a self-conscious life, of authentic self-realization, and of autonomy – a humanism that is not bent on self-assertion.'[6]

In May 1987, Habermas and his wife travelled to Denmark, where he was awarded the Sonning Prize of Copenhagen University. He was the first German citizen to receive the prize, and it was given to him explicitly for his academic work and for his commitment as an intellectual. In his acceptance speech, which was published in the *Frankfurter Rundschau* the next day (15 May), the laureate spoke about the way political identities emerge in democratic societies, and towards the end he suggested that, in democratically constituted societies, such identities do not form through identification with traditional views of a glorified past. Rather, the bonds between individuals and their political community are established via the universalizable norms of justice and solidarity.

A year later, a long interview with Habermas, conducted by the legal scholar Rainer Erd, appeared in the *Frankfurter Rundschau* (11 March 1988). The topic was the political culture twenty years after the student revolution. Interestingly, Habermas comes across in this interview as optimistic, all in all, concerning the contemporary political situation. He said there were progressive tendencies, even a 'fundamental liberalization', which had to be seen as a long-term consequence of the cultural revolution triggered by the student movement, whose effects were evident even at the conservative end of the political spectrum. In addition, after thirteen years, the social–liberal coalition 'behind the screen of institutions and structures has changed more in the weak flesh of motivations and mentalities . . . than in the hard rock of bureaucracy.' For Habermas, the new orientation towards post-material values and the success of the Green Party showed a sensibility among the citizenry for all those achievements that come with a state under the rule of law and with democracy. 'The new perspective is that of a cultural society, in which autonomous public spheres multiply and are able to form subversive counterweights to a highly organized public sphere suffused with power.' However, he added, in Germany it was still common for political opponents to be declared enemies within and for generally left-wing intellectuals to be defamed, especially at times when the country was ruled by conservative forces in government. He mentioned the 'Social Darwinism of the two-thirds society' as a new social and political problem.[7]

Habermas had long since become a 'travelling philosopher' who jetted halfway around the world year after year in order to present lectures and, from time to time, to receive awards and be honoured. A short survey of his itinerary for 1988 illustrates this. In the spring, he became a member of the Academia Europaea in London and a member of the Serbian Academy of Science in Belgrade. In April, he was invited by Harvard University's Center for Human Development to present a lecture on the American moral philosopher and developmental psychologist Lawrence Kohlberg. In August, he spoke about the pragmatist George Herbert Mead at the World Congress of Philosophy in England and, shortly afterwards, about his idea of communicative rationality in Finland. This was followed by a talk on Heidegger and National Socialism in Milan. In September, he packed his bags for a series of lectures in the USA, where he talked about various philosophical and sociological topics in Berkeley, Baltimore and Chicago. Finally, towards the end of the year he presented his recent research on the 'normative concept of the public sphere' at the Forum Philosophie in Bad Homburg.

Add to such intense lecturing activities – which usually took place outside of term time – Habermas's teaching commitments, and it becomes clear that there was hardly time even to consider writing a new monograph. However, over the space of ten years the series of *Kleine Politische Schriften* [Short political writings], containing his lectures, speeches and conversations, grew from five to eight volumes.

Although Habermas maintained Starnberg as his main place of residence, he had by now become a citizen of Frankfurt again – so he began looking for a second home in the Westend part of the city. Initial plans to purchase a flat with some money of his own and a loan were discarded because he found a flat to rent at Myliusstraße 31, within walking distance of the university, which perfectly suited his needs: it was in a comfortable position, in a quiet location, and not far from the university, the train station, and the city's cultural establishments. Ever more frequently, he would spend stretches of more than two days on his own in the city, while his wife lived for the most part in Starnberg until their younger daughter, Judith, completed her Abitur.* The married couple had to put up with this geographical separation until Ute finally moved with kit and caboodle (and the family cat) into the flat in Frankfurt, which she had already furnished. Ute and Jürgen usually passed the months of the summer break in Starnberg, and the whole family continued to spend their winter holidays in Sils Maria, in the Upper Engadin –

---

* The German equivalent to A-levels.

both Ute and Jürgen are keen skiers. In the summer, they travelled more and more often to the South of France, where they rented a holiday home in Joucas, a small place near Apt.

In September 1988, there was an international conference in Baltimore on 'The Contemporary German Mind', organized by Steven Muller, president of Johns Hopkins University and himself of German descent.[8] Habermas spoke about the 'Development of the Social Sciences and Humanities in the Federal Republic'. Muller had set the conference the question: '. . . from Luther to Marx, from Leibniz to Küng, von Goethe to Grass, German ideas had a formative influence on the culture of their time – and today?' Presenting alongside speakers such as Hans Magnus Enzensberger, Wolf Lepenies, Hartmut von Hentig, Peter Sloterdijk and Karl Dietrich Bracher, Habermas defended those critical traditions of thought which had become influential after the return of exiles to the Federal Republic. The elitist self-image of the German mandarins, he said, had been broken. The contemporary threats to reason originate from the neo-conservative hostility to intellectuals and from the various versions of the postmodern critique of rationality. And yet, the lesson had been learned 'that moral universalism is not the opposite of individualism and self-realization, but a precondition for autonomy and solidarity being able to complement each other.'[9]

'Dionysos' During his time in Frankfurt, quite apart from all his teaching and research commitments, Habermas was also involved in a now legendary discussion group. The group met once a month in a back room of the Greek restaurant Dionysos in the Bockenheim district of Frankfurt. This was just before the first SPD–Green coalition in Hesse. The idea for the discussion circle had resulted from a 'lively evening conversation' between Habermas and Joschka Fischer, who would later, in December 1985, be sworn in as Hesse's minister for the environment.[10] It was organized by, among others, Helmut Dubiel, Axel Honneth and Günter Frankenberg. Depending on the theme, the group would invite representatives from the worlds of politics, the media or academia in order to participate in what were often very politically charged discussions.[11] At the first meeting, Habermas presented on 'Der neue Revisionismus in der Geschichtsschreibung des Nationalsozialismus' [The new revisionism in the historiography of National Socialism]. He used the 'Dionysos meetings', which were well attended (with forty to seventy participants), as an opportunity to present his views in the form of long statements. It was not always easy for those chairing to interrupt him mid-flow and to moderate his debates with, say, Joschka Fischer or Daniel Cohn-Bendit, who were both among the regular attendees. In retrospect, Fischer, later foreign minister in the Red–Green government, said that this discussion group had been

'altogether productive' for the Red–Green political constellation.
'The major social topics were discussed – for instance, "The future
of pensions" or "The future of the welfare state". That was during
the pre-globalization era. Sometimes the discussions took place at
an academic level, sometimes at a political one.'[12]

In January 1989, Habermas joined an initiative set up by the candidate for the post of mayor of Frankfurt, Volker Hauff: together
with Helmut Böhme, the president of the Technische Hochschule
Darmstadt, and Kasper König, the director of the 'Städelschule',* he
campaigned for the creation of an Academy of Science in Frankfurt,
the 'hub of European intellectuals', as he called it. However, the project
disintegrated in the course of the election campaign for the position
of mayor.[13] So Habermas invested all the more energy in starting the
series 'Forum Humanwissenschaften' [Forum for the humanities] in
the *Frankfurter Rundschau*, a new special section of the newspaper
that would concentrate on controversial debates about the state of
the humanities and social sciences. It was intended as an alternative
to the 'Geisteswissenschaften' [Humanities] section of the *Frankfurter
Allgemeine Zeitung*, which was edited by Henning Ritter and, according to Habermas, informed by neo-historicism. Habermas described
it as 'a kind of reaction to the advance of social scientific methods
and perspectives in the humanities. This reaction also perceives itself
as a return to the important nineteenth-century traditions of the
humanities in Germany. The central keyword is the rehabilitation
of narration – i.e., the narrative representation of events as opposed
to claims to theoretical explanation.'[14] The correspondence with
Werner Holzer, editor-in-chief of the *Frankfurter Rundschau*, shows
that this new project of the 'Forum Humanwissenschaften' was very
close to Habermas's heart. The background to this was

> a certain irritation regarding the selectivity of the 'FAZ-
> Geisteswissenschaften'; the failure of *Die Zeit* to respond to this; the
> end of the period of resignation on the left, with a new and younger
> generation emerging that was open and politically alert; annoyance
> over the rather too brash behaviour of some right-wing intellectuals
> in the wake of the 'Wenderegierung' after the political turn from left
> to right; etc.[15]

Habermas attached a great deal of importance to daily journalism
because, '[w]ithout the opposition of the left liberals – and occasionally even of the left intelligentsia . . . a sense of *zivilisierter Bürgersinn*
[civil sense of being a citizen], or a civic mentality as such, would
never have been able to develop in the Federal Republic.'[16]

---

* School of Fine Arts of the Städel arts museum in Frankfurt.

In the meantime, Suhrkamp had acquired the rights for *The Structural Transformation of the Public Sphere* and *Theory and Practice* from Luchterhand, as Unseld wanted to reissue them in revised editions. And Habermas was also keen that his books would be adequately visible in the various Suhrkamp series. Three years later, he would sign a 'general contract' with Siegfried Unseld which gave the publisher full rights for the works already published and preferential rights on all future works of the author. At the same time, Unseld offered Habermas fixed payment terms which came into force in 1991.

In spring 1989, the Department of Philosophy organized a major conference marking the 100th anniversary of Ludwig Wittgenstein's birth. The event was supported by Suhrkamp and organized by Habermas. In his opening address, on 'Wittgenstein as a contemporary',[17] Habermas emphasized a parallel between Wittgenstein, Heidegger and Adorno: all three, in accordance with their *'esoteric self-understanding'*, were philosophically radical thinkers but, at the same time, turned their backs on 'institutionalized science and the political public'. In conclusion, he pointed out that Wittgenstein would have 'rejected any solemnity in a birthday celebration'.[18] Was this a not so subtle hint, perhaps, in light of his own forthcoming sixtieth birthday?

Sixtieth birthday Siegfried Unseld suggested to his author that he might want to mark the date 18 June 1989 with festivities to be held in the guesthouse of the Goethe University, but Habermas decided on a more private affair with his family and some friends in Starnberg. The birthday party met a day earlier in the Forsthaus Ilkahöhe, an inn near Tutzing with a splendid view over Lake Starnberg and the Bavarian Alpine peaks. The next day, the family home in Ringstraße was bursting at the seams when the guests arrived late in the evening to present the sexagenarian with a Festschrift, hot off the press: *Zwischenbetrachtungen: Im Prozeß der Aufklärung* [Intermediary reflections: within the process of enlightenment]. The volume was dedicated to 'the philosopher, sociologist and theoretician of modernity, but also to the intellectual who publicly defended enlightened positions, continually and relentlessly, in a country which is still again and again threatened by surges of counter-enlightenment.'[19] The collection of texts – more than thirty authors discussing Habermas's work – opens with a personal letter from Leo Löwenthal which says: 'As the last person from the group that stood at the beginning of Critical Theory,* it fills me with pride

---

* Löwenthal uses the term 'Gründergruppe'. However, 'founding group', or 'group which founded', seems to suggest too much of a consolidated, intentional and momentary act, given the actual history of Critical Theory à la Frankfurt.

and satisfaction to see that the towering figure of the second generation is not an epigone, as is so often the case with the successors to
philosophical and other scientific schools.' After midnight, following the presentation of the Festschrift (and with Habermas already
complaining about how expensive the book was), Unseld did not
want to miss the opportunity of making a speech. He spoke about
his first encounter with Habermas on the occasion of Adorno's sixtieth birthday celebrations in Frankfurt. Unseld also touched upon
the international reception of Habermas's works, which had by then
been translated into many languages, and acknowledged his influence on the publication policies of Suhrkamp.

> And in this context, a word about Habermas the author. The pecu-
> liar 'uncoerced force of persuasion' that Habermas has identified in
> communicative action comes through in his own books and lectures
> by dint of his literary ability. He is capable of writing prose in a way
> which presents conclusions and theses in a linguistic form that makes
> following the reflective paths of this intellectual continent at times a
> pleasure, without avoiding objective-thematic subtlety. I would like to
> take the liberty of repeating what, back then, I said about Adorno's
> use of language. Each sentence of Adorno's – and likewise each sen-
> tence of Habermas – follows the contours of the state of affairs it
> expresses, but at the same time points beyond it.[20]

The press also took notice of this special birthday. In the
Frankfurter Hefte, the SPD politician Peter Glotz congratulated
Habermas, paying tribute to him as a 'crucial figure of the second
German Republic'.[21] On 16 June, *Die Zeit* printed an article by
Gunter Hofmann which delved into Habermas's biography and
emphasized the fact that, during the German autumn of 1977, he had
successfully defended himself against the neo-conservative slander
about critical theorists being the spiritual fathers of terrorism. In
the *Frankfurter Allgemeine Zeitung* of the same day, Gustav Seibt
stressed the point that Habermas had reconstructed Critical Theory,
turning it from a theory of despair into a 'radical theory of democracy'. Oskar Negt, by then professor of sociology in Hannover,
apologized in the features section of the *Frankfurter Rundschau* for
having edited, many years ago, the book *Die Linke antwortet Jürgen
Habermas* [The left responds to Jürgen Habermas]. And, in *Merkur*,
Ralf Dahrendorf wrote: 'He is most of all a warm-hearted, caring
and compassionate friend whose irony never gets the better of his
cordiality. ... It is simply a pleasure to talk with and be in the
company of Jürgen Habermas.'[22] In response, Habermas thanked
Dahrendorf in a handwritten letter for his 'friendly bond, which has
held out over long distances and which has naturally formed over
the course of decades.' He was proud, he wrote, of Dahrendorf's rec-

ognition, because 'nothing is more complicated and more unlikely than recognition among peers,* who move through life independently of each other and exert their efforts on the same themes but in very idiosyncratic ways.'[23] The minister of the Saarland, Oskar Lafontaine, congratulated Habermas in a personal letter, which honoured him as a pioneer in the battle for a better and more democratic society and as someone who had warned 'against the excesses of a leftist rigorism'.[24]

In the months before and after his sixtieth birthday, Habermas was positively showered with public expressions of recognition. The New School for Social Research had already awarded him an honorary doctorate in 1980. Now, the Hebrew University of Jerusalem, in June 1989, and the University of Buenos Aires, in September of the same year, did the same. The award certificate presented to Habermas in Jerusalem, in the presence of the Israeli Foreign Minister Moshe Arens and the former president of Israel, Yitzhak Navon, thanked Habermas for 'his friendship towards Israel and the Jewish people'. Habermas expressed the particular importance that the award held for him in a letter to the sociologist Erik Cohen, who spoke at the award ceremony, writing that, throughout their extended stay, he and Ute had learned more about the 'painfully beautiful present' of Jerusalem but also about the conflicts. 'A suggestive memory', he says,

> is the afternoon in the arena: the desert at the rear, the not altogether young students and an attentive audience in front; next to me, colleagues who, despite the informal character of the event, could not altogether ignore the seriousness of the occasion. In the mood of this almost Brechtian friendliness, I felt the award certificate's ceremonial sentence ('in token of his friendship for Israel and the Jewish people')† was an exact expression of my sentiment.[25]

Finally, on 14 December, the University of Hamburg honoured Habermas by awarding him the title *Doctor rerum politicarum honoris causa* – the first time an honorary doctorate of that kind had been awarded in Germany. In the overflowing main lecture hall, the speech honouring Habermas was given by the political scientist Udo Bermbach. In his acceptance speech, titled 'Wie soll der Adressat bei einer solchen Rede nicht erröten?' [How can an addressee not blush in the face of such a speech?], Habermas explained that honour is a category which 'has lost its place in life'. At the end, he pointed out that the university was honouring someone whose scientific

---

* 'Peers' in English in the original.
† Quotation in brackets in English in the original.

position [*wissenschaftliche Position*] was anything but uncontroversial.[26] Further 'honours', both at home and abroad, would follow in the years to come: awarded by Utrecht University, Northwestern University at Evanston, the universities of Athens, Tel Aviv, Bologna, Paris, Cambridge, etc.

In 1992, the tenth anniversary of Gershom Scholem's death, Suhrkamp produced the first publication in German of his biography of Sabbatai Zevi, the 'mystic Messiah' of Smyrna.[27] In February 1993, Habermas and György Konrád discussed the history of the heretical kabbalist's work at an event organized by the Jüdischer Verlag, which had been brought back to life by Siegfried Unseld under the umbrella of Suhrkamp. In his presentation, Habermas traced the analogy between Sabbatai's heresy and Scholem's negative theology, which, he holds, deals with the dawning of the Messianic age. Habermas expressed his conviction that Scholem 'believed in the gift of mystic illumination. Admittedly, as he once told me, he had encountered such a capacity for inspiration only once in his life – in the person of his friend Walter Benjamin.'[28]

Under the spell of the philosophy of law

When the German Research Foundation awarded the Gottfried Wilhelm Leibniz Prize for the first time in 1986, Jürgen Habermas was one of the recipients, as was, incidentally, the later Nobel Prize winner Christiane Nüsslein-Volhard.[*] Habermas used the generous prize money of 2 million Deutschmarks, which recipients are allowed to spend on a project entirely of their choosing, to create a research group on the philosophy of law. Among its members were Rainer Forst, Günter Frankenberg, Klaus Günther, Ingeborg Maus, Bernhard Peters and Lutz Wingert. Helmut Dubiel and Axel Honneth also frequently participated in the research colloquia. At the centre of the broadly conceived research agenda were questions regarding morality, law and democracy. More than two decades later, Klaus Günther expressed the sense of unique opportunity which the members of this research association felt they had been granted:

> We met in Jürgen Habermas's Frankfurt flat in Myliusstraße in order to talk about a research programme. While he was making coffee, I read a letter congratulating him on the award of the Leibniz Prize of the German Research Foundation. I was amazed at the unusually

---

[*] A German biologist, born in 1942, who, together with Eric Wieschaus and Edward B. Lewis, was awarded a Nobel Prize in 1995 for work on genetic control in the development of *Drosophila melanogaster*.

generous prize money, running into the millions . . . Habermas imag-
ined the foundation of a small group of younger female and male
researchers who would be working on questions in the theory of law
and democracy. It was the birth of the 'AG Rechtstheorie'.[29]

Habermas himself would later remark that he experienced this work
environment as 'unusually stimulating and instructive'.[30] His final
report, written for the German Research Foundation in May 1991,
bears witness to this. It highlights four problem areas that were clarified over the course of project: first, the relationship between law
and morality, where it was established 'that the principles of morality and of law are co-original with and rest on a discourse principle
which expresses the conditions for a post-conventional justification
of practical questions'. Second, the group succeeded in developing in
broad outline 'a de-substantialized concept of popular sovereignty',
according to which this sovereignty finds its expression in a procedure that satisfies democratic principles. And, third and fourth,
they established the status of law as a mechanism for integration
in complex societies and the connection between legal guarantees
for communicative freedom and the 'pragmatic conditions for an
intersubjective practice of reaching understanding'.[31]

Morality and law

Between Facts and Norms. The five years of research conducted in
this association produced a whole series of important publications.
Habermas himself published his *Erläuterungen zur Diskursethik* in
1991,* and the autumn of 1992 saw the publication of his study in
the philosophy of law, *Faktizität und Geltung.*† Before that, he travelled to the USA and presented the results of his research, first at an
international symposium in New York at the Benjamin N. Cardozo
School of Law (Yeshiva University), on 'Habermas on Law and
Democracy: Critical Exchanges', and then in Chicago and Evanston
at Northwestern University.

In *Between Facts and Norms*, Habermas extends the range of
application of his discourse ethics by trying to solve the problem of
how discursive conflict resolution may be successfully institutionalized in modern societies. The central focus is the question of how the
intertwining of democracy and the Rechtsstaat through the system
of rights may be conceived in such a way that the Rechtsstaat cannot
be played off against democracy, or vice versa. To his publisher,

---

* English edition: *Justification and Application: Remarks on Discourse Ethics*, Cambridge,
1993.
† English edition: *Between Facts and Norms*, Cambridge, 1996.

Habermas wrote: 'I think I have brought something off one more time.'[32]

Habermas is guided by the conviction that law and morality remain connected, despite having separated into independent spheres in the course of modernity and the process of secularization. According to Habermas, legal norms require moral legitimation in order to be valid as norms, and they acquire this legitimation by being presentable as the result of a consensus formed by way of argumentation. In other words, legal norms are legitimized by the approval of the communicative community, which, in turn, is guided by moral considerations. The norms agreed to are those that are convincing on account of their justification by way of argument in practical discourses.

A system of rights that is legitimized in this fashion guarantees not only private autonomy but also public autonomy – i.e., equal opportunity for all to participate in the processes of political opinion and will-formation. The thesis that private and public autonomy are co-original puts the emphasis on citizens' self-legislation. According to Habermas, the concrete realization of self-legislation takes place within the practices of discursive will-formation. Within the space of politics, the principle of discourse ethics, which stipulates that '[o]nly those norms can claim to be valid that meet (or could meet) with the approval of all affected in their capacity as participants in a practical discourse',[33] becomes a principle of democracy: 'The discourse principle is intended to assume the shape of a principle of democracy ... by way of legal institutionalization. The principle of democracy is what then confers legitimating force on the legislative process.'[34] This means that, in a democracy, the practice of legislating and of legal findings must be modelled on argumentative justification. Only this understanding of the law is in line with the principle of neutrality which informs the democratic state under the rule of law and which prohibits the implementation of any specific ethical preferences regarding what constitutes the good life. Nevertheless, an 'ethical impregnation of the Rechtsstaat' cannot be avoided because the rights which are agreed by a legal community against the background of its specific lifeworld are never free of specific ethical ideas. However, these value preferences cannot take on the status of generally accepted legal norms, as the latter are formed on the basis of rules that are generally binding.

The distinction between law and morality, as Habermas first presents it in *Between Facts and Norms*, rests essentially on three points. Firstly, he clarifies that legal norms, as opposed to moral norms – in the sense of categorically binding propositions ('oughts') – contain an element of coercion. This is connected to the fact that the law, apart from securing subjective freedom, is also an organizational means of domination. Whoever violates laws must reckon with the coercive sanctions that come into effect independently of any awareness of injustice on their part. As soon as moral norms become the content of positive legal norms, we must assume that violations are punished.

Secondly, it is characteristic of law that it leaves open the question of the attitude [*Gesinnung*] with which individuals, as bearers of subjective rights, follow it. Subjective rights used by private legal subjects, such as the freedom of contract, entitle their bearers to engage in strategic behaviour. Moral motivations may, but need not, play a role. Habermas speaks of legal norms as allowing for the motivational neutrality of obedience to the law. 'Whereas morality appeals to insight and a good will, law restricts itself to requiring action in conformity with the law. This uncoupling of behaviour in conformity with law from the motive of "respect for the law" also explains why legal norms can apply essentially only to "external behaviour".'[35]

Thirdly, moral and legal norms differ in that laws, which taken together constitute the system of positive law, have been created in a rule-governed process. They 'stem from the decisions of a historical legislature; they refer to a geographically delimited legal territory . . .'.[36] In contrast to a moral community, a legal community is a delimited collective with rules for defining citizenship – i.e., for distinguishing clearly between citizens and non-citizens. The members of a legal community are, on the one hand, bearers of subjective rights which grant them individual autonomy: 'Private autonomy extends as far as the legal subject does *not* have to give others an account or give publicly acceptable reasons for her action plans. Legally granted liberties [*subjektive Handlungsfreiheiten*] entitle one to *drop out of* communicative action . . .; they ground a privacy freed from the burden of reciprocally acknowledged and mutually expected communicative freedoms.'[37] On the other hand, the members of a legal community can appeal to general human rights which they possess independently of their status as members. Among these human rights that have been positively formulated as basic rights are 'four absolutely justified categories of civil rights'. These are, first, 'the *right to the greatest possible measure of equal individual liberties*'; second, rights regarding 'the *status of a member* in a voluntary association of consociates under law'; third, rights regarding 'individual *legal protection*'; and, fourth, rights 'to equal opportunities to participate in processes of opinion- and will-formation in which citizens exercise their *political autonomy* and through which they generate legitimate law.'[38] For Habermas, what is distinctive about general human rights, whose content is moral and so universal, consists in the fact that, as moral principles, they are the result of social learning processes. Human rights – for instance, the right to life and to freedom of opinion and expression – accord with

the generalizable interests of all and express a level of moral consciousness that has stripped itself of its allegiance to conventions.

In order to be legal, laws must be constructed in accordance with
legal norms. By contrast, there is no analogous constructive procedure for the creation of moral norms, although moral-practical
discourses that are egalitarian and free of repression make it possible in principle to reach an understanding about the prescriptive
validity [*Sollgeltung*] of moral norms. This is the case, at least, where
there is a need for establishing understanding. Moral consciousness depends on a specific, historically accumulated socio-cultural
self-understanding of individuals who feel themselves to be part of
a moral community. For Habermas, the moral sentiments of such
individuals are always internally bound up with good reasons, a fact
that explains the immediate social efficacy of moral judgements as
well as their cognitive character. By contrast, legal norms are the
expression of a rationally motivated agreement. However, despite
all their formal differences, there is only one possible procedure
for the justification of morality and the creation of law, and that is
discourse: 'Just those action norms are valid to which all possibly
affected persons could agree as participants in rational discourses.'[39]
Both moral and legal norms carry a 'time and knowledge index'
[*Zeit- und Wissensindex*],* even after their claim to validity 'has
passed the universalization test'.[40] If, in the light of new experiences
or new knowledge, counter-arguments arise, a norm that has been
established as correct, in the sense of being rationally acceptable,
can – indeed, *must* – be considered problematic again.

In the age of modernity, an ever more complex system of law
increasingly has the task of compensating for the cognitive, motivational and organizational weaknesses of morality. Thus, the law
contributes to social integration at the level of legal consociates as
bearers of abstract freedoms. The law, in a manner of speaking,
compensates functionally for the loss of a universalist morality and
stabilizes social expectations regarding behaviour through its coercive character. As it has come about through a discursive procedure,
and thus is legitimate law, it also mediates the opposition between
private and public autonomy. Private autonomy is juxtaposed to
the public autonomy of the citizen. Thanks to the latter, the citizen
is also legislator of, and not merely subject to, the law. The expectation is that the citizen, in this role, will also act for the common
good, although this cannot be legally enforced. The law thus generated through discursive processes is an expression of the principle
of democracy, which 'derives from the interpenetration of the discourse principle and the legal form'.[41]

---

* 'Remarks on Discourse Ethics', in *Justification and Application*, pp. 19–112, here: p. 37.

Habermas also reconstructs the normative substance of democracy on the basis of discourse theory: it derives from the fact, he says, that all political decisions are tied to basic democratic processes of justification which function according to the demanding model of practical discourses.[42] These discourses take place in a civil society that is placed between the spheres of the economy and the state, and whose members make social grievances public. For this reason, the citizens' public autonomy as community members must coexist with their private autonomy if their authority is to be effective. According to Habermas, this co-originality constitutes the normative self-understanding of the democratic Rechtsstaat. He is therefore critical of the tendencies towards the concentration of power that he observes in the public sphere and its media, within the political parties and the parliaments, as well as in the administrative apparatuses. There is only one remedy for such uncontrolled proliferation of power: lived democracy.

With cameras rolling   In early spring 1995, Habermas met with Ronald Dworkin for a two-day seminar with colleagues and invited journalists at the Centre for Interdisciplinary Research at Bielefeld in order to discuss his fully developed legal theory. Given that Habermas is not exactly a friend of the 'semantically degenerate public sphere which is preoccupied with images and visual realities', and that he usually remains faithful to his maxim that he 'write[s] for the public but [does] not appear in public',[43] it was remarkable that this debate took place with cameras rolling and was later turned by Ulrich Boehm, an editor at the Westdeutscher Rundfunk, into a forty-five minute programme – 'Regiert das Recht die Politik? Habermas meets Dworkin'.[44] That Habermas was more relaxed in his attitude towards television, or, to be more precise, towards appearing on television, probably resulted from the positive experiences he had had with Boehm earlier that year. In February 1995, he had permitted Boehm to accompany him during a lecture series at Stanford University in Palo Alto, south of San Francisco. The resulting film – with the title 'Einladung zum Diskurs' [Invitation for discourse] – was first shown on television by the Westdeutscher Rundfunk on 10 December 1995 and repeated several times by other stations. It shows Habermas on campus in discussion with American students, at lectures and in debate at seminars, and visiting the university bookshop, where, upon being shown a selection of his books, he remarked: 'These are the small gratifications in a life where all one gets is criticism.' At the end of the film, we see Habermas wandering through the Museum of Modern Art in San Francisco and as a guest in the apartment of Carl Djerassi, the 'inventor' of the contraceptive pill and a colleague at Stanford University, who shows him his remarkable collection of paintings by Paul Klee.

The documentation of the debate between Habermas and Dworkin, conducted in English, is less colourful in comparison. It was broadcast by the Westdeutscher Rundfunk on 25 June 1995. The topics were the relationship between law and morality, the compatibility of freedom and equality, and democracy and the Rechststaat. Their agreements and differences soon became apparent, even though they simply spoke past each other at times. The legal scholar Erhard Denninger summed it up in the *Frankfurter Rundschau* (17 October 1995):

> Although both authors, Habermas as well as Dworkin, agree on the fundamental idea that the Rechtsstaat and democracy (the constitutional state and majority rule) require and complement each other, there are nevertheless obvious differences between their conceptions of democracy. Dworkin assumes the community of a people 'into which' the individual is 'born'; and this membership makes the demand for obedience to the law legitimate, albeit with some further qualifications. . . . For Habermas, the given, 'natural' community is of secondary importance for the concept of democracy. What is crucial is that a group of people decides to solve their social problems through the medium of law. Therefore, everything depends on the quality of the procedures: only if the democratic discourse which generates the law can be successfully organized in such a way that the results form 'exclusively under the uncoerced force of the better argument' can discourse justify the assumption that these results are reasonable and thus the law legitimate.

Jan Roß's commentary in the *Frankfurter Allgemeine Zeitung* (27 June 1995) differed somewhat:

> Dworkin needs objectivity in order to be able to establish the guarantee of freedoms and social rights independently of the majority principle. Habermas, by contrast, who still wants to risk more democracy, is afraid of objectivity as a kind of intellectual authority [*geistiger Obrigkeit*]. It appears Wilhelminian to him. Where he sees the threat of authoritarian postulates, Dworkin recognizes the chance of legally enforceable claims.

9

Battles over the Politics of Ideas[*]

> The intellectual should have the ability to get worked up – and yet
> should have sufficient political judgement not to overreact.[1]

The communicative power of intellectuals. Karl Mannheim characterizes the figure of the socially free-floating intellectual – someone
who neither comes from nor can be assigned to a specific group – as
a person falling between two stools, structurally without a fixed
place, transcendentally homeless.[2] You are destined to become an
intellectual neither by birth nor heritage, nor can the intermittent,
unpredictable practice of the intellectual be professionalized. It is a
rather rare phenomenon altogether and thus culturally conspicuous.
Whereas Mannheim sees intellectuals as characterized structurally
by being positioned at a social distance, M. Rainer Lepsius refers
to a specific linguistic practice and form of writing – namely, what
he calls 'incompetent but legitimate criticism' – as the most striking
feature of this social type. Ralf Dahrendorf and Michael Walzer also
stress the characteristic behaviour of the intellectual: his resistance
to extreme ideologies and his moral incorruptibility; his particular
capacity for compassion and his sense of proportion.[3]

Since the Dreyfus affair shook the Third French Republic around
1900, individuals have been called 'intellectuals' when they have
taken the risk of publicly voicing their opposition to something.[4]
Publicly expressed criticism is what turns a potential intellectual
into an actual intellectual. This is not 'critique' in the sense in which
Kant, for instance, speaks of a 'critique of pure reason' – i.e., a
method of analysing and measuring limits; it is, rather, a name
for repeated interventions in topical, practical-political problems,
interventions that are mostly born out of moments of crisis and
are temporally limited. Intellectuals typically possess a deep-seated

---

[*] The terms 'Ideenpolitik' and 'ideenpolitisch' refer to an approach that focuses on the
overlapping of political theory and the history of political ideas.

tendency to vacillate between distance and commitment, and they are said to be able to recognize and evaluate global social processes and historical crises. Intellectuals make use of their capacities by – visibly and audibly – detecting and putting their finger on the raw wounds of society.

Intellectuals must keep their distance by insisting on, and convincingly demonstrating, their relative independence as scientists, writers or artists, so as to be recognized as independent authorities amid the clamour of voices. Commitment is needed in order to leave the 'protected sphere' of science and be heard. To be effective in social and political debate, an intellectual's statements must be clear and to the point. And above all, despite their momentary and interventionist character, they must have a normative 'line' so that the intellectual can position herself within the field of contradictory political interests. This orientation towards values of justice and self-determination, towards the communicative ideal of discursive conflict resolution (and so the possibility of identifying instances in which this ideal is not being followed), is Habermas's actual motivation for taking on the role of the intellectual.

In his 1986 lecture on Heinrich Heine, previously mentioned, Habermas reflects on the social figure of the intellectual. It is the task of the intellectual to 'stand up for violated rights and repressed truths, for overdue developments and delayed progress, with rhetorically pointed arguments'.[5] For this he is dependent on a functioning public sphere, where public sphere means a 'medium and amplifier of democratic will-formation. It is here that the intellectual finds his place.'[6] Later, in conversation with Angela Brauer, he distinguishes between two opposing types of intellectuals. In Germany, 'the mandarin with his great gestures ... enjoys an uncritically granted advance of trust.' Scientists, by comparison, are met with scepticism and 'in their role of intellectuals attract the suspicion that their political commitment is incompatible with the hard-headed search for truth.' On the one hand, the public do not need authorities who display the 'posturing of the great thinker. On the other hand ... the guild of academics should be able to live with the political commitment of its members without showing resentment.'[7] When an intellectual publicly voices his opinions outside of his own field of expertise, Habermas says, he leaves his professional role. And yet, there must be affinities between his political evaluations and his fundamental theoretical beliefs. In other words, and with Habermas's own theory of communication and discourse in mind, the intention behind his interventions is also to prove the productive force of communication in a practical context – i.e., to demonstrate that 'communicative power' is able to determine the political culture. This is completely compatible with his understanding of himself as one active citizen among many, who engages in political matters part-time, unsolicited and without a political mandate – a self-understanding Habermas has expressed in various places. His commitment, he says, rests on a 'responsibility for the whole', not on an ambition to gain personal political power.[8]

According to Habermas's ideal, intellectuals do not strive to exert strategic influence on the political struggle for power but, instead, want to help create an autonomous and pluralist public sphere through communication. A citizen gains the status of an intellectual not by being an expert authority or a professional know-it-all but by being a participant in discourses and by trying to do what others could also do: that is, provide convincing arguments for or against something. The recognition of an intellectual as *public intellectual,** therefore, is a consequence of the quality of his or her arguments, which must win through and prove themselves in the back and forth of public debate. Intellectuals, for Habermas, do not impose a certain interpretation of events. Rather, 'those addressed' should always 'have the clear option of accepting or rejecting the interpretations being offered under appropriate circumstances – i.e., without being coerced. Enlightenment which does not terminate in insight [*Einsicht*] – i.e., in interpretations which are accepted without coercion – is no enlightenment.'[9] But does Habermas's own practice as an intellectual meet these standards? Which overall picture would emerge from a recapitulation of the most important stages of his 'career as a public intellectual'?

Habermas's birth as an intellectual has already been described above. As early as 1953, he invoked the 'role of public critique as guardian' when he expressed his indignation over Heidegger's silence after the war. In the following years, he not only participated in various academic disputes, such as the positivist dispute, the debates over systems theory and the philosophy of postmodernism, etc., from the early 1960s he also fought at the front line of the battle for a democratization of the universities and the implementation of equal opportunities within the educational system overall. His commitment to being both a part and a critic of the '68 movement gained him enemies in almost all political factions. In this context, he did not handle his opponents with kid gloves – nor they him. He openly says that he is 'a polemical talent'; and he made thorough use of this talent, especially at times when, as he says in retrospect, the interpretive battles over the democratic self-understanding of his country 'took place under less than peaceful conditions'.[10] His coinage of the term 'left-wing fascism' certainly marked a pivotal point in his engagement with radical positions on the left between 1967 and

---

* 'Public intellectual' in English in the original.

1969. His battles over intellectual authority in political discussions, in which he engaged with various representatives from groups of a liberal and liberal-conservative persuasion, spanned almost two decades, beginning with the time when the gap between 'risking more democracy' and the 'decree against radicals' began to widen.

The economic and oil crisis of 1973–4, the financial crisis of the state and the accompanying reduction in the welfare state, as well as the emerging awareness that there are limits to economic growth (Club of Rome), put an end to the euphoria over modernization in Germany. In West Germany, the era of Brandt came to an end, and his politics of transformation were replaced by the crisis management of Helmut Schmidt's chancellorship, which saw the nightmarish events of the German autumn, discussed in detail above. These events set the tone for the intellectual debates of the time. Habermas feared that the autumn of 1977 might prove to be a turning point. In a letter to the historian Ulrich Herbert, he wrote in retrospect: 'In my experience, at no other point did we have such a pogrom-like atmosphere. The well-known old resentments and stereotypes surfaced again.'[11]

Opinion leader* of the New Left?

Polemics On 18 November 1970, an article appeared in the *Frankfurter Allgemeine Zeitung* that led to a cascade of reactions, some of which were quite vehement. The author of the article was the Austrian philosopher Ernst Topitsch, who had taught at Heidelberg between 1962 and 1969 before moving to Graz, and who not only was a staunch critic of Marxism but also approached any kind of ideology with an extreme scepticism. The fact that he had already taken a stance in the positivist dispute, namely against Adorno and Habermas and with Popper and Albert, may have some bearing on what took place between him and Habermas at the end of 1970. In any case, in his article Topitsch asked whether the concept of 'humanity' might not have lost its innocence, as historically it had not proved resistant to ideological abuse: 'Power, battle, and violence' were justified as humanistic by left-wing forces 'insofar as they lead to the [ultimate] removal of power, battle, and violence.'[12] Topitsch summarized his experiences teaching in Heidelberg during the 'hot phase' of student protest by saying that this 'militant ideology of humanism' was currently put into practice by the self-appointed avant-garde of the student revolt, which was at the same time on the way towards conquering the educational

---

* 'Opinion leader' in English in the original.

institutions in order to 'expand them into bases from which to attack the constitutional order'.

Scarcely two weeks later, Habermas published a forceful reply in the same newspaper.[13] He begins by setting out the names of those who – he suspects – form the conservative community of like-minded individuals [*konservative Gesinnungsgemeinschaft*] behind Topitsch: Armin Mohler, Rüdiger Altmann, Hanno Kesting, Reinhart Koselleck, Hermann Lübbe and Roman Schnur. 'The question . . . that exercises me, dear Mr Topitsch, is what may have moved an intrepid liberal thinker like yourself to throw in his lot with the argumentative contexts currently being built up consider-ably in our counter-enlightenment traditions.'[14] In response to the moralizing radicalism of the left, he wrote, there is now a flourish-ing of 'the resentment of the lapsed liberals who take refuge in militancy and conspiracy theories'. He described this latter group as the 'renegades of the middle ground'[15] and accused them of avoid-ing a serious engagement with the reasons for the student protests. As a consequence, they tended 'to evaluate situations in terms far removed from reality', especially as regards the new conditions at the reformed universities. The reduction in status of the old Ordinarien* within the context of mass universities produces resent-ment in them, which they now direct at those who hold dear the idea of democratizing educational institutions. What really infuriates Habermas is Topitsch's claim that there was a lack of national pride [*Nationalbewusstsein*] and that this had to do with the German guilt complex. Habermas makes it clear that he would certainly not desist in his efforts in helping 'establish an official opinion which protects us from the worst kind of Teutonic ethnocentrism . . . by relentlessly referring to the most recent past'.[16]

In August 1972, Robert Spaemann published an essay on 'Die Utopie der Herrschaftsfreiheit' [The utopia of freedom from domi-nation] in *Merkur*. Through Gadamer, Habermas was personally acquainted with Spaemann, a philosopher of religion teaching in Munich, and he held him in high regard. In his essay, Spaemann compared Habermas's position both with Ralf Dahrendorf's theory of democracy as based on conflict and with Niklas Luhmann's social systems theory. He criticized the idea of domination-free under-standing on the grounds that its inventor could apparently not make up his mind as to whether it was meant to be a transcendental idea or the anticipation of a form of life to come. He also raised the objection that uncoerced discourses can be operative only in the spe-cially protected space of science, not in that of politics, where there

* An 'Ordinarius' was a full professor before the reform of the universities, a position invested with far-reaching authority.

are time pressures and the need to make decisions. Spaemann finally comes to the quite provocative conclusion that the 'aim of replacing domination with domination-free consent'* becomes 'a theory legitimizing unlimited and uncontrolled domination'.[17]

Habermas's reply appeared in the form of an open letter in the same journal four months later. The format is rather unusual in the context of scientific debates: it is an explicit invitation to enter into a dialogue but also contains an element of compulsion. Habermas countered Spaemann's arguments directly with a vivid description of colonial domination, which he took from Frantz Fanon's famous manifesto of the anti-colonial revolution *Les Damnés de la terre* [The wretched of the earth]. The example of colonialism, he said, showed that legitimate domination could be a façade concealing outrageous injustice. 'The phenomenon to be explained is thus how an illusory justification can in effect be established which guarantees the non-violent acceptance of the factually existing institutions. What I try to do is explain this structural violence as a systematic limitation of discourses of will-formation.'[18] A colonial system of domination can never reckon with the uncoerced consensus of all affected persons. This fact will show up once discourses become a social reality – i.e., once everyone has the same right to participate in the political processes through which decisions are reached.

The rules of democracy, Habermas argued, are in force to the extent that such participation is realized, and to that extent nothing prevents discursive will-formation from taking the place of domination. And yet, not all is discourse; rather, 'discourses . . . are always islands in the sea of practice.'[19]

In his essay, Spaemann had also objected that, under conditions of the practical everyday necessity of making decisions, discourses are too demanding, and that not everyone is capable of entering into them at all times in the sense Habermas envisages. It is therefore unavoidable that decisions are taken on the basis of legitimate domination that is distributed across various authorities. Habermas responded:

What allows you to assume that the holders of positions of domination – who, as a rule, are privileged not only through the position of power – are less likely to pursue particularistic interests than the masses of the population who are not privileged or who are underprivileged? This is not a matter of anthropological pessimism or optimism. I think that it is altogether impossible to give an anthropological answer to the question of how far discursive will-formation can be established as

---

* The German term, here and in the following paragraph, is 'Herrschaft', which can mean both 'rule' and 'domination'. While the translation is 'domination' throughout, it may be useful to keep this ambiguity in mind.

an organizational principle of society before the capacity of personality structures to engage in this are exhausted.[20]

Spaemann did not publicly respond to the open letter, but he
did dedicate a whole section of his book *Zur Kritik der politischen
Utopie* [Towards a critique of political utopia] to discourse theory.[21]
He accuses it of committing the fundamental mistake of assuming
that all individuals who, for various reasons, are not in a position
to participate in discourses, or who do not find an advocate for
their interests, therefore remain without a voice or influence, and
he reaches the conclusion that the idea of discursively produced
freedom from domination is 'only a specific form of domination'.[22]

In 1974, Spaemann made a public appearance at a congress at the
Bavarian Academy of the Fine Arts in Munich, which was organized
by the minister for culture of Baden-Württemberg, Wilhelm Hahn
(CDU). Other participants at this congress on the 'Tendenzwende'
[ideological turn] included Hermann Lübbe and Golo Mann.
Spaemann joined his fellow campaigners from the Bund Freiheit der
Wissenschaft [Association for the Freedom of Science] in claiming
that the 'discourse of the left, felt to be hegemonic', was responsible
for the 'disintegrating consensus' and for the 'dwindling of commitment'.[23] He also used the occasion to mount a renewed attack on
the emancipatory teachings of the left. At this point, his tone was
comparatively mild. But that would soon change.

Sontheimer In October 1977, Jürgen Habermas wrote another open
letter, this time to Kurt Sontheimer, who had claimed that there was
a causal link between left-wing terrorism and Critical Theory. The
substance of this controversy has already been discussed,[24] but it is
instructive to look at it further in terms of the way the opponents
within the battle over political ideas acted towards one another at
the time. These were, it should be noted, battles within the liberal
camp, namely between left-liberals and liberal-conservatives. One of
their striking features is that they were highly personalized disputes
in which combative polemics and arguments entered into a peculiar
admixture. They would end up leaving a lot of blood on the carpet.

In his open letter to Sontheimer, Habermas did not shy away
from slurs. He belittled Sontheimer's recently published *Das Elend
unserer Intellektuellen* [The misery of our intellectuals] as 'tenden-
tious literature' because the author uses weapons from the arsenal
of the counter-enlightenment. Sontheimer, he said, made himself
a lackey for reactionary forces by presenting a simplified picture
of left-wing theory and constructing a direct link from this theory
to terrorism, implicit in his demand for an exertion of ideological
control [*Gesinnungskontrolle*] through penal law and for the limitation of the basic rights of radical opponents to the system. And yet,

everyone knew 'that there was no bridge leading from the political theories of the New Left to the political psychology of the RAF.'[25] In striking contrast to his own polemical tone, Habermas advocated 'the values of fraternal conduct', and – in an attempt at objectivity, so to speak – he went on to ask the question of the historically specific experiences which feed into terrorists' psychological motivation.[26]

Habermas explicitly positioned himself as the mouthpiece of the non-dogmatic left, and it was precisely this point which Sontheimer picked up on in his reply to the letter. He asks Habermas, with some irony, whether he believed he had 'an intellectual command over the whole of the New Left, comparable to the pope'.[27] At the same time, he affirmatively quoted Habermas's 'idiots on the left' formula, using it to question the scientific quality of 'left-wing publications' as well as left-wing professors who contributed to 'the excessive defamation of our democracy'.[28] Sontheimer demanded of Habermas, but also of the left as a whole – those idiots of which there were far too many – that they unequivocally distance themselves from terrorism. He saw such a distancing as a matter of the defence of the republic, a task for which he was prepared to join hands with Habermas. In his reply, again in the form of an open letter printed in the *Süddeutsche Zeitung* (26–7 November 1977), Habermas expressed his fear that the left might be demoralized by ideological control [*Gesinnungskontrolle*] and intimidation. In vivid colours, he painted a picture of how intellectuals close to the Social Democrats were at risk of being deformed under 'the massive pressure from the New Right' – clearly an attempt at convincing Sontheimer, himself a social democrat.[29]

A further escalation followed after a forum on the 'Courage to Educate', which took place in January 1978 at the newly founded Centre of Science in the Bad Godesberg area of Bonn under the aegis of the Federal Republic's president, Walter Scheel, and in the presence of the president of the national parliament, Karl Carstens, and about three hundred invited guests. The event was the prelude to the ideological turn [*Tendenzwende*] in education. It was based on a programmatic text in the form of nine theses on pedagogy at schools and on political education, which clearly bore the stamp of Hermann Lübbe, a renowned representative of the school of right Hegelians headed by Joachim Ritter.[30] Among those who commented, Friedrich H. Tenbruck, Nikolaus Lobkowicz, Golo Mann, Christa Meves, Hans Maier, Thomas Nipperdey, Alexander Schwan and Robert Spaemann, most were members of the Association for Freedom in the Sciences. The first three theses downplayed the importance of maturity [*Mündigkeit*], emancipation and individual fulfilment as goals of education, in order for the following theses, four to six, to insist on the educational necessity of teaching virtues

such as diligence, discipline, order and the willingness to make sac-
rifices. The remaining theses formulate demands which essentially
aim to retain the school as a place that protects traditional values.
Habermas was not mentioned by name, but it was obvious that
the text intended to turn the page on an idea of educational reform
connected with him. The theses were signed by Hermann Lübbe,
Wilhelm Hahn, Nikolaus Lobkowicz, Hans Bausch, Golo Mann
and Robert Spaemann.

The first reaction came not from Habermas himself but from the
philosopher Ernst Tugendhat, who at the time was a member of
Habermas's group at the Max Planck Institute in Starnberg, and
who also taught ethics on the side at a Bavarian secondary school.
Six months after the publication of the nine theses in *Die Zeit*, he
presented a strongly worded criticism of them in which he spoke
of a relapse into the times before Kant's notion of maturity, of a
complete forfeit of the capacity for critique, and of a 'totalitarian
tendency'. It almost seemed, he wrote, as if the authors of the theses
took 'the type of Adolf Eichmann' as the norm to be achieved by
education.[31]

Tugendhat's criticism was met with a vigorous response in the
form of six letters to the editor published in the weekly's edition
of 23 June 1978. The letters were supported by two articles from
Golo Mann and Robert Spaemann, which had also originally been
written as letters to the editor. Golo Mann, in his piece, referred
to the Rahmenrichtlinien [framework directives] of Hesse, which
Habermas had co-authored, as amounting, in essence, to nothing
but the teaching of 'thousands and thousands of teachers'. The
'advocates of continual emancipation in theory' have to accept that
they no longer hold the monopoly on opinions. Spaemann, in his
piece titled 'Ein Pamphlet' [A pamphlet], claimed that Tugendhat
lacked competence and that, in contrast to Habermas, he was 'not
even interested in anything like having a rational discourse'. His
insinuation that the authors had taken Eichmann 'as the norm to be
achieved in our educational system', he said, was malicious. Four
weeks later, Habermas joined the debate with aplomb. He affirmed
the 'astute' critique of the educational counter-enlightenment given
by his 'friend Tugendhat',[32] saying this counter-enlightenment
threatened 'to return pedagogy to the times before moral thinking guided by principles'. Habermas put the theses of 'this cartel
of right-wing professors' into the context of a political rather than
a scientific agenda and attacked Spaemann directly: 'It seems
that Spaemann does not realize what he is doing when he signs
himself up to an ideological community [*Gesinnungsgemeinschaft*].'
'No argument can be had', he said, over the claim that those who
'educate children to practise critique' are 'ideological know-it-alls
and seducers', 'because here the ground of a common logos on

which a dialogue can take place has already been vacated.' He continued: 'In no other Western country, as Tugendhat rightly mentions, would theses like these, which mock any tradition of reason, even receive any attention. In our country, they are elevated to the status of an administrative creed by loyal ministers of culture [*gesinnungsfreundliche Kultusminister*].' Finally, Habermas appears to meet Spaemann halfway by saying that Tugendhat should 'not have referred to Eichmann. This name stands for a dimension of horror which can only suffocate any argument.' Instead, Habermas suggested a more fitting comparison, that with the type of Filbinger:*

> An education teaching a conventional morality has to put up with the fact that individuals who follow 'what is given' will obey any existing order, even if it turns into inhumanity, especially as such a turn may not be conspicuous on the face of that order's normality. It can only be hoped that – thanks to the 'white-wash certificates'† recently issued for him by Spaemann's colleagues – we shall be able to enjoy Filbinger remaining in his post for a long time to come, as a shining example.

The media fanned the flames of this controversy, but it was also carried out in private correspondence, where neither Habermas nor Spaemann refrained from invective in dealing with each other. Behind a polite and respectful tone, they accused each other of having influenced the editorial office of the weekly newspaper via friends, and thus of having orchestrated the publication of letters to the editor and other statements. The controversy threatened to turn into a personal feud. In a letter to Spaemann of 12 September 1978, Habermas made some concluding comments on the dispute which make clear whom he saw as the main actor and adversary:

> I must, however, ask you please to be clear that it was Mr Lübbe who overstepped the mark of what I had until then considered to be academic decency with the organization of the congress in Munich (and its declared intention) as well as with . . . the thesis of a transcendental terrorism, which has been repeated frequently since then. Apparently, Lübbe wants to wage civil war within the academic world.[33]

In his open letter to Sontheimer, and elsewhere, Habermas referred to 'the repressed tradition of the Enlightenment from

---

* Hans Karl Filbinger was a CDU politician and minister of Baden-Würtemberg who resigned from his political posts in 1978 after protracted controversies over his involvement with Nazi Germany. He had been a judge in the German navy, and opinion about his behaviour in this role, and his attitude to National Socialism in general, is still divided. Filbinger died in 2007.

† 'Persilscheine' – a colloquial expression in post-war Germany for 'de-Nazification certificates'.

Lessing to Heine and Marx, in all its breadth'. Maybe this was one of the reasons why, in 1980, a group of individuals around the philosophers Lübbe and Spaemann participated in a conference on 'Aufklärung heute' [Enlightenment today] organized by the Hanns Martin Schleyer Foundation.[34] The proceedings were published shortly after the event.[35] It may also have been an attempt to offer a counterweight to the two volumes of *Stichworte zur 'Geistigen Situation der Zeit'* [Notes on the intellectual situation of the time] that Habermas had just published to significant, if mostly negative, reaction in the media. In any case, the main thread running through the conference as well as the proceedings was the intention to show that, within the politics of ideas, the Enlightenment was a tradition that the left certainly had no right to claim exclusively for itself – a point which, of course, further deepened the divide between the two rival ideological groups [*Gesinnungsgemeinschaften*]. Habermas was perfectly clear about the fact that the intellectual field was one of rivalries, and, indeed, the idea that such rivalries and provocations not only annoyed but also positively stimulated him is probably not altogether implausible. As in so many instances in the past, and some still to come, he did not try to avoid this dispute but reacted quickly and actively to it in the form of his acceptance speech for the Adorno Prize at the Paulskirche in Frankfurt. The speech was dedicated to the idea of modernity as an 'incomplete project', and towards its end he spoke about the various types of conservative thought: apart from the conservative thought of an older generation – here, he named Gottfried Benn and Ernst Jünger – there existed, in his mind, a young conservatism in Germany, especially in circles close to alternative cultures. Further, the group of new conservatives on both sides of the Atlantic consisted of defected liberals and American intellectuals such as Daniel Bell and Irving Horowitz. They blamed the negative consequences of capitalist modernization on a cultural modernity whose principle of self-realization, they claimed, released hedonistic motivations.[36]

In a lecture given in October 1982 at a forum of the Friedrich Ebert Foundation, which is close to the SPD, Habermas pursued this theme in more detail, speaking about 'Die Kulturkritik der Neokonservativen in den USA und in der Bundesrepublik' *See 'Neoconservative Cultural Criticism in the United States and West Germany', in *The New Conservatism*, pp. 22–47. And at a conference on 'Die Zukunft der Aufklärung' [The future of Enlightenment], organized by Peter Glotz in December 1987 at the Jewish Community Centre in Frankfurt, he was one of the presenters, together with the historians Dan Diner and Jürgen Kocka, the theologian Jürgen Moltmann, and the sociologist M. Rainer Lepsius. Here, Habermas again defended the critical tradition of an Enlightenment which continuously renews itself against attempts by the young or new conservatives to question its universalism or to discredit it as the expression of a logocentric reason that makes itself absolute.[37]

In hindsight it is clear that, in substance, the long dispute with the liberal conservatives was about the concept, the interpretation and the role of the Enlightenment within modernity. Both the political climate and the long pre-history – which actually went right back to the positivist dispute, during which certain enduring battle lines were drawn – meant that it was more than just an academic quarrel. The fact that the dispute was carried out mostly in public, and thus quickly acquired a dynamic that resembled a classic cultural struggle, was also a contributing factor. The debate moved quickly into the maelstrom of fundamental moral questions. The threshold for irritability plunged rapidly on both sides, allies were gathered, and personal invective flew. In the heat of such battles, which can easily escalate from factual disputes into quarrels between opponents and fights between irreconcilable enemies, it is rare for someone to end up affirming his opponent's perspective. Perhaps this is simply asking too much, given how much is at stake from the points of view of the different sides. In any case, there is a great danger of falling short of the ideal of discourse ethics,[38] and, of course, the person who had put that ideal at the centre of his theory was far from immune to that danger. On the contrary, in the role of the public intellectual, Habermas frequently and consciously made use of the arsenal of weapons used in ideological warfare. He worked with dramatization, generalization and other rhetorical means of intensification, knowing full well that the politics of ideas he thus practised would have a polarizing effect, would simplify the arguments, and would thus contradict his ideal of enlightenment. Here, it seems, the end did justify the means. And to a certain extent it does, for ideological controversies are not primarily about the formation of convictions; those directly involved have long since established their convictions. Rather, they are about gaining an audience for one's convictions and winning public opinion over to one's side. 'The statements of political contemporaries about topical issues', Habermas writes in the preface to *The New Obscurity*, 'follow rules which are less restrictive than those of academic business.'[39] Thus, it lies partly in the nature of things – i.e., the practice of intellectual debates as such, or rather their intrinsic dynamic – that on both sides the 'orientation towards understanding' recedes into the background, and, all the more so, the more ferociously the two competing factions fight with and against each other.[40]

Instead of talking to each other, they intentionally use the media in order to talk about each other. Although matter-of-fact discussions and the politics of ideas are not necessarily mutually exclusive, the more thoroughly contributions to a debate are laden with political ideas, the more battle lines harden and disagreement becomes almost a forgone conclusion. While truthfulness is implicitly assumed by both parties in the context of matter-of-fact discussions, in the context of ideological quarrels it becomes an explicit topic: it is stressed in one's own case, and it is denied to the opponent.[41] 'There is a relatively simply touchstone', Habermas wrote in a letter to Ulrich Herbert in 1999, 'for the polarization within my generation (which does not coincide with an "a priori division into political factions"): the feeling of wanting either to make a clean break with "German" continuities or to "save" the ruined reputation of the (intellectual) fathers and grandfathers.'[42]

The historians' debate

> The historians' debate has set landmarks in the field of memory politics which . . . Germany's political elites no longer try to dislodge.[43]

The politics of the past. In May 1985, the American president, Ronald Reagan, a conservative Republican, visited Europe and, for the second time, Germany. The reason for Reagan's trip was the fortieth anniversary of the Allied victory in the Second World War. Following a visit to the memorial site of the former concentration camp at Bergen-Belsen on 5 May, Chancellor Helmut Kohl had organized for an official ceremony to be held at the Kolmeshöhe military cemetery, near the city of Bitburg in the Eifel Mountains. The commemoration of those fallen in the Second World War was to take place in front of the Wehrmacht soldiers' graves, among them many members of the Waffen SS. This arrangement had caught the attention of the media on both sides of the Atlantic even before it took place and had led to protests by some Jewish organizations in the USA. It was all part of the new politics of history of the trained historian Kohl, as was his 'holding of hands' at Verdun (with the French president, François Mitterrand), the plans for the 'Haus der Geschichte' [House of history] in Bonn, and the 'Mahnmal für die Opfer der Kriege und der Gewaltherrschaft' [Memorial for the victims of the wars and of violent rule] to be erected in Berlin. By contrast, the much noticed speech of the president of the Federal Republic, Richard von Weizsäcker, in the plenary hall of the German parliament on 8 May ran counter to the conservative spirit of the times and its 'intellectual-moral turn'. Von Weizsäcker emphasized that 8 May 1945 was not a day of defeat but a 'day of liberation from the inhuman system of National Socialist violent rule', and he concluded with the words: 'Let us today, on the 8th of May, look the truth in the eye as well as we can.'[44]

Like many others, Jürgen Habermas was deeply impressed by this speech, which has been called a 'great moment in Germany's post-war history'. And he was outraged by the spectacle at Bitburg. In an article published in *Die Zeit* (17 May 1985) with the title 'Entsorgung der Vergangenheit' [Disposal of the past], he interpreted the demonstrative handshake between Reagan and Kohl in the Eifel Mountains as 'a turn away from a destabilizing way of coming to terms with the past and a demonstration of being brothers in arms'. And he adds that this official state ceremony was intended to show not only that Germany had always stood on the right side in the fight against the threat of communism but that 'Kohl wanted a return to German continuities. And this intention of his was well understood.'[45] It is certainly no coincidence that this article began and ended with remarks on Hermann Lübbe. The controversy over Bitburg was a continuation of the quarrels with the neo-conservatives, and it was the prelude to the 'historians' debate' which would stir emotions in 1986 (and beyond), and which would have a lasting impact on the Federal Republic. It was triggered by Habermas, who launched direct, public attacks on historians such as Michael Stürmer, Andreas Hillgruber and Ernst Nolte, or more specifically on their views on National Socialism. It was predominantly (but not exclusively) historians of various persuasions who participated in this debate over the crimes committed in Germany's name. In the course of these exchanges, which took place mostly in newspapers, political factions soon formed on both left and right.[46]

It began with an article in the *Frankfurter Allgemeine Zeitung* in April 1986, titled 'Geschichte in geschichtslosem Land' [History in a land without history]. The author, Michael Stürmer, who was an academic advisor to Helmut Kohl at the time, made a plea for a new interpretation of the National Socialist past. The perspective on German history, he said, needed to be informed by a stronger national self-confidence. Only on that basis – i.e., that of a view of history that gave meaning to it – could a national identity emerge. Stürmer came to the conclusion that, 'in a land without history, the future is controlled by those who determine the content of memory, who coin concepts and interpret the past.' This was wholly in line with the 'politics of history' practised by the conservative government of Helmut Kohl, whose plans for a museum of history involved Stürmer.

Around the same time, Andreas Hillgruber published a book with the title *Zweierlei Untergang: Die Zerschlagung des Deutschen Reiches und das Ende des europäischen Judentums* [Two kinds of decline: the destruction of the German Reich and the end of European Jewry]. In this book, the historian – who would be referred to as 'a constitutional Nazi' by Rudolf Augstein in *Der Spiegel* six months later – called for historiographical research to pay more attention to the geopolitical situation of Germany as a centrally positioned country, to accept the concrete fate of the Germans which resulted from this, and to identify with what German troops in the East achieved 'through their desperate efforts'.

Finally, on 6 June 1986, an article by Ernst Nolte, titled 'Vergangenheit, die nicht vergehen will' [The past that will not pass] and subtitled 'Eine Rede, die geschrieben, aber nicht gehalten werden konnte' [A speech that could be written but not delivered], appeared in the features section of the *Frankfurter Allgemeine Zeitung*, edited by Joachim Fest. In this article, the author questioned the singularity of the Holocaust. And he went even further by interpreting National Socialism as a secular counter-movement against Bolshevism and by claiming that the 'murder of an entire class' by the communists was the forerunner of the 'racial murder' of the Nazis. Thus, the Soviet extermination camps were more original [*ursprünglicher*]* than Auschwitz.

On the very same day this text was published, Habermas polemicized against Nolte at the Römerberg Talks† on the theme of 'Politische Kultur – heute?' [Political culture – today?]. Nolte had originally been invited to the meeting by the cultural magistrate of the city of Frankfurt, Hilmar Hoffmann, but was then replaced by the historian Wolfgang Mommsen, who himself was to give a talk with the title 'Die Vergangenheit, die nicht vergehen will' [The past that won't go away]. When Habermas rose to speak on the second day of the Römerberggespräche, he referred critically to Nolte's attempt to prepare the ground for a trivializing historical relativism.

What we have here is an attempt at exceptionalizing Auschwitz, partly by indicating that what the National Socialists did, with the sole exception of the technical procedure of gassing, had already been described in a rich literature in the early 1920s. Nolte presents German fascism, in its 'excesses', purely as a response and reaction to the Bolshevist threat of destruction, using the beautiful, almost Heideggerian‡ words: 'Wasn't the Gulag more original [*ursprünglicher*] than Auschwitz?' The reactualization of anti-communism can then be understood as the other side of the coin of this argument.[47]

---

* On this formulation, see footnote ‡ below.

† The 'Römerberggespräche' are named after the location of Frankfurt's City Hall on the Römerberg. They were initiated by Hilmar Hoffmann and H. W. Wirth in 1973 and are described by the city as 'conversations among experts for an interested urban public' (www.roemerberggespraeche-ffm.de).

‡ '... mit den schönen, fast heideggernden Worten': Habermas turns the proper name into the present participle of the verb 'to heidegger', implying that Nolte's use of the term 'ursprünglicher' betrays a slip from a claim regarding temporal precedence to a metaphysical primordiality.

These rather succinct comments would not be Habermas's last word on the topic, for it had clearly got under his skin. On 11 July 1986, *Die Zeit* published his article 'A Kind of Settlement of Damages', announced on the front page by the editor of the features section, Karl-Heinz Janßen, as a 'declaration of war'. In various argumentative strands, Habermas explicitly opposed what he saw as the latest revisionist and relativizing tendencies in the way that recent German history was viewed and made a plea for a 'critical appropriation of traditions'. Simply drawing a line under the past was out of the question. He attributed to Hillgruber a heroicization of the defensive battles of the German troops in the East, while he accused Stürmer of pursuing ideological plans and Nolte of a complete lack of instinct. Nolte, he wrote, engaged in a shameful falsification of history by delivering into the world the claim that the singularity of the destruction of the Jewry was limited to the technical detail of gassing. He insisted on the collective responsibility (in Jaspers's sense of the term) of the Germans for the crimes committed by National Socialism, and thereby the duty of keeping the memory of those murdered by the Germans alive.

> These dead, first of all, have a right to the weak anamnetic force of a solidarity which those born late can practise only in the medium of an ever renewed, often desperate, in any case restless remembrance. If we ignore this legacy from Benjamin, Jewish fellow citizens, any son or daughter of one of those murdered, would no longer be able to breathe in our country.[48]

The moral integrity of the Germans, he said, is tied to the 'acknowledgement of a responsibility resulting from a joint liability'.[49] Against any kind of apologetic attitude towards history, he held on to the view that national self-confidence after Auschwitz 'can result only from an appropriation of the better of our historical traditions, an appropriation which is not blind, but critical.' Such an attitude towards history is a sign that Germans had learned from their history and that a post-conventional identity had emerged. This, he said, is associated with a patriotism which can only be conceived as a post-national constitutional patriotism: '[a] commitment to universalistic constitutional principles which is anchored by conviction'.[50] These principles are, according to Habermas, a political achievement of West Germany and can be looked on with pride.

When a day later *Die Tageszeitung* published a critical review of Hillgruber's book by Micha Brumlik, and shortly thereafter the *Frankfurter Allgemeine Zeitung* began to open a front against Habermas, the debate had begun in earnest. Nolte and Stürmer responded in short letters to the editor of the *Frankfurter Allgemeine Zeitung*; Klaus Hildebrand attacked Habermas in a longer article in which he claimed that the latter generally had a troubled relationship with historical research and that his one-sidedness had 'even totalitarian features'.[51] Frank Schirrmacher and Joachim Fest tried to prove that Habermas used historical concepts in an indiscriminate fashion and, more generally, was ideologically biased. By the end of August, the debate had spread across all major newspapers.

Over the course of the summer, as the tone of the controversy became ever more bitter, Habermas was in touch by phone with an editor at *Die Zeit*, Robert Leicht, who at first reacted with restraint, kept his distance, and recommended that Habermas contact the *Frankfurter Allgemeine Zeitung*, as the newspaper which had triggered the debate, in relation to the publication of his responses. Habermas thereupon sought the support of the editor-in-chief and one of the newspaper's main editors, Marion Gräfin Dönhoff. In a three-page letter he sent in September 1986, he tried to win her over to his position and, at the same time, defended himself against the 'hair-raising accusations' that had been made both in the *Frankfurter Allgemeine Zeitung* by Fest and by Hillgruber – in particular the claim that he had engaged in an 'academic character assassination' directed at the historians.[52]

> It is obvious that I am only interested in certain interpretations of the historical events that, at the present time, spread into the wider public, rather than the character traits of authors I have never met in person. If, solely on the basis of the texts in question, I were to engage in speculations regarding the latter, I would, for instance, consider Nolte to be a particularly morally sensitive individual. At least, this is how one might try to explain, among other things, the fervour with which he is trying to detect a causal nexus between the mass murder of the Nazis and those of the Bolsheviks.

In his letter, Habermas attached importance to the fact that he does not approach the public as a trained historian but, rather, as a layman who intervenes in a debate. And such a 'literary-political polemic does not belong in a beginners' seminar in history.'[53] Indeed, this was another bout in the politics of ideas, fought with the gloves off – despite the fact that, as Habermas formulated it in his concluding remark on the debate in *Die Zeit*, it was a matter 'in which it is not possible [for anyone among us] to be a disinterested party.' Such a dispute, he added, 'one should not confuse . . . with discussions between scientists. . . . The pompous outrage over an alleged mixing of politics and science shunts the issue onto completely the wrong track.'[54]

Like the heated controversies over the intellectual roots of left-wing terrorism during the German autumn, the historians' debate was a prototypical contest over the politics of ideas, characterized by sharp polarizations and black-and-white intellectual factions. The spokesperson of the left-liberals was Jürgen Habermas, whose position was, more or less, supported by historians such as Martin Broszat, Eberhard Jäckel, Jürgen Kocka, Hans and Wolfgang Mommsen and Hans-Ulrich Wehler, as well as Heinrich August Winkler. The opposing faction, comprising Andreas Hillgruber, Ernst Nolte and Michael Stürmer, was supported by Joachim Fest, Klaus Hildebrand, Horst Möller, Thomas Nipperdey and Hagen Schulze. These skirmishes in print were about political and cultural hegemony. According to Volker Ullrich in the *Frankfurter Rundschau* (5 September 1987), at the end of this controversy over the uniqueness of the genocide of the Jews, the view of the democratic left had won out.[55]

Déjà vu Twenty-five years later, it seemed as if, incredibly, the historians' debate might flare up once again. But, the short-lived debate, which again began in the *Frankfurter Allgemeine Zeitung*, was from the very beginning little more than a damp squib and had something absurd about it. The background was a volume in preparation entitled *Singuläres Auschwitz?* [Auschwitz – a singularity?], which was to contain ten contributions looking back at the historians' debate after a quarter of a century.[56] In his 'slightly unusual preface', the editor Mathias Brodkorb complained that the 'important philosopher' who had been contacted in writing and invited to participate several times had refused to enter into a 'discourse free of domination' with Ernst Nolte, which could have served the purpose of discussing the old 'differences in substance in a public forum and at an academic level'. Further, he had avoided clarifying matters with the editor. However, Brodkorb said, he was able to explain for his readers without any difficulty what Habermas preferred to remain silent about. Habermas, he said, in his own practice did not adhere at all to the discourse theory that he nevertheless 'invented'. This might not say anything about the quality of the theory, but it did say something about its 'inventor'.

This storm in a teacup was triggered by a pre-publication of a section of the Auschwitz book. On 13 July 2011, the *Frankfurter Allgemeine Zeitung* published an abbreviated version of the contribution by Egon Flaig in the 'Geisteswissenschaften' section.[57] Flaig taught ancient history at the University of Rostock. In his piece, he surprised his readers with a full-frontal attack on Habermas, suggesting that he had falsified quotations 'in order to make denunciatory judgements. ... Habermas used journalistic tricks of a kind usually reserved for rogue journalism.' At the end of his broadside, Flaig referred to the thesis of the singularity of Auschwitz and wrote: 'And when I make the claim that the democracy of Athens was just as unique as the Shoah, I can give a good reason for it: because it is more important to me than the Shoah.'[58]

A week later, Heinrich August Winkler commented on the matter in *Die Zeit* (21 July 2011). He gave a short summary of the positions within the historians' debate and criticized both Flaig's attempt at downplaying the singularity of the murder of the Jews as a 'trivial truth' and his insinuation that the abnormality of the Germans was to be maintained so as to assert their 'mythical uniqueness'. At the same time, he cautiously but clearly defended Habermas's perspective on the historians' debate.[59] Curiously, Winkler also has an article in the volume edited by Brodkorb.[60]

Habermas remained silent in this strange and brief revival of the historians' debate.[61] In any case, the majority of commentaries in the printed media took his side, and in addition he probably thought that he had said all he had to say in this debate, which had been extremely gruelling for him personally. Now, other themes took centre stage – first and foremost, Europe.

Habermas as a sceptic towards reunification

Unification hasn't been understood as a normatively willed act of the citizens of both states, who in political self-awareness decided on a common civil union.[62]

A new nationalism? In the exciting months of 1989, as radical transformations took place in the countries of actually existing socialism, as the Berlin Wall fell in November and the Brandenburg Gate was opened, Habermas remained silent, at least to begin with. He tried to keep a distance from these dramatic, historical turning points. The swift pace of reunification worried him, and his old fears resurfaced of a rebirth of ideas about being a great nation and power, even if he was convinced that modern societies develop into post-national entities. Like Günter Grass, he welcomed the unification more than the unity itself. At the same time, the Federal Republic's integration into the West was important to him as a guarantee 'that the trend of our post-war development will not be reversed'.[63] For Habermas, all these were good reasons for regarding the initial process of unification of the two German states, and the 'destruction of the Bonn Republic', largely from a critical distance.[64] In his first statement on the events, 'Die Stunde der nationalen Empfindung: Republikanische Gesinnung oder Nationalbewußtsein?'[The hour of national sentiment: republican conviction or national consciousness?] – written just two weeks after the borders had opened but initially circulated only among a small circle of friends – he was very concerned about the way in which the unification, referred to as an 'accession', was being carried out. In this process, he said, East Berlin was on a financial drip feed from Bonn. At the same time, he expressed his fear that a new mentality would prevail and painted a gloomy picture of a Federal Republic using its economic power in order to force East Germany into a pure annexation. However, when he saw how the East Germans streamed across to West Berlin on 9 November 1989, his

> heart filled with joy at the moment of regained freedom, a freedom to move that transformed into a run. There was also a shocked pause: all of a sudden, the monstrosity, absurdity, surreality of everything the Wall stood for was laid bare. For sure, when it was erected in 1961 it was thought brutal as well. But that feeling was soon seized by anti-communism and rhetorically worn down . . . Only now, with the shell of habituation cracked open, can the unnaturalness step out again like something long forgotten.[65]

Nevertheless, Habermas was mistrustful of the new demonstrations of national emotion and of that 'speechless power of sentiment' he thought he could detect in the teary eyes of Willy Brandt in parliament. As an antidote to the intoxication of the national, Habermas recommended a sober constitutional patriotism: the 'consent to a political order that is constituted by rights for self-determination in contradistinction to the idea of an order based on an ethnic, cultural, collective "community of fate".'[66]

Habermas believed that the citizens of East Germany should be included in a democratic decision-making process. He was sceptical about the hectic pace of Helmut Kohl's 'policies of self-imposed deadlines and the commandeering of the organizational networks of the bloc parties'.[67] The failure of actually existing state socialism, in his opinion, was primarily a result of the hypertrophic bureaucracy of the totalitarian state apparatus and its disregard for the democratic principles of the rule of law, but it was also because of the prioritization of increasing productivity in the sphere of social labour at the expense of quality of life.

Habermas interpreted the lasting mass demonstrations in Leipzig, with their key slogan 'We are the people', as a 'belated revolution' with the general aim of gaining political freedom and achieving economic well-being. However, the fixation on the economic model of capitalism revealed the 'almost complete absence of innovative ideas for the future'.[68] Against this background, the representatives of Marxism in the West, who had allegedly been put on the defensive, had 'no reason to wear sackcloth and ashes'. But the non-communist left, of which Habermas considered himself to be a part, 'likewise cannot pretend that nothing has happened'.[69]

At the outset of his first substantial article on the topic of German unity, which appeared in *Die Zeit* at the end of March 1990 under the title 'Der DM-Nationalismus' [DM nationalism], Habermas asked:

'What will happen with Germany's identity?'[70] His reservations are directed against 'a kind of national economic attitude [*Gesinnung*]' that 'overpowers the republican consciousness' and against a nationalism based on financial power: 'Only *one* unit in which to express *all* topics. German interests are weighed and enforced in German Marks.' He criticized both the 'alliance for Germany' that Helmut Kohl was pursuing in spite of all the resistance and his 'faits accomplis' approach to politics. Habermas pleaded for unification according to Article 146 of the Basic Law, which stipulates that a new constitution, freely decided upon by the German people, has to be the basis for the process of unification. To proceed according to Article 23, by contrast, would mean that the citizens would only passively 'suffer' unification,* although admittedly this would be to the advantage of the citizens of the German Democratic Republic, who would be presented with the social and currency union as a gift.[71]

Almost a year later, Habermas again commented in *Die Zeit* on the problem of reunification. The overtones of this article show that its author now distinguished more clearly between 'us' – that is, 'we, in the West' – and 'them' in the former GDR. That in the course of its short history progressive ideas had been discredited by political rhetoric was 'one of the evil aspects of the GDR's legacy', according to Habermas. It almost seems as if he wanted to point out to those on the left in the West who had considered actually existing socialism a viable alternative what an illusion they had been under – an illusion, he was ready to admit, that had been promoted by the anti-communism which had characterized West Germany's early years. He also admitted that he had only ever had a minimal interest in the GDR state and that apart from short trips to East Berlin he had first set foot on GDR soil in 1988, after being granted permission to enter the country for the first time. 'Their history was not our

---

* Before the events of 1989, Article 23 listed the individual federal states in which the law is 'zunächst' [initially] valid, and then concluded: 'It shall be put into force for other parts of Germany on their accession' (www.cvce.eu/content/publication/1999/1/1/7fa618bb-604e-4980-b667-76bf0cd0dd9b/publishable_en.pdf). After 1989, the old text of the paragraph was deleted, and the new version now covers the relationship with the European Union, the protection of basic rights, and the principle of subsidiarity. Article 146 is the final article of the Basic Law and concerns its duration: 'This Basic Law, which since the achievement of the unity and freedom of Germany applies to the entire German people, shall cease to apply on the day on which a constitution freely adopted by the German people takes effect' (https://www.btg-bestellservice.de/pdf/80201000.pdf). Article 23 applied, for instance, in 1956 when the Saarland joined the Federal Republic. However, while it had clearly been formulated with the possibility of reunification in mind, Article 146 would have allowed for a 'symmetric' coming together under a joint constitution, rather than one state 'asymmetrically' joining the other. Regardless of which article has the better arguments on its side, the historical circumstances can certainly, and ironically, be viewed as a prime example supporting Spaemann's argument regarding time pressures in politics (see p. 256 above).

history. This is true perforce for my children and their generation.
. . . We must be allowed to say this without sentimentality.'[72]

The crux of this article, which was based on conversations with
the publicist Michael Haller,[73] was again a critique of the way in
which the Federal Republic's government dealt with the GDR. It
was a case of 'land-grabbing territorial fetishism . . ., as if we could
appropriate some ground of tradition with the annexation of the
GDR. These triumphal tones regarding an alleged gain in intellectual greatness have made me rather nervous.'[74] The fact that
spaces in which public communication could flourish were increasingly shrinking or being limited, Habermas said, severely damaged
national self-confidence and rendered impossible a process of unification that would be at least to some extent symmetrical. Habermas
did not think that the 'belated revolution' of the GDR citizens threw
new light on the old problems confronting Germany.

> The devaluation of our best and most fragile intellectual traditions
> is, for me, one of the most evil aspects of the legacy that the GDR
> brings into the expanded Federal Republic. . . . It's clear that reified,
> textbook dialectical materialism [Lehrbuch-DiaMat] was from the
> beginning a legitimation ideology tailored to Stalin's Soviet imperial-
> ism. But until 1953 the emigrants who had returned to the GDR from
> the West, such as Brecht, Bloch, Hans Mayer, Stefan Heym or Anna
> Seghers, testified to the GDR's willingness, at least on the surface, to
> stand up for those progressive traditions that had always had a par-
> ticularly rough time in Germany. . . . If you're asking me about the
> normative orientations that are worth preserving, you have to think
> back not so much to the GDR of the Free German Youth and party
> convention speeches as to the GDR of the early DEFA films, to some
> of the publishing programmes from the early 1950s, or to a span of
> one or two generations of left-wing oppositional writers extending to
> Heiner Müller and Christoph Hein.[75]

In a third article for Die Zeit in April 1992, Habermas went
deeper into his views on the totalitarian aspects of the GDR past,
to which he had already alluded in his conversations with Michael
Haller, saying: 'You slay a dragon, but an octopus just perishes –
however, it doesn't let go of everything in its grip. Therefore some
things survive that really aren't worth preserving.'[76] He considers
working off the GDR's past to be a 'multidimensional undertaking'
which needs to be informed by a differentiation between public discourse, juridical judgement and personal justification. GDR society,
he holds, suffers from a deficit in coming to terms with the past on
account of its ideological imprint, '[b]ecause the anti-fascist figures
which provided the legitimation for the old regime rather stood in
the way of a deeper engagement with the NS past.'[77] The fact is

that, after the GDR finally joined the Federal Republic, following the 'two-plus-four talks', 'turncoats [*Wendehälse*] and opportunists climbed up. This revolution does not devour its children; it does not have any. Everything points to the fact', Wolfgang Herles writes in his *Eine andere Geschichte Deutschlands* [A different history of Germany], 'that the revolution in the GDR was the cause of a minority. The majority wanted the prosperity of the West under conditions of the East.'[78] As regards West Germany, Habermas identified a renewed shift to the right. Liberal-conservatives moulted and became Deutschnationale,* and young conservatives agreed with right-wing extremists. 'Today, hardly a single voice is raised against industrious historians who emphasize, apparently without qualms, the continuity of the Bismarck Reich or who weigh up the shift in modernization brought about by National Socialism against its mass crimes.'[79]

For Habermas, any equation between National Socialism and the GDR is ruled out entirely. One reason for this is that the 'GDR is not responsible for a world war with 50 million victims or for the extermination of an entire people through industrialized mass destruction.'[80] Another is the fact that the totalitarian regime of the GDR, because of its long existence and the entanglement of the individual 'in the bureaucratic net of domination', profited from the emergence of 'a kind of normality'. And there had at least been a potential for critique and, along with it, a hope for democratization.[81] Against this background, Habermas warned against a mentality of revenge and staged tribunals. 'In the West's slick magazines we find a confluence of many things, for purely technical reasons, so to speak, and as if by chance, because the former GDR had not had time to develop its own public sphere with its own infrastructure and discourses. That is why intellectuals from the East are frequently manipulated by journalists in the West . . ..'[82] After two years of an expanded Federal Republic, it was far too soon to speak of a unified Germany, even if 'the constitutionally established unification signifies that both sides have opted for a common future and a reciprocal understanding with regard to the two different post-war histories . . ..'[83]

Ralf Dahrendorf was the best known of the liberals who forcefully criticized the 'talk' about 'DM nationalism' as 'based on the erroneous belief that money is necessarily disreputable, the state, by contrast, potentially positive.' It was precisely the German Mark that had not only liberated the former GDR from the Wall for good but also made it 'citizen-friendly and hostile to power'.[84] For Habermas, by contrast, the level of freedom in a society is indicated

---

* Literally 'National Germans', a right-wing faction in Weimar Germany.

in the first place not by the existence of a functioning market, or by the existence of a welfare state, but rather by the modes and subjects of the communication that takes place in it, and how this is reflected in its democratic procedures.

Christa Wolf. In November 1991, a correspondence developed between Habermas and Christa Wolf, the writer and dissident from the former GDR.[85] Like Habermas, she was initially critical about a premature unification of the two parts of Germany, but in contrast to him she sympathized with a socialist alternative, with socialism as a third way.

Both were interested in an exchange of ideas. The correspondence came about in the wake of a discussion at the East Berlin Academy of the Arts at Robert Koch Platz 7, which still existed as an independent institution at the time. Habermas was there in November 1991, although he was not part of the panel, and immediately after his return to Starnberg he wrote a personal letter to Wolf in which he problematized, among other things, the contemporary tendency to force the two dictatorships – Nazi Germany and the GDR – into the same mould. The vanishing point of the democratization process in Germany, he wrote, had been the integration into the West, which had fostered its development. By contrast, there had been the abuse of progressive ideas by the SED regime. The achievements of West German democracy are sacrosanct for Habermas: '[w]e in West Germany lived under conditions that made possible . . . an intellectual orientation towards the West that was . . . experienced as emancipatory. This orientation towards the West did not mean a bending of the German soul but an exercising of the upright gait.'[86]

Christa Wolf had visited Habermas and his wife in the Myliusstraße apartment in Frankfurt a year after the fall of the Wall, and they had enjoyed long discussions after dinner lasting well into the night. Now, she responded to Habermas's letter swiftly with a matter-of-fact reply.[87] She expressed her irritation over the demarcation of two political cultures she detected in Habermas's position. At the same time, she regretted that a 'zero hour' was not available, and precisely for this reason she saw a need to talk about the respective histories as well as individual biographies. Wolf vehemently denied that the intellectuals in the East lacked familiarity with the culture and life of the West, as Habermas, she said, seemed to assume.

This was a point also contradicted by Richard Schröder, the theologian and leader of the SPD faction in the first freely elected Volkskammer [parliament] of the GDR. In particular, he took exception to Habermas's accusation of a 'territorial fetishism'. Further, he interpreted his demand for a plebiscite as a demand for a decision about whether GDR citizens should become citizens of the Federal Republic at all. In truth, Schröder wrote, 'the majority of the Federal Republic's citizens have also welcomed unification under the mode of accession, and they did not require that there should first be a test of whether hard- heartedness can gain a majority in the Federal Republic.'[88] Friedrich Dieckmann, a writer born in 1937 and raised in Dresden and Berlin, criticized Habermas's statements in similarly plain terms. It is erroneous, he wrote, to claim that the histories of the Federal Republic and of Germany took parallel and unconnected courses. 'The fact that a thinker as important as this one could delude himself over this points unmistakably to the illusory character of the state consciousness associated with the Federal Republic.'[89] The accusation that he had fallen for the West German state's own self-delusions – that was a new one even for Habermas.

10

Against Germanomania* and Nationalism

L'Espresso: What does it mean for you to be a German today?
Habermas: To make sure that the fortunate date of 1989 does not let
us forget the instructive date of 1945.[1]

Relapse into megalomania? Jürgen Habermas has always feared
that a renaissance of the nation-state could follow in the wake of
German reunification. Thus, in the early 1990s he began to look
into the theme in more philosophical detail, not least because speculative suggestions that Germany would or should again strive for
political or economic supremacy became more and more frequent.
'As if today this kind of national state still existed', he wrote as
early as 11 December 1992 in *Die Zeit*, 'on which the ideological
halo of the nineteenth century could rest; and as if the old, yet new,
Federal Republic, which is more deeply implicated in the network
of mutual political and economic dependencies than any other state,
could be pruned back in the image of that antiquated model.'[2] In
those years, Hamburg-based *Die Zeit* was Habermas's preferred
medium for his political statements and interventions. This did not
stop Frank Schirrmacher trying to secure him as an author for the
features section of the *Frankfurter Allgemeine Zeitung*. Habermas's
response, however, was unambiguous: with regard to this newspaper, he wrote to Schirrmacher, he would prefer to limit 'his role to
that of a reader who notes with interest the unashamedly pro-fascist
articles of your correspondent in Rome, a right-wing radical defence
of Carl Schmitt's "imperative of homogeneity", and the exculpa-
tion of Gentile, the fascist political philosopher, by a former PCI
intellectual – this is the yield of just a few days.'[3]

Habermas's scepticism towards both the nation-state, when
understood as based on ethnic unity, and nationalism as a source

---

* The German term is 'Deutschtum', which simply means 'Germanness'; however, the
implication in the use of this term is that of an exaggerated and/or distorted emphasis on
Germanness.

of identity is deep-seated and rooted in his biography. He had experienced German nationalism turn into a murderous megalomania that was responsible for millions of deaths and a Europe in rubble. Moreover, that same nationalism had ensured that after the end of 'total war' there was neither a sovereign German state nor a nation as a territorially delimited and legally constituted unity. He could not ignore that historical fact, either then or later, and he tried to justify the claim that no one should be able to ignore it by investigating what actually constitutes the troubling aspects of 'nation and state'. Following reunification, the nation-state became a topic in his political-philosophical reflections; as we shall see, the idea of a post-national Europe played a prominent part in these from the very beginning.

Solidarity between citizens. In a lecture at the Clinic for Psychiatry and Psychotherapy in Littenheid, Switzerland, on 'Staatsbürgerschaft und nationale Identität' [Citizenship and national identity],[4] Habermas claimed that, in parallel to the formation of the European Union, there needed to be an international, deliberative politics in which the post-national public spheres of the European countries opened themselves up to each other and interacted. The loss of national sovereignty after the turning point of 1945, he said, did not inhibit but, rather, promoted the arduous process of democratization set in motion by the 'commitment to the Western culture of enlightenment'.[5] However, the epochal change of 1989,[6] and a fixation – born of power-political strategizing – on the nation-state, may now pose a threat to the stability of existing democratic institutions. This, he said, would awaken spectres long thought dead, against which the post-traditional consciousness of a later-born generation, with its 'more sober political identity' that had left behind 'the background of a past centred on national history', would hopefully know how to protect itself.[7] 'The abstract idea of a generalization of democracy and human rights forms . . . the solid core by which the rays of national tradition are refracted – the language, the literature, and the history of one's own nation.'[8]

A symposium organized jointly by the Institute for Social Research, the Fritz Bauer Institute and the Jewish community in Frankfurt also had this topic as its subject. It took place between 1 and 3 December 1995 under the title 'Bürgergesellschaft im Ernstfall' [Civil society in the state of emergency]. Habermas had just returned with Ute to the city on the Main from a conference at the University of California in Santa Cruz, which was attended by Ronald Dworkin, Amy Gutmann, Thomas Nagel and John Rawls, along with a number of American disciples of Rawls.[9] The conference focused on Rawls's *Theory of Justice*, which had been published twenty-five years earlier. Under the title '"Reasonable" versus "True", or the Morality of Worldviews', Habermas spoke about the differences between Rawls's political liberalism and his own Kantian republicanism.[10] On his return flight to Boston, Rawls suffered a stroke, and until his death in 2002 Habermas did not have another chance to meet his colleague, whom he held in high esteem. In November, Habermas gave an acceptance speech for the Karl Jaspers Prize in Heidelberg.[11] The paper he presented at the symposium in Frankfurt was published on 30 December 1995 in the features section of the *Frankfurter Rundschau*. The title was 'Aufgeklärte Ratlosigkeit: Warum die Politik ohne Perspektiven ist: Thesen zu einer Diskussion' [Enlightened perplexity: why politics is without perspectives: some theses on a discussion]. This time, he did not speak about the dangers of a renationalization but about the effects resulting from the de-nationalization of national economies – i.e., from the erosion of national sovereignty. His suggested solution: the 'tiger's leap'* into a common supranational politics.

One of the sections in Habermas's *The Inclusion of the Other: Studies in Political Theory* is subtitled 'Is There a Future for the Nation-State?' The volume, published in 1996, also contains an appendix on 'Faktizität und Geltung' [Facticity and validity] and pieces on Rawls's political liberalism, but its core is formed by texts on the question of the nation-state, on human rights and on deliberative politics. In the fourth essay, 'The European Nation-State: On the Past and Future of Sovereignty and Citizenship', Habermas retraces the historical phases in the development of the modern nation-state; the latter, he says, is not without its achievements but also contains certain risks. These are rooted in 'the tension between the universalism of an egalitarian legal community and the particularism of a community united by historical destiny' which 'is built into the very concept of the national state.'[12] While the idea of a nation based on a people is always in danger of being used for the justification of violent action both domestically and abroad, the republican and at the same time cosmopolitan idea of a nation of citizens aims at a solidaristic life within a legal community. Political cohesion on the basis of the state's self-understanding as a nation-state is replaced with 'solidarity between the citizens'.[13] Notwithstanding the historical importance of the nation-state in shaping the political integration and democratic self-determination of citizens, it is obvious today that nation-states' political room

---

* The German 'Tigersprung' is an allusion to Walter Benjamin's 'Theses on the Philosophy of History': 'Fashion has a flair for the topical, no matter where it stirs in the thickets of long ago; it is a tiger's leap into the past. This jump, however, takes place in an arena where the ruling class gives the commands. The same leap in the open air of history is the dialectical one, which is how Marx understood the revolution'. Benjamin (1999), *Illuminations*, p. 253.

to manoeuvre has actually become increasingly limited: domestically, by multicultural conditions of life and the increasing ethnic
diversity of populations, and externally, by the inexorable dynamic
of globalization, which undermines the sovereignty of individual
states. For Habermas, the only candidate for a functional replacement of the nation-state is the democratic process itself. The circles
of communication that form a political public sphere, that is to say,
the democratic processes of opinion and will-formation, would need
to act as a kind of 'deficiency guarantee' for social integration.[14]
The integration of the polity, Habermas says, comes about through
the mutual recognition of forms of life and by including them in the
organization of culture and politics as much as possible. Among the
means for such a 'difference-sensitive inclusion', or 'coexistence with
equal rights', Habermas counts 'above all guarantees of cultural
autonomy, group-specific rights, compensatory policies, and other
arrangements for effectively protecting minorities'.[15]

Habermas's ambiguous attitude towards military interventions

The war experience had made me a pacifist.[16]

Escaping the logic of war. At the beginning of 1991, about three years
after the end of the first Gulf War between Iran and Iraq, the second
Gulf War, also referred to as the first war in Iraq, broke out. Its pre-
history was the invasion of Kuwait by Iraqi troops in early August
1990 in the wake of a conflict over oil production. Within a matter
of hours, the UN Security Council reacted by passing Resolution
660, which condemned the invasion and demanded the immediate
withdrawal of Iraqi troops. Another half dozen resolutions and economic sanctions would follow before Resolution 678 authorized the
member states of the United Nations 'to use all necessary means'
should Iraq not adhere to Resolution 660 – i.e., withdraw completely
from Kuwait. Iraq disregarded the ultimatum and the military intervention of allied forces, Operation Desert Storm, ensued shortly
after the ultimatum had elapsed. Under the supreme command of the
American general Norman Schwarzkopf, thirty-four states took part
in the operation. Across Europe, people took to the streets – 200,000
in Germany alone – to demonstrate against the air and land offensive
and the destruction of Baghdad and Basra, as well as against the
devastation of Kuwait and the rocket attacks that Saddam Hussein's
regime had launched against Israel.

Habermas followed events in international politics attentively;
however, he remarked on them only infrequently, at least by his
standards. During the crisis in Libya in the spring of 1986, which
reached its peak with the bombing of Tripoli and Benghazi by the

US air force in April,[17] he sided with protesters. In a newspaper interview in May, he referred to the 'action' against Libya, which the Americans called Operation El Dorado Canyon, in the course of defending the universalist core of morality. Regarding the general validity of morality, he said, one need not be sceptical from the outset. 'There is, after all, hardly any constitution these days which does not have a written or unwritten component on basic rights.' In light of this, it was clear that the operations of the American military under the leadership of Ronald Reagan had violated international law, because the lives of innocent people had wilfully been put at risk. This imperialist behaviour by the world power, he said, was the reason that he 'joined a demonstration again, after many years'.[18]

Habermas's statements on the Gulf War are far more visible and extensive. As early as 15 February 1991, he published an article in *Die Zeit*, titled 'Wider die Logik des Krieges' [Against the logic of war]. He criticized the manner in which the UN resolution had been acted upon, although he considered the resolution itself perfectly justified. He spoke of the 'obsolescence of war as a category of world history' and reached the following general conclusion: 'The aim of abolishing war is a demand of reason.'[19] But he also wrote: 'There can be worse evils than war.'[20] His recommendation for the German government was a 'politics of restraint', but he also argued for the unconditional support and protection of Israel.

Habermas's attitude towards military intervention is nuanced and cautious. In his conversations with Michael Haller, which were published around this time, he stressed that the 'obscene connection between the German export of technology into Iraq and Scud missiles . . . was a particular challenge for the political morality of Germans.'[21] From the perspective of world politics, he said, the conflict in the Gulf demonstrated the need to strengthen the authority of the UN in order to enforce international law. And this point of view, for him, leads to clear restrictions on military operations such as Desert Storm. They have to be recognizable as policing actions under a UN mandate and, accordingly, must not pursue the purely national interests of the war-waging parties, such as interests in natural resources. In a central passage of the article in *Die Zeit* of February 1991, he said: 'I consider the interventions as such to be justified. At the same time, I harbour grave doubts as to whether the campaign, in its present form, would hold up under scrupulous examination. There is only one decisive judgement I am confident to make: that we should not hesitate to help Israel.' He found two contradictory emotions at play in the German debate over the war: 'never again anti-Semitism' and 'never again nationalism and war'. In the end, his personal plea was unambiguous: 'Despite all reservations, the blatant violation of international law [by Iraq; S. M.-D.] and the corresponding UN resolutions justify the limited use of military force in the Gulf.' His statements in *Die Zeit* make it very clear that he feels a special obligation towards Israel (a fact that has not changed since), an obligation that should prevent all Germans from 'rejecting the Gulf War outright'. This position earned him a great deal of criticism, as is evident from the letters to the editor in the following issue of the paper. One of the letters reached the following conclusion: 'To escape from the logic of war can therefore only mean to do without war.' Another letter says: 'But in 1968, Habermas still recognized the character of US imperialism in Vietnam. Today, 1991, he can no longer see that the war in the Gulf serves only the purpose of defending the strategic interests of American capitalism.'[22] Habermas showed understanding for the restraint of the German government and for the hesitation shown by Helmut Kohl: 'But whatever our government did wrong, at least its policy of refusing to send German Tornados to attack Baghdad was, God knows, no mistake. In memory of the global ambitions of a German *Reich* that plunged Europe into two world wars, the policy was also the expression of a historically well-grounded inhibition.'[23]

Cosmopolitan law. In the 1990s, the conflict in the Balkans escalated as a consequence of the attempts by various parts of the former Yugoslavia to gain autonomy after the collapse of 'actually existing socialism' in Eastern Europe. Military confrontations took place in all of the new republics formed on the territory of the former Yugoslavia, with the war in Bosnia and the massacre in Srebrenica in particular prompting worldwide horror. In the spring of 1998, Serbian security forces began an offensive against the liberation army of the Serbian province of Kosovo, the UÇK. In the face of the ruthlessness of the Serbs under the leadership of President Slobodan Milošević, NATO threatened Belgrade with the possibility of military intervention and pressed for negotiations between Kosovo Albanians and Serbs, which took place in Rambouillet, near Paris. After negotiations failed, the allies began Operation Allied Force on 24 March 1999. From the first day of the operation, German soldiers were involved – the first foreign deployment of soldiers in post-war German history. The previous autumn, there had been a change of government in Berlin when, after sixteen years, the coalition of the CDU/CSU and the FDP, and along with it Chancellor Helmut Kohl, whom Habermas had almost grown fond of towards the end,[24] had been ousted from power in the national elections. Thus, although the vote on German military involvement had already taken place before the new parliament was constituted and the new SPD–Green coalition took office, the responsibility for implementing the decision now rested with two left-wing parties with strong pacifist streaks. Chancellor Gerhard Schröder of the SPD and Foreign Minister Joschka Fischer from the Green Party had their

1 Jürgen Habermas in his study in Starnberg in 2009

2 On holiday at Timmendorfer Strand in August 1931: the two-year-old
Jürgen with his parents Ernst and Grete Habermas

3 Autumn 1937: Grete Habermas and her three children, Hans-Joachim (on the left), Jürgen, and Anja, who is just a few weeks old.

Als Jürgen Habermas auf die „Oberschule für Jungen" kam, sah die erste Seite des Klassenbuchs seiner Klasse (42 Schüler) so aus.

4 The first page of the 'Klassenbuch' [class book] at the secondary school for boys in Gummersbach which Habermas attended from autumn 1939 until his 'Abitur', the final school leaving examinations.

Habermas ist entschieden der begabteste und der am bewußtesten auf seine geistige Entwicklung bedachte Schüler der Klasse. Er ist ein selbständiger Denker, der das Bedürfnis empfindet, in eigenem Arbeiten mit selbstgestellter Aufgabe Klarheit über weltanschauliche und literarische Fragen zu gewinnen und seine Gedanken in guter Form wiederzugeben. Sein angeborener Arbeitseifer wurde vielleicht durch die psychische Wirkung eines Geburtsfehlers, der ihn besonders in den Unterklassen sichtlich belastete, und dem damit verbundenen Willen zur Ausgleichsleistung noch erheblich gesteigert. Seine früher etwas gedrückte und empfindsame Haltung hat er durch einen gesunden Humor überwunden, der auch vor der eigenen Person nicht haltmacht und nur auf dem Grunde einer echten Bescheidenheit erwachsen sein kann.
Ganz ausgesprochen ist seine Begabung für <u>philosophische Fragen</u>, zu denen er ohne äußere Anregung von selbst kommt. Schon als Sekundaner vertiefte er sich in philosophische Werke und ruhte nicht, bis er ihnen selbständig gegenüberstand. Seine <u>Aufsätze</u> durften oft im Hinblick auf ihre geistige Höhenlage sehr gut genannt werden. Sie standen unter großen Gesichtspunkten und gingen in die Tiefe; auch in ihrer stilistischen Haltung war ein stetiger Aufstieg zu beobachten, sein Bemühen um eigenständige Ausdrucksweise und anschauliche Fassung der Gedanken machte zusehends Fortschritte. <u>In der Geschichte</u> zeigte er großes Interesse für historische Probleme, insbesondere auf verfassungsrechtl. Gebieten, für Theorien des Staatsrechts und der wirtschaftl. Entwicklung, die seiner philosophischen Neigung Nahrung boten. In der Erwerbung konkreten geschichtl. Wissens hätte er mehr Sorgfalt beweisen können. <u>In Latein und Englisch</u> trat sein scharfes logisches, oft eigenwilliges Denken und die Fähigkeit, sich entsprechend auszudrücken, hervor. In der <u>Mathematik</u> hielt er mit Einwendungen, die er geschickt und klar zu formulieren wußte, nicht zurück. Seine Fähigkeit zu einem Problem Stellung zu nehmen und klar zu urteilen, war allerdings größer als sein Tatsachenwissen. Auch in der <u>Chemie und in Biologie</u> war er bemüht, die philosophische Grundlage zu erkennen, er förderte durch eigene Gedanken das Unterrichtsgespräch.

5 'His talent for philosophical questions is altogether exceptional ...': evaluation of his class teacher for Habermas's final examinations at Easter 1949.

6 Jürgen Habermas in 1942, the
year that marked the turning
point of the war when the
Sixth Army was marooned in
Stalingrad and the Allies landed
in Africa.

7 Final mobilization: the Hitler Youth is marching off to be deployed at
the Siegfried Line in August 1944. Jürgen Habermas is in the foreground
with flowers attached to his cap.

8 Karl-Otto Apel around 1955

Mit Heidegger gegen Heidegger denken

Zur Veröffentlichung von Vorlesungen aus dem Jahre 1935

Martin Heidegger *(Photo)*

Theater-Notizen

9 Beginnings of a career as a public intellectual: 'It appears to be time to think with Heidegger against Heidegger.'

10 Frankfurt on Main 1956: Assistant of Theodor W. Adorno at the Institute for Social Research

11 Birth of a classical text: *The Structural Transformation of the Public Sphere* is published by Luchterhand Verlag in 1962.

12 Theodor W. Adorno and Jürgen Habermas at the annual meeting of
sociologists in Heidelberg in April 1964

JOHANN WOLFGANG GOETHE-UNIVERSITÄT
Frankfurt am Main

Am Montag, 28. Juni 1965, 12 Uhr c. t. findet in der Aula der Universität die feierliche Antrittsvorlesung des Ordinarius für Philosophie und Soziologie,

Herrn Professor Dr. phil. Jürgen Habermas,
über das Thema

„Erkenntnis und Interesse"
statt.

Wir beehren uns, hierzu einzuladen.

Frankfurt am Main, den 10. Juni 1965

Franz	Kluke
Rektor	Dekan der Philosophischen Fakultät

Die Vorlesungen fallen in der Philosophischen Fakultät von 12–13 Uhr aus.

13 Inaugural lecture at the Goethe University on the topic of 'Knowledge and Interest'

14 Page from the manuscript of *Knowledge and Human Interests*: 'That we disavow reflection, that *is* positivism.'

I 2064. 18

Oct. 1 [1967]

Liebe Margarete, lieber Alexander, wir haben das jüdische Neujahrsfest im Park mitgefeiert als gehörten wir dazu: mit Luftballons, ...

15 ' ... black power, New Left, hippies': letter, dated 1 October 1967, sent from New York to Margarete and Alexander Mitscherlich.

16 In conversation with Rudolf Augstein in the late 1960s

17 At the refectory of Frankfurt University: Habermas speaking at the
students' and pupils' congress on 1 June 1968, criticizing the SDS, the
alliance of socialist German students.

18 Special offprint of the *Sechs Thesen über Taktik, Ziele und Situationsanalysen der oppositionellen Jugend* [Six theses on the tactics, aims and the situational analysis of the oppositional youth]: 'The fight is directed against a depoliticized public sphere within which will formation cannot take a democratic form.'

```
              demokratie im notstand
              aktionskomitee


theodor w. adorno. juergen habermas. alexander mitscherlich.
walter ruegg. siegfried unseld.
----------------------------------------------------------------


                                 frankfurt, den 25.mai 1968

sehr geehrte kollegen,
die notstandsgesetze werden voraussichtlich am kommenden
mittwoch und donnerstag vom bundestag in dritter lesung
verabschiedet. hier wird ein gesetz 'durchgepeitscht'
das grundrechte einschraenkt. es verbindet regelungen
fuer den aeusseren notstand, die wir bejahen, mit
regelungen fuer inneren notstand und spannungsfalls,
die unsere demokratische ordnung gefaehrden koennen,
und die tendentiell das grundgesetz aushoelen. diese
notstandsverfassung kann durch ihre  blosse existenz
dazu fuehren die buerger einzuschuechtern.
deshalb fordern wir schriftsteller, professoren,
kuenstler, publizisten und verleger auf zu einer


              kundgebung demokratie
              im notstand.


wir wollen unsere argumente gegen teile der gesetzgebung
noch einmal vortragen und unsere entschlossenheit be-
kunden, in zukunft alles zu tun, damit diese gefaehr-
lichen gesetze niemals als instrument der unterdrueck-
kung anwendung finden koennen.
```

19 Resistance at the time of the first Great Coalition: a call to attend the
Kundgebung Demokratie im Notstand [Rally about democracy in a state
of emergency] at the broadcasting studio of Hessischer Rundfunk

20 'Homage to the architectural language of the avant-garde of classical modernism': the private home of the Habermas family in Starnberg, designed by Christoph Sattler, viewed from the side

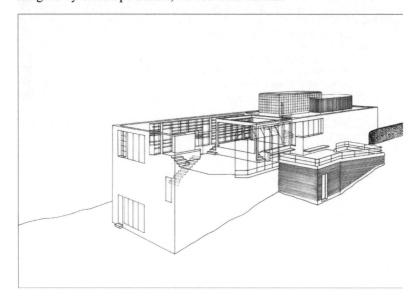

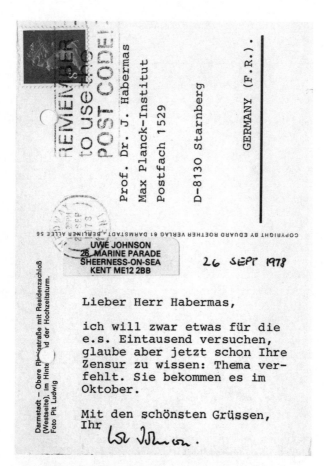

REMEMBER
to use the
POST CODE!

Prof. Dr. J. Habermas
Max Planck-Institut
Postfach 1529

D-8130 Starnberg

GERMANY (F.R.).

UWE JOHNSON
26 MARINE PARADE
SHEERNESS-ON-SEA
KENT ME12 2BB

26 SEPT 1978

Darmstadt – Obere R̶i̶n̶gstraße mit Residenzschloß
(Westseite), im Hinte̶r̶̶d̶ der Hochzeitsturm.
Foto Pit Ludwig

Lieber Herr Habermas,

ich will zwar etwas für die
e.s. Eintausend versuchen,
glaube aber jetzt schon Ihre
Zensur zu wissen: Thema ver-
fehlt. Sie bekommen es im
Oktober.

Mit den schönsten Grüssen,
Ihr

21 'Off-topic': postcard from Uwe Johnson
[The text of the postcard reads: 'Dear Mr Habermas,
I intend to try to write something for the e.s. one
thousand, but think I know already which mark you
will award it: off-topic. You will receive it in October.
With best wishes, your U. J.]

Stichworte zur

›Geistigen Situation der Zeit‹

1. Band: Nation und Republik

edition suhrkamp

SV

22 'e.s. one thousand': *Stichworte zur 'Geistigen Situation der Zeit'* [Notes on the intellectual situation of the time]

23 Siegfried Unseld with Ute and Jürgen Habermas, probably in the winter of 1977–8

24 Max Frisch, Hildegard Unseld, Jürgen Habermas, Martin Walser and Ute Habermas in early June 1977 in Nußdorf am Bodensee, watching the returning swimmer, Siegfried Unseld

25 Award ceremony of the Theodor W. Adorno Prize at the Paulskirche in Frankfurt am Main in 1980; to the left of the laureate is Walter Wallmann, then lord mayor of Frankfurt.

Jürgen Habermas
Theorie des
kommunikativen
Handelns
Band 1
Handlungsrationalität
und gesellschaftliche
Rationalisierung
Suhrkamp

Jürgen Habermas
Theorie des
kommunikativen
Handelns
Band 2
Zur Kritik der
funktionalistischen Vernunft
Suhrkamp

26 The magnum opus

27 'I would very much like to say something on the, if you like, elementary role of my wife; but, whatever I would say, it would not pass the threshold of domestic censorship.' Mr and Mrs Habermas on a visit to Switzerland in the spring of 1990

Die Linke und die Revolutionen
in Osteuropa und der DDR

Jürgen Habermas

Foto: Isolde Ohlbaum

Die revolutionären Vorgänge in der DDR, in Mittel- und
Osteuropa halten uns in Atem, während der anfängliche
Enthusiasmus eher Furcht und Skepsis gewichen ist.
Die Ereignisse verändern die internationale und die
innerdeutsche Szene beinahe täglich. Aber die nachholende
Revolution wirft kein neues Licht auf unsere *alten* Probleme.

Die nachholende
Revolution

Bisher nicht angeboten. Erscheint im Mai 1990.
edition suhrkamp 1663. 240 Seiten. DM 14,-

edition suhrkamp

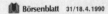

28 Notification of the publication of edition suhrkamp 1663: *Die
nachholende Revolution* [The belated revolution] in the *Börsenblatt* (18
April 1990)

31 Habermas receives the Peace Prize of German Publishers and Booksellers on 14 October 2001 in the Paulskirche in Frankfurt; the speech honouring Habermas was given by Jan Philipp Reemtsma.

29 'Three elderly gentlemen constitute a self-referential and closed
system ...': the laureates of the Hessischer Kulturpreis 1999 – Jürgen
Habermas, Siegfried Unseld and Marcel Reich-Ranicki

30 With Jacques Derrida in Lecture Hall VI of Goethe University
(23 June 2000)

32 An oeuvre travels the world.

33 On the eve of Habermas's eightieth birthday: Alexander Kluge gives
the official speech in the German National Library at the opening of the
exhibition '… die Lava des Gedanken im Fluß' [The lava of thought in
flow …].

34 Starnberg 1999: the painting in the background, titled *Wiesengrund*, is by Günter Fruhtrunk.

work cut out for them in trying to win support for the deployment, not only within their own parties but also among the wider German public.[25] At the Greens' special party convention on Kosovo in Bielefeld, paint was thrown at Joschka Fischer; within the SPD, opposition came from Oskar Lafontaine and representatives of the party's left, as well as from former chancellor Helmut Schmidt. And the public was divided, too. The problem was that NATO, and thus also the Bundeswehr, went into the mission without a mandate from the UN Security Council. In a television address on 24 March 1999, Gerhard Schröder sought to justify the operation, which he said was not a war but a humanitarian intervention.

A little over three weeks later, on 29 April 1999, a contribution by Habermas appeared in large format on the front page of *Die Zeit*. The title was 'Bestialität und Humanität: Ein Krieg an der Grenze von Recht und Moral' [Bestiality and Humanity: a war on the border between law and morality]. The play on Carl Schmitt's cynical formula 'humanity, bestiality' was, of course, intentional.[26] However, when he published this intervention as part of his *Kleine Politische Schriften IX* [Short political writings IX] in 2001, he chose another title: 'From Power Politics to Cosmopolitan Society'.

Habermas, who had recently received the Theodor Heuss Prize for his contributions to the development of political culture, began by noting with relief that the participation of the Bundeswehr in a war had not triggered any superpower fantasies in Germany: 'During the Gulf War, the rhetoric of national emergency and invo-cations of state pathos, of dignity, tragedy, and manly courage were still being marshalled against a vociferous peace movement. Not much remains of either this time. . . . No special German path or consciousness.'[27] He then went on to mention possible reasons to oppose the military operation: the lack of diplomatic skill which left military intervention as the only option, the assumed utility of the military strikes, and the political goals, which stood in no propor-tionate relation to the means being employed. Finally, he revealed his own position, interpreting the war purely from the perspective of legal philosophy – i.e., as a 'significant advance on the road from classical international law between states to the cosmopolitan law of a society of world citizens'. To the extent that such a society could be realized, 'violations of human rights would [not] be judged and combated immediately in accordance with moral standards; instead they would be persecuted like criminal acts within national legal systems.'[28]

Habermas made a subtle distinction between two types of paci-fism: a pacifism based on conviction [*Gesinnung*] and a pacifism based on law. This allowed him to consider the military interven-tions, which were devastating for the affected populations, in the light of an 'under-institutionalization of cosmopolitan law'.[29] As soon as this deficit is removed, the world would no longer need a power to play 'the role of hegemonic guarantor of global order'. Looking ahead, he anticipated a 'cosmopolitan order, beyond the divisions of the current military conflict', which he saw as the result of 'a learning process to be mastered collectively'. The interventions, which were in his view peacemaking operations, were justified because they represented a necessary act on the way towards the juridification of international relations within a cosmopolitan order and served to protect a persecuted minority and prevent a 'murderous ethno-nationalism'.[30] At the end of this process, during which the state of nature between states, so to speak, is transformed into a legal state – i.e., the legal state of cosmopolitanism – Habermas envisaged not a world state with a world government but, rather, a security council and an international criminal court, a general assembly of government representatives from all states and a representation of citizens of the world. And: 'Only when human rights have found their proper "place" in a global democratic constitutional order, analogous to that of the basic rights in our national constitutions, will we be able to assume that the addressees of these rights can also regard themselves as their authors at the global level.'[31]

Habermas's comments on Kosovo irritated many and were met with consternation even from his son Tilmann and some close friends. War as a necessary means to advance cosmopolitanism? Habermas faced an immense amount of criticism. There were letters to the editor in the following edition of *Die Zeit*.[32] In two short articles in the *Frankfurter Allgemeine Zeitung* of 4 May and 9 June, Christian Geyer expressed his astonishment at the fact that Habermas had not placed more emphasis on the lack of a UN endorsement of the aerial bombardments. In *Die Tageszeitung* of 5 May, Christian Semler criticized the 'abstract-normative' character of Habermas's arguments and the absence of any concrete suggestions about how air strikes might be avoided in the future. Habermas's *peers* reacted even more bitterly.* The legal philosopher Reinhard Merkel, for instance, wrote: 'This war is illegal, illegitimate and, despite its high moral aims, morally reprehensible' (*Die Zeit*, 12 May 1999). He saw the aerial attacks as 'beyond any possible justification' because 'the "cosmopolitan right" to a homeland of the one is maintained by destroying the right to life of the other!' The criticism from the jurist Dieter Simon in the *Frankfurter Allgemeine Zeitung* of 18 June 1999 was even more polemical. Habermas, he claimed, wanted to enforce the envisaged cosmopolitan state and the establishment of human rights as subjective rights – 'if necessary with the help of

---

* 'Peers' in English in the original.

bombs'. His polemic culminated in the final sentence: 'The missionary zeal of enlightenment universalism optimistically closes its eyes
before the "whole enormity of war, the crime of all crimes" (Thomas
Bernhard).'*

With a keen, analytic focus, the legal scholar Thomas Blanke
examined whether Habermas's discourse theory passes the test of its
application in public debates. He concluded that it is understandable that Habermas does not put international law at the centre of
his argument, because it stands in a tense relationship with human
rights and there are therefore good reasons for overcoming it in its
present form. However, Blanke rejects the legalistic way envisaged
by Habermas as unrealistic.[33]

As might have been expected, there was a storm of criticism from
the field of peace research. Lutz Schrader noted that Habermas
entirely ignored the political mistakes that were made and observed a
striking convergence between the foreign policies of the Red–Green
federal government and the perspective adopted by Habermas.
Schrader did not mention it explicitly, but it was no secret that
Fischer and Habermas had known and been close to each other
for some time. Habermas, Schrader said, gave too much credit to
NATO's war propaganda, to the government and to the media, and
not enough to the concerns expressed in large parts of the peace
movement and wider civil society. And he had not said a word
about the consequences of the war, even though a military deployment, despite being sold as an act of civilization, was bringing about
'a dramatic return to international anarchy'.[34] Schrader asked: 'Is
he just doing his bit to make sure that the coalition doesn't collapse
over the question of the war?'[35]

Literary authors also spoke out: György Konrád, a personal
acquaintance of Habermas, wrote at the end of a long article in the
Frankfurter Allgemeine Zeitung (30 April 1999): 'Who protects us
from our own errors, from the demons which lead our own power
into temptation?' And Peter Handke attacked the philosopher in
the *Süddeutsche Zeitung* (18 May 1999) as an apologist for wanton
violence.

Habermas was thus facing strong headwinds. In particular, they were coming from his own 'ideological community'
['*Gesinnungsgemeinschaft*']. There is a lot of evidence to suggest that
he revised his judgement on the war in Kosovo very quickly. In his
short reply to Handke, which appeared in the very same edition of
the paper, he admitted: 'In the meantime, the utility and propor-
tionality of the means being employed has become so questionable

---

* The Bernhard quotation is from a volume of his autobiography: 'An Indication of the
Cause', in *Gathering Evidence*, trans. David McLintock, London, 2003, pp. 75–141; here:
p. 109.

that I consider the demand of the Green Party for a temporary ceasefire reasonable.' However, he would hold on to his legal philosophical arguments, even if he admitted that the '[a]spects of the operation that had been problematic from the beginning – the paper-thin legitimacy according to international law, the disproportionate use of military force and the unclear political aims – had been thrown into even sharper relief by the subsequent course of events.' 'Nevertheless', Habermas said, 'I still defend the Kantian perspective of a transition from international to cosmopolitan law from which I sought to justify the intervention in principle at the time.'[36] That he maintained this position is clear from an interview conducted by Eduardo Mendieta in November 2003 – i.e., after the terror attacks of 9/11 and in the light of the 'war on terror' in Afghanistan and Iraq.[37]

Criticizing US policy. When the USA became the victim of several spectacular terrorist attacks on 11 September 2001, the world – which watched the events unfold live on television – was in shock. Immediately after the attacks, there was an almost global outpouring of solidarity with the Americans, including from Germany. This changed very quickly, however, once the Bush administration declared the 'war on terror' and made first Afghanistan and later Iraq its targets.

As chance would have it, the Börsenverein des Deutschen Buchhandels* awarded Habermas its Peace Prize that very same year. The award ceremony at the Paulskirche in Frankfurt on 14 October 2001, which took place in the shadow of the New York attacks and also, by then, the military intervention in Afghanistan, was accompanied by unusually tight security and demonstrations by opponents of the war. After a laudatory speech by Jan Philipp Reemtsma (upon Habermas's request), Habermas gave his acceptance speech, which was published the following day in the *Frankfurter Allgemeine Zeitung*, and the day after that in the *Frankfurter Rundschau*: 'When restricted in the choice of one's subject by the depressing current events, one is severely tempted to compete with the John Waynes among us intellectuals to see who is the fastest shot.' He resisted this temptation insofar as he did not comment on the war in Afghanistan directly but only warned against the 'language of retaliation'. He then philosophically examined the fraught relationship between faith and knowledge in post-secular societies, bearing in mind that 'the suicidal murderers who made living bombs of civil aircraft, directing them against the capitalist citadels of Western civilization, were motivated by religious

---

* The Association of German Book Sellers and Publishers, based in Frankfurt.

beliefs.'* He would later comment directly on the third war in the Gulf, the Iraq War, and would partly revise his attitude towards military operations.

After Saddam Hussein's Iraqi government failed to comply with the UN Security Council resolution demanding that they destroy their weapons of mass destruction (which, as we now know, did not exist), President Bush announced in his January 2002 State of the Union address that he would take strong action against Iraq – which, together with North Korea and Iran, formed what he dubbed the 'axis of evil'; as the world would find out a year later, he was prepared to do so even without a mandate from the Security Council. The Bush doctrine was for the United States to use pre-emptive strikes to defeat potential aggressors before they could attack. The restrained reactions of France and Germany, who did not participate in the military operations carried out by the 'coalition of the willing', led US Secretary of Defense Donald Rumsfeld to make derogatory remarks about 'old Europe'. As one might have expected, 'old Europe' reacted to this insult with indignation. Habermas too was irritated and published a short article in the *Frankfurter Allgemeine Zeitung* (24 January 2003) in which he defended 'old Europe' as, in fact, progressive and new, if looked at from the perspective of how democratic forms of life had established themselves there (that is, here) – wholly in accordance with the American ideals of the eighteenth century. In today's Europe, he wrote, 'a normative kind of interpretation has won out over old mentalities – over the hard-boiled cynicism of those practising realpolitik, over the conservative cultural criticism of sensitive minds [*der Feinsinnigen*], and over the anthropological pessimism of those who placed their hopes in violence and powerful institutions.' The fact that 'old Europe' sided with the human rights policies of the United Nations was to the moral credit of those states, Habermas wrote.

Before ground troops entered Iraq as part of Operation Iraqi Freedom, massive demonstrations in cities all over the world took place on 15 February, and Habermas was among the demonstrators.

> These demonstrations were not an answer to the attack of 11 September, which immediately inspired impressive displays of solidarity among Europeans. Rather, the demonstrations gave voice to the impotent, infuriated outrage of a highly diverse mass of citizens, many of whom had never before taken to the streets. The anti-war appeal

---

* An English translation of the speech, 'Faith and Knowledge', is appended to *The Future of Human Nature*, Cambridge, 2003, pp. 101–15; here: pp. 101f.

was directed unambiguously against the mendacious and illegal policies of certain of the allied governments. I regard this mass protest as no more 'anti-American' than our Vietnam protests were in their day . . .. So I was glad that my friend Richard Rorty spontaneously joined in our initiative of May 31 with an article . . .[38]

Habermas here referred to a statement the American philosopher published in the *Süddeutsche Zeitung* of 31 May 2003, in which he welcomed the manifesto published jointly by Derrida and Habermas on the same day and demanded the formation of a unified core Europe as a counterweight to the hegemonic unilaterism of the USA.[39] A month after the invasion of Iraq by American and British troops, Habermas published another essay, again in the *Frankfurter Allgemeine Zeitung*, in which he expressed his feelings about the military intervention and the toppling of Saddam Hussein. The brutal facticity of an illegal war was shocking, but the liberation of a country from a dictator, he said, was a relief. He tore to shreds the political ambition of a new American world order, as the United States ignored UN prohibition on wars of aggression – this prohibition being, for Habermas, an important 'step on the way toward a cosmopolitan legal order'. His final judgement with regard to the USA was damning: '[t]he normative authority of the United States of America lies in ruins.'[40] He then returned to the war in Kosovo, which he had once thought justified despite many commentators judging it to be in contravention of international law:

Nor does a comparison with the intervention in Kosovo provide any mitigation. Granted, authorization by the Security Council was not forthcoming in this case either. But three circumstances of that intervention offered legitimation after the fact: first, the aim of preventing ethnic cleansing, which was known at the time to be taking place; second, the *erga omnes* provision in international law which mandates intervention to provide emergency aid in such cases; and finally, the undisputed democratic and constitutional character of all the states participating in the vicarious military coalition. Today, by contrast, the normative disagreement is dividing the West itself.[41]

The critical analysis of the Bush doctrine and its rigorous implementation after 9/11 led Habermas to a critique of the unilateralism of American plans for a new global political order. The plans, he argued, were bound to fail: it is folly to want to steer a complex global society centrally. Apart from that, the effects of hegemonic policies based on the police, the military and secret services are dangerous, as they undermine the foundations of the state under the rule of law. Habermas summarized his counter-arguments as follows:

Precisely the universalistic core of democracy and human rights forbids their unilateral imposition at gunpoint. The universal validity claim which binds the West to its 'basic political values', that is, to the procedure of democratic self-determination and the vocabulary of human rights, must not be confused with the imperialist claim that the political form of life and the culture of a particular democracy – even the oldest one – is exemplary for all societies.[42]

For this criticism, some people accused Habermas of anti-Americanism,[43] which is ironic given that he held as sacrosanct the integration into the West since the era of Adenauer, regularly taught at American universities, had lived in the country, and held the tradition of America's democratic constitution as exemplary. Years later, Joschka Fischer still saw his 'I am not convinced' attitude confirmed by Habermas* and defended him against this accusation: 'When a convinced Westerner . . ., a friend of and expert on the liberal America – I intentionally say: the *liberal* America – such as Jürgen Habermas, distances himself so energetically from the US, then this confirms our rejection of the course taken by America towards the war in Iraq.'[44] Habermas himself sees his criticism as one that 'measures itself against the better traditions of the United States itself'.[45] He has not forgotten that his generation 'acquired their faith in the civilizing power of international law from the Americans who founded the United Nations'.[46] His hope is that 'the US once again positions itself at the forefront as the driving force of the movement' that will, through the juridification of international relations, establish the cosmopolitan order which he sees as the democratic alternative for the future. From this perspective, he views anti-Americanism as a problematic phenomenon: 'In Germany, it has always allied itself with the most reactionary movements.' Europeans seeking legitimately to criticize Washington need to ally themselves with internal American opposition. 'If we can point to a protest movement within the United States itself, the counter-productive charge of anti-Americanism leveled against us also loses its force.'[47]

---

* 'I am not convinced' in English in the original. At a security conference in Munich in 2003, Fischer deviated from the prepared German speech and, turning directly to Rumsfeld, explained in English that, if you want to go to war, you must make a case for it on the basis of reasons in which you actually believe. And, since he did not believe in the reasons given, he could not defend the decision vis-à-vis the public. In the course of his emphatic explanation, he said: 'Excuse me, I am not convinced', an impromptu translation of a common rhetorical phrase in German: 'Es tut mir leid, aber . . .', which usually comes up at a point in a discussion where the spade turns and disagreement cannot be overcome.

The asylum debate

I can recall no other issue that has been so zealously dragged out and kept alive in the public media and yet, at the same time, has been made so obscure and unrecognizable regarding what is truly at stake. Behind the smoke screen of this deceitful asylum debate, the mentality of the old Federal Republic has changed more profoundly and more rapidly in the last quarter of 1992 than it did in the preceding fifteen years.[48]

Criticizing the chauvinism of affluence. Until 30 June 1993, an unlimited right to asylum, to which any individual could appeal, was in force in the Federal Republic of Germany. This right made it the duty of the state to grant asylum to those who were politically persecuted. This exceptionally liberal asylum regime had been part of the Basic Law since 1949: an immediate reaction on the part of the members of the parliamentary council to the experience – for some, the first-hand experience – of the deprivation of rights and the persecution during the Nazi era. But it also acknowledged the fact that Germany had become a country of immigration from the end of the nineteenth century onwards. During the years of the economic miracle, policies were in place to encourage immigration; but in 1973, because of the economic crisis and the growing number of unemployed people, the further employment of 'guest workers' was halted. From the mid-1980s onwards, the number of foreigners living in Germany began to fall and the number of refugees from countries where civil wars were raging was on the rise. 'This', writes Hans-Ulrich Wehler, 'made the multi-ethnic character of some major cities more pronounced; these cities became hotspots for immigration.'[49] Policies on foreigners and asylum-seekers increasingly became a focus of controversy and political debate during this time, not least because, after the national elections of 1987, the CDU/CSU made the question of asylum a recurring theme. These debates intensified further after the elections of 1990, when, with the support of the Springer press, the CDU/CSU pushed for a change in the Basic Law. Arnulf Baring, for instance, who at the time was a professor of contemporary history and international relations at the Free University in Berlin, demanded the immediate abolition of the right to asylum because 'our soft social security legislation has become a magnet which attracts the poor from around the globe' (*Bild*, 13 October 1990). In this climate, right-wing parties were able to achieve a string of successes in regional state elections, and the number of violent xenophobic acts rose rapidly. In early 1990, there was a spate of racist incidents – especially, if not exclusively, in the 'new federal states'. The riots in Hoyerswerda in September 1991 and in Rostock-Lichtenhagen in August 1992 became infamous, even outside Germany.[50] Against this background, the CDU/CSU, SPD and FDP negotiated an agreement on asylum law, which significantly limited the fundamental right to asylum. The agreement stipulated that refugees who entered Germany via a third country considered to be safe could not appeal to the fundamental right to asylum. The necessary change to the Basic Law was passed with the required two-thirds majority by the German parliament on 6 December 1992 and came into force in mid-1993. An intense debate occurred around this vote; Habermas was, of course, involved in the debate.

The first time Habermas commented on the matter was in November 1992. In an interview in the Italian journal *L'Unità*, founded by Antonio Gramsci, he spoke out in favour of retaining a liberal immigration policy in Germany as a matter of principle and condemned any attempt at making foreigners themselves responsible for xenophobia and sealing Germany off from immigration. On 14 November, the *Frankfurter Allgemeine Zeitung* published a short note on the interview, with a remark from Habermas about the threat of a right-wing turn in German politics. He elaborated on his fears in an article in *Die Zeit* on 11 December – i.e., shortly after the parliamentary vote had taken place. Under the title 'Die zweite Lebenslüge der Bundesrepublik' [The second fundamental self-deception of the Federal Republic], he explicitly attacked the 'hypocritical asylum debate' that the parties had used in order to distract 'from the real problems of a botched unification process'. Habermas condemned the reactions to the burning of asylum-seekers' homes and the continuing acts of violence carried out by right-wing extremists as entirely inadequate. Instead of mourning for the victims, there was concern over Germany's reputation abroad. It is high time, he said, that the political parties took note of the fact that Germany cannot be a fortress; the transformation into a country of immigration had been well established. The predominant 'mentality of chauvinistic affluence' stood in the way of a rational solution.

For all that, Habermas conceded, there were still mass protests against xenophobia in German cities, which he welcomed as defending 'the standards of civilized social intercourse which has been rehearsed in the old Federal Republic and has become something that can be more or less taken for granted. The population is better than their politicians and spokespersons.'[51] When 350,000 people took to the streets of Berlin on 8 November 1992 in protest at the planned change to the Basic Law, Habermas was among them.[52] More of his published interventions attest to the seriousness with which he viewed the matter. There was, for instance, an article in *Die Zeit* of 28 May 1993, which took up a whole page, in which – following on from a lecture on the same topic in Paris on

14 January[53] – he again discussed immigration policy and the compromise over the asylum law.[54] At the beginning of this article, 'Die Festung Europa und das neue Deutschland' [Fortress Europe and the new Germany], he explored the extent to which a nation of citizens has the right to self-determination and to affirm its own identity and reached the conclusion that the democratic state under the rule of law is authorized to preserve the integrity of its citizens' form of life by requiring that immigrants assimilate.

Habermas had two levels of assimilation in mind: one concerns the agreement with the constitutional principles of the receiving country; the other relates to the preparedness for further acculturation to the practical mode of life within society. However, the state may demand only political assimilation, not the surrender of the immigrants' cultural form of life. Habermas is clear that integration into the Rechtsstaat rules out immigration from fundamentalist cultures. However, any demands for a kind of integration above and beyond the requirement to respect the principles of democratic culture would be excessive; the 'self-affirmation of the cultural form of life dominant in the country' is the wrong kind of touchstone. It is likely, he said, that an open polity of this kind will gradually change as a result of immigration. However, this also involves a broadening of horizons, or a change in the 'context in which the citizens' ethical-political discourses aiming at reaching self-understanding take place'.[55]

On the question of who has a right to immigrate, Habermas emphasized the general moral duty to provide assistance, which spontaneously emerges from the continuously growing interdependencies within global society. From these interdependencies follows a fundamental 'moral obligation for having a liberal immigration policy that opens one's own society to immigrants and regulates the flow of immigration in relation to existing capacities.'[56] At that point in time, European societies, in his view, were still far from having reached the limit of this capacity.

From these considerations, it was only a small step to the rejection of the compromise on asylum which, according to Habermas, ignored the difference between political asylum and poverty-driven migration and shirked Europe's responsibility towards refugees from impoverished regions of the world. The compromise on asylum, he said, was also influenced by the 'desire for normalization of those who did not want to accept the caesura of 1945'[57] – an allusion not only to the mood in the new federal states but also to certain sections of the old Federal Republic. The only antidote to this 'brewing revisionism', as Habermas saw it, was the Federal Republic's commitment to its integration into the West, which, from the very beginning, meant a break with old German traditions:

The orientation of the old Federal Republic to the West pointed the way for a shift in mentality that affected broad segments of the public after the youth revolt of 1968 under the favourable conditions of an affluent society, a shift that made it possible for democracy and the constitutional state *to take* political and cultural *root* in German soil for the first time.[58]

Habermas adopted a similar tone in an essay published in *Der Spiegel* under the title 'Gelähmte Politik' [Paralyzed politics]. It targeted the inability of the political class to react appropriately to accumulating social problems such as integration, violent crime, unemployment, and the ecological limits of economic growth. As a consequence, citizens abstain from voting in elections and disillusionment with politics increases. It was therefore necessary to 'set the entangled mobile of public communication . . . into motion in such a way that relevant themes and contributions, suitable definitions of the problems and suggestions for solutions can float freely and enter into public consciousness.' An essential part of this is 'the awareness that the basis of our right to citizenship must be altered from the principle of descent to the territorial principle, if only because it would enable the naturalization (and the possibility of dual citizenship) for those foreigners who are already residents.' In Western Europe, multiculturalism, he wrote, is not an option but a necessity. The classical nation-state is not able to face the new challenges of the twenty-first century.[59]

A memorial to the murdered Jews

The goal of the memorial is to challenge future generations to take a stand, to take a stance on what the memorial expresses, what Auschwitz means for German identity a half century after the event.[60]

The politics of the past and memory culture. The 'decision on the German capital' involved a protracted, confused and extremely controversial debate which culminated in the decision to move the seat of the German government to Berlin, which had already been declared the capital of the united Germany as part of the Unification Treaty of 1990. Part of the intense parliamentary debates was the question of how the memory of German history could be kept alive at the new place of government and parliament.[61] At a panel discussion in 1988, the publicist and television journalist Lea Rosh had already asked how the rupture of civilization, the murdered Jews of Europe, might be remembered in the form of a memorial. She had pleaded for the erection of a 'memorial as a visible confession of the deed' [*sichtbares Bekenntnis zur Tat*]. The same month, Rosh, together with Eberhard Jäckel, took the initiative and petitioned for the construction of a memorial, either on the former grounds of the Gestapo in the Kreuzberg area of Berlin or north of the former Reich chancellery on what had been the ministers' gardens in the Third Reich. Willy Brandt was the first to sign the appeal of the sponsors, who then, after some toing and froing that went on until spring 1992, eventually gained the support of the federal government and Chancellor Helmut Kohl. For Habermas, this was 'the first time in the 50-year history of the Federal Republic that a federal vote for such a manifestly future-oriented sign of a purified German collective identity has moved into the realm of possibility.'[62]

By mid-1995, the first proposals for the memorial had been received, and the city council, the state and the sponsors agreed on a design by Christine Jackob-Marks. Helmut Kohl, however, did not agree, and as a consequence a second, time-consuming competition had to be initiated. In the course of the passionate controversies about the project and the various proposals, a design developed jointly by the internationally renowned architect Peter Eisenman and the artist Richard Serra emerged as the favourite. Still, though, discussions around their design continued, and it had to be modified several times upon the request of various parties, including the federal government. Because of these changes, Serra withdrew from the project in 1998. In the same year, the federal government, a coalition of the SPD and the Greens, decreed that the German parliament should have the final word on the memorial. After several hearings and still further exhibitions of proposals, in June 1999 the parliament voted with a large majority for a 'memorial to the murdered Jews' on the basis of Eisenman's design: a 'field of stelae' at the historical centre of Berlin on an area of 19,000 square metres near the Brandenburg Gate. This memorial, which would cost about 30 million euros, was to be accompanied by a 'place of information' about the victims. On 10 May 2005, the memorial and the place of information were opened to the public in the presence of 1,200 guests from Germany and abroad.

Even though the 'politics of the past' is an exceptionally important topic for Habermas, he intervened only once in the gruelling decision-making process. The article 'The Finger of Blame: The Germans and Their Memorial', which appeared on 31 March 1999 in *Die Zeit*,[63] is the most important document about his attitude towards the genocide of the European Jews and on the question of how the Germans should deal with it today[64] – about which more later.

Rift with Martin Walser. Habermas wrote the article of March 1999 in part to vent his anger about the acceptance speech given by his former friend Martin Walser on 11 October 1998 on receiving the Peace Prize of the Association of German Book Sellers and Publishers in the Paulskirche in Frankfurt. What was going on?

In his address 'Experiences While Composing a Sunday Speech', the literary author confessed to the crowd of assembled political and cultural notables that he was irritated by the routines of remembrance concerning the Holocaust. 'Twenty times, easily', he said,

> I have averted my eyes from the worst filmed sequences of concentration camps. No serious person denies Auschwitz; no person who is still of sound mind quibbles about the horror of Auschwitz; but when this past is held up to me every day in the media, I notice that something in me rebels against this unceasing presentation of our disgrace.[65]

And he went even further, claiming of a particular group of intellectuals that they instrumentalize 'our disgrace'.* In this context, he also quoted verbatim from 'Die zweite Lebenslüge der Bundesrepublik: Wir sind wieder "normal" geworden' [The second lifelong delusion of the Federal Republic: we have become 'normal' again], Habermas's article published in 1992 in *Die Zeit*.[66] According to Walser, the article's charge that the Germans lack sensibility regarding the monstrosity of their own past, the genocide committed by the Nazis, serves only to harm, self-harm, a population confronted 'incessantly' with the 'disgrace' of National Socialism. Walser's blanket description for the 'intellectuals' (the term, incidentally, he uses most frequently in the speech) was 'warriors of conscience led by vanity', 'soldiers of public opinion' who, 'with moral pistol extended, force the writer into the service of opinion'. And he asked: 'Could it be that in doing so the intellectuals who hold this disgrace up before us fall prey to the illusion for a moment that, because they have laboured once more in the grim service of memory, they have relieved their own guilt somewhat, that they are even for a moment closer to the victims than to the perpetrators?' For Walser, what was crucial was the reconciliation of the Germans with their history – a rejection of moral responsibility. He said the planned Holocaust memorial would involve 'paving over the centre of our capital to create a nightmare the size of a football field', calling it a 'monumentalization of our disgrace'. Walser, then, came out emphatically against 'the erection of a monumental place of remembrance'.[67]

Habermas was not present at the event itself, as he was still in the USA, at Northwestern University in Evanston, where, between 1994

---

* The passage runs: '. . . I am almost happy when I believe I can discover that often the motive is no longer keeping the memory alive, or the impermissibility of forgetting, but rather the exploitation of our disgrace for present purposes. Always good and honourable purposes – but still exploitation.' Walser (2008), 'Experiences while Composing a Sunday Speech: The Peace Prize Speech (1998)', p. 90.

and 2006, he regularly spent six weeks at a time as a visiting professor.[68] But Walser's speech in the packed Paulskirche was greeted with applause from the thousand-strong crowd. Only Friedrich Schorlemmer, a Protestant theologian and civil rights activist in the GDR, and Ignatz Bubis, the chairman of the Central Council of Jews in Germany, did not applaud.[69] Bubis, whose father, brother and sister were killed by the Nazis, accused Walser of 'intellectual arson'. Walser's speech, he said, was an attempt to repress the terrible side of German history and extinguish the memory of it in order to be able to refer once again to a past unalloyed by such horrors.[70] Walser's reference to the 'moral cudgel Auschwitz' led in short order to an intense media dispute. The provocations of the historian Heinrich August Winkler, in particular, reverberated through the debate: his article of 4 August in *Der Spiegel* – presumably endorsed by the paper's editor Rudolf Augstein[71] – attributed a 'fixation with the Holocaust' and a 'negative nationalism' to left-wing intellectuals. And Augstein himself wrote on 3 November 1998 in *Der Spiegel*:

> Now in the centre of the recently recovered capital of Berlin, a memorial is supposed to be erected as a reminder of our perpetual shame. Such a way of dealing with the past would be alien to other nations. A suspicion arises that this memorial of shame is directed against the capital and the new Germany that is forming in Berlin. However, even if the muscles flex, no one will dare keep the centre of Berlin free of such a monstrosity, mindful of the New York press and the sharks in lawyers' suits.

In autumn of the same year, the 'Walser–Bubis' debate led to a heated dispute between Klaus von Dohnányi, Richard von Weizsäcker, Reinhard Baumgart, Micha Brumlik and others, which played out mostly in the pages of the *Frankfurter Allgemeine Zeitung* – moderated, in effect, by Frank Schirrmacher. Habermas did not immediately or directly enter into the controversy, but in his *Die Zeit* article on the memorial, mentioned above, he returned to Walser's spectacular remarks and the waves they had caused in the media. He called them 'gasses from an undigested past which emanate periodically from the stomach of the Federal Republic' from which public political discussion 'only managed to free itself . . . by virtue of the civil courage – this is what is disturbing – of a prominent Jew.'[72] And he continued: 'Anyone who views Auschwitz as "our shame" is more interested in the image others have of us than in the image German citizens retrospectively form of themselves in view of the breakdown in civilization, in order to be able to look each other in the face and show each other respect.'[73]

The polemical tone at the outset of the article indicates that the friendship between Habermas and Walser had definitely been damaged. The rift is even more apparent in another statement the philosopher made on the events of autumn 1998: 'Recently, even respected members of the political and social elite have been making a public display of their inability to distinguish between what belongs in the Paulskirche and what belongs on the analyst's couch. On live television, they accord a writer who no longer wants to be reminded of "our shame" a standing ovation.'[74]

The relationship between Walser and Habermas had been a very close one for a long time. It began in the mid-1960s after they were introduced by Hilde and Sigfried Unseld. Their families, including the daughters, became friends, and they would often visit one another and do things together, for instance in 1976 during a stay in the USA at Haverford and West Virginia.[75] Three years before Walser's 'Sunday speech', however, he had already provoked Habermas's ire. When the Romance scholar Victor Klemperer was posthumously awarded the Hans and Sophie Scholl Prize for his diaries,* Walser, who had promoted the publication of the diaries, gave a speech in honour of Klemperer at the main auditorium of the Ludwig Maximilian University in Munich on 27 November 1995; Habermas was in attendance. 'He who sees everything as a path that can lead only to Auschwitz', Walser said, 'turns the German–Jewish relation into a catastrophe of fate that would have happened under any circumstances. That appears absurd to me. And, quite apart from being absurd, it would mean that there could be no German–Jewish flourishing in the present and future.'[76] Habermas, by contrast, sympathized with the attitude of Gershom Scholem, who had 'raised awareness of the political and social downsides of a carelessly invoked German–Jewish symbiosis'.[77] According to Walser's biographer Jörg Magenau, it is very likely that, in this speech, 'the thematic field of the Paulskirche speech [had already been] ... prepared. The media-baiting emotive and provocative terms [medialen Reizworte] had been identified. Walser needed only to combine and apply them.'[78]

While listening to Walser's speech, Habermas already had a sense of its potentially explosive character. In a lecture published by the Frankfurter Rundschau in December 1995, 'Aufgeklärte Ratlosigkeit' [Enlightened perplexity], he took a position on the matter, without mentioning Walser by name – but the target was obvious nonetheless. The diaries of Victor Klemperer, Habermas explained, record,

---

* The diaries were published in English in three volumes, titled *I Shall Bear Witness (1933–1941)*, *To the Bitter End (1942–1945)* and *The Lesser Evil (1945–1959)*, in 1998, 1999 and 2003, respectively.

from the very first minute, the cold and bureaucratic process of exclusion, which proceeds step by step to the point of complete isolation and destruction – a process whose brutality any neighbour was able to watch. On the side of the one subjected to the process, who tries to take flight into the risky role of a diarist bearing witness, his notes reflect the disillusionment of the assimilated Jew, which progresses together with growing misery and leaves his illusory trust in German culture utterly disappointed. The fact that at the recent posthumous award of the Sophie and Hans Scholl Prize to Victor Klemperer this dimension was able to disappear behind the pompous and self-congratulatory celebration of an obscenely harmonized German-Jewish culture is a symptom of a change in consciousness. Since 1989, a reversal has taken place in the way the National Socialist period is being dealt with. Before then, public discourses needed first to break through a wall of silence. But now everyone garrulously partakes in the meta-discourse on the permissibility and character of that discussion. Thus, today, the process of coming to terms with the past suffocates in the blithely employed medium of public discourse. In this respect, the New Right has prevailed. It has successfully established a broad coalition reaching right into the features section of the *Frankfurter Allgemeine Zeitung*, and which in a rising *he goat song** denounces the 'resentful demagogy' of the 'professional copers [i.e., with the past]' as an excretion of 'political correctness'. If it is politically correct to deal with what the archives tell us in such a way that we do not hurt the victims and do not have to feel ashamed ourselves, then one wishes to know just what 'censorship' these rebels against political correctness want to be liberated from.[79]

Habermas, who was later unflatteringly parodied in Walser's controversial 2002 novel *Tod eines Kritikers* [The death of a critic],[80] was depressed about all this ill will in their relationship. A few years later, he and his wife stopped off in Nußdorf at Lake Constance while returning from their holidays in the South of France specifically to talk to Walser and try – for the sake of an old friendship, and despite all their differences – to rekindle a 'normal' relationship with him. But their attempt was in vain. Walser, who would many years later, in 2012, criticize what he called the 'tense atmosphere of having to be right',[81] intentionally avoided the visitors. And his wife, who usually tried to mediate, was not at home.

The complex enterprise of destruction as a whole   By the time Habermas spoke about the controversy over the Holocaust

---

* 'Anschwellender Bocksgesang' was the title of an essay by the writer Botho Strauß in *Der Spiegel* (8 February 1993). The title uses the literal translation of the Greek 'tragodia': tragos = he goat; and 'ode' = song.

memorial in his *Die Zeit* article at the end of March 1999, Walser's attitude towards the politics of the past played only a minor role. Something else now took centre stage: Habermas, despite all his agreements with the Red–Green coalition, criticized Gerhard Schröder, accusing his government of officially 'disposing of the past'. In his 'telegenic-trivializing fashion', the 'chancellor of the media', he wrote, succeeded in doing what Kohl, 'in his pompously historicizing fashion in Bitburg', had failed to achieve. Schröder 'does not give a hoot about anything normative . . . if it requires public argumentation and cannot be "got across" via a short appearance on a talk show.'[82]

However, such polemical sideswipes really feature only as asides in the text, which deals principally with the reasons why a monument in Berlin for the murdered Jews of Europe seems appropriate, even necessary. For Habermas, such a monument is on the one hand a symbol of self-critical remembrance and of the imperative 'Auschwitz: never again'. On the other hand, it expresses 'the will to abandon habits of thought embedded in the continuity of our own traditions that have led us astray'. A break with these continuities 'is the precondition for recovering our self-respect'. In that sense, it is not only the remembrance of the Jewish victims of German crimes that is at stake: 'With this memorial, the present generation of descendants of the perpetrators professes a political self-understanding into which is branded the deed – the crime against humanity committed and tolerated under the National Socialist regime – and *therewith* the anguish over the unspeakable crimes inflicted upon its victims, as a permanent source of disquiet and admonition.'[83]

Habermas sees those erecting the memorial as 'those citizens who find themselves as the direct heirs of a culture in which "that" was possible.' However, he considers the foundation of the memorial not just in a material sense but also in the sense in which such a memorial establishes a relationship 'to the perpetrators, to the victims, and to the victim's descendants'.[84] And he adds: 'How we retrospectively apportion blame and innocence . . . also reflects the norms in terms of which we currently express our respect for each other as citizens of this republic.'[85] Habermas also warns against instrumentalizing the remembrance of the victims, who can only be remembered for their own sake. A memorial stylized into a monument of shame through narcissistic self-reference, he says, destroys the 'value of the weak, indeed vain, force of anamnetic solidarity' – it is not the 'shame' that should disturb us but, rather, 'the rupture of civilization as such'.[86] And it could also not be the purpose of the memorial 'to elevate the Holocaust to the "founding myth of the Federal Republic"'. Rather, the memorial is the result of citizens seeking 'a symbolic expression of their political self-understanding which is essentially characterized by the historical reference to Auschwitz.'[87]

'The purpose of the memorial is to challenge future generations to take a stand. . . . In this way, the memorial [*Denkmal*] . . . becomes an admonition [*Mahnmal*].'[88]

Habermas explicitly welcomed the artistically abstract form of the design, writing: '[O]nly an uncompromising form of art can provide it with an appropriate language. Anyone who wants something more comfortable or more discursive has not grasped the meaning and the point of the project.'[89] The 'abstract, formal language of modern art . . . still provides the best protection against embarrassments and trivialization.'[90] Habermas also welcomed Eisenman's design. The envisaged field of stelae he described as a silent, 'vaguely troubling wave', which would not, however, fill visitors 'with awe in the manner of monumental art'.[91]

Habermas expected that not everyone would agree with the monument. But: 'If we really want such a memorial, then it must also be as a barometer for the sentiments we wish to overcome – otherwise we betray the project itself.'[92] Habermas considered it important that the monument should not draw attention to the victims in a reverential way. Objections against its abstractness raised by, for instance, Hermann Lübbe, Rudolf Augstein or Martin Walser (though Walser would later declare himself to be highly impressed by the monument and called Eisenman a 'genius') he thought were grounded in 'the tradition of the cult of sacrifice, which, still during my own youth, was devoted to the image of the heroic dead, of the supposedly voluntary sacrifice for the "higher" good of the collective. The Enlightenment had good reasons for wanting to abolish sacrifice.'[93] And he recommended 'a de-centered collective self-understanding that includes the injured others',[94] and whose core is the 'moral universalism of equal respect' for everybody.[95] 'In this way, nations also begin to feel the impact of the postnational constellation.'[96]

Moral universalism – whose time, Habermas thinks, has long since come – also prohibits any kind of 'differential treatment of victims'. He welcomed the influence of those historians who 'have repeatedly drawn attention to the universalist intuition that we should resist "establishing hierarchies among different groups of victims".' He saw the memorial's exclusive reference to the Jews as problematic, however, because such a particularization can, at least potentially, do injustice to other groups of victims. The Jewish culture had a great influence on the German past, but a differential treatment of victims is morally illegitimate. It is clear what Habermas is calling for: the great importance of the German–Jewish relationship must not 'neutralize the unconditional moral obligation to show equal respect in commemorating all victims', and the perpetrator-centred dimension of the memorial must not come at the expense of the victim-centred dimension. Habermas presented arguments for a non-exclusive dedication of the memorial. The term 'Holocaust', he says, has the advantage of expressing 'the complex enterprise of destruction as a whole'.[97]

On 16 December 1998, Habermas wrote a letter to the architect Eisenman in New York in which he encouraged him to hold on to the formal quality of his design for the memorial at all costs, and under no circumstances to consider the compromises suggested by Michael Naumann, the then minister for culture and the media: 'You are in any case well aware of the simple argument against Mr Naumann's proposal to replace a lasting monument by [sic!] some sort of institution for historical instruction. Such a place can tacitly turn into something else, once the climate shifts.'[98] The criticism that the memorial might encourage a possible renationalization of remembrance by Germans for Germans apparently did not impress Habermas.[99] The same applied to Peter Eisenman, who, in an interview with Michael Mönninger for the *Berliner Zeitung* (21 December 1998), said: 'The Walser debate showed the danger of anti-Semitic undertones springing up in the discussions about the memorial. . . . Now, Jürgen Habermas has expressed his concern to me that the debate among Germans might turn into a dispute between Germans and Jews.' Eisenman declared explicitly that he would not change anything about his design.

> It was an enormously difficult task to design a place to be built that has no hierarchy, no entrance, no readable shape. In contrast to the multitude of representations and symbols serving the remembrance of the dead, I wanted to create an emptiness, an incision into the city and its history that can be physically experienced. . . . Jürgen Habermas wrote to me saying: Please, do not make any more compromises.

What, then, did Habermas make of the memorial near the Brandenburg Gate, with its almost 3,000 concrete blocks, when he saw it for the first time in the summer of 2005? In the press, we find the following:

> A gentleman with snow-white hair is standing a few metres from the ice cream van. He is wearing black pleat-front trousers and a grey jacket. His hand is pensively holding his chin. He is looking at the people surging amid the stelae, the catch-me-if-you-can games of the pubescent, the photo-shooting fathers, exhausted pensioners. The man is standing there in silence. He looks like – actually it is: Jürgen Habermas. . . . Habermas is standing there as if he were watching a sociological experiment. He looks dissatisfied. As if the whole scene

was a shade too friendly. What is he thinking? '*No comment*', says Habermas.* He does not want to talk about it in public, not yet. He excuses himself and leaves. For some time, his white hair can still be seen among the crowd.[100]

---

* 'No comment' in English in the original.

PART IV

Cosmopolitan Society and Justice

The cosmopolitan condition is just the condition of peace made permanent.[1]

11

Critique as a Vocation: The Transition into the Third Millennium

Having a sense of oneself as free means, in the first place, being able to initiate something new.[1]

Professor emeritus. On 22 September 1994, three months after his sixty-fifth birthday, almost to the day, Jürgen Habermas's leave-taking was marked by a reception hosted by the prime minister of Hesse, Hans Eichel, in his official residence in Wiesbaden. Present on that pleasant late summer day were the minister for science and culture, Evelies Mayer, and numerous colleagues. In a short speech, Habermas made no secret of the fact that he did not consider retirement a cause for celebration. And, in any case, he would continue his work as before, including giving lectures at the University of Frankfurt, albeit now only every other term. At least that was his plan.

Habermas's sixty-fifth birthday and retirement was the occasion for numerous appreciations in the press. In retrospectives on his work, both the philosopher Walther C. Zimmerli (*Süddeutsche Zeitung*, 18 June 1994) and Thomas Assheuer (*Frankfurter Allgemeine Zeitung*, 18 June 1994) retraced his intellectual path. Assheuer concluded:

> With an admirable, unflagging insistence Jürgen Habermas has staged this one hope, that 'humanity is the audacity which is left to us in the end'. Democracy and right, self-reflexive morality and the reason embedded in language provide for him the answer to those who want to use the myth of class or, more recently, the myth of the nation in order to nationalize society and violently redirect modernity.

In September 1993, Habermas met with Adam Michnik, the editor-in-chief of the largest Polish newspaper, *Gazeta Wyborcza*, for a debate about the situation in the reunified Germany. The debate, moderated by Adam Krzemiński, and published in *Die Zeit* in mid-December and a few weeks later in the *New Left Review*,[2] prompted a most remarkable response in early 1994. Michnik had been a member of the anti-communist opposition in Poland since the 1960s, and in the 1980s he was, among other things, an advisor to the independent trade union Solidarność. When he asked Habermas why he had never commented critically on Stalinism, his reply was succinct: he simply had not felt called upon to write about the matter. And, apart from that, the left had wanted to avoid the danger of being made a mouthpiece for virulent anti-communism in Germany. This remark led Wolfgang Kraushaar of the Institute for Social Research in Hamburg to publish in March 1994 an article in *Die Zeit*, which used Habermas as an example of what he saw as the 'blindness' of left intellectuals 'to the communist system as such, and the SED regime in particular. Not that Habermas would have harboured any illusions regarding the political situation in the Soviet Union or in the GDR – rather, he left the Stalinist system out of his social-theoretical analysis so as not to provide ammunition for those he considered the real danger.'[3] Habermas's response was not long in the making. In a letter to the editor of *Die Zeit* (25 March 1994), he clarified that from the time of his early philosophical studies he had 'unambiguously dealt with the Stalinist orthodoxy', but that in the face of the tendency towards restoration in post-war Germany it had been important for democratic development to concentrate on the fascist potential within his own society. At the same time, he had openly confessed his sympathy for dissidents in the countries of actually existing socialism. Insofar as he had always kept his distance from Stalinism, he saw no personal reason for any symbolic settling of scores.[4]

Kraushaar, in turn, responded to Habermas's letter to the editor in *Die Zeit* with a lengthy letter to Habermas, some passages of which are rather sharp in tone (*Die Zeit*, 26 April 1994). Differences in the interpretation of post-war anti-communism in Germany were at the heart of the letter. These differences related to whether the role of the '68 protest movement had been one of stabilizing democratic self-understanding or one of fostering left-wing totalitarianism; the role of dissidents in Eastern European states; and, finally, the responsibility of left-wing intellectuals. In his reply of 9 May 1994, which he kept short, Habermas defended himself against the 'suggestion of "being born into a [Stalinist] complex of guilt" as an undogmatic leftist. I consider this, frankly, hokum. If the anti-authoritarian left . . . at the time had actually moved towards the course of radical reform which I favoured, it would have saved me ten years of not very amusing defamation.'[5]

The retired professor had just begun to prepare for his departure from Frankfurt when, on 8 May 1995, he found himself on the rostrum of the Paulskirche once again, giving a speech on the fiftieth anniversary of the end of the war. In his speech, Habermas explained the Federal Republic's process of democratization, which he now also finally deemed successful, as the result of the fact that it had been possible over many years to engage in critical discourse about the past. A couple of weeks later he travelled to Tel Aviv, where he was awarded an honorary doctorate by the city's university on 21 May. The justification for this distinction, which acknowledged in particular his role in the historians' debate, states that Habermas merited the award for 'resisting tendencies in the German historiography of the 1980s which aimed at lightening the burden of the politics of the Third Reich'.[6]

On 26 September, Habermas gave his acceptance speech for the Karl Jaspers Prize awarded to him by the university and city of Heidelberg. He spoke about 'The Conflict of Beliefs: Karl Jaspers on the Clash of Cultures'. The philosopher Reiner Wiehl, an erstwhile assistant to Gadamer, also gave a speech, reconstructing what he called the 'tense relationship' between Habermas and Jaspers's philosophy of existentialism. He was also open about the fact that some colleagues at the university had not agreed with awarding the prize to Habermas, not least because of his support of the university reforms in the 1960s and his unambiguous political statements, which had led to a polarization between left and right. Wiehl, who had a Jewish mother and had been sent to a camp as late as 1945, found the courage to defend Habermas's support for the students' efforts at reform. 'If there have been voices saying that the years from 1968 to 1970 were as bad as the Nazi period, then the response must be that those who say this cannot possibly have had any genuinely bad experiences during the NS period.' He further explained that Habermas's partisanship rests on two 'foundational solidarities': 'the solidarity of the citizens in a free and democratic polity and the incontrovertible solidarity of all human beings for which discourse ethics aims to provide the justification.'[7]

In his acceptance speech, Habermas spoke about the problems of intercultural communication. He referred to the distinctions between different faiths [Glaubensmächte] (Islam, Judaism and Christianity) and interpreted their ethical conceptions of life as 'communities of interpretation' – surely a subtle nod to Hans-Georg Gadamer in the audience – 'each of which is united around its own conception of the good life.'[8] Although their engagement with each other promotes understanding, he says, it does not lead to agreement.

In the spring of 1996, Habermas went on longer lecturing tours to the Baptist University in Hong Kong, where he spoke about 'Kant's Idea of Perpetual Peace',* and – upon the invitation of the Korean Society for Philosophy – to Seoul, where he spoke on 'National

---

* Title in English in the original.

Unification and Popular Sovereignty'.* He was at first a little taken aback by the level of interest in his moral philosophical interpretations of Kant and his analysis of modernity. As part of the Seonam Lectures, he gave talks on the nation-state and on popular sovereignty at the National University of Seoul. His visit came amid bloody student protests in Seoul. Uwe Schmitt, reporting on them for the *Frankfurter Allgemeine Zeitung* (21 August 1996), suggested a connection between the protests and the lectures given by Habermas. Habermas reacted with irritation, writing in a letter to the editor:

> [T]his infamous claim fits well into a structure of prejudices which the *FAZ* has fostered for decades, but contrasts with the liberal tenor of my numerous academic engagements in Korea and also with the press conference . . .. I have just received a fax in which Professor Sang-Jin Han of the National University in Seoul, one of the leading intellectuals of his country, assures me that no one in Korea would dare make a similarly absurd claim: 'It is perfectly absurd to try to relate your speeches and interviews during your stay in Korea to the student violence at Yonsei University. Your message has clearly been received as pointing in the opposite direction.'9

Following a trip to London, where Habermas spoke about moral philosophy at the University of London's Senate House, in the autumn he once more went as a visiting professor to Northwestern Universtity in Evanston. He also spoke at a conference on globalization at Saint Louis University, Missouri. In early 1997, he received an honorary doctorate from the Sorbonne and taught seminars on legal philosophy and his concept of a democratic public sphere in Paris.

The Goldhagen debate. In March 1997, the American historian Daniel Jonah Goldhagen was awarded the Democracy Prize of the *Blätter für deutsche und international Politik* for his book *Hitler's Willing Executioners: Ordinary Germans and the Holocaust*, which had appeared in German translation the previous year, sparking highly charged debates both in academic circles and among the public at large.10 Habermas spoke at the event alongside Jan Philipp Reemtsma, under the title 'On the Public Use of History: Why a Democracy Prize for Daniel Goldhagen?' In a speech delivered to a 2,000-strong audience in the Beethovenhalle in Bonn, Habermas maintained that the public controversies triggered by Goldhagen's theses reflected the disagreement between those historians who

---

* Title in English in the original.

viewed the Holocaust as a natural event, to be explained by the circumstances surrounding it, and those who saw it as the result of actions by individuals who are responsible for what they did. He saw the value in Goldhagen's approach, especially in the fact that he did not concentrate on the idea of human beings as evil by nature, and referred instead to specific traditions and mentalities in order to explain German eliminationist anti-Semitism.[11]

In his speech, Habermas once again expressed his personal attitude towards the question of how one should deal with the fateful German past:

> Here, in an ethical-political discourse, the question is not primarily the guilt or innocence of the forefathers but rather the critical self-assurance of their descendants. The public interest of those born later, who cannot know how they themselves would have acted in the same situation, has a different goal than the zeal of morally judgmental contemporaries of the Nazi years, who find themselves in the same context of interaction and demand a moral reckoning from each other. Painful revelations of the conduct of one's own parents and grandparents can only be an occasion for sorrow; they remain a private affair between those intimately involved. On the other hand, as citizens, members of subsequent generations take a public interest in the darkest chapter of their national history with regard to themselves. They are not pointing a finger of blame at anyone else. They are trying to bring about some clarity concerning the cultural matrix of a burdened inheritance, to recognize what they are collectively liable for, and what is to be continued, and what revised, of those traditions that once had formed such a disastrous motivational background. An awareness of collective liability emerges from the widespread guilty conduct of individuals in that is simply incoherent on conceptual grounds alone.[12]

Following this speech, Ulrich Raulff, the then editor of the features section of the *Frankfurter Allgemeine Zeitung*, sneered at the fact that Habermas and Reemtsma – neither a trained historian – had the confidence to pass judgement in public on Goldhagen's book, which had prompted damaging accusations from his fellow historians.[13]

In those days of rapidly progressing globalization, Habermas turned more and more towards an analysis of the contemporary situation in order to work against what he called (in a contribution for the *Frankfurter Rundschau* on 13 December 1995) 'enlightened perplexity'. He identified three tendencies which he thought would shape the future:

> [1] The social-liberal project of the post-war era, which until recently has been successful, can no longer be continued under the same

premises. In our own interest, we must realize that we are confronted
with tasks set by social policies on a global scale. [2] The perception
of a dialectic between borders and globalization determines today's
ideological alternatives between market and nation. Instead, politics
should follow the markets. [3] Just as there is no alternative to the
Federal Republic's political integration into the West, so there is no
alternative to its cultural integration. However, in the future the latter
will most likely have to stabilize itself without the stimulus which ema-
nated from coming to terms with the NS past.*

In the spring of 1998, Habermas delivered a lecture entitled
'Learning from Catastrophe? A Look Back at the Short Twentieth
Century' at the American University in Cairo.[14] He also used his first
short stay in Egypt – it lasted just four days – to visit the cultural
sites of the country, including the Egyptian Museum in Cairo, the
pyramids at Giza and the Ibn Tulun Mosque, in the company of the
philosopher Ernst Wolf-Gazo. To his audiences at the University
of Cairo and the American University he expressed his hope that
the new experiences he had had in discussions with intellectuals
and others in the country would lead to a modification in his own
Eurocentric perspective.

Habermas followed the development of democracy in the West
with a critical eye. Not surprisingly, he registered a progressive normative erosion at the heart of politics during those years. Politics,
he said, increasingly followed a neo-liberal agenda, a fact that had
led not only to a deregulation of the labour market but also to a
dismantling of the welfare state. There was a risk of an explosion in
social inequality within society. Such a trend became all the more
likely as state policies became more and more dependent on a globally connected market economy.[15]

In the summer of 1998, during a lively election campaign,
Habermas was again invited to the Cultural Forum of the Social
Democrats, as he had been in 1983. He urged the comrades to bid
farewell to their traditional core themes of justice and solidarity, to
close their eyes to the actual looming crises of poverty, social insecu-
rity, disintegration and exclusion. In the course of the development
of a transnational economic system, he said, precisely those conditions that once made the welfare state compromise possible were
now under threat. Despite not being a party member, and although
he did not shy away from criticizing Gerhard Schröder's political
style (in the full knowledge that it might well win him the election, in
which he was vying to be chancellor), he nevertheless openly put his
reputation in the service of the SPD:

---

* Numbering has been added here to identify the three tendencies more clearly.

I would not be sitting here if I did not wish for an election victory for the Social Democrats in September, solely for the simple reason that it would be the first time in the Federal Republic for a party to come into government from the opposition benches.* With this element of democratic normality a process would come to completion that has filled the entire history of my adult life – the development of a democratic political culture in this country.[16]

The press were astonished by the encounter between Habermas and the candidate for the chancellorship. In *Die Zeit* (10 June 1998), Gunter Hofmann stated that their meeting was

> swathed in ironies; the concepts of politics are so different, and the roles are also so incompatible, that it is ultimately propped up only by the functional idea behind it. . . . While the candidate intones the melody of 'German interests' that need to be brought to the fore more strongly in Europe, the philosopher grabs the bull 'Europe' by the horns and seeks a 'political alternative to a European Union that is frozen into the neo-liberal shape of a Europe of a common market.' . . . The change of roles is baffling. The philosopher, not the politician, sketches a federal European state that is capable of acting in terms of social and economic policy. . . . No, there is no closing of ranks taking place. While Schröder, the election campaigner, occasionally drops a few snappy remarks about how one might kick out criminal foreigners quickly, Habermas puts on record that he considers the erosion of the basic right to political asylum as unconstitutional. . . . [H]e also considers it to be 'damaging to the central elements of political culture, which had a difficult enough time in forming in the Federal Republic in the first place.'

In *Die Tageszeitung* (8 June 1998), Thomas Groß stated that Schröder's reply had been 'an enormous intellectual slump compared to the previous speaker' which had made his 'ventriloquizing all the more striking'. Claus Offe, who was a participant at the event, also shared the impression that Habermas had allowed himself to be pressed into the service of Schröder's politics, and that Schröder had 'reaped a reputational return'. To Offe's surprise, Habermas had introduced him to Schröder as a high-calibre political advisor. Nothing, Offe states, had been further from his mind.[17] Regarding the Red–Green coalition which would eventually be formed after

---

* This claim may sound surprising. However, in previous changes of government at least one of the parties continued in office after the elections. Hence, 1998 was indeed the first time that a complete change in government took place. The following website contains a diagram which illustrates this fact: https://de.wikipedia.org/wiki/Liste_der_deutschen_Bundesregierungen.

the SPD came first in the national elections at the end of September, Habermas later stated with relief:

> In a democracy, citizens must have the conviction that, at certain turning points, their decision in voting can, after all, influence a state-centred, isolated political practice. In the old Federal Republic, it took a few decades before such a democratic attitude actually took hold of people's minds. I have the impression that this process is now, so to speak, sealed.[18]

After the national elections in 1998, and the defeat of Chancellor Helmut Kohl, Habermas interpreted the results, in a remarkably long interview for *Die Zeit*, as a sign of the political self-confidence of the citizens. When asked about his attitude towards the former chancellor, Habermas acknowledged that his 'historical achievement was to link the reunification of Germany with the unification of Europe', and that, for him, 'his deflation of empty claims and trivialization of public representation made him into a sympathetic figure.'[19] Kohl's programme for an intellectual-moral turn had met with resistance and thus, in effect, had contributed to the country's becoming more liberal. That, he said, improved the electoral chances of a Red–Green coalition in government, and now what mattered was that the new government would use this opportunity to show the required energy in developing alternatives to the 'deregulation competition' and implement these domestically and also beyond the national framework. Habermas had high hopes about the new foreign minister, Joschka Fischer, whom he called a 'solid European'. 'I have known him for long enough and well enough – the handover of European policy from Kohl to Fischer is a stroke of luck.'[20] Asked about the ways in which the political parties were developing within the mediatized society, he painted a rather gloomy picture. The parties were fixated on personalities and devoted less and less time to the work of politically convincing people. And, Habermas said, the public sphere 'takes its cues from the commercialized mass media'.[21] At the end of the interview, Habermas formulated his own political programme:

> I believe that we all would like to live in a civilized country which has opened itself up in a cosmopolitan manner and takes its place among the other nations in a cautious and cooperative spirit. We would all like to be surrounded by fellow citizens who are accustomed to respecting the integrity of foreigners, the autonomy of individuals, and diversity, be it regional, ethnic, or religious. Moreover, the new Republic would do well to remember Germany's role in the catastrophic history of the twentieth century, but also preserve the memory of those rare moments of emancipation and the achievements

of which we can be justly proud. Quite unoriginally, I would wish for a mentality that is suspicious of high-flown rhetoric and rejects the aestheticization of politics, while remaining alert to the limits of trivialization when it comes to the integrity and the distinctiveness of intellectual creations.[22]

On 9 December 1998, Habermas gave a lecture on 'Symbolic Expression and Ritual Behaviour: Ernst Cassirer and Arnold Gehlen Revisited', having been invited by the Sonderforschungsbereich* 'Institutionalität und Geschichtlichkeit' [Institutionality and Historicity] at the Technical University of Dresden.[23] A few days later, an anonymous commentary appeared in the *Frankfurter Allgemeine Zeitung*, which said hardly a word about the content of the lecture but made allusions to Habermas's speech defect and his allegedly incomprehensible academic language. In the following weeks, the paper published two letters to the editor, one by Alexander Kluge and another by Karl-Siegbert Rehberg (23 and 30 December), which expressed their outrage over the 'disgraceful' reporting and the 'tastelessness' and 'injurious lack of dignity' it showed. Before these, Habermas had defended himself in a letter of 16 December to Frank Schirrmacher, in which he wrote: '[I] talk not about polemic but about resentment and a violation of fundamental rules of journalism.'[24]

Quarrel with Sloterdijk. The same year, Habermas intervened for the first time in the debate about bioethics, which interested large swathes of the public. In two newspaper articles, he chose strong words to express what it means genetically to determine human beings: 'arrogation and enslavement'.[25] To begin with, the tone in this public debate over the moral dimensions of genetic engineering, and in particular cloning, remained entirely matter of fact. But in the summer of 1999 it escalated when the Karlsruhe philosopher Peter Sloterdijk, with a speech he gave at an international conference on philosophy and theology on Schloss Elmau in Upper Bavaria, triggered a controversy, bordering on scandal, which lasted until the end of the year.[26] The title of the speech, which he had in fact already presented two years earlier in Basle, was 'Regeln für den Menschenpark: Ein Antwortschreiben zum Brief über den Humanismus – die Elmauer Rede' [Rules for the human park: a reply to the Letter on Humanism – the Elmau speech]. *Die Zeit* printed it on 16 September 1999,[27] and four weeks later it was published as a special edition in the edition suhrkamp series under the slightly different title *Regeln für den Menschenpark: Ein*

---

* Special research areas funded by the German Research Foundation.

Antwortschreiben zu Heideggers Brief über den Humanismus. In response to the trenchant criticism that his demand for a domestication of human beings through 'anthropo-technologies' had received from Thomas Assheuer in the *Hamburger Wochenzeitung* and from Reinhard Mohr in *Der Spiegel*,[28] Sloterdijk launched a frontal attack on Habermas, which culminated in the accusation that the latter had very deliberately 'ordered some alarming articles to be written'; such an attempt at exerting influence amounted to nothing less than the death of Critical Theory, a version of 'the tyranny of virtue'. And he pointedly wrote: 'The era of the hyper-moral sons of National Socialist fathers is drawing to a natural close.' A freer generation was succeeding them – a generation to which a culture of suspicions and accusations meant very little, Sloterdijk said.[29]

Habermas's response came hot on the heels of this provocation. In the meantime, he had looked at Sloterdijk's arguments but had avoided making any public statements about them. However, a private letter to Lutz Wingert, dated 14 August 1999, shows what he thought of them: 'What irritates me is the fascist core of a Social Darwinist call for breeding, which may have some traction in an age of neo-liberalism and increasing inequality, just as it did in the first phase of industrialization in the late nineteenth century: Sloterdijk, a reincarnation of Eugen Dühring?' Further, he wrote:

> Sloterdijk's anthropology (of the 1940s) consists of a simple dialectic between the 'world-disclosing' natural history of hominization and the dwelling-taming cultural history. The counter-movement of the production of linguistic 'environments', however, should no longer be transfigured into civilization, in humanistic fashion; rather, it should at long last (Konrad Lorenz, Gehlen, etc.) be unveiled as 'a matter of training and of breeding'.

The letter closes with the worry that the time may have come for 'the "super-humanists" . . . who bank on the Übermensch'.[30]

In his only public statement on the debate, a letter to the editor in *Die Zeit* (16 September) titled 'Post vom bösen Geist' [Mail from the evil spirit], Habermas complained that, instead of discussing the substantial and urgent arguments associated with the ethical problems of cloning, mere suspicions were being bandied about in the media. Behind all of this, there were motives – 'tussles over reputation' – and he attributed to Sloterdijk a 'neo-heathen' attitude [*Gesinnung*] and the 'air of an initiated and chosen one', which he found suspicious. Apart from that, he said, Sloterdijk had overestimated Habermas's ability to exert undue influence over the press. Sloterdijk, he wrote, 'not only forms a projective image of the nature of my ambition and my motivations. Most of all he overestimates my interest in his work and the time and effort I have invested in reading his lecture.' At the end, he stated with self-confidence: 'To be short and succinct: my generation has abolished the tone of superiority in philosophy which had already irked Kant and Heine.'

Christian Geyer (*Frankfurter Allgemeine Zeitung*, 16 September 1999) stated as fact what had been floating around as rumour, namely that, before the debate, Habermas had sent a letter to Thomas Assheuer in which he had described Sloterdijk's Elmau speech as 'genuinely fascistic'.[31] The article continued:

> The fact that Habermas in his reply intentionally does not talk about the lecture is unsatisfactory. Of course, one would like to know what exactly it is about the speech that had such a 'devastating' effect on Habermas that he felt compelled, after reading it, to draw it to the attention of the responsible editor at the Suhrkamp Wissenschaftsprogramm and ask him 'to have a quick look at the text'. . . . Given the scope of such a fear, one would at least have expected a sketch of an engagement with the speech, such as is allegedly also contained in the letter to the editor of *Die Zeit*. Without any publicly formulated justification, in any case, Habermas's most recent conclusion hovers peculiarly in mid-air.

With respect to Sloterdijk, Geyer raises the question of whether his 'Rules for the human park' had been designed 'to provoke critical responses so that he could then lambast them as undercover operations by Jürgen Habermas.' In an open letter to Sloterdijk, published in *Die Zeit* (23 September 1999), Manfred Frank, the chair of philosophy at Tübingen, also accused Sloterdijk of 'provoking the audience': 'Trying to extract from the lecture a clear thesis, a conviction, not to mention a rational recommendation for a particular course of action, is about as easy as nailing custard to the wall.' The idea of the death of Critical Theory, he wrote,

> is so comical that I wonder whether the suspicion of rampant hubris on your side might not be a rampant exaggeration, or at least a lack of humour, on mine; . . . No, Critical Theory is not bedridden; it is as fit as a fiddle. It is no more than a sober statement of fact when I say that no other philosophical voice of post-fascist German philosophy . . . is taken as seriously around the world as that of Habermas.

It is obvious that this war of the Diadochi* was exactly what the public and the media were craving. But Habermas wanted to avoid a media spectacle at all costs, even if Sloterdijk subsumed

* The wars of the Diadochi were fought following the death of Alexander the Great in 323 BC between various of his generals to decide who would rule over his empire.

him under 'the inhumane heritage of the intellectual style of ideology critique',[32] because he was under no illusions about the likely result of a public quarrel between two representatives from different generations and with different philosophical positions, both of whose pride had been wounded. As a theoretician who attaches importance to the distinction between discourse and dispute,[33] he studiously concentrated on turning the discussion towards the real ethical problems of genetic engineering.

However, it is worth mentioning something of an epilogue to the debate. In *Die Zeit* of 24 February 2000, Rudolf Walther reported on the way in which Sloterdijk judged Habermas in the French press and quoted from an interview published by the journal *L'Événement*. Walther accused Sloterdijk of engaging in 'vulgar psychological speculations' with his remarks on the sons of great fascists, and of leavening these speculations with '"facts" to make them suitable for the media'. Following on from this, an extensive interview conducted with Sloterdijk by Hans-Jürgen Heinrich appeared in *Lettre International* (1 March 2000). With regard to Habermas, Sloterdijk spoke of 'discourse hegemony' and the 'power of mentality'. Pointedly he added: 'One might go so far as to say that the whole left-liberal block consists of faint Habermasians. It is typical of this large majority that it understands itself as a persecuted minority, and that it practises its cultural hegemony, which is almost never threatened, in the style of self-defence against an overpowering opponent.' Critical Theory 'in Habermas-style', he said, is 'a crypto-theological version of logical absolutism that is the product of a monologically overstretched concept of truth which takes great pains to appear in dialogical camouflage . . . At bottom, Habermas has always remained nothing but a theoretician of re-education.'*

To mark Habermas's seventieth birthday, all the major daily and weekly newspapers, throughout June 1999, featured articles assessing his work. In the *Süddeutsche Zeitung*, Hans-Georg Gadamer, by then ninety-nine years of age, emphasized the independence of Habermas's judgement and the political commitment of the public intellectual; it was no coincidence, he wrote, that the concept of communicative reason was central to his philosophy. In the same paper, Pierre Bourdieu described Habermas's reception in France, where his 'moral version of democracy' and the idea of 'communication without repression' were important; however, against the latter he objected that it 'remains silent about that form of domination which is potentially immanent to all communication'.

Richard Rorty wrote very personally in the *Frankfurter Rundschau*

---

* 'Re-education' in English in the original.

that, at 'seventy, Habermas has maintained the intellectual curiosity of a twenty-year-old.' Like his American colleague Hilary Putnam writing in the *Neue Zürcher Zeitung*, Rorty saw his friend, who is almost the same age as him, as standing in the tradition of the radical democratic pragmatist John Dewey.[34] A certain closeness to Habermas can be felt in Axel Honneth's essay for *Die Zeit*, in which Habermas's former assistant and successor to the chair in Frankfurt discussed his life and work, concluding that his intellectual presence and his public use of reason had contributed substantially to raising the intellectual culture in Germany to a higher level of a self-critical openness.[35] Congratulating Habermas in *Der Tagesspiegel*, Oskar Negt stated: 'I have never again in my life met a person who, in trying to find the truth, attaches as much weight to the exchange of arguments as Habermas.'[36]

On 18 June, the *Frankfurter Allgemeine Zeitung* published a collage of heterogeneous views – from philosophers and sociologists, theologists and literary scholars – on the seventy-year-old intellectual under the heading 'Answers to Jürgen Habermas', accompanied by two photographs showing Habermas in the library of his Starnberg home. A mixed picture emerges. While Wilhelm Hennis, for instance, accused him of political errors, false interpretations of situations, and a certain lack of judgement, and the former Bavarian Minister for Culture Hans Maier requested that Habermas tell us to which childhood experiences we owe his 'tone of zealous instruction', Martin Seel's contribution characterized him affectionately as the 'exception of a philosopher who has a system, without the system having him'.[37]

What would be an appropriate way to acknowledge the seventieth birthday of a scholar of such stature? His disciples from Frankfurt, led by Klaus Günther and Lutz Wingert, organized a symposium in his honour at the Johann Wolfgang Goethe University in July 1999 with a large number of renowned Anglo-American and German speakers as participants. The papers more or less took their leads from Habermas's various books and focused on three thematic complexes: epistemology and the philosophy of language; morality and ethics; and the public sphere, democracy and law. Habermas would later say that the title of the symposium, which would also become the title of the published proceedings – *Die Öffentlichkeit der Vernunft und die Vernunft der Öffentlichkeit* [The public sphere of reason and the reason of the public sphere] – was a particularly fortunate one, 'because the public sphere as a space of reasoned communicative exchanges is the issue that has concerned me all my life. The conceptual triad of "public space," "discourse," and "reason," in fact, has dominated my work as a scholar and my political life.'[38] At the end of the conference, a 'belated celebration of Jürgen Habermas's seventieth birthday' took place at the university's guesthouse, organized by Ute Habermas-Wesselhoeft and Suhrkamp. The small print on the back of the invitations read: 'Jürgen Habermas thinks that this should not be an occasion for presents.'

Even before he turned seventy, Habermas had been dealing with health problems, brought on partly by stress. For some time he had been afflicted with tinnitus. In a letter of 24 June 1999 to Wolf Lepenies, in which Habermas thanked him for his birthday wishes, he complained about his poor health and added: 'On the other hand, I feel so intimidated by the publicity of the previous days that I somehow feel I should not leave the house for some time.' And in a letter of 15 July to a colleague in Frankfurt, the philosopher Matthias Lutz-Bachmann, he wrote that he 'trudged with some effort through the spring and summer', that he had cancelled trips to China, Italy and Spain, and that the 'normal progress of work' had been disrupted.[39] Through the following year, Habermas indeed refrained from committing himself to lectures and travel. For instance, he declined the opportunity to speak on the topic of European identity in the European Parliament. The summer holidays, which he and his wife, as so many times before, spent in southern France, were also exclusively dedicated to recuperation. He even tried to limit the time he spent daily on his correspondence to a minimum. However, he did go to New York and continue his visiting professorship at Northwestern University.

And he also continued with his role as advisor to the Suhrkamp publishing house. Disagreements with Unseld over the direction of the programme caused Friedhelm Herborth, the head of the academic section, to leave Suhrkamp after twenty-five years. The long-standing editor Horst Brühmann resigned with him, effective from 30 September 1999, after the two of them had finished planning the programme for the forthcoming six months. At the first signs of disagreement with Unseld, Habermas had tried to protect Herborth, and he continued to do so until Herborth made critical comments about Unseld's ideas for the future of the academic programme in a conversation with the cultural correspondent of the *Neue Züricher Zeitung*, Joachim Güntner, which appeared in the paper on 15 October 1998.[40] When the vacant post was to be filled at the end of 1999, Unseld asked Habermas to help him choose the right person. In a letter of 14 March, Habermas suggested that the current profile of the academic programme should be maintained.[41] One would hope, he wrote, that there would be no 'softening of the brain of the "suhrkamp wissenschaft"', and that a gradual deterioration of the current high standards of the stw [suhrkamp taschenbuch wissenschaft], and a loss of substance, should be avoided at all costs. And Habermas registered serious doubts over Unseld's intention to put editorial responsibility in the hands of the philologist Raimar Zons, who had been in charge of the programme of the well-respected Wilhelm Fink Verlag since 1981, first as editor-in-chief and later as publishing director. From Habermas's perspective, Zons was responsible for a programme with a preponderance of French philosophy and conservative thinkers. Zons would later remember that Peter Sloterdijk suggested to Unseld that he should get in touch with him, and that Christoph Buchwald, Suhrkamp's publishing director, did just that. At that point, Habermas sent Zons a long list of questions he intended to ask the applicant. A conversation with Unseld and Buchwald in Frankfurt followed in which they discussed which authors might be of interest for the academic programme. Unseld was immediately convinced that he had found the right person in Zons and offered him a contract straightaway. Zons also remembers a conversation with Habermas at the time which was far from harmonious – and says that, in the end, despite being seriously interested in the job, he eventually turned down the offer because, for reasons of ill health, his old publisher Ferdinand Schöningh desperately needed him to stay on at Fink. Finally, in November 1999 the press department of Suhrkamp announced that Bernd Stiegler, also a philologist, would be in charge of the academic programme (together with Annette Wunschel to begin with).[42] Stiegler had applied to Suhrkamp on his own initiative, and Buchwald had invited him to Frankfurt for an interview in spring 1999. At a lunch, where Unseld was also present, Habermas first got to know the new editor, who would then make a habit of travelling to Starnberg once or twice each year in order to discuss plans, programmes and authors. Stiegler recalls this cooperation as having been pleasant, constructive and informed by trust.[43]

In December 1999, Jürgen Habermas was awarded the Hessischer Kulturpreis along with the literary critic Marcel Reich-Ranicki and Siegfried Unseld. The prize is unique insofar as, at the ceremony, each of the three laureates is expected to give a speech honouring the other two. Habermas described this media-friendly set-up as a 'self-referential system' in which 'three old men' held up mirrors to one another in order to put each other in perspective. He praised the unpretentious language of *Mein Leben*,* Reich-Ranicki's recently published autobiography, in which he describes, among other things, his memories of the Warsaw Ghetto. But Habermas also praised the 'challenging value judgements' of his literary reviews. Unseld's merit, Habermas said, is that he maintains friendships 'with those authors who eternally revolve around themselves' – idiosyncratic spirits such as Adorno and Bloch, Johnson and Enzensberger, Handke and Frisch, whom he 'brought ... back together again

---

* English edition: *The Author of Himself: The Life of Marcel Reich-Ranicki* (London, 2001)

and again in changing constellations'. While Unseld characterized Habermas as a philosopher whose theoretical designs are sparked by pre-scientific intuition, Reich-Ranicki thanked his co-laureate for his unyielding attitude in the historians' debate and honoured him in his 'role as a central moral and intellectual authority'.[44]

How did all this sit with Habermas's image of himself? Several times he had made it clear that he had no sympathy for the idea of a moral authority that judges from above, or, as he called it, the 'key-holder attitude' of the philosopher or intellectual. 'The citizens, not the philosopher, are to have the final word.'[45] But, of course, ethical and moral motivations always played a major role in his thinking and acting as a philosopher and public intellectual, for instance in his contributions to the debate on biopolitics. He is horrified 'by the prospect of chimera created by genetic engineering'. Because he is of the opinion that a postmetaphysical withdrawal from questions of value is not an option when the 'ethical self-understanding of subjects capable of language and action as such is at stake', he introduces the concept of an 'ethics of the species'.[46] The first time he dealt with this theme was on 9 November 2000 in an acceptance speech in the main lecture hall of the University of Zurich, having just received the prize of the Dr Margrit Egnér Foundation, which is endowed with 25,000 Swiss francs. He later covered it in more detail as part of his Christian Wolff Lectures at the University of Marburg.

A plea for freedom of the will and the inviolability[*] of the person

The scientistic belief in a science that will one day not only supplement but replace the self-understanding of actors as persons by an objectivating self-description is not science, but bad philosophy.[47]

Bioethics. The conceptual framework of discourse ethics, which Habermas had already developed in the 1980s, provides the perspective from which he comments extensively on the future possibilities for targeted genetic modification. The point of departure for his criticism of genetic engineering is his distinction between ethics and morality – that is, between the good, understood as an existential self-understanding, and the just. In order to justify his bioethical

---

[*] The German is 'Unverfügbarkeit', a term that oscillates interestingly between not being at one's disposal as a matter of fact and not being negotiable for moral or legal reasons. One may even argue that the term straddles the divide between an 'is' and an 'ought'. It is sometimes also translated as 'unavailability'; see the title of Habermas's lecture at the Adorno conference 2003 (see p. 336 below).

position, Habermas reconsidered this opposition, which he had previously taken to imply that philosophy must not interfere with the concrete content of ethical self-understanding. Discourse ethics was meant to be limited to securing the external – i.e., as Habermas puts it, the formal and procedural conditions of discourse – so that, in an ideal case, the process of presenting reasons and counter-reasons within an argument would yield a nearly consensual decision regarding the recognition of norms and the moral maxims associated with them.

However, in light of the technical possibilities for intervening in human nature opened up by the biological sciences, for instance as a consequence of pre-implantation genetic diagnosis, Habermas came to think that questions about what constitutes an individual ethical life were not of primary concern. Rather, central aspects of the normative orientation of the human species as such needed to be clarified. What is at stake is nothing less than the '*uncontrollability* of the contingent process of human fertilization that results from what is now an *unforeseeable* combination of two different sets of chromosomes.'[48]

Habermas goes so far as to interpret the 'subjugation of our body and our life to biotechnology' as a 'third decentration of our worldview', following the previous 'destruction of our geocentric and our anthropocentric worldviews'.[49] He speculates about the future in order to set the successes of genetic engineering in a broader context. In a conversation with journalists from *Die Zeit* on 24 January 2002, he said clearly:

> I distrust those experts who make light of things, and only want to take the next step. So far the development of biotechnology generates a dynamic which again and again overtakes the time-consuming processes through which society reaches a self-understanding about its moral aims. The shorter the temporal horizon we take into consideration, the greater the power of the created facts will be.

The premise of Habermas's bioethical argument is an anthropological claim: the randomness of the human genetic make-up is a precondition for the formation of individual identities as well as for the fundamental equality in the relations between human beings. Interventions in the human genome and the manipulation of genetic material therefore threaten the inviolable status of persons by treating them as if they were objects. The medical use of genetics potentially substitutes the individual uniqueness and autonomy of a newborn with heteronomy, thus creating a new kind of inequality between human beings. Those techniques of cloning that may turn genetic material into an artificial product of dispositions realized through genetic engineering undermine 'the conditions of symmetry in the relations of adult persons to one another'.[50] Thus, a 'person who sets himself up as master over the genetic material of another' revokes the very reciprocity through which human beings acknowledge each other as autonomous.[51]

Habermas wants to open people's eyes to the fact that traditional ethical sentiments are being violated. He is worried that this new type of interpersonal relationship 'constitutes a foreign body in the legally institutionalized relations of recognition in modern societies'.[52] The manipulation of genetic material overrides a person's self-responsibility for what she is by nature, a self-responsibility based on the fact that persons 'regard themselves as the sole authors of their own life history'.[53]

In order to avoid misunderstanding, it might be useful to point out that Habermas's critique is directed against a very specific idea of practical eugenics. His target is what he terms 'liberal eugenics' – i.e., methods of genetic engineering that are freely accessible on unregulated markets and that manipulate traits in accordance with parents' wishes. He does not reject biotechnological interventions as a matter of principle. Rather, he wants to give the otherwise vague fears often associated with a possible future of biotechnological programming a clear articulation using the concepts of moral theory. Habermas sees very clearly the clinical opportunities provided by therapeutic cloning within the framework of what he calls 'negative eugenics' (such as, for instance, the eradication of hereditary diseases). Genetic interventions are permissible, in his view, if one may assume (in theory) that they would subsequently be accepted by those concerned. In the case of 'positive eugenics', by contrast, where children are equipped through direct control by gene technology with the traits desired by their parents, reification of the embryo cannot be ruled out. Because the borders between interventions aimed at preventing the development of diseases and those aimed at optimizing programming of genetic material are not clear-cut, Habermas insists on a distinction 'between the nature we *are* and the organic equipment we *give* ourselves'.[54] Habermas fears that, in the course of the combination of reproductive medicine with gene technology (cloning), and as a consequence of the possibilities offered by pre-implantation genetic diagnosis, a regressive tendency towards a de-differentiation between subject (what has grown) and object (what has been made) is carried further forward – a de-differentiation between 'the categories of what is *manufactured* and what has *come to be by nature*'.[55] It would fit in with this tendency, he says, that the peculiarities of the natural fortunes (of the organism) and the fortunes of socialization (of the person) are increasingly levelled out.

The conclusions are obvious: 'A genetic intervention offers no communicative scope for the projected child to be addressed as a second person and to be involved in a process aimed at reaching understanding.'[56] Instead, 'a relationship emerges that is asymmetrical in more than one respect – a specific kind of paternalism.'[57]

The inviolability of human nature. Habermas's argument involves a species-ethical imperative of the inviolability of subjective nature, or of pre-personal human life. Such subjective nature develops its unique individual shape 'in the public sphere of a linguistic community' in which a 'natural creature [develops] into both an individual and a person endowed with reason.' For this reason, the possibility of an intentional 'quality control' of the embryo is morally explosive: it intervenes in the unpredictability of natural endowments and in the interactive process in which the self emerges. Thus, it has implications for fundamental questions of value, specifically for 'our self-understanding as members of the species'.

This is why, for Habermas, we require an ethics of the species, the fundamental premise of which is the 'being able to be oneself' of the person. An essential part of this is 'that the person be at home, so to speak, in her own body', which 'has to be experienced as something natural'. Another fundamental dimension of being able to be oneself is the possibility of maintaining interpersonal relations on the normative grounds of mutual recognition. The purpose of bioethics, for Habermas, is to draw attention to these two conditions of being able to be oneself. And he considers this to be necessary 'as long as belonging to a moral community remains a vital interest to us'. In order to warn against the danger of a voluntary surrender of our ethical self-understanding, and to illustrate the anticipated risks of a liberal eugenics, Habermas repeatedly refers to the 'slippery slope' we shall end up on if, along with the self-commitments of an ethics of the species, 'morality itself [starts] slipping'.[58] Habermas acknowledges that, with his concept of a species ethics, he 'leave[s] the path of deontological virtue',[59] since such a conception identifies anthropological conditions for a person's ability to act morally and contains substantial determining factors on which all moral persons draw – i.e., 'a prior ethical self-understanding of the species, which is shared by all moral persons.'[60]

Habermas's intense preoccupation with liberal eugenics serves almost as a paradigm for the way in which he approaches social questions. At the beginning, there is an impression or an intuition – in this case that there are deep-seated fears of the possibility of cloning human beings. In the next step, he tries to identify the rational core of these fears. This rational core is then the impetus for (in this case) ethical reflections for which, in yet another step, he provides an argumentative basis. The final stage is going public, usually via the media, in order to stimulate a discussion in the political realm, which, in turn, he uses to develop and concretize his own position even further.

Free will. In his critique of biotechnology, Habermas had not given a precise definition of free will as a property of intentional agents. Such a definition then became the subject of his engagement with the claims of the neurosciences, which continues to the present day. In October 2002, Habermas first had the opportunity to test his position regarding the nature of human beings and free will at a top-level forum of the Kulturwissenschaftliches Institut in Essen, where, in the presence of Richard Rorty and Michael Tomasello, among others, he entered into a confrontational debate with the neuroscientist Wolf Singer. Reporting on the event in the *Frankfurter Allgemeine Zeitung* (14 September 2002), Christian Geyer said one would not have expected of the 'highly renowned neuroscientist' that he would 'have so little to say philosophically. . . . It seems that Habermas, for instance, thought for a long time about how to set Singer straight without having to offend him.'

As is well known, many neuroscientists side with Wolf Singer in claiming that our consciousness of possessing free will can be revealed as an illusion. All mental acts, they say, are determined by the natural causality of neuronal states. Such a naturalism trusts blindly in science and accepts explanations only in terms of causal chains governed by natural laws, thus ignoring the meaningfulness of motivations for social actions. Against this, Habermas relates his systematically grounded concept of free will to conditions of responsible agency under which persons act intentionally. Part of the horizon of conditions for this free will – which accompanies a person in all their activities (as the inviolability of their own body) – is, on the one hand, the reflection on one's own intentions and on the factors characterizing a specific action situation and, on the other, the conviction that there are always alternative courses of action. An actor must eventually internalize the reasons that appear rational to her as subjective motives, so as to be able to act genuinely out of conviction on the basis of them. Habermas deciphers free will '*as the mode of how one binds one's own will on the basis of convincing reasons.* Freedom of the will characterizes a mode of being – the mode in which agents exist within the space of reasons and are responsive to culturally transmitted and socially institutionalized reasons.'[61]

Free will, Habermas argues, is always a conditioned form of freedom – conditioned by that symbolically structured 'space of obligating reasons',[62] as well as by the natural endowment of the subject, its life history and the contingent constellation of a historical situation. 'But the actor makes all of these factors her own, as it were, so that they no longer operate on the formation of her will like external causes and disrupt her sense of freedom.' In this context, Habermas speaks of a 'soft' naturalism in which the free will is subsumed not under the sphere of the intelligible but, rather, under the experience of the organic body as one's own flesh [*Leib*]. Although the 'point of reference of selfhood' for a person is 'its organic roots in the lived nature of [its] bodily existence', the free will only manifests itself in the 'exchange of reasons'. In this way, the transcendental subject is transformed 'into a multitude of subjects capable of speech and action'.[63]

In a speech at the Ludwig Maximilian University marking the end of the German Philosophy Congress in mid-September 2011, Habermas addressed the question of how human language and culture, and with them the space of reasons, emerged. In front of some 2,000 listeners 'in a rapt grand auditorium',[64] he spoke 'Über die Verkörperung von Gründen' [On the embodiment of reasons][65] and explained the prominent role of reasons in everyday communication as well as in the practice of discourses. In general they have, 'in processes aiming at reaching understanding, a double-edged function: as both the supporting solid rock and the loose rubble – they can support a consensus as well as shake it.'[66] Reasons, he said, can become embodied in cultural, psychosocial and material ways. Insofar as they have solidified into cultural traditions and institutionalized forms of behaviour, they form parts of the life-world, which he calls the 'space of symbolically embodied reasons'. At the climax of his speech, Habermas summarized his conclusions from the perspective of evolutionary anthropology, which he was studying intensely at the time: 'Everyday communication produces the weak normativity of a trans-subjective logos which makes the human spirit sensitive to reasons. Communication with the [sacred] powers of salvation and misfortune* produces and renews the strong normativity of social solidarity.'[67]

The philosophers listening to this would hardly have failed to notice that it amounted to a fundamental modification to the speaker's linguistic theory: 'Apparently, the discursive practices which submit controversial utterances to the non-coercive force of the better argument ultimately also move within a horizon of impenetrable and opaque experiences, which may be iconically represented

---

* 'Heil und Unheil' might also be translated as 'salvation and doom'. The phrase, Habermas says in a footnote, follows Martin Riesebrodt's 'general definition of religious practices' (Habermas (2012), *Nachmetaphysisches Denken II*, p. 69). The reference is to Martin Riesebrodt (2010), *The Promise of Salvation: A Theory of Religion* (Chicago). In his preface, Riesebrodt points out that, while the functions of religions are highly variable, their promise 'remains astonishingly constant': 'Religions promise to ward off misfortune, to help cope with crises, and to provide salvation.' Interestingly, Riesebrodt wants to offer neither 'an "essential" definition of religion', nor a 'theory of religious development . . . from religious to scientific thinking'; instead he looks at religion to 'discover something new about humans, society, history, and "actual, existing modernity".' He 'does not seek to prove that all religions are "ultimately" the same, but rather to make it possible to compare them in relation to a structure of meaning that underlies them' (p. xiii).

but cannot be discursively captured and explained [*aufgeklärt*] in their entirety.'[68] Habermas concluded: 'The space of symbolically embodied meaning [*Sinn*] still extends into the periphery of sedimented meanings [*Sinnsedimenten*], which goes beyond the space of reasons that are explicitly at our disposal.'[69] Does Habermas here allude to certainties by which human beings are intuitively led, and which are thus not exclusively owed to the logic of the better argument? In any case, he holds that there are dimensions of experience, for instance aesthetic experiences, which are 'rooted [in] *communication that is symbolic, but not linguistic*', and which precede the logic of argumentation and accompany it.[70] The *Süddeutsche Zeitung* commented on this thesis:

> While Habermas's fascinating new approach, it seems, describes the process of secularization, conversely, the liberal constitutional state and its norms become religiously charged – against a world of wild contingency. . . . The development from the old to the new Jürgen Habermas is apparently, if both allow us the comparison, almost like the one from the early to the late Plato. The massive final applause from the audience in Munich was thus given not only to an argument but also to an old and wise man.[71]

The philosopher as globetrotter

In the first year of the new millennium, Hans-Georg Gadamer celebrated his 100th birthday at the University of Heidelberg. Anyone who was anyone in German philosophy was there, gathered at this historic place in honour of this mediator between philosophical generations. Habermas dedicated two congratulatory messages to his erstwhile mentor, a personal one which appeared in *Der Tagesspiegel* (1 February 2000) and one focusing on his work in the *Neue Züricher Zeitung* (12 February 2000).

After having scaled back his activities for a while, at least with regard to larger overseas trips, Habermas travelled with Ute to China for two weeks in April 2001. The original invitation from the Academy of Social Sciences, which is under the control of the State Council of the People's Republic of China, had been extended a few months earlier. As part of the trip he gave lectures to large audiences at the Tsinghua University in Beijing and at the Fudan University in Shanghai. 'I expected conversations among academics. Now, I am suddenly speaking in front of huge audiences. It is all much more political than I thought.'[72]

Habermas witnessed China's rapid process of modernization firsthand. He completed a huge programme of events: in two weeks, he gave eight lectures, speaking about globalization and the postnational constellation, as well as about human rights. In addition, he answered questions at six meetings in academies and informal discussion groups. His main works had already been translated into Chinese at that point, and in China he found a well-informed audience that was familiar with Western philosophy. In *Die Zeit* of 26 April 2001, the correspondent Georg Blume reported on the lectures at the universities: 'To begin with, the students want to know whether Habermas's discourse theory is valid across cultural borders.' Asked about the idea of socialism, he responded that the intention of socialism had been 'to provide social roots for solidarity'. In a discussion with Chinese artists and intellectuals, moderated by Blume and documented in *Die Zeit* (10 May 2001), it is striking that the Chinese partners expressed themselves in such critical terms about the modernization policies of their regime and that they saw Habermas as a voice supporting their democratic demands.

Of course, Habermas also spoke about human rights. He stated that universal human rights have absolute priority over the sovereignty of individual states. At the same time, he explained his belief that the West must not use human rights as a kind of instrument of power in foreign policy. Habermas turned down an invitation for a longer visiting professorship in Beijing.[73] Later, the Chinese social philosopher and translator Cao Weidong, who had accompanied Habermas during those two weeks, would state in an interview that, thanks both to this visit and to better translations of books such as *The Theory of Communicative Action* and *Between Facts and Norms*, a real 'Habermas fever' had broken out in China.[74] For his part, Habermas felt 'in China like a "barbarian" in the ambiguous Greek sense of the word – as someone ignorant of the language and culture who aimed not at instructing, but at an intercultural dialogue between equals.'[75]

Peace Prize. Shortly after Habermas's return from China, the media in Germany reported that the philosopher and sociologist had been awarded one of the most prestigious honours in Germany, the Peace Prize of the German Book Trade. According to the reasons given by the Association of German Publishers and Booksellers, the award honoured him as a contemporary figure 'who has accompanied the path of the Federal Republic critically as well as with commitment . . . and who is perceived by a worldwide readership as the central German philosopher of the era.'[76] The award ceremony in the Paulskirche (where only a few weeks earlier, in the presence of Habermas, Jacques Derrida had received the Adorno Prize)[77] traditionally took place on the last day of the Frankfurt Book Fair. That year – 2001 – this happened to be on 14 October, and the attacks of 9/11 were still fresh in everyone's minds. There were big expectations ahead of the day. Jan Roß wrote in *Die Zeit* of 11 October under the heading 'Hegel der Bundesrepublik' [The Hegel of the Federal Republic]:

> Against this background, we may eagerly await the speech Jürgen Habermas will give on Sunday in Frankfurt's Paulskirche. This may sound like a trivial phrase, but, as far as political statements or other occasional contributions from German intellectuals are concerned, it is not at all something to be taken for granted. If we leave aside Günter Grass, who is officially notable, so to speak, by virtue of his Nobel Prize, there are only two other candidates one might think of, apart from Habermas, whose interventions always meet with interest and also reach a European audience, and who may as naturally and informally make an appearance in *The Independent*, in *Le Monde*, or in the *Corriere della Sera* as they would in the German press – and these are Hans Magnus Enzensberger and Ralf Dahrendorf.

For the award ceremony in Frankfurt, Habermas flew in from New York, where he had been giving lectures. Among the thousand guests, there were a particularly large number of state representatives: the president of the Federal Republic, the chancellor, the foreign minister, the minister of the economy, the president of the Constitutional Court and the secretary for culture. Jan Philipp Reemtsma spoke at the ceremony, at Habermas's request, emphasizing the open and unfinished nature of the construction of Habermas's theory. In his 'eagerly awaited' acceptance speech, titled 'Faith and Knowledge', Habermas himself used the attacks of 9/11 as an occasion to reflect publicly on the conditions of modernity and of successful processes of secularization. Like many others, just thirty-three days earlier, in his hometown of Starnberg, Habermas had followed the attacks on the World Trade Center live on television.[78] It soon emerged that Osama bin Laden's terror network, al-Qaeda, was responsible for the deaths of nearly 3,000 people. In the days that followed, many people all over the world remembered the victims of *Nine Eleven** with moments of silence and memorial ceremonies.

Right at the beginning of 'Faith and Knowledge', Habermas explained the fundamental approach informing his reflections: on 11 September, the 'tension between secular society and religion exploded in an entirely different[†] way.'[79] After telling his audience that they should not expect a 'Sunday speech' from him (an allusion to the acceptance speech Martin Walser had given in the same place four years earlier), the laureate pleaded for a sense of proportion,

---

* 'Nine Eleven' in English in the original.
† I.e., as the context of the speech explains, it is different from the way it appears in the controversy between religion and science in the case of genetic engineering.

asking that the Western world take account of its own process of secularization. At the end of the speech, during which he frequently deviated from the script, he received a standing ovation.

Shortly after the award ceremony Habermas returned to New York. The young philosopher Giovanna Borradori took the opportunity to engage him in an extensive conversation on the topic of 'Fundamentalism and Terror'. The conversation was subsequently published as part of a book titled *Philosophy in a Time of Terror*, which also contained an interview with Jacques Derrida.[80] The French philosopher was at the time visiting the New School for Social Research as a guest of the philosopher Richard J. Bernstein, and Derrida and Habermas met for private conversations over dinner in Bernstein's New York apartment. After their meetings in Evanston, Paris and Frankfurt, the once tense relationship between the two had become more amicable.[81]

Habermas looks for the causes of the madness of global terrorism perpetrated by self-described 'holy warriors'. In so doing, he not only considers fundamentalist appeals to Islamism as a dogmatic certainty of faith; he also holds that part of the attraction of fundamentalism stems from the ethical weakness of Western culture: 'The West confronts other cultures . . . only through the provocative and trivializing aura of a banal materialistic consumerist culture. . . . Let's admit it – the West presents itself in a form bereft of any normative core as long as its concern for human rights only extends to promoting free markets abroad.'[82] Habermas interprets the growing readiness to use violence – on the part of the terrorists *and* those fighting them alike – as a manifestation of disturbed communication, which prevents mutual recognition and drives a spiral of increasing mistrust. He hopes that this spiral of violence and counter-violence can be broken by a transformation of international law into a transnational legal order.

On 3 December 2001, the American philosopher Richard Rorty was awarded the newly established Meister Eckhart Prize in Berlin, and Habermas travelled to the capital in order to give a speech at his friend's award ceremony. In the spring of 1999, the German translation of a new book by the American philosopher had appeared under the title 'Stolz auf unser Land' [Proud of our country].* Habermas defended his friend's critical discussion of the American left; in particular he sought to defend it against a possible neoconservative appropriation of Rorty's theses on the usefulness of patriotic attitudes as a defence of national pride. In a review of the book, Habermas emphasizes that, for Rorty (as for Habermas himself), 'the nation signifies the self-creation of a deliberating civil

---

* See note 34 of this chapter.

society – a work in progress, not a gift of nature. National identities only take shape in the current of discourses.'[83]

In his speech, Habermas stressed Rorty's attempt at dissolving the concept of truth and at giving 'back [to philosophy] its significance for practical life' by giving up the goal of 'finding the essence or nature of things'.[84] He did not mention the philosophical disagreements between him and the laureate. Rorty, for instance, disputed the idea that communicative reason is a 'natural human endowment'. Rather, he saw it as

> a set of social practices ... To agree with Habermas that reason is communicative and dialogical ... is to substitute responsibility to other human beings for responsibility to a non-human standard. ... By hanging on to it [i.e., the ideal of universal validity], it seems to me, Habermas remains in thrall to the philosophical tradition that burdened us with the idea of reason as a human faculty that is somehow attuned to the really real.[85]

Walser and Bohrer. In the spring of 2002, a debate over anti-Semitism flared up in the media. It was triggered by Martin Walser's latest novel, *Tod eines Kritikers* [Death of a critic], which the author had personally offered to the *Frankfurter Allgemeine Zeitung* for serialization before publication. As soon as he had read the proofs, Frank Schirrmacher wrote an open letter to Walser which was published in the features section of the paper: 'I have to inform you that your novel will not appear in this newspaper ... Your novel is an execution', wrote Schirrmacher. His letter provided only a rough indication of the actual content of the book: a story about power and subordination within the literary world in the course of which a rumour about the alleged murder of the powerful Jewish literary critic André Ehrl-König causes a stir; Ehrl-König, however, turns up again safe and sound.[86] In this figure, Schirrmacher wrote, the reader could easily recognize the literary critic Marcel Reich-Ranicki, who was well known, particularly through his television appearances. Schirrmacher stated: 'What is at stake is not the murder of a critic as a critic ... What is at stake is the murder of a Jew ... The repertoire of anti-Semitic clichés is unfortunately obvious.' Just four years earlier, Schirrmacher had spoken at the award ceremony when Walser received the Peace Prize of the German Book Trade, an event that would be remembered in the media for Walser's 'Sunday speech'. Now, Schirrmacher ended his open letter with the remarkable sentence: 'You, dear Mr Walser, have said often enough that you wanted to feel liberated. Today, I think your freedom is our defeat.'[87]

The charge of anti-Semitism against Walser sparked an avalanche of commentary in the German media. While one group of critics diagnosed in Walser an aversion to anything Jewish, others praised his courage in confronting a German taboo. Unsurprisingly, Habermas was drawn into this debate, especially as another of the figures in Walser's novel, Professor Wesendonck, was clearly intended as a caricature of him. But, in fact, this did not play a role in his intervention, which was published by the *Süddeutsche Zeitung* on 7 June 2002 under the title 'Tabuschranken: Eine semantische Anmerkung: Für Marcel Reich-Ranicki, aus gegebenen Anlässen' [Taboos: a semantic note: for Marcel Reich-Ranicki, in light of various recent events]. Habermas explained, among other things, that 'the charge of anti-Semitism, whether it is justified or not . . . relates to the violation of a value which is by now anchored in our political culture. To call such behaviour the "breaking of a taboo" is misleading.' To remain relaxed in the face of anti-Semitic tendencies, Habermas wrote – in order, perhaps, 'finally to find a freer relationship to one's own history' – is a sign not of courage but of a lack of 'sensitivity towards the victims of past excesses'. Such sensitivity, in turn, was the 'transparent result of a reflection on the necessary conditions for restoring our self-respect and a civilized communal life'. To dignify a turn away from this attitude as a 'breaking of a taboo' amounted to a 'semantic confusion'.

The reaction followed hastily in the features section of the *Frankfurter Allgemeine Zeitung* (10 June 2002) in the form of a trenchant attack on Habermas by Karl Heinz Bohrer. The latter accused Habermas of an 'obsession with regulation' and criticized his 'style of insinuation, which he adopts not for the first time, and the associated method of conceptual determinism – i.e., the undifferentiated reference to various mindsets which only appear to hang together under one generic term.' Habermas, he said, had not understood the difference between 'political correctness' and the 'removal of history' [*Geschichtsentsorgung*], and falsely characterized the 'removal of taboos' [*Enttabuisierung*]

> as though a new de-sublimated wilfulness would violate vulnerable political and civil norms. . . . And this lack of distinction enables you wrongly to relate the specificity of the object of Walser's contempt to the generality of a historically founded principle of communication [*Verständigungsgebot*]. These are the framework conditions for your renewed formulation of a national pedagogy. At this point, it becomes clear how you want to instrumentalize the Walser debate in the interest of your anti-fascistic tilting at windmills.

'What is at stake', says Bohrer, 'is not the abolition of appropriate civilized principles' but the

> use of civilized speech: namely in the form of a rejection of the torch-bearers of doctrinal certainties of faith which are held up against

the sober recognition of reality. . . . Walser's excesses in particular, however good or bad they might be in literary terms, betoken a liberal society: not because one should be infinitely lenient as if everything were permitted, as among crooks, but because the tonic of literature is also hatred. You speak of 'stuffiness'. What would be more stuffy than this 'putting under suspicion' as it was practised by the dozen?

Bohrer ends his letter with the words: 'Not without nostalgia. Your K. H. B.'

Bohrer's sign-off alludes to the fact that there had once been a friendly relationship between him and Habermas. As Bohrer stated in a recent interview, Habermas was among those who protested when he had to give up his post as the chief literary editor at the *Frankfurter Allgemeine Zeitung* to Marcel Reich-Ranicki, who was favoured by the new publisher Joachim Fest.[88] Over the years, their friendship began to turn sour, especially after Bohrer took over Hans Schwab Felisch's role as editor-in-chief at *Merkur* at the end of the 1970s and quickly steered the cultural journal in the direction of a cultural politics that Habermas rejected. The two differed mainly with regard to their attitudes towards German intellectual history, French post-structuralism and the future of a reunified Germany.[89] Habermas's reaction to Bohrer's open letter shows just how strained the relationship between the two intellectuals was at the time of the debate over Walser's novel.[90] In a short letter to the editor of the *Frankfurter Allgemeine Zeitung* (11 June 2002), he replied succinctly that Bohrer was agitated over 'his own projections'. However, he accused the editorial board of the paper of having published a 'denunciation' because the readership was not able to verify what Habermas had actually written in his original article, which had appeared elsewhere. Finally, Ulrich Raulff intervened in the dispute in a piece in the *Süddeutsche Zeitung* (15 June 2002). The historian, who would become the director of the German Literature Archive in Marbach in 2004, pointedly remarked that there was a 'poverty of aesthetic criticism' because it was being replaced with 'moral-political judgements, a critique of mentalities [*Gesinnungskritik*]'. The 'grandchildren of Critical Theory', in particular, 'found it easiest to part with its aesthetic heirs. . . . The criticism of aesthetic works is replaced with the examination of the authors' mentalities [*durch die Gesinnungsprüfungen der Autoren*].' Habermas did not react to these accusations – he simply let the matter rest.

In June 2002, Habermas accepted an invitation from Mohammad Khatami, the then Iranian president and the founder of the International Centre for Dialogue among Civilizations, to spend a week in Iran. He visited the University of Tehran, which he found to possess an 'open-minded academic atmosphere', and gave two public lectures in which he spoke to a large, mostly academic audience about the 'secularization in the post-secular societies of the West' and the universal validity of human rights. He related his impressions of the country in a conversation with the *Frankfurter Allgemeine Zeitung* (13 June 2002): 'The picture of a centrally directed society, controlled by a secret service, mute, simply does not fit – at least, it does not fit with the impressions I got from my encounters with intellectuals, with citizens of an unintimidated, spontaneous and self-confident urban population.' But Habermas also remarked that 'support for Hezbollah cannot simply be glossed over.' 'However, what was irritating at first sight were the enormous banners with the heads and slogans of the two spiritual leaders of the revolution, which somehow reminded you of Honnecker's GDR.' He added: 'When you travel with little intellectual baggage from West to East, you enter into the usual asymmetrical communicative situation in which the role of the barbarian is awaiting us: they know more about us than we do about them.' On 19 June, the *Frankfurter Allgemeine Zeitung* reported on the reactions of the 'anti-reform Iranian press', according to whom Habermas had 'ended up in between the camps of domestic politics in Iran':

> The conservative newspaper *Entechab* used Habermas's remarks to attack not so much the philosopher himself as his host, the Centre for Dialogue among Civilizations, which is close to the reformist President Mohammad Khatami. . . . Under the heading 'The surprising effect we had on Habermas', *Entechab* complained that the centre brought Habermas, 'who has a lot to say about the philosophy of secularism', in touch only with reformers. . . . Contrary to the actual reality, Habermas had put the freedom of religious minorities in Iran in doubt.

Habermas as a defender of religious intolerance? He actually grappled with the problem of a philosophical justification of tolerance, which had occupied him since his early days as a student in Göttingen, during a three-day colloquium in the second week of March 2002 at the University of Lucerne and then at the Leibniz Congress of the Academy of Science in Berlin. For him, tolerance as a virtuous form of behaviour towards alien ethical orientations principally implies the complete legal inclusion of all citizens in the polity. The members must reach a mutual and uncoerced agreement about the rules of tolerance in such a way that everyone can see themselves as being tolerated and at the same time as tolerating others.[91] Regarding the question of how tolerant a democracy should be towards its opponents, Habermas registers his doubts over attempts to protect the constitution 'in a paternalistic way' that could involve curtailing the space for civil disobedience and defining the limits of tolerance too narrowly. Tolerance, he says, is more than just openness and the absence of prejudice; it is a form of behaviour, or even an imposition that becomes necessary 'when the parties with good reason neither seek agreement concerning controversial beliefs nor think agreement is possible.'[92]

Partings. 2002 was also a year of great personal loss for Habermas. In January, news of the death of the French sociologist Pierre Bourdieu reached him; on 13 March, Hans-Georg Gadamer died, and on 26 October his close companion Siegfried Unseld also passed away. In *Die Zeit*, Habermas remembered Gadamer's 'seemingly non-coercive authority'. For him, Gadamer had been one of those teachers 'who, by looking closely at the break with corrupted traditions, taught us to make distinctions and, through this critique, to appropriate what had been left unharmed.'[93] In the *Süddeutsche Zeitung*, he published a final letter to Unseld, which ends with the words:

> Dear Siegfried, you are leaving behind a great emptiness, because you were such a huge presence. But you occupied this space not in order to take it away from others but, rather, to create a universe. Movement was the mode of your existence. To keep alive by moving, that was the trauma of those distressing hours in the Black Sea, when the fleeing soldier, exhausted almost to the point of death, kept swimming and swimming for his life. The trauma transformed, you transformed it, into the archetype of the unexpectedly saved life.

Habermas also remembered Unseld's patience with 'narcissistic-quarrelsome' authors, his openness in the face of the reluctant attitude of philosophical authors, his special affection for Ernst Bloch. 'Did he not give philosophical honour to the source of your courage for life with his *Principle of Hope*?'[94] Habermas was unable to attend Unseld's memorial ceremony and funeral because, as in every other year, he was in Evanston at Northwestern University for six weeks as a visiting professor, and attending would have entailed flying to Europe and back in two days.

In December 2002, Rainer Rochlitz died at the age of just fifty-six. The philosopher, art historian and director of research at the Centre national de la recherche scientifique and at the École des hautes études en sciences sociales had been the French translator of Habermas's works. In the *Frankfurter Allgemeine Zeitung* (17 December 2002), Habermas wrote: 'His lean and lanky, always somewhat harried appearance retained the moving aura of a burdened, a dangerous life – as if Rochlitz did not want to, or could not, leave behind the role of a German emigrant in Paris, the historical shadow of a long sequence of famous predecessors.'

2003 – a hectic year On 18 March 2003, Christian Geyer reviewed the *Memoirs* of the philosopher Hans Jonas, which had been published only days earlier, for the 'new non-fiction books' section of the *Frankfurter Allgemeine Zeitung*.[95] Geyer pointed out that Jonas, born in 1903 and author of *The Imperative of Responsibility*, had not been able to feel at home again after resettling in Germany, and that he found too little recognition. 'Symbolically, he saw his alien status best confirmed by the fact "that Jürgen Habermas, who is well disposed towards me and views me with a certain respect, blocked me from receiving the Adorno Prize, as he told me himself, but was much taken with the notion that I should receive the Sophie and Hans Scholl Prize, and at a dinner at his house said Yes, that fits. Given the conservative spirit which you represent."'* In a letter to the editor (21 March), Habermas commented on the passage Geyer quoted:

Geyer speaks of a 'haggling over prizes in the Habermas home'. There was nothing to 'haggle' over. Wallmann had invited me as one of the earlier recipients to join the jury for the Adorno Prize. After Norbert Elias had received the prize, and Hans Jonas and Günter Anders had been suggested, I justified my proposal of choosing someone younger instead, namely Alexander Kluge, with the argument that the history of Adorno's reception should be taken into account. As we know, Günter Anders received the prize in the end. Jonas must have learned about these discussions through somebody's indiscretion. I am still baffled as to why this usually confident character, free of any vanity, would have asked me at all about this internal procedure in the course of such a friendly dinner.[96]

Shortly afterwards, Habermas took aim at recent US foreign policy in an article titled 'Was bedeutet der Denkmalsturz?' [What is the significance of the toppling of the monument?] (*Frankfurter Allgemeine Zeitung*, 17 April 2003). The hegemonic unilateralism of the USA, he wrote, meant that it had stopped being the pacemaker for a cosmopolitan legal order. Its normative authority lay in tatters; it had 'given up the role of guarantor of international law'. His criticism focused on the superpower's military strikes aimed at removing the Iraqi dictator Saddam Hussein and combating al-Qaeda; for Habermas, these were neither defensive actions nor humanitarian interventions. He welcomed the anti-war demonstrations staged by

---

* Hans Jonas (2008), *Memoirs*, p. 204. The context of the quoted passage is Jonas's alleged Aristotelianism, one result of which was that 'those who consider themselves members of the Frankfurt School see me as conservative, the more so because I can't be assigned to any of the current camps in German philosophy and thus seem to be an outsider. *That* becomes visible symbolically in the fact that . . . etc.' (ibid.; emphasis added).

peace movements all over the world. It is a contradiction in itself, he wrote, that a leading power attempts to enforce the universalist core of democracy and human rights with fire and sword.

In September 2003, Theodor W. Adorno would have celebrated his hundredth birthday, and events marking the occasion were held throughout the whole year, among them an international conference 'Dialektik der Freiheit' [Dialectics of freedom], organized by the Institute of Social Research and its director Axel Honneth.[97] On the afternoon of 25 September, Jürgen Habermas gave the opening lecture to a packed Lecture Hall VI – '"I Myself am Part of Nature" – Adorno on the Intrication of Reason in Nature'. In the evening, Jan Philipp Reemtsma spoke about 'Adorno und die Literatur' [Adorno and literature]. Habermas's lecture discussed the antinomy of freedom and determinism against the background of Adorno's notion of an uncontrolled '"first" nature' and the naturalistic image of a '"second" nature' that has become completely controllable, 'determined through and through in accordance with laws'.[98] Freedom, he explained, is indeed conditioned in a twofold way: through an individual's nature and through an individual's life history in the social world. 'Reasons and the exchange of reasons constitute the logical space in which the free will is formed.'[99] This space, in turn, is threatened by a society which has become an independent 'second nature' and in which the principle of a self-preservation gone wild is on the rise.[100]

In October 2003, Habermas travelled to Oviedo in northern Spain, where he received the Prince of Asturias Award for Social Science, which came with an endowment of 50,000 euros, from the Spanish Crown Prince Felipe. In his acceptance speech at the Teatro Campoamor, Habermas warned against a failure of the constitutional process in Europe. After talks at the Goethe Institute in Madrid, he received the gold medal of the Círculo de Bellas Artes.

The hectic year of 2003 was full of vexations for Habermas. The Jonas affair in March was followed by a scandal in the summer concerning a book by the Canadian-British philosopher Ted Honderich, which had appeared in 2002 with Edinburgh University Press. As a member of the board of trustees (established only in June 2002) of the Siegfried and Ulla Unseld Foundation, which is the majority owner of the Suhrkamp publishing house, Habermas had recommended the translation and publication of Honderich's treatise on the consequences and causes of the 9/11 attacks, titled *After the Terror*. The book appeared in German as *Nach dem Terror: Ein Traktat* in the anniversary series '40 years of edition suhrkamp'. Micha Brumlik, a professor of education at the Johann Wolfgang Goethe University and director of the Fritz Bauer Institute, which is dedicated to documenting and researching Nazi mass crimes, in particular the Holocaust, published an open letter in the *Frankfurter*

Rundschau (5 August 2003). Brumlik unambiguously demanded that the publisher take the book off the market because it advocated an 'anti-Semitic anti-Zionism' by justifying the murder of Jewish civilians in Palestinian suicide attacks. The following day, Harry Nutt published a commentary, 'On the Honderich Dispute', in the *Frankfurter Rundschau*. It was a case, he said, of 'a kind of casual anti-Semitism', but the main theme of the book was 'the demand for a redistribution of life chances'. Nevertheless, it was surprising 'that Suhrkamp let such a text pass'. On this point, Habermas expressed himself in the same paper and on the same day:

> Micha Brumlik's letter startled me. I did recommend the book by Ted Honderich for the edition suhrkamp, and thus carry my part of the responsibility for a publication which, Brumlik thinks, must 'be taken off the market at once'. . . . When Honderich's manuscript came into my hands at the end of last year, I had just returned in a depressed mood from my annual stay in the USA. I was depressed by the public atmosphere in that liberal country, where the government was preparing for the war against Iraq even in the media. It appealed to the fears of an understandably deeply worried population, while the voices of the opposition had fallen almost completely silent. I breathed a bit more easily when I found that the manuscript of a respected English colleague presented an entirely different perspective. The text reveals the pathos of justice of an old social democrat who has thought for a long time about the concrete consequences which a monstrously uneven distribution of earthly goods has on the life expectancy, life chances and life histories of those tired and exhausted populations in the marginalized parts of the world, and who now sees an opportunity to rattle the social conscience of 'normal citizens' in the Western world. . . . Of course, it is a casual pamphlet, one with which a philosopher well versed in theory wants for once to reach a broader audience. The one-sided sketch of the history of the conflict which began with the foundation of the state of Israel, of which the author explicitly approves, is far from satisfactory in terms of doing justice to history. . . . However, there are also generalizing sentences which make me cringe: 'Having been the principal victims of racism in history, some Jews seem now to have learned from their abusers.'* Such sentences,

---

* The new, revised and extended German translation of Honderich's book correctly gives: 'Als die vornehmlichen Opfer von Rassismus in der Geschichte scheinen einige Juden heute von ihren Peinigern gelernt zu haben.' Honderich ([2003] 2004), *Nach dem Terror* (Neu-Isenburg), p. 49. Habermas quotes: 'Als Hauptopfer von Rassismus in der Geschichte scheinen die Juden von ihren Peinigern gelernt zu haben.' = 'As the principal victims of racism in history, the Jews seem to have learned from their abusers.' Apparently, the original translation by Suhrkamp omitted the qualification 'some', a small but in this context not negligible omission, as it turns a (problematically suggestive) qualified statement into an (untenable) generalization.

when removed from their argumentative context without exercising any hermeneutic charity, can always be used for anti-Semitic purposes, even against the intentions of the author.

Again on the same day, Christian Geyer reported in the *Frankfurter Allgemeine Zeitung* that Suhrkamp had announced that they would not reprint the book – which in the meantime had sold out – and that they would hand back the rights. In the *Neue Züricher Zeitung* (7 August), Andreas Breitenstein insisted that, although Honderich is an 'old leftist', he is certainly no 'anti-Semite of the old school. . . . While today programmatic racism constitutes intellectual suicide, there has nevertheless spread a smart kind of anti-Semitism, which hides its fundamental rejection of Jewishness behind seemingly plausible arguments, open declarations and witty allusions.' Breitenstein concluded: 'No, Honderich's book really has no place in an "edition" which always had the aspiration that Habermas himself denies the treatise in his reply: "to contribute to the disentanglement of complex causalities".'

The year ended with another unpleasant matter. In December, the entire board of trustees of the Suhrkamp publishing house resigned. Apart from Habermas, its members were Hans Magnus Enzensberger, Alexander Kluge, Adolf Muschg and Wolf Singer. Shortly before his death, Siegfried Unseld had established the board, which was meant to advise the family foundation so as to ensure some continuity in the publisher's policies. There was plenty of speculation about the reasons behind this spectacular resignation. Rumours were circulating about differences regarding the management reorganization following the exit of the publishing director Günter Berg. The central statement in the declaration of the board of trustees also pointed in that direction: 'As members of the board of directors of the Siegfried and Ulla Suhrkamp Family Foundation, we have been confronted with serious decisions that have been taken without our involvement and against our advice. The issue does not concern individuals, but the managerial structure of the publishing house.' They further clarified that their resignation did not in any way affect the loyalty 'which we, as authors, continue to feel towards the publishing house.'[101] In the *Frankfurter Allgemeine Zeitung* (4 December 2003), Hubert Spiegel remarked that the members of the board had to answer the question of 'which part they played in the breakdown in cooperation. Did serious differences regarding fundamental questions lead to the separation, or was it the consequence of a belated realization of their own powerlessness?' Apparently, the members of the board of trustees had indeed overestimated their potential influence.

Many honours and an affair

In the spring of 2004, two issues gripped the German public. One was the Agenda 2010, Gerhard Schröder's programme of reforms for his second period in office, which met with strong resistance from both the right and the left and led to several defeats for the SPD in local and state elections, some of them heavy. This prompted the chancellor, in 2005, to ask parliament for a vote of confidence in order to trigger early elections. The other issue was the imminent election of a new president. There were two candidates for the office, Gesine Schwan, a political scientist and president of the Europa Universität Viadrina in Frankfurt an der Oder, and Horst Köhler, acting director of the International Monetary Fund (IMF) and an experienced and internationally respected finance and economic expert, who, incidentally, had been suggested for the IMF post by Schröder. About the forthcoming election, Habermas wrote in *Die Zeit* (13 May 2004): 'Because what is at stake is the use of symbolic capital, the political calibre of the candidate is more important than usual.' With this in mind, he criticized 'the power games', the way in which the leaders of the Christian Democrats and the Liberal Party had furtively conjured up a candidate to be elected by the Federal Assembly. 'Not only did these political string-pullers not give a hoot about the institution of the federal president, they also did not give a hoot about the citizens' justified interest in the person that would represent all Germans on the global stage.' Habermas complained that the public and the citizens did not have sufficient opportunity to form a concrete picture of the two candidates, both of whom were political newcomers without experience in professional politics. Habermas made no secret of his sympathies for the political independence and passion of the Social Democrat candidate, while he accused Horst Köhler of toeing the lines of the parties responsible for his nomination in the run-up to the election. In the end, Horst Köhler was elected as the ninth president of the Federal Republic on 23 May.

But Habermas also reproached the Red–Green coalition (whose days, it would soon turn out, were numbered) for their neo-liberal and fainthearted policies regarding Europe. In an interview published in the *Süddeutsche Zeitung* on 18 June 2004, one day before his seventy-fifth birthday, Habermas said: 'The economic glance at the voters is a *déformation professionelle* of election analysts.'* He recommended that the Social Democratic Party 'remember their

---

* 'Der ökonomische Blick auf die Wähler ist eine *deformation professionelle* der Wahlforscher.' What is meant, presumably, is that it is a professional deformation of election analysts to assume that voters are interested only in economic matters – a mistake here said to be repeated by left-wing parties.

programmatic virtues [and] opt for political goals that go beyond the scope for action of individual nation-states.' The real problem, he said, is 'the voluntary abdication of politics in the face of objective constraints which politics itself unleashed in the first place.' The interview, by Andreas Zielke, ended with Habermas's remark that, even in a secularized Europe, the normative self-understanding was informed by the spiritual sources of world religions. Habermas reached a conclusion that also threw light on himself: 'Atheists are no heathens.'[102]

On 18 May 2004, *The Divided West* appeared in the edition suhrkamp as Volume X of the *Kleine Politische Schriften* [Short political writings]. Four weeks later, Habermas celebrated his seventy-fifth birthday. Again, the occasion was widely covered in the media. Perhaps the most personal birthday wishes came from Jacques Derrida, who told 'the story of a friendship with obstacles' in the *Frankfurter Rundschau* (18 June 2004) under the heading 'Unsere Redlichkeit!' [Our honesty!]. He emphasized their 'political closeness in more than one area', especially with respect to the future of Europe. Derrida ended with the sentence: 'But I wish from my heart that the word, the writings and the person of Jürgen Habermas will continue to lighten our hopes for much longer, in these times of powerlessness and in view of the dark threats that announce themselves.' A little later, the publisher Philo would bring out the small volume *Philosophy in Times of Terror*, which contained the conversations between Derrida and Habermas led by Giovanna Borradori in New York. And the first account of Habermas's life, written by Rolf Wiggershaus, appeared in Rowohlt's legendary 'Monographien' series.

Yet more prizes. Around the same time, Habermas was virtually showered with prizes and honours. First, in 2004, the year of his seventy-fifth birthday, he was awarded the internationally renowned Kyoto Prize of the Inamori Foundation, in recognition of his life's work. He received the generously endowed prize in November at an imperial ceremony in Kyoto. Habermas gave an academic lecture in which he again rejected the claim that the neurosciences are able to demonstrate that human free will and self-responsibility are mere illusions.[103] After Kazuo Inamori, founder of the Japanese technology corporation Kyocera, asked Habermas to '[p]lease, talk about [himself], Habermas, for the very first time, reflected in public about his own life, or, more precisely, about the 'biographical roots' of his thinking and his political commitments – i.e., the traumatic operations on his palate in early childhood, his speech impediment and the 'feelings of dependence and vulnerability' associated with it, the caesura of 1945, the awareness of the rupture in civilization, the dismay at how the National Socialist crimes were dealt with immediately after the war, and his impulse to intervene publicly, which was fuelled by the permanent fear of a political relapse.[104] Nevertheless, he said, the position of the philosopher must not be overestimated. A philosopher's life 'in general . . . is rather poor in external events'; it is

> not the stuff that the lives of saints are made of . . . Indeed, in our field, we treat those thinkers as 'classics' whose works have remained contemporary for us. The ideas of such a classical thinker are like the molten core beneath a volcano that has deposited biographical rings of hardened lava. The great thinkers of the past whose works have stood the test of time impress this image upon us. By contrast, we, the many living philosophers – who are in any case more professors of philosophy – are merely the contemporaries of our contemporaries.[105]

And, in the role of an intellectual, it is the philosopher's task 'to improve the deplorable discursive level of public debates'. At the end of his speech, Habermas spoke about the standards of communicative reason on which a philosopher and intellectual draws: 'It is hardly surprising that we generally fail to live up to these standards; but that in no way devalues the standards themselves. For if there is one thing that intellectuals – a species that has so often attacked its own kind and pronounced its demise – cannot allow themselves, then it is to become cynical.'[106] Like all laureates of the Kyoto Prize, Habermas was asked to formulate a maxim for the youth. His was: 'Never compare yourself to a genius, but always strive toward criticizing the work of a genius.'

When Habermas left the University of Bonn after having completed his doctorate, he was twenty-four years of age. Fifty years later, in November 2004, the Rheinische Friedrich Wilhelms Universität honoured him with a 'Golden Doctorate'. Again, the laureate accepted his honour with a biographical speech in which he looked back at his philosophical beginnings: at the years as a student in Bonn; the influence of his academic teachers; his own philosophical interests at the time, which sometimes ran counter to those of his teachers; and encountering Karl-Otto Apel, under whose influence, he said, he had begun to develop an interest in the philosophy of language and in pragmatism.

The next prize came from Norway and had been endowed by the Norwegian parliament with a prize fund of 585,000 euros. He received the International Holberg Memorial Prize in November 2005 in Bergen[107] for, among other things, his 'path-breaking theories of discourse and of communicative action, which also open up new perspectives on law and democracy'. 'Religion in the Public Sphere' was the topic of his acceptance speech, as well as of the Holberg Prize Seminar, whose invited respondents included Arne

Johan Vetlesen, Gunnar Skirbekk, Cristina Lafont, Craig Calhoun, Thomas M. Schmidt, Hauke Brunkhorst and Tore Lindholm.[108] A year later, Habermas was invited by the Norwegian ambassador to present a further talk associated with the Holberg Prize at the Academy of Art in Berlin. This time he spoke on the topic of free will.

When receiving the Bruno Kreisky Prize in Vienna in March 2006, Habermas dealt with two very different topics. One was Europe; the other was the role of the intellectual.[109] He predicted that the new figure of the alert, telegenic, self-promoting media intellectual would bring about its own downfall. 'Perhaps', Habermas said, 'this is why the groups of politicians, experts, and journalists invited by one of those fabulous talk-show hostesses do not leave any room to be filled by an intellectual. We don't miss the intellectual because her role is already performed better by the other participants.'[110]

The transformations towards a media society would continue to occupy Habermas. In June 2006, he attended the World Congress of the International Communication Association in Dresden. The ICA was founded in 1950 and has about 3,500 members who work on communication and mass media at an academic level. Habermas presented a paper in English, 'Does Democracy Still Have an Epistemic Dimension? The Impact of Normative Theory on Empirical Research', which marks an important development in his work because here he updates his theory of mass communication from the perspective of deliberative democracy. The published version of the talk, which appeared in 2008 in *Ach, Europa* (Volume XI of *Kleine Politische Schriften*), is dedicated *in memoriam* to one of his most important disciples in this area, Bernhard Peters, a social theorist and expert on the public sphere who taught at the University of Bremen, who had died in 2005. Habermas's essay contains his most up-to-date reflections on his theory of the public sphere and democracy.

Is the omnipresence of mass media compatible with a model of deliberative democracy? Taking this question as his point of departure, Habermas discusses, on the one hand, empirical results from research in communication which demonstrate the cognitive effects of public discourses. On the other hand, he complains that communication mediated by the press, radio and television is abused in the course of its commercialization. By contrast, he says, internet communication, it seems, offers the new possibility 'of counterbalancing the weakness associated with the anonymous and asymmetrical character of mass communication because it makes it possible to reintegrate interactive and deliberative elements into an unregulated exchange between partners who communicate with one another as equals, if only virtually.'[111] However, this is juxtaposed with tendencies towards an increasing fragmentation of the public sphere, which, as research in communication has shown, can be explained by the compression and acceleration of information flows. But this would not rule out the model of deliberative democracy because, at all three levels – the central political system, a dispersed mass communication, and decentralized communication in everyday life – there was, after all, a functional coherence. For that reason, the circulation of information within the public sphere as an intermediate system of communication remains intact, without the sources of democratic legitimation drying up. However, Habermas also analyses the gap that opens up between what is democratically required and what emerges as a reality within the political sphere. He criticizes not only the mixing of politics and entertainment through the mechanisms of personalization and scandalization but also the lack of openness in the media when it comes to providing a space for the voices of civil movements and their opposed perspectives. As in the *Structural Transformation of the Public Sphere* of 1962, Habermas argues that 'radio and television audiences are not only consumers, that is, market participants, but also citizens who have a right to partake in culture, to follow political events, and to be involved in the formation of political opinions.'[112]

In November 2006, Habermas received the Staatspreis des Landes Nordrhein-Westfalen from the minister of North Rhine-Westphalia, the CDU politician Jürgen Rüttgers, at the Petersberg guesthouse near Königswinter. The philosopher Wolfram Hogrebe, who teaches in Bonn, honoured the laureate in carefully chosen words as a thinker with 'the power to analyse discourses and at the same time an enormous power to initiate discourses'. The former leader of the Social Democratic Party, Hans-Jochen Vogel, highlighted the fact that Habermas's discourse theory as well as his political commitment had been 'good for democracy'. 'You have acquired intellectual power, power of the mind, and used it in the interest of our polity.' The minister of North Rhine-Westphalia, who spoke last, amused the audience by remarking that only someone from the Rhineland was capable of writing a thousand pages on communication. In his acceptance speech, Habermas criticized the neo-liberal mainstream and complained that European unity was no longer at the very top of the political agenda. Rather, we saw a 'global politics characterized by uninhibited Social Darwinism'. Habermas again promoted the development of classical international law into a politically constituted global society.[113]

The affair over an allegedly swallowed document. Günter Grass's memoir, *Peeling the Onion*, appeared in September 2006. In it, he admitted that, as a seventeen-year-old, he had joined the Waffen SS towards the end of the war.[114] That September also saw the publication of the autobiography of the historian and publicist Joachim

Fest, *Not Me: A German Childhood,* in which a rumour that had circulated in various publications was now presented as fact: Jürgen Habermas – who, despite not being mentioned by name, is obviously who Fest means to refer to – chewed and swallowed a letter that had turned up by chance, written when he was a member of the Hitler Youth, which demonstrated his enthusiasm for the Nazis and for 'final victory'.[115] This passage from Fest's book[116] was taken up by the journalist Jürgen Busche and used for an article in the cultural magazine *Cicero,* bearing the title 'Hat Habermas die Wahrheit verschluckt?' [Did Habermas swallow the truth?]. In an alleged 'search for evidence', he investigated the rumour and insinuated that Habermas did, indeed, dispose of the piece of evidence of his involvement in National Socialism in this peculiar way. Ralf Dahrendorf responded in the *Neue Züricher Zeitung* (16 November 2006): 'Whoever believes such nonsense has suspended his normal powers of judgement; there would, indeed, be simpler methods of getting rid of a piece of paper, if that were necessary.' The whole affair is indeed bizarre: the rumour was not new, and had been circulating since the 1970s.

Hermann Lübbe, in his book *Politischer Moralismus* [Political moralism], is generally thought to be the source of the rumour about the allegedly swallowed document:

> An intellectual who consistently uses the opinions of others regarding current political, moral or historical questions as criteria for judging the degree of their emancipation from German history was on one occasion, with the best of intentions, handed a document which showed him, when he was a Pimpf* . . . to have for a short time been in agreement with this role. Instead of adopting, on that occasion, the appropriate attitude towards this biographical episode in his life, the man took the document in question and ate it. That is what one may call, quite literally, repression, i.e., through ingestion, and in a metaphorical sense a refusal to count incriminating parts of one's own past as belonging to one's originary identity.[117]

It was disgraceful, however, of Fest and Busche to rekindle this rumour despite the fact that they knew it to be false, since the person to which everyone was referring, Hans-Ulrich Wehler, had long since publicly denied its truth on several occasions. On 4 April 2006, Joachim Fest turned to Wehler, whom Habermas had known since his adolescence and been friendly with since the 1960s, asking him for accurate information about the matter. In his reply of 18 April,

---

* 'Pimpfe' were members of the Hitler Youth aged six to ten, which does not fit with the further details behind the rumour.

Wehler unambiguously and comprehensively described what had actually happened. And in *Der Spiegel* of 30 October 2006, as well as in *Die Zeit* of 2 November, Wehler repeated his description. A Hitler Youth form from their time together in Gummersbach had turned up by chance when Wehler was going through his wartime diaries, and it contained a reminder from Habermas to the recipients to attend the first aid courses he ran. Much later, Wehler had sent this curious document to Habermas. During a holiday they spent together on Elba in the summer of 1974, he had asked Ute Habermas what had happened to this piece of mail, 'and on the beach Ute Habermas answered ironically: "You know Jürgen, he swallowed it."'

Through his lawyers, Habermas obtained an injunction against Fest's book. The publisher Rowohlt was threatened with a fine of 250,000 euros if he continued to publish the passage in question, which constituted a deliberate defamation. An appeal by the publisher was rejected by the courts. Habermas did not accept the compromise suggested by Rowohlt of adding a correction to the copies of the book that were already printed. Thus, 20,000 copies were pulped.[118]

Habermas also made the following clarifications in a letter to the editor of *Cicero* (25 October 2006): The 'by now famous "document"' had been

> one of the common 'requests' at the time – a pre-printed form which I sent out back then in order to ensure the participants of my courses kept attending. Otherwise, I would have had to discontinue them. And then I would have had to turn up again for the regular HY 'duty', as it was called, which I detested. . . . Where else but in the waste paper bin should it [the document; S. M.-D.] have landed?

Although the 'form affair' was gratefully picked up by the publishing media, most commentators agreed that the real scandal consisted of the accounts given by Fest and Busche. Thus, Christian Geyer, for instance, wrote in the *Frankfurter Allgemeine Zeitung* (27 October): 'Is the intention to produce a suggestive impression of Habermas in the shadow of the Grass affair? How cheap, how tasteless, how historically revisionist this is. Busche is not able to add even one new fact about the rumour that would make it anywhere near verifiable.' The same day, in the *Süddeutsche Zeitung*, Andreas Zielcke remarked that Joachim Fest knew long before he died that the anecdote was not true in the form in which it had been told to him. Zielcke's conclusion was clear-sighted: 'The wounds which the historians' debate had caused must have been deep and open to the present day if they are to explain *such* attacks that ignore any kind of historical fairness.' Robert Leicht, in *Die Zeit*

(2 November 2006), wrote that Fest's need 'to denounce [Habermas] as a moralistic person who had a National Socialist skeleton in the closet' must have been so great that he even 'used an empty rumour against his better judgement'. Also writing in *Die Zeit*, Thomas Assheuer called Busche's article 'a neat little piece of loathsome denunciation'. The edition of *Cicero* in question didn't hold back: it had 'Forget Habermas!' written in large letters across the front page and prophesied the imminent end of political philosophy. This mostly caused irritation or was met with rejection. '*Cicero* presents Germany's new thinkers', the magazine announced, in an allusion to a 1977 monograph by Jean Baudrillard with the title *Oublier Foucault*. Inside, the following candidates were presented as possible successors: Peter Sloterdijk, who, according to a caption, was 'about to take up the position of the leading German intellectual', then Peter Bieri, Dominik Perler, Armin Grunwald, and the two 'disciples of Habermas' Rainer Forst and Lutz Wingert. Apart from Sloterdijk, they all protested against being stylized in this fashion in a joint declaration which appeared on the *Cicero* homepage and in the November edition: 'However, the situation becomes unacceptable for us when we are meant to be instrumentalized in the context of a campaign of political denunciation against our colleague Jürgen Habermas.' In the following December edition of the magazine and on the homepage, Wolfram Weimer, the editor-in-chief of *Cicero*, apologized to Habermas in an open letter. His earlier statement on *Deutschlandradio Kultur* on 27 October had already struck a similar tone.

12

The Taming of Capitalism and the Democratization of Europe

Of course, the theoretical foundations of Marx's critique of capitalism have been superseded. But an impartial analysis of the simultaneously liberating and uprooting, productive and destructive effects of our economic organization on the life-world is more essential than ever before.[1]

Looking back: Marx and the critique of capitalism. How can totalitarian worldviews and forms of rule be prevented? It should by now be sufficiently clear that this question forms the core of Jürgen Habermas's overall social-theoretical project, as well as his commitments as an intellectual. The aim is to develop a normatively grounded theory of democracy and to work towards a practice of democracy that is based on civil society.[2] But how does his (deliberative) concept of democracy, which will be discussed later, relate to capitalism? For, as we know: 'Whoever doesn't want to talk about capitalism should also remain silent about fascism.'[3]

Of course, Habermas did not remain silent about capitalism. Rather, very early on he had already concerned himself, in particular, with Marx's theory of capitalism and the concept of alienation, for instance in the article 'Dialektik der Rationalisierung' [Dialectics of rationalization], published in 1954. (As mentioned before, Habermas himself said that this article anticipated motifs that he later developed more fully in his social theory.)[4] Or, for instance, in his 'Marx in Perspektiven' [Perspectives on Marx] of 1955, where he claims, contra Marx, that it would be a mistake to assign an emancipatory potential to the forces of production.[5] This insight essentially determined the future path of Habermas's reception of Marx.

During his time as a researcher at the Institute for Social Research in Frankfurt in the mid-1950s, Habermas intensified his efforts at clarifying his position with regard to historical materialism and to Marx's critique of capitalism, and he reached the conclusion that the crisis-induced self-sublation of the capitalist economy, as predicted by Marx, was not a foregone conclusion.[6] Although he retained

Marx's critique of the one-sided distribution of private control over the means of labour and material resources – i.e., over the means of production – as well as Marx's insights into the causes of the uneven distribution of income and into the anarchic character of the capitalist process of self-valorization and accumulation, Habermas fairly quickly moved away from the economistic perspective which characterizes Marx's thought.

At the beginning of the 1970s, Habermas began to concentrate more and more on the project of a crisis theory, at which point the deficiencies of a Marxian critique of political economy were clearly at the forefront of his mind. As he himself put it in a 1978 interview with the Italian social scientist Angelo Bolaffi:

> The point on which I differ from the traditional Marxist analysis is that, today, when we use the means of the critique of political economy, we can no longer make clear predictions: for that, one would still have to assume the autonomy of a self-reproducing economic system. I do not believe in such an autonomy. Precisely for this reason, the laws governing the economic system are no longer identical to the ones Marx analysed. Of course, this does not mean that it would be wrong to analyse the mechanism which drives the economic system; but, in order for the orthodox version of such an analysis to be valid, the influence of the political system would have to be ignored.[7]

Late capitalism. In his lecture 'Some Conditions for Revolutionizing Late Capitalist Societies', given in August 1968 at the Korčula Summer School, in the former Yugoslavia, as well as in 'Technology and Science as "Ideology"' of the same year, Habermas focused on an analysis of the transformational processes of capitalistically organized societies. What distinguishes contemporary late capitalism from the capitalism of the end of the nineteenth century, he argued, is that, on the one hand, in the case of the former there is increased state involvement through economic and social policies aimed at the prevention of looming crises. On the other hand, today we witness the merging of technology and domination, with the result that the continuous progress in applied research, along with innovative labour-saving technologies (which, from the perspective of the employee, shorten working hours), can guarantee economic growth: technology and science, Habermas said, become the 'leading productive force', and a technocratic consciousness becomes the new form of ideology. As a consequence, Habermas concluded,

> [i]t no longer makes sense to calculate the amounts of capital for investments in research and development on the basis of the value of unskilled (simple) labour power, because institutionalized scientific-

technical progress has become the basis of an indirect surplus value production, compared to which the only source of surplus value Marx considered – the labour power of the immediate producers – has less and less importance.[8]

It is likely that some members of his audience, which included Marxists such as Ernst Bloch, Alfred Sohn-Rethel and Herbert Marcuse, would have been perturbed to hear this.[9] Habermas continued:

> The stabilization of the state-regulated capitalist social system depends on the loyalty of the masses being linked to a non-political form of social compensations (of income and leisure time) and on ensuring that there is a screening out of their interest in the solution of practical questions concerning a better and good life. For this reason, however, the social system of state-regulated capitalism rests upon a *very weak legitimation basis*.[10]

As his analysis of capitalism progressed, Habermas tried to resolve the uncertainties which result from the oscillations between relative stability and potential instability in late capitalist systems by way of a more precise diagnosis: in the face of state budget deficits, recession and unemployment following the onset of the social liberal era in the 1970s, he identified *Legitimationsprobleme im Spätkapitalismus* [Legitimation problems in late capitalism],* which he interpreted as side effects of modern, functionally differentiated societies that are both capitalistically and democratically organized. Even in the mid-1970s, Habermas still dedicated a whole book to disassembling and reassembling historical materialism with the aim of making it useful for a theory of social evolution. Marx's theory of capitalism, Habermas argued, should be considered part of such a theory. In this book, he repeats his central criticism of historical materialism in its classical form, a critique aimed at three theoretical points which, in his view, are untenable: the primacy of the analysis of the capitalist process of accumulation; the dialectic between the forces of production and the relations of production; and the determination of the superstructure by the economic base.[11]

Half a decade later, in his *Theory of Communicative Action*, Habermas made another attempt at a reinterpretation of Marx. In this work, he seeks to link Marx's analysis of the value-form as commodity–money relations to a sociological theory of reification, which, in

---

* The English translation of this text turns the plural 'problems' into a singular 'crisis': *Legitimation Crisis*, Cambridge, 1988.

turn, is based on his own conceptual dualism between system and lifeworld.[12] In the second volume in particular, entitled *Lifeworld and System: A Critique of Functionalist Reason*, Habermas uses elements of Marx's critique of political economy in order to develop a contemporary theory of the sub-system 'economy', a system that has the function of regulating labour and the processes of distribution within society according to its own logic. For Habermas, the economic system of modern societies is characterized not only negatively, by the fact that it periodically produces crises which lead to political destabilization, but also positively, by the fact that, as it is based on benefit-oriented market economy principles, it functions according to criteria of economic efficiency and prosperity.

The focus of Habermas's variety of the critique of capitalism is not the specific character of the globalized capitalist economy, but what he calls the 'monetarization of the lifeworld' and what he identifies as a manifestation of a reduced form of system rationality that has become autonomous.[13] As he sees it, as long as money circulates only within the economic system, it is not problematic to have it function as the independent mediator that secures the production and distribution of goods. However, in the further course of his analysis of capitalism he reaches the conclusion that, because of its profit-driven tendency towards expansion, the economic system, with the help of the steering medium of money, penetrates into the communicative practices of everyday life. As a result, social relations become reified. It is worth noting that Habermas does not consider reification an inescapable consequence of the systemic logic of capitalism. Rather, it is to be understood as the result of capitalism's undue expansion into normatively independent spheres of social relations, such as the upbringing of children, care within the family, friendships, etc. – spheres which belong to the lifeworld and in which the ascendancy of money relations triggers pathological side effects such as, for instance, the loss of meaning or social disintegration.

Democratic politics – a counterbalance to capitalism?

The crisis of the welfare state. However, Habermas's critique of reification is not intended to resuscitate ideas of a completely domination-free society. He is as sceptical towards Marxist-inspired concepts of a 'politicized society of workers' as he is towards the old 'radical democratic promises' of the unions or the idea of 'workers' self-governance'.[14]

Rather, he is interested in working out the tensions between capitalism and democracy, insofar as the two are bound up with conflicting principles of social integration and organization.[15] While accepted democratic norms require that decisions within the political sphere be legitimized by consent, the operations of *homo oeconomicus* are guided by the maxim of achieving maximum benefit with minimal use of resources under conditions of incompatible interests among actors.

Habermas's analysis aims at relating these two sides to each other and establishing the primacy of democratically legitimized norms. His aim is to show that, within social practice, these norms prove to be successful as normative restrictions on the formation of economic power and political domination, or at least that they should prove to be so.

According to Habermas, the threat of the reification of social relations does not follow solely from the dynamic of economic growth and the laws of the regime of accumulation, but derives also from the intrinsic logic of the actions of states using the medium of power. What becomes manifest as bureaucratization in the case of the state, he says, effects the already mentioned monetarization of public and private spheres of life in the case of the economy. Because the economy and the state depend on each other, and yet have to obey their own imperatives, the possibility of conflict cannot be excluded. In addition, the political system is under pressure not only to offset the negative effects of recurring economic crises but also to produce mass loyalty in the interest of securing its own continued existence. This, Habermas says, is done, on the one hand, through ever more comprehensive political strategies for the prevention and management of crises and, on the other, through strategies that aim at raising practical-political questions to the status of special problems to be dealt with by expert elites. The political elite then tends to declare that there are no alternatives to the proposed solutions to these problems in order to avoid a public debate about them. Thus, the 'establishment of basic political rights in the framework of mass democracy means, on the one hand, a universalization of the role of the citizen and, on the other hand, a segmenting of this role from the decision process, a cleansing of political participation from any participatory content.'[16]

These strategies, which fundamentally amount to a depoliticization, have an analogue in the political system, which preventatively intervenes in the lifeworld through regulations. This tendency of the state administration towards juridification is the subject of Habermas's much noted speech on 'The Crisis of the Welfare State and the Exhaustion of Utopian Energies', which he gave in November 1984 to the Cortes Generales at the invitation of the president of the Spanish parliament. In this speech, he clearly expressed the nature of a politics of expanding welfare policies with its administrative practices of planning which cover everyday life with increasingly dense nets of legal regulation. Given this threat of a proliferation of state functions, Habermas considered it a matter of urgency that the mechanisms of democratic participation in society – in this context he spoke of 'solidarity' as a resource – are 'in a position to assert [themselves] against the "forces" present in the two other steering resources, money and administrative power.'[17]

Civilizing capitalism. The development of a global banking, financial and economic crisis out of the crisis in the US real-estate sector in the summer of 2007 went some way to confirming Habermas's worries. Now, the whole world was asking how the capitalist dynamic could be civilized and tamed. Habermas's answer was: capitalism must be put in its place by democratic means – i.e., those of a democratically legitimized and publicly practised politics. As there is no alternative to capitalism; capitalism needs to be regulated.[18]

Habermas also stressed this point in an interview with *Die Zeit*, which appeared under the heading 'Nach dem Bankrott' [After the bankruptcy].[19] In response to an initial question about his concerns over the crisis in the financial markets, he said:

> What worries me most is the scandalous social injustice that the most vulnerable social groups will have to bear the brunt of the socialized costs of market failure. The mass of those who are in any case not among the winners of globalization will now have to pick up the tab for the impact on the real economy of a predictable dysfunction of the financial system.

One could already feel the consequences of an agenda which

> recklessly prioritizes the interests of investors and is indifferent to increasing social inequality, to the emergence of a precariat, to child poverty, to a low wage sector, and so on . . . With its mania for privatization, this agenda hollows out core functions of the state, it sells out the remnants of a politically deliberating public sphere to financial investors who aim to improve their returns, and it makes culture and education dependent on the interests and whims of sponsors who are dependent on market cycles.

Habermas opposed this agenda: 'In a state with a democratic constitution there are also some public goods, for example undistorted political communication, which cannot be tailored to the profit expectations of financial investors.' And because '[s]ince 1989–90, it has become impossible to break out of the universe of capitalism', Habermas said, 'the only remaining option is to civilize and tame the capitalist dynamic from within.' In order for this to happen, the steering potential of democratically legitimized politics must be enhanced.

Thus, Habermas is interested in the primacy of politics, more precisely the *'idea of an action-upon-self programmed by laws'*. According to Habermas, this idea 'appears plausible only on the supposition that society as a whole can be represented as an association writ large, which governs itself through the media of law and political power.'[20]

Habermas indicated obliquely how this might be possible in a talk he gave in Berlin at the end of March 2012 at a symposium on 'Liberal Democracy in Hard Times: Transitions, Dilemmas, and Innovations'.* The symposium took place in honour of the retiring political scientist Claus Offe at the Hertie School of Governance. Habermas spoke about 'Dilemmas of Democracy',† using the seemingly unending crisis of the European Union as his example. If a common European politics fails, he argued, this would mean that an epoch-making opportunity has been missed: the opportunity for a supranational authority to oppose the hegemony of a global capitalist economy and the solidarity-eroding effects of deregulated markets.

The day after his talk, Habermas travelled to Wuppertal, where the conference 'Habermas und der Historische Materialismus' [Habermas and historical materialism] took place at the Bergische Universität. One of the highlights of the event was to be a debate between Karl-Otto Apel, who had just turned ninety, the Hungarian philosopher Agnes Heller, and Habermas about the explanatory value of Marx's analysis of capitalism in the light of the ongoing financial crisis. The discussants, however, completely neglected their intended topic and limited themselves to marking out their divergent philosophical positions against one another. However, Habermas referred to 'historical materialism' in the context of spontaneous remarks on the numerous individual papers presented by philosophers and sociologists. He had never been interested in an orthodox reading of historical materialism, he said, but rather had used Marx's theory in order 'to solve problems' of social theory. This was his response to the accusation that he was responsible for a social democratic deflation of Marx's theory of capitalism, in particular by ignoring the theory of money. Habermas today agrees with the Marxist diagnosis that capitalism time and again threatens its own existence. There can be no talk of a capacity of capitalism to stabilize itself economically, because, as was becoming clear, it is inevitable that nation-states become overstretched in their capacity for steering and intervention. And yet, despite this permanent threat, a 'third way' between capitalism and communism,

---

* Title in English in the original.
† Title in English in the original.

he admitted, would be an illusion at present. However, 'to think against desperation', as he put it in a contribution to the discussion, 'that is ultimately not just a motif, but a responsibility, because in many situations we could otherwise no longer act, but only freeze.'[21] This responsibility is supported by a 'communicative reason' which operates 'as a force of revenge in history'.[22] It by no means stopped short of naming those injustices which capitalism produced from its very beginnings.[23]

The Gordian knot. At the end of an interview that Habermas gave in 1990, he spoke of a 'remnant of utopia' which his sober philosophy has retained, namely the idea 'that democracy – and the public struggle for its best form – is capable of hacking through the Gordian knots of almost insoluble problems.' This focus on democratic decision-making, and the reference to 'almost insoluble problems' – i.e., the 'blindnesses' of 'occidental rationalism', but also the irrationalism of a capitalist economy with which the state struggles in vain – make it very clear that democracy must bear a significant burden.[24] But of what, exactly, does democracy consist? In short, Habermas identifies three fundamental elements: constitutionally embedded and legally secured basic rights; a functioning public sphere; and a package of rights regarding political and social participation.

Habermas derives these three fundamental elements of a democratic legal order, and in addition the principle of majority rule, as well as separate state institutions exercising legislative, executive and judicative powers, from various traditions in intellectual history. While the liberal tradition emphasizes the freedom of the citizens, the republican tradition sees their political participation as central. The concept of deliberative democracy, by contrast, highlights public debate:

> Thus the deliberative model is concerned more with the reasonableness of discourses and negotiations than with the fair aggregation of the motives of success-oriented individuals or with the authentic character of the common will of a nation. Here we find the cooperative search for shared solutions to problems of the aggregated interests of private individuals or of the collective ethos of the citizen body.[25]

The crucial point here is that Habermas translates the notion of popular sovereignty as we find it in the classical theories of democracy into the terms of a theory of communication. 'Set communicatively aflow, sovereignty makes itself felt in the power of public discourses. . . . [S]uch power originates in autonomous public spheres . . . Communicative power is exercised in the manner of a siege.'[26]

What does all this mean for the project of saving capitalism from itself? How, exactly, could this be achieved politically with the help of democratically legitimized regulatory measures, especially under conditions of a globalized economic system? Habermas knows full well that the operational space of nation-states has become increasingly limited under globalization. This, he says, is shown not least in the fact that, following the crisis of the financial market and the ensuing debt crisis in Europe, the states of the European Union were barely capable of implementing successful policies against the 'markets' in order to save the euro – despite permanent multilateral negotiations at the highest level and the introduction of various fiscal measures and monetary policies in the form of rescue packages and criteria for stability. Habermas puts the collapse of the financial system down to the limitations placed on policies of individual states, which, however, he argues could be overcome by a transnational expansion of the basis for their legitimacy.

Habermas would certainly reject Albrecht Wellmer's claim that democracy has run its course because its existing forms 'have become captives of existing capitalism'.[27] 'Before norms of domination could be accepted *without reason* by the bulk of the population, the communication structures in which our motives for action have formed up until now would have to be thoroughly destroyed. Of course, we have no metaphysical guarantee that this will not happen.'[28] And yet he understands the normative substance of constitutional guarantees in democratic states as a legal expression of the level of communicative reason that has been reached and from which we cannot really regress.

To this day, Habermas holds on to his programmatic point: democracy must find political ways of taming the economy. However, in many of his more recent statements, he emphasizes that his perspective has widened because, in view of a globally functioning, deregulated economy, a supranational expansion of democratic structures is urgently needed. As already alluded to, his hopes in this respect rest largely with a united Europe that could provide an impetus for international acceptance of democratic political standards. For '[o]nly regionally comprehensive regimes like the European Community can still affect the global system along the lines of a coordinated world domestic policy.'[29]

European integration

We will only be able to meet the challenges of globalization in a reasonable manner if the postnational constellation can successfully develop new forms for the democratic self-steering of society.[30]

The model of supranational integration, which Habermas had tire-lessly promoted since the 1980s, and even more so in the 1990s and up to the present, is for him more than just an alternative to a system of rivalling nation-states. Rather, it is bound up with hopes for a mobilization of forces which may oppose the weakening of democ-racy that he fears.[31] This, in turn, is one of the crucial conditions for being able to contain the dangerous potential of the globally con-nected economic system through democratically legitimized forms of political regulation. The idea of setting up a unified and democ-ratized Europe as a consolidated communicative power, as it were, which would represent a counterweight to the destructive tenden-cies of a globalized capitalist economy, is the result of a long-term process of reflection and learning on Habermas's part. Of course, as a politically interested contemporary, he attentively followed the European project, from the very beginning of the Treaty of Rome in 1957 and the Maastricht Treaty of 1992, to the signing of the Treaty of Lisbon by the heads of the European states in December 2007, which was meant to end several years of negotiations over institu-tional reforms within the EU – although even today this 'reform treaty' still lacks the status of a definitive constitution. But only since it had become clear that the process of political unification was stagnating, that the European Parliament remained without decision-making authority, and that the European Union could not be transformed into a European society of citizens because of the particularist interests of individual nations, did Europe become the topic that would get Habermas most 'worked up', as he himself put it.[32] He consistently intervened in his capacity as a public intellec-tual in the discussions over the unification and democratization of Europe, indeed more so than in any other debate.[33]

During the 1950s, when, thanks to Adenauer, the European idea was relatively popular, Habermas was only moderately interested in it (perhaps *because* of Adenauer's role). Despite his aversion to all things nationalistic, which was already strong at the time, the young Habermas was not an avid 'European'. To begin with, he consid-ered the formation of a European Union of the kind the chancellor was striving for as a predominantly economic matter which mostly enhanced the liberalization of trade and thus benefited capitalist market interests. As late as 1979, he said in an interview: 'I am not a fan of Europe, and also wasn't one when it was fashionable.'[34] And in a later interview for the German Press Agency (dpa) in 2007, he complemented this as follows:

> I must admit that, regarding domestic politics fifty years ago, I was more passionately interested in the question of a nuclear armament of the Bundeswehr than in the foundation of the European Economic Community. I did not understand at the time that this customs union

had already been equipped with elements that were akin to constitutional institutions, and thus already opened up the perspective of a political unification of the countries of Western Europe. On the other hand, the pacifist motivation which drove the followers of the peace movement within the national context were in harmony with the motivation which drove the six founding states and the main actors Adenauer, de Gasperi and Schumann: never again war between the nation-states that had torn each other apart in two world wars and, of course, the integration of Germany, which had instigated the war and was burdened with the monstrous crime of the destruction of the Jewry.[35]

Apart from the hope of civilizing capitalism through a global network of legal regulations, Habermas's commitment to the European idea is fuelled primarily by the insight that nation-states have a limited capacity to act. In an interview with the Hungarian *Budapester Zeitung* (17 May 2009), which is published in German, he said that, for him, the European Union

> since 1989 has become a dominant topic, for national, European and international reasons. Only a sense of Europeanness [*ein europäisches Bewußtsein*] could protect the justified joy over national unification in Germany against a false nationalistic exuberance. . . . And within today's multipolar global society, in which the USA calls the shots but is no longer the all-dominant superpower, only a politically and economically united Europe, a Europe that is capable of following its own foreign policies, is able to maintain the specificity of its multifarious cultures and to pursue the programme of a society modelled on the welfare state.

Because of the fundamental changes brought about by globalization, 'we must try to carry further the republican legacy of the nation-state on a European level.'[36]

Habermas suggests making a distinction between the nation-state and the nation of citizens – i.e., between a community by descent and a legal community based on a shared constitutional culture – where the latter 'need by no means depend on all citizens sharing the same language or the same ethnic and cultural origins',[37] and yet could be the source of a patriotism that would provide cohesion. A European constitution – that is his vision – would give 'Europe as a whole . . . a *second* chance'[38] of reinventing itself as a community of solidarity.*

---

* Habermas's point is that history so far has granted empires only one appearance. Europe, by contrast, might have a second chance, though 'not on the terms of its old-style power politics but only under the changed premises of a nonimperialist process

In 1995, in his dispute with Dieter Grimm, who at the time was professor of public law at the University of Bielefeld (later at the Humboldt University in Berlin), as well as a judge at the First Senate of the Federal Constitutional Court, Habermas challenged the objection that the creation of a European constitution would be problematic because there is no European people who could play the role of the collective subject in the constitutional process.

> I see the point of republicanism in the fact that the forms and procedures of the constitutional state, together with the democratic mode of legitimation, simultaneously forge a new level of social integration. Democratic citizenship establishes a comparatively abstract, in any case legally mediated solidarity between strangers. This form of social integration, which first emerges with the nation-state, is realized in the form of a *communicative context* which stretches right into political socialization.[39]

In his 'Hamburg Lecture' at the end of June 2001, Habermas tried to convince his listeners that Europe, as a diverse cultural area with a specific legal history, needs a constitution of its own. The 'constitution-founding process itself represents a unique medium of transnational communication' which acts as a *'self-fulfilling prophecy'** insofar as a European identity would emerge through the process itself.[40]

On 31 May 2003, a few weeks after President Bush had declared the second Iraq War a 'mission accomplished', a joint manifesto by Jacques Derrida and Jürgen Habermas appeared in the *Frankfurter Allgemeine Zeitung* and in the French daily newspaper *Libération*. 'Nach dem Krieg: Die Wiedergeburt Europas' [After the war: the rebirth of Europe]† was a long-planned, concerted initiative prompted by the two philosophers and supported by independent statements from other renowned European intellectuals published at the same time. There were statements by Umberto Eco in *La Repubblica*, by Adolf Muschg in the *Neue Züricher Zeitung*, by Fernanda Savater in *El País*, and by Gianni Vattimo in *La Stampa*.[41] Habermas and Derrida began their manifesto by reminding their readers of the date 15 February 2003, when large numbers of people took to the streets 'in London, Rome, Madrid, Barcelona, Berlin, and Paris' in order to protest against the Bush government's rush towards

---

of reaching understanding with, and learning from, other cultures.' *Between Facts and Norms*, p. 507.

* 'Self-fulfilling prophecy' in English in the original.

† The title was chosen by the newspaper. Published in English as part of *The Divided West* under the title 'February 15, or: What Binds Europeans' (see note 42). Habermas, in an interview, speculated whether the *Frankfurter Allgemeine Zeitung* 'wanted to downplay the importance of the demonstrations' (*The Divided West*, p. 89).

war and against the European governments supporting him. They wrote: 'The simultaneity of these overpowering demonstrations – the largest since the end of World War II – may go down in future history books as a signal for the birth of a European public.'[42] They go on to demand, among other things, a strengthening of cooperation between the old continental European states because:

Europe must throw its weight onto the scales at the international level and within the UN in order to counterbalance the hegemonic unilateralism of the United States. At global economic summits and in the institutions of the WTO, the World Bank, and the International Monetary Fund, it should bring its influence to bear in shaping the design of a future global domestic politics.[43]

When the ratification of the 'Treaty Establishing a Constitution for Europe', which had been drafted by a European Convention and ceremoniously signed by the heads of state or government of the EU member states at the end of October 2004, failed as a result of the referenda in France (end of May 2005) and the Netherlands (beginning of June 2005), the dream of a European constitution evaporated, at least for the time being. The Lisbon Treaty, which was ratified with significant difficulty some four years later, did not change anything about that. Habermas interpreted the rejection of the European constitution in the referenda as a lesson delivered by the citizens to the political elites about what happens when European issues are not publicly negotiated but, rather, made a matter for an exclusive expertocracy. Instead of risking conflicts over political aspects of the unification process, this expertocracy favours the abuse of European elections for dealing with national issues.[44]

On 23 November 2007, Habermas was invited by the Social Democratic Party to take part in a discussion with the foreign minister and vice-chancellor at the time, Frank-Walter Steinmeier, at the Willy-Brandt-Haus in Berlin. In the discussion, Habermas said that the stagnation, even 'devolution', of the process of European integration had to do with the fact that it had become a project of the political elite: 'It is not the populations but the governments who are the stumbling block', as they reacted to the historical fact of the loss of power of individual nation-states over financial and economic policy 'since the end of embedded capitalism' by putting their emphasis on, of all things, national interests.[45] *Die Zeit* summed up the discussion, saying: 'They met – but they spoke past each other.'[46] Steinmeier defended the Lisbon Treaty as a constitutional compromise because it had prevented 'institutional chaos'. Other commentators also more or less agreed that the two gentlemen were, ultimately, talking at cross purposes. Then, in August 2008, Habermas received the first official honour that explicitly recognized his commitment to Europe. The Swiss Hans Ringier Foundation awarded him the 'European Prize for Political Culture'. Sigmar Gabriel, the then minister for the environment, gave a speech at the award ceremony praising the laureate as a great European intellectual.

In the years to come, Habermas regularly made statements on Europe, for instance in an article for *Die Zeit* (20 May 2010) in which he argued for an 'effective coordination of [European] economic policies', which he said would 'involve an increase in the powers of the parliament in Strasbourg'.[47] On 6 April 2011, he participated in a panel discussion on 'Europe and the Rediscovery of the German Nation-State' at the Berlin branch of the European Council on Foreign Relations, an independent pan-European think tank. The other participants were the former foreign minister Joschka Fischer, the economist and political scientist Henrik Enderlein, and the expert on European law Christian Calliess. In the course of the discussion, Habermas complained that the 'governments of this economically successful republic' make themselves dependent 'on the two imperatives which more or less every state has to follow today, namely that of making the economy competitive enough, within the limits of certain social considerations, so as to allow the output to provide enough legitimacy to avoid any political problems that might hinder one's re-election.' Asked whether one should anticipate a return of the 'German question', he answered:

> I do not think so. Back then, the politicians had the Second World War and the mass crimes to deal with, and the categories of the nineteenth century in their heads. The intention at the time was to prevent a renewal of power politics practised by a giant state in the centre of Europe through integration, an important motive. I do not see a similar situation existing today.[48]

Two months later, on a scorching June day in 2011, Habermas spoke about 'The Crisis of the European Union in Light of a Constitutionalization of International Law' in the crowded main lecture hall of the Humboldt University in Berlin. Finally, at the beginning of November 2012, he again energetically promoted a European constitution at a forum of the annual meeting of German Jurists in Berlin, dedicated to the theme of 'Limits of European integration':[49] 'According to my ideas, the aim would be a draft constitution for a supranational democracy, which – *without taking the shape of a federal state* – would allow for common governance.'[50]

Shortly afterwards, Habermas travelled to Paris and presented his ideas on European politics first in a lecture hall of the Université Paris Descartes and then, two days later, at the Goethe Institute. His talks were peppered with trenchant criticisms of the crisis management of the German chancellor, Angela Merkel, and the French president, Nicolas Sarkozy: 'I detest the political parties. Our politicians have for a long time been incapable of seeking anything but re-election, of representing anything of substance, of having any convictions.' And he continued: 'I speak here as a citizen. I would much rather sit at home at my desk, trust me. But this is too important. It must be clear to everyone that we are facing enormous, fundamental decisions. That is why I am committed to this debate. This project of Europe can no longer be carried forward just by elites.'[51]

Habermas develops the outlines of a transnational order in Europe on the basis of the universalist spirit of democracy in his book *The Crisis of the European Union.** The book prompted a flurry of responses upon its publication on 9 November 2011; apart from the former chancellor Helmut Schmidt and the leader of the Social Democratic Party Sigmar Gabriel, the former president of the European Parliament, Hans-Georg Pöttering, the Italian prime minister at the time, Romano Prodi, and the socialist candidate for the French presidency and later president, François Hollande, all made clear references to Habermas's reflections.[52]

As in texts such as *Europe: A Faltering Project*, here Habermas opposes the idea of deciding on Europe's future on the basis of market imperatives, and he attacks the 'executive federalism' of Merkel and Sarkozy.[53] He sets out four more constructive points: first, he argues for stronger political integration and the gradual expansion of the European Union on the basis that living in a global society characterized by mutual dependencies means that, in the case of political questions of transnational significance, the likelihood of decisions that conform to his criterion of reasonableness – i.e., decisions to which all could generally agree – increases with the size of the group of states that have to reach mutual understanding.[54] As Habermas had already noted in his contribution to the Frankfurt conference on international relations, this is true in particular because 'neither deliberation nor the public sphere . . . have national borders by their own nature', a point he would continue to emphasize.[55]

Habermas's second point relates to his plea for participation and deliberation on the basis of discourse theory. He wants to demonstrate that, under the conditions of progressive globalization, there is no alternative to the practice of 'governing beyond

---

* The German title *Zur Verfassung Europas* is deliberately ambivalent and can mean both 'On Europe's constitution' and 'On the condition of Europe', or even 'On the state that Europe is in'. The English title, taken from that of the book's main essay, emphasizes this last meaning.

the nation-state'.[56] As previously mentioned, he sees the process of European unification as a counter-project to the formation of communities on an ethnic basis. The nation of citizens takes the place of the nation as a community of origin. And through the constitution of 'Europe' as a nation of citizens, its members gradually develop a collective identity related to that nation. In this context, it is of only marginal significance that this collective identity is something yet to be created, because the citizens of the European continent will identify with the emerging Europe if the required solidarity of this Europe is established with some measure of 'orientation towards understanding' – ideally in the form of a constitutional process in which all are involved.[57] Apart from that, he argues that Europe should not allow itself to be taken over and must protect the specificity of its cultures and forms of life. This, too, could best be guaranteed by a transformation of the sovereignty of individual states into a supranational association. In *The Divided West*, he already had written: 'Thus the question is not whether a European identity "exists", but whether the national arenas can be so opened up to each other that a self-propelling process of shared political opinion- and will-formation on European issues can develop above the national level.'[58]

The third point refers to the constitution of a transnational public sphere by means of a 'Europeanization' of the processes of political opinion- and will-formation. This would promote a constitutional patriotism at the European level, which 'heightens an awareness of both the diversity and the integrity of the different forms of life coexisting in a multicultural society.'[59] Habermas talks about all governments and parties 'risking more democracy' at the European level; they must try to gain the vote of every European citizen in a Europe-wide election campaign. For Habermas, such a shift of political emphasis away from nation-states would not mean that the latter become superfluous: 'They are the irreplaceable elements out of which international organizations are composed. . . . Who, if not the nation-states, would guarantee equal rights for all citizens on their territories?'[60]

Finally, the fourth point concerns the possible role of a strong Europe in the world. Habermas would wish for the European states to bring their weight to bear on the solutions for the problems of a globalized world in which ecological, military and economic risks pay no heed to territorial borders.

Habermas seems to be a supporter of the model of flexible integration (a 'two-speed Europe') that has been discussed since the 1980s and, much like Joschka Fischer in his well-received Humboldt speech in 2000 before him, appeals for an 'avantgardistic core Europe' which exerts a pulling influence – i.e., which functions as an engine for integration. For Habermas, part of a future Europe is –

alongside the European Parliament and the European judiciary – a European government which acts as the executive power within the federation and can appeal to a constitutional treaty and a charter of basic rights.[61]

A crisis of politics? In early August 2012, Habermas was persuaded by Sigmar Gabriel to work on a statement on the government policies of the Social Democrats alongside the philosopher and former state minister for culture Julian Nida-Rümelin and the economist and 'economic sage'* Peter Bofinger. Their jointly authored text appeared on 4 August 2012 under the heading 'Einspruch gegen die Fassadendemokratie' [An objection to pseudo-democracy] in the features section of the *Frankfurter Allgemeine Zeitung*, with a note added by the newspaper: 'The programme [of government policies] is written no longer in a "closed shop" but in exchange with scientists and intellectuals.' The 'objection', which was also published in *La Repubblica*, contains sustained diagnostic passages and some shorter prognostic ones, as well as a catalogue of political demands. The European crisis, it says, is a consequence of a lack of power in political policy formation. The effects are felt by countries such as Greece, Spain, Portugal and Italy, which have ended up in a severe recession. As a result of the fragmentation within the community of states, there is no concerted resistance to the global financial industry. The solution would be to pool the resources of the continent, to deepen integration, to hold on to the common currency, and to hand over sovereignty from individual states to the community. In order to limit the risk of insolvency for individual countries, a shared liability for government bonds within the eurozone must be instituted, combined with a control over national budgets exercised by the community.

On the way to a democratically constituted world order

I make no demands; I simply register that we can no longer get by as solitary nation-states.

Alliances on the basis of international treaties are also no longer sufficient for solving the problems we now face.[62]

Globalization. For Jürgen Habermas, the correct response to the epoch-making process of globalization is the integration of

---

* 'Wirtschaftsweiser' – a colloquial expression for a member of the 'Council of experts for the evaluation of overall economic development', which is charged by the federal government with producing an annual report on the state of the economy.

Europe. He writes: 'By "globalization" is meant the cumulative processes of a worldwide expansion of trade and production, commodity and financial markets, fashion, the media and computer programs, news and communications networks, transportation systems and flows of migration, the risks generated by large-scale technology, environmental damage and epidemics, as well as organized crime and terrorism.'[63] What emerges is what he calls a 'postnational constellation',[64] which carries with it a number of risks. First, globalization as the elimination of economic boundaries and the interconnection of markets has led to an enormous increase in the mobility of capital. As a result, the fiscal basis of individual states is shrinking, and this weakens their capacity to function as political legitimated systems that guarantee legal certainty.

Second, the loss of significance of the nation-state and the blurring of territorial boundaries means that societies lose their democratic centre and their legal and constitutional points of reference for trying to fashion their polity democratically. The line between domestic and foreign policies, which is fundamental for nation-states, also becomes blurred.[65] This results in entirely new steering problems and, in particular, substantial legitimation problems: 'With the deregulation of markets and the globalization of flows of traffic and information . . . a need for regulation arises that is being absorbed and processed by transnational networks and organizations. Their decisions . . . make deep inroads into the public life of nation-states without being connected with processes of legitimation at the national level.'[66]

Third, Habermas questions whether a residual solidarity among citizens can be secured without a reconnection with the experience of national community. Such solidarity is necessary if the citizens of multicultural societies are to stand up for one another.

In this connection, the fourth risk Habermas identifies is that weakened nation-states may no longer be capable of fulfilling their function as intervening welfare states that protect democratic rights of participation: 'But to remain a source of solidarity, the status of citizenship has to maintain a use-value: it has to *pay* to be a citizen, in the currency of social, ecological, and cultural rights as well.'[67]

For Habermas, everything depends on the question of whether 'the *social* forces of nature that have been unleashed at the transnational level' can be successfully controlled.[68] For that to happen, he says, transnational steering capabilities would need to be created that are capable of dealing with the mechanisms of the global capitalist economy, and which have sufficient – meaning transnational – democratic legitimacy and are secured by the rule of law. Such a transnationalization – elsewhere he speaks of a 'division of sovereignty' [*Soveränitätsteilung*]* – is what Habermas has in mind with regard to the European Union. It is already the case, he says, that its citizens have a double role to play because they participate in the democratic process of legitimation as citizens of the Union and as citizens of their states.[69] This division of sovereignty can be justified by the fact that the 'respective nation-states . . . *continue to perform their constitutional role* as guarantors of law and freedom.'[70]

Global society. Europe is one issue, but it is not the end of the story – and of course Habermas is perfectly aware of that. The process of European unification is but a first step towards a political community of world citizens within a 'horizontally juridified international community that is legally obligated to cooperate'.[71] His utopia is a cosmopolitan association of world citizens who should decide in a world parliament – a general assembly – about those political matters that are of global significance. Again, individuals – but, this time, all individuals – would have a double role to play as citizens of their states and as citizens of the world.

Habermas imagines a federal world republic, including global civil rights that are the rights not of states but of individuals. He dreams of 'a politically constituted global society that reserves institutions and procedures of global governance for states at both the supra- and transnational levels.'[72] Part of this cosmopolitan condition would be that the 'normative framework of constitutions beyond the state . . . must remain tied at least indirectly to processes of legitimation within constitutional states.'[73] This normative framework, he writes, requires the

> 'backing' from the kinds of democratic processes of opinion- and will-formation that can only be fully institutionalized within constitutional states . . . Only within constitutional states do administrative mechanisms exist to insure the equal inclusion of citizens in the legislative process. Where these are lacking, as in the case of constitutions of international organizations, there is always the danger that the 'dominant' interests will impose themselves in a hegemonic manner under the guise of impartial laws.[74]

Habermas wants not a world government that would hold the monopoly on violence but, rather, a 'multilevel political system'

---

* As the translator of *The Crisis of the European Union* rightly points out, 'Souveränitätsteilung' may mean either 'shared' or 'divided sovereignty', and Habermas himself notes that the expression is ambiguous (p. 37). However, his argument suggests that 'division' is closer to his intended meaning. In the case of the EU, he says: 'The division of the constituent power divides sovereignty *at the origin of a political community which is going to be constituted,* and not only *at the source of the already constituted political community'* (p. 38).

which does not bear the character of a state.[75] He characterizes his conception, which follows on from Kant,[76] as a 'global domestic politics [*Weltinnenpolitik*] without a world government', or a 'world society without a world government'.[77] Within a democratically constituted 'world society', the UN, as an already existing supranational organization, would concentrate primarily on securing peace, human rights and the environment, although it would need to be strengthened further. Alongside the UN, or rather below it, there would be regional bodies responsible for world domestic politics, which would need to be, 'on the one hand, designed to overcome the extreme disparities in wealth within the stratified world society, reverse ecological imbalances, and avert collective threats while, on the other, endeavouring to promote an intercultural discourse on, and recognition of, the equal rights of the world civilizations.'[78] And it goes without saying that, for Habermas, all authorities within the multilevel federal system, including the UN, must be democratically legitimized.

Of course, within a world society the universal validity of human rights should become effective.[79] For this to be more than just lip service, Habermas believes a change of perspective is necessary – i.e. the juridification of international relations would need to be complemented by a transformation of international law into a cosmopolitan constitution. The time of classical international law, a law which recognizes only states as legal subjects, and which 'reflects the contours of the European state system which took shape following the Peace of Westphalia and remained in place roughly until 1914', is over.[80] The Charter of the 193 member states of the UN was already the first step towards a development of international law into a kind of world constitution, because it committed the international community to guaranteeing basic rights and to respecting human rights. Thus, when Habermas speaks of a constitutionalization of international law, this can be related to the UN Charter of 26 June 1945 – i.e., the emergence of a constitution with valid legal principles which govern the relations between sovereign states and international organizations according to the maxim of equality. 'This shift in perspective from classical international law to the political constitution of world society is no longer a purely intellectual construction. Social reality is itself imposing this shift in perspective on contemporary consciousness.'[81] An important consequence of the transformation of international law into a global constitution, or a 'constitution of a community of states', is that the distinction between just and unjust wars is replaced with the 'procedural distinction between legal and illegal wars'.[82] However sceptical one may be about aspects of the political practices of the UN, there are useful conclusions to be drawn from it regarding a politics without a world government. Habermas, indeed, formulated an agenda of reforms for the UN. The Security Council, for instance, would need to be made more independent to provide it with more power to act; this would mean member states providing the requisite financial resources to allow for the execution of resolutions. In addition, the authority of the International Court of Justice would need to be expanded and the *jus in bello* 'developed into a law of intervention that would protect affected populations against UN operations in a way analogous to the protection enjoyed by private citizens against domestic police operations.'[83] Finally, the legitimation of, and level of agreement with, decisions of the Security Council and the General Assembly could be improved by tying them to a well-informed global public sphere, because '[t]he pressure of problems generated by an increasingly globalized society will sharpen the sensitivity to the growing need for regulation and fair policies at the transnational level.'[84]

As in the case of Europe, Habermas considers a transnational expansion of civic solidarity to be possible at the global level if the transnationally negotiated global domestic politics is tied to a world parliament.[85] However, the notion that a world society would develop a 'shared political culture' of the kind he sees as existing in the case of Europe is a chimera: 'world citizens do not form a collective that would be held together by a political interest in the *self-assertion* of a way of life that shapes their identity.'[86]

As mentioned above, relations within a polity of world citizens require a juridification which has a civilizing power, especially at this international level. In this context, Habermas refers directly to Kant and his treatise on *Perpetual Peace*. However, whether this constitutes a return to a 'material philosophy of history', as Micha Brumlik (*Die Tageszeitung*, 18 November 2011) and Christian Schlüter (*Frankfurter Rundschau*, 30 December 2011) suppose, is questionable. In any case, Habermas does not stipulate a new subject of history; rather, he presents his reflections as a counter-agenda to a normatively deprived politics.[87]

13

Philosophy in the Age of Postmetaphysical Modernity

Today, in contrast, the experience of contingency is a whirlpool into which everything is pulled: everything could also be otherwise . . .[1]

In the mid-1980s, a controversy flared up between Dieter Henrich and Jürgen Habermas over the viability of a postmetaphysical philosophy of the kind Habermas had defended since his *Theory of Communicative Action*.[2] According to Habermas, postmetaphysical thinking, which begins with Kant, is the only possible approach that contemporary philosophy can take after its transformation from a philosophy of consciousness to a philosophy of language:[3]

> The development points, first, in the direction of a de-centred conception of the world as the totality of states of affairs and events that can be described by physics; second, in the direction of a separation of theoretical and practical reason; and, finally, in the direction of a fallibilistic, but not sceptical, understanding of theoretical knowledge. Of course, these tendencies point back to our own hermeneutic point of departure, that is, to a postmetaphysical understanding of the world and of ourselves which emerged from the seventeenth and eighteenth centuries onwards.[4]

Against this background, Habermas published a response to Henrich's article 'Was ist Metaphysik, was Moderne? Thesen gegen Jürgen Habermas' [What is metaphysics, what modernity? Theses against Jürgen Habermas] in *Merkur*. Henrich's article, in turn, discussed a review by Habermas that had been published in October 1985, also in *Merkur*, under the title 'Rückkehr zur Metapysik – Eine Tendenz in der deutschen Philosophie?' [Return to metaphysics – a tendency in German philosophy?].[5] The differences between Habermas and Henrich, who is close to the Marburg school of hermeneutics,[6] are evident in their evaluations of contemporary philosophy. Whereas for Henrich philosophy still has the task of a total clarification of the world through integrative thinking, Habermas takes a sceptical stance towards speculative interpretations of the world as a totality. Even if philosophy with its self-reflective attitude does not dissolve into science, it nevertheless must prove itself in relation to the results produced by the empirical sciences.[7] The core of Habermas's objections aims at the Kantian distinction between appearance and the thing-in-itself, as well as the epistemological status of self-consciousness. With respect to the latter, Habermas denies that it provides a 'specific kind of certainty'.[8] Habermas no longer grounds self-consciousness with reference to the concept of a transcendental subject. Self-consciousness is 'not a phenomenon inherent in the subject'[9] but, rather, the result of linguistically mediated social practices in which subjects are embedded. His argument uses the idea of a 'transcendence from within', or, in other words, the concept of reciprocal recognition and an intact intersubjectivity.[10]

Habermas's use of the label 'postmetaphysical thinking' is meant to express, in particular, that the insight into the transcendental status of language renders meaningless the idea that 'we could somehow step in between the linguistic realm of concepts and "naked" reality, purified, as it were, of all subjective components.' As he put it in a lecture presented at a conference on 'Putnam and the Tradition of Pragmatism' in June 2000 in Münster: 'In coping intelligently with what we encounter in the linguistically disclosed world, we can certainly revise our language. But we cannot step outside the horizon of language itself.' Because of this primacy of language, the

> transcendental subject forfeits its status beyond space and time and is transformed into many subjects capable of speech and action and situated in the cooperative contexts and practices of their linguistically articulated lifeworlds. . . . Transcendental reason has come down from its supersensible pedestal and has sedimented itself in the pores of the practices and forms of life of historical linguistic communities.[11]

According to Habermas, the 'vanished transcendental subject' leaves no gap behind,[12] because its place is taken by the interplay between world-disclosing language and the practices of the lifeworld, which establishes enduring learning processes. In other words, the introduction of the philosophical paradigm of language as a third category between mind and matter, and the disclosure of its general formal structure, makes metaphysics obsolete.

For Habermas, postmetaphysical thinking abstains from approaching ethical questions and limits itself to treating those aspects of validity inherent in the pragmatics of speech. It is the preliminary endpoint of philosophical forms of reflection which in antiquity took 'being' and in modern times 'consciousness' as their object. Both idealism, equating being and thinking, and identity thinking, with its claim to be able to explain the world in its totality from a single principle, have to be overcome.

Although a postmetaphysically disenchanted philosophy leaves behind the identity of being and thinking, as well as the idea of transcendental subjectivity and idealism's claim to have access to a binding and, in this sense, powerful theory of the good life, to the absolute, it nevertheless takes it upon itself 'to justify morality and right, the normative content of modernity as such, on the basis of reason alone'.[13] Thus, postmetaphysical thinking defends what Habermas calls a 'non-defeatist' concept of reason, which he understands as a kind of procedural rationality. Discursive processes offer the unique opportunity of identifying good reasons, bearing in mind that there are 'always better and worse reasons; there is never the "one and only right" reason.'[14] 'Rationality (Rationalität) is reduced to something formal insofar as the rationality (Vernünftigkeit) of content evaporates into the validity of results.'[15]

Postmetaphysical thinking, Habermas says, is suspicious of various kinds of holistic interpretations of the world; rather, it respects the pluralism of worldviews that characterizes modernity. The 'unity of reason' finds expression in the 'diversity of its voices' alone.[16] The hypothetical character of the way in which postmetaphysical thinking understands the world is manifested in the practices of argumentation. Their openness, Habermas holds, is associated with a renunciation of the idea of any privileged access to truth. The 'fallibilistic consciousness' of postmetaphysical philosophy – i.e., the general doubt regarding the existence of statements that are irrefutable – forecloses any possibility of providing ultimate justifications. Postmetaphysical philosophy gives up any claim to be able to establish indubitable conditions of knowledge.[17] Metaphysical certainties are replaced with the assumption that with every speech act there is the possibility of reaching understanding within the open space of reasons. The greater the number and weight of the reasons, the greater the need for their discursive clarification: 'More discourse means more contradiction and difference. The more abstract the agreements become, the more diverse the disagreements with which we can *non-violently* live.'[18] In line with this, metaphysical thinking resists the claims of religious teachings without, however, simply ignoring their cognitive content. It also objects to the alleged supremacy of the objective-scientific type of knowledge.

Postmetaphysical thinking is based on the assumption – and herein, one may say, lies a residual essentialism – that the mind is constituted intersubjectively and is guided by norms. The 'constitution of the human mind' has its 'origin in the triadic relationships *between* actors who, by coordinating their actions through communication, jointly relate *to something* in the world.'[19] The roots of this postmetaphysical programme, which structures all of Habermas's philosophy, reach back to the 1960s, when he began to investigate epistemological questions.

What can I know?
Linguistic pragmatics as a form of naturalism and realism

Cheques which we issue on the truth of a statement can be cashed only in the currency of reasons.[20]

What is knowledge? It was not just the intellectual fashion of the time that sparked the young Habermas's interest in questions of epistemology in the 1960s. This was part of the regular business of philosophy for him: 'I was interested in the problem of meaning and understanding in connection with questions from the logic of the social sciences. This provided an impulse for engaging with the analytic theory of science.'[21] This engagement did not only involve taking a stance in the positivist dispute with his critique of Karl Popper's and Hans Albert's Critical Rationalism; with his literature review *On the Logic of the Social Sciences* of 1967, he also began a methodological debate about the status of a sociology that understands society in terms of the meaningful structures of everyday life and therefore approaches its object hermeneutically. *Knowledge and Human Interests*, published a year later, was then an explicit attempt to go a step further and practise epistemology as a critique of society. The book's interpretation of the structural model of psychoanalysis in terms of a theory of communication prepared the way for the later foundation of sociology on a theory of language centred round the linguistically mediated intersubjectivity of actors. From the late 1960s, Habermas abandoned the concept of epistemological interest. This approach had failed because, in the manner of a philosophy of history, it tried to explain 'the normativity of knowledge and the analytic force of self-reflection with respect to a learning subject on a grand scale'.[22]

Another conception Habermas would soon revise was the consensus theory of truth he held in the early 1970s, at which time it was still somewhat novel and original. It tried to formulate a discursive justification for truth claims and differed substantially from other theories of truth, such as the correspondence theory, the coherence theory, and the evidence theory of truth.[23] According to Habermas's consensus theory, truth claims about facts are true, and normative propositions are correct, if the validity claims they raise can be argumentatively redeemed in practical discourses, resulting in a general, non-coercive and justificatory consensus.[24] Prompted in part by objections raised by Cristina Lafont and Albrecht Wellmer,[25]

Habermas came to reassess his theory, saying that he had allowed himself to be tempted into an

> overgeneralization of the consensus-based explanation for the validity of norms as oughts. . . . However, in the assimilation of propositional truth into the validity of moral judgements and norms, the sense in which statements referring to objects of an objective world that exists independently of its description are true – a sense which *transcends the justification* for these statements – is lost.[26]

The necessary revision led to 'a concept of unconditional truth, of truth that is not epistemically indexed. . . . Only once they make the transition from action to discourse do participants take a reflective attitude and dispute the now thematized truth of controversial propositions in the light of reasons for and against it.'[27] Thus, it is clear that the concept of rational discourse 'retains its status as a privileged form of communication that forces those participating in it to continue decentering their cognitive perspectives. . . . Argumentation remains the only *available* medium of ascertaining truth since truth claims that have been problematized cannot be tested in any other way.'[28] However, on account of the necessary epistemological realism, Habermas argues, propositional truth must not be aligned to rational acceptability under near ideal conditions. Rather, a stricter distinction between truth and correctness must be drawn and conceptually elaborated in light of the relationship between theoretical and practical reason – something Habermas pursued in his central essay on this matter, 'Rightness versus Truth: On the Sense of Normative Validity in Moral Judgments and Norms'.[29]

In this context, a particular distinction becomes important for Habermas, namely the one between the validity of judgements, insofar as they refer to something that exists empirically, and a validity which results from the fact that certain judgements deserve intersubjective recognition because they could be accepted as right. If the difference between validity and social acceptance is discarded, 'what we are entitled to is assimilated to what we are merely accustomed to.'[30] According to Habermas, truth in the sense of validity applies to the descriptive content of facts as well as to the prescriptive content of norms, because:

> On the one hand, we discover the rightness of moral judgments in the same way as the truth of descriptions: through argumentation. We no more have direct access unfiltered by reasons to truth conditions than we do to the conditions under which moral norms merit universal recognition. In either case, the validity of statements can be *established* only through discursive engagement using available reasons.[31]

However, moral and empirical convictions must not be equated: moral rightness lacks those references to an objective world of objects that exist independently of their description which characterize statements of fact that are claimed to be true. Nevertheless, 'the *projection* of a moral world and the *presupposition* of an objective world are functionally equivalent',[32] and Habermas introduces these equivalents as points of reference that transcend justification for correct judgements and true statements. This, he says, does not change anything about the fact that, 'with the reference to the objective world, moral validity claims lose a touchstone that extends beyond discourse and transcends the insightful self-determination of the will of the participants.'[33] For Habermas, moral facts are created by social practices. Nevertheless, there remains the possibility of assessing moral judgements and norms as correct or incorrect because the social world acts as a constraining factor, albeit in a different way from that in which the objective world determines which statements can be true or false.

Language and the fact of learning. Two interconnected problems arise from the projection of a moral world and the assumption of an objective world. How can the normativity of the lifeworld be explained within the framework of the developmental processes of natural history? And how can the assumption of a reality that can only be approached through a world-disclosing language be reconciled with the need to assume the existence of an objective world that is the same for everyone? Habermas approaches these questions in several stages. As a first step, he offers his fundamental insight into the philosophy of language, namely that language and reality are intertwined: 'Facts can be explained only by recourse to factual statements, what is real only by appeal to what is true. . . . We cannot confront our sentences directly with a reality that is not already permeated by language.'[34] According to Habermas, we understand language because we are members of a linguistically constituted lifeworld. We always already move within the space of language while at the same time making use of it.

Habermas further assumes that the two aspects of language are bound up with each other: the semantic side, which serves the functions of world-disclosing and of representing facts, and the pragmatic side, which establishes a relationship between a speaker and a hearer who reach an understanding about something in the world. Because of this 'equiprimordiality', Habermas says, 'there is an *internal* connection between successful communication and the representation of facts.'[35] This, however, also implies that our 'linguistic knowledge' makes possible our 'knowledge of the world' and that, in contrast to the latter, the former has a revisionary power: 'This power of revision is explained by the discursive processing of action-related experiences. We have such experiences either in pragmatically coping with an objective world, which we presuppose as the same for and independent of all of us, or in our interactive coping with members of a social world that we presuppose to be shared.'[36]

The thesis of the revisionary power of a knowledge that is embodied in language corresponds to the idea that it is '[n]ot language as such' but, rather, the 'communicative use of linguistic expressions ... that contains a peculiar rationality. ... This *communicative rationality* is expressed in the compounding force of speech orientated towards reaching understanding ... '.[37]

In the second step of his argument, Habermas makes use of a theorem he developed during his years in Starnberg. The theorem is that 'subjects capable of speech and action, who can be affected by reasons, can learn – and in the long run even "cannot not learn."'[38] This theorem, he holds, can illuminate our behaviour towards the world insofar as it is independent of us, as well as the moral orientations of subjects in their relationships with each other. Thus, Habermas explains knowledge in this twofold sense as a function of learning processes. The task of epistemology is therefore to 'explain the learning process, complex *from the very beginning*, that sets in when the expectations that guide our actions are problematized.' This 'transcendental fact of learning'[39] allows us to relinquish Kant's idea of a transcendental subject that is situated in the sphere of the intelligible; this transcendental consciousness 'has come down to Earth in the form of everyday communicative practice, which is no longer sublime.'[40] Thus, the conditions of knowledge, which for Kant have a transcendental status, are for Habermas 'embodied in practices. These practices are characteristic of our sociocultural forms of life, which have evolved naturally';[41] Kant's view is simply a metaphysical residue. This brings into play the concept of the lifeworld. Within the lifeworld, the learning processes mentioned above fall on fertile soil: 'This architectonic of "lifeworld" and "objective world" goes hand in hand with a methodological dualism of understanding and observation. This dualism more or less echoes the distinction between transcendental and empirical cognition.'[42]

Ever since the critique of the concept of a unitary science he voiced in the positivist dispute, Habermas has maintained the view that different scientific cultures also have different forms and aims of cognition: 'In the natural sciences ... theoretical strategies are directed towards discovering deterministic or probabilistic laws and towards nomological explanations of physically measurable processes; in the humanities and social sciences, theoretical strategies are directed towards explicating and interpreting semantic and empirical connections among hermeneutically disclosed data.'[43]

Finally, Habermas draws some conclusions from his theoretical premises. Even if he discards the idea of a transcendental subject of knowledge, he retains the transcendental question and formulates it in a new way. For cognition, the essential mode of problem-solving is that which enables learning processes to take place and, together with justifications, leads to an increase in knowledge. In this, there is an interplay between spatial, social and temporal dimensions:

> In the spatial dimension, knowledge is the result of working through experiences of frustration by coping intelligently with a risk-filled environment. In the social dimension, it is the result of justifying one's ways of solving problems against the objections of other participants in argumentation. And in the temporal dimension, it is the result of learning processes fed by the revision of one's own mistakes.[44]

Habermas, of course, has presented himself as a staunch critic of the self-objectification of the neurosciences* and of that kind of naturalism represented by Willard Van Orman Quine's belief that all knowledge can be explained in terms of the methods of the natural sciences. However, in his recent writings, Habermas nevertheless defends what he calls a 'weak' or 'soft' naturalism with regard to epistemological questions, a naturalism which he distinguishes sharply from scientism. Based on the assumption of a continuity between nature and culture, he affirms the view 'that the biological endowment and the cultural way of life of *Homo sapiens* have a "natural" origin and can in principle be explained in terms of evolutionary theory.'[45]

More recently, concepts from natural history and natural evolution have increasingly become part of Habermas's philosophical horizon. At the centre is the question of 'how the "nature" of natural history, broadly understood, differs from the nature of the natural sciences which it exceeds.'[46] Habermas assigns epistemic priority to the fact that subjects cannot transcend the horizon of the lifeworld; the ontological priority of their objective world is demonstrated by the fact that it can be felt within human practices as challenging certain descriptions and motivating learning processes. Cultural learning, he says, is the result of the acquisition of language and replaces the genetic mechanism of evolution.[47] Habermas calls his epistemological position a 'realism without representation'. Facts are facts, but they can only be opened up in the medium of language, and can only be appropriated linguistically. This position

---

* 'Selbstobjektivierung der Neurowissenschaften': the term describes the fact that the neurosciences proceed as if the brain and its functions can be described entirely from the perspective of an observer, turning even the self into an external (physical) object.

is compatible with the assumption that 'those structures of the life-world that constitute our personal self-understanding, as well as our cognitive access to the objective world, have themselves emerged from an evolutionary *learning* process.'[48] Referring to George Herbert Mead's interactionism and, more recently, to research carried out by the developmental psychologist Michael Tomasello, Habermas holds that the ability to take the perspective of the other and the possession of language are the crucial evolutionary factors in this learning process.

What should I do?
From the demand of virtue to the assumption of rationality

A political justice that stands on its own moral feet no longer needs the support of the truth of religious or metaphysical comprehensive doctrines.[49]

Modernity. In *The Theory of Communicative Action*, and elsewhere, Habermas describes modernity as an (ongoing) historical phase during which a complex society characterized by diverse concep-tions of life and by individual designs of life has emerged.[50] This society, a capitalistically organized Rechtsstaat, produces out of itself the sort of rationality typical of Western culture that Max Weber had already described, from the perspective of a universal history, as a 'disenchantment of the world' – the intellectualization of all areas of life and the calculability of all things. Apart from the systemic mechanisms of economic and bureaucratic power struc-tures, Habermas also counts the modern sciences, positive law, and secular, principle-governed ethics among the rational structures of such a society. Secular ethics takes the place of sacred law, and with this a utilitarian ethics replaces the idea that the world is a cosmos ordered by God.

To the extent that modernity forces individuals to be reflective, Habermas argues, religious convictions become a private matter. Thus, we can speak of secular ethics since – in parallel with the processes of rationalization – multiple worldviews have emerged which stand on an equal footing with one another. The liberation of human beings from traditional interpretations of the world is associated with the loss of a general and taken-for-granted interpre-tation of one's relation to self and world,[51] which Habermas speaks of as 'a decentred, even fragmented public consciousness'. With this development a risky dynamic has set in: within modern societies, there is a growing danger of a kind of centrifugal disintegration. This 'risk of dissension', Habermas says, results from the fact that social coherence can no longer be established by a generally binding communal ethos in the form of a 'bewitching authority' [*faszinierende Autorität*].[52]

In Habermas's view, it is not only the foundations of the legitimacy of the social order that have changed. The claims of philosophy, which once saw itself as called upon to provide comprehensive interpretations of the world as a totality, have also become more modest in the course of these changes. In 'the role of an interpreter', philosophy is unable 'to reclaim some sort of access to essential insights that is *privileged* in relation to science, morality, or art; it now disposes only over knowledge that is fallible.'[53] However, Habermas sees it as a legitimate task of present-day philosophy not only to express preferences for more just living conditions and for democratic procedures in decision-making but also to justify them. Philosophy sensitizes people to the *moral point of view** without relieving them of the burden of practical responsibility for their ethical decisions. It cannot issue any prescriptions regarding the question of what the individual and his or her peers ought to do because 'the moral philosopher does not have a privileged access to moral truths.'[54] The individual's decision about what to do, his or her own ethical self-understanding, is, in the first instance, a matter for personal, but also collective, processes of self-clarification. In an essay of 1997 with the title 'The Relationship between Theory and Practice Revisited', which was first published in the Italian journal of philosophy *Paradigmi* and then included as the last piece in *Truth and Justification*, Habermas expresses himself unequivocally on this point: 'If in liberal societies everyone has the right to develop and pursue her own conception of the good life, or of a life that is not misspent, then ethics must confine itself to *formal* aspects.'[55]

In light of this, Habermas argues, the protection of social integration under conditions of modernity – where the ideas of self-consciousness, self-determination and self-realization are embedded in institutions – requires a type of legal norm that has two sides to it: legal norms must be recognized and followed both because they are coercive and because they possess legitimate validity. That the law is simultaneously coercive and recognized, Habermas says, is an exclusive feature of modernity. The law is the medium in which the rights to freedom as such are given because it produces the legal subject and because, through it, citizens organize their free communal living in the form of self-legislation. Political power also operates through the medium of law, but as the result of a democratic process. This means: 'On this premise, the deployment of political power, even

---

* 'Moral point of view' in English in the original.

for cognitively quite demanding steering processes, *is still* subject to constraints that result directly from the juridical form of collectively binding decisions.'[56]

Law, morality, ethics. Legal norms must be recognized as binding by all members of a legal community. They are, Habermas says, the result of a democratically organized legislative process that takes place within a political community of equals. By contrast, moral norms demand universal validity; they apply to all human beings qua members of the human community. Accordingly, the validity of moral norms is based on an agreement which results from a shared 'we' perspective that is put into practice. The distinction between norms and values becomes plausible from this perspective: 'Norms are either valid or invalid, whereas values compete for priority over other values and must be brought into a transitive order *in each case. . . .* How we assess our values and decide what is "good for us" and what is "better," at a given time, changes every day.'[57] Thus, the validity of norms is the subject of debate only once it becomes apparent that they have lost the unquestioned acceptance that comes from the principle of intersubjective generalization on the basis of rational processes of justification.[58]

In his early sketch of 1983, 'Discourse Ethics: Notes on a Program of Philosophical Justification', and later in his Howison Lectures at Berkeley in 1988,[59] Habermas expressed the difference between ethics and morality, and between values and norms, in clear terms: 'the universalization principle acts like a knife that makes razor sharp cuts . . . between the good and the just. While cultural values may imply a claim to intersubjective acceptance, they are so inextricably intertwined with the totality of a particular form of life that they cannot be said to claim normative validity in the strict sense.'[60] The sphere of the good comprises values that are desirable for the individual and for groups and these values can be put into practice in various ways. In contrast to moral norms, which belong to the realm of justice, existential ethics cannot lay claim to a universal validity, only to a partial one.

Values do not wear their particularist nature on their sleeve; this only emerges in the course of empirical controversies that occur when ethical conflicts flare up within societies and between cultures. According to the legal standards of modern societies, Habermas argues, various types of discourse[61] are the appropriate ways of reaching an understanding about what can be accepted as 'equally good for all', and this does not contradict the criterion of justice as the highest political value, which is universalist at its core.[62] The norm of justice is related to the good insofar as Habermas interprets the former 'as what is equally good for all'.[63]

Habermas and Rawls. Habermas explicitly resists the idea of a restoration of traditional virtues and thus distinguishes his position from approaches as diverse as Hans Jonas's ethics of responsibility, Alasdair MacIntyre's virtue ethics, or the communitarianism of Charles Taylor or Michael Walzer.[64] In an interview with the Danish social scientist Torben Hviid Nielsen for the journal *Acta Sociologica*, Habermas clarified that, for him, justice is 'nothing substantial, not a specific "value", but a dimension of validity'.[65]

The core of his moral philosophy consists in the substitution of the demand for virtue with an assumed rationality.[66] With this move, Habermas continued the tradition in moral philosophy originally set in motion by John Rawls in his seminal *A Theory of Justice* of 1971. However, Habermas also pointed out differences, although he called them merely 'family disputes',[67] as early as the summer of 1992 at a conference of the Philosophical Society in Bad Homburg. Habermas wanted to insist that their commonalities far outweigh their differences: both are guided by Kant's idea of man as an autonomous and rational being and by the conviction that, faced with a pluralism of values, justice can only be justified discursively. Their differences consist in the fact that Rawls tries to ground justice in fairness, and Habermas tries to ground it procedurally.[68] In times of postmetaphysical abstinence, justice, according to Habermas, cannot be understood in substantial terms, such as, for instance, the common good based on a general consensus on principles of political and social justice, but only procedurally: the task is to find out, through a process of argumentation, which interests can be generalized.

Rawls contrasts this type of procedural justice with a distributive justice based on contractual arrangements. This egalitarian conception of justice entails that basic goods are redistributed in favour of those that are the least well-off. Against Rawls, Habermas insists on the need to provide justifications for claims of justice, including their moral substance, if they are meant to gain the acceptance of citizens. Habermas contrasts this intersubjective validity of morality with the merely subjective commitment of ethical values. He criticizes Rawls for not distinguishing clearly enough between justice and the good. In addition, he holds that Rawls's theory of justice, with its priority of subjective civil liberties, does not attach enough importance to the practice of self-determination of citizens. By contrast, his own theory would take account of the latter by postulating the coeval origin of public and private autonomy. Thus, in his paper in Bad Homburg, he summarized that his theory

is at the same time more and less modest than Rawls's theory. It is more modest in that it focuses exclusively on the procedural aspects of the public use of reason and derives the system of rights from the idea of its legal institutionalization. It can leave more questions open because it entrusts more to the *process* of rational opinion- and will-formation. Philosophy shoulders different theoretical burdens when, as on Rawls's conception, it claims to elaborate the idea of a just society, while the citizens then use this idea as a platform from which to judge existing arrangements and policies. By contrast, I propose that philosophy limit itself to the clarification of the moral point of view and the procedure of democratic legitimation, to the analysis of the conditions of rational discourses and negotiations. In this more modest role, philosophy need not proceed in a constructive, but only in a *reconstructive* fashion. It leaves substantial questions that must be answered here and now to the more or less enlightened engagement of participants, which does not mean that philosophers may not also participate in the public debate, though in the role of intellectuals, not of experts.[69]

Habermas considers it a distinguishing feature of modernity that morality is a morality of reason. Values, by contrast, form a realm of their own. Decisions regarding values are ideally made within the context of ethical and existential discourses aiming at reaching self-understanding,[70] while legal norms as well as moral questions are the subject of justificatory discourses which require 'a break with all of the unquestioned truths of an established, concrete ethical life, in addition to distancing oneself from the contexts of life with which one's identity is inextricably linked.'[71] Habermas is convinced that

> Higher-level intersubjectivity characterized by an intermeshing of the perspectives of each with the perspectives of all is constituted only under the communicative presuppositions of a universal discourse in which all those possibly affected could take part and could adopt a hypothetical, argumentative stance toward the validity claims of norms and mode of actions that have become problematic.[72]

Even though ethical questions can be discussed with discursive means – without, however, reaching a final and binding agreement – discourse ethics, despite what the name suggests, has only a limited relevance for ethics.[73] As a procedure for the intersubjective construction of norms, discourse ethics is responsible for a morality guided by principles, and beyond that for positive law, both of which, in turn, have their own functional areas and areas of validity and their own modes of action within functionally differentiated societies.

Ethical cognitivism. Processes oriented towards reaching under-standing are the source of rational solutions to social conflicts, the source of solidarity 'among strangers – strangers who renounce violence and, in the cooperative regulation of their common life, also concede one another the right to *remain* strangers.'[74] In explaining his procedural concept of integration, Habermas writes that the democratic process of intersubjective understanding can serve, metaphorically speaking, as a 'deficiency guarantee' for the 'social integration of an increasingly differentiated society'.[75]

How does Habermas explain the discrepancies between moral judgements and moral actions, as well as the motivational preparedness to act as a moral person? Despite his cognitivist conception, he does not deny the importance of feelings:

> Firstly, moral feelings play an important role in the *constituting* of moral phenomena. We will not perceive certain conflicts of action as being at all morally relevant if we do not *feel* that the integrity of a person is being threatened or violated. Feelings form the basis of our own *perception* that something is moral. Anyone who is blind to moral phenomena has blind feelings. He lacks the sensor, as we would say, for the suffering of a vulnerable creature which has a right to the protection of both its physical self and its identity. And this sensor is clearly closely related to sympathy and empathy.
>
> Secondly, and most importantly . . . moral feelings guide us in our *judgement of particular moral instances.* . . . Moral feelings are a reaction to problems arising in the mutual respect between subjects or in interpersonal relations in which actors are involved, be it from the first, second or third person point of view. That is why the structure of moral feelings is such that they reflect the system of personal pronouns. Thirdly, moral feelings clearly play an important part, not just in the application of moral norms but also in their *justification*. At the very least, empathy, that is, the ability to feel one's way across cultural distances into alien and prima facie incomprehensible ways of living, predispositions to react and interpretive perspectives, is an emotional prerequisite for ideal role-taking which requires everyone to assume the point of view of all the others.[76]

In the interview with Torben Hviid Nielsen from which this quotation is taken, Habermas describes his concept of discourse ethics in summary fashion as deontological, universalist, cognitivist and formalist. Discourse ethics, like Kant's moral philosophy, is deontological because it prioritizes the just over the good; it is universalist because the moral principle is not culturally specific but universally valid; it is cognitivist because it assumes that matters of what is normatively correct can be justified and decided on in as rational a fashion as those regarding what is true; and it is formalist because it limits itself to a procedure without prescribing any substantial value ethics.[77]

Habermas's ethical cognitivism makes strong claims: normative questions can be answered in terms of true and false, and hence legal and moral norms can be universalized. However, the test of universalizability must not be misunderstood, as it is in Kant, as a monological undertaking of an individual subject trusting their good will. Rather, it must be continued in the form of an inter-subjective process of argumentation until a consensus is reached. 'Which argument convinces [within a discourse] is decided not by private insight but by the stance that, bundled together in a ration-ally motivated agreement, is adopted by everyone who participates in the public practice of exchanging reasons.'[78] Thus, Habermas explicitly takes up Kant's ethics but develops it along the lines of a theory of communication. 'The emphasis shifts from what each can will without contradiction to be a general law, to what all can will in agreement to be a universal norm.'[79]

Habermas asserts the criterion of an 'ideal speech situation' for discourses,[80] according to which all participants as subjects capable of speech and action have the same chance to speak. They can all make use of the opportunity to make assertions and to ask for jus-tifications, and they are all guided by the principle of truthfulness, with respect both to themselves and to others. Coercive mechanisms, acting from within or from outside the discourse, are to be excluded. Only such norms as can be accepted by all participants in a dis-course that takes place in a speech situation free of domination can be regarded as valid – valid in the sense of the rational acceptability that Habermas posits as the crucial criterion. The conditions of an ideal speech situation that regulate the discourse and find expression in the principle of universalizability are not arbitrary assumptions but inescapable rules, because whoever engages in argumentation makes use of them. They are, according to Habermas, 'presupposi-tions'; as such they serve as a kind of foil, allowing us to recognize and criticize forms of systematically distorted communication.

In the course of the 1980s, Habermas revised and refined his idea of the ideal speech situation as an anticipation of a form of life for which we should strive. He confessed that the concept of an ideal speech situation is 'somewhat too concrete a term for the set of general and unavoidable communicative presuppositions'.[81] In *Between Facts and Norms*, he discarded the concept, which had provoked many misunderstandings and criticisms, and replaced it with the concept of the ideal communication community – which, however, has the status of a mere methodological fiction.[82] In the previously mentioned conversations with Michael Haller in spring 1991, Habermas clarified that he does not appeal to ideals 'that the solitary theorist sets up in opposition to reality; I am referring only to the normative contents that are encountered in practice . . .'.[83]

Although Habermas assumes in principle that argumentation is a reflective form of communicative action, it would be 'a concretis-tic fallacy to assume that an emancipated society could consist in nothing but "communication free from domination".'[84] And yet, Habermas is convinced that the rules of discourse are more than just methodological fictions; taken together, they form a pragmatic kind of presupposition, an 'unavoidable counterfactual assumption', which is 'operatively effective'.* Habermas assumes that '[c]ounterfactual presuppositions become social facts. This critical thorn sticks in the flesh of any social reality that has to reproduce itself via action oriented towards reaching understanding.'[85] Whoever agrees to enter into argumentation necessarily honours those communicative presuppositions of argumentative speech that Habermas has formalized as discursive rules.[86] These express, Habermas holds, what can be stated normatively from a discursive perspective as the good of a social order. They are, Habermas said in his speech before the Spanish parliament in January 1985, the necessary and universal 'conditions for a communicative praxis of everyday life and for a process of discursive will-formation which would put participants *themselves* in a position to actualize concrete possibilities for a better and less endangered life, in accord with their *own* needs and insights, and on their *own* initiative.'[87]

What may I hope?
Religion in a post-secular society

I have grown old, but not pious.[88]

The coexistence of faith and knowledge. In the introduction to the collection of essays published as *Between Naturalism and Religion* (2005), Habermas writes that we currently observe a 'spread of naturalistic worldviews', but, at the same time, the countervailing trend of a 'growing political influence of religious orthodoxies' in the form of an aggressive Islamism, a Hindu nationalism or the Protestant fundamentalism of the USA.[89] The resulting ideological, and sometimes violent, conflicts are certainly one of the reasons why Habermas has become increasingly concerned (again) with problems of religious philosophy.[90]

Habermas's point of departure is the question of whether – and, if so, on what basis – the modernity of the present can be described as 'post-secular'. He stresses the fact that he uses the term from a sociological perspective in order 'to describe modern societies that have to reckon with the continuing existence of religious groups and the continuing relevance of the different religious traditions,

---

* The German 'operativ wirksam' is no less tautological. Presumably, it is meant to stress the fact that something which is a mere assumption is nevertheless 'effective' in reality.

even if the societies themselves are largely secularized.'[91] In a conversation with the philosopher Eduardo Mendieta, Habermas says: 'Insofar as I describe as "postsecular," not society itself, but a corresponding change of consciousness in it, the predicate can also be used to refer to an altered self-understanding of the largely secularized societies of Western Europe, Canada, or Australia.'[92] Even if the trend towards post-secular societies should continue, there is no doubt, Habermas says, that a secular consciousness will remain predominant. Philosophically, it is reflected in the form of a post-metaphysical thinking whose attitude towards religious truths is both tolerant and aims at reaching understanding, while at the same time insisting on the difference between faith and knowledge, even as it is critical of any instrumentally reduced notion of a reason that is not interested in its own history, as in the case of the naturalism that is dominant today. 'This form of radical naturalism devalues all types of statements that cannot be traced back to empirical observations, statements of laws, or causal explanations, hence moral, legal, and evaluative statements no less than religious ones.'[93] Of course, this does not mean that the postmetaphysical thinker of an anti-scientist persuasion would be inclined towards piety or that her philosophy would lose its fundamentally agnostic streak: 'Postmetaphysical thought does not dispute determinate theological affirmations; instead it asserts their meaninglessness.'[94]

Stages in Habermas's philosophical reflections on religion.   Even though some recent commentators have sneered at the spectacle of one of the most outspoken defenders of a reason-based morality turning towards religion, of all things, Habermas's interest in questions concerning the philosophy and sociology of religion is already evident in his early work and does not signal a new turn in his late work.[95] In his 1971 essay 'Does Philosophy Still Have a Purpose?', and also a little later in one of the last chapters of *Legitimation Crisis* in 1973, Habermas analysed the function of religious systems from a sociological perspective. These systems

> originally connected the moral-practical task of constituting ego- and
> group-identities . . . with the cognitive interpretation of the world . . .
> in such a way that the contingencies of an imperfectly controlled
> environment could be processed simultaneously with the fundamental
> risks of human existence. I am thinking here of crises of the life-cycle
> and the dangers of socialization, as well as of injuries to moral and
> physical integrity (guilt and loneliness, sickness and death).[96]

In November 1974, a working group on 'Theology and Politics' including, among others, Dorothee Sölle, Hans-Eckehard Bahr and Traugott Koch, visited the Max Planck Institute in Starnberg for a discussion of the 'Frage nach dem "Mehr" der Theologie' [The question of the 'surplus' of theology]. Habermas's suggested thesis for discussion was

> that an objectivist, pre-Enlightenment concept of a transcendent God, accompanied by the idea of an immortal soul, was necessary, not only in a contingent but in a logical sense, in order to form an emphatic concept of individuality. The idea of a soul which is co-extensive with God in the temporal dimension, at once eternal and temporal, might have been necessary in order to grasp the idea of the irreplaceability of the individual.[97]

At the end of the 1980s, when neo-conservatism flourished and postmodernism and its cheerful nihilism had its heyday, Habermas intensified his engagement with the relationship between philosophy and religion, between secular reason and religious faith. He was about to elucidate further his programme of postmetaphysical thinking when he was invited to present his views on the status of religion in modernity; in February 1988, on the initiative of Matthias Lutz-Bachmann, an open discussion took place at the philosophical faculty of the Cusanus Foundation* in Frankfurt in which Habermas took part, following talks on that topic in Aarhus, Utrecht and Halle. He explained that, for him, religion is a form of the human spirit which lays claim to shaping the course of a life in its entirety. The religious images which interpret the world help individuals to cope with the experience of contingency. Habermas saw the core of religious practice in providing comfort in existentially difficult situations of need, in contrast to 'the complete absence of comfort in philosophical thinking'.[98] Some three years later, Habermas's own experience would bear out this statement, as he would go on to mention in a later publication. On 4 April 1991, Max Frisch died, a few weeks before his eightieth birthday. Habermas attended the funeral ceremony, which, in accordance with Frisch's wishes, took place in the Stiftskirche St Peter in Zurich. 'No priest, no blessing. The mourners were made up of intellectuals, most of whom had little time for church and religion. Frisch himself had drawn up the menu for the meal that followed.' But with his choice of location, Habermas continued, Frisch, the committed agnostic, demonstrated the fact that 'the enlightened modern age has failed to find a suitable replacement for a religious way of coping with the final *rîte de passage* which brings life to a close.'[99]

In a lecture at the Divinity School of the University of Chicago in September 1988, Habermas separated religious experience from

---

* Foundation of the Catholic Church providing academic scholarships for students.

postmetaphysical philosophy and demanded that the process of revelation be integrated into the context of argumentation on the basis
of reasons: 'At those fracture points where a neutralizing translation
of this type can no longer succeed, philosophical discourse must
confess its failure.'[100] And 'Themes in Postmetaphysical Thinking',
probably the most programmatic of the texts in *Postmetaphysical
Thinking*, also published in 1988, concludes by saying:

> Philosophy, even in its postmetaphysical form, will be able neither
> to replace nor to repress religion as long as religious language is the
> bearer of a semantic content that is inspiring and even indispensable,
> and as long as this content (for the time being?) eludes the explana-
> tory force of philosophical language and still awaits translation into
> reasoning discourses.[101]

From then on, Habermas would defend various forms of this thesis
in a variety of contexts.

One such occasion was his speech on 'Faith and Knowledge'
upon receiving the Peace Prize in 2001, in which he emphasized that
religions that offer a path to salvation and the promise of redemption provide important impulses for ethical self-realization. They
also promote those moral discourses through which modernity at
present, as a community of communication, reaches an understanding about its internal normative commitments. The utterances of
believers, therefore, have to be taken seriously as contributions to a
pluralistic public sphere. While those of faith are obliged to express
the content of religious traditions and the certainties of faith in the
medium of a secular language, the other side must be open to the
discursive deliberation of religious convictions as providing ethical
orientation in life:

> The religious side must accept the authority of 'natural' reason as the
> fallible results of the institutionalized sciences and the basic princi-
> ples of universalistic egalitarianism in law and morality. Conversely,
> secular reason may not set itself up as the judge concerning truths of
> faith, even though in the end it can accept as reasonable only what
> it can translate into its own, in principle universally accessible, dis-
> courses. The one presupposition is no more trivial from a theological
> perspective than the other is from that of philosophy.[102]

Within a democratic community, religious and secular citizens
cannot avoid undergoing 'complementary learning processes'.
Those who have faith must tolerate that, in the context of public
debates, their religiously non-committed fellow citizens insist on
making a distinction between certainties of faith and criticizable
validity claims – i.e., between faith and knowledge. Ideally, a person

who thinks in postmetaphysical terms, in turn, 'is prepared to learn from religion while at the same time remaining agnostic'.[103] Even if the religious conscience of believers is an important factor guiding their views when taking part in the public process of opinion- and will-formation, they must respect that, within the sphere of institutionalized politics – i.e., in parliament, courts, ministries, and the like, only decisions that are justified in secular terms are legitimate.

In his speech on Leibniz Day at the Berlin Brandenburg Academy of Science in July 2002, Habermas's central theme was tolerance, especially the idea of religious tolerance as a 'respect for the ethos of others'. Religious tolerance, he said, provides a model for dealing with ideologically opposed groups that do not speak a common language. It lies beyond prejudices and discrimination and becomes 'necessary . . . only when the parties with good reason neither seek agreement concerning controversial beliefs nor think agreement is possible'.[104] Believers, in particular, must be tolerant because, within a pluralist, democratically constituted society, they must not only set limits to their religious forms of life but must also accept that their faith is to be understood as just one possible value orientation among others.

Habermas and Ratzinger. In recent years, Habermas has repeatedly engaged with prominent representatives of Western religious philosophy and theology. Among these conversations, his dialogue with Joseph Ratzinger, who later became pope, certainly stands out. It must have been obvious to Habermas that a discussion with an official dignitary of the Catholic Church would give rise to wild speculations and the most serious misunderstandings. Nevertheless, he accepted the invitation for a discussion with the cardinal on the evening of 19 January 2004 at the Catholic Academy in Munich. The handpicked audience included the Archbishop of Munich and Freising, Friedrich Wetter, Cardinal Leo Scheffczyk, the theologians Johann Baptist Metz and Wolfhart Pannenberg, the philosopher Robert Spaemann, and the politicians Hans-Jochen Vogel and Theo Waigel. At the time, Ratzinger was still the prefect of the Congregation for the Doctrine of the Faith, whose task it is to protect the Church against heresy – in earlier times, they would have used the word 'inquisition' in this context.[105]

On this evening,[106] Habermas, the philosopher of postmetaphysical thinking, was introduced by the director of the academy, Florian Schuller, 'as the most influential German philosopher since Marx, Nietzsche and Heidegger', whose 'role is that of a public conscience of the political culture in this country'.[107] As guest at the Catholic Academy, Habermas spoke first; he presented a talk based around five theses, which were then also used as the structure for Ratzinger's talk, before the evening ended with a discussion between the two main protagonists and the audience. In his first thesis, Habermas emphasized that it is constitutive of democracies that they create their ethical life and their normative and motivational presuppositions out of themselves through a democratic process of uncoerced and egalitarian deliberation. Because the democratic process is characterized by the fact that the legitimacy of state power emerges from a legal constitution that is created by the citizens themselves, there can be no vacuum to be filled by a general, pre-political ethical life in the form of a religion, be it an ecclesiastically or a civilly constituted Church. Nevertheless, the democratic process presupposes the civic virtue of citizens, such that they participate in the political process; this virtue needs to be learned.[108] This learning process, Habermas said, results from the liberation of communicative freedom and from the representation of individual and collective interests promoted by self-determination. In this context, the idea that a society must be organized on the basis of the principles of justice finds acceptance to the extent that the value of civil liberties is experienced in real life.

Habermas's second thesis was that the integration of individualistic societies depends on its citizens possessing a certain moral self-understanding that is informed by ethical sources, prominent among which is a Judeo-Christian understanding of a religious life, including the ideas of the integrity of the person and of neighbourly love in the sense of respect for human dignity. Something special is held in the Holy Scriptures: authentic images of the persistent ills in the world and the wish to redeem them. Philosophy, too, has kept itself open to these 'intuitions of lapse and redemption', and it must continue to do so. 'The translation of the theological doctrine of creation in God's image into the idea of the equal and unconditional dignity of all human beings constitutes one such conserving translation.'[109]

However, as Habermas set out in his third thesis, the importance of religion in society is by no means limited to its symbolic content being an indispensable resource for the creation of meaning.

Indeed, in the face of the present demands of an accelerating, one-dimensional modernization, moving towards conditions of a global market and competition characterized by increasing economic and social inequalities, the attitude of solidarity is gradually disappearing, and – as Habermas poignantly put it in his fourth thesis – disappearing, only to be replaced by a self-seeking privatism of the bourgeois citizen.

In his last thesis, Habermas expressed the hope that the religious ethos and the moral attitudes associated with it might also promote those political virtues which translate into the preparedness to act and to show empathy, into the virtues of the good, which 'are only "levied" in small change' within states under the rule of law.[110] Apart from that, the potential of religions for providing meaning may turn out to be an antidote to the irrational tendencies of a radicalized critique of reason as well as to the regression into the 'intellectual configurations of a new heathenism' that can be observed today.[111]

Ratzinger's presentation took its lead from Habermas's, featuring as its themes religion, reason, the management of new forms of power, human rights and interculturality. He praised the previous speaker for presenting an 'impressive picture' of the 'strict rationality' of a 'secular culture'. And, like Habermas, he pleaded for a mutual 'willingness to learn from each other' on the part of reason-based morality and Christian ethics. He demanded that 'reason, too, must be warned to keep within its proper limits', and that this must be done by the counter-forces of faith and religion. He spoke of the 'mutual relatedness' of Christian faith and Western secular rationality and appealed for a principled openness towards other cultures and religious persuasions.[112]

Many commentators noted the circumspect behaviour of both the 'guardian of discourse' and the 'guardian of dogma', and that Habermas did not, as some had expected, show any deference to spiritual authority. Rather, in the ensuing conversation he contradicted the cardinal in phrases 'whose diplomatic subtlety was second to none'.[113]

In September 2007, the Italian Society for Political Philosophy invited Habermas to a three-day conference at the Capitol in Rome. In his paper, he spoke about 'The Resurgence of Religion – A Challenge for a Secular Self-Interpretation of Modernity?'[114] Joseph Ratzinger, who had by then become Pope Benedict XVI, was residing nearby but did not participate in the conference. A few days earlier, however, he had referred to Habermas and his concept of reason in a speech on Europe at the Hofburg in Vienna, even going so far as to quote him, if in truncated form:

> For the normative self-understanding of the modern period Christianity has been more than a mere catalyst. The egalitarian universalism, which gave rise to the ideas of freedom and social coexistence, is a direct inheritance from the Jewish notion of justice and the Christian ethics of love. Substantially unchanged, this heritage has always been critically reappropriated and newly interpreted. To this day an alternative to it does not exist.[115]

Habermas had not exactly been taken with Ratzinger's earlier speech in Regensburg on 12 September 2006, in which he had set out supposed differences between Christianity (as guided by reason) and Islam (as prepared for violence).[116] And now, he was angry that the pope had quoted selectively from his work, leaving out the description of Christianity as a 'precursor' to the 'normative self-understanding of modernity', as well as his reference to the fact that the 'autonomous conduct of life, . . . human rights, and democracy' arose out of 'egalitarian universalism'.[117]

During this time, Habermas repeatedly lectured on the question of what the revitalization of the world religions means for the self-understanding of modernity; he spoke, for instance, before a packed auditorium at the University of Münster and, a little later, upon the invitation of the Nexus Institute, at the University of Tilburg in the Netherlands. On the latter occasion, he argued for the thesis that the multicultural global Church of Roman Catholicism has adapted better to globalization than the national Protestant churches, which have emerged as the great losers. The only remedy for the new global ideological tensions, he said, is a secular reason that, as a practice of argumentation, can convince individuals across ideological divides. In this lecture, Habermas again pleaded for an agnosticism that is prepared to learn and which accepts the convictions of people of faith.[118]

Following lectures on the philosophy of religion Habermas gave at Yale University in 2008,[119] another conversation with Eduardo Mendieta took place in 2009. First published in *Deutsche Zeitschrift für Philosophie* in 2010, one of the topics of this dialogue, which is dominated by Habermas, is the question of whether religion in the form of reflective faith is a kind of 'wellspring' for attitudes of solidarity and 'civic engagement'.[120] Habermas criticized those philosophical movements which, in his view, were guilty of devaluing religion, that is, of possessing a 'secularistic self-understanding'. He accused them of overlooking the motivational potential inherent in the world religions, which, he added, had also exerted an influence on the development of postmetaphysical thinking. Habermas concluded: 'Consciousness-raising critique joins a rescuing remembrance, so to speak.'[121] It is highly problematic, he said, if the secularization of the state and the secularization of civil society are not sharply distinguished.[122] The secularization of state power requires a constitution that is neutral with respect to worldviews. 'But a constitutional democracy, which explicitly *authorizes* citizens to lead a religious life, may not at the same time discriminate against these citizens in their role as democratic co-legislators.'[123]

In this conversation Habermas anticipated motifs from, as he put it, a *work in progress** concerned with an analysis of the perplexing constellation of scientism, philosophical reason and religion in a global multicultural society.[124] Central to this analysis is the idea that religions are kept alive by a common cultural practice of rituals: 'Religions do not survive without the cultic activities

---

* 'Work in progress' in English in the original.

of a congregation. That is their "unique distinguishing feature" [*Alleinstellungsmerkmal*].'[125]

There is another reason why rituals are of interest to Habermas, and that has to do with the evolution of language.[126] In his interpretation of research in cultural anthropology, 'in terms of developmental history, ritual is older than mythical narratives, which require a grammatical language.'[127] This raises the question of whether ritual forms of behaviour based on gestures and other non-linguistic signals are an evolutionary precondition for the development of propositionally differentiated languages. For Habermas, language in general is based on the human use of symbols that have the same meaning for everyone within an intersubjectively shared space of semantic content. He draws on recent research by Michael Tomasello to corroborate his conviction that language has a triadic structure consisting of a speaker and a hearer who refer to something in the world with a mutually shared intention. For Habermas, human beings have a monopoly on this type of communication, and it distinguishes *Homo sapiens* from their biological relatives.[128]

A conference on 'Muslims and Jews in Europe'* at Schloss Elmau in Bavaria (June 2008) led to a flurry of interest in the media. It was organized by Michael Brenner, professor for Jewish history and culture in Munich, and John Efron, who teaches Jewish history at Berkeley. Interest was sparked less by the academic conference as such than by the remarkable encounter between Habermas and the Egyptian-born scholar of Islam Tariq Ramadan, one of the most prominent campaigners for the rights of Muslims in Europe. The articles of Alan Posener in *Die Welt* (29 June 2008) and Julia Encke in the *Frankfurter Allgemeine Zeitung* (26 June 2008) both mentioned how impressed Habermas had been by Ramadan's remarks, and that Habermas had pointed out how difficult it is for the Christian and secular majority culture in Europe to be tolerant. He is reported to have said that the distrust of this majority culture towards non-Christian religions has its roots, in part, 'in a distrust of itself'. In his extensive contribution to the discussion, Habermas also reminded the audience of the opportunism shown by some German Christians in 1933, and of the reservations of Catholics about liberal democracy, which were overcome only with the Second Vatican Council of 1962.

Another conference, organized by Hans Joas at the Max Weber Kolleg in Erfurt (3–5 July 2008) on 'The Axial Age and its Consequences for History and for the Present', dealt with questions in the philosophy of religion in a narrower sense. At this conference, internationally renowned philosophers and sociologists, among

---

* Title of conference in English in the original.

them Jan Assmann, Johann Arnason, Robert N. Bellah, Shmuel Eisenstadt and Charles Taylor, discussed Karl Jaspers's thesis that, independently of one another, the great world religions of China, India and the Occident underwent a simultaneous cognitive shift between 800 and 200 BC, around the middle of the millennium, which complemented the mythical with a theoretical picture of the world. In his presentation, Habermas spoke about this cognitive shift and suggested that one might re-examine the relationship between philosophy and religion in light of the idea of the Axial Age. At the same time, according to the report on the conference by Thomas Assheuer (*Die Zeit*, 14 July 2008), Habermas warned that a fixation on the concept of the Axial Age might result in a 'blindness to the specificity of the present time, to the drama between progress and modernity. Non-Western civilizations responded to the pressures of modernization by mobilizing and radicalizing the substance of their cultural legacy [*Erbmasse*]. And thus, behind the outbreaks of religious violence, there also lurks a lot of anger about outrageous injustices, about the uneven distribution of power and wealth, and about the general "Social Darwinism of world politics"'.

What is man?
Language and intersubjectivity

Persons *are* symbolic structures; by contrast, the symbolically structured natural substrate is experienced as one's own body, but – as nature – it remains as external to the individual as all of the material natural basis of the lifeworld.[129]

In the beginning: anthropology. In an interview conducted by Karl-Siegbert Rehberg in 2008, Habermas described how he developed a particular interest in philosophical anthropology during his early years as a student in Bonn. Apart from Helmuth Plessner's work on the 'eccentric position' of man, which impressed and influenced him with its dialogical concept of the ego,[130] Habermas was especially taken with Arnold Gehlen's *Man, His Nature and Place in the World* of 1940, which fascinated him because it was based on a theory of action – even if Habermas was, as he put it, 'personally and politically suspicious' of its author.[131]

In the same interview, Habermas said that, during his studies, he looked at anthropological approaches from the perspective of Humboldt's philosophy of language[132] and that he was also inspired by the tensions between anthropology and the philosophy of history: 'Since my schooldays, I had occupied myself . . . with Herder's and Kant's – and, incidentally, also already with Marx's – thoughts on the philosophy of history, and later in Bonn I had to bring these matters together with my interest in anthropology.'[133] This latter interest was the reason why Habermas contributed an article on 'Anthropology' to Alwin Diemer's philosophical dictionary in 1958, during his time as Adorno's assistant.[134] Ivo Frenzel, the editor-in-chief at the Fischer publishing house at the time, had invited him to participate. In the second half of this article, Habermas formulates a critique of Gehlen's anthropologically grounded theory of culture. By putting the emphasis on the constant aspects of human nature, Gehlen's theory is not far from 'a dogmatism with political consequences, which is all the more dangerous where it claims to be value-free science.'[135] Habermas argues, against the institutionalism of Gehlen's *Urmensch und Spätkultur* [Primordial man and late culture], that man's nature has become historical and is shaped by culture. 'A disquieting fact for an anthropology, which deals ... with the "nature" of man.'[136] Habermas argues, *contra* Gehlen, that man is not condemned to be forever reliant on repression:

> *Gehlen's* anthropological theory of invariants promotes the discipline and severity of archaic institutions, the strictness of imposed renunciation, and the violence of coerced suppression of the drives, beyond what is suggested by the historical findings, to the status of something natural and therefore desirable. In any case, irrational institutions of coercion and discipline are meant to subsume individuals in such a fashion that they lose any intention [*Bestimmung*] and inclination to be subjects.[137]

Habermas further developed his critique of Gehlen in the previously mentioned essay in *Merkur* in 1970, published on the occasion of the publication of Gehlen's *Moral and Hypermoral* [Morality and hypermorality].[138]

Despite all his scepticism towards philosophical anthropology, Habermas was still attracted to the topic and, when he took up Max Horkheimer's chair in Frankfurt, offered a lecture course on 'Problems of a Philosophical Anthropology' in the winter term 1966–7.[139] It is noteworthy that, in the very first of these lectures, he picked up a theme which would occupy him up to the present day, namely the congruence between Kant's epistemology and Darwin's evolutionary theory regarding the question of 'how the emergence of culture' is to be conceived.[140] Along these lines, he discussed the various anthropological conceptions of Darwin, Gehlen, Plessner and others and tried to explain the special organic status of man within the evolution of the species. He was interested in using an evolutionary perspective to provide a foundation for the idea that labour, interaction and the use of symbols are anthropological invariants. As evolutionary achievements, culture, language and communicative action result from the species-specific traits of man, he explained. It is characteristic for man that culturally mediated learning processes take the place of organic adaptation. Natural evolution has produced the basis for culture, defined as the connection between the use of symbols, labour and interaction.

In this lecture course, Habermas defined culture as the essence of what *Homo sapiens* can produce through the use of tools and language. In the course of the evolutionary process, the natural environment is transformed into a socio-cultural lifeworld that is adapted to the needs of the species. Under the influence of culture, the organism itself changes, within certain limits. Habermas mentioned five characteristics that are decisive for the special position of man: the upright gait; the size of the brain and the interaction of head and hand; naturally being born prematurely and the resulting expansion of the period of dependency; the de-differentiation of the motivational system; and the family structure, which is indispensable because of premature birth. Habermas discussed these characteristics in light of the thesis that culture is a form of life through which man, the 'deficient being' [*Mängelwesen*] (Gehlen), tries to secure the conditions necessary for his existence. Reciprocal interactions, which are necessary for the formation of family structures, and thus, in combination with the incest taboo, for securing the survival of vulnerable offspring, are conditions for the formation of culture. The exchange of intentions and wishes – here Habermas employs the concept of an 'intersubjectivity of understanding' – emerges simultaneously with language, a form of communication which is based on the use of symbols. Language, he argued, is not only the medium of the collective memory of the species but also possesses the power to give orientation to actions and regulate norms.

In this early lecture, the young Habermas was already enquiring into the relationship between ritual practices and the origin of language. Do ritual forms of behaviour and taboos appear as initial institutions which stabilize a state of consciousness triggered by linguistic interactions?[141] Perhaps surprisingly for a lecture on anthropology, at the end Habermas came to talk about Marx. The development of society, he said, is determined by the constellation between social labour as the essence of the system of purposive-rational action, on the one hand, and the forms of symbolically mediated interaction, on the other.

This anthropology lecture, given half a century ago when Habermas was just thirty-six years old, is instructive, as it lays out, even if in slightly different terminology, an astonishing number of the motifs that he would later develop in his theory of language, and that he continues to pursue to this day. He also went into more detail regarding some of the ideas in his inaugural lecture on 'Knowledge and Interest', which he had given two terms previously. He then gave his anthropological epistemology its definitive shape in the monograph of 1968, *Knowledge and Human Interests*; however, he would later admit that the book's attempt to derive deep-seated epistemological interests from the conditions of the self-constitution of the human species was a dead end.[142]

In his work on socialization and identity theory of the 1970s, carried out in part while he was still in Frankfurt, and in part later in Starnberg, it is already clear that Habermas associates a normative substance with the construction of the autonomous subject, namely that of a 'rational identity' at the end of a successful process of socialization. This identity is the result of processes of maturation and of learning processes, in the course of which subjects internalize those value orientations 'that enable them *to play* social *roles*'[143] in such a way that they achieve a balance between social and personal identity and between a role distance and role flexibility. Habermas judges the system of social roles according to the degree of its repressivity and rigidity, as well as the level of control over behaviour it imposes. In light of these criteria, the conditions of primary and secondary socialization, as given, for instance, by the psychosocial system of the family and the system of basic roles, can be critically analysed and evaluated by asking whether they promote or inhibit individuation and autonomous behaviour. According to Habermas, individuation and autonomy are expressed in the 'specifically human' interpenetration of linguistic competence, cognitive competence and role competence.[144]

> The degree of individuation can be measured by the preservation of ego identity in the process of an increasing differentiation between personal and social identity. The latter, in turn, depends on the differentiation of the system of roles and on a 'rationalization' of the institutional frame (in the sense of decreasing repression, the disappearance of rigidity, and increasing flexibility in the control of behaviour).[145]

Individuation takes place within a system of demarcations of the ego against the objectivity of outer nature, the normativity of society and the intersubjectivity of language.

In this phase of his work, Habermas describes individuation as a 'symbolic organization of the ego'. On the one hand, it requires universal validity, because it is embedded in the structures of formative processes as such. On the other hand, an autonomous ego organization is far from being the assured outcome. Habermas later systematically summarized this conception in his 'Notizen zur Entwicklung der Interaktionkompetenz' [Notes on the development of interactive competence] of 1974. In these notes, he assumed that the 'ego forms its identity by inner nature learning to reflect on itself in the course of an integration into the gradually developing structures of cognitive, linguistic and interactive exchange with the environment. Inner nature learns at the same time to preserve its unity – i.e., to satisfy requirements of spatial and temporal consistency.'[146]

Individual and society. Some two decades later, Habermas introduced some shifts in emphasis into his conception of interactive competence. Within the context of his mature theory of rationality and communication, the concept of interactive competence acquires the broader meaning of intersubjectivity.[147] On the basis of the theorem of intersubjectivity, Habermas now wanted to show how subjective structures develop simultaneously with social structures within the symbolic medium of grammatically differentiated languages. In view of these interdependencies, any 'anthropological' talk about man as such is avoided from the outset. Instead, the dialectic between individual and society takes centre stage, and the idea that subjectivity is constituted intersubjectively is emphasized.

It is a normative demand of modernity that the individual is self-determined, engages in self-realization, and develops a 'post-conventional' ego identity. These achievements, Habermas says, are socially expected and must be accomplished by each individual. In this context, he envisages society as an unlimited 'communication community in which everyone is capable of taking up the perspective of everyone else and is willing to do so.'[148] As the individual develops within the linguistic community, he learns of his own accord to behave in conformity with norms and at the same time to maintain his individuality. This is because the individual wants both to be like everyone else and to be unique, Habermas claims. 'Only to the extent that we grow into these social surroundings, do we constitute ourselves as accountably acting individuals; by internalizing social controls, we develop for *ourselves*, in our own right, the capacity either to follow or to violate the expectations that are held to be legitimate.'[149]

Habermas presented these complex thoughts on the intersubjective constitution of the ego in a lecture on George Herbert Mead's theory of subjectivity given at the 18th World Congress of Philosophy in Brighton, England, in August 1988. What is remarkable about this lecture is that Habermas shifts the focus from the individuation of an autonomous subject to intersubjectivity.[150] What are the conditions under which the individual may become a subject, and what role do intersubjective relations play in this? Mead's theory of symbolically mediated interaction, Habermas argued, provides a basis on which these questions can be addressed,[151] because from his 'social behaviorism' follows the 'genetic primacy of society in relation to socialized individuals'.[152]

According to Mead, the uniqueness of humans as a species capable of language consists in the use of symbols in order to express things to one another. The meaning of significant symbols that are understood by all is constituted in interactive processes. Symbolically mediated actions take their orientation from mutual expectations of actors regarding their behaviour. In that sense, an individual action can be conceived of only as part of the comprehensive social context of action.[153] Mead explains the capacity of one person to take the perspective of the others with the model of the appropriation of social roles. Thus, the socio-cultural structuring of behaviour through the internalization of norms for actions within processes of socialization takes the place of merely instinctive regulation.[154]

In short: Mead provides Habermas with a theoretical framework within which he can draw his own conclusions regarding identity formation:

> The ego-identity of the adult proves its worth in the ability to build up new identities from the shattered or superseded identities, and to integrate them with old identities in such a way that the fabric of one's interactions is organized into the unity of a life history that is both *unmistakable* and *accountable*. An ego-identity of such nature simultaneously makes possible self-determination *and* self-realization . . . . To the extent that the adult can take over and be responsible for his own biography, he can come back to himself in the narratively preserved traces of his own interactions. Only one who takes over his own life history can see in it the realization of his self. Responsibly to take over one's own biography means to get clear about *who one wants to be*, and from this horizon to view the traces of one's own interactions as *if* they were deposited by the actions of a responsible author, of a subject that acted on the basis of a reflective relation to self.[155]

His insight that individuation is owed to a mutual dialogical relation, and that identity finds expression in the continuity of a life history for which the subject is responsible, leads Habermas to the conclusion that subjectivity is 'anchored in relations of intersubjective recognition'.[156] Subjectivity must be explained from the perspective of the relation between speaker and listener. It is, he holds, the 'participant perspective from which alone the self-experience of the freely acting subject is accessible'.[157]

One specific feature of humans, according to Habermas, is the fact that they can store and pass on to the next generation the experiences they have undergone in the context of learning processes. That, he says, makes them cultural beings. He agrees with Tomasello and others that shared knowledge about objects arises out of the 'we' perspective of intersubjective relations. By one person taking the perspective of the other, an interpersonal relation is formed on the basis of a shared practical knowledge which is sedimented in symbolic systems. At an evening lecture of the German Philosophy Congress in October 2008 in Essen, Habermas again emphasized that the world is only accessible through language, and that language at the same time is the medium in which intersubjective relations are established. The use of language enables us to appropriate experiences and cumulatively to process new knowledge. 'World-disclosure and immanent learning processes interlock through communicative action.'[158] And in his speech on Michael Tomasello on the occasion of the latter's receiving the Hegel Prize in 2009, he said: 'What distinguishes man from the apes is a kind of communication which enables the intersubjective *bundling* of cognitive resources and their reworking, as well as their *transmission* across generations.'[159]

More recently, Habermas has dealt with a question of evolutionary theory: whether 'contexts of cooperation as . . . points of the origin of language' are the only important factor in the formation of a society through communication. Elementary speech acts in which the truth of a proposition as well as the sincerity of the speaker's intention are expressed can be explained with the help of the model of cooperation – i.e., with the necessity 'of reaching agreement among those involved under a pressure to act'.[160] But, in order to make claims to correctness on the basis of recognized norms, an awareness [*Vergegenwärtigung*] and appropriation of ritual practices was once necessary. In *Postmetaphysical Thinking II*, Habermas explains the 'linguistification of the sacred' – a thesis he had first developed in *The Theory of Communicative Action*[161] – as a 'transfer of meaning from the sources of communication of the sacred to ordinary language'. He now distinguishes more sharply 'between ordinary and non-ordinary communication'. Accordingly, he assumes that normative substance is 'first detached from its encapsulation in ritual and then transferred into the semantics of ordinary language'. Apparently, Habermas has in mind a translation process with multiple steps: from ritual to myth, and from myth to ordinary language. In other words:

> The achievement of mythical, religious and metaphysical worldviews consists in releasing the semantic potential encased in cultic practices into the language of mythical narratives or dogmatically formed teachings and, at the same time, on the basis of the worldly knowledge available at a given time, in processing them into an interpretative system that stabilizes identity.[162]

In the lecture on anthropology in the 1960s, the physical body of humans [*Leiblichkeit*] played an important role. Helmuth Pessner was certainly influential for Habermas in this respect. Habermas was rather enthusiastic about Plessner's anthropology because it performed 'with great determination the naturalistic turn, but without thereby having to pay the price of a naturalism'.[163] At the time, Habermas was of the opinion, *contra* Plessner, that 'the double aspect of animate body [*Leib*] and physical body [*Körper*]' might be understood as 'merely [representing] the double structure of language'. Nevertheless, in more recent times, Habermas has continually revisited the question of human beings' embodied nature: first in his critical engagement with biogenetic research and the application of genetic engineering to humans in his *The Future of Human Nature*, mentioned above, and then in his lecture at the Adorno Conference in Frankfurt in 2003, where, in considering the idea of the freely acting person, he mentioned such a person's 'somatic existence', 'the organic substrate of the body'. A responsible agent, he says, must identify 'with the physical body as its own animate body'.[164]

14

Books at an Exhibition

Eightieth birthday. On 10 June 2009, the weekly newspaper *Die Zeit* splashed the preposterous headline 'World Power Habermas' in huge letters across its front page, probably in allusion to Thomas Mann.[1] Below, in smaller letters, it continued: 'If there is anyone today who can explain reality to us, it is Jürgen Habermas. On his eightieth birthday, Germany's most influential philosopher is in demand on all five continents.'[2] This message was accompanied with an equally tabloidesque coloured photograph showing Habermas surrounded by a library of world literature arranged in the form of an arena, his gaze seemingly wandering into the distance, his face looking stern.

Habermas himself refrained from commenting on this coverage, but certain discreet hints allow us to conclude that he might have found it sensationalist. At least, he did not contradict his publisher when she stated publicly that a world power 'which relies exclusively on the non-coercive force of the persuasiveness of the better argument has so far not appeared in world history.'[3]

A few years later, Habermas expressed himself along similar lines in an interview in the *Rheinische Post* (10 December 2012), saying that the lead story had been a 'bad joke'.

> Intellectuals may at best exert a certain influence with their public statements, but they do not have any power. Power is tied to positions with the ability to push through a determined will against others. By contrast, the diffuse influence of intellectuals depends not on empowerment but on the persuasiveness of their words, as well as on the aura of the media through which the words are disseminated. Since I, for instance, express myself only in newspapers, my influence is limited for that reason alone.

In the middle sections of the paper, *Die Zeit* covered Habermas's birthday in a more serious fashion. Thomas Assheuer pointed out, among other things, the central role played by language in Habermas's philosophy, and he ended by saying that Habermas 'has welded together the Republic even through the disputes he has caused and has changed his own arguments as well as those of his opponents in the process.' A further page contained congratulatory messages from colleagues and intellectuals from all over the world. Ronald Dworkin, for instance, wrote: 'Jürgen Habermas is not only the most famous living philosopher on earth. His fame itself is famous.' The Turkish sociologist Ahmet Çiğdem noted: 'Habermas possesses an eminent sensitivity for the threats facing all thinking – for instance by universities that are "managed" like companies; by media that disempower the word; or by a politics that does no more than distinguish between what is bad and what is the worst.' And Richard Sennett summarized: 'For us, Habermas is a contemporary, not an intellectual hero, and thus his position within the history of German thought interests us less than his capacity to provoke debate.'[4]

Of the large number of birthday wishes, the one published by Michael Krüger in the *Süddeutsche Zeitung* on the very day, 18 June, stands out. In his article, Krüger, who at the time was still working for the Hanser Verlag in Munich, had long been friendly with Habermas and his wife. He wrote of his frequent visits to their home in Starnberg, about Ute and Jürgen's hospitality, about the fact that 'the man of the house himself insists on fetching culinary delight after culinary delight from the kitchen', and about the lengthy conversations:

> Jürgen Habermas is usually either just coming back from somewhere or just preparing to go somewhere. Chicago, Arabia, China, Cologne, Barcelona, even Berlin on occasions. When he talks about his travels – and he is an excellent narrator – you get the impression that there are decent people everywhere in the world, although not too many of them. What surprises him most is that everyone has read his books. Even in China? Especially there. When he is not travelling, he is writing, although one cannot help suspecting that he also works while travelling, given the large number of his publications. Most of the time, he writes for something, for human rights, for a just society, for the survival of newspapers, for the affirmation of reason, for Europe. As he keeps everything in his head and does not forget anything, he occasionally also writes against something. Then, he can become brusque. No one can get as nicely worked up as he does, especially in conversation. The way he then tugs at his thick white hair gives you a rough impression of what he might do to the person who has agitated him. But before it gets dicey, he begins to laugh. As philosophers have little to laugh about, he keeps philosophical laughter alive! Compared to his laughter, that of Gargantua is a tired giggle.

Ute: Not so loud! Do you want the whole world to hear what you are thinking about it? . . . Perplexity and lethargy are repugnant to him, as is bragging or an elitist demeanour. For a few years now, he has not been a complete stranger to melancholia, which reassures me. . . . Then, there is dessert. A conversation about apricot dumplings is also part of communicative competence. When you leave, he is standing in the doorway – upright, with his head slightly tilted forward – as if he had stepped out of the cave like Plato. Above him the starry skies, next to him Ute.[5]

Frankfurt, the metropolis on the Main and the hub of Habermas's teaching activities, came up with an original way of marking the start of his ninth decade. At the German National Library, an exhibition – curated by the philologist Wolfgang Schopf on behalf of the Goethe University – was dedicated explicitly to the author and political commentator Habermas. Apart from a very few photographs there were only Habermas's books and other printed matter on display, for instance a hundred dust jackets from books he had published with both German and foreign publishers. This approach of a 'withheld biography' in favour of the written word, Schopf said, had been Habermas's condition for agreeing to the project. The exhibition bearing the title '. . . die Lava des Gedanken im Fluss' [The lava of thought in flow . . .][6] was an impressive demonstration of the visible traces left behind by the levels of theoretical reflection.

The exhibition highlighted the history of an author's work. Habermas himself speaks of his books as 'handrails' he holds on to.[7] The twenty-five cabinets containing first editions also displayed documents relating to how the books developed and how they were received. A collection of the articles he had published in newspapers and journals since the early 1950s showed how Habermas had influenced the political climate in his role as an intervening public intellectual. They were distributed as facsimiles across tables in order to be read by visitors. The 134 documented titles of his seminars and lectures gave an impression of his lifetime achievement as an academic. At the opening of the exhibition, Habermas, who, together with Ute, had seen the exhibition of his work for the first time only a few minutes earlier, said: 'I feel like a painter in the halls of a museum presenting the first retrospective on his work.'[8] In the *Frankfurter Rundschau* (18 June 2009), Christian Schlüter concluded:

What this 'exhibition of works' shows in particular is the fact that, and the degree to which, the so-called Suhrkamp culture must be credited to Jürgen Habermas. Unseld relied almost entirely on the advice of the politically interested and committed philosopher. The latter, in turn, knew how to make good use of the publisher's reputation for his strategic theoretical purposes.

After the opening of the exhibition on the afternoon of 17 June, Ulla Unseld-Berkéwicz hosted a celebration at the house in Klettenbergstraße that had been occupied by the family until Siegfried Unseld's death in October 2002, and which is still regularly used today for the publisher's events and receptions. Topics of conversation that evening revolved around not only the exhibition at the National Library and the speeches that had just been given but also the publishing house's plans to relocate from Frankfurt to Berlin. In his thank-you speech at the opening of the exhibition, Habermas had referred in passing to Unseld-Berkéwicz's extraordinary plans when he spoke of a 'departure to new shores':

> I can understand, and reluctantly comprehend, this – if not without some melancholy. On the other hand, no one knows better than you that publishing houses cannot renew themselves without remembering their history. And because every memory is *rooted* in a specific spatial and temporal context, it will – I hope – be possible to save the material memory of the *Suhrkamp- and Unseld-Verlag* from becoming uprooted.[9]

On the afternoon of his birthday, Habermas took part in a discussion at Frankfurt University's Campus Westend, which was moderated by Axel Honneth and covered by the Zweites Deutsches Fernsehen. Young researchers from various countries, who utilized parts of Habermas's work in their doctoral dissertations, were given the opportunity to put their questions to Habermas in person. The day ended with a large reception at the university guesthouse, with the university's president Werner Müller-Esterl and the Suhrkamp Verlag as official hosts. About 200 guests came together in Ditmarstraße and celebrated late into the night, enjoying delicacies from Hesse and Rheingau wines. Following the welcome from the university's president, Ulla Unseld-Berkéwicz thanked her author for his commitment to the scientific programme and to the publisher's public profile over many decades. Later, after an entertaining speech by the music and literary critic Joachim Kaiser, Hauke Brunkhorst presented Habermas with a copy of the *Habermas Handbuch* [Habermas handbook], which he had edited alongside Regina Kreide and Cristina Lafont.

Welcoming the guests, Habermas made a point of addressing his 'oldest friend', Karl-Otto Apel: 'Dear Karl-Otto, I would like to use this opportunity in order also to say in public what you know anyhow: as far as my philosophical arsenal of thoughts is concerned, without you I would not have become the person I am today.' However, the main part of his short speech was dedicated to the personal importance for him of the Johann Wolfgang Goethe University. Its influence, he said, is personified 'in the unusual figure of Adorno, the only genius I have met in my life.' Rather unexpectedly given the context, Habermas praised the academic institution of the traditional seminar, saying: '[I]t rewards precisely thoughts and information which, within the space of reasons, topple coherent structures of order and create new ones.' He concluded by mentioning the central experience of his academic life, 'that things were going the right way only as long as the professor could also learn something from his assistants, the teacher from his students', and with a thank-you to his collaborators, most of whom were present.[10]

Four weeks before his birthday, the Suhrkamp Verlag published a five-volume edition of Habermas's *Philosophische Texte* [Philosophical texts], a collection of essays spanning four decades, which Habermas had compiled himself. More precisely, as he writes in the preface, it is a

> systematic collection of texts . . . each of which has to stand in for an *unwritten* monograph. I have not written whole books on the important themes which concern my philosophical interests in the narrower sense – neither on the foundations of sociology in the theory of language, nor on the conception of language and rationality grounded in formal pragmatics, nor on discourse ethics or political philosophy, nor on the status of postmetaphysical thinking. I have come to realize this strange fact only in retrospect.[11]

Christian Schlüter, somewhat prematurely, classified this edition as Habermas's 'philosophical legacy' (*Frankfurter Rundschau*, 13 June 2009) and commented: 'Habermas no longer opens up new front lines; rather, he is interested in the unitary architecture of his thought. . . . In this context, he even admits mistakes, if occasionally and through gritted teeth; but still – he does.' Christian Geyer (*Frankfurter Allgemeine Zeitung*, 20 May 2009) noted that the five volumes 'contain fifty further books'. The design of Habermas's theory, he wrote, becomes visible. 'Slightly misconstrued corners, or stones sticking out, are made to fit in the introductions to the volumes, and left-over mortar is removed. Habermas uses the opportunity to correct crude readings, interpreting them in hindsight as misreadings and integrating them into a systematic order. Lines of continuity are marked out where one had suspected ruptures.'

Consciousness-raising and rescuing critique

Contemporary philosophy lacks Benjaminian words which go beyond mere cultural criticism.[12]

Keeping the rhythm. After the birthday celebrations and a holiday in the South of France, Habermas and his wife, together with Toni, the younger of their two grandchildren, travelled to the USA, where Habermas taught for six weeks at Stony Brook University. He held one seminar per week and gave a public lecture, 'On the Concept of Human Dignity and the Realist Utopia of Human Rights', a new theme for him.[13]

Regarding human dignity, Habermas explained that its normative substance has a 'disclosive function' [*Entdeckungsfunktion*] in identifying living conditions under which human beings are suffering. The moral source of the moral surplus value of human rights, he says, is human dignity. At the same time, this source has a catalytic function in the legally binding codification of human rights. In spite of this, human rights are Janus faced because they relate both to morality and to the law. In addition, there is the tension between the constitutional ideal and the constitutional reality. This may be ameliorated by, for instance, combining the recognition of human dignity with legal guarantees which safeguard everyone's status as a citizen, with its concomitant enforceable rights. This status would therefore need to be created through positive law. As a moral principle, human dignity applies to everyone. Brought into a legal form as, for instance, a basic right enshrined in the constitution, only the members of the corresponding legal community can appeal to it. For that reason, Habermas insists on adopting the perspective of a cosmopolitan legal condition whose creation would require a novel kind of constitutional assembly.[14]

On 22 October, during the last weeks of his stay in the USA, Habermas met with Charles Taylor, Judith Butler, and the theologian and activist Cornel West in New York for a discussion on 'The Power of Religion in the Public Sphere'. This was a public colloquium with an audience of over 1,000 gathered in the historical Great Hall of the Cooper Union, jointly organized by New York University, the Social Science Research Council and Stony Brook University. Habermas again argued for his theses on the relationship between communicative reason and faith. Craig Calhoun moderated a conversation between him and Charles Taylor, whose recent *A Secular Age* had just caused something of a furore. Habermas clarified that, for him, the status of religious certainties of faith is the same as that of secular reason as far as individuals' self-understanding is concerned. However, he maintained his claim that a distinction needs to be drawn between general principles of justice and individual decisions in the realms of existential, ethical and religious convictions. Taylor, however, rejected Habermas's differentiation between morality, ethics and religion; further, he doubted whether a rational clarification of questions of faith through public discourse is even possible and defended the intrinsic importance of the profound experiences on which religions are based.[15]

Back in Europe, Habermas was invited to an event at the Felix Meritis cultural centre in Amsterdam, organized by the Goethe Institute, which took place in the afternoon of 5 November 2009 and was moderated by Harry Kunneman. As in the discussion with Charles Taylor in New York, it became very clear that dialogue is Habermas's preferred form of engagement. He was on top form in his short replies to five questions from politicians, sociologists and philosophers; he explained to the first questioner, Job Cohen, the social democratic mayor of Amsterdam, that the increasing potential for conflict in Western societies, characterized as they are by heterogeneous religious communities and cultural traditions living alongside one another, can be reduced only by policies which are open to this pluralism and by liberal immigration policies. Habermas argued for cosmopolitan forms of life with striking brio, insisting that ties with the national traditions of the country of origin are of secondary importance. Forms of communication which transcend borders, he said, had long since developed into habitual everyday practices, as he had experienced first-hand with his fifteen-year-old grandchild Toni, Rebekka's daughter.

On 16 November 2009, Habermas was a speaker at the UNESCO conference on 'Philosophy in Dialogue with Cultures', organized by the Russian Academy of Sciences in Moscow. At the centre of his lecture on 'The International Relationship between Human Dignity and Human Rights' was again the concept of human dignity. In a discussion with the philosophers Abdusalam Guseynov and Nelly Motroshilova, he argued that, with the help of this morally charged concept, the maxims of human rights could be transformed into an ethical attitude. And in his essay 'On the Concept of Human Dignity and the Realist Utopia of Human Rights', he writes:

> The struggle to implement human rights continues today, in our own countries, as well as, for example, in Iran and China, in parts of Africa, or in Russia, Bosnia or Kosovo. Whenever an asylum seeker is deported at an airport behind closed doors, whenever a ship carrying refugees capsizes on the crossing from Libya to the Italian island of Lampedusa, whenever a shot is fired at the border fence between the United States and Mexico, we, the citizens of the West, confront one more troubling question. The first human rights declaration set a standard which inspires refugees, people who have been thrust into misery, and those who have been ostracized and insulted, a standard which can give them the assurance that their suffering is not a natural destiny. The translation of the first human right into positive law gave rise to a *legal duty* to realize exacting moral requirements which has become engraved in the collective memory of humankind.
>
> Human rights constitute a *realistic* utopia insofar as they no longer paint deceptive images of a social utopia which guarantees collective

happiness but anchor the ideal of a just society in the institutions of constitutional states themselves.[16]

Interventions. In an article for the *New York Times* (28 October 2010), Habermas discussed changing political mentalities in Germany. The piece was titled 'Leadership and Leitkultur', and a little later it was also published by *Le Monde*, as 'L'Europe malade de la xénophobie'. Habermas highlighted three symptoms that were typical of the time: a stereotypical hostility towards immigrants, especially those of Islamic origin; the attraction exerted by a new kind of politician who remains loftily on the sidelines of party political discussions; and, finally, the reactions to spontaneous political protest movements which push for greater involvement in decisions on important, large-scale matters. He drew the attention of his readers in the USA and in France to the recent xenophobic trends in Germany, which he sees as incompatible with the constitution of a country that considers itself liberal, and where, in any case, there has been more emigration than immigration in the past. Habermas criticized the demands from populist commentators and politicians that, for instance, Muslim immigrants should adopt the Jewish-Christian tradition not only as based on a limited, namely ethnic, understanding of liberal democracy but also as an arrogant appropriation of the Jewish religion that disrespects the fate suffered by the Jews in Germany in the past. He leaves it an open question as to whether or not the popularity of political figures presenting themselves as enlightened figures [*Lichtgestalten*], rising above party-political differences, is a symptom of new forms of anti-democratic and authoritarian dispositions. Towards the end of his article, he sounds a rather more optimistic note, pointing out that the strong call for more citizen participation, for instance in connection with the planned new train station in Stuttgart or regarding the question of the phasing out of nuclear energy, is a sign that a formal and truncated understanding of the democratic process is meeting with growing resistance.

In the late autumn of 2010 there appeared a study of the Federal Foreign Office during the time of the National Socialist dictatorship and the post-war period, edited by an international commission of historians.[17] The commission had been set up by the then foreign minister, Joschka Fischer, following a row over obituaries for diplomats.* Among other things, the study dispelled the myth that the Foreign Office had been a pocket of resistance between 1933 and 1945, and it established the complicity of the

---

* In 2003, Fischer had passed a decree which prohibited the ministerial journal *Intern AA* (AA = Auswärtiges Amt, that is, 'foreign office') from publishing detailed obituaries for diplomats who were former members of National Socialist organizations.

service in the crimes of the regime – although it was published at a time former office-holders could no longer be expected to face any legal repercussions. Still, it prompted a highly charged debate, in particular around its methodology, that is to say, its scientific value.[18]

At the height of the debate, which played out in all the major daily and weekly newspapers as well as in academic journals, a discussion took place at the Catholic Academy in Munich in January 2011 between one of the authors of the study, the historian Norbert Frei, and the contemporary historian Christian Hacke, who had criticized the study. Hacke had argued that the study's primary concern was not coming to terms with the past but, rather discrediting the old elite of German foreign policy.[19] Habermas and his wife were guests at the event in Munich and listened to the presentations given by the two historians. In the heated discussion that ensued, Habermas intervened and defended Frei against Hacke by asking whether one could really explain the conformism of the members of the Foreign Office by referring to the fact that human beings, by their very nature, seek orientation in reality. Is it not necessary in this case, too, to seek explanations for the emergence of anti-Semitic and National Socialist mentalities? Habermas suggested that the vehement reactions provoked by the book were symptoms of the fact that the core of an apologist intellectual mindset was still active, years after an anti-communism that had served the purpose of repressing the past and after the historians' debate.[20]

A conference on 'Jewish Voices in the Discourse of the 1960s' took place at Schloss Elmau at the end of June 2011, and one of the underlying concerns was the problem of racist and religious discrimination. In a conversation focusing on intellectual history with the literary scholar Rachel Salamander on 'The (Re)migrated Philosophers and the Intellectual Life of the Federal Republic', Habermas reminded the audience that in the 1950s and 1960s it had been, for the most part, Jewish emigrants returning to Germany who had been most sensitive to the ways in which German culture had discredited itself. To that extent, he had himself been the 'beneficiary of an improbable gift which Jewish emigrants as teachers of a younger generation, despite everything, had presented to the homeland which had expelled them.'[21]

In May 2012, Ute and Jürgen Habermas travelled to Israel for a week. Habermas had been invited by the Israel Academy of Sciences and Humanities to present the first Buber Memorial Lecture. As a topic he chose 'A Philosophy of Dialogue'. He began by setting out the significance of Martin Buber as a representative of the 'modern Jewish national culture' during the years of the Weimar Republic. Together with Franz Rosenzweig, he had played an important role at the Jüdisches Lehrhaus in Frankfurt and then again in post-war Germany, where 'the reconciliatory religious interlocutor was the antipode of the implacable historian Gershom Scholem, who, during the 1960s, opened our eyes to the downside of the casual invocations of the so-called German-Jewish symbiosis.' In the following passages of this lecture, Habermas attempts to provide an interpretation of Buber's dialogical philosophy from the perspective of a theory of intersubjectivity, pointing out that Buber's philosophy is, indeed, consistent with the linguistic turn in philosophy. The communicative relationship, the recognition of the other in dialogue, is associated with an egalitarian individualism, which does not exhaust itself in 'self-objectification': 'The phenomenon of self-consciousness is derived from dialogue.' That Buber generally discards objectifying attitudes towards the world, Habermas sees as a fallacy of cultural criticism. In the role of a religious writer, Buber pursued the goal of justifying Zionism with arguments drawn from a humanist philosophy. His political goal was 'a single state that would unite citizens of Jewish and Arab nationality on an equal footing'.[22]

At the beginning of his lecture at the Carl Friedrich von Siemens Foundation in Munich (19 June 2012), Habermas declared that the good must be decoupled from the idea of justice. The lecture formed part of a series on 'Politics and Religion', moderated by the philosopher Heinrich Meier. Habermas also entered into discussion with the Protestant theologian Friedrich Wilhelm Graf, who, on that evening, characterized himself as an 'intellectual of religion' for whom 'religion is the "most dangerous mental substance" you can imagine'.[23] Habermas was concerned about the potential for violence that lies dormant in religious fundamentalism, and he insisted that this potential must not be allowed 'to ignite because of the spark of the dynamics of worldviews'.[24] The Western cultures that invoke their Enlightenment legacy have to open themselves up to the perspectives from which other cultures regard them. These perspectives 'make the West become aware of the provincialism of Eurocentric generalization by reminding us of the imperial conquests and colonial atrocities, of the crimes which have been committed in the name of our high ideals.' And, at the end, Habermas renewed his plea for an acceptance of the intrinsic rights of religions and for treating them with respect, because it is impossible to know whether the 'continuing process of the translation of the unrealized potential of religious meaning has exhausted itself.'[25]

In the *Frankfurter Allgemeine Zeitung*, Christian Geyer wrote that at this event Habermas 'spoke coolly ... and yet very cautiously, like a good surgeon who does not want to cause any unnecessary pain.' Habermas, Geyer said, at first raised only minor objections to Heinrich Meier, whose interest in religion was of a purely sociological nature, by pointing out that his own interest was to examine religion 'as a resource . . . for a philosophy that does not refute itself through a narrow naturalistic and scientistic approach but, rather, tries to make full use of its semantic potential. In this context, Habermas signalled more sympathy for Dieter Henrich and Robert Spaemann than for the Heideggerian* approach of Agamben.'[26] Habermas's 'masterfully performed role of someone who, despite being tone-deaf to religion, tries to strengthen the cause of theology' imparted 'magic to the evening at the Siemens Foundation'. However, in the end he nevertheless performed the decisive 'cut' with a single question posed to the theologian Graf: 'Given that the claims to religious truth apply not only to doctrines, and that religious knowledge is actualized in the form of religious socialization, as a path to salvation – why, then, Habermas asked, do theologians increasingly decouple themselves from the ritual practice of the community?'[27]

'Prize trips'. In recent years, as more and more honours are heaped upon him, a considerable amount of Habermas's time has been spent composing acceptance speeches and lectures. In June 2010, he received the Ulysses Medal in Dublin; in May 2012, he received two prizes in Vienna, the Erwin Chargaff Prize for Ethics and Science in Dialogue and the Honorary Prize of the Viktor Frankl-Fonds of the city of Vienna. In September 2012, Habermas travelled to Wiesbaden, where he received the Georg-August Zinn Preis zur Förderung von Rechtsstaatlichkeit, Demokratie und sozialem Zusammenhalt [Georg-August Zinn Prize for the promotion of the rule of law, democracy and social cohesion] awarded by the Social Democratic Party of Hesse. A few weeks later, on 14 December, he was awarded the Heinrich Heine Prize of the city of Düsseldorf, which came with an award of 50,000 euros, for his life's work as a philosopher. Munich awarded him the city's Cultural Prize of Honour in January 2013, and Kassel the Citizens' Prize 'Das Glas der Vernunft' [The glass of reason] at the end of September 2013. And, finally, Habermas received the Erasmus Prize of the Praemium Erasmianum Foundation, with 150,000 euros in prize money, presented to him by King Willem-Alexander at the Royal Palace in Amsterdam on 7 November. The prize is awarded to thinkers from the disciplines of sociology, philosophy and politics.

Before the award ceremony in Dublin, Habermas conducted a seminar at University College Dublin and gave a public lecture on the topic of 'The Political: The Rational Meaning of a Questionable Inheritance of Political Theology'.[28] At the start of the lecture, he asked what meaning could be gleaned from the concept of the politi-

---

* '. . . für den heideggerisierenden Agamben': the formulation uses Heidegger's name as a verb in the continuous form, giving it an ironic and polemic tone.

cal, understood as 'the symbolic medium of self-representation of a society',[29] given the 'force of systemic imperatives' which seem increasingly immune to intentional interventions.[30] Following a survey of the conceptual and theoretical history of the notion of the political and a comparative look at the theories of Carl Schmitt and John Rawls, he argued that a secularized state is not necessarily forced to make a strict distinction between the political and religion. Religiously motivated contributions to the processes of political will-formation within the public sphere are perfectly legitimate. He went even further to say: 'The discursive encounter with religious tradition, especially the attempt at rationally capturing unrealized semantic potentials, forms points of resistance to a purposive rationality wedded to the principle of maximizing gain.'[31]

Habermas's thank-you speech in the Town Hall of Vienna discussed eugenic interventions in the human genome and whether they are justified. Before addressing his topic, he mentioned the psychiatrist Frankl and the chemist and author Chargaff, who contributed to the decoding of DNA; both, he said, had realized early on that scientific progress would raise the question of its ethical justification. 'I am not', Habermas said, 'one of those specialists [of biotechnology, S. M.-D.]. But when a famous colleague, Ian Hacking, attached the neologism of "bio-conservative" to me, I replied: although I find it hard to imagine that I would ever accept the charge that I am a "conservative" in any political sense, I could happily accept being called a bio-conservative.'[32]

When speaking in front of the Social Democratic Party in Wiesbaden, Habermas began with recollections of his first year in Frankfurt, when he had been working as Adorno's assistant and lived 'in a climate of compressed contemporaneity'. 'In retrospect, these were the most intense years of my adult life.' After that, he again took the government to task for its fixation on the nation in matters pertaining to Europe. This attitude, he said, was a capitulation in the face of the powers of globalization and was not suited to escape the 'vicious circle whereby the euro countries are blackmailed by the financial markets'.[33]

Upon receiving the Heinrich Heine Prize in Düsseldorf, Habermas spoke about the euro crisis. He opened his talk by remarking that he would like to see intellectuals commenting on Europe in droves. Today's timidity, he said, is the exact opposite of Heinrich Heine's commitment. Instead of nurturing revolutionary hopes, we keep our heads down: 'We are all cowering under the demands of the financial markets and, by keeping still, are confirming the seeming impotence of a mode of politics that makes the bulk of the taxpayers pay for the damage of the financial crisis instead of the speculators. Heine would have poured scorn over the bookkeepers of privatized profits and socialized costs.'[34]

Habermas had last engaged with Heine more than two decades ago.[35] Now, he described him with words that Heine himself had used for Lessing: 'Lessing was the living criticism of his time, and his whole life was a polemic.'[36] He explained Heine's influence in post-war Germany by saying that, after 1945 he 'contrasted even more sharply with everything that had led to the German catastrophe'. Habermas sees Heine's contemporary relevance in the latter's commitment as an author to the political struggles of his times: as a kind of 'mentality-shaping tribune'. Heine's commitment, Habermas says, owes its persuasiveness to 'the pathos of truth of a sensitive poet'; Heine was sensitive to the impulse of rescuing critique – 'the desire to rescue a vulnerable, because non-renewable, human heritage'.[37]

Since 1972, Habermas has lived with Ute near Munich. Munich University twice refused to give an honorary professorship to the then director of the Max Planck Institute. In 1985, he was awarded the Sophie and Hans Scholl Prize of the city of Munich. When the Social Democratic lord mayor of Munich, Christian Ude, now presented him with the city's Cultural Prize of Honour, endowed with 10,000 euros, at the Old Town Hall, Habermas must have felt gratified. As he himself put it, it was an 'act of embrace' from a city which had not always welcomed him with open arms, a fact also emphasized by Julian Nida-Rümelin in his speech at the ceremony. Habermas opened his acceptance speech with a short reflection on the concept of solidarity and then quickly made a link with the half-hearted politics of solidarity with the indebted countries in Europe. However, at the centre of his short deliberations was an entertaining look back on previous recipients of the prize and on Habermas's personal experiences as a citizen moving back and forth between Starnberg, his place of residence, and the municipal centre of a culturally attractive metropolis.[38]

In his speech in Kassel, Habermas reminisced about his first visit to the *documenta* in the 1950s, speaking about his 'encounter with that transatlantic modernity which Arnold Bode and Werner Haftmann laid out before us at the Museum Fridericianum at the time. It was intoxicating suddenly to be confronted with the overwhelming large-scale formats of Jackson Pollock and Barnett Newman, with the unusual colour compositions of Rauschenberg, Mark Rothko and Motherwell.' And he added: 'The capacity to meet contemporary art with open eyes is a measure of one's own contemporaneity.'[39]

His wife, his three children and their partners, his two grandchildren, and his older brother, Hans Joachim, all accompanied Habermas to the award ceremony in Amsterdam, which was conducted according to a stringent protocol. Habermas was urged to keep strictly to the text of his fifteen-minute speech, which he had submitted in advance, and to keep to the time limit. Before the ceremony, he had had discussions with students at the university and with Dutch colleagues at a non-public event of the foundation. The day after the award ceremony, Habermas could be spotted with his wife at the Rijksmuseum, which had reopened only six months previously.

A conclusion. In mid-2013, the twelfth and final volume of *Kleine Politische Schriften* [Short political writings] appeared under the title *The Lure of Technocracy*. Forty-five years ago, Habermas had published his first volume in the edition suhrkamp series. The *Kleine Politische Schriften* were begun in 1981 with a hardcover volume dedicated to his son Tilmann. According to its preface, this book showed Habermas being 'politically and journalistically active in a somewhat bourgeois sense'.[40] In the preface to the present volume, which is announced as the last of the *Kleine Politische Schriften*, he writes:

> 'A full dozen'* – normally, this is an expression of relief at the end of a project. In my case, one might speak of an ending but not of a completion accompanied by relief, because this kind of public importunity does not have a goal; it is nothing but an attempt at an uninvited argumentative contribution to the ongoing process in which public opinion forms.

Although the first volumes also had the 'apologetic purpose' of 'defending [him] against insinuations which made the rounds in the heated academic atmosphere of the 1970s', the *'basso continuo'* of all volumes 'is the battle over the normative self-understanding first of the old, and then of the expanded Federal Republic.' In his view, his interventions did not in fact have the 'intended effect' – an opinion some may wish to dispute – because the division he practised between 'the "interventions" of an intellectual and the academic work of a professor' is not accepted, and 'academics baulk at the price to be paid for committing themselves publicly on an issue.'[41] Alexander Cammann in *Die Zeit* also commented on the series in the same vein: '[W]hat a show; a one-man performance in the service of the *res publica*!'

The centrepiece of volume XII is a text with the subtitle 'A Plea for European Solidarity', in which Habermas criticizes not only the lack of solidarity among European states but also the manner in which *'the delayed democratization* is presented as a promise in the

---

* 'Das Dutzend vollmachen' is an idiomatic expression used to mark the end of a task or activity.

manner of a light at the end of the tunnel.'[42] Habermas's analysis stands out because he renders more precise the concept of solidary action in the sphere of international politics: solidary action, he says, is an ethical commitment which depends 'on the predictability of reciprocal conduct – and on confidence in this reciprocity over time'.[43] Solidarity differs from both law and morality on account of its 'peculiar reference to a "joint involvement" in a network of social relations. That involvement grounds both the demanding expectations of one side . . . and the confidence on the other side that its behaviour will be reciprocated in the future if need be.'[44] Connected to this is the proactive character of solidary action – i.e., 'the *proactive character* of striving to fulfil a promise that is implied in the claim to legitimacy of any political order.'[45] When looking back on the idea of solidarity it becomes clear, he says, that what is at stake is 'a *redemptive reconstruction* [*rettende Rekonstruktion*]* of relations of solidarity that were familiar but had become hollowed out by the more far-reaching processes of modernization.'[46] The topic of solidarity was also the focus of Habermas's lecture on 'Demokratie, Solidarität und die europäische Krise' [Democracy, solidarity and the European crisis], which he delivered at the Pieter De Somer auditorium of the Catholic University in Leuven in Belgium. The president of the European Council, Herman Van Rompuy, was in attendance; Habermas took the opportunity to demand that the Council be democratized. Habermas also expressed his preference for more balanced economic policies and investment programmes targeted more accurately at specific regions and countries. He rejected the power fantasies of a German Europe: 'As Germans, we should have learned from the catastrophes of the first half of the twentieth century that it is in our national interest permanently to avoid the dilemma of a semi-hegemonial status.'[47] The report on the lecture in *Süddeutsche Zeitung* (29 April 2013) ended with a reference to Habermas's warning against the danger

> that the 'technocratic dynamic of the crisis' might lead to dubious forms of democracy that are in conformity to the market. . . . In order to avoid this, all resolutions have to be legitimized by the European committees. After two hours, there was a *standing ovation*† for the 83-year-old philosopher – who, visibly moved, apologized for having spoken for so long.[48]

---

* The expression 'rettende Rekonstruktion' is an allusion to Benjamin, as well as to Adorno's reading of Kant's 'rescuing urge'. See Habermas (2012), 'Walter Benjamin: Consciousness-Raising or Rescuing Critique', in *Philosophical-Political Profiles*, pp. 129–63, and Theodor Adorno (2001), *Kant's Critique of Pure Reason* (Cambridge). In the latter, 'Rettung'/'retten'/'rettend' are translated as 'salvage', 'salvaging', 'urge to salvage', etc.

† 'Standing ovation' in English in the original.

'A master thinker despite himself'. In the summer of 2012, a special event took place at the Ludwig Maximilian University in Munich. On the suggestion of the academic assistant Jörg Noller, some advanced philosophy students invited Habermas to lead a 'master class' on his book *Between Facts and Norms*. The agreement was that Habermas would respond to introductory presentations on five themes, a format which must have been to his liking: contact with the next academic generation has always been of high importance to him, especially in recent years. The students prepared a report on their experiences of the course, which contains remarkable characterizations of Habermas and his style:

> And after only two days of argumentative discussions with Habermas, we certainly feel justified in saying the strangest opinion that has ever circulated about him is probably that the worldwide fame of his theoretical work is owing to his clever self-presentation. Rather, in parallel to his insistence on the primacy of the force of the better argument, the impression one gets of Habermas's personality is that he is not a charismatic figure. We never experienced any rhetorically incisive statements or any of the charming tolerance that bends over backwards to achieve compromise and accepts any statement, no matter how absurd, which is so common in the humanities today. However, nor did we experience any posturing in the style of a grand master. When Habermas thinks – and, at some point, he thought so intensely that he apologized for his "stuttering" – you always get the impression that he is, in fact, entering into an intellectual wrestling match with a problem.[49]

For Habermas, rescuing [*Rettung*] as the final horizon of critique is a political category, because behind the 'motive of a rescuing appropriation'[50] lies the intention to preserve and protect the levels of normativity that have been achieved as a consequence of learning processes, without which any orientation regarding questions of moral correctness, or of justice, would lack foundation. 'But in any case, philosophy today is less concerned with the idealistic transfiguration of a reality in need of salvation than with indifference towards a world flattened out by empiricism, and rendered normatively mute.'[51]

Belligerence, or: what makes Habermas such a provocative figure? For more than six decades, Habermas has been a constant presence as a political writer and critical intellectual. He has intervened and often made his mark on often heated public debates and controversies. If 'as an intellectual you take a public stance regarding polarizing questions', as Habermas said in conversation with the *Abendzeitung* (18 June 2004), then 'you pay a price. You have to learn to live with animosity. And sometimes you are exposed to malice for decades.'

Through his 'actively taking sides in public',[52] such controversies were condensed into communicative events which caused strong reactions. However, the public perception of Habermas as someone who rarely turns down an opportunity to put his point across in the opinion pages, and who courts controversy with the stances he takes, is not just down to the sheer number of eye-catching interventions he has made. It is also, and especially, because of his communicative strategy. That is, this public perception is owed to the manner in which he uses the art of polemic in his journalistic interventions in order to gain the public's attention and at the same time influence the public agenda. Jürgen Kaube (*Frankfurter Allgemeine Zeitung*, 24 June 2009) rightly states, under the heading 'Die Kräche, die ihr kanntet' [The quarrels you've known], that 'conflict' has a first-rate news value: 'In most cases, quarrels, morally tinged quarrels in particular, save you the trouble of further having to justify their reporting. In that sense, a symbiotic relationship between Habermas and the media has developed over many years, a relationship which, in contrast to symbiosis in the animal kingdom, has included, and made use of, strong aversions.'

Within the political arena, Habermas's behaviour is anything but restrained. When he says of Heinrich Heine that he polarized his readers 'because he wrote his works in the expectation of provoking dissonant reactions',[53] this can also be read as an indirect characterization of himself. In his political interventions, and when taking sides in specific disagreements, Habermas displays a tendency towards attack rather than defence. The reasons for this are specific political motivations and ambitions. These are the driving force behind his offensive stance within the political public sphere, where he uses the weapons of intellectual dispute and strategically deploys language in order to take up his political position.[54] In the battle of ideas between the left-liberal and the liberal-conservative camps in particular, Habermas uses any rhetorical means at his disposal in order to establish interpretive authority for his own perspective.[55] A format he likes to use in this context is the open letter. Despite the mutual expression of respect and acceptance as partners in discourse that goes along with the letter form, the exchanges previously mentioned (especially those with Ernst Topitsch, Robert Spaemann and Kurt Sontheimer) reveal each participant adopting a polarizing perspective on the other. In these cases, too, Habermas appears as a belligerent opponent who does not shy away from disagreement, who dismantles his opponents' concepts through exaggerated characterizations or negative evaluations, and thereby ends up provoking an intense backlash. As far as disputes with his political enemies are concerned, he does not hesitate to use crude evaluations and simplifications, or irony and sarcasm, which he deploys in a scathing tone and, at times, *ad hominem*. Strategically, it is one of his main objectives to establish his claim to interpretive authority. In most cases, developments in daily politics are the concrete trigger for his public remarks; in such cases the decision to make an intervention in the first place must be seen as motivated by the politics of ideas. In these contexts, the dissensus between intellectual positions exceeds that of the business of daily politics; it is rather the result of ideational battles that stretch over longer periods of time.

There are many examples of Habermas's urge to attack. We may think back to the article he published in *Der Spiegel* on 10 October 1977 under the title 'Probe für Volksjustiz' [Testing popular justice]. It was an immediate reaction to a programme broadcast by Bavarian television in which the CDU politician Alfred Dregger had claimed that Critical Theory had intellectually paved the way for terrorism. Habermas chose a dramatic opening for his piece:

So now it is the 'Frankfurt School's' turn. On the first Sunday of October, the Lord Mayor of Frankfurt, a member of the CDU, on the occasion of the Adorno Prize being awarded to Norbert Elias, wanted to see not only the laureate but Adorno himself being honoured. Then, on Wednesday evening, the ARD* broadcast a propaganda programme of the Bayerischer Rundfunk in which Mr Mühlfenzl [i.e., Heribert Mühlfenzl, from 1969 the editor-in-chief at the BR's television section; S. M.-D.] tested the popular justice recommended by Strauß. Mr Dregger also made an appearance in the programme and flatly declared that the 'Frankfurt School' was one of the causes of terrorism. . . . Both obscure the fact that, in the 1960s, left-wing professors were the ones who were particularly conscious of intellectual causalities. But Strauß and Dregger would rather construct objective lines of responsibility in a manner that is elsewhere popular only within the sphere of influence of Stalinist bureaucracies. . . . Do not worry; we shall not call Mr Strauß a fascist. We shall study his speeches, observe his behaviour, and pursue our suspicions, now that Spain has finally lost its Franco, that Strauß intends to 'Francoize' the Federal Republic.[56]

In this article, Habermas consciously opens up a front between the 'good' democratic left and the 'evil' authoritarian right (he even uses the word 'fascist'). At the same time, he uses a personalizing generalization, ascribing certain characteristics to a group ('left-wing professors') – i.e., being 'particularly conscious of intellectual

---

* Arbeitsgemeinschaft der öffentlich-rechtlichen Rundfunkanstalten der Bundesrepublik Deutschland: a consortium of regional public radio and television stations.

causalities'. Towards the end, when he comes to talk about Franz Josef Strauß, explicitly saying he is 'not a fascist', and thus precisely implying that he is, this almost sounds like a threat. In interventions of this sort, where the irreconcilability of the positions comes to the fore, it is almost unavoidable that standpoints take the place of arguments, because the opponents are trying to gain authority over certain concepts in order to launch a particular political use of language that expresses their own convictions.

A more recent example of this is the article in *Der Spiegel* of 5 August 2013, titled 'Ein Fall von Elitenversagen' [A case of failing elites], which injected some controversy into an otherwise lacklustre national election campaign in 2013. In this piece, Habermas launched an attack on the minister of finance, Wolfgang Schäuble, and in particular Chancellor Angela Merkel:

> Her public persona seems to lack any normative core. Ever since the beginning of the Greek crisis and the regional elections in North Rhine-Westphalia, which were ultimately lost, she subordinates each of her well-considered decisions to the opportunism of staying in power. Since then, the clever chancellor has navigated her way on the basis of clear thinking but without any recognizable principles, depriving a national election of any controversial topic for the second time – not to mention her policies on Europe, which she keeps far from public view.

The liberal-conservative coalition's policies, which follow the credo of a liberal market capitalism that 'ruthlessly' utilizes 'the economic and demographic supremacy' of Germany, he wrote, mean that 'the countries of Europe that are less competitive and heavily indebted are disciplined, and that Germany, at the same time, denies its responsibility towards all of Europe.'

Habermas pushed this overtly negative judgement on Merkel's policies even further in another statement, published in *Die Zeit* on 5 September 2013, just three weeks before election day. There, he called the chancellor 'pusillanimous and lacking any perspective', and claimed both that she had behaved 'opportunistically in the interest of keeping power' and that she was incapable of reacting adequately to the crisis in the eurozone. Prompted by the newspaper, he gave his recommendation as to whom people should vote for:

> In the present situation, Peer Steinbrück suggests himself as a politician of an entirely different stature – able to assert himself, with a clear orientation towards the future, and prepared to take responsibility, a character who has a sense of what is important. I trust Red–Green to have the courage to be open about the alternatives and to win over France for a genuine change in policy.

On 2 February 2014, Habermas gave a speech at a closed meeting of the Social Democratic Party in Potsdam. The background to this speech, apart from the forthcoming European election campaign, was the fact that, despite (or maybe because of?) the formation of a Grand Coalition in November 2013, there had still been no change in governmental policy. Habermas, who was introduced by the leader of the party, Sigmar Gabriel, as a 'critical companion', savaged the Grand Coalition's policies regarding the crisis. Under the heading 'Für ein starkes Europa – aber was heißt das?' [For a strong Europe – but what does that mean?], he criticized the government for being blind to the 'causes of the crisis'. He noted a 'change in mentality' in favour of a national attitude which was finding expression in misguided, egocentric policies aiming at the assertion of specifically German interests. The lack of legitimacy of a 'casually pushed through management of the crisis', and the striking absence of 'common economic policies', would fuel the 'mutual scapegoating . . . in national public spheres . . . caused by the division of Europe into donor and recipient countries'. It was high time, he said, that a 'common method' was finally adopted in earnest – a 'change in policies which includes transfer payments across national borders'. However, at the end of his speech, Habermas evinced some optimism: 'Luckily, in today's Europe we have intelligent populations, and not the kind of welded together grand national subjects which right-wing populism is trying to sell to us.'[57] Despite ending on this positive note, the speakers following Habermas, among them Martin Schulz and Sigmar Gabriel, disputed the negative aspects of Habermas's analysis.[58]

Resonances. Habermas's style of thinking and his conceptual tools are so idiosyncratic, so unmistakable, that strictly speaking we cannot talk about an unambiguously identifiable Habermas 'school' with a geographical centre. Nevertheless, his academic teaching and his writings have had a decisive and enduring influence on numerous academics. Philosophers and sociologists, as well as representatives from other disciplines, refer to his categories and models. His name is among those cited most often in the Social Sciences Citation Index, and the secondary literature on his oeuvre is enormous – a mountain that keeps growing.[59]

Habermas's theoretical conceptions, in particular his ideas of communicative freedom and communicative reason, have led to a broad and sustained academic discussion and, needless to say, have provoked objections. In certain areas of philosophy it is almost impossible to avoid engaging with his work. This is especially true of the theory of rationality, of political philosophy, and of legal theory and the theory of democracy. His analyses of the contemporary world still find a broad audience both within and outside academic circles, even if he himself might not see it this way. For Habermas, good academic practice means treating objections to one's reflections as opportunities to counteract the cognitive provinciality of a finite mind. He replied to many critical statements with extensive responses. Attempts by various groups of his opponents to distance themselves from him often had the unintentional effect of revealing them to be opposed, and in that sense independent, intellectual currents. For instance, one might go so far as to say that the formation of a liberal-conservative intellectual community [*Gesinnungsgemeinschaft*] within German philosophy was in part a consequence of tireless efforts at rejecting the claims of, say, discourse ethics.[60] With these criticisms of the paradigm of understanding, what are at stake are not the front lines drawn by those who oppose Habermas in principle and accuse him of, for instance, '*wishful thinking*', 'linguistic communism', 'linguistic idealism' and 'normative essentialism'. Rather, the objections from a number of philosophers, such as Dieter Henrich, Robert Spaemann and Hermann Lübbe, question the very core of his concept of reason.

Faced with this phalanx of critics, Habermas has repeatedly insisted that his method is that of a rational reconstruction. Such a method aims at disclosing the implicit knowledge that is embedded in the structure of intersubjectivity and the practices of everyday communication. Indeed, this methodological principle is diametrically opposed to the desire to present a generally binding and substantive conception of what is ethically good: 'Nothing makes me more nervous than the *imputation* – repeated in a number of different versions and in the most peculiar contexts – that ... the theory of communicative action ... proposes, or at least suggests, a rationalistic utopian society. I do not regard the fully transparent society as an ideal, nor do I wish to suggest *any* other ideal.'[61]

Robert Spaemann again expressed his scepticism regarding what he sees as the rationalism of discourse theory in a conversation in 2011 with Stephan Sattler, the former editor of the culture section of *Focus*:[62] 'Rational discourse always already presupposes reason, rather than the other way around ... In contrast to ideal discourses in a utopian world, real discourses, if they are meant to be relevant for action, are subject to limiting conditions. Their freedom must first be secured by a protective form of rule [*herrschaftliche Sicherung*].'[63]

Axel Honneth criticizes the concept of communicative reason from a different angle, pointing out that social inclusion, in the sense of belonging to society, does not result primarily from the experience of participation in processes of opinion- and will-formation. Rather, according to Honneth, the precondition of communicative action is the experience of social recognition. Honneth shifts the analytic focus from relations in which understanding is reached to relations of recognition or, rather, to the uncovering of the social causes of the systematic violation of recognition.[64] Habermas, by contrast, concentrates entirely on the rational potential of the practices through which understanding is reached, and as a consequence, Honneth says, the 'everyday experiences of actors within the context of social life' are ignored.[65]

Beyond the general question of how a critical theory of society might be developed further, the deliberative model of democracy also led to heated debates.[66] One of the objections raised against it by, for instance, Ronald Dworkin, is that the substantial implications of the socio-cultural conditions for political participation are not taken into detailed consideration beyond the assumption of a 'favourable political culture'. As mentioned before, Dworkin rejects the procedural and purely formal model of justification through norms and insists on substantial legal principles, such as, for example, the principle of autonomy as a universal value that must be assumed as a basis of democracy. According to Dworkin, law and morality cannot be separated out from each other; for him, the just life and the good life form a unity.

Richard Rorty also took up a position against Habermas. Rorty's 'radicalization of the pragmatic turn'[67] involves the idea of knowledge as social practice, and for him moral practices are historically limited and contingent. He defends a concept of truth in which truth remains tied to specific contexts: 'The world is out there, but descriptions of the world are not. Only descriptions of the world can be true or false. The world on its own – unaided by the describing activities of human beings – cannot. . . . The world does not speak. Only we do.'[68] Rorty's main point of contention is that understanding based on the search for good reasons is not a universally valid normative concept. Rather, he holds that truth and correctness must be defined in terms of what counts as a justifiable claim for the members of an epistemic community. At least to this extent, Habermas agrees with his friend; he admits that validity claims must be made in concrete situations and must be accepted by communities with particular standards for justification. But, for Habermas, the other side of this particular coin is that validity claims must be defendable 'in all possible contexts, that is, at any time and against anybody', because 'argumentation of its very nature points beyond all particular forms of life.'[69] And this very fact constitutes its moment of unconditionality, a moment which, however, 'is not an absolute, or it is at most an absolute that has become fluid as a critical procedure.' It consists, Habermas says, in the assumption of ideal conditions of justification.[70] 'For this reason, the process of justification can be guided by a notion of truth that *transcends justification*, although it is *always already operatively effective in the realm of action*.'[71] Habermas's objection to Rorty's anti-realism is that we must assume the existence of an objective world, a world about which true claims can be made, and which is the same for all – or, rather, which grounds the practical certainties of everyone, no matter how we conceive of access to this world.

Jean-François Lyotard was one of the first of the postmodern philosophers to oppose the theory of a domination-free discourse and the claim that the rules of discourse are universally valid. The philosopher Manfred Frank summarized Lyotard's critique in a 'Spectral conversation between Lyotard and Habermas' as follows:

> Even domination-free consensus, if it is not kept alive by the freedom of an endlessly controversial and continuing discussion, does not escape his [i.e., Lyotard's; S. M.-D.] suspicion that it is, in truth, a bureaucratic institution for the avoidance or arrest of discussion. More specifically, the suspicion is that the rules which are declared to be formal, in truth, imply substantial conditions which, because of their universalist ambitions, are not suited to keep totalitarian tendencies at bay.[72]

Lyotard points to the diversity of language-games and the possibility of one type of discourse suppressing another. The antagonism between types of discourse, he holds, is irreducible because there is no universally valid meta-rule.[73] While Habermas does not deny the irreconcilability of the opposed language-games of parties in conflict with each other, he nevertheless maintains that argumentative speech is the only way of avoiding violent confrontation. And the alleged ideal nature of discourse consists not

> in a harmony among all partners in conversation which would suffocate all contradiction but in a right that everyone has in principle to question the consensus at any given moment. . . . Thus, the consensus theory is actually no more averse to conflict than Lyotard's plea for an agonistic discourse. It only puts the emphasis on the fact that all speaking with one another . . . takes place with a counterfactual view towards reaching understanding.[74]

Habermas never tried to evade his main opponent in the area of social theory, despite the fact that in conversation this opponent sometimes chose to adopt the ironically distanced tone of a 'sober enlightener' talking to an 'old European thinker'. Niklas Luhmann recommended that the tradition of Enlightenment based on the idea of reason should 'be put away in the museum for sociological archaeology'.[75] In accordance with his fundamental assumption of an autopoiesis of communication,[76] Luhmann considers the concept of 'rational understanding' unfounded and rejects the claim that one can derive 'an ideal norm of the endeavour to reach agreement from language itself'.[77]

Habermas thought intensely about the paradigm of systems theory, according to which societies must be understood as operatively closed systems. His main objection to Luhmann can no longer be reduced to the terms of the controversy of the 1970s, that is, 'theory of society or social technology?' Against the systems theorist, Habermas insists that social theory, beyond pure observation and description, must take a position on whether or not the prevailing conditions in a society comply with the criteria for freedom, justice and solidarity. One of his main objections to Luhmann is that the functionalist reason of systems theory is limited to the reduction of complexity and is based on 'an objectivistic self-understanding of human beings and their world'.[78] The assumption that society as a whole is a system that describes itself, and that within functionally differentiated societies there can be no viewpoint that could lay claim to being a meta-position, would necessarily leave us, Habermas says, 'without any point of reference for a critique of modernity'.[79]

Epilogue: The Inner Compass

Who really knows the true motives of their speculations?[1]

Biographical experiences. Habermas himself says of his life that it has been one lived for science. And that what is left of the life of a philosopher 'is at best a new and often enigmatic thought, formulated in an idiosyncratic language, with which later generations continue to struggle.'[2] Of course, Habermas also stood on the shoulders of giants and developed his own thinking in imaginary conversations and in critical engagement with the great minds of the past, whose works are interpretations of their experiences of the world. Habermas understands the construction of theories as a learning process, as work on an open and fallible project, pursued in the spirit of a critique of the status quo, a project which needs to be continued in the light of new historical and scientific experiences.

The *Archimedean point* of his social theory lies in the idea of a critical standard that can be found in the rational potential of speech oriented towards reaching understanding. The fact 'that something is deeply amiss in the rational society'[3] marks the *sensitive spot* and the driving force for the critique of society. The goal of leading a self-determined life, which is grounded in mutual recognition, in the respect shown by every individual to every other, is the *normative vantage point* for Habermas's programme in social theory:

> The motivating thought concerns the reconciliation of a modernity that has fallen apart, the idea that without surrendering the differentiations which have made modernity possible . . . , one can find forms of living together in which autonomy and dependency can truly enter into a non-antagonistic relation, that one can walk tall in a collectivity that does not have the dubious quality of backward-looking substantial forms of commonality.[4]

In various passages of his writings and in numerous interviews Habermas addresses the question of how a philosopher and social theorist can be sure that the problems he subjectively registers are in fact the crucial ones, and that the traditional approaches he makes use of are indeed the ones that lead to progress. Clearly, historically and biographically determined intuitions play a large role in this. They are like the needle of an inner compass which 'of course . . . can only give the direction; it cannot ensure that the right path will be chosen or that it will be consistently pursued.'[5]

Habermas has provided some information on the biographical roots of his thinking. As mentioned previously, in his speech upon receiving the Kyoto Prize, he referred to the fact that *three* personal, biographical facts about his early life left impressions on him that influenced his intuitions and appear as leitmotifs in his theories of communication, discourse and morality. First, the operations during his early childhood, made necessary by his cleft palate, made him realize that human beings are mutually dependent on one another. This insight ultimately led him to 'those approaches that emphasize the intersubjective constitution of the human mind'.[6] Second, his speech defect and the discrimination he suffered as a consequence created certain sensitivities in him. Habermas cites his nasalization as the reason why, throughout this life, he valued the written word over the spoken. 'The written form disguises the taint of the spoken word.'[7] Habermas himself says this 'taint' and the experiences associated with it explain his strong interest in pursuing the conditions under which linguistic communication is successful or fails, and in investigating the genesis and effects of the moral principles and social norms governing communal life.

It is hardly surprising that Habermas, more than any other thinker, insists on the 'acid bath of relentless public discourse'[8] as the touchstone for the seriousness of claims and is sceptical towards the epistemic value of intuitions. And yet, he is aware of the importance of intuition as a spur to reflection, as a kind of hinge between biographical experience and the emergence of thoughts. Habermas says of his intuitions that they represent the 'dogmatic core', but that he would 'rather let go of science altogether than allow this core to melt'. These are intuitions, he says, which he did not 'acquire through science, that no person ever acquires that way',[9] but through the fact that a person 'grows up in an environment with people with whom one must come to terms, and in whom one recognizes oneself.'[10] It is not science which forms the inner voice and the thoughts it creates; rather, these are '[a]t times . . . no more than an expression of the biography from which they spring.'[11]

Thus, it is the lived life, both of the particular individual and of the collective, which forms the fertile ground for intuitions to grow and provide the stimulus for theoretically reflected convictions and for intellectual exertions. Habermas says that he always wanted 'to do something in life into which one can bring, and in which one can clarify, one's basic intuition'.[12] This clarification, in his case, takes place 'through the medium of scientific thinking, or through philosophy'. In other words, intuitions are not yet truths. One cannot 'produce truths outside of the sciences'.[13]

The fallibility of truth and morality. Science is essentially an error-prone, open-ended process of seeking the truth, and for Habermas this process plays itself out in the experimental laboratory of the argumentative testing of validity claims. Such claims thus have a hypothetical character. Compared to the rationality or irrationality [*Vernünftigkeit/Unvernünftigkeit*] of arguments, which is established through discursive procedures, intuitions appear vague. They need to be continuously translated into intersubjectively accessible reasons if they are to 'survive' in the long term. They acquire the status of a 'de-subjectivized' consensus only once they have passed the test of discursive universalizability.

This does not exclude the possibility that the participants in a discourse are being led by their intuitions. But the point of discourse, including ethical and existential discourses, consists precisely in the fact that, where necessary, one revises even those of one's views one thought unassailable due to subjective intuition and existential experience. In the course of argumentation and processes of gaining self-understanding, what stood at the beginning of the cognitive process may turn out to have been an error. We may even say that the whole discursive game begins with a doubt that sets in motion the search for what may count as true and correct. 'Which argument does convince is not decided by private insight but by the stances that, bundled together in a rationally motivated agreement, are adopted by everyone who participates in the public practice of exchanging reasons.'[14] Habermas believes that this criterion also applies to those specifically ethical and existential discourses in which one clarifies one's personal values.[15]

Thus, at the beginning of discourse, uncertainty reigns, and yet a 'moment of unconditionality ... is preserved in the discursive concepts of a fallibilistic truth and morality', a moment Habermas characterizes as 'an absolute that has become fluid as a critical procedure'.[16] Is this an expression of the solidarity of postmetaphysical thinking with 'metaphysics at the moment of its fall'?[17] Habermas's response is:

> Only with this residue of metaphysics can we do battle against the transfiguration of the world through metaphysical truths – the last trace of '*Nihil contra Deum nisi Deus ipse*'. Communicative reason is of course a rocking hull – but it does not go under in the sea of contingencies, even if shuddering in high seas is the only mode in which it 'copes' with these contingencies.[18]

Answers to seven questions. At the end of December 2006, a letter from a school class at the Liceo Scientifico Galileo Galilei in Lanciano, a remote Italian community in the region of Abruzzo, arrived at the Ringstraße in Starnberg. The pupils asked Habermas to answer seven questions, which they also wanted to put to the pope:

1   What can we know of the other?
2   When and how do we know that we have recognized the truth?
3   Is the only way to recognize the truth dialogue, or are there also other ways?
4   Why do we want to gain knowledge, and how do we tell that we are content with our knowledge?
5   Do we have a reason for claiming that life is meaningful?
6   How do we recognize the truth?
7   Is the meaning of a dialogue with another person or persons the claim: 'I am the you that you make of me'?

In a letter of 4 January 2007, Habermas sent his answers:

1   That which the other, consciously or unconsciously, makes us understand about him.
2   The human mind can always err.
3   If we want to reach understanding about the truth, or about what we take to be the truth, we should rely on the discursive way of gaining knowledge, that is, we should give good reasons.
4   We can never be satisfied with what we know or think we know.
5   Throughout the history of mankind, many reasons have been presented in order to show that our life, and the life of all human beings, is meaningful. What else is there to do but examine these reasons one by one?
6   The truth does not exist in the singular. If we are lucky, we find some knowledge about which we can be reasonably certain.
7   In dialogue between human beings, this statement makes sense only if the one can say it about the other just as much as the other can say it about the one.[19]

To conclude, a story told by the actor Josef Bierbichler:

Half a year ago, I was sitting in my local inn, in the corner where I always sit, when Habermas entered the room, accompanied by another person. His companion looked at me and then said to Habermas: 'Isn't that the famous actor?' Habermas replied: 'That's what an actor wants to hear', whereupon I replied: 'No, Mr Habermas, I really do not need that any longer. But you know that yourself. Or do you still need praise?' Habermas grinned and shook his head, and then murmured: 'No. I no longer need that.'[20]

Notes

Preface

1 The quotation is taken from the prose piece 'Das Kind (III)', in *Sämtliche Werke in zwanzig Bänden*, vol. 8 (1995), p. 74.
2 *Die Zeit*, 16 June 2004; *Süddeutsche Zeitung*, 18 September 1999; *Frankfurter Allgemeine Zeitung*, 23 January 2003, *Die Zeit*, 11 October 2001; *Frankfurter Allgemeine Zeitung*, 23 January 2003; *Frankfurter Allgemeine Zeitung*, 13 October 2001; *Frankfurter Allgemeine Zeitung*, 18 June 1999; *Die Welt*, 13 October 2001. In the *Frankfurter Allgemeine Zeitung* of 24 June 2009, Jürgen Kaube raises the question of the 'newsworthiness' that Habermas holds for the print media and claims that it consists in the fact that you can rely on him to start 'morally tinged controversies'.
3 Max Frisch, *Gantenbein*, San Diego (1998).
4 For a list of the various archives, including a comprehensive description of my own, see the appendix, p. 543.

Prologue

1 Habermas (1981), *Kleine Politische Schriften I–IV*, p. 517.
2 Adorno (1997), open letter to Max Horkheimer, *Gesammelte Schriften*, vol. 20.1, p. 163.
3 Here, and in other places, I refer to a number of conversations I had with Habermas.
4 Habermas (1986), 'The Dialectics of Rationalization', in P. Dews (ed.), *Autonomy and Solidarity*, p. 98.
5 Ibid., p. 97 (trans. modified).
6 Ibid.; Habermas (1980), 'Max Horkheimer', in *Philosophisch-politische Profile*, p. 415.
7 Habermas (2009), *Philosophische Texte*, vol. 4: *Politische Theorie*, p. 13.
8 Habermas (2009), *Philosophische Texte*, vol. 3: *Diskursethik*, p. 177.
9 Habermas (1998), *A Berlin Republic*, p. 70.
10 Habermas (1992), 'The Unity of Reason in the Diversity of its Voices', in *Postmetaphysical Thinking*, pp. 115–48; here: pp. 145f.
11 Habermas (1999), *The Inclusion of the Other: Studies in Political Theory*, p. xxxvi.
12 Habermas (1986), 'The Dialectics of Rationalization', p. 127.

Part I Catastrophe and Emancipation

1 Habermas ([1997] 2001), *The Liberating Power of Symbols*, p. 118.

Chapter 1 Disaster Years as Normality

1 Habermas (1987), *Eine Art Schadensabwicklung*, p. 140.
2 Wehler (2003), *Deutsche Gesellschaftsgeschichte 1914–1949*, pp. 481f.
3 See Nolzen (2010), 'Der Durchbruch der NSDAP zur Massenbewegung seit 1929', p. 48.
4 Habermas (1992), 'Bürgersinn und politische Kultur', pp. 22 and 26.
5 Notes from a personal conversation with Habermas.
6 For important information regarding family history, I rely on an extensive genealogy which Friedrich Wilhelm Fernau, the brother-in-law of Jürgen Habermas, compiled and kindly made available to me.
7 He was the first-born son of Ernst Friedrich Habermas (1833–1897), who was a teacher and cantor near Eisenach, and his wife, Auguste, *née* Struth (1841–1915).
8 The success of the NSDAP in the region was owed not least to intensive propaganda activities,

> which were pushed ahead decisively by the head of the NSDAP-Gau Rheinland-Süd, Robert Ley, with a high degree of personal commitment as a speaker, founder of a newspaper and organiser. After the doctor of chemistry, who came from the locality of Niederbreidenbach, Homburg, had lost his position at the Bayer works in Leverkusen for making radically anti-Semitic remarks, he moved to his in-laws' farm in Straße, a part of Marienberghausen. ... After two years, the party had acquired a well-established organizational structure in the area south of the Agger, and as early as 1929 the NSDAP had its own regional newspaper, the 'Oberbergische Bote'. (Pomykaj (2001), 'Von 1918 bis 1948', pp. 69f.)

9 Ibid., pp. 73 and 80.
10 Ibid., pp. 115–20.
11 Ibid., p. 114.
12 Ibid., pp. 98f.
13 I make use of information provided by the Deutsche Dienststelle für die Benachrichtigung der nächsten Angehörigen von Gefallenen der ehemaligen deutschen Wehrmacht in Berlin, on 12 July 2007, and by Hugues Courant, the Attaché de conservation at the Archives municipales et communautaires de Brest, on 30 May 2007.
14 At the time of the defence of Brest, Ernst Habermas was assigned to the military unit of the command at Brest Fortress [*Festungskommandantur*] for three months, as stated in a letter of the 'Deutsche Dienststelle' of 12 July 2007: 'according to report of 10 June 1944 and of 30 August 1944 Commander at Brest Fortress'. The journalist Erich Kuby wrote a report of his experiences during the months in which Brest was at first defended and then destroyed: Kuby (1959), *Nur noch rauchende Trümmer*.
15 See Young-Bruehl (1982), *Hannah Arendt. For Love of the World*, pp. 108f. [German edn: pp. 115ff. and pp. 167f.].
16 Wiese (1982), *Ich erzähle mein Leben*, p. 180.

17 Habermas ([2005] 2008), 'Public Space and Political Public Sphere – The Biographical Roots of Two Motifs in my Thought', in *Between Naturalism and Religion*, pp. 11–23; here: p. 15.

18 Ibid., p. 13.

19 Ibid., p. 15 (trans. modified).

20 See ibid., pp. 13–17.

21 Under the influence of National Socialist ideology, the medical profession considered a cleft palate, also called a harelip or 'Wolfsrachen' [wolf's jaw], to be a 'sign of degeneration'. Cf. Weygandt (1936), *Der jugendliche Schwachsinn*, pp. 31f. and 69. Everything indicating a weakness of the 'body of the German people' was meant to be 'eradicated'.

22 Letter from Josef Dörr to the author, dated 17 January 2012.

23 See Wehler (2003), *Deutsche Gesellschaftsgeschichte, 1914–1949*, p. 762.

24 See Reese (2010), 'Zum Stellenwert der Freiwilligkeit'.

25 *Berliner Zeitung*, 30 October 2006, and *Frankfurter Allgemeine Zeitung*, 1 November 2006.

26 See Habermas's comments in an open letter to *Cicero*, dated 1 December 2006, p. 12. In the aftermath of the historians' debate, Ernst Nolte, in an interview with the Italian journal *Panorama* (22 January 1989), expressed the opinion that Habermas had been an 'enthusiastic leader of the Hitler Youth'. In his own letter to the editor, Habermas pointed out: 'Even if I had wanted to become this, someone like me – a boy with a cleft palate, a "birth defect" was the term used at the time – would hardly have identified with the aims of a biological ideology and would also not have had the option of pursuing one of the usual H.-Y. careers.'

27 Wehler (2006), *Eine lebhafte Kampfsituation*, p. 26.

28 Pomykaj (2001), 'Von 1918 bis 1948', p. 145.

29 Wiggershaus (2004), *Jürgen Habermas*, p. 11. Habermas later corrected his statement: the Americans actually arrived on 11 April.

30 Kristian Buchna, in a study of the Free Democratic Party in North-Rhine-Westphalia between 1945 and 1953, has shown that this regional branch of the party campaigned vehemently for a general amnesty for NS perpetrators and was infiltrated by former National Socialists. The influence of Friedrich Middelhauve and of the jurist Ernst Achenbach was crucial in this regard. As the former head of the political section of the German embassy in Paris, Achenbach had been one of those responsible for the deportation of Jews from France, and he had acted as a defence lawyer at the Nuremberg trial. Buchna (2010), *Nationale Sammlung an Rhein und Ruhr*; Herbert (1996), *Best*, pp. 461ff.

31 Quoted after Hamburger Institut für Sozialforschung (1995), *200 Tage und 1 Jahrhundert*, p. 28.

32 Herbert (1996), *Best*, p. 434.

33 Peter Sloterdijk was feeding the rumour mill when, in an interview with the French magazine *L'Événement du jeudi* (no. 13/2000), he called Jürgen Habermas the 'son of a great Nazi'. In *Die Zeit* of 9 September 1999, Sloterdijk wrote with regard to Habermas as a representative of Critical Theory: 'The era of the hyper-moral sons of National Socialist fathers approaches its temporal end.' ['Greatest commander of all times' translates 'größter Feldherr aller Zeiten', a Nazi propaganda term of the early years of the war referring to Hitler, but also often quoted with ironic intention.]

34 Wild (2002), *Generation des Unbedingten*.

35 Habermas (1981), *Kleine Politische Schriften I–IV*, p. 511.
36 I draw on a remark made by Habermas in conversation with me.
37 See Broszat et al. (1983), *Deutschlands Weg in die Diktatur*, and in particular the contribution by Lübbe: 'Der Nationalsozialismus im politischen Bewusstsein der Gegenwart', pp. 329–49. See also Frei (1996), *Vergangenheitspolitik*.
38 Habermas ([2001] 2006), *Time of Transitions*, p. 41 (trans. modified).
39 Letter from Habermas to Paeschke, dated 15 March 1955 (Marbacher Literaturarchiv).
40 Habermas, '"Morgengrauen" – morgen das Grauen' [Dawn of the 'morrow' – and tomorrow dawns the horror], *Süddeutsche Zeitung*, 2–3 October 1954.
41 Habermas ([1990] 1994), *The Past as Future*, p. 64.
42 Mannheim ([1928] 1964), 'Das Problem der Generationen'. See also Mannheim ([1927] 1954), 'Das konservative Denken', pp. 409ff.
43 'The term "Flakhelfer-Generation" refers exclusively to the male part of the youth.' Some of the Flakhelfer-Generation were 'pupils of intermediate and secondary schools born between 1926 and 1929, those born during those years and already in work at the time, and those born in 1930, or even 1931 or 1932, who were deployed in units of the "Volkssturm"'. Bude (1987), *Deutsche Karrieren*, p. 39. According to the expert in the didactics of history Rolf Schörken, the expression '1945 generation' comprises all those 'who experienced the defeat and the occupation of Germany with all its consequences, and then the new beginning, during the most sensitive time of their youth'. Schörken (2004), *Die Niederlage als Generationserfahrung*, p. 19. See also Moses (2000), 'Eine Generation zwischen Faschismus und Demokratie'; Wehler (2008), *Deutsche Gesellschaftsgeschichte, 1949–1990*, pp. 185ff.; Wild (2002), *Generation des Unbedingten*, pp. 847ff.; Specter (2010), *Habermas*, pp. 34ff.
44 See Schörken (2000), 'Sozialisation inmitten des Zusammenbruchs', pp. 123ff.
45 Habermas, 'Jahrgang 1929', *Frankfurter Allgemeine Zeitung*, 2 May 2009.
46 Habermas (1969), *Protestbewegung und Hochschulreform*, p. 49.
47 Habermas (2002), 'Meine gymnasiale Schulzeit', p. 51. The Mont Pelerin Society, founded in Switzerland in 1947, is a network of liberal intellectuals dedicated to organizing discussions between liberals and socialists. Among its members were Raymond Aron, Bertrand de Jouvenel, Karl Popper, Ludwig von Mises, Milton Friedman and Michael Polanyi. See Fischer and Mandell (2009), 'Die verborgene Politik des impliziten Wissens', pp. 540ff.
48 Based on my own notes from conversations with Habermas.
49 Wehler (1992), 'Späte Liebeserklärung an meine Schule', p. 32.
50 Habermas in an open letter to *Cicero*, 1 December 2006, p. 12.
51 See Ueberschär and Müller (2005), *1945*, pp. 43ff.
52 Wehler (2008), *Deutsche Gesellschaftsgeschichte, 1949–1990*, p. 186.
53 Habermas (2001), *Zeit der Übergänge*, p. 22.
54 Habermas (1981), *Kleine Politische Schriften I–IV*, p. 512.
55 Ibid.
56 See Schörken (2004), *Die Niederlage als Generationserfahrung*.
57 Habermas (1990), *Die nachholende Revolution*, p. 32. On the wider context see Frei (1996), *Vergangenheitspolitik*.

58 I draw on my notes from a conversation with Habermas. See also Habermas (2009), *Philosophische Texte*, vol. 4: *Politische Theorie*, p. 9; Habermas ([2005] 2008), *Between Naturalism and Religion*, pp. 17–19.
59 Wehler (2008), *Deutsche Gesellschaftsgeschichte, 1949–1990*, pp. 188ff.
60 Wehler (2006), *Eine lebhafte Kampfsituation*, p. 188.
61 Habermas (2002), 'Meine gymnasiale Schulzeit', p. 52.
62 See Specter (2010), *Habermas*, pp. 77f. The historian Matthew Specter explains the orientation of Habermas's political theory with reference to the fact that he always wanted to defend the constitutional democratic Rechtsstaat, as the great achievement of 1949, against its detractors from both left and right.
63 Habermas ([2005] 2008), *Between Naturalism and Religion*, p. 17.
64 Habermas (1985), *The New Conservatism*, pp. 207ff.
65 Habermas (2002), 'Meine gymnasiale Schulzeit', p. 52.
66 Letter from August Dresbach to Ernst Habermas, 18 June 1948, Nachlass Dresbach, in Archiv des Oberbergischen Kreises.
67 According to the philosopher Dieter Henrich (born in 1927), philosophers, despite their similarities, may be characterized 'in equal measure' by 'the capacity for distanced reflection, a sense for matters of principle and a non-intuitive relationship with life as such'. Henrich (2006), *Die Philosophie im Prozeß der Kultur*, p. 58.
68 Habermas (2002), 'Meine gymnasiale Schulzeit', p. 52.
69 See ibid., pp. 51–3, and also Schörken (2004), *Die Niederlage als Generationserfahrung*, pp. 115ff.
70 Habermas (2002), 'Meine gymnasiale Schulzeit', p. 51. It is worth mentioning that the art teacher's daughter later became the wife of the philosopher Karl-Otto Apel. Habermas would later meet Apel in Bonn and be greatly influenced by him.
71 Ibid., p. 52.
72 Ibid.
73 Archive of the Städtische Gymnasium Moltkestraße in Gummersbach. The author would like to thank Jürgen Woelke for providing him with information and the documents. There are two more substantial essays by Habermas in the school's archive, both written as part of the Abitur [A-level] examination and marked 'good' to 'very good'.
74 See Alsberg (1985), *Der Ausbruch aus dem Gefängnis* – a re-edition of *Das Menschheitsrätsel* under a different title.
75 Habermas (2002), 'Meine gymnasiale Schulzeit', p. 52.
76 Berger and Müller (1983), *Lebenssituationen 1945–1948*.
77 Quoted after Wiggershaus (2004), *Jürgen Habermas*, p. 13.
78 Habermas ([1990] 1994), *The Past as Future*, p. 66. See Frei (1996), *Vergangenheitspolitik*.
79 From the 'Epilogue' in Bertolt Brecht (1981), *The Resistible Rise of Arturo Ui*, trans. Ralph Manheim, London, p. 99 [trans. D.S. The German original is 'Der Schoß ist fruchtbar noch, aus dem das kroch'; the excellent English translation deviates slightly, and the final line becomes 'The Womb he crawled from still is going strong.']
80 Habermas (2009), *Philosophische Texte*, vol. 4: *Politische Theorie*, pp. 9f.

Chapter 2 At University in Göttingen, Zurich and Bonn

1 Habermas ([2005] 2008), 'Public Space and Political Public Sphere – The Biographical Roots of Two Motifs in my Thought', in *Between Naturalism and Religion*, pp. 11–23; here: p. 18.
2 Ibid., p. 19. (trans. substantially modified).
3 Habermas (1981), *Kleine Politische Schriften I–IV*, p. 513 ['reeducation' in English in the original].
4 Habermas, 'Demokratie auf der Schlachtbank', in *Der Fortschritt: Parteifreie Wochenzeitung für neue Ordnung*, 13 August 1953. On the democratic discourse on participation during the post-war years, see the study by Forner (2007), 'Für eine demokratische Erneuerung Deutschlands', pp. 243ff. The author refers to Dolf Sternberger, Eugen Kogon, Walter Dirks and Alfred Weber.
5 Wiggershaus (2004), *Jürgen Habermas*, p. 18.
6 Wehler (2008), *Deutsche Gesellschaftsgeschichte, 1894–1990*, p. 269. See also Doering-Manteuffel (1988), *Die Bundesrepublik Deutschland in der Ära Adenauer*, pp. 7ff. and 206ff.; Dubiel (1999), *Niemand ist frei von Geschichte*, pp. 35ff.
7 Habermas (1981), *Kleine Politische Schriften I–IV*, pp. 512f.
8 Quoted from Claus Grossner, 'Der letzte Richter der Kritischen Theorie', *Die Zeit*, 13 March 1970, pp. 8–10.
9 Habermas (2002), 'Meine gymnasiale Schulzeit', p. 51.
10 Habermas, 'Traditionalist der Moderne: Glossen und Assoziationen zu Sean Scully' [Sean Scully, the traditionalist of modernity: glosses and associations], *Neue Züricher Zeitung*, 28 December 2002.
11 Habermas ([1990] 1994), *The Past as Future*, pp. 34f.
12 Habermas (1981), *Kleine Politische Schriften I–IV*, p. 467.
13 See ibid.
14 Habermas ([1990] 1994), *The Past as Future*, p. 48. In the *Neue Züricher Zeitung* of 22 May 1999, the historian Heinrich August Winkler wrote the following about the nationalistic tendencies within the major popular parties of the Federal Republic:

> After 1945, the moderate forces of the centre-right, represented by the bourgeois coalition led by Adenauer, pursued policies of supranational integration, while the moderate social democratic left under the leadership of Kurt Schumacher and Erich Ollenhauer focused on the nation and tried to present itself as the party that gave primacy to German unity. Thus, Adenauer faced not a 'national opposition', an anti-democratic opposition from the right, as in the times of Weimar, but an opposition that was simultaneously democratic, anti-communist and national. If things had been different, it would hardly have been possible to push through Germany's integration with the West. Seen in this light, the national role of the social democrats was almost a condition of the possibility of Adenauer's supranational politics – a dialectic of which those involved were most likely not fully aware.

15 See George (2010), *Studieren in Ruinen*.
16 Habermas ([1997] 2001), *The Liberating Power of Symbols*, p. 69.
17 Ibid., pp. 68f. (trans. modified).
18 Apel (1988), *Diskurs und Verantwortung*, p. 371.

19 Based on personal notes from a conversation with Karl-Otto Apel on 12 May 2011.

20 See Keulartz (1995), *Die verkehrte Welt des Jürgen Habermas*, pp. 83ff.

21 Wolters (1999), 'Der "Führer" und sein Denker', pp. 231ff. See also Wolters (2004), *Vertuschung, Anklage, Rechtfertigung*; and Laugstien (1998), *Philosophieverhältnisse im deutschen Faschismus*.

22 Becker (1963), *Dasein und Dawesen*. See also Hogrebe (2006), 'Von der Hinfälligkeit des Wahren und der Abenteuerlichkeit des Denkens', pp. 234ff.

23 Ibid., p. 221.

24 Wolters (2004), *Vertuschung, Anklage, Rechtfertigung*, p. 14. See also Keulartz (1995), *Die verkehrte Welt des Jürgen Habermas*, p. 121.

25 Quoted from Wolters (2004), *Vertuschung, Anklage, Rechtfertigung*, pp. 23ff.

26 Ibid., p. 18. See Stöwer (2011), *Erich Rothacker*.

27 See Habermas ([1997] 2001), *The Liberating Power of Symbols*, pp. 66–78.

28 See Keulartz (1995), *Die verkehrte Welt des Jürgen Habermas*, pp. 106ff.

29 See ibid., pp. 106–34: 'The core concept of cultural anthropology is "style of life", and the guiding thought is that a historically acquired way of living forms the prism, so to speak, through which the members of a culture perceive and judge reality' (p. 108). Habermas would later develop a theory of epistemological interests on this basis, interests which are invariant and 'anchored in the "natural history of the human species"' (p. 131).

30 This seminar paper, which Habermas today considers one of the 'sins of [his] youth' (note from personal conversation), is preserved in Erich Rothacker's posthumous papers at the Universitäts- und Landesbibliothek der Rheinischen Friedrich-Wilhelms-Universität Bonn, Abteilung Handschriften und Rara. NL Rothacker XIV, Mappe 23. Roman Yos brought the existence of this seminar paper to my attention.

31 The quotation is from p. 24 of the seminar paper.

32 Ibid., p. 28.

33 Ibid., p. 39. Around the same time, Habermas wrote another paper, a text that he apparently corrected again and again. Its title is: 'Von der doppelten Wurzel der Moral: Schelers Ethik heute' [On the twofold root of morality: Scheler's ethics today] (Bestand Na 60, Vorlass Jürgen Habermas, Archivzentrum der Universitätsbibliothek J. C. Senckenberg Frankfurt am Main). Habermas considers this text another of his 'youthful sins'.

34 Habermas (1973), *Kultur und Kritik*, pp. 107ff.

35 Habermas (1970), *Arbeit, Erkenntnis, Fortschritt*, pp. 70ff.

36 Habermas (1985), 'A Philosophico-Political Profile', p. 76.

37 Habermas (1954), 'Das Absolute und die Geschichte: Von der Zwiespältigkeit in Schellings Denken' (dissertation, Bonn).

38 Ibid..

39 See ibid., p. 346. See also the synopsis in Frank (2009), 'Schelling, Marx und Geschichtsphilosophie'; and Keulartz (1995), *Die verkehrte Welt des Jürgen Habermas*, pp. 36ff.

40 Habermas (1954), 'Das Absolute und die Geschichte', p. 9.

41 Ibid., pp. 368f.

42 Habermas (2015), 'Jewish Philosophers and Sociologists as Returnees in the Early Federal Republic', p. 107. Löwith's *Von Hegel zu Nietzsche: Der revolutionäre Bruch im Denken des neunzehnten Jahrhunderts* was first published in 1941, with a second edition following in 1950. [The first English edition was published in 1964.]

43 Habermas (1963), *Theorie und Praxis*, p. 215.
44 In an interview in November 2000, Habermas commented on Schelling again:

> By the way, I think that Schelling is closest to the revolutionary potential of romanticism neither in his early philosophy of nature, nor in his later philosophy of mythology, but during the intermediary phase – at two points in particular. In his 'System des transzendentalen Idealismus' of 1800, Schelling explains the cognitive role of the work of art, as the *organon* of an intuitive grasp of the absolute, with the help of the conception of the 'unconscious' – long before Freud. While our dreams express unconscious contents of the human soul, works of art articulate a kind of 'higher' unconscious to which we submit in contemplation. And 10 years later, 1810, is the only time that Schelling develops, in his 'Stuttgarter Privatvorlesungen', a radical, almost anarchistic view of the state as a repressive agency that is to be overcome. (Interview with Habermas (2000), 'Globalism, Ideology and Traditions', p. 9)

45 Quoted after Dahms (1994), *Positivismusstreit*, p. 372. The grade *egregia* used to be awarded to doctoral theses of exceptional quality and corresponds to *summa cum laude* [the highest of three possible grades].
46 Letter from Habermas to Rohacker, 11 March 1958, Universitäts- und Landesbibliothek Bonn, Abt. Handschriften und Rara. The correspondence between Rothacker and Habermas consists of ten letters, six of which are by Habermas.
47 I refer to a written report by Rohrbach of 24 June 2013. Rohrbach got to know Habermas in the summer term of 1951 in Bonn and a friendship quickly developed. Habermas, Rohrbach recalls, was a social and life-loving character at the time and remains so up to the present day.
48 See Tietgens (1982), 'Studieren in Bonn nach 1945', pp. 720–44.
49 Personal notes from a conversation with Sabine Berghahn.
50 Habermas, 'Wie ist nach dem Historismus noch Metaphysik möglich? Zum 100. Geburtstag Hans-Georg Gadamers', *Neue Züricher Zeitung*, 12–13 February 2000.
51 Dews (1986), *Autonomy and Solidarity*, p. 191.
52 Letter from Habermas to Paeschke, 12 January 1955, Marbacher Literaturarchiv.
53 Karl Korn, born on 20 May 1908 in Wiesbaden, 'discovered artists, authors, critics, and a whole generation of journalists from Karl Heinz Bohrer and Maria Frisé to Eduard Beaucamp.' Frank Schirrmacher recalls that Korn wanted 'to bring a whole new choir of inner voices to speak out: from Habermas to Alfred Andersch, from Heinrich Böll and Claude Chabrol to Ingmar Bergman.' Schirrmacher, 'Der Zivilisationsredakteur', *Frankfurter Allgemeine Zeitung*, 17 May 2008.
54 Bohrer and Scheel (1996), 'Zum fünfzigsten Jahrgang', p. 1.
55 In the obituary he wrote for Hans Paeschke in the *Frankfurter Rundschau* of 8 October 1991, titled 'Das Genie eines selbstlosen Regisseurs', Habermas emphasizes the *Merkur* editor's talent for making his journal a forum for politically opposed voices: 'Paeschke's temperament was characterized by a young conservatism. He never was just liberal; his tolerance was mixed up with a headstrong will.'

56 Habermas, 'Im Lichte Heideggers' [In the light of Heidegger], *Frankfurter Allgemeine Zeitung*, 12 July 1952.
57 Habermas ([1954] 1970), 'Die Dialektik der Rationalisierung', in *Arbeit, Erkenntnis, Fortschritt*, p. 15.
58 Habermas's report on the meeting appeared in the *Handelsblatt* of 28 October 1955 under the title 'Der Geist geht zu Fuß' [The spirit walks]. See Laak (1993), *Gespräche in der Sicherheit des Schweigens*, p. 44.
59 Habermas (1970), *Arbeit, Erkenntnis, Fortschritt*, p. 53.
60 See Keulartz (1995), *Die verkehrte Welt des Jürgen Habermas*, pp. 58ff. Keulartz demonstrates that Habermas adopts Heidegger's critique of technology during this period and develops his critique of Marx from that perspective.
61 Personal notes from conversations with Habermas.
62 Wehler (2008), *Deutsche Gesellschaftsgeschichte, 1949–1990*, pp. 270ff.
63 Kraushaar (1998), *Frankfurter Schule und Studentenbewegung*, vol. 2, p. 106.
64 Habermas ([1981] 2012), *Philosophical-Political Profiles*, p. 42. See also Habermas, 'Die (re)migrierten Philosophen und das Geistesleben der Bundesrepublik' [The (re)migrated philosophers and the intellectual life of the Federal Republic], unpublished manuscript (Elmau conference, 26 to 29 June 2011). In this paper, Habermas criticizes the 'passive-pandering tone' when talking about the commonalities between Jewish and German traditions:

> The melancholy recognition that there remains after all an *unbridgeable* gap nowhere became clearer to me than in the friendly relations with someone like Saul Friedländer, with whose views one wholly agrees: precisely in his conciliatory politeness a moment of inexorable distance can still be felt. … Scholem's painful recognition that the so-called German-Jewish symbioses were, from the very beginning, a misalliance is sociologically and politically correct; it illuminates an asymmetry in the giving and taking of the two sides the existence of which is denied again and again.

65 Ebbinghaus (1947) *Die große Not*, pp. 30–5.
66 Habermas (2008), 'Ich bin alt, aber nicht fromm geworden' [I have become old, but not devout], in Funken, *Über Habermas*, p. 190.
67 Habermas (1978), *Politik, Kunst, Religion*, p. 7.
68 Habermas (1981), *Kleine Politische Schriften I–IV*, p. 515.
69 Habermas (1991), *Texte und Kontexte*, p. 74.
70 Habermas (1993), 'Martin Heidegger: On the Publication of the Lectures of 1935', p. 195 (trans. modified) [German edn: 'Martin Heidegger: a) Zur Veröffentlichung von Vorlesungen aus dem Jahre 1935 (1953)', in *Philosophisch-politische Profile* (1981), pp. 65–72, here: p. 70. This text is not included in the English translation of that book, *Philosophical-Political Profiles*.]. In the chapter on 'The Undermining of Western Rationalism through the Critique of Metaphysics: Martin Heidegger', in his lectures on *The Philosophical Discourse of Modernity* ([1985] 1987), p. 157, Habermas writes:

> The basic concepts (left unchanged) of fundamental ontology were given a new content by Heidegger in 1933. If he had hitherto used 'Dasein' in

an unmistakable way for the existentially isolated individual on his course toward death, now he substitutes for this 'in-each-case-mine' Dasein the collective Dasein of a fatefully existing and 'in-each-case-our' people [*Volk*]. All the existential categories stay the same and yet with one stroke they change their very meaning – and not just the horizon of their expressive significance.

In a footnote, Habermas adds that Oskar Becker had already drawn his attention to this shift in meaning during his student days (see ibid., p. 403).
71 The political dimension of the intellectual constellations during the postwar era, for instance the significance of existentialism, is described by Müller (2013), *Das demokratische Zeitalter*, pp. 211–88 ['mainstream' in English in the original].
72 Habermas ([2005] 2008), 'Public Space and Political Public Sphere', p. 20.
73 See Payk (2008), *Der Geist der Demokratie*, pp. 25ff. and 208ff.; and Schild (1999), *Zwischen Abendland und Amerika*.
74 Habermas (1991), *Texte und Kontexte*.
75 Heidegger was born in 1889 and taught at Freiburg from 1928. After 1945, he was banned from teaching until his retirement.
76 Habermas (1993), 'Martin Heidegger: On the Publication of the Lectures of 1935', p. 197 (trans. modified) [see note 70 above] [German edn, p. 72].
77 I agree with the thesis put forward by Roman Yos in an outline for his doctoral dissertation according to which Habermas was, indeed, shocked by the fact that Heidegger republished his lectures of 1935 without any further commentary, but that this shock did not immediately bring about a complete distancing from Heidegger's thinking of Being [*Seinsdenken*]. As evidence for this thesis, Yos points to Habermas's dissertation on Schelling, which, he says, shows that Habermas was deeply attached to Heidegger's philosophy but at the same time was in the process of breaking away from it.
78 Habermas ([1981] 2012), 'Martin Heidegger: The Great Influence', in *Philosophical-Political Profiles*, pp. 53–60; here: pp. 53 and 56.
79 Habermas (1993), 'Martin Heidegger: On the Publication of the Lectures of 1935', p. 196 [German edn, p. 71.]
80 *Frankfurter Allgemeine Zeitung*, 12 July 1952, p. 23.
81 *Frankfurter Allgemeine Zeitung*, 14 August 1953.
82 Heidegger (1977), 'The Question Concerning Technology', p. 35.
83 Ott (1988), *Martin Heidegger*; Víctor Farías (1989), *Heidegger and Nazism*. See also Bourdieu (1991), *The Political Ontology of Martin Heidegger*. Bourdieu analyses the linguistic form of Heidegger's philosophy and, together with his habitus and discursive field, lays open his intellectual style, which corresponds to a *völkisch* mood. See also Adorno (2003), *The Jargon of Authenticity*; Löwith (1986), *Heidegger – Denker in dürftiger Zeit* Around the beginning of 2014, it emerged that Peter Trawny would edit Heidegger's so-called Schwarze Hefte [Black notebooks] for Vittorio Klostermann, to be published in spring 2014. These notebooks contain Heidegger's thoughts from the 1930s and 1940s. One of the volumes contains notes that illuminate his attitude towards National Socialism, towards Hitler, and towards the Jews. The announcement of this publication rekindled the debate over the question Habermas had already asked in 1953, namely whether there is an 'intimate connection between Heidegger's NS commitment and his thought'. See Thomas Assheuer,

"'Er spricht vom Rasseprinzip": Nach seinen jetzt bekannt gewordenen Ausfällen gegen die Juden lässt sich Heidegger nur noch schlecht verteidigen' ['"He speaks of the principle of race": After the abusive comments about the Jews we now know Heidegger can hardly be defended'], *Die Zeit*, 27 December 2013. This edition of *Die Zeit* also contains comments by Peter Trawny and an interview with the French philosopher Emmanuel Faye, both of whom confirm that an anti-Semitic resentment can be found in Heidegger. While Trawny speaks of an 'anti-Semitism that was kept secret', Faye claims that Heidegger tries to 'elevate anti-Semitism into something metaphysical'. Faye concludes: 'In the *Schwarze Hefte*, Heidegger elevates the "uprootedness" he deliberately ascribes to the "World Jewry" to a matter of metaphysics.' Two weeks later, in an interview printed in the same paper, François Fédier fundamentally contradicts this claim: 'Neither anti-Semitism nor any other anti-stance can be integrated into Heidegger's thought.'

84 Habermas (1991), *Texte und Kontexte*, p. 76.
85 Ibid., p. 58; emphasis in the original.
86 Ibid., p. 50; emphasis in the original.
87 [Translation by D.S.]; emphasis in the original. Cf. Habermas ([1985] 1987), *The Philosophical Discourse of Modernity*, p. 156.
88 See Görtemaker (2005), 'Thomas Mann und die Politik', in Stachorski, *Fragile Republik*.
89 See Weidmann (2008), 'Karl Jaspers'. See also Payk (2008), *Der Geist der Demokratie*, pp. 25ff and 208ff; Schild (1999), *Zwischen Abendland und Amerika*.
90 [My translation; this text is not part of the English edition.] German edn: Habermas ([1966] 1981), 'Karl Jaspers: Über den moralischen Notstand in der Bundesrepublik', in *Philosophisch-politische Profile*, pp. 96f.
91 See Forner (2007), 'Für eine demokratische Erneuerung Deutschlands'. See also Kießling (2012), *Die undeutschen Deutschen*, pp. 48f.
92 Adorno (1981), 'Cultural Criticism and Society', p. 34.
93 Adorno (1986), 'Die auferstandene Kultur', p. 460. See also Müller-Doohm and Ziegler (2008), 'Professionell Heimatloser', pp. 63–84.
94 Arendt (1993), *Besuch in Deutschland*.

Part II Politics and Critique

1 Habermas (2006), 'February 15, or: What Binds Europeans', p. 46.

Chapter 3 *Education intellectuelle* in Café Marx

1 See Reijen and Schmid Noerr (1988), *Grand Hotel Abgrund*.
2 See Tiedemann (1993) *Frankfurter Adorno Blätter II*, pp. 28ff.
3 Habermas (1986), 'Life-Forms, Morality and the Task of the Philosopher'. The *Merkur* article prompted the sociologist Helmut Schelsky to write a 'response to Jürgen Habermas' of more than 160 pages, which, however, remained unfinished and was never published. On 14 March 1973, Schelsky sent the manuscript to Habermas along with a two-page letter, in which he wrote that the response was also intended to gain clarity about his own past role in social philosophy. He returns to this early publication by Habermas,

he says, because he is convinced that it touches on recurring motifs which also form the basis of his later work. At the beginning, Schelsky speaks of an excessive level of reflection on Habermas's part, which finds an expression in his repetition of obsolete criticisms, for instance of technology as overpowering, with new terminological tools and on a high level of abstraction, while at the same time using this repetition as an opportunity to introduce objections which could then be elegantly invalidated. Apart from this 'intellectual trick', as Schelsky called it, he first criticizes Habermas for deriving the diagnosed pauperism in the spheres of work and consumption from technology and industry in general and trying to explain this causality with reference to historical periods of time which lie in the distant past and have been overcome. Second, he charges Habermas with equating the contemporary human being with the proletarian as described by Marx and, third, he accuses him of employing a dichotomy between human being and system, which belongs to a problematic tradition in which a positively characterized community is played off against a society characterized as abstract. As a consequence, Schelsky concludes, Habermas unites the Marxist critique of alienation with the critique of civilization in bourgeois idealism. In a central passage of the manuscript, he says:

> If there is something like a 'Frankfurt School' of 'critical theory' at all, then this identification of a bourgeois-romantic with a Marxist-humanist critique of contemporary time would have to be considered one of its characteristics; we would need to emphasize, though, that Habermas formulated this position very early on and before he had any contact with 'Frankfurt', although it allowed him to make 'Frankfurt' his home later.

The manuscript is kept at the Universitäts- und Landesbibliothek Münster, Nachlass Schelsky, 16,012 and 16,015. I owe the reference to this manuscript to Roman Yos. See also Kießling (2012), *Die undeutschen Deutschen*, pp. 334–9.

4 Bestand Na 60, Vorlass Jürgen Habermas, Archivzentrum der Universitätsbibliothek J. C. Senckenberg, Frankfurt am Main.
5 Ibid.
6 Ibid.
7 Habermas (1970), *Arbeit, Erkenntnis, Fortschritt*, p. 29.
8 *Merkur*, 8(8), pp. 701–24. Habermas (1970), *Arbeit, Erkenntnis, Fortschritt*, pp. 7–30.
9 Ibid., p. 9.
10 Habermas, 'Autofahren: Der Mensch am Lenkrad', *Frankfurter Allgemeine Zeitung*, 27 November 1954.
11 Letter from Habermas to Adorno, 13 December 1955, Bestand Na 60, Vorlass Jürgen Habermas, Archivzentrum der Universitätsbibliothek J. C. Senckenberg, Frankfurt am Main.
12 See Rammstedt (1986), *Deutsche Soziologie 1933–1945*.
13 Habermas, 'Jahrgang 1929', *Frankfurter Allgemeine Zeitung*, 2 May 2009.
14 Habermas, 'Der Soziologen-Nachuchs stellt sich vor: Zu einem Treffen in Hamburg unter Leitung von Professor Schelsky', *Frankfurter Allgemeine Zeitung*, 13 June 1955.
15 See Sonnenfeld (2010), 'Ein Fundstück aus dem IfS-Archiv'. Habermas later expanded and summarized his theoretical ideas regarding leisure activities in his essay 'Soziologische Notizen zum Verhältnis von Arbeit

und Freizeit' [Sociological notes on the relationship between work and leisure], which he wrote for Erich Rothacker's Festschrift *Konkrete Vernunft*, published in 1958. The essay can also be found in Habermas (1970), *Arbeit, Erkenntnis, Fortschritt*, pp. 56–74.

16 Habermas (1981), *Kleine Politische Schriften I–IV*, p. 516.
17 Habermas ([1981] 2012), 'Theodor Adorno: The Primal History of Subjectivity – Self-Affirmation Gone Wild', in *Philosophical-Political Profiles*, pp. 99–109; here: pp. 102f. (trans. modified).
18 See Demirović (1999), *Der nonkonformistische Intellektuelle*, pp. 339ff.
19 Habermas (2007), 'Die Zeit hatte einen doppelten Boden', pp. 19f.
20 Ibid., p. 18.
21 Ibid.
22 'Vier Jungkonservative beim Projektleiter der Moderne', *Die Tageszeitung*, 21 October 1980.
23 Based on my own notes from conversations.
24 See Müller-Doohm (2005), *Adorno: A Biography*, pp. 325–87.
25 Adorno, 'The Meaning of Working through the Past', p. 93.
26 I draw on remarks by Spiros Simitis in an interview conducted on 11 May 2011.
27 Habermas (1986), 'The Dialectics of Rationalization', p. 97 (trans. modified).
28 Letter from Habermas to Paeschke, 5 April 1956, Deutsches Literaturarchiv Marbach.
29 Habermas (1991), 'Eine Generation von Adorno getrennt', p. 50.
30 Ibid.
31 See Gretel Adorno and Walter Benjamin (2007), *Correspondence 1930–1940*.
32 Habermas (2000), '50 Jahre Suhrkamp', p. 22.
33 Habermas ([1981] 2012), 'Consciousness-Raising or Rescuing Critique', in: *Philosophical-Political Profiles*, pp. 129–163. ['Bewußtmachende oder rettende Kritik', in Unseld (1972), *Zur Aktualität Walter Benjamins*, pp. 173–223].
34 The French philosopher Georges Bataille hid the painting, which Benjamin had bought in 1921, among the latter's posthumous papers at the Bibliothèque nationale in Paris. From there it came to Adorno, who passed it on to Gershom Sholem, as requested in Benjamin's last will. Until Scholem's death, it hung in his apartment. Today it is kept at the Israel Museum in Jerusalem. See Palmier (2009), *Walter Benjamin*, pp. 323f.
35 Habermas (1991), *Texte und Kontexte*, p. 101.
36 See Müller-Doohm (2005), *Adorno: A Biography*, pp. 366f., and Müller-Doohm (2003), *Adorno: Eine Biographie*, Frankfurt am Main, p. 947 [a table of Adorno's teaching is omitted from the English edition].
37 Habermas, 'Die Zeit hatte einen doppelten Boden', p. 18.
38 Habermas (1986), 'Life-Forms, Morality and the Task of the Philosopher', p. 192.
39 Habermas, 'Die Zeit hatte einen doppelten Boden', p. 21.
40 Habermas (2011), 'Die (re)migrierten Philosophen und das Geistesleben der Bundesrepublik' [The (re)migrated philosophers and the intellectual life of the Federal Republic], unpublished MS, Elmau conference 'Jewish Voices in the German Sixties', 26–9 June 2011. See also Habermas (2015), 'Jewish Philosophers and Sociologists as Returnees in the Early Federal Republic', p. 116.

41 Kleinspehn (1999), 'Ein öffentlicher Intellektueller: Der Philosoph und streitbare Demokrat', Radio Bremen, unpublished MS, p. 8. Apart from *Hegel's Ontology and the Theory of Historicity* [original German title: *Hegels Ontologie und die Grundlegung einer Theorie der Geschichtlichkeit*] of 1932, Habermas is thinking in particular of Marcuse's articles in the *Zeitschrift für Sozialforschung*. See Marcuse (1965), *Kultur und Gesellschaft*, vol. 1 (this volume contains four essays from the years 1934 to 1938: 'Der Kampf gegen den Liberalismus in der totalitären Staatsauffassung' [The battle against liberalism in totalitarian notions of the state]; 'Über den affirmativen Charakter der Kultur' [On the affirmative character of culture]; 'Philosophie und Kritische Theorie' [Philosophy and critical theory]; and 'Zur Kritik des Hedonism' [Towards a critique of hedonism]).

42 Habermas, 'Triebschicksal als politisches Schicksal: Zum Abschluß der Vorlesungen über Sigmund Freud an den Universitäten Frankfurt und Heidelberg' [The fate of drives as political fate: on the completion of the Sigmund Freud lecture series at the universities of Frankfurt and Heidelberg], *Frankfurter Allgemeine Zeitung*, 14 July 1956.

43 Habermas (1980), 'Psychic Thermidor and the Rebirth of Rebellious Subjectivity', p. 80. [This text is not part of the English edition of *Philosophical-Political Profiles*.] A handwritten letter dated 10 July 1978, wishing Marcuse a happy birthday, demonstrates Habermas's high esteem. Not only, he writes, was Marcuse one of the reasons why he had discovered the theory of psychoanalysis and learned to read 'Freud systematically', but it was Marcuse's philosophical thought which helped him build the bridge between social theory and political practice. 'Back then I invented the term "Heideggermarxism" for you. Of course, this term also contains a distancing from my own philosophical past.' Bestand Na 60, Vorlass Jürgen Habermas, Archivzentrum der Universitätsbibliothek J. C. Senckenberg, Frankfurt am Main.

44 Habermas (1981), *Kleine Politische Schriften I–IV*, p. 469. The lecture series was published in 1957, under the title *Freud in der Gegenwart* [Freud in the contemporary world], as vol. 6 of the *Frankfurter Beiträge zur Soziologie*.

45 Personal notes from a conversation with Habermas.

46 Habermas (1991),*Texte und Kontexte*, p. 104.

47 Habermas (1989), 'Ein Brief', p. 393.

48 Dahrendorf recalls having made a 'fleeting acquaintance' with Habermas at the institute, which had 'resulted in mutual sympathies without any consequences'. In the 1950s, Habermas had begun 'a spectacular as well as a long-lasting career', he says. Dahrendorf (2002), *Über Grenzen*, pp. 182f. In conversation, Habermas corrected this as a lapse of memory on Dahrendorf's part, saying he actually never met him at the Institute for Social Research. In an article which he published in 1989 in *Merkur* on the occasion of Habermas's sixtieth birthday, Dahrendorf reports on his brief acquaintance with Horkheimer, who, he writes, made use of individuals 'with the mentality of a Swabian entrepreneur of the early capitalist period'. Of Habermas, Horkheimer is meant to have said: 'He's got a cleft palate and thus he can't teach, so is only any good for research.' Dahrendorf concludes: 'It did not do Jürgen Habermas any harm that he was being associated with this world [of the Institute for Social Research], but he did not belong to it. For that he was, and is, too honest, too critical and too practical. In his academic wanderings he circled Frankfurt but

never became fully one with the epicentre either.' Dahrendorf (1989), 'Zeitgenosse Habermas', pp. 478f.

49 See Rammstedt (1986), *Deutsche Soziologie 1933–1945*, p. 25.
50 Habermas (1970), *Arbeit, Erkenntnis, Fortschritt*, p. 80.
51 Hans-Georg Gadamer, 'Der Meister der Kommunikation', *Südeutsche Zeitung*, 18 June 1999.
52 See Marcuse (1957), *Soviet Marxism: A Critical Analysis*.
53 Habermas (1963), *Theorie und Praxis*, p. 276 [trans. D.S. The existing English translation is based on the 1971 re-edition of *Theorie und Praxis*, which differs substantially from the original edition of 1963. But see Habermas (1974), 'Between Philosophy and Science: Marxism as Critique'].
54 Habermas (1963), *Theorie und Praxis*, pp. 306 and 311. [Habermas's formulation 'empirisch überprüfbare Geschichtsphilosophie in praktischer Absicht' is an allusion to Kant's text of 1784 'Idee zu einer allgemeinen Geschichte in weltbürgerlicher Absicht' – 'Idea for a Universal History with a Cosmopolitan Purpose'].
55 Ibid., p. 289.
56 Ibid., p. 277.
57 Ibid., p. 269.
58 Horkheimer (1988), *Gesammelte Schriften*, vol. 14: *Nachgelassene Schriften 1949–1972*, pp. 82ff.
59 Horkheimer (1996), *Gesammelte Schriften*, vol. 18: *Briefwechsel 1949–1973*, p. 443.
60 Ibid., pp. 440, 443, 445f., and 448.
61 Ibid., pp. 445ff.
62 Ibid., p. 443.
63 Ibid., p. 446.
64 See the editorial comments on this letter by Gunzelin Schmid Noerr, ibid., pp. 449ff. Cf. also Adorno and Horkheimer (2006), *Briefwechsel*, vol. 4, pp. 508-524.
65 See Adorno's letter to Horkheimer, dated 15 March 1960, ibid., pp. 616–22.
66 Ibid., p. 620.
67 Horkheimer (1996), *Gesammelte Schriften*, vol. 18: *Briefwechsel 1949–1973*, p. 438.
68 Habermas (2009), *Philosophische Texte*, vol. 4: *Politische Theorie*, p. 10.
69 See Gunzelin Schmid Noerr, 'Aus der Vorgeschichte eines gesellschafts-theoretischen Paradigmawechsels – Horkheimers Kritik an Habermas', *Konkret* 9 (1996), pp. 43–5. Schmid Noerr writes:

At first sight this looks like a piece of evidence for a late Oedipal drama: a young disciple appropriates the ideas of his foster father in such a way that the father sees his life's work threatened and tries to get rid of the disciple. At first, he succeeds in doing so, but now the drama will really take its course, as we know not only from Sophocles but also, in retrospect, from the history of the Frankfurt School as it unfolded. Precisely because the young one is cast out by the old one, he gathers the strength to remove the old one, in turn, and take his place. (pp. 43f.)

70 Letter of 22 February 1977, Bestand Na 3, Nachlass Herbert Marcuse Archivzentrum der Universitätsbibliothek J. C. Senckenberg, Frankfurt am Main.

71 Habermas (1989), 'Ein Brief', pp. 392f.
72 Habermas (2010), interview with Karl-Siegbert Rehberg, unpublished MS.
73 Habermas et al. (1961), *Student und Politik*, p. 44.
74 Horkheimer (1996), *Gesammelte Schriften*, vol. 18: *Briefwechsel 1949–1973*, p. 447.
75 Adorno and Horkheimer (2006), *Briefwechsel*, vol. 4, pp. 570 and 619.
76 Bestand Na 1, Nachlass Max Horkheimer, Archivzentrum der Universitätsbibliothek J. C. Senckenberg, Frankfurt am Main, MHA V 83.
77 Letter dated 11 June 1960, Deutsches Literaturarchiv Marbach, Handschriftenabteilung, Briefwechsel Merkur, Mappe 2.
78 Personal notes from conversations.
79 See Müller-Doohm (2005), *Adorno: A Biography*, pp. 368ff.
80 Habermas, 'Partisanenprofessor im Lande der Mitläufer' [The partisan professor in the country of the 'Mitläufer'], *Die Zeit*, 29 April 1966.
81 See Demirović (1999), *Der nonkonformistische Intellektuelle*, pp. 239ff.
82 See Albrecht et al. (1999), *Die intellektuelle Gründung der Bundesrepublik*, pp. 413–42.
83 Bestand Na 1, Nachlass Max Horkheimer, Archivzentrum der Universitätsbibliothek J. C. Senckenberg, Frankfurt am Main, MHA V 83. Letter of 29 March 1965. The exact wording in the original letter, which was written in English, is: 'Jürgen Habermas, by the way, is one of the former members of the Institute and now my successor, not in die [*sic*!] Board of Directors but in the department of Philosophy. I would say he is one of the most promising intellectuals in Western Germany.'
84 Habermas (1982), *Zur Logik der Sozialwissenschaften*, pp. 77ff. [The paper is not part of the English translation of *Zur Logik der Sozialwissenschaften*, which is based on the 1970 edition].
85 Letter from Habermas to Horkheimer, 10 January 1969, Bestand Na 1, Nachlass Max Horkheimer, Archivzentrum der Universitätsbibliothek J. C. Senckenberg, Frankfurt am Main.
86 Habermas (1985), 'A Philosophico-Political Profile', p.78. [The dedication is actually not a verbatim quotation but an allusion to the last sentence of Benjamin's essay on Goethe's Elective Affinities (Quoted by Marcuse at the end of his book): 'It is only for the sake of those without hope that hope in given to us.']
87 Habermas (1968), *Technik und Wissenschaft als 'Ideologie'*, p. 147.
88 Letter from Horkheimer to Habermas, 10 August 1965, Bestand Na 1, Nachlass Max Horkheimer, Archivzentrum der Universitätsbibliothek J. C. Senckenberg, Frankfurt am Main.
89 Horkheimer (1996), *Gesammelte Schriften*, vol. 17: *Briefwechsel 1941–1948*, p. 172.
90 Habermas (1968), *Technik und Wissenschaft als 'Ideologie'*, p. 163.

Chapter 4 Under the Aegis of Conflicting Personalities

1 See Rammstedt (1986), *Deutsche Soziologie 1933–1945*, pp. 25ff.
2 Habermas (1985), 'Wolfgang Abendroth in der Bundesrepublik', in *Düsseldorfer Debatte*, p. 55. One of the reasons for Abendroth's interest in the topic of Habermas's Habilitation was the dissertation of one of his former doctoral students, Rüdiger Altmann, who, in 1954, had written

on 'Das Problem der Öffentlichkeit und seine Bedeutung für die moderne Demokratie' [The problem of the public sphere and its significance for modern democracy]. This dissertation shows affinities with Carl Schmitt's statism. Altmann later came to prominence as one of Chancellor Erhard's advisors. This leaves open the question of whether *The Structural Transformation of the Public Sphere* was also a kind of anti-Schmittian project. See Laak (1993), *Gespräche in der Sicherheit des Schweigens*, pp. 217ff.

3 Habermas (2008), 'Der Hermann Heller der frühen Bundesrepublik: Wolfgang Abendroth zum 100. Geburtstag [The Hermann Heller of the early Federal Republic: For Wolfgang Abendroth on his 100th birthday], in *Ach, Europa*, pp. 11–14; here: p. 12 [this text is omitted from the English translation: *Europe: the Faltering Project*].

4 Habermas ([1966] 1981), 'Wolfgang Abendroth: Der Partisanenprofessor', in *Philosophisch-politische Profile*, pp. 249–52; here: p. 249 [this text is not part of the English edition].

5 Habermas (2008), *Ach, Europa*, p. 13.

6 *Die Zeit*, 29 April 1966.

7 Habermas (2008), *Ach, Europa*, p. 13.

8 Universitätsarchiv der Philipps-Universität Marburg, UniA Marburg 307d Nr. 2912.

9 Letter from Habermas to Paeschke, 7 June 1961, Deutsches Literaturarchiv Marbach, Handschriftenabteilung, Briefwechsel Merkur.

10 Habermas (1974), 'The Classical Doctrine of Politics in Relation to Social Philosophy', in *Theory and Practice*.

11 Ibid., p. 44 (trans. modified).

12 Ibid., pp. 77f.

13 Habermas (1966), 'Soziologie', in *Evangelisches Staatslexikon*, pp. 2108–13.

14 Habermas (1981), *Kleine Politische Schriften I–IV*, p. 516.

15 Habermas (1985), *'A Philosophico-Political Profile'*, p.76.

16 Gadamer (2001), *Die Lektion des Jahrhunderts*, pp. 88ff. Quoted after Wiggershaus (2004), *Jürgen Habermas*, p. 56.

17 Gadamer (1999), 'Der Meister der Kommunikation', *Süddeutsche Zeitung*, 18 June 1999.

18 Habermas (1963), *Theorie und Praxis*, p. 160.

19 Habermas (1974), 'Between Philosophy and Science', in *Theory and Practice*, p. 196.

20 Ibid., pp. 241f. (trans. modified).

21 Ibid., p. 233.

22 Habermas (1981), *Kleine Politische Schriften I–IV*, p. 517.

23 Habermas (2000), 'Wie ist nach dem Historismus noch Metaphysik möglich? Zum 100. Geburtstag Hans-Georg Gadamers', *Neue Züricher Zeitung*, 12–13 February 2000.

24 Habermas ([1981] 2012), 'Hans-Georg Gadamer: Urbanizing the Heideggerian Province', in *Philosophical-Political Profiles*, pp. 189–97.

25 See Grondin (1999), *Hans-Georg Gadamer: Eine Biographie*, pp. 334ff.

26 Habermas ([1981] 2012), 'Hans-Georg Gadamer: Urbanizing the Heideggerian Province', p. 196.

27 Habermas (2000), 'Der liberale Geist', p. 51 (emphasis in the original).

28 See Habermas (1982), *Zur Logik der Sozialwissenschaften*, pp. 331–66 [this section is not part of the English *On the Logic of the Social Sciences*, which is based on the text published by *Philosophische Rundschau* (February 1967)]. Habermas focuses on the hermeneutic concept of tradition [*Überlieferung*]

and points out that an agreement based on tradition may rest on power relations. What is needed is a kind of meta-hermeneutics which establishes the conditions of possibility for analysing distorted communication. See ibid., pp. 348ff. and 358ff. The condition for such a meta-hermeneutics would, in turn, be the development of a theory of communicative competence. On the debate about hermeneutics, see the volume *Hermeneutik und Ideologiekritik* (1971), which contains contributions by Karl-Otto Apel, Claus von Bormann, Rüdiger Bubner, Hans-Georg Gadamer, Hans-Joachim Giegel and Jürgen Habermas.

29 Habermas (1990), *Die nachholende Revolution*, pp. 155f.; emphasis in the original.
30 Quoted after Gondin (1999), *Hans-Georg Gadamer*, p. 343.
31 Gunter Hofmann, 'Denker in der Arena', *Die Zeit*, 25 June 1989.
32 Habermas (1974), 'Hegel's Critique of the French Revolution', in *Theory and Practice*, pp. 121–41; here: p. 139.
33 Oskar Negt, 'Autonomie und Eingriff', *Frankfurter Rundschau*, 16 June 1989.
34 Oskar Negt (2009), 'Einheimischer und Welterklärer? '.
35 Habermas (2000), 'Der liberale Geist', p. 52.
36 Habermas ([1981] 2012), 'Karl Löwith: Stoic Retreat from Historical Consciousness', in *Historical-Political Profiles*, p. 94.
37 Ibid., p. 85.
38 See Laak (1993), *Gespräche in der Sicherheit des Schweigens*, pp. 53ff.
39 See Forner (2007), 'Für eine demokratische Erneuerung Deutschlands'. See also Kießling (2012), *Die undeutschen Deutschen*, pp. 225ff. [And see the recently published Sean A. Forner (2014), *German Intellectuals and the Challenge of Democracy*].
40 See Mitscherlich (1983), *Ein Leben für die Psychoanalyse*, pp. 189ff.; Dehli (2007), *Leben als Konflikt*, pp. 237ff.
41 'Ute und Jürgen Habermas gratulieren Margarete Mitscherlich zum 70. Geburtstag', *EMMA*, 1 July 1987, pp. 26–8.
42 See Schülein (2000), 'Von der Kritik am "szientistischen Selbstmißverständnis"'.
43 Habermas, 'In memoriam Alexander Mitscherlich', *Psyche*, 36, pp. 1060–3.
44 Ibid., p. 1063.
45 Habermas (2010), 'Kultur des Gegenwartssinns', p. 38.
46 I refer to the voluminous correspondence on the Theory series between Habermas and the publishing house represented by Siegfried Unseld and Karl Markus Michel. The letters dating from the period between November 1964 and 1966 were kept in the archive of the Peter Suhrkamp Foundation. In 2009, in connection with the relocation of the Suhrkamp publishing house from Frankfurt to Berlin, the archival documents, all in all about 9,000 boxes, were sold to the Deutsches Literaturarchiv Marbach for an estimated €7 million.
47 Schopf (2003), *'So müßte ich ein Engel und kein Autor sein'*, pp. 456f.
48 Undated letter from Habermas to Unseld (probably January 1964), Bestand Na 60, Vorlass Jürgen Habermas, Archivzentrum der Universitätsbibliothek J. C. Senckenberg, Frankfurt am Main. The original is in the Peter Suhrkamp Foundation, Frankfurt am Main.
49 Ibid.
50 Ibid.
51 See Michalzik (2002), *Unseld*, pp. 148ff.

52 In a letter of 28 August 1965, Enzensberger asks Habermas for a contribution on sociolinguistics. Habermas responds to say that he is working on the subject at the moment and could not say anything about it yet.

53 Letter from Habermas to Michel, 4 February 1966, Bestand Na 60, Vorlass Jürgen Habermas, Archivzentrum der Universitätsbibliothek J. C. Senckenberg, Frankfurt am Main.

54 Blumenberg's attitude can be gleaned from the correspondence between Blumenberg and Taubes. In a longer letter to Taubes, dated 11 September 1970, Blumenberg mentions the reason for his leaving the editorial team:

> Since our 'Theorie' meeting on 17 July, it has become clear that I cannot continue as a member of the editorial circle. Mr Unseld has come up with an idea for how to further intensify the special treatment for which he has singled me out among those in the group of editors for some time now; and I am simply fed up with exposing myself to the arbitrary behaviour of the publisher. Maybe you will understand when I briefly tell you the course of events. During the meeting in July, I said that I would not enter into any new agreements with the Suhrkamp Verlag because, compared to the treatment of the other editors of the 'Theorie', the publishing house had discriminated against me for years. Thereupon, Mr *Unseld* asked me for a conversation in private, where he expressed his regret over the fact that, since 1 February 1968, I had been excluded from the payment of fees without having been informed or given any reasons, and he offered to establish parity in retrospect. After considering the offer for a week, I accepted it and retracted my reservation regarding a new agreement. Thereupon, Mr *Unseld* acknowledged my willingness to enter into a new agreement but at the same time withdrew his offer of establishing retrospective parity again. I told him as a final response that I could only accept the result of our conversation on 17 July in its entirety. (Blumenberg and Taubes (2013), *Briefwechsel 1961–1981*, pp. 161f.)

55 Taubes and Schmitt (2012), *Briefwechsel mit Materialien*, pp. 44 and 96. In a review of this correspondence, published in the *Süddeutsche Zeitung* (30 January 2012), Hans-Martin Lohmann remarked that Taubes was 'structurally incapable of turning his thoughts into discourse' and that he displayed a 'striking lack of respectability'. 'Name-dropping and the spreading of rumours were among his specialities.'

56 Habermas (1966), 'Nachwort', in Hegel, *Politische Schriften*, pp. 343ff.

57 Letter from Taubes to Arendt, 22 December 1966, Collection of the Manuscript Division, Library of Congress. The exact words of the invitation are: 'the editors Blumenberg, Habermas, Henrich and myself would like to persuade you to comment on the work of Sartre. . . . Regarding the honorarium, I can only report that the rates of the "Kursbuch", which pays the highest honoraria in Germany, are also meant to apply to "Theorie".'

58 Unseld (2010), *Chronik*, vol. 1, p. 267, fn. 2.

59 See Fellinger and Schopf (2003), *Kleine Geschichte der edition suhrkamp* (2003).

60 Habermas (1970), 'Über das Verhältnis von Politik und Moral' [On the relationship between politics and morality], in *Arbeit, Erkenntnis, Fortschritt*, pp. 219–42; here: p. 238.

61 Ibid.

62 For a better result, the FDP had to wait until 2009, when it received 14.6 per cent of the second votes. [Within the electoral system of the FRG, each elector has two votes. The first is a vote for an individual candidate, the second a vote for a party. If the percentage of a party's second vote does not cover the number of its directly elected candidates, the directly elected candidates nevertheless enter the Bundestag on a so-called *Überhangmandat* – an overhang mandate or seat.]

63 Four years earlier, the campaign slogan 'No experiments!' won Adenauer's CDU a triumphant victory in the national elections.

64 Reichel (1981), *Politische Kultur in der Bundesrepublik*, pp. 148f. See also Müller (2013), *Das demokratische Zeitalter*, pp. 217ff. The author is of the opinion that the 'innovative institutions' of West German democracy 'are justified in terms of a decidedly traditional moral and political vocabulary'. It was tempting, he writes, 'to represent the post-war era not as a new beginning, but as a return to something long since familiar'.

65 *Magnum – die Zeitschrift für das moderne Leben* [Magnum – journal for modern life] was published between 1954 and 1966 by M. Dumont Schauberg and was considered to be one of the most important cultural journals of the German-speaking area. In the bimonthly volumes, which appeared in large-size format, distinguished writers, scientists and artists published on all aspects of political and cultural life. Famous photographers, such as Robert Capa, Henri Cartier-Bresson or Andreas Feininger, contributed high-class photo reportage.

66 Habermas (1961), 'Die Bundesrepublik – eine Wahlmonarchie?', *Magnum*, 1 January 1961, p. 28.

67 The first to review the book was Kurt Sontheimer, who waxed lyrical about it in the *Frankfurter Allgemeine Zeitung* of 26 September 1962. In particular, the book's language appeared 'in a very unique way as a medium of an intense thinking whose richness and differentiating power one cannot help but admire.'

68 At the beginning of the 1960s, the analysis of the public sphere was clearly exercising many people, as shown not only by Hannah Arendt's *Vita Activa* (the German version appeared in 1960) but also by the efforts of Wilhelm Hennis, who belonged to the same generation as Habermas. He considered working on the public sphere almost at the same time as Habermas. When it became apparent that the latter was ahead of him, he limited his output to two articles, one on the 'Begriff der öffentlichen Meinung' [Concept of 'public opinion'] and one on 'Meinungsforschung und representative Demokratie' [Opinion research and representative democracy], both of which Habermas referred to critically. See Schlak (2008), *Wilhelm Hennis*, pp. 51ff. and 75ff.

69 Habermas ([1962] 1989), *The Structural Transformation of the Public Sphere*, p. 142.

70 Ibid., p. 170.

71 Habermas (199), *Strukturwandel der Öffentlichkeit*, p. 28 [the English translation is of the 1962 edition, and thus does not contain this preface].

72 Habermas ([1962] 1989), *The Structural Transformation of the Public Sphere*, p. 209. An important source of inspiration for Habermas was an article of 1954 by the Gießen-based professor of public law and the science of politics Helmut Ridder, titled 'Meinungsfreiheit' [Freedom of opinion]. In an interview conducted by Joachim Perels in 2005, Ridder, a legal scholar with a critical attitude towards legal positivism who worked in the

tradition of left-wing democratic jurists from the Weimar period such as Hermann Heller, Otto Kirchheimer, Franz Neumann, and Ernst Fraenkel, remembered that Habermas sat in the lectures he gave during his time in Frankfurt (1951–9) and that the two were acquainted. Ridder and Perels (2005), 'Stationen im Leben eines Juristen', p. 373.

73 Habermas ([1962] 1989), *The Structural Transformation of the Public Sphere*, p. 248.
74 Habermas (1990), *Strukturwandel der Öffentlichkeit*, p. 21.
75 See Schlak (2008), *Wilhelm Hennis*, pp. 76ff.
76 See Dahms (1994), *Positivismusstreit*, pp. 361ff.
77 Habermas (1970), *Zur Logik der Sozialwissenschaften*, p. 9 [this text is not part of the English edition].
78 Ibid., pp. 15ff. and 45ff.
79 Ibid., p. 18.
80 Ibid.
81 See Dahms (1994), *Positivismusstreit*, p. 394.
82 Albert and Popper (2005), *Briefwechsel 1958–1994*, pp. 62, 137, 141 and 146. [*Hexeneinmaleins*, literally 'the witch's multiplication table', is a reference to a scene from Goethe's *Faust* in which the witch cooks a rejuvenating potion for Faust:

> Hear how it's done!
> Make ten from one
> And let two be
> And also three
> And then you're rich!
> Forfeit the four!
> From five and six,
> So says the witch,
> Make seven and eight.
> The end's in sight!
> And nine is one
> And ten is none.
> The witch's times-table is done!
> Goethe (2005), *Faust*, Part 1, ll. 2540–51.]

83 Adorno (2005), 'Progress', p. 150.
84 Habermas ([1963] 1981), 'Theodor W. Adorno: Ein philosophierender Intellektueller', in *Philosophisch-Politische Profile*, p. 161 [this text is not part of the English edition].
85 See Habermas (1963), *Theorie und Praxis*, pp. 215–30 [this text is not part of the English edition].
86 Habermas (1969), *Protestbewegung und Hochschulreform*, p. 91.
87 See Kraushaar (1998), *Frankfurter Schule und Studentenbewegung*, pp. 192f.
88 *Der Spiegel*, 18 September 1963. See Liehr (2002), *Von der Aktion gegen den Spiegel zur Spiegel-Affäre*; Ellwein et al. (1966), *Die Spiegel-Affäre*, vol. 2: *Die Reaktion der Öffentlichkeit*.
89 See Kraushaar (1998), *Frankfurter Schule und Studentenbewegung*, vol. 1, pp. 194ff.; see also Bering (2010), *Die Epoche der Intellektuellen 1898–2001*, pp. 354ff.
90 Habermas (1987), *Eine Art Schadensabwicklung*, p. 48.
91 *Merkur*, 17(7) (1963), p. 716.

450   Notes to pages 117–122

92 *Blätter für deutsche und internationale Politik*, no. 4 (1964), pp. 335–40.
93 *Die Zeit*, 18 September 1964.
94 Undated letter from Habermas to Paeschke, Bestand Na 60, Vorlass Jürgen Habermas, Archivzentrum der Universitätsbibliothek J. C. Senckenberg, Frankfurt am Main.
95 Habermas, 'Vom Ende der Politik – oder die unterhaltsamen Kolportagen des Kriminalberichterstatters Hans Magnus Enzensberger', *Frankfurter Allgemeine Zeitung*, 17 October 1964. See Lau (1999), *Hans Magnus Enzensberger*, pp. 185ff.
96 Habermas, 'Vom Ende der Politik', *Frankfurter Allgemeine Zeitung*, 17 October 1964.
97 Altmann completed his doctorate under the supervision of Wolfgang Abendroth in 1954. The topic of his dissertation was the public and democracy. Later, when he was an advisor to Chancellor Ludwig Erhard, he coined the phrase *formierte Gesellschaft* [formed society].
98 See Demirović (1999), *Der nonkonformistische Intellektuelle*, pp. 210ff.
99 Habermas, 'Das chronische Leiden der Hochschulreform', *Merkur*, no. 109 (1957), p. 272; Habermas (1969), *Protestbewegung und Hochschulreform*, pp. 62f.
100 Habermas (1970), 'Vom sozialen Wandel akademischer Bildung', *Arbeit, Erkenntnis, Fortschritt*, pp. 246 and 249.
101 Ibid., p. 251.
102 Ibid., p. 255.
103 Schäfer (2000), 'Die nivellierte Mittelstandsgesellschaft'.
104 I refer to the correspondence between Schelsky and Habermas during the years 1962 to 1970, in particular to Schelsky's letters to Habermas, dated 26 March 1963, 4 June 1963, and 17 June 1970, Bestand Na 60, Vorlass Jürgen Habermas, Archivzentrum der Universitätsbibliothek J. C. Senckenberg, Frankfurt am Main.
105 Habermas (1970), 'Pädagogischer "Optimismus" vor Gericht einer pessimistischen Anthropologie: Schelsky's Bedenken zur Schulreform' [Educational 'optimism' stands trial before a pessimistic anthropology: Schelsky's reservations regarding the school reform], in *Arbeit, Erkenntnis, Fortschritt*, pp. 181–218; here: pp. 204f. See also 'Vom sozialen Wandel akademischer Bildung', pp. 243–57.
106 See Habermas, 'Nachgeahmte Substantialität', *Merkur*, no. 24 (1970), pp. 313–27; Habermas ([1970] 2012), 'Arnold Gehlen: Imitation Substantiality'. The correspondence with Helmut Schelsky, which is held in the *Vorlass* of Jürgen Habermas, would warrant closer scrutiny and interpretation. The long letters from Schelsky are particularly remarkable. Again and again, he attempts to come to terms with aspects of Habermas's thought concerning anthropology, educational theory and university politics. Compared to Schelsky's advances, Habermas's comments are rather restrained. Roman Yos drew my attention to the fact that the Schelsky archive in Münster holds a voluminous manuscript documenting an intense occupation with Habermas's publications.
107 Habermas (1971), 'Kritische und konservative Aufgaben der Soziologie', in *Theorie und Praxis*, p. 306 (fn. 25); Habermas, 'Theodor Adorno: The Primal History of Subjectivity', p. 106.

Chapter 5 Back in Frankfurt

1 On the following, see Hammerstein (2012), *Die Johann Wolfgang Goethe-Universität Frankfurt am Main*, vol. 2, pp. 602ff.

2 Bestand Na 1, Nachlass Max Horkheimer, Archivzentrum der Universitätsbibliothek J. C. Senckenberg, Frankfurt am Main, MHA V 83.

3 Liebrucks argued that, since Habermas was of the opinion that philosophy had reached its end, he was actually unsuitable for a chair in philosophy. See Hammerstein (2012), *Die Johann Wolfgang Goethe-Universität Frankfurt am Main*, p. 602.

4 Ibid., p. 604.

5 Letter from the dean to the Hessian Minister for Culture and Education, dated 26 July 1963, Universitätsarchiv Frankfurt.

6 Bestand Na 1, Nachlass Max Horkheimer, Archivzentrum der Universitätsbibliothek J. C. Senckenberg, Frankfurt am Main, MHA V 83.

7 Ibid., MHA V XIX,4.

8 Ibid., MHA V 83,166a-c.

9 Letter from Habermas to von Friedeburg, 18 November 1965, Vorlass Habermas.

10 A letter by Habermas, dated 15 October 1964, says: 'Upon the request of my deceased friend Dr Wilfried Berghahn and his wife Susanne, *née* Mattner, I am happy to take on the guardianship for their children Sabine and Martin.' Vorlass Habermas.

11 My private notes from conversations.

12 Hammerstein (2012), *Die Johann Wolfgang Goethe-Universität Frankfurt am Main*, vol. 2, pp. 611ff. Klaus Reichert published an impressive portrait of Szondi with the title 'Zum Bilde Szondis' in the *Neue Züricher Zeitung*, 19–20 February 2005.

13 On the 'affair', see the contribution by Klaus von See: 'Peter Szondi und die Frankfurter Universität: Eine Recherche aus aktuellem Anlaß', *Deutsche Vierteljahresschrift für Literaturwissenschaft und Geistesgeschichte*, 79 (2005), pp. 341–58.

14 Habermas (2008), 'Zum Gedenken an Gajo Petrović', unpublished MS, p. 2.

15 Ibid.

16 Gunter Hofmann, 'Denken in der Arena: Die Rolle des "öffentlichen Intellektuellen"', *Die Zeit*, 16 June 1989.

17 Oevermann (2009), 'Der akademische Lehrer – eine Erinnerung', pp. 42–5. See also Oevermann (2010), 'Der Gegenbegriff von Natur ist nicht Gesellschaft, sondern Kultur'; Offe (2005), 'Die Bundesrepublik als Schattenriß zweier Lichtquellen'.

18 Letter from Habermas to the dean of the Faculty of Philosophy, 4 December 1964, Universitätsarchiv Frankfurt am Main.

19 Löwenthal and Kracauer (2003), *In steter Freundschaft*, p. 256. In a letter of 3 June 1965, Habermas wrote to his lector Karl Markus Michel: 'I was in the end not able to visit Marcuse, despite his generous invitation and energetic insistence, because I had to have my appendix removed in California, and thus did not make it to Boston.' Bestand Na 60, Vorlass Jürgen Habermas, Archivzentrum der Universitätsbibliothek J. C. Senckenberg, Frankfurt am Main.

20 'Vier Jungkonservative beim Projektleiter der Moderne', *Die Tageszeitung*, 21 October 1980, p. 9.
21 Bestand Na 1, Nachlass Max Horkheimer, Archivzentrum der Universitätsbibliothek J. C. Senckenberg, Frankfurt am Main, MHA V 188 204.
22 Habermas (1982), *Zur Logik der Sozialwissenschaften*, p. 309 [this text is not part of the English edition].
23 Ibid., p. 240 [this text is not part of the English edition].
24 Reinhart Klemens Maurer's literature review *Jürgen Habermas' Aufhebung der Philosophie* [Jürgen Habermas's sublation of philosophy], which was published as a special issue of the *Philosophische Rundschau* (vol. 24, Beiheft 8) in 1977, contains an extensive reconstructive and critical discussion of Habermas's early publications up to 1976. The guiding thread running through this review, by a philosopher who was close to the school of thought associated with Joachim Ritter in Münster, is the attempt to explain the meaning in Habermas of the concepts 'critique', 'utopia' (domination of nature, reconciliation with nature, freedom from domination), 'emancipation' and 'discourse'. Habermas's later development of his work on the basis of the philosophy of language and legal philosophy, which had long since bid farewell to the idea of the human species as the subject of world history, would probably thereby have avoided Maurer's questions and objections. Nevertheless, as an example of a specific type of criticism current at the time, it is still informative, even if Maurer's claim that the early version of Habermas's discourse theory has 'the same structure' as the 'Marxist-Leninist theory of the avant-garde' (ibid., p. 35) must be seen as purely polemical.
25 Dietrich Deininger, 'Befreiung – aber wie? Jürgen Habermas über Technik, Wissenschaft und Lebenspraxis', *Frankfurter Allgemeine Zeitung*, 31 May 1969.
26 Habermas ([1968] 2004), *Knowledge and Human Interests*, p. 310.
27 Ibid., p. 308; emphasis in the original.
28 Ibid., p. 311 (trans. modified).
29 See Apel (1971), 'Szientistik, Hermeneutik, Ideologiekritik. See also Apel (1998), *Auseinandersetzungen in der Erprobung des transzendentalpragmatischen Ansatzes*, pp. 649–837.
30 Habermas ([1968] 2004), *Knowledge and Human Interests*, p. 371; emphasis in the original.
31 Ibid. [emphasis added, following the German original].
32 Ibid., p. 55.
33 Ibid., p. 62.
34 Ibid., p. 284.
35 Ibid., p. 287.
36 Letter of 26 November 1968 from Karl-Otto Apel and letter of 2 February 1969 from Niklas Luhmann to Habermas. Both letters are in Bestand Na 60, Vorlass Jürgen Habermas, Archivzentrum der Universitätsbibliothek J. C. Senckenberg, Frankfurt am Main.
37 Habermas ([1968] 2004), *Knowledge and Human Interests*, p. 351 [emphasis added, following the German original].
38 Ibid., p. 377.
39 *Der Spiegel*, 28 May 1973, pp. 141f.; *Der Spiegel*, 18 June 1973.
40 Habermas (2000), 'Nach dreißig Jahren', p. 15.
41 Habermas ([1990] 1994), *The Past as Future*, pp. 48f.

42 Habermas (1969), *Protestbewegung und Hochschulreform*, p. 104.
43 Habermas ([1968] 2004), *Knowledge and Human Interests*, p. 284.
44 The failure to address urgently needed reforms with sufficient seriousness was one of the things that motivated the protest movement, and members of the generation that constituted it, to act.

> As soon as the new generation, which had grown up entirely in the Adenauer era, began to take the propositions offered by the political education and ideology of their time seriously – i.e., as soon as they took them literally – their separation from the *status quo* began: they were, after all, little burdened by the inwardness shown by the generation of their fathers and mothers; they did not have to *forget* the division of Germany and the national socialist past. They *remembered*. To that extent, the generation of those born from 1940 onwards were, in a particular sense, a *new* generation. (Brückner (1978), *Versuch, uns und anderen die Bundesrepublik zu erklären*, p. 151; emphases in the original)

Jan-Werner Müller, in his analysis of the '68 movement, reaches the conclusion that a political goal was the guiding principle:

> Direct democracy was meant to replace the extremely cautious and limited conception of democracy which had been supported by the European elites after 1945 . . . An important value, maybe even the core concept of the international '68 movement, was that of autonomy . . . It was autonomy, understood as individual as well as collective self-determination, that stood in the most obvious opposition to a post-war world ruled by technocrats and bureaucrats. (Müller (2013), *Das demokratische Zeitalter*, pp. 300 and 313)

45 The conference took place on 22 May 1966 at the Goethe University in Frankfurt. See Kraushaar (1998), *Frankfurter Schule und Studentenbewegung*, vol. 1, pp. 226 and 228.
46 Habermas made these remarks at a panel discussion organized by the Sozialdemokratischer Hochschulbund [Social Democratic University Association] in December 1966 in Frankfurt. Ibid., vol. 1, p. 239.
47 Ibid., vol. 1, p. 216.
48 'What else would you have expected from the bodies of a state in the case of a nation whose avant-garde had turned Europe into a concentration camp between 1933 and 1945, and had declared the murder of minorities to be socially appropriate behaviour?' Brückner (1978), *Versuch, uns und den anderen die Bundesrepublik zu erklären*, p. 153.
49 Sebastian Haffner (1967), 'Nacht der langen Knüppel: Der 2 Juni 1967 – ein geplanter Pogrom', *Der Stern*, no. 26 (June 1967). See also the documentation in 'Der nicht erklärte Notstand: Dokumentation und Analyse eines Berliner Sommers', *Kursbuch*, no. 12 (1968).
50 See Richter (2008), 'Die Außerparlamentarische Opposition in der Bundesrepublik Deutschland 1966 bis 1968'.
51 Habermas (1969), *Protestbewegung und Hochschulreform*, p. 141. See Fichter and Lönnendonker (1977), *Kleine Geschichte des SDS*, pp. 106–10. See also the film *Ruhestörung* by Hans Dieter Müller and Günther Hörmann, Institut für Filmgestaltung (1967); a DVD of this film is part of the special edition of *Protestbewegung und Hochschulreform* (2008).

52 Habermas (1969), *Protestbewegung und Hochschulreform*, pp. 145f.
53 Fichter and Lönnendonker (1977), *Kleine Geschichte des SDS*, p. 107.
54 Ibid., p. 148.
55 Negt (1968), 'Studentischer Protest – Liberalismus – Linksfaschismus', pp. 182, 187 and 189.
56 Offe (2005), 'Die Bundesrepublik als Schattenriß zweier Lichtquellen', p. 153.
57 Habermas, *Kleine Politische Schriften I–IV*, p. 519; emphasis in the original.
58 The correspondence on which I draw here is stored in the Frankfurt University archives.
59 Mitscherlich-Archiv, Archivzentrum der Universitätsbibliothek J. C. Senckenberg, Frankfurt am Main.
60 Letter from Habermas to Heide Schneider, 7 September 1967, Bestand Na 60, Vorlass Jürgen Habermas, Archivzentrum der Universitätsbibliothek J. C. Senckenberg, Frankfurt am Main.
61 See Neumann (1996), *Uwe Johnson*, pp. 626ff.
62 Habermas, 'Und dann erfuhr ich die philosophische Produktivität des weiblichen Blicks', *Du: Die Zeitschrift der Kultur*, 60/710 (2000), p. 53.
63 Letters from Habermas to Hans Paeschke, 9 March and 21 March 1966, Deutsches Literaturarchiv Marbach, Handschriftenabteilung, Mappe 3. See Habermas ([1966] 1981), 'Hannah Arendt: Die Geschichte von den zwei Revolutionen', in *Philosophisch-politische Profile*, pp. 223–8 [this text, the *Merkur* review, is not part of the English edition]. See also Canovan (1983), 'A Case of Distorted Communication'.
64 Habermas (1969), *Protestbewegung und Hochschulreform*, p. 170.
65 Pol, 'Die Proteste der Studenten: Ein Vortrag des Frankfurter Soziologie-Professors Jürgen Habermas in New York', *Frankfurter Allgemeine Zeitung*, 5 December 1967.
66 Bestand Na 60, Vorlass Jürgen Habermas, Archivzentrum der Universitätsbibliothek J. C. Senckenberg, Frankfurt am Main.
67 Letter from Habermas to Meyersohn, 14 March 1968, ibid.
68 Dutschke died on Christmas Eve 1979. His death was ultimately a consequence of his injuries, as a result of which he suffered from epileptic fits. He drowned in the bath.
69 See Kraushaar (1998), *Frankfurter Schule und Studentenbewegung*, vol. 1, p. 338. A good chronicle of the events can be found in Gilcher-Holtey (2008), *1968: Eine Zeitreise* and *1968: Vom Ereignis zum Mythos*.
70 Enzensberger (1969), 'Entrevista'. In his own unique way, Alexander Kluge has made use of the events at the Hessischer Rundfunk and in the meeting hall of Bettinaschule in his take on 'Die Tage der Politischen Universität' [The days of the political university], in Kluge (2000), *Die Chronik der Gefühle*, vol. 2, pp. 204–41.
71 *Bild*, 7 February 1968.
72 Bestand Na 60, Vorlass Jürgen Habermas, Archivzentrum der Universitätsbibliothek J. C. Senckenberg, Frankfurt am Main.
73 See Habermas, (1969), *Protestbewegung und Hochschulreform*, p. 248.
74 Ibid., p. 196.
75 Ibid., p. 199.
76 Abendroth and Negt (1968) *Die Linke antwortet Jürgen Habermas*. The volume contains contributions by Wolfgang Abendroth, Peter Brückner, Furio Cerutti, Klaus Dörner, Ekkehart Krippendorff, Herbert Lederer,

Wolfgang Lefèvre, Klaus Meschkat, Oskar Negt, Arnhelm Neusüss, Claus
Offe, Reimut Reiche, Claus Rolshausen, Helmut Schauer and Frank Wolf.
77 Ibid., p. 18.
78 Ibid., p. 20.
79 Ibid., pp. 63 and 66.
80 Ibid., p. 39; emphasis in the original.
81 Ibid., pp. 63 and 66.
82 Ibid., p. 91.
83 Ibid., p. 109.
84 Ibid., pp. 202 and 207; emphasis in the original.
85 *Der Spiegel*, 24 February 1969, p. 146.
86 Kraushaar (1998), *Frankfurter Schule und Studentenbewegung*, vol. 2, pp.
   465f.
87 Unseld (2010), *Chronik*, vol. 1, p. 25.
88 See ibid., p. 29. In the *Chronik der Lektoren* [Chronicle of the editors],
   Karlheinz Braun, one of its authors, wrote:

> If, on the other hand, I read the report on the so-called editor's revolt in
> Siegfried Unseld's *Chronicle of a Conflict*, I feel as if I am taking a glance
> into another life. As if there is a stranger, who allegedly said or did this or
> that back then. As if that notorious 'revolt of the editors' had taken place
> without me. Although I was a part of it, I did not play the role Unseld
> describes. I reputedly have said sentences such as 'it is high time now to
> expropriate the publishing house' (now vehemently denied by Marianne
> Frisch, who is Unseld's alleged source for this sentence). 'Expropriate
> Springer' was a common slogan at the time, an expropriation demanded
> for political reasons – but why expropriate the Suhrkamp publishing
> house? I am also meant to have elevated myself (together with other
> editors) to the position of a self-appointed elite above the other employees
> of the company and to have pursued my own selfish interests? An attempt
> by Unseld to mobilize the other employees of the house against the editors
> which is all too easy to see through. And was I not also to have made
> authors, who considered this well-functioning publishing house their
> livelihood, nay their home, feel insecure? That is how the publisher saw
> it. I must have been a different person, back then. (Boehlich et al. (2011),
> *Chronik der Lektoren*, p. 60)

See also the detailed review of Unseld's *Chronik* by Sandra Kegel in the
Frankfurter Allgemeine Zeitung, 16 October 2010.
89 Boehlich et al. (2011), *Chronik der Lektoren*, p. 98.
90 Unseld (2010), *Chronik*, vol. 1, p. 32.
91 *Der Spiegel*, 28 April 1969, p. 210.
92 Sebastian Haffner, 'Apropos Habermas', *Konkret*, 16 June 1969, p. 54.
93 Karl Korn, 'Der radikale Reformist', *Frankfurter Allgemeine Zeitung*, 14
   June 1969, p. 77.
94 Oevermann (2010), 'Der Gegenbegriff zur Natur ist nicht Gesellschaft,
   sondern Kultur', p. 373.
95 Habermas (1969), *Protestbewegung und Hochschulreform*, pp. 245–8.
96 Kraushaar (2008), 'Ein Seminar im Brennspiegel der Ereignisse'.
97 Habermas (1969), *Protestbewegung und Hochschulreform*, pp. 247f.
98 Verheyen (2007), 'Diskussionsfieber', p. 214. See Zoller ([1969]), *Aktiver
   Streik*, pp. 29–30.

99 Letter from Habermas to Marcuse, 5 May 1969, Bestand Na 3, Nachlass Herbert Marcuse, Archivzentrum der Universitätsbibliothek J. C. Senckenberg, Frankfurt am Main.

100 Lorenz Jäger, 'Komödie der Weisheiten', *Frankfurter Allgemeine Zeitung*, 30 May 1998. When Jäger, in a letter of 1 November 1992, asked Habermas to write a contribution for a book on the performance artist Imhoff, Habermas declined, with the words: 'In those days, when eggs and firecrackers were flying around the lecture halls, I felt hurt only once, when Mr Imhoff aimed below the belt. That is hardly the right background for a contribution to a kind of celebratory publication.' Letter of 16 November 1992, Bestand Na 60, Vorlass Jürgen Habermas, Archivzentrum der Universitätsbibliothek J. C. Senckenberg, Frankfurt am Main.

101 Letter from Habermas to Brandt, 8 December 1970, Vorlass Habermas.

102 Habermas (1968), *Antworten auf Herbert Marcuse*, p. 16; emphases in the original [the text is also contained in the 1981 German edition of *Philosophisch-Politische Profile*, under the title 'Herbert Marcuse: Einleitung zu einer Antifestschrift' (Introduction to an anti-Festschrift), pp. 253–9; here: p. 259].

103 Habermas (2012), 'The Primal History of Subjectivity – Self-Affirmation Gone Wild', p. 102 (trans. modified).

104 Habermas (1986), 'The Dialectics of Rationalization', p. 96.

105 Habermas, 'The Primal History of Subjectivity – Self-Affirmation Gone Wild', p. 102.

106 Habermas, *Kleine Politische Schriften I–IV*, pp. 448f.

107 Habermas ([1970] 2012), 'Arnold Gehlen: Imitation Substantiality', p. 121 [No one against God but God himself].

108 For Habermas, speech acts are actions that are carried out by uttering a sentence. Thus, a linguistic utterance is itself an action that serves the purpose of establishing an interpersonal relation.

109 Habermas (1971), *Theorie der Gesellschaft oder Sozialtechnologie*, p. 201.

110 'Often we lack the words to say what we feel; and this in turn places the feelings themselves in a questionable light.' Habermas ([1981] 1986), *Theory of Communicative Action*, vol. 1, p. 93.

111 *Merkur*, no. 264 (1970), p. 313. The title of the review is 'Imitation Substantiality', and it was reprinted in *Philosophical-Political Profiles* (see note 107 above). Wolf Lepenies, in a critical commentary on this dispute, draws attention to the fact that in Gehlen we find a different 'relationship between anthropology, institutional theory and the approach to ethics', which Habermas notes but does not place at the centre of his discussion. 'While for Gehlen the relocation of ethics from institutional theory into anthropology is what matters, for Habermas it is the recourse to anthropology as such. . . . Habermas . . . has reached the point himself where he formulates an outline for an anthropology.' While Gehlen resigns himself to biology, Lepenies says, Habermas develops a utopian communication free of coercion. Lepenies, 'Anthropologie und Gesellschaftskritik', in Lepenies and Nolte (1971), *Kritik der Anthropologie*, pp. 77–102; here: pp. 85f.

    Habermas's article in *Merkur* prompted Rudolf Augstein to publish a statement in *Der Spiegel*, no. 23 (1970), under the title 'Wir Mundwerksburschen: Arnold Gehlens antiintellektuelle Wissenschaft' [We journeymen of the mouth: Arnold Gehlen's anti-intellectual science].

Further issues of *Merkur* (nos. 266 and 267) contain reactions by Rüdiger Altmann and Margret Boveri. In a letter to Habermas dated 17 June 1970, Helmut Schelsky gave a detailed explanation of his own critical attitude to Gehlen's *Moral und Hypermoral*, in which he distanced himself from its author. Schelsky mentions that the model of communication free from coercion could be given a concrete form on the basis of an ethics of brotherhood rooted in the family. He also defends Habermas's conception of ethics against the accusation of being left-wing intellectualism, saying:

> This brings me to the only point in your discussion I actually consider to be wrong: that you declare your position to be that of 'a left-wing intellectual' and thus, in the end, accept the confrontational stance into which Gehlen wants to push you and others. Your own ethical conception, standing in the tradition of Kant, Schelling, Hegel, even mobilizing Max Weber (!) against Gehlen, and reaching its climax in a mutuality of I and Thou which is assumed to be free from institutional influences, without inhibitions, and spontaneous, you cannot possibly call 'left-wing', much less monopolize, without underrating it. If you are 'left-wing', then it is for political reasons which are not mentioned here. (Universitäts- und Landesbibliothek Münster, Nachlass Schelsky, 16,012 and 16,015)

In his reply of 9 July 1970, Habermas meets Schelsky halfway:

> I wholly agree with you that the initial conditions of anthropology represent constants which must be permanently put to use. However, I would distinguish between language and symbolically organized types of action, such as labour and interaction, and the corresponding forms of consciousness as emergent properties of cultural systems, on the one hand, and the traits of our biological equipment, which are part of the heritage from natural history that is put to use by way of cultural universals at this new organizational form of life, on the other. (Bestand Na 60, Vorlass Jürgen Habermas, Archivzentrum der Universitätsbibliothek J. C. Senckenberg, Frankfur am Main)

112 Altmann (1970), 'Brüder im Nichts? Zur Auseinandersetzung Jürgen Habermas mit Arnold Gehlens Ethik'.
113 Such as the lament of a right-wing, intellectual, bourgeois elite about the cultural revolution of 1968, which 'has become a litany': 'Private well-being corrupts the readiness to take risks; the primacy of the social corrupts the politics of the great individuals; the social interest corrupts the substance of the state.' Habermas ([1970] 2012), 'Arnold Gehlen: Imitation Substantiality', p. 121.
114 Ibid., p. 118 (trans. modified).
115 Ibid., p. 119; see also p. 120.
116 Ibid., pp. 119f.; emphasis in the original.
117 Habermas (1981), *Kleine Politische Schriften I–IV*, p. 525.
118 Wellershof (2008), *Zwischenreich: Gedichte*, p. 36. The poem, written in 1971, is untitled.

Chapter 6 In the Ivory Tower of Social Scientific Research

1 Habermas (1984), *Vorstudien und Ergänzungen zur Theorie des kommunikativen Handelns*, p. 7. [The quotation is from the preface, which is omitted in the English edition.]

2 Kraushaar (1998), *Frankfurter Schule und Studentenbewegung*, vol. 2, p. 718.

3 Hammerstein (2012), *Die Johann Wolfgang Goethe-Universität Frankfurt am Main*, vol. 2, pp. 803f.

4 Bestand Na 60, Vorlass Jürgen Habermas, Archivzentrum der Universitätsbibliothek J. C. Senckenberg, Frankfurt am Main.

5 Von Weizsäcker (1981), *Der bedrohte Friede*, p. 464; see also pp. 472f.

6 Letter from Habermas to Max Horkheimer, 22 April 1971, Bestand Na 60, Vorlass Jürgen Habermas, Archivzentrum der Universitätsbibliothek J. C. Senckenberg, Frankfurt am Main.

7 Letter from Habermas to Herbert Marcuse, 14 April 1971, Bestand Na 3, ibid.

8 Letter from Marcuse to Habermas, 23 April 1971, ibid.

9 Letter from Habermas to Claus Offe, 29 May 1970, Bestand Na 60, ibid.

10 These names are mentioned on page 5 of the consulted letter.

11 Claus Offe (2005), 'Die Bundesrepublik als Schattenriß zweier Lichtquellen', p. 152.

12 Letter from Habermas to Wellmer, 16 December 1971, Bestand Na 60, Vorlass Jürgen Habermas, Archivzentrum der Universitätsbibliothek J. C. Senckenberg, Frankfurt am Main.

13 In a letter to Habermas dated 26 September 1994, Wellmer discusses in detail the various points where the two philosophers differed in substance despite the predominant agreement between them. See Albrecht Wellmer (1986), *Ethik und Dialog*, sections VII and VIII, pp. 51–102; also his *Sprachphilosophie* (2004), pp. 228ff.

14 Habermas's letter was titled 'Ermordung der Theorie?' [The assassination of theory?']. Kraushaar (1998), *Frankfurter Schule und Studentenbewegung*, vol. 2, pp. 744f.

15 Habermas signed the contract with the Max Planck Society for the Advancement of Science on 9 August 1971. His annual salary, including all allowances, according to the stipulations of the state of Lower Saxony for the payment of civil servants, was DM 63,019.92. Paragraph 7 states: 'Mr Habermas may terminate his service at any time, with the notice to take effect at the end of the next calendar half year and a period of notice of six months.'

16 This arrangement is referred to in the correspondence between Unseld and Habermas during that period. The correspondence was part of the Peter Suhrkamp Foundation and is now kept at the German Literature Archive in Marbach.

17 Hilmer and Sattler (2000), *Bauten und Projekte*, pp. 77–82.

18 Padilla (1971), *Außerhalb des Spiels*, p. 111.

19 See Unseld (2014), *Chronik*, vol. 2, pp. 395f.

20 Habermas's lecture was first published in the conference volume edited by Unseld in 1972. See Habermas (1972), 'Bewußtmachende oder rettende Kritik – die Aktualität Walter Benjamins'. It is reprinted in Habermas (1981), *Philosophisch-politische Profile*, pp. 336–76, as well as in Habermas (2006), *Politik, Kunst, Religion*, pp. 48–95. [The subtitle

is omitted from the 1981 extended edition of *Philosophisch-politische Profile*, as well as in the English translation (see note 24 below)]. Two decades later, a review of the correspondence between Adorno and Benjamin, which had just been published, appeared in *Die Zeit* of 23 September 1994. In the review Habermas, quoting Gershom Scholem, refers to Benjamin's 'metaphysical genius', to 'the aura of an intellectual habitus as auspicious as it is mysterious', and to Benjamin's *Arcades Project*, which remained a fragment. 'The enthusiastic expectations which Adorno associated with it carried projective traits in both senses of the word. Without a shimmer of rhetoric, he expected Benjamin to deliver 'our destined piece of *prima philosophia*' and 'the decisive philosophical word which must find utterance today'. And yet, Adorno criticized Benjamin's intention to rescue the origins that have been lost in the course of history. 'Adorno does not permit himself recourse to anything primordial which would prove modernity *altogether* wrong, to which, after all, it belongs.' For Habermas, Adorno was, of the two of them, the better acquainted with the philosophical tradition and the demands of dialectical thought and the one who, 'faced with a Benjamin who collected and arranged quotations, insisted on the theoretical penetration of the material, while at the same time de-theologizing the speculative thought-provoking impulses he received from it, in order to . . . construct a negativistic philosophy of history out of them' (emphasis in the original).

21 See Neumann (1996), *Uwe Johnson*, pp. 661f. Karl Heinz Janßen, 'Walter Benjamin 80 – Eine würdige Geburtstagsfeier in Frankfurt', *Die Zeit*, 7 July 1972.

22 Habermas (2010), 'Kultur des Gegenwartssinns' [A culture of sense for the contemporary], *Du: Die Zeitschrift der Kultur*, no. 803, January/February, pp. 36–9.

23 Regarding the notion of an aesthetic reconciliation of man and nature, Habermas takes up ideas from Walter Benjamin, namely that art is

> the resource for the satisfaction, albeit only virtual, of the needs which become, so to speak, illegal within the material process of bourgeois society: what I have in mind is the need for a mimetic relationship with nature, external nature as well as that of one's own life; the need for living together in solidarity, more generally for the happiness of experiencing communication which is free from the imperatives of purposive rationality, and which leaves a playful space for the imagination as well as for spontaneity in one's actions. (Habermas (1973), *Kultur und Kritik*, p. 318)

24 Habermas (1972), 'Bewußtmachende oder rettende Kritik – die Aktualität Walter Benjamins', pp. 219f.; Habermas (2012), 'Consciousness-Raising or Rescuing Critique', in *Philosophical-Political Profiles*, pp. 129–64; here: p. 158.

25 Habermas (1972), 'Bewußtmachende oder rettende Kritik – die Aktualität Walter Benjamins', p. 220; Habermas (2012), 'Consciousness-Raising or Rescuing Critique', p. 158.

26 Letter from Habermas to Unseld, 27 January 1973, Bestand Na 60, Vorlass Jürgen Habermas, Archivzentrum der Universitätsbibliothek J. C. Senckenberg, Frankfurt am Main. Unseld offered to provide the loan, but in the end Habermas did not make use of the offer.

27 The reference is to the manuscript of Habermas's speech on the occasion of receiving the Kultureller Ehrenpreis der Stadt München [cultural prize of honour of the city of Munich] on 22 January 2013. The title of the speech is 'Aus der nahen Entfernung' [From a close distance], and it can be found in Habermas (2013), *Im Sog der Technokratie*, pp. 189–93. [The speech is omitted from the English edition.]

28 The historian Ariane Leendertz has researched in detail the eventful development of Starnberg's Max Planck Institute for the Study of Living Conditions in the Scientific and Technical World, evaluating numerous documents, such as correspondence, working papers, memoranda and protocols in the institute's archive. See Leendertz (2010), *Die pragmatische Wende*, esp. pp. 14–50. See also the retrospective by, a former collaborator from the Weizsäcker group, Michael Drieschner (1996), 'Die Verantwortung der Wissenschaft'.

29 Michael Haller, 'Habermas in Starnberg', *National-Zeitung Basel*, 19 January 1974.

30 Habermas (1968), *Technik und Wissenschaft als 'Ideologie'*, p. 114.

31 Habermas (1981), *Kleine politische Schriften I–IV*, pp. 527f.

32 Habermas ([1973] 1988), *Legitimation Crisis*, p. xxv (trans. modified).

33 Ibid., p. 73.

34 Ibid., p. 47.

35 In 2013, with reference to the acute problems of the global economy of an interdependent world society and the 'transformation of the tax state into the debt state', Habermas wrote, in the *Blätter für deutsche und internationale Politik*:

> Its starting point is a justified critique of the crisis theory that Claus Offe and I developed in the early 1970s. Inspired by the Keynesian optimism concerning government regulation that was prevalent at the time, we assumed that the economic crisis potentials mastered by politics would be *diverted* into conflicting demands on an overstrained governmental apparatus and into 'cultural contradictions of capitalism' (as Daniel Bell would put it a couple of years later), and that they would *find expression* in a legitimation crisis. Today, we are not (yet?) experiencing a legitimation crisis, but we are witnessing a palpable economic crisis.

> This crisis, Habermas wrote, came about not despite but because of the policies of neo-liberal reform, in the course of which 'corporatist negotiation constraints were relaxed and the markets deregulated'. Habermas ([2013] 2015), 'Democracy or Capitalism? The Abject Spectacle of a Capitalistic World Society Fragmented along National Lines', in *The Lure of Technocracy*, pp. 85–104; here: pp. 85f. (emphases in the original).

36 Habermas ([1973] 1988), *Legitimation Crisis*, p. 70; emphasis in the original.

37 Habermas and Hennis opened the debate at the congress of political scientists in Duisburg in the autumn of 1975. See Kielmansegg (1976), *Legitimationsprobleme politischer Systeme*; Schlak and Hacke (2008), 'Der Staat in Gefahr'.

38 Hennis (1976), 'Legitimität'. See also Hennis (2000), *Politikwissenschaft und politisches Denken*, pp. 250–88.

39 Hennis criticized Habermas's conception of democracy in the strongest terms as unrealistic because it aimed at self-determination and participa-

tion. 'The idea', Hennis wrote, quoting Habermas, 'that "all politically consequential decisions" are to be subjected to democratic will-formation is . . . simplistic – bad arm-chair philosophy – and, flowing from the pen of an author as influential as Habermas, simply irresponsible.' Hennis (1976), 'Legitimität', p. 33.

40 Ibid., p. 16.

41 Ibid., p. 28.

42 Habermas did not defend his theses on the dynamics of late capitalist crises only against Hennis. At the centre of a second controversy in the mid-1970s, instigated mainly by Wolfgang Fach, were questions regarding the plausibility of Habermas's model for the testing and the satisfaction of validity claims in practical discourses, rather than questions regarding the theory of capitalism and crises. See Habermas (1976), *Zur Rekonstruktion des Historischen Materialismus*, pp. 329ff.; Fach (1974), 'Diskurs und Herrschaft – Überlegungen zu Habermas' Legitimationslogik'; Fach and Degen (1978), *Politische Legitimität*.

43 Habermas (1991), *'Legitimation Problems in the Modern State'*, p.185.

44 Ibid., p. 197.

45 Von Weizsäcker (1981), *Der bedrohte Friede*, pp. 472f.

46 Conversation with Claus Offe (18 May 2009). Conversation with Günter Frankenberg (11 May 2011).

47 See Habermas (1976), *Zur Rekonstruktion des Historischen Materialismus*, pp. 49–62.

48 Habermas (1993), 'Remarks on the Development of Max Horkheimer's Work'; German original in Schmidt and Altwicker (1986), *Max Horkheimer heute*, pp. 163–80, and in Habermas (1991), *Texte und Kontexte*, pp. 91–109.

49 Habermas (1981), *Kleine Politische Schriften I–IV*, p. 420.

50 The 'Radikalenerlass' was a common resolution passed in January 1972 by all heads of government of the federal states and the chancellor, Willy Brandt. Brandt later called it a mistake. See Brandt (1986), *'. . . wir sind nicht zu Helden geboren'*.

51 Letter from Habermas to Hans Maier, 15 June 1973, Bestand Na 60, Vorlass Jürgen Habermas, Archivzentrum der Universitätsbibliothek J. C. Senckenberg, Frankfurt am Main.

52 Habermas, '". . . And to Define America, her Athletic Democracy"': In Memory of Richard Rorty', pp. 3f.

53 '"Sie werden nicht schweigen können": Ein Briefwechsel zwischen J. H. and W. R. Beyer', *Die Zeit*, 13 September 1974, p. 22.

54 The work of this group is documented in Döbert et al. (1977), *Entwicklung des Ichs*; see esp. pp. 9–30 ('Moralentwicklung und Ich-Identität'). Habermas (1973), 'Notizen zum Begriff der Rollenkompetenz', in *Kultur und Kritik*, pp. 195–231. See also the papers produced in connection with two seminars which Habermas taught on 'Soziologie der Jugendkriminalität' [Sociology of juvenile delinquency] (winter term 1968–9) and on 'Totale Institutionen' [Total institutions] (summer term 1969): Habermas Arbeitskreis (1972), *Jugendkriminalität und Totale Institutionen*.

55 Among the titles published by Suhrkamp are Böhme et al. (1978), *Die gesellschaftliche Orientierung des wissenschaftlichen Fortschritts*; Guldimann et al. (1978), *Sozialpolitik als soziale Kontrolle*; Ronge (1979), *Bankenpolitik im Spätkapitalismus*; and Fay et al. (1980), *Strukturveränderungen in der kapitalistischen Weltwirtschaft*.

56 Habermas (1976), *Zur Rekonstruktion des Historischen Materialismus*, p. 44.

The Quotation is from the last paragraph of the introductory 'Historischer Materialismus und die Entwicklung normatives Strukturen', which has been omitted from the English translation; 'Historical Materialism and the Development of Normative Structures', in *Communication and the Evolution of Society*, pp. 95–129.

57 Ibid., p. 248; emphasis in the original.

58 Habermas (1991) 'Toward a Reconstruction of Historical Materialism', p.148.

59 Habermas (1984), 'Notizen zur Entwicklung der Interaktionskompetenz' [Some notes on the development of interactive competence], in *Vorstudien und Ergänzungen zur Theorie des kommunikativen Handelns*, pp. 187–225; here: p. 192. 'Following on from Piaget', Habermas writes in these fragmentary notes, presented as a working paper at Starnberg, 'I imagine that these general structures of the capacity for knowledge, language and action form in the course of a subject's simultaneously constructive and adaptive engagement with its environment, where this environment is differentiated into *external nature, language* and *society*' (pp. 191f.; emphasis in the original).

60 Habermas (1991), *'Toward a Reconstruction of Historical Materialism'*, p. 177.

61 Habermas (1976), *Zur Rekonstruktion des Historischen Materialismus*, p. 235; emphasis in the original.

62 Habermas (1991) 'Historical Materialism and the Development of Normative Structures', p. 120.

63 *Der Spiegel*, 19 September 1977, pp. 227–39.

64 Notes on a personal conversation.

65 Frisch (1986), *Gesammelte Werke in zeitlicher Folge*, vol. 6, p. 595.

66 Habermas (1981), *Kleine Politische Schriften I–IV*, pp. 340–63.

67 Ibid., p. 333.

68 Wehler (2008), *Deutsche Gesellschaftsgeschichte, 1949–1990*, p. 319. See also Herles (2008), *Neurose D*, pp. 158ff.

69 Kraushaar (2006), 'Der nichterklärte Ausnahmezustand', p. 1023.

70 Ibid., p. 1021.

71 Habermas (1985), *Die neue Unübersichtlichkeit*, pp. 180f. [my translation; see 'The Dialectics of Rationalization', p. 106].

72 Habermas (1990), *Die nachholende Revolution*, p. 22.

73 See Bering (2010), *Die Epoche der Intellektuellen*, pp. 406–44. [The German expletives 'Pinscher', 'Ratten' and 'Schmeißfliegen' are meant to evoke the idea of small, low, noisy and worthless creatures.]

74 The undeclared state of emergency of the executive was staged on the political proscenium, accompanied by a

> symbolic civil war in which the political consequences of the National Socialist heritage for the Federal Republic were at present the subject of relentless debate. As images of history, anti-fascism and anti-totalitarianism were ultimately mutually exclusive. For the anti-fascists, the political and economic functional elites of the Federal Republic were continuous with the National Socialist past; and, similarly, within the context of the anti-totalitarian worldview, the terrorists of the RAF were 'Hitler's children' – i.e., the contemporary representatives of National Socialist history. This irreconcilable dispute was fought out in many social areas. (Dubiel (1999), *Niemand ist frei von der Geschichte*, pp. 147f.)

See also Müller (2013), *Das demokratische Zeitalter*, pp. 289–339, especially pp. 338f.

75 Bestand Na 60, Vorlass Jürgen Habermas, Archivzentrum der Universitätsbibliothek J. C. Senckenberg, Frankfurt am Main.

76 On 2 May 1977, *Der Spiegel* reported that every other citizen in the Federal Republic was in favour of reintroducing the death penalty; 35,000 people signed a petition demanding a reintroduction. See Dubiel (1999), *Niemand ist frei von der Geschichte*, pp. 145–82.

77 Habermas (1981), *Kleine Politische Schriften I–IV*, p. 372.

78 Ibid., p. 379.

79 Ibid., pp. 378f.; emphasis in the original.

80 Ibid., p. 388.

81 Quoted after ibid., p. 389.

82 Ibid., p. 393.

83 See Kailitz (2007), *Von den Worten zu den Waffen*, pp. 190ff., especially p. 199.

84 Habermas (1981), *Kleine Politische Schriften I–IV*, p. 402.

85 Bestand Na 60, Vorlass Jürgen Habermas, Archivzentrum der Universitätsbibliothek J. C. Senckenberg, Frankfurt am Main.

86 See Bering (2010), *Die Epoche der Intellektuellen*, pp. 406–44.

87 *Neue Rundschau*, 89 (1978), pp. 142–7.

88 *Die Zeit*, 13 October 1978. See Habermas (1981), *Kleine Politische Schriften I–IV*, pp. 367–406. Habermas, among others, had written a letter to the editorial office of *Die Zeit* in support of Raddatz, who had been sacked from his post for a misquotation in an article on the Frankfurt Book Fair. See Raddatz (2010), *Tagebücher 1982–2001*, pp. 93f.

89 *Die Zeit*, 13 October 1978.

90 See Brückner (1977), *Die Mescalero-Affäre*. In 2001, the author of the 'obituary', a schoolteacher of German by the name of Klaus Hülbrock, revealed his identity in *Die Tageszeitung*.

91 Habermas (1981), *Kleine Politische Schriften I–IV*, p. 442. See also Krovoza et al. (1981), *Zum Beispiel Peter Brückner*, pp. 13f.; Spiller (2006), 'Der Sympathisant als Staatsfeind'.

92 Frisch (1986), *Gesammelte Werke in zeitlicher Folge*, vol. 7, p. 37.

93 Bestand Na 60, Vorlass Jürgen Habermas, Archivzentrum der Universitätsbibliothek J. C. Senckenberg, Frankfurt am Main.

94 See Habermas (2008), 'Ich bin alt aber nicht fromm geworden' [I have grown old but not pious], in Funken (2008), *Über Habermas*, pp. 181 and 188.

95 Habermas et al. (1978), *Gespräche mit Herbert Marcuse*, p. 32.

96 Ibid., p. 37.

97 *Deutsche Zeitung*, 3 September 1975.

98 Letter to the editor, *Deutsche Zeitung*, 24 October 1975.

99 *Die Zeit*, 3 December 1977.

100 'Letter to Tito', *New York Review of Books*, 6 February 1975.

101 Habermas (2007), 'Begegnungen mit Gershom Scholem', p. 15.

102 See Habermas ([1981] 2012), 'Gershom Scholem: The Torah in Disguise', in *Philosophical-Political Profiles*, pp. 199–211.

103 Ibid., p. 379 (trans. modified).

104 Habermas, 'Wo bleiben die Liberalen?', *Die Zeit*, 5 May 1978.

105 Letter dated 11 May 1978, Bestand Na 60, Vorlass Jürgen Habermas, Archivzentrum der Universitätsbibliothek J. C. Senckenberg, Frankfurt am Main.

106 *Merkur*, no. 374, July 1979, pp. 648–65. An extended version can be found in Bonß and Honneth (1982), *Sozialforschung als Kritik*, pp. 87–126.

107 Bestand Na 60, Vorlass Jürgen Habermas, Archivzentrum der Universitätsbibliothek J. C. Senckenberg, Frankfurt am Main.

108 Habermas (1989), 'Über Titel, Texte und Termine oder wie man den Zeitgeist reflektiert' [On titles, texts and dates, or: how to reflect the spirit of the age], in Habermas and Pehle (1989), *Der Autor, der nicht schreibt* [The author that does not write], p. 4.

109 Letter dated 5 April 1979, Bestand Peter Suhrkamp Stiftung, Frankfurt am Main, Korrespondenz Siegfried Unseld, Deutsches Literaturarchiv Marbach.

110 See Michalzik (2002), *Unseld*, pp. 251f.

111 Letters from Habermas to Unseld, dated 5 April, 11 October and 19 December 1979, Bestand Peter Suhrkamp Stiftung, Frankfurt am Main, Korrespondenz Siegfried Unseld, Deutsches Literaturarchiv Marbach.

112 Letter dated 5 April 1979, ibid.

113 Letter dated 15 October 1979, ibid.

114 Letter dated 19 December 1979, ibid.

115 Letters dated 17 October and 3 December 1979, ibid.

116 Habermas (2007), 'Begegnungen mit Gershom Scholem', p. 9. Unseld mentions the birthday party in his travel diary in an entry on the period from 15 to 19 June 1979: 'Friendly atmosphere, dominated by the "children", but the celebration lacks a focus. Wherever Scholem was, there was the centre – he usurped the conversation; at one point, I tried to channel this: in a circle – Marcuse, Walser, Hamm, Baumgart – everyone told the story of his first publication.' About the reception in the Hotel Bayerischer Hof the following day, he writes: 'It was a very pleasant event. I expressed to Jürgen Habermas that it had been arranged in order to ease the burden on Ute Habermas and assured him of the Suhrkamp publishing house as his production base for as long as he wanted it and however he wanted it. He understood my allusion.' Unseld (2010), *Reiseberichte*, pp. 35f.

117 Habermas (2007), 'Begegnungen mit Gershom Scholem', p. 9.

118 Habermas (1979), *Stichworte zur 'Geistigen Situation der Zeit*, vol. 1, p. 9.

119 Habermas (1981), *Kleine politische Schriften I–IV*, p. 426.

120 Habermas (1979), *Stichworte zur 'Geistigen Situation der Zeit*, vol. 1, pp. 22–3; emphasis in the original.

121 See *Die Zeit*, 16 April 1976, and *Der Spiegel*, 5 April 1976, pp. 207f.

122 My remarks are based on personal conversations with Claus Offe and Günter Frankenberg, both academic members of the institute. Frankenberg, who held a doctorate in law, also represented Habermas's section at the institutional board from 1974 onwards.

123 There is no evidence in support of Dirk Baecker's claim in the *Luhmann-Handbuch* that Niklas Luhmann was considered as a co-director of the Starnberg Institute. See Dirk Baecker (2012), 'Niklas Luhmann, der Werdegang', pp. 1f.

124 See 'Auf die Qualität kommt es an: Warum das Starnberger Institut nicht weitergeführt wird – Ein Gespräch mit Reimar Lüst', *Die Zeit*, 9 May 1980. In this conversation, Lüst clarifies as follows:

> Maybe I should set one thing straight. There is again and again public talk about the closure of the Starnberg Institute, in particular by Mr Picht. However, Mr von Weizsäcker's area is at issue. This area will not be continued. The area which Mr Habermas introduced to Starnberg, however, will be continued and expanded. Thus, in effect, we will create a

new institute for the social sciences which makes a part of the programme of the Max Planck Institute visible to the outside world. This, in turn, is not meant to be a conventional institute for social sciences of the type that already exists at many universities, but is meant to complement the research done at universities.

125 See Leendertz (2010), *Die pragmatische Wende*, pp. 29–44.
126 *Rheinischer Merkur*, 25 January 1980, p. 28.
127 Letter from Habermas to von Weizsäcker, 29 January 1981, Bestand Na 60, Vorlass Jürgen Habermas, Archivzentrum der Universitätsbibliothek J. C. Senckenberg, Frankfurt am Main.
128 Leendertz (2010), *Die pragmatische Wende*, pp. 46f.
129 *Die Zeit*, 8 May 1981, p. 42.
130 Baumgart (2003), *Ein Leben in Deutschland 1929–2003*, pp. 324ff.
131 Ibid., p. 326. In a letter to Habermas, dated 1 February 1992, Baumgart regretted that ten years of friendship had been gambled away 'carelessly and insensitively'. He acknowledged his part 'in this venomous story'. On 4 February 1992, Habermas replied: 'Regarding the disagreeable status quo of our relationship, I feel similar sentiments to yours. After such a long time it is not possible to reconstitute anything, but maybe one might return to a more normal relation.' Bestand Na 60, Vorlass Jürgen Habermas, Archivzentrum der Universitätsbibliothek J. C. Senckenberg, Frankfurt am Main.
132 Weizsäcker (2002), *Lieber Freund! Lieber Gegner!*, p. 220.
133 Habermas in an interview with Karl-Siegbert Rehberg (2010), MS.
134 Peter Iden (1980), 'Alles Linke auf seine Kappe nehmen: Ein Gespräch mit Jürgen Habermas – aus Anlaß seiner Auszeichnung mit dem Adorno-Preis', *Frankfurter Rundschau*, 11 September 1980.
135 Tilman Reitz takes the opposite view regarding the existence of a 'Habermas School': 'Kreise mit schwachen Meistern', in Kroll and Reitz (2013), *Intellektuelle in der Bundesrepublik Deutschland*, pp. 173f.

Part III Science and Commitment

1 Jürgen Habermas, '. . .And to define America, her athletic Democracy: In Memory of Richard Rorty', in: *Europe. The Faltering Project*, trans. by Ciara Cronin, Polity (Cambridge) 2009, pp. 3–16; here: p. 13. [The quotation is taken from the following passage: 'Private edification is of course just one half of the business of philosophical communication. Public commitment is the other, even more important task of philosophy.']

Chapter 7 Genius Loci

1 Habermas (2009), speech on 17 June 2009 at the opening of the exhibition: '. . . die Lava des Gedankens im Fluss' [The lava of thought in flow. . .], p. 1.
2 Theunissen (1981), *Kritische Theorie der Gesellschaft*, pp. 41–57; here: pp. 42f., 47 and 49ff.
3 Habermas ([1990] 1997), 'Modernity: An Unfinished Project', p. 53. First published in German in *Die Zeit*, 19 September 1980.
4 Ibid., pp. 54 and 53.
5 Ibid., p. 54.

6 'Vier Jungkonservative beim Projektleiter der Moderne' [Four young conservatives visit the manager of the modernity project], *Die Tageszeitung*, 3
October 1980, pp. 8f.
7 In another interview, Habermas spoke about socialism in more detail:

> Socialism meant an attempt, wherever possible a fallibilistic attempt,
> aiming at self-correction, at least to reduce the suffering, injustice and
> avoidable repression that can be identified by collective efforts – i.e., to
> solve problems – which are anyway dealt with on a continuous basis –
> from a specific perspective. In abstract terms, this perspective is easily
> identified: namely, it aims to arrest the destruction of life-forms based on
> solidarity and to create new forms of solidarity – that is, life-forms allow-
> ing for expressive behaviour, offering a flexible space of moral-practical
> orientations, that is to say life-forms which offer a context within which
> one's own identity and that of others can develop in less problematic and
> less damaging ways. This perspective has emerged from the self-criticism
> of today's dominant life-form which has established itself in the course of
> capitalist modernization. Socialism, therefore, first and foremost, means
> knowing what one does not want, what one wants to get rid of: a life-
> form in which all questions pertaining to life keep being redefined until
> they fit into the pattern of abstract labour prescribed by industry, profit-
> orientation, bureaucracy and domination. (Hans Ulrich Reck, 'Über die
> Vernunft des Wollens', *Basler Magazin*, 7 January 1984)

8 Habermas, 'Ein wahrhaftiger Sozialist', *Die Zeit*, 4 January 1980;
Habermas (1981), *Kleine Politische Schriften I–IV*, pp. 304–7. In a letter
dated 7 July 1992, Rudi Dutschke's son, Hosea-Che, who was studying
political science at the University of Aarhus at the time, asked Habermas
for a contribution to a volume which was to show his father's 'life in the
mirror of the secret services'. On 20 July 1992, Habermas declined for
'objective' and 'personal' reasons:

> Objectively, it would probably be preferable to ask someone who is better
> acquainted with the life of your father than I am. . . . The personal reason
> is a rather trivial one. Because of writing a book, I have to work my way
> down such a long list of overdue commitments that before the end of next
> year I would not be able to find the time to engross myself in these matters,
> which are alien to me [i.e., the penetration of the private life by the secret
> services, S. M.-D.]. (Bestand Vorlass Habermas)

9 Habermas (1980), 'Psychic Thermidor and the Rebirth of Rebellious
Subjectivity', p. 83.
10 The title of the paper he gave at the conference, organized by Robert Bellah,
Norma Haan and Paul Rabinow, was 'Reconstruction and Interpretation
in the Social Sciences'. It can be found in Habermas ([1983] 1990), *Moral
Consciousness and Communicative Action*, pp. 21–42; here: p. 30. The
topic of his opening lecture at the 20th meeting of the German Society for
Sociology in September 1980 in Bremen was 'Konstruktionsprobleme der
Gesellschaftstheorie' [Problems of construction in social theory].
11 Habermas (1986), 'The Dialectics of Rationalization', pp.104 and 108. The
interview was partly conducted by correspondence.
12 Ibid., p. 100 (trans. modified).

13 Ibid., p. 115 (trans. modified).
14 Ibid., p. 126.
15 Ibid., p. 129.
16 Habermas ([1984] 2003), *On the Pragmatics of Social Interaction*, pp. 85f.
17 Letter, from Habermas to Wehler, 1 July 1982, Bestand Na 60, Vorlass Jürgen Habermas, Archivzentrum der Universitätsbibliothek J. C. Senckenberg, Frankfurt am Main.
18 Habermas ([1981] 1987), *The Theory of Communicative Action*, vol. 2, p. 397.
19 Habermas ([1981] 1986), *The Theory of Communicative Action*, vol. 1, p. xli.
20 Habermas ([1999] 2003), *Truth and Justification*, p. 1.
21 Habermas ([1981] 1986), *The Theory of Communicative Action*, vol. 1, p. 392.
22 I discuss Habermas's concept of validity claims on pp. 159ff. and pp. 214ff.
23 Habermas ([1981] 1986), *The Theory of Communicative Action*, vol. 1, p. 289; emphases in the original (trans. modified).
24 Ibid., p. 95.
25 Ibid., p. 101; emphasis in the original.
26 Habermas ([1981] 1987), *The Theory of Communicative Action*, vol. 2, p. 126.
27 Ibid., pp. 122f.; emphasis in the original.
28 Ibid., p. 145.
29 Ibid., p. 160; emphasis in the original.
30 Ibid., p. 152; emphases in the original.
31 Ibid., p. 153.
32 See ibid., pp. 305 and 318.
33 Ibid., p. 155.
34 Letter from Habermas to Brunkhorst, 27 October 1982, Bestand Na 60, Vorlass Jürgen Habermas, Archivzentrum der Universitätsbibliothek J. C. Senckenberg, Frankfurt am Main.
35 The letters to Wellmer and Jaeggi are in Bestand Na 60, ibid.
36 Habermas ([1983] 1990), *Moral Consciousness and Communicative Action*, p. 14. [The English translation omits the qualification preceding 'philosophical idea', 'wenn das Wort überhaupt einen Sinn hat': 'if the expression is meaningful at all'.]
37 Habermas (2011), 'Er zeigt auf unseren blinden Fleck' [He points at our blind spot], *Frankfurter Allgemeine Zeitung*, 16 February 2011.
38 Ibid.
39 Habermas (2007), 'Begegnungen mit Gershom Scholem', p. 16. See also Habermas (1982), 'Tod in Jerusalem: Am Grabe von Gershom Scholem'.
40 Habermas, 'In memoriam Alexander Mitscherlich', p. 1061.
41 Habermas (1991), *Texte und Kontexte*, p. 175.
42 See Mohal (1983), 'Vernunftspiel über die Grenzen', *Süddeutsche Zeitung*, 22 August 1983; Peeters (2013), *Derrida: A Biography*, pp. 570ff.
43 Universitätsarchiv Frankfurt am Main, Abt. 14, Nr. 1201, Bl. 68.
44 I refer here to the 'Contract of employment between the county of Hesse, represented by its minister for culture, and Prof. Dr Jürgen Habermas', dated 27 September 1982, Universitätsarchiv Frankfurt am Main, Abt. 14. [In Germany, you become a civil servant for life; hence the relevance of this clause.]
45 Habermas (1985), *Die Neue Unübersichtlichkeit*, p. 211.

46 Against the French philosophers, Habermas maintains that the project
   of modernity is threatened by failure not because of a surfeit, but because
   of a lack, of reason. In his lectures, he defends the project of modernity
   as founded by Kant and conceptually defined by the young Hegel. The
   phalanx of detractors of modernity, he says, find it hard to accept what
   is actually modern about modernity – i.e., the fact that society can no
   longer take the standards for its orientations from the example of previous
   epochs – but must create its normativity out of itself. The way in which this
   might be done is shown by the paradigm of understanding [*Verständigung*]
   which depends on the intersubjective relationships between subjects who
   recognize each other. Eight years later, Habermas returned to the question
   of the reception of Heidegger's and Adorno's critiques of reason in France
   in an interview with Roger-Pol Droit and Jacques Poulin for *Le Monde*. As
   could be expected, he differentiated between the two philosophers:

   > I would not mention Adorno and Heidegger in the same breath. Of course,
   > both of them dramatize their diagnoses of our time by means of a com-
   > prehensive historical perspective of decline. . . . However, Adorno knew
   > that even the most radical critique of reason is dependent on the power
   > of negation, which derives from reason itself. Unlike Heidegger, he never
   > became an opponent of Enlightenment.

   And he continued:

   > At present a rather undialectical critique of Enlightenment is dominant,
   > from which we cannot learn very much. When Adorno and Horkheimer
   > spoke of 'instrumental reason', they did not mean that reason could
   > simply be equated with a self-asserting subject's objectivizing act of
   > understanding. The point they were trying to make was that a form of
   > understanding that has ballooned into a totality is usurping the place that
   > properly belongs to reason.

   Habermas's conclusion was: 'There is neither a higher, nor a lower reason
   to which we can appeal, only a procedurally sobering reason – a reason
   that proceeds solely on sufficient grounds; a reason that also puts itself on
   trial. That is what Kant meant: the critique of reason is the work of reason
   itself.' Habermas (1998), 'French Views, French Anxieties: An Interview
   with *Le Monde*', pp. 59ff. (trans. modified).
47 See Geuss (1987), 'Reviewed Works: *Der philosophische Diskurs der
   Moderne* by Jürgen Habermas'; Ingram (2003), 'Foucault and Habermas';
   Ostowoch (1987), 'Der philosophische Diskurs der Moderne', pp. 631f.
48 Habermas (1986), 'The Dialectics of Rationalization', p. 129.
49 Habermas ([1985] 1987), *The Philosophical Discourse of Modernity*, pp.
   185–210.
50 Ibid., p. 208.
51 Ibid.
52 Ibid., p. 209.
53 See Habermas (1981), *Kleine Politische Schriften I–IV*, pp. 340–63.
54 'An utterance can be poetic to the extent that it is directed to the linguistic medium itself, to its own linguistic form.' Habermas holds that the
   '*aestheticizing of language . . . is purchased with the twofold denial of the
   proper senses of normal and poetic discourse.*' Habermas ([1985] 1987),

The Philosophical Discourse of Modernity, pp. 200 and 205; emphasis in the original. See Gottfried Gabriel, 'Logisches und analogisches Denken: Zum Verhältnis von wissenschaftlicher und ästhetischer Weltauffassung', in Demmerling et al. (1995), *Vernunft und Lebenpraxis*, pp. 157–74.

55 The examples in this sequence [except for 'ossuary'; *Schädelstätte*] can be found in the following texts by Habermas: *Vorstudien und Ergänzungen zur Theorie des kommunikativen Handelns* (1984), p. 489; *Moral Consciousness and Communicative Action* ([1983] 1990), p. 15 ['Sprengsatz', here translated as 'detonator']; and *The Philosophical Discourse of Modernity* ([1985] 1987), p. 117 ['Schädelstätte' here rendered as 'ossuary'] and p. 86 [Habermas uses the actual expression from the *Tractatus* 'wegwerfen', which is usually translated as 'throw away' rather than 'cast away'].

56 In cognitive acts of categorizing states of affairs, metaphors may take on various pragmatic functions. As provocations, they may initiate a dissolution of rigidified semantic schemata; they may provide a foundation for new cognitive structures and experiences; they may conceptualize new abstractions; they may linguistically objectify states of affairs which are altogether new; they may talk about states of affairs which are categorically outside of all sensual or empirical experience in analogous fashion; they may simplify complex and obscure states of affairs in the form of models. (Köller (1975), *Semiotik und Metapher*)

57 Robin Celikates argues that Habermas categorically discards rhetoric as purely a means for manipulation and persuasion. 'Rhetoric . . . from the very beginning is seen as a form of strategic action which is alien . . . to language in the proper sense. In this way, Habermas creates an abstract and artificial opposition between the speech of reason, which allegedly is free of passion and neutral, and pure rhetoric, which is always characterized by irrational emotions and partisan.' Celikates (2010), 'Habermas: Sprache, Verständigung und sprachliche Gewalt', p. 281.

58 See Müller-Doohm (2008), 'Sagen, was einem aufgeht'.

59 See Habermas (2013), *Im Sog der Technokratie*, p. 7. [In his preface to the German edition, Habermas speaks about the division between 'the "interventions" of an intellectual and the scientific work of a professor'. For the English edition (2015), he wrote a new preface, concentrating on the European Union: *The Lure of Technocracy*, pp. vii–xi.

60 According to Habermas, erudite language [*Bildungssprache*] is distinguished 'from everyday language by the discipline in written expression and by a more differentiated vocabulary, which also includes technical words. On the other hand, it is distinct from professional languages by being principally open to everyone who is able to acquire a certain knowledge and orientation [*Orientierungswissen*] by means of a general education at school.' Habermas (1981), *Kleine Politische Schriften I–IV*, p. 345.

61 Habermas ([2011] 2012), *The Crisis of the European Union*, p. 52; Habermas ([2001] 2003), *The Future of Human Nature*, *passim*; Habermas ([2008] 2010), 'An Awareness of What is Missing' [Ein Bewußtsein von dem, was fehlt], in Reder and Schmidt, *An Awareness of What is Missing*, pp. 15–23.

62 My claim is based on verbal communication with Axel Honneth. See also Honneth (2008), 'Wie man sich einen Professor vorstellt'.

63 Jürgen Habermas, verbal communication.

64 Marco Meier in *Die Weltwoche*, 3 November 1983. Meier's article details the criticisms of the Adorno conference that were published in *Der Pflasterstrand*. On 17 June 1983, Habermas had published a review of Peter Sloterdijk's *Critique of Cynical Reason* in the alternative newspaper. In it, he praised the 'literary brilliance with which philosophical essayism and analysis of the contemporary times are combined'. Sloterdijk, he says, is not a neo-conservative because he insists on the reflective power of enlightenment on which the '68 generation had placed their hopes. However, he holds that the author does not succeed in overcoming subject-based philosophy and does no more than 'gesture at an exit from it', just as the Cynic philosopher – and this is what Sloterdijk considers himself to be – as a matter of principle exits 'from the communicative community of those practising reason'. Habermas (1983), 'Sloterdijk zwischen Heine und Heidegger'.

65 'Konservative Politik, Arbeit, Sozialismus und Utopie heute: Hans Ulrich Reck sprach am 2 April 1983 in Starnberg mit Jürgen Habermas' [Conservative politics, labour, socialism, and utopia today: Hans Ulrich Reck in conversation with Jürgen Habermas in Starnberg on 2 April 19983], *Basler Magazin*, 7 March 1984.

66 Ibid.

67 Habermas (1985), *Die Neue Unübersichtlichkeit*, p. 84.

68 Habermas, 'Ungehorsam mit Augenmaß: Der Rechtsstaat braucht des Bürgers Mißtrauen', *Die Zeit*, 23 September 1983, p. 9. See also the article by Kurt Reumann, 'Schon vor 15 Jahren hielt Jürgen Habermas Regelverletzungen für geeignet: Eine Diskussion über zivilen Ungehorsam', *Frankfurter Allgemeine Zeitung*, 24 September 1983.

69 Habermas (1985), *Die neue Unübersichtlichkeit*, p. 137.

70 Habermas (1989) 'Taking Aim at the Heart of the Present: On Foucault's Lecture on Kant's What is Enlightenment?', p. 176.

71 Thomas Biebricher (2005) provides an instructive comparison of their theories in his *Selbstkritik der Moderne*.

72 Habermas ([1985] 1986), 'The New Obscurity', p. 16.

73 See Honneth and Wellmer (1986), *Die Frankfurter Schule und die Folgen*.

74 See Mehring (2014), *Carl Schmitt: A Biography*, p. 291 [for the quotation, see Kennedy (1986), 'Carl Schmitt und die "Frankfurter Schule"', p. 380].

75 Kennedy (1986), 'Carl Schmitt und die "Frankfurter Schule"', p. 402.

76 See Habermas (1985), *Die neue Unübersichtlichkeit*, pp. 79ff.

77 See Kennedy (1986), 'Carl Schmitt und die "Frankfurter Schule"', p. 415.

78 Ibid., p. 416.

79 Lindner, 'Philosophie ohne Pathos', *Süddeutsche Zeitung*, 29–30 December 1984, p. 15.

80 Söllner (1986), 'Jenseits von Carl Schmitt', pp. 517ff.

81 Jay (1987), 'Les extrêmes ne se touchent pas', pp. 553f. See also Becker (1994), *Die Parlamentarismuskritik bei Carl Schmitt und Jürgen Habermas*, pp. 132ff. Becker's comparison reaches the conclusion that the analyses of parliamentarism in the *Structural Transformation of the Public Sphere* are in part influenced by Schmitt's critique and that of his disciples Ernst Forsthoff and Werner Weber. However, in contrast to Kennedy's claim, he sees no commonalities between Habermas's and Schmitt's understandings of democracy. 'Their divergent concepts of the public sphere demonstrate their different intellectual attitudes [*die unterschiedliche Geisteshaltung*].' Becker (1994), p. 161; see also pp. 142ff.

82 Habermas's review appeared in *The Times Literary Supplement* on 26
   September 1986, while Kennedy's letter appeared on 31 October 1986. See
   Specter (2010), *Habermas: An Intellectual Biography*, pp. 179ff.
83 Habermas (1987), *Eine Art Schadensabwicklung*, p. 17.
84 Ibid., p. 50.

Chapter 8 New Projects

1 In the preface to the third German edition of *The Theory of Communicative
  Action*, Habermas writes that the re-publication comes

> at a time when a serious reception has begun. The first reactions of resent-
> ment and incomprehension have ebbed away. Within professional circles,
> polemic and rather defensive reflexes also give way to objective engage-
> ment. The criticism so far follows lines which are not surprising, given the
> contemporary context. The philosophy of consciousness is being defended
> against the paradigm shift which has been introduced; in particular,
> the phenomenological concept of the lifeworld is defended against its
> attempted reformulation in terms of a theory of communication. Richard
> Rorty has raised objections against the claim to universalism, which a
> reconstruction of the concept of reason in the sense of communicative
> rationality must hold on to, even if it turns away from the justificatory
> fundamentalism of traditional transcendental philosophy. Against the
> procedural concept of rationality, T. McCarthy insists on an aspect
> from the Hegelian heritage by not being satisfied with the disintegration
> of reason into different rational complexes and corresponding validity
> claims. The renewed criticism of ethical formalism – i.e., the defence of
> ethical life against pure morality – also belongs in this context. (Habermas
> (1995), *Theorie des kommunikativen Handelns*, vol. 1, p. 3 [The preface is
> not part of the English edition.])

2 Habermas (1991), *Erläuterungen zur Diskursethik*, pp. 9–30. [The English
  edition, *Justification and Application. Remarks on Discourse Ethics* (1994),
  omits some of the chapters of the German edition, has one additional
  chapter, and changes the sequence of chapters.] Some of the papers
  presented at the Centre of Interdisciplinary Research can be found in
  Honneth and Joas (1986), *Kommunikatives Handeln*.
3 See Müller (1985), 'Habermas im Zentrum'. On 1 March 1987, a generally
  critical discussion of the *Theory of Communicative Action* appeared in the
  journal *Kommune: Forum für Politik, Ökonomie und Kultur* (which was
  discontinued in 2012). Here, the philosopher and politician of the Grün-
  Alternative Liste Hamburg [Green alternative list Hamburg] Willfried
  Maier criticized Habermas's concepts of nature, communication and
  politics against the backdrop of Gregory Bateson's *Mind and Nature* and
  Hannah Arendt's *The Human Condition*. He not only accused Habermas
  of ignoring the 'by now crisis-ridden relationship between society and
  nature' but also claimed that there was no way his theory might be
  applied to ecological questions. Sensuousness and corporeality, he said,
  are excluded by Habermas because of a 'thorough subjectivization of
  needs, wishes and feelings'; his concept of rationality is truncated because
  rationality is seen as something belonging exclusively to subjects and tied

up with language. Maier continues: 'Because Habermas looks only at what elevates humans above nature, and not at the same time what unites them with nature, his model of communication and of communicative action becomes incorporeal and airy. But not just that, his *lifeworld*, as a sedimentation of communicative action, also appears strangely ethereal and bottomless.' He further levelled the charge against Habermas that, inspired as he is by Luhmann's systems theory, the function of securing the conditions for social life rests exclusively with the two systems of the state and the economy. He concluded:

> The 'Theory of Communicative Action' is normative in the sense that what exists and acts must justify itself with regard to ends which are shown to be rational by way of discussion. It is a theory of the *domination* of the rational, not a theory which establishes the right of existing particularities and investigates their connections with other such particularities. It is therefore justified to confront it with a critique which suspects that there is still a secret totalitarianism of reason at work in it. (Maier (1987), 'Stimmen ohne Körper', pp. 40, 42, 48 and 56)

4 In an interview given to the philosophical journal *Hohe Luft* in May 2012, John R. Searle was critical of Habermas's theory of language. It is false, he said, to assume that the purpose of language is communicative action.

> The purpose of language is to perform speech acts. His [i.e., Habermas's, S. M.-D.] idea of communicative action consists of reaching understanding by way of rational discussion. There is a certain irony in this because Habermas grew up in the Third Reich where another theory was dominant: the 'Führungsprinzip' [*sic*!]. And that did not consist of general agreement being built from below. It consisted of leadership from above. The theory of communicative action says that we should all come together as equals – 'herrschaftsfrei' [free of domination] – and then are meant to find agreement. That is very nice. But it is not essential to language. The Third Reich had language all along: 'Ein Volk, ein Reich, ein Führer' [One people, one Reich, one Führer]. That was not communicative action in Habermas's sense. Thus, it is possible to have societies who do not believe in reaching agreement through rational discussion. (Interview with John R. Searle by Tobias Hürter and Thomas Vašek, *Hohe Luft*, 23 May 2012, pp. 73–9; here: p. 80. [In this interview, the expressions in German are preceded by '(deutsch)', indicating that Searle actually used the German expression. I here retranslate, as the English original of the interview was not available to me.]

See Searle (2010), *Making the Social World*, pp. 61f.
5 Manfred Schröder reported on this event under the heading 'Gipfeltreffen der Philosophen' [Summit of the philosophers], *Süddeutsche Zeitung*, 2 April 1987.
6 Habermas ([1988] 1992), *Postmetaphysical Thinking*, pp. 115–48; here: pp. 145f.
7 *Frankfurter Rundschau*, 11 March 1988, p. 11. [The expression 'two-thirds society' – 'Zweidrittel-Gesellschaft' – was a catchword of the 1980s, referring to a situation in which significant parts of the population are in long-term unemployment and poverty.]

8 Steven Muller, born in Hamburg in 1927, had quickly to flee from Germany after the November pogroms in 1938, as his father Werner Adolph Müller was of Jewish descent. The family emigrated to Britain, and in 1940 went from there to the USA. In 1972, Muller became the president of Johns Hopkins University in Baltimore. As a political scientist, he fostered transatlantic dialogue.

9 Habermas (1991), *Texte und Kontexte*, p. 215. In *Die Zeit*, 14 October 1988, Marion Gräfin Dönhoff [publisher of *Die Zeit*] reported on the conference under the heading 'Ob unser Geist noch weht? So übel fällt die Antwort deutscher Intellektueller nicht aus' [If our spirit still blows? The answers from German intellectuals are not all that negative'.

10 In the autumn of 1985, serious confrontations took place in the streets of Frankfurt in the wake of the death of Günter Sare. Sare, a member of the governing board of an autonomous youth centre, had been fatally wounded when he was run over by a police vehicle carrying a water cannon during a demonstration against a meeting of neo-Nazis in the Gallus community centre, the building in which the Auschwitz trials took place in 1963. Reinhard Mohr reported on the 'Turnschuh-Revolution' [trainers revolution] in the *Frankfurter Allgemeines Sonntagsblatt* of 2 February 2014. [Joschka Fischer was wearing a pair of trainers when he was sworn in as minister for the environment in the Hessian parliament and was subsequently labelled the 'Turnschuh-Minister', the 'trainers minister'.

11 I refer to a letter of 12 February 1986 from Habermas to Joschka Fischer, minister of state, Ministry for the Environment and Energy, Bestand Na 60, Vorlass Jürgen Habermas, Archivzentrum der Universitätsbibliothek J. C. Senckenberg, Frankfurt am Main.

12 Fischer (2008), 'Gründungsfigur des demokratischen Deutschland', pp. 48f.

13 See *Frankfurter Allgemeine Zeitung*, 19 January 1989.

14 Habermas (1989), 'Grenzen des Neohistorismus: Gespräch mit Jürgen Habermas', *Frankfurter Hefte*, 36(4), pp. 370–4; here: p. 370.

15 Bestand Na 60, Vorlass Jürgen Habermas, Archivzentrum der Universitätsbibliothek J. C. Senckenberg, Frankfurt am Main.

16 Habermas ([1990] 1994), *The Past as Future*, pp. 48f.

17 See Habermas (1991), *Texte und Kontexte*, pp. 84–90.

18 Ibid., pp. 86 and 90; emphases in the original. See also the conference proceedings McGuinness (1991), *'Der Löwe spricht . . . und wir können ihn nicht verstehen'* ['The lion speaks . . . and we cannot understand him'; the title is based on *Philosophical Investigations*, Part II, §327: 'If a lion could talk, we wouldn't be able to understand it.'].

19 Honneth et al. (1989), *Zwischenbetrachtungen: Im Prozeß der Aufklärung*, p. 9.

20 The script of the speech, titled 'Die Versöhnung der mit sich selbst zerfallenen Moderne' [The reconciliation of a modernity that has fallen out with itself], is kept in the archive of the Peter Suhrkamp Stiftung, Frankfurt am Main, which is now located in the Deutsches Literaturarchiv Marbach.

21 Glotz (1989), 'Im weichen Fleisch der Motive und Mentalitäten'.

22 Ibid., pp. 483f.

23 Letter from Habermas to Dahrendorf, 4 June 1989, Bestand Na 60, Vorlass Jürgen Habermas, Archivzentrum der Universitätsbibliothek J. C. Senckenberg, Frankfurt am Main.

24 Letter from the minister of the Saarland to Jürgen Habermas, 13 June 1989, ibid.
25 Letter from Habermas to Erik Cohen, 29 June 1989, Korrespondenzbestand Vorlass Habermas.
26 Here, I refer to records in the Siegfried Unseld Archiv of Suhrkamp Verlag and also to the typewritten script of the thank-you speech which is kept at the Archivzentrum der Universitätsbibliothek J. C. Senckenberg, Frankfurt am Main (Bestand Na 60, Vorlass Jürgen Habermas).
27 Scholem (1992), *Sabbatai Zwi: Der mystische Messias.*
28 *Frankfurter Rundschau*, 21 February 1992. Habermas ([1997] 2001), 'Tracing the Other of History in History: On Gershom Scholem's Sabbatai Sevi', in *The Liberating Power of Symbols*, pp. 57–65; here: p. 58.
29 Günther (2009), 'Im Umkreis von Faktizität und Geltung', pp. 58f.
30 Habermas ([1992] 1996), *Between Facts and Norms*, p. xliii.
31 See Habermas (1991), 'Schlußbericht der AG Rechtstheorie' [Final report of the working group on legal theory] (Leibniz programme), Universitätsarchiv Frankfurt am Main, Abt. 14 Nr. 1201, Bl. 217.
32 Letter to Unseld, 10 September 1992, Bestand Na 60, Vorlass Jürgen Habermas, Archivzentrum der Universitätsbibliothek J. C. Senckenberg, Frankfurt am Main.
33 Habermas ([1983] 1990), 'Discourse Ethics: Notes on a Program of Philosophical Justification', p. 93.
34 Habermas ([1992] 1996), *Between Facts and Norms*, p. 121.
35 Habermas ([2005] 2008), 'On the Architectonics of Discursive Differentiation: A Brief Response to a Major Controversy', in *Between Naturalism and Religion*, pp. 77–97; here: p. 91.
36 Habermas ([1992] 1996), *Between Facts and Norms*, pp. 124.
37 Ibid., p. 120; emphases in the original.
38 Ibid., pp. 122f.; emphases in the original.
39 Ibid., p. 107.
40 Ibid., p. 120.
41 Ibid., p. 121.
42 This model corresponds to the idea of a society which acts on itself through political means. Within this model, deliberation provides a counter-position to decisionism.
43 The quotation 'I write for the public . . .' is taken from the television documentary 'Philosophie heute: Einladung zum Diskurs' (WDR 1995). See also Habermas ([1996] 1999), *The Inclusion of the Other*, p. 175. In a letter of 30 October 2006 to the cultural editor Matthias Hoenig, Habermas explained his attitude as follows: 'Some journalists do not seem to understand that, according to my taste, I enjoy too much and not too little publicity (although I avoid television as a matter of principle). I experience the customs of media society as a burden and not as an opportunity.' Korrespondenzbestand Vorlass Habermas.
44 Broadcast on 25 June 1995 by Westdeutscher Rundfunk as part of the television series 'Philosophie heute' [Philosophy today]. [Regiert das Recht die Politik? = Does the law rule over politics? 'Habermas meets Dworkin' in English in the original.]

Chapter 9 Battles over the Politics of Ideas

1 Habermas ([2008] 2009), *Europe: The Faltering Project*, p. 5.
2 See Mannheim (1955), *Ideology and Utopia*, pp. 155ff. See also Jung (2008), 'Wächter zu sein in finsterer Nacht: Karl Mannheims denksoziologische Bestimmung des Intellektuellen'.
3 See Lepsius (1964), 'Kritik als Beruf: Zur Soziologie des Intellektuellen', p. 88; Dahrendorf (2006), *Versuchungen der Unfreiheit*; Walzer (2002), 'Die Tugenden des Augenmaßes'; Schlich (2000), *Intellektuelle im 20. Jahrhundert*.
4 See Gilcher-Holtey (1997), 'Menschenrechte oder Vaterland?', pp. 61ff. Jacob Taubes writes:

> The 'Manifesto of the intellectuals' of 1898, in the middle of the Dreyfus affair, was essentially supported by the École normal superieure, and it created the conditions for the 'Republic of professors' which represented the Third Republic during the first decades of the twentieth century. The Dreyfus affair had unambiguously divided opinion, with the forces of the *ancien régime*, the Church and the military on one side and the bearers of the revolutionary tradition and the intellectuals on the other. . . . That is the reason why the French intellectuals, to the present day, are more homogeneously standing on the left than is usually the case. (Taubes (1996), 'Die Intellektuellen und die Universität', in *Vom Kult zur Kultur*, pp. 327f.)

5 Habermas ([1986] 1987), 'Heinrich Heine und die Rolle des Intellektuellen in Deutschland', in *Eine Art Schadensabwicklung*, p. 29.
6 Ibid.
7 '"Wider den Fundamentalismus der Endlichkeit": Ein Gespräch mit Jürgen Habermas von Angela Brauer', *Neue Züricher Zeitung*, 12 June 1999.
8 Habermas (1987), *Eine Art Schadensabwicklung*, p. 28.
9 Habermas (1981), 'Die Utopie des guten Herrschers', in *Kleine Politische Schriften I–IV*, p. 327.
10 Habermas (2008), 'Ich bin alt, aber nicht fromm geworden', p. 181.
11 Letter from Habermas to Ulrich Herbert, 31 July 1999, Bestand Na 60, Vorlass Jürgen Habermas, Archivzentrum der Universitätsbibliothek J. C. Senckenberg, Frankfurt am Main.
12 Ernst Topitsch (1970), 'Machtkampf und Humanität', *Frankfurter Allgemeine Zeitung*, 28 November 1970.
13 Habermas (1981), *Kleine politische Schriften I–IV*, pp. 311–17.
14 Ibid., p. 311.
15 Ibid., p. 312.
16 Ibid., p. 316.
17 Spaemann (1972), 'Die Utopie der Herrschaftsfreiheit', p. 752.
18 Habermas (1981), *Kleine politische Schriften I–IV*, pp. 319f.
19 Ibid., p. 324.
20 Ibid., p. 320.
21 Spaemann (1977), *Zur Kritik der politischen Utopie*, pp. 104–41.
22 Ibid., p. 123.
23 On this complex, see the study by Hacke (2006), *Philosophie der Bürgerlichkeit*, pp. 106 and 109. See also Moses (2007), *German Intellectuals*

and the Nazi Past, pp. 187–218; Wehrs (2008), '"Tendenzwende" und Bildungspolitik'.

24 See pp. 188ff. above.

25 Habermas (1981), *Kleine politische Schriften I–IV*, p. 375.

26 Ibid., p. 383.

27 The exchange of letters, published in the *Süddeutsche Zeitung* of 26–7 November 1977, can also be found in Habermas (1981), *Kleine politische Schriften I–IV*, pp. 367–406; here: p. 389.

28 Ibid., p. 391.

29 Ibid., p. 403.

30 On Ritter's school in Münster, Hermann Lübbe says: 'The practical options which resulted from . . . the practical philosophy which, to the present day, people like to connect with the name of Joachim Ritter factually implied anti-Marxism. Corresponding to this, there was agreement concerning the critique of the neo-Marxist variants of Western intellectual culture, including the socialist romanticism of the Frankfurt School.' Lübbe (2004), *Modernisierungsgewinner*, pp. 58f.

31 Ernst Tugendhat (1978), 'Totalitäre Tendenz: Es wird eine Schule anvisiert, die Untertanen, nicht Bürger erzieht', *Die Zeit*, 2 June 1978.

32 *Die Zeit*, 21 July 1978. Habermas (1981), *Kleine politische Schriften I–IV*, pp. 407–10.

33 Letter from Habermas to Spaemann, 12 September 1978. Habermas is probably referring to an essay by Lübbe, titled 'Freiheit und Terror' [Freedom and terror], which was first published in *Merkur* and then in a collection of essays. See Lübbe (1978), *Praxis der Philosophie, Praktische Philosophie, Geschichtstheorie*, pp. 78–96; esp. p. 92.

34 See Hacke (2006), *Philosophie der Bürgerlichkeit*, pp. 100ff.

35 See Zöller (1980), *Aufklärung heute: Bedingungen unserer Freiheit*.

36 Ibid., pp. 448f.

37 Rüsen et al. (1988), *Die Zukunft der Aufklärung*. Habermas's presentation is titled 'Die neue Intimität zwischen Politik und Kultur' [The new intimacy between politics and culture], pp. 59–68. He sets out from the observation that politics is entering the cultural sphere and uses cultural means for the purpose of producing self-presentations.

38 This is Hermann Lübbe's conviction:

> Intellectual discussions in which the leadership in opinion within the media is gained or lost do not follow the irresistible evidence of compelling arguments at all. Rather, they trigger the formation of ideological communities [*Gesinnungskommunitäten*] whose members affirm each other publicly [in their opinions], and thus support each other, and trigger anxieties over a progressive loss of repute of one's own founding communicative tradition. (Lübbe (2004), *Modernisierungsgewinner*, p. 16)

39 Habermas (1985), *Die neue Unübersichtlichkeit*, p. 7.

40 I refer to a project supported by the German Research Foundation, and directed by myself, on 'Ideenpolitische Kontroversen in der publizistischen Öffentlichkeit'. See Hartwig Germer, Stefan Müller-Doohm and Franziska Thiele, 'Intellektuelle Deutungskämpfe im Raum publizistischer Öffentlichkeit', *Berliner Journal für Soziologie*, no. 23 (2013), pp. 511–20.

41 Ibid.

42 Bestand Na 60, Vorlass Jürgen Habermas, Archivzentrum der Universitätsbibliothek J. C. Senckenberg, Frankfurt am Main.

43 Habermas (2008), 'Ich bin alt, aber nicht fromm geworden', p. 188 ['memory politics' in English in the original].

44 'Ansprache des Bundespräsidenten Richard von Weizsäcker am 8 Mai 1985 in der Gedenkstunde im Plenarsaal des Deutschen Bundestages', web-based archive of the German parliament, available online at: www. bundespraesident.de/SharedDocs/Reden/DE/Richard-von-Weizsaecker/ Reden/1985/05/19850508_Rede.html?nn=1892504.

45 Habermas (1985), *Die neue Unübersichtlichkeit*, p. 262.

46 A detailed and systematic account of the historians' debate, in which historians were not the only participants, can be found in Steffen Kailitz (2001), *Die politische Deutungskultur im Spiegel des 'Historikerstreits'*. See also Große Kracht (2005), *Die zankende Zunft*, pp. 91ff.

47 Kraushaar (1998), *Frankfurter Schule und Studentenbewegung*, vol. 1, pp. 594–5. It should be mentioned that the Spanish author Jorge Semprún, who gave the opening talk, not only spoke about German reunification as a necessity but also called for a critical debate about Soviet communism. He adapted a dictum of Horkheimer: 'Whoever does not want to talk about Stalinism should remain silent about fascism as well.' See ibid., pp. 594f. (Horkheimer had originally said: 'Wer aber vom Kapitalismus nicht reden will, sollte auch vom Faschismus schweigen' [Whoever doesn't want to talk about capitalism should remain silent about fascism as well], in Horkheimer ([1939] 1988), 'Die Juden und Europa', in *Gesammelte Werke*, vol. 4, pp. 308f. Many of the texts from the historians' debate are collected in Knowlton and Cates (1993), *Forever in the Shadow of Hitler?* – for instance, Stürmer's 'History in a Land without History' (pp. 16–23), from which the quotation in the main text is taken (p. 16).

48 Habermas (1987), *Eine Art Schadensabwicklung*, p. 141. [This title, a collection of essays, should not be confused with the original article in *Die Zeit*, which has been translated into English: see note 50 below.]

49 Ibid., p. 13.

50 Habermas, 'A Kind of Settlement of Damages (Apologetic Tendencies)', *New German Critique*, no. 44 (1988) [special issue on the *Historikerstreit*], pp. 25–39; here: p. 39. On the term 'Verfassungspatriotismus' [constitutional patriotism], see the study by Jan-Werner Müller (2010), *Verfassungspatriotismus*.

51 Augstein et al. (1987), *'Historikerstreit'*, p. 89. [This is a collection of major contributions to the debate, with some additional rejoinders by major protagonists.]

52 Habermas expressed himself along similar lines in a longer interview published under the title 'Epilogue inédit à une querelle d'Allemands', in *L'Express*, 5 February 1988. He rejects the accusation levelled against him by Hillgruber that he wanted to dictate to the historians what they could and could not do, and he suggests that some historians might be well advised to pay more attention to their scholarly independence.

53 Letter from Habermas to Marion Gräfin von Dönhoff, 5 September 1986, Bestand Na 60, Vorlass Jürgen Habermas, Archivzentrum der Universitätsbibliothek J. C. Senckenberg, Frankfurt am Main.

54 Habermas, 'Concerning the Public Use of History', in *New German Critique*, no. 44 (1988) [special issue on the *Historikerstreit*], pp. 40–50; here: p. 47 (trans. modified). [The full German title of the article in *Die Zeit* (7 November 1988) was 'Vom öffentlichen Gebrauch der Historie: Das

offizielle Selbstverständnis der Bundesrepublik bricht auf' – 'Concerning the public use of reason: the official self-understanding of the Federal Republic begins to crack open'. The English translation omits the qualification 'in der es *unter uns* Unbeteiligte nicht geben kann', here restored in square brackets.]

55 See Kailitz (2001), *Die politische Deutungskultur im Spiegel des 'Historikerstreits'*, pp. 287ff., 294ff.; Wehler, 'Kampf um kulturelle Hegemonie: Gespräche mit Rainer Erd über Ziele und Folgen des Historikerstreits', *Frankfurter Rundschau*, 11 February 1988; Wehler (1988), *Entsorgung der deutschen Vergangenheit?*

56 Brodkorb (2011), *Singuläres Auschwitz?*

57 Flaig (2011), '"Die Habermas-Methode" und die geistige Situation ein Vierteljahrhundert danach: Skizze einer Schadensaufnahme', ibid., pp. 67–93.

58 *Frankfurter Allgemeine Zeitung*, 23 July 2011.

59 Heinrich August Winkler, 'Hellas statt Holocaust: Vergangenheit, die nicht vergehen will: Egon Flaigs wundersame Wiederbelebung des westdeutschen Geschichtsbildes der fünfziger Jahre', *Die Zeit*, 21 July 2011.

60 A further curiosity regarding this attempted resuscitation of the historians' debate, long since presumed dead, is the rumour that the article by Flaig had ended up in the *Frankfurter Allgemeine Zeitung* with the help of Lorenz Jäger, who just two months later would claim that he had been referred to by Habermas as the 'well-known right winger of the features section'. In the same breath, he publicly dissociates himself from the politics of the conservatives and all forms of right-wing populism. See *Frankfurter Allgemeine Zeitung*, 5 October 2011.

61 The work of the American historian of Eastern Europe Timothy Snyder, among others, has led to new insights into the places and geographical spaces where the intentional destruction of 14 million lives took place in Europe's twentieth century. 'Spatial turn' has become the familiar term for such research, which gives a new impetus to comparative studies in genocide. However, experts have rightly remarked that, in his book *Bloodlands*, Snyder avoids 'the pitfall of another historians' debate by speaking of an "overlapping" and an "interaction" between the Stalinist and the National Socialist terror, while, however, avoiding any relativizing comparison of the systems.' Ahlrich Meyer, 'Comeback der Totalitarismustheorie?', *Neue Züricher Zeitung*, 27 July 2011. See Snyder (2010), *Bloodlands*.

62 Habermas ([1990] 1994), *The Past as Future*, p. 44.

63 Habermas (1990), *Die nachholende Revolution*, pp. 98 and 100.

64 Herles (2008), *Neurose D*, p. 200.

65 Habermas (1990), *Die nachholende Revolution*, p. 157.

66 Habermas, 'Der DM-Nationalismus', *Die Zeit*, 30 March 1990. See also Müller (2010), *Verfassungspatriotismus*, pp. 36ff.

67 Habermas ([1990] 1994), *The Past as Future*, p. 41.

68 Habermas (1990), *Die nachholende Revolution*, p. 181.

69 Ibid., pp. 188 and 203.

70 Habermas, 'Der DM-Nationalismus', *Die Zeit*, 30 March 1990.

71 See Herles (2008), *Neurose D*, pp. 207f. The opinion polls carried out at the time, which Habermas would hardly have missed, were clear:

At the end of March, 65 per cent of the Federal Republic's citizens want to have a say in the question of unification through a referendum. Two-thirds of West Germans consider the speed of developments as too extreme, only 23 per cent consider reunification to be an urgent task of the government (it takes fifth place after labour, pensions, protection of the environment, and the building of homes), and only a quarter of the population would be prepared to accept a rise in state debt and taxes for the sake of unification. It is thus likely that unification would fail if all Germans were allowed to vote on it on the basis of all available information on the actual situation in the GDR. Therefore, the motto now is: unity takes precedence over democracy. (Ibid., pp. 208f.)

72 Habermas, 'Die andere Zerstörung der Vernunft', *Die Zeit*, 10 May 1991. Also in Habermas (1994), *The Past as Future*, p. 35 (trans. modified).
73 Ibid., pp. 33–72.
74 Ibid., p. 36 (trans. modified).
75 Ibid., pp. 37f.
76 Ibid., pp. 33f. (trans. modified).
77 Habermas, 'Bemerkungen zu einer verworrenen Diskussion', *Die Zeit*, 3 April 1992. See also Habermas ([1995] 1997), *A Berlin Republic: Writings on Germany*, pp. 17–40.
78 Herles (2008), *Neurose D*, p. 215.
79 Habermas ([1995] 1997), *A Berlin Republic*, p. 22 (trans. modified).
80 Ibid., p. 24.
81 Ibid., pp. 24f.
82 Ibid., p. 37 (trans. modified).
83 Ibid., p. 40.
84 Dahrendorf (1990), 'Politik: Eine Kolumne: Eine Mark für Deutschland', p. 580.
85 The correspondence is published under the heading 'The Leftover Baggage from German History', in Wolf (1997), *Parting from Phantoms*, pp. 109–23. The letter from Habermas can also be found in Habermas ([1995] 1997), *A Berlin Republic*, pp. 95–105.
86 Ibid., p. 102 (trans. modified).
87 The actual reason for her visiting Frankfurt was an event at the Paulskirche on the continuation of the so-called roundtable that had been started by the civil movement in the GDR. In a letter of 18 June 1991, she thanked Habermas for the invitation and remarked: 'How little even we know each other, how little we know about each other. That will be a long process, and I shall certainly make sure you remember me by inviting you to the Academy in Berlin.' On 16 December 1991, Habermas wrote to Wolf:

> Dear Christa Wolf, many thanks for your understanding letter which corrects my perspective somewhat. Of course, my controversial sentence was aimed at certain aspects of the official practice of the GDR administration, and not at all at the productions of intellectuals whose attitude towards those practices was as critical as mine – and at a time when their situation was much more difficult than ours. (Korrespondenzbestand Vorlass Habermas)

88 Richard Schröder, 'Es ist doch nicht alles schlecht', *Frankfurter Rundschau*, 14 September 1991.
89 Friedrich Diekmann, 'Die Deutschen und die Nation', *Die Zeit*, 31 May 1991.

Chapter 10 Against Germanomania and Nationalism

1 The quotation is taken from the German version of an interview which Stefano Vastano conducted with Habermas in March 1995 for the journal *L'Espresso*. Bestand Na 60, Vorlass Jürgen Habermas, Archivzentrum der Universitätsbibliothek J. C. Senckenberg, Frankfurt am Main.

2 Habermas (1992), 'Die zweite Lebenslüge der Bundesrepublik: Wir sind wieder "normal" geworden', *Die Zeit*, 11 December 1992. See also Habermas ([1990] 1994), *The Past as Future*, pp. 69–72.

3 Bestand Na 60, Vorlass Jürgen Habermas, Archivzentrum der Universitätsbibliothek J. C. Senckenberg, Frankfurt am Main. 'PCI' stands for Partito Comunista Italiano, the Communist Party of Italy.

4 Habermas (1991), *Staatsbürgerschaft und nationale Identität*.

5 Habermas (1987), *Eine Art Schadensabwicklung*, p. 162.

6 See Habermas ([1995] 1997), *A Berlin Republic*, pp. 161ff.

7 Habermas (1987), *Eine Art Schadensabwicklung*, p. 168.

8 Ibid., p. 174.

9 On the various debates between Habermas and Rawls, see Finlayson and Freyenhagen (2010), *Habermas and Rawls*, pp. 2–21 and 283–304. Habermas's most recent statement on Rawls can be found under the title 'Rawls' Politischer Liberalismus: Replik auf die Wiederaufnahme einer Diskussion' [Political liberalism: reply to the resumption of a discussion] in Habermas (2012), *Nachmetaphysisches Denken II*, pp. 277–327.

10 Habermas ([1996] 1999), '"Reasonable" versus "True", or the Morality of Worldviews', in *The Inclusion of the Other*, pp. 75–101.

11 His acceptance speech is titled 'The Conflict of Beliefs: Karl Jaspers on the Clash of Cultures', and is published in Habermas ([1997] 2001), *The Liberating Power of Symbols*, pp. 30–45.

12 Habermas ([1996] 1999), *The Inclusion of the Other*, p. 115.

13 Ibid., p. 115. See also Thumfart (2009), 'Staat, Integration und Solidarität'.

14 Habermas ([1996] 1999), *The Inclusion of the Other*, p. 159 (trans. modified).

15 Ibid., pp. 145f.

16 Habermas (1981), *Kleine Politische Schriften I–IV*, p. 513.

17 This had been preceded by, among other things, an operation of the US Marines against Libyan ships in the Mediterranean and a whole series of terrorist attacks in Europe suspected of having been masterminded by the Gaddafi regime, among them one carried out at the discotheque La Belle in Berlin, which was mostly frequented by American soldiers at the time. The bombing of a Pan Am flight from London to New York, which crashed in the Scottish town of Lockerbie on 21 December 1988, is widely believed to have been an act of retaliation by Libya against Operation El Dorado Canyon, to which Habermas refers here.

18 'Das Schicksal der Moderne' [The fate of modernity], interview with Habermas by Helmut Hein, *Die Woche*, 15 May 1986.

19 Some of the reflections from this article in *Die Zeit* have found their way into the essay 'Does the Constitutionalization of International Law Still Have a Chance?', in Habermas ([2004] 2006), *The Divided West*, pp. 113–93.

20 Habermas, 'Wider die Logik des Krieges: Ein Plädoyer für die Zurückhaltung, aber nicht gegenüber Israel' [Against the logic of war: a plea for restraint, but not when it comes to Israel], *Die Zeit*, 15 February 1991.

21 Habermas ([1990] 1994), *The Past as Future*, p. 9.
22 *Die Zeit*, 8 March 1991. The quotations are from letters to the editor by Stephan Teuber (Heidelberg) and Harald Martens (Bochum).
23 Habermas ([1990] 1994), *The Past as Future*, p. 25.
24 See Habermas ([2001] 2006), *Time of Transitions*, pp. 3f.
25 See Lampe (2002), 'Medienfiktionen beim NATO-Einsatz im Kosovokrieg'.
26 See Schrader (2000), 'Krieg für Menschenrechte? Der Krieg um Kosovo und der kosmopolitische Rechtspazifismus des Jürgen Habermas', p. 35. In an essay in which he comments critically on Habermas's article on the war in Kosovo, Thomas Blanke writes about the reference to Carl Schmitt:

> Schmitt polemically rejected all approaches that would try to commit the battle for political power within and between sovereign states to humane standards, and thus make them 'more human'. He intended his thesis 'humanity, bestiality' as a response to them, saying that moralization necessarily implied bestialization ('whoever invokes humanity wants to cheat'). According to Habermas, the exact opposite is the case. From the perspective of a 'cosmopolitan state', he claims, to continue on the arduous path of civilizing the political by committing it to be respectful of human rights remains an unfulfilled goal of international politics and international law. (Blanke (2000), 'Theorie und Praxis: Der Philosoph im Handgemenge', pp. 496f.)

[The Carl Schmitt quotation is from *The Concept of the Political*, Chicago, 1997, p. 54.]
27 Habermas ([2001] 2006), *Time of Transitions*, 19f.
28 Ibid., p. 26.
29 Ibid., p. 27.
30 Ibid., pp. 30 and 22.
31 Ibid., p. 28.
32 Josef Lang (Zug, Switzerland), for instance, asks: 'Does the juristically illegal, morally questionable, and in terms of realpolitik wholly misplaced bombing campaign not rather further a general devastation of the law?' Norbert Hoerster (Reichenberg) notes: 'Only a war that is permitted by valid international law can justify the deliberate acceptance of the death of innocent individuals. No philosophical rhetoric can detract from this unambiguous legal situation.' And Bernhard H. F. Taureck of the Technische Hochschule Braunschweig asks:

> But how does Habermas know when a humanitarian war becomes necessary? Diplomatic, moral, economic, cultural and educational forms of conflict resolution are not less but probably more in agreement with maxims such as 'genocide is to be condemned' or 'no more genocide'. Instead, Habermas's hyper-diplomacy is trying to convince us that military emergency aid follows directly from the 'No' to genocide.

Fite Saß (Cologne):

> What a toothless tiger Habermas has become! The 'transformation of international law into cosmopolitan law [is] on the agenda'? What a beautiful dream! What about the cheap justifications of the two ministers Scharping and Fischer, of all things, causes Habermas to have such hope?

The war fought by NATO is in breach of international law and our Basic Law. The way in which NATO proceeds weakens the UN. The conduct of the federal government betrays the foreign policy aims of the SPD's and Green Party's election manifestos and of the coalition agreement. What is on the agenda now is the reduction of international law to a kind of NATO-Caesarism and a militarization of international relations. (*Die Zeit*, 20 May 1999)

33 Blanke introduces an interesting comparative perspective: as Habermas appeals to an 'extra-legal legitimacy' derived from moral norms, a comparison of this strategy with the justification of civil disobedience may be instructive, he suggests. What this would show is that the criteria for the justification of acts under the principle of civil disobedience are formulated in far stricter terms than those used for the evaluation of NATO operations. This difference in the demands being placed on the legitimacy of the military enforcement of human rights policies and of civil disobedience is to be explained by the lagging moral development of international law, which would not stand up to a comparison with the constitutional law of democratic states.

Civil disobedience is a demonstrative expression of a refusal to obey the law within a legal order which is generally considered to be, and actually is, legitimate. A war, by contrast, that protects citizens who are persecuted on ethnic grounds against the crimes of their own government is conducted within a legal framework which, so far, has not made the respect for human rights and the requirement of democratic self-determination part of its very foundations, and which therefore has not yet incorporated the tension between legality and legitimacy into the legal system as such.

Within a democracy, the barriers against acts of resistance are higher than those against violations of an international legal order, which is comparatively underdeveloped. However, such violation must follow strict moral principles and constitute a move in the right direction. 'Which, in turn, raises the question: whence does the philosopher receive this wisdom?' Blanke (2000), 'Theorie und Praxis. Der Philosoph im Handgemenge', pp. 516f.

34 Schrader (2000), 'Krieg für Menschenrechte?', in Bilek et al., *Welcher Friede? Lehren aus dem Krieg um Kosovo: Beiträge der Friedensforschung*, p. 45.

35 Ibid., p. 42.

36 Habermas ([2001] 2006), *Time of Transitions*, p. 17.

37 See Habermas ([2004] 2006), *The Divided West*, pp. 85f.

38 Ibid., p. 89.

39 Derrida and Habermas made a public statement in the form of a manifesto, titled 'Unsere Erneuerung: Nach dem Krieg: Die Wiedergeburt Europas' [Our renewal: after the war: the rebirth of Europe], published on the occasion of the imminent invasion of Iraq by American and British troops and the worldwide anti-war demonstrations on 15 February 2004. See Habermas ([2004] 2006), *The Divided West*, pp. 39–48. [The English translation has been given the title 'February 15, or: What Binds Europeans'].

40 Ibid., p. 29.

41 Ibid.
42 Ibid., p. 34f.
43 An essay by Gerd Langguth, 'Alte neue Ressentiments: Habermas, die deutschen Intellektuellen und der Antiamerikanismus', published in 2004, serves as an example. In an article in the *Neue Züricher Zeitung* of 12 August 2003, Langguth had already accused Habermas of anti-Americanism, or, rather, of an 'anti-Americanism disguised as anti-Bushism', with regard to his theses on Europe.
44 Fischer (2008), 'Gründungsfigur des demokratischen Deutschland', p. 49; emphasis in the original.
45 Habermas ([2004] 2006), *The Divided West*, p. 50.
46 Ibid., p. 57.
47 Ibid., p. 110f.
48 Habermas ([1990] 1994), *The Past as Future*, p. 127f. (trans. modified).
49 Wehler (2008), *Deutsche Gesellschaftsgeschichte, 1949–1990*, pp. 40–7; here: p. 43.
50   The rise in right-wing extremist violence gives cause for concern. Even more worrying is the fact that large parts of the population silently sympathize with it and the restraint shown by police and the judiciary. In Hoyerswerda (1991) and Rostock (1992), local residents applauded pogroms lasting several days and arson attacks against asylum-seekers. For the first year of the united country, over a hundred arson attacks were counted. (Herles (2008), *Neurose D*, pp. 217f.)

In 1990, at least six people died as a result of right-wing extremist violence; the following year, the figure was seven, and in 1994 it even rose to twenty-four. See Staudt and Radke (2012), *Neue Nazis*.
51 Habermas (1992), 'Die zweite Lebenslüge der Bundesrepublik: Wir sind wieder normal geworden', *Die Zeit*, 11 December 1992. See Habermas ([1990] 1994), *The Past as Future*, pp. 121–41.
52 See Gunter Hofmann (1992), 'Der Abstieg ins Provinzielle droht', *Die Zeit*, 13 November 1992.
53 The lecture was titled 'The Asylum Debate' and can be found in Habermas ([1990] 1994), *The Past as Future*.
54 See also Habermas (1992), 'Struggles for Recognition in the Democratic Constitutional State', in Taylor, *Multiculturalism and 'The Politics of Recognition'*, pp. 107–48. And Habermas ([1996] 1999), *The Inclusion of the Other*, pp. 239–64.
55 Habermas (1993), 'Die Festung Europa und das neue Deutschland', *Die Zeit*, 18 May 1993. Habermas ([1996] 1999), *The Inclusion of the Other*, pp. 229, and see pp. 246ff. (trans. modified).
56 Ibid., p. 231.
57 Ibid., p. 236. See also the article of 1993, 'Das Bedürfnis nach deutschen Kontinutitäten' [The urge for German continuities], *Die Zeit*, 3 December 1993, in which Habermas reviews a study of Carl Schmitt's, whose theory, he says, contains resources for 'quenching the renewed thirst for German continuities'.
58 Habermas (1993), 'Die Festung Europa und das neue Deutschland', *Die Zeit*, 18 May 1993; emphasis in the original. [See also Habermas ([1996] 1999), *The Inclusion of the Other*, p. 236.]
59 Habermas, 'Gelähmte Politik', *Der Spiegel*, 12 July 1993.
60 Habermas ([2001] 2006), *Time of Transitions*, p. 44 (trans. modified).

61 See Dubiel (1999), *Niemand ist frei von der Geschichte*, pp. 249–56. Also Moses (2007), *German Intellectuals and the Nazi Past*, pp. 219–45.
62 Habermas ([2001] 2006), *Time of Transitions*, p. 73.
63 See ibid., pp. 38–50.
64 From a critical perspective, see Tjark Kunstreich, 'Retter der Republik', *Jungle World*, 22 April 1999. See also Rensmann (2004), 'Bausteine der Erinnerungspolitik: Die politische Textur der Bundestagsdebatte über ein zentrales "Holocaust-Mahnmal"'.
65 Walser, 'Experiences While Composing a Sunday Speech', p. 89; the following quotations from this text are on pp. 92, 93, 89 and 91.
66 Habermas, 'Die zweite Lebenslüge der Bundesrepublik: Wir sind wieder "normal" geworden', *Die Zeit*, 11 December 1992; repr. in Unseld (1993), *Politik ohne Projekt? Nachdenken über Deutschland*, pp. 283–97.
67 On Martin Walser's Paulskirchen speech in general, see *Frankfurter Rundschau*, 12 October 1998. See also Saul Friedländer (1998), 'Die Metapher des Bösen: Über Martin Walsers Friedenspreis-Rede und die Aufgabe der Erinnerung', *Die Zeit*, 26 November 1998.
68 Victor Gourevitch from the Department of Philosophy, and Thomas McCarthy, who was teaching at Wesleyan University from 1985 onwards, had made efforts to secure Habermas as a visiting professor.
69 In an appreciation of Ignatz Bubis after his sudden death in August 1999, Habermas wrote:

> Bubis had the desperate will – to which, after all, his life bore witness – to live as a Jew among Germans again, as a citizen among citizens. His last will to be buried in Israel is an expression of resignation and at the same time a message: that the lonely scene in the Paulskirche – in which he had to see how everyone else jumps up and applauds while he remains seated – may not be repeated. (*Die Welt*, 18 August 1999)

70 See Brumlik et al. (2004), *Umkämpftes Vergessen*, pp. 6–12 and 55–126.
71 See Merseburger (2007), *Rudolf Augstein: Biographie*, pp. 530f. On Augstein's position in this matter, Habermas writes:

> When Rudolf Augstein laments (in the last but one issue of *Der Spiegel*) that 'Now, in the center of the recently recovered capital of Berlin, a monument is supposed to be erected as a reminder of our enduring shame,' then this is an expression of the resistance of the particularist consciousness of the German, which is afraid of the embarrassing scrutiny of others, against the universalistic demand for a form of inclusion that transcends borders. Hermann Lübbe says openly what Martin Walser thinks: 'One can't erect a monument to one's own shame.' Three members of the same generation among themselves. (Habermas ([2001] 2006), *Time of Transitions*, pp. 55f.; trans. modified)

72 Habermas, 'The Finger of Blame: The Germans and Their Memorial', ibid., pp. 38–50; here: p. 38.
73 Ibid., p. 42 (trans. modified).
74 Habermas ([2001] 2006), 'Richard Rorty, *Achieving our Country*', ibid., pp. 138f.
75 See Walser (2010), *Tagebücher 1974–1978*.

76 Walser (1997), 'Das Prinzip Genauigkeit: Über Victor Klemperer', pp. 780ff.
77 I refer to a manuscript by Habermas (2012), '"A Philosophy of Dialogue" – First Buber Memorial Lecture: The Israel Academy of Science and Humanities', MS, p. 4. See also Magenau (2005), *Martin Walser: Eine Biographie*, p. 462.
78 Magenau (2005), *Martin Walser: Eine Biographie*, p. 462.
79 Habermas (1995), 'Aufgeklärte Ratlosigkeit: Warum die Politik ohne Perspektiven ist: Thesen zu einer Diskussion', *Frankfurter Rundschau*, 30 December 1995.
80 See Walser (2002), *Tod eines Kritikers*, pp. 55 and 73. Walser writes:

> But because Wesendonck, a radical critic of the system, had from the very beginning understood his legitimacy as grounded in anti-fascism, they were, so to speak, natural allies. The fact that Wesendonck's anti-fascism . . . was a consequence of the National Socialist undertones of his childhood only made it more serious. Hence the alertness, the sensitivity with which they reacted to any symptom of a weakening anti-fascism. (p. 55)

In a letter of 3 June 2002, Habermas reacted to Walser's book:

> Dear Martin, because it has to do with me, I would like to draw your attention to a little detail. I am sure you will remember the biology text-book which we both, at roughly the same time, used at secondary school. In it, there were three photographs which, for the purpose of the general health of the people [*Volksgesundheit*], were meant to provide a striking illustration of incriminating hereditary diseases: next to the depiction of a 'madman' and someone with a clubfoot, there was a photo of a 'Wolfsrachen' [wolf's jaw], as a cleft palate was called in those days. Even without knowledge of the plans the Nazis had for dealing with people belonging in those categories, the memory of the schoolboy should have been enough for him to know that this was not exactly a favourable condition in which to pursue a 'career' at the time. However, your much praised 'feeling for history' probably blesses you with soothing lapses in memory. The present communication you could well take as an occasion for another indecency. 'Arrogation of the victim's role', I presume, would be the key phrase within the new jargon of suspicion. This is why, as a precaution, I would like to add that I considered myself – and all of us, yourself included – *always* as the undeserving beneficiaries of a histori-cal constellation that fell to us in post-war Germany. Would you please give greetings to Käthe. (Bestand Na 60, Vorlass Jürgen Habermas, Archivzentrum der Universitätsbibliothek J. C. Senckenberg, Frankfurt am Main; emphasis in the original)

In an interview with Martin Oehlen (*Frankfurter Rundschau*, 12 March 2010), Walser came to talk about his friendships. The interviewer asked him about a note in his diary which refers to Habermas as one of the few with whom he got along. Walser's answer: 'Yes. I liked him the most.' [Er war mir der Liebste.]
81 Walser (2012), *Über Rechtfertigung, eine Versuchung*, p. 163.
82 Habermas, 'Der Zeigefinger: Die Deutschen und ihr Denkmal', *Die Zeit*,

31 March 1999. See also Habermas ([2001] 2006), *Time of Transitions*, pp. 38–50. The first paragraph of the version of the text included in *Kleine Politische Schriften IX* deviates from the text of the article in *Die Zeit*. [So does the English version, which does not contain the formulation translated here.]

83 Habermas ([2001] 2006), *Time of Transitions*, pp. 40f.

84 Ibid., p. 41 (trans. modified).

85 Ibid., pp. 41f.

86 Ibid., p. 42.

87 Ibid., p. 43.

88 Ibid., p. 44 (trans. modified).

89 Ibid.

90 Ibid., p. 45 (trans. modified).

91 Ibid., p. 46.

92 Ibid.

93 Ibid.

94 Ibid., p. 47.

95 Ibid.

96 Ibid.

97 Ibid., p. 48.

98 See Michael Mönninger, 'Mein Mahnmal ist ein Ort des Nichts', *Berliner Zeitung*, 21 December 1998. See also Michael Naumann (1999), 'Blick in die Tiefe der Täterschaft', *Frankfurter Allgemeine Zeitung*, 1 April 1999. For a comprehensive documentation of the whole debate, see Heimrod et al. (1999), *Der Denkmalstreit – Das Denkmal? Die Debatte um das 'Denkmal für die ermordeten Juden Europas'*. Habermas's English letter to Eisenman: ibid., p. 1185. See also Thünemann (2003), *Das Denkmal für die ermordeten Juden Europas*, and Moses (2007), *German Intellectuals and the Nazi Past*, pp. 229–83.

99 See the argument between Henryk M. Broder and Wolfgang Menge 'Das ist die Fortsetzung des Dritten Reichs: Was soll, was kann, was hilft das Berliner Holocaust Mahnmal?', *Der Tagesspiegel*, 9 June 2005.

100 Henning Sußebach (2005), 'Ein weites Feld', *Die Zeit*, 2 June 2005. See also the interview with the architect of the memorial, Peter Eisenman: 'Es ist kein heiliger Ort', *Der Spiegel*, 10 May 2005.

Part IV Cosmopolitan Society and Justice

1 Habermas ([2004] 2006), 'Does the Constitutionalization of International Law Still Have a Chance?', p. 121; emphasis in the original. In 1986, Habermas described the political role of social theory as follows:

> A theory of society which has renounced all the certainty of a philosophy of history without having renounced its claims to having a critical edge can perceive its *political* role to rest only in heightening, with somewhat sensitive diagnoses of the times, the attention we pay to the substantial ambivalencies displayed by the contemporary historical situation. Only a knowledge of structurally anchored developmental trends that run in opposite directions can help one become aware of possibilities for practical interventions. (Habermas (1991), 'A Reply', in Honneth and Joas, *Communicative Action*, p. 260)

Chapter 11 Critique as a Vocation

1 Habermas ([2005] 2008), '"I Myself am Part of Nature" – Adorno on the Intrication of Reason in Nature: Reflections on the Relation between Freedom and Unavailability', in *Between Naturalism and Religion*, pp. 181–208; here: p. 186.
2 *Die Zeit*, 17 December 1993. 'Overcoming the Past', *New Left Review*, no. 203, January/February 1994, pp. 3–16.
3 *Die Zeit*, 11 March 1994.
4 *Die Zeit*, 25 March 1994.
5 Correspondence in Vorlass Habermas.
6 *Frankfurter Allgemeine Zeitung*, 22 April 1995.
7 Wiehl (1996), 'Karl-Jaspers-Preis 1995: Laudatio auf Jürgen Habermas'. The *Stuttgarter Zeitung* reported on the award ceremony on 28 November 1995.
8 An abbreviated version of the acceptance speech appeared in *Die Zeit* under the title 'Wahrheit und Wahrhaftigkeit' [Truth and truthfulness] on 8 December 1995. Habermas (2001), 'The Conflict of Beliefs: Karl Jaspers on the Clash of Cultures', p. 42.
9 *Frankfurter Allgemeine Zeitung*, 28 August 1996.
10 The thesis proposed by the American historian, that the murder of European Jewry was the consequence of an 'eliminationist anti-Semitism' which is typical of the Germans, was criticized by several fellow historians. In the media, in particular in *Die Zeit*, a long debate ensued and was branded a new historians' debate. See Ullrich, 'Hitlers willige Mordgesellen: Ein Buch provoziert einen neuen Historikerstreit', *Die Zeit*, 12 April 1996. No fewer than nineteen contributions on the subject appeared in *Die Wochenzeitung*; among the authors were Christopher R. Browning, Julius H. Schoeps, Raul Hilberg, Gordon A. Craig, Hans-Ulrich Wehler, Ulrich Herbert and Hans Mommsen. See Scherf (2009), *Deutsche Diskurse: Die politische Kultur von 1945 bis heute in publizistischen Kontroversen*, pp. 152–6.
11 Habermas (2001), 'On the Public Use of History'.
12 Ibid., p. 31.
13 *Frankfurter Allgemeine Zeitung*, 12 March 1997.
14 Habermas (2001), 'Learning from Catastrophe? A Look Back at the Short Twentieth Century'.
15 Habermas (2000), 'Globalism, Ideology and Traditions'; Habermas (2000), 'Globalization's Valley of Tears'. Apparently, Habermas's critique of neo-liberalism caught the attention of the French sociologist Pierre Bourdieu, who, in the summer of 1989, had already invited him to participate in the foundation of the European journal *LIBER*, which he intended to be a centre for a European public sphere. Habermas, who had just returned from a long trip to South America, responded promptly to the invitation. His letter begins with the preliminary remark 'that in Europe we live in provincial innocence on a small island, without having in front us the real problems of the 21st century.' Habermas declared himself in favour of creating an awareness in European countries which would make it possible to view the political and economic problems of all citizens with the same salience. Because the new journal cooperated with the *Frankfurter Allgemeine Zeitung*, something Habermas had refused to do in any shape or form since the 1970s, he wanted, rather, 'initially to observe [*LIBER*] a little from a distance'.

16 Nida-Rümelin and Thierse (1998), *Philosophie und Politik*, vol. 3: *Jürgen Habermas und Gerhard Schröder über die 'Einbeziehung des Anderen'*, p. 51.
17 Conversation between the author and Claus Offe, 18 May 2009.
18 '"Es gibt doch Alternativen!" Jürgen Habermas antwortet auf Fragen nach den Chancen von Rot–Grün, der Ära Kohl und der Zukunft des Nationalstaates', *Die Zeit*, 8 October 1998.
19 Habermas ([2001] 2006), *Time of Transitions*, pp. 3f.
20 Ibid., pp. 8 (trans. modified).
21 Ibid., p. 9.
22 Ibid., p. 15. Habermas's political dream contrasts with a prolonged political scandal in the wake of secret donations which were passed on to the Christian Democrats via their chairman, the former Chancellor Kohl. Habermas's outrage over this led him to write an article on the sordid affair for the *Süddeutsche Zeitung* (18–19 March 2000). His criticism was aimed at the typical attitude shown by leading representatives in politics towards constitutional obligations within a Rechtsstaat. At the heart of the scandal, said Habermas, was the fact that leading political representatives did not understand the constitution as 'a convincing and lived norm which informs their own behaviour as a matter of course'.
23 Habermas ([2001] 2006), *Time of Transitions*, pp. 53–70.
24 Correspondence, Vorlass Habermas.
25 *Süddeutsche Zeitung*, 17 January 1998; *Die Zeit*, 19 February 1998.
26 The title of the conference, co-organized by the Van Leer Jerusalem Institute and the Franz Rosenzweig Minerva Research Centre in Jerusalem, was 'Jenseits des Seins – Exodus from Being: Philosophie nach Heidegger'.
27 Rainer Stephan, among others, had previously reported on Sloterdijk's lecture in the *Süddeutsche Zeitung* of 29 August 1999. He summarized its theses: 'Being faced with the new possibilities of "anthropo-technologies", philosophers cannot take refuge in the innocence of refusal. Whoever does not select will be selected. Thus, it should be the philosophers – or at least the knowledgeable elite among them – who take control of the concepts which regulate gene-technological human breeding. An absurd joke? Not at all: just applied ontology.'
28 The article of 2 September 1999 by Assheuer carried the title 'Das Zarathustra-Projekt: Der Philosoph Peter Sloterdijk fordert eine gentechnische Revision der Menschen' [The Zarathustra Project: the philosopher Peter Sloterdijk demands a gene-technological revision of the human being]. The author discussed the position taken by Sloterdijk as a philosopher and remarked that the latter exerted an influence on the Suhrkamp programme, 'as the closest advisor of Siegfried Unseld', next to Ulrich Beck and Jürgen Habermas. Assheuer wrote that Sloterdijk

> envisages a community of true philosophers and appropriate genetic engineers who work outside of democratic processes, and who no longer discuss moral questions but take practical action. This elite group has the task of using selection and breeding in order to begin the genetic revision of the history of the species. . . . As a first measure, he considers a transition from 'the fatalism of birth' to 'optional birth' and 'prenatal selection'.

In *Der Spiegel* (6 September 1999), Reinhard Mohr identified 'traits of fascist rhetoric' in Sloterdijk and called him a 'breeder of the over-man' [*Übermensch*]. In addition, he claimed that Suhrkamp offered a forum to authors 'who make passionate anti-democratic, anti-Western, even totalitarian-fascistic [*totalitär-faschistoide*] confessions: Peter Sloterdijk and Peter Handke.' Michael Mayer reconstructed the temporal dynamic and discursive strategies of the debate in the *Frankfurter Rundschau* (27 September 1999). *Die Zeit* of 30 September 1999 dedicated a whole section to the debate: 'Worum geht es? Ein Philosoph hält einen Vortrag und die Republik streitet'. In his opening address at the Congress of Philosophy (4 September 1999), Jürgen Mittelstraß gave his opinion on Sloterdijk's remarks. A short report in the *Deutsche Presse-Agentur* said that Sloterdijk 'naively, and in unsound fashion, ignored all scientifically and philosophically justifiable limits.' Nennen (2003), *Philosophie in Echtzeit*, pp. 182ff.

29 *Die Zeit*, 9 September 1999.
30 Letter from Habermas to Lutz Wingert, 14 August 1999, correspondence, Vorlass Habermas.
31 Nennen (2003), *Philosophie in Echtzeit*, p. 24, points out that the charge of fascism first entered the debate with the article by Reinhard Mohr in *Der Spiegel*, on 6 September 1999. In his book, Nennen analyses the more than 100 publications on the topic which appeared in the media.
32 Bernd Ulrich in *Der Tagesspiegel* (24 September 1999), for instance, stylizes the debate, which was stoked up by the media, as the 'Habermas Debatte: Deutsche Denker danken ab' [The Habermas debate: German thinkers abdicate]. As the title implies, Ulrich thought Habermas's influence was petering out.

> For a long time, they [Habermas and his disciples, S. M.-D.] took care that the Germans always remained conscious of their historical guilt. With popular appeal, they picked on a favourite opponent each year who would be convicted of dangerous right-wing thinking – Martin Walser, Botho Strauß, Ernst Nolte. . . . For a long time, this worked. Until they picked on the philosopher Peter Sloterdijk. This time, the result is not the dismantling of the opponent, but the weakening of Habermas's system.

33 On the theme of discourse and dispute, Habermas (1971) writes:

> A dispute, as a strategic means for realizing a goal that is defined by the distribution of roles, is not a discourse. A discourse, rather, serves the aspiration of a cooperative search for truth – i.e., in principle, an unlimited communication free of coercion which only serves the purpose of reaching understanding, where understanding is a normative concept which needs to be defined counterfactually. A discourse is not an institution; it is a counter-institution par excellence. (*Theorie der Gesellschaft oder Sozialtechnologie*, p. 201)

34 A few weeks earlier, Habermas had reviewed the German translation of Rorty's new book *Stolz auf unserer Land* [Proud of our country; the original English title was *Achieving our Country: Leftist Thought in Twentieth-Century America*, 1998]: 'Rorty's patriotischer Akt: Aber vor Analogie wird gewarnt' [Rorty's patriotic act: but beware of analogies], *Süddeutsche Zeitung*, 27 February 1999. See also Habermas (2009), '". . . And to define America, her athletic democracy": In memory of Richard Rorty'.
35 Axel Honneth, 'Unsere Kritiker', *Die Zeit*, 17 June 1999.

36 Oskar Negt, 'Der große Kommentator', *Der Tagesspiegel*, 18 June 1999.
37 *Frankfurter Allgemeine Zeitung*, 18 June 1999.
38 Habermas (2008), 'Public Space and Political Public Sphere – The Biographical Roots of Two Motifs in my Thought', pp. 12f. See Wingert and Günther (2001), *Die Öffentlichkeit der Vernunft und die Vernunft der Öffentlichkeit: Festschrift für Jürgen Habermas*.
39 Correspondence, Vorlass Habermas.
40 In the *Neue Züricher Zeitung* of 15 October 1998, Joachim Güntner reported on a visit he paid the 'theory-enthusiastic editor' of Suhrkamp, for whom nothing is more practical than a good theory. On 22 December 1998 the same paper reported: 'As the editor of Suhrkamp, Siegfried Unseld, tells us, "a loss of trust has occurred in the last couple of years" between him and Herborth. The separation took place "by mutual agreement". The programme of the academic section for which Herborth is the chief editor is to be continued after his departure "with the same quality and breadth".' In a longer report, again in the *Neue Züricher Zeitung*, Herborth is reported as quoting Unseld, who had further fanned the flames:

> 'The programme is narrowly conceived. I do not want that. I want another programme.' Friedhelm Herborth remembers well: those, he says, had been the exact words Unseld had said about the 'suhrkamp taschenbuch wissenschaft' (stw) series. . . . The fact that, apart from Jürgen Habermas, whose judgement Unseld had always trusted, Ulrich Beck and Peter Sloterdijk would now advise the publishing house on authors and proposed books for stw did not calm the spirits. The 'Süddeutsche Zeitung' speculated that 'stw' would now specialize more on 'non-fiction light', on 'zeitgeist literature' and on 'life-style sociology'.

41 Correspondence, Vorlass Habermas.
42 I refer to information provided by Friedhelm Herborth, Reimar Zons and Bernd Stiegler in personal conversations. See also Peter Michalzik, 'Stachel im Fleisch des Denkenden', *Süddeutsche Zeitung*, 23 November 1999.
43 I refer to information provided by Friedhelm Herborth, Reimar Zons and Bernd Stiegler.
44 *Frankfurter Allgemeine Zeitung*, 20 December 1999.
45 Habermas (1999), '"Reasonable" versus "True", or the Morality of Worldviews', p. 95.
46 Habermas ([2001] 2003), *The Future of Human Nature*, pp. 3 and 1.
47 'Faith and Knowledge', ibid., p. 108 (trans. modified).
48 Ibid., p. 13; emphasis in the original.
49 Ibid., p. 54.
50 Habermas ([1998] 2001), 'An Argument against Human Cloning: Three Replies', in *The Postnational Constellation*, pp. 163–72; here: p. 169.
51 Ibid., p. 165.
52 Habermas ([2001] 2003), *The Future of Human Nature*, p. 14.
53 Ibid., p. 79.
54 Ibid., p. 22; emphasis in the original.
55 Ibid., p. 46; emphasis in the original.
56 Ibid., p. 62 (trans. modified).
57 Ibid., pp. 63f.

58 Ibid., pp. 35, 30, 69, 57f., 73 (trans. modified), 67.
59 Ibid., p. 125
60 Ibid., p. 40.
61 Habermas (2007), 'The Language Game of Responsible Agency and the Problem of Free Will', p. 19; emphasis in the original.
62 Ibid., p. 15.
63 Habermas ([2005] 2008), *Between Naturalism and Religion*, pp. 30, 161f., 188, 191.
64 *Süddeutsche Zeitung*, 17–18 September 2011.
65 Habermas (2012), *Nachmetaphysisches Denken II*, pp. 54–76.
66 Ibid., p. 57; emphasis in the original.
67 Ibid., p. 69.
68 Ibid., pp. 73f.
69 Ibid., p. 76.
70 Ibid., p. 75; emphasis in the original.
71 *Süddeutsche Zeitung*, 17–18 September 2011.
72 *Die Weltwoche*, 26 April 2001.
73 See Rudolf Walther, 'Unter Hegelianern: Als Barbar unterwegs: Jürgen Habermas über die Eindrücke seiner China-Reise', *Frankfurter Rundschau*, 10 May 2001.
74 'Habermas, China und die "halbierte Moderne": Im Gespräch mit dem chinesischen Sozialphilosophen und Übersetzer CaoWeidong', *Forschung Frankfurt* no. 2 (2009), pp. 78–81.
75 *Frankfurter Rundschau*, 10 May 2001.
76 Börsenverein des Deutschen Buchhandels, in Habermas (2001), *Friedenspreis des Deutschen Buchhandels 2001*, p. 10.
77 In an interview, Habermas commented that Derrida

> gave a very subtle lecture in the Paulskirche in Frankfurt upon receiving the Adorno Prize, which revealed the intellectual affinity between these two thinkers in an impressive way. Such a gesture does not leave one unmoved. Moreover, aside from all political questions, what unites me with Derrida is the philosophical reference to an author like Kant. Admittedly, we part ways over the later Heidegger – even though we are roughly the same age, our life histories have been very different. Derrida assimilates Heidegger's ideas from the Jewish-inspired standpoint of a Levinas. I encounter Heidegger as a philosopher who failed as a citizen, in 1933 and especially after 1945. But he is suspect for me even as a philosopher because, during the 1930s, he interpreted Nietzsche precisely in the neo-pagan fashion then in vogue. Unlike Derrida, whose reading of '*Andenken*' (lit. 'remembrance') accords with the spirit of monotheistic tradition, I regard Heidegger's botched '*Seinsdenken*' (lit. 'thinking of being') as a leveling of the epochal threshold in the history of consciousness which Jaspers called the 'Axial Age.' On my understanding, Heidegger betrayed that caesura which is marked, in different ways, by the prophetic awakening of Mount Sinai and by the enlightenment of Socrates. (Habermas ([2004] 2006), *The Divided West*, p. 88.

In an article for the *Süddeutsche Zeitung* (21 September 2001), Ulrich Raulff used the occasion of the award ceremony to discuss the ambivalent relations between Critical Theory and French structuralism, including those intellectuals who had made early efforts at a mediation between the two traditions. Such efforts, however, were in vain, as the German side, Raulff writes, is characterized by 'a pronounced perception of enmity', caused by a

> deep-seated need for security which is fed by the political history of the twentieth century and permanently urges authors to strive toward the safe, the right side of the discourse. . . . The thinkers of Critical Theory in particular, all of them sworn enemies of Carl Schmitt, have often perceived the world in terms of friend and enemy, an attitude which is at home in the pre-philosophical realm.

Habermas did not let this accusation, which was also directed at him, rest unchallenged for long. In a letter to the editor of 22 September 2001 in the same paper, he remarked that philosophical discussions were being brought down to the level of academic rumours rather than concentrating on arguments and counter-arguments. In his biography of Derrida, Benoît Peeters claims that the award of the Adorno Prize contributed to the reconciliation between the French deconstructionist and Habermas – a reconciliation that, according to their own testimony, had already taken place. See Peeters (2013), *Derrida: A Biography*, p. 502. See also Derrida, '"Unsere Redlichkeit!" Jeder in seinem Land, aber beide in Europa: Die Geschichte einer Freundschaft mit Hindernissen – Jürgen Habermas zum 75. Geburtstag' ['Our honesty!' Each in his country, but both in Europe: the history of a friendship with obstacles – for Jürgen Habermas on his 75th birthday], *Frankfurter Rundschau*, 18 June 2004.

Habermas had invited Derrida for a lecture in Frankfurt even before he published his discussion of his work in *The Philosophical Discourse of Modernity*, and Derrida had accepted. After Habermas's critique in the seventh chapter of that book had appeared, both philosophers kept a distance from each other until Habermas broke the silence in 1996. While he was teaching at Northwestern University in November that year, a reception for Derrida took place there, and Habermas made contact with him; both agreed to have lunch in Paris on 13 January 1997. This encounter in Paris quickly took on a friendly atmosphere. Two years later, Derrida was invited for a lecture in Frankfurt by Axel Honneth, and Habermas introduced him on that occasion. The following day, Derrida and Habermas met for an exchange at the Suhrkamp publishing house, at which only personally invited guests were allowed to be present, and which therefore was spoken of as the 'secret meeting'. Habermas later returned the favour of Derrida's lecture in Frankfurt with a visit to Paris, where between 3 and 5 December 2000 he took part in an international colloquium on the subject of 'Judéités: questions pour Jaques Derrida' [Jewishness: questions for Jacques Derrida] at the Jewish community centre. See Habermas ([2008] 2009), 'How to Answer the Ethical Question: Derrida and Religion', in *Europe: The Faltering Project*, pp. 17–36.

78 A fourth plane was probably meant to hit the government district in Washington, DC, but came down over Shanksville, Pennsylvania, before reaching its target destination.

79 Habermas (2003), 'Faith and Knowledge', p. 101.

80 Habermas and Derrida (2003), *Philosophy in a Time of Terror*, pp. 25–44 and 85–136. The interview with Jürgen Habermas, 'Fundamentalism and Terror', can also be found in *The Divided West*, pp. 3–25.

81 See Peeters (2013), *Derrida: A Biography*, pp. 502 and 505.
82 Habermas ([2004] 2006), *The Divided West*, p. 12.
83 Habermas ([2001] 2006), 'Richard Rorty: *Achieving our Country*', in *Time of Transitions*, pp. 136–41; here: p. 138.
84 Habermas (2008), 'Richard Rorty und das Entzücken am Schock der Deflationierung' [Richard Rorty and the pleasure about the shock of deflation], in *Ach, Europa*, pp. 15–23; here: pp. 17f. [The speech is not part of the English translation of this book, *Europe: The Faltering Project*].
85 Rorty (2007), *Philosophy as Cultural Politics*, pp. 77f.
86 See Magenau (2005), *Martin Walser: Eine Biographie*, pp. 524–43.
87 Years later, in his acceptance speech for the Joseph Neuberger Medal, Schirrmacher emphasized 'that the measure of pain which Germany caused the Jews is too enormous to tolerate even one false word.' *Frankfurter Allgemeine Zeitung*, 23 September 2012.
88 Karl Heinz Bohrer, 'Ich habe einen romantischen Blick: Gespräch mit Sven Michaelsen', *Süddeutsche Magazin*, 5 October 2012.
89 This is the impression one gets from excerpts of the correspondence between Habermas and Bohrer, which is preserved in Habermas's Vorlass. In an article in *Merkur* (December 2011), Bohrer writes that, in January 1990, he received a letter from Habermas 'in which he ended his cooperation with *Merkur*. The reason was a conflict over the question of a possible reunification of the two parts of Germany which had developed between Habermas and myself after the fall of the Berlin Wall.' At issue was a text by Bohrer which Habermas did not want to see published, but which then appeared in the *Frankfurter Allgemeine Zeitung*. 'In light of our friendly relationship which began in 1967 and has had its ups and downs, but – despite all foreseeable theoretical differences – appeared to be stable, I was all the more hit by this reaction, as I could not follow Habermas's arguments.' Karl Heinz Bohrer, 'Ästhetik und Politik: Eine Erinnerung an drei Jahrzehnte des *Merkur*', *Merkur*, 751 (2011), pp. 1091–103; here: pp. 1095f.
90 In a later interview, published in *Die Welt* (30 July 2012), Bohrer expressed himself in far more relaxed terms about Habermas:

> Habermas was the astute left-liberal analyst of the social situation *par excellence*, clearly distinct from the majority of utopians. . . . Habermas was the appearance of the candid intellectual of the kind never seen in Germany before! At once witty and serious, lively and strict. And he had enormous style in his somewhat frustratingly difficult diction. Thus, a man full of tensions, which I liked.

91 Habermas ([2005] 2008), 'Religious Tolerance as Pacemaker for Cultural Rights', in *Between Naturalism and Religion*, pp. 251–70.
92 Ibid., pp. 255 and 261.
93 *Die Zeit*, 21 March 2002.
94 *Süddeutsche Zeitung*, 28 October 2002.
95 Jonas (2008), *Memoirs*.
96 Habermas, 'Indiskretion und Jonas' [Indiscretion and Jonas], letter to the editor, *Frankfurter Allgemeine Zeitung*, 21 March 2003.
97 The rich programme, 'Theodor W. Adorno 100. Geburtstag 2003', included a festive concert, readings, and events on Adorno's philosophy of music and his style as a composer, in the context of the event 'Musikalische Analyse und Kritische Theorie' [Musical analysis and Critical Theory], at

the Holzhausenschlösschen; a symposium on the question of 'Was wäre eine "Assoziation freier Individuen"?' [What would an 'association of free individuals' be?] at the Literaturhaus; a matinee organized by Suhrkamp at the Bockenheimer Depot; and an exhibition of the Universitätsarchiv J. C. Senckenberg. See Honneth (2005), *Dialektik der Freiheit*. See also Ziegler (2008), 'Auswahl-Bibliographie zu Theodor W. Adorno ab dem Jahr 2003'; and *Literaturen: Das Journal für Bücher und Themen*, no. 6 (June 2003), an edition with the theme 'Adorno: Luxus des Denkens' [Adorno: the luxury of thinking].

  98 Habermas ([2005] 2008), '"I Myself am Part of Nature" – Adorno on the Intrication of Reason in Nature', in *Between Naturalism and Religion*, pp. 181–208; here: pp. 199f.

  99 Ibid., p. 191.

100 Ibid., pp. 203f. and 208.

101 *Frankfurter Allgemeine Zeitung*, 3 December 2003.

102 'Wähler sind nicht nur Kunden' [Voters are not just customers], interview by Andreas Zielke in the *Süddeutsche Zeitung*, 18 June 2004.

103 Habermas ([2005] 2008), 'Freedom and Determinism'.

104 Habermas ([2005] 2008), 'Public Space and Political Public Sphere'.

105 Ibid., pp. 11f.

106 Ibid., pp. 22f.

107 Before his visit to Bergen, Habermas gave an interview in Starnberg which was recorded on video, and which is instructive not least because it provides some biographical background to his intellectual ideas:

> When I look back, democracy can be identified as at least one major issue. It was the obvious alternative to the regime under which I had been living until my fifteenth birthday. I am also a product of what was called at that time re-education. Thus, democracy is a leitmotif in my work from the beginning until what I am interested in at the present, for instance legal philosophy or international law. I was always convinced that there is a cognitive dimension to this democratic procedure. And that is why I am one of the first and most vigilant defenders of deliberative democracy. And deliberative democracy obviously leads to the second major issue of my work: communicative rationality. (www.youtube. com/watch?v=jBl6ALNh18Q [I give here a mildly edited transcription of Habermas's interview in English.])

108 See Holberg Prize Seminar (2007) *The Holberg Prize Seminar*.

109 Habermas (2009), 'An Avantgardistic Instinct for Relevances'.

110 Ibid., p. 54.

111 Habermas (2009), 'Political Communication in Media Society', p. 157.

112 Habermas (2009), 'Media, Markets and Consumers', p. 133.

113 Habermas (2008), 'Europa und seine Immigranten' [Europe and its immigrants], in *Ach, Europa*, pp. 88–95; here: p. 90 [the speech is not part of the English edition]. I further quote from the manuscript of the speeches made available to me by the press office of the event's host.

114 In a conversation with Frank Schirrmacher and Hubert Spiegel in the *Frankfurter Allgemeine Zeitung* of 11 August 2006, Grass admits that 'the Waffen SS was not abhorrent to me at first.' He saw it as an elite troop 'which was always deployed in critical situations, and which, word got around, had the most casualties.'

115 In 2004, the philosopher Gereon Wolters had already tried to correct the facts on the basis of information provided in letters from Hans-Ulrich Wehler and Jürgen Habermas, establishing unambiguously even back then that the rumour was unfounded. See Wolters (2004), *Vertuschung, Anklage, Rechtfertigung*, p. 33. Despite Wolters's correction and the rectifications in Wehler's letter, Joachim Fest picked up the rumour again in his autobiography, *Ich nicht: Erinnerungen an eine Kindheit und Jugend* [*Not Me: A German Childhood*, 2012]. In chapter 11, he talks about the 'communicative silence' about guilt in post-war Germany and, at the same time, is ironic about the lamentations of the 'self-accusers'. On p. 342 [of the German edition], it says:

> Indeed, there have been innumerable escape paths and side paths. One of them is being reported about one of the leading intellectual figures of this country. He was an HY leader in the last days of Hitler's Reich and allied to the regime with every fibre of his existence. At a birthday party in the 1980s, it is said, an erstwhile subordinate gave him, as his former HY superior, a letter, written in the spring of 1945 by the latter, which expressed a passionate commitment to the Führer and an unshakable belief in final victory. Without looking any closer at the document, the story continues, according to the testimony of several of those present and those in the know, the addressed crumpled up the paper, stuffed it into his mouth, and swallowed it, not without some gulping up and down. One may see a kind of settlement of damages in this, a removal of the personal burdens of the past.

In the November edition of *Cicero*, Jürgen Busche refers to Habermas's and Wehler's past and mentions that both studied with professors who had been faithful to the NS regime. The journalist identifies these facts as the 'environment from which the rumour entered into the public' (*Cicero*, 11/2006, pp. 72–7; here: p. 73). He mentions Gereon Wolters's attempt to correct the fact. Wolters, he says, made an effort to 'take the disgrace away from the rumour'. From Ute Habermas's 'humorous' answer [*launige Antwort*] he concludes: 'This confirms the core of the story – if one does not want to interpret the word humorous as an indication of fictionality' (p. 75). Busche further speculates:

> This seems plausible when looking at it from the end of the story, but not when looking at it from its beginning. The piece of paper may have ended up in the diary of the under-age Wehler and stayed there, and the diary may have survived all the tumult of the times. If the document was remembered in the course of a conversation after such a long time, if it was considered to be worth taking the trouble to return it to its original sender, and if the busy professor of history then asked after its whereabouts, then it is likely that more was written on it than printed matter. (p. 76)

On 25 October, Habermas responded to the article by Busche with a letter to the editor-in-chief of *Cicero*, which he requested be published:

> If one recollects the circle of individuals of whom one knows that they spread the rumour – Fest, Lübbe, Koselleck and (only now?) Busche – one recognizes the renewed denunciation for what it is: the continuation of a political smear campaign of the *Frankfurter Allgemeine Zeitung* to which

I was exposed in particular during the 1970s and 1980s. Apparently, Fest took offence at my criticism of those vanguard thinkers of the NS regimes whom he rehabilitated in his paper. How do you defend yourself against a denunciation which has the obvious aim of removing, along with Grass, an inconvenient generation of intellectuals that was committed to a self-critical identification of the traditional background for the approval of NS rule which also, and in particular, existed in academic circles? (Habermas, 'Vergiftetes Klima' [Poisoned atmosphere], *Cicero*, 12/2006, p. 12)

116 Joachim Fest did not live to see the publication of his book and the subsequent affair around Habermas. He died after a severe illness on 11 September 2006 in Kronberg im Taunus.
117 Lübbe (1989), *Politischer Moralismus*, p. 72.
118 Joachim Güntner, 'Ohne Kompromiss: Die Causa Habermas gegen Rowohlt vor dem Hamburger Landgericht', *Neue Züricher Zeitung*, 18 November 2006.

Chapter 12 The Taming of Capitalism and the Democratization of Europe

1 Habermas ([1995] 1997), 'The Adenauer Restoration's Debts: An Interview with the *Kölner Stadtanzeiger*', p. 87. The interview by Markus Schwering was first published in the *Kölner Stadt-Anzeiger* on 18 July 1994.
2 I refer to two works by Habermas which were published quite some time apart, that is, his study 'Über den Begriff der politischen Beteiligung' [On the concept of political participation] of 1961 and his lecture 'Does Democracy still have an Epistemic Dimension?' of 2008. See Habermas et al. (1961), *Student und Politik* [Students and politics], pp. 11–51, and Habermas (2009), *Europe: The Faltering Project*, pp. 138–83.
3 See Horkheimer (1988), *Gesammelte Schriften*, vol. 4: *Schriften 1936–1941*, pp. 308f.
4 'The key ideas in this article contain the kernel of much of what I later came to write in *The Theory of Communicative Action*.' Dews (1986), *Autonomy and Solidarity*, p. 187.
5 Ibid., p. 94.
6 The 'four facts' which Habermas puts forward against Marx are his failure to shed enough light on the role of the state, the problematic primacy given to the development of the forces of production, his obsolete prognosis about the emergence of a revolutionary class consciousness, and the fact that he overlooks the economic system's capacity for self-correction. Habermas fundamentally questions the validity of the labour theory of value and the law of the tendency of the rate of profit to fall on the basis that Marx did not consider the rationalization of the labour process brought about by science and technology. See Habermas ([1963] 1974), *Theory and Practice*, pp. 195ff. and 222ff.
7 Habermas (1981), *Kleine Politische Schriften I–IV*, pp. 500f.
8 Habermas (1983), 'Some Conditions for Revolutionizing Late Capitalist Societies [1968]', p. 35.
9 See Künzli (1968), 'Marxismus im Trockendock: Ein Bericht von der internationalen marxistischen Sommerschule auf der Insel Korčula', *Frankfurter Rundschau*, 14 September 1968.

10 Habermas (1983), 'Some Conditions for Revolutionizing Late Capitalist Societies [1968]', pp. 38–9; emphasis in the original (trans. modified).

11 One passage succinctly states: 'I consider the . . . attempts to "derive" the juridical and political "forms" of the capitalist state from the forms of economic exchange, and ultimately from the commodity form, as mistaken.' Habermas (1976), *Zur Rekonstruktion des Historischen Materialismus*, p. 267, fn. 1.

12 Marx's labour theory of value explains the real abstraction which takes place in acts of exchange: the value of commodities – i.e., the amount of social labour necessary for their production – makes it possible for the parties involved in exchange to compare different objects while neglecting their concrete properties. The commodity form thus points towards a social paradox – i.e., that needs which are based on use value become subordinated to an abstract form of mediation, one that is linked to exchange value. With money becoming an independent commodity, the production of surplus value for the sake of surplus value becomes a process with its own dynamic. See the critical but constructive discussion of Habermas's interpretation of Marx by Cerutti (1983, 'Habermas und Marx'), who, according to Habermas's 'Reply', 'has defended Marx against the objections [Habermas] had raised in a philologically well-founded article'. Habermas (1991), 'A Reply', in Honneth and Joas, *Communicative Action*, p. 263.

13 See Habermas ([1981] 1987), *The Theory of Communicative Action*, vol. 2, pp. 332ff.

14 Habermas ([1992] 1996), 'Popular Sovereignty as Procedure', pp. 463–90, esp. pp. 477–83; here: p. 479. In an interview in 1981, Habermas explained that the abolition of private ownership of the means of production would by no means remove class structures as such: 'Personally, I no longer believe that a differentiated economic system can be democratically transformed from within in accordance with the simple recipes of workers' self-management.' Habermas (1985), *'A Philosophico-Political Profile'*, p.103.

15 See Habermas ([1981] 1987), *The Theory of Communicative Action*, vol. 2, pp. 345ff. See also Ingram (2010), *Habermas: Introduction and Analysis*, pp. 260ff.

16 Habermas ([1981] 1987), *The Theory of Communicative Action*, vol. 2, p. 350.

17 Habermas, 'The New Obscurity: The Crisis of the Welfare State and the Exhaustion of Utopian Energies', trans. Phillip Jakobs, *Philosophy and Social Criticism*, 11 (January 1986), pp. 1–18; here: pp. 14f.

18 Habermas, 'Kommunikative Rationalität und grenzüberschreitende Politik', in Niesen and Herborth (2007), *Anarchie der kommunikativen Freiheit*, p. 428.

19 *Die Zeit*, 6 November 2008, and Habermas (2012), 'After the bankruptcy: an interview', in *The Crisis of the European Union*, pp. 102–18; here: pp. 102f., 105 (trans. modified) and 106 (trans. modified).

20 Habermas ([1992] 1996), 'Popular Sovereignty as Procedure', p. 482; emphasis in the original.

21 Rapic (2014) *Habermas und der Historische Materialismus*.

22 Habermas (1984), *Vorstudien und Ergänzungen zur Theorie des kommunikativen Handelns*, p. 489.

23 I refer to personal notes taken at the conference. Habermas has checked the notes on his statements. See also Rapic (2014), *Habermas und der Historische Materialismus*.

24 Habermas ([1990] 1994), 'Europe's Second Chance', in *The Past as Future*, pp. 96f. (trans. modified).
25 Habermas (2009), 'Political Communication in Media Society: Does Democracy still have an Epistemic Dimension?', in *Europe: A Faltering Project*, pp. 138–83: here: p. 144 (trans. modified); see pp. 144–6. See also Habermas ([1996] 1999), *The Inclusion of the Other*, esp. the chapter 'Three Normative Models of Democracy', pp. 239–52. And see also Forst (2002), *Contexts of Justice*.
26 Habermas ([1992] 1996), 'Popular Sovereignty as Procedure', p. 486.
27 Wellmer (2009), 'Erinnerung an die Anfänge und eine späte Antwort auf einen fast vergessenen Brief'. On the question of the stability, or instability, of democracy, see Nancy (2010), *The Truth of Democracy*; Crouch (2004), *Post-Democracy*.
28 Habermas (1991), 'Legitimation Problems in the Modern State', in *Communication and the Evolution of Society*, pp. 178–206; here: p. 188.
29 Habermas ([1996] 1999), 'Does Europe Need a Constitution? Response to Dieter Grimm', in *The Inclusion of the Other*, pp. 155–61; here: p. 158.
30 Habermas ([1998] 2001), 'The Postnational Constellation and the Future of Democracy', in *The Postnational Constellation*, pp. 58–112; here: p. 88.
31 The current reasons for 'democracy's loss of substance' are discussed by Colin Crouch (2004), *Post-Democracy*, pp. 6f.
32 Habermas (2009), 'An Avantgardistic Instinct for Relevances: The Role of the Intellectual and the European Cause', in *Europe: A Faltering Project*, p. 56. [The full sentence runs: 'Others find my main current preoccupation, the future of Europe, abstract and boring.' This deviates significantly from the German: 'Was mich heute am meisten aufregt, die Zukunft Europas nämlich, finden andere abstrakt und langweilig.' (*Ach, Europa*, p. 85) = 'What I get most worked up about these days, the future of Europe, others find abstract and boring'.]
33 See Müller-Doohm (2008), *Jürgen Habermas: Leben, Werk, Wirkung*, pp. 130–8.
34 Habermas (1981), *Kleine Politische Schriften I–IV*, p. 524.
35 Matthias Hoenig conducted the interview for dpa: see www.perlentaucher. de/essay/wacht-auf-schlafende-mehrheiten-fuer-eine-vertiefung-der-euro paeischen-union.html.
36 Habermas (1998), '1989 in the shadow of 1945: On the normality of a Future Berlin Republic', in *A Berlin Republic*, pp. 161–81; here: p. 181 (trans. modified). See Habermas (1996), 'Citizenship and National Identity (1990)', in *Between Facts and Norms*, pp. 491–515.
37 Ibid., p. 500.
38 Ibid., p. 507.
39 Habermas (2006), 'Does Europe Need a Constitution?', in *Time of Transitions*, pp. 89–110; here: p. 159 (emphasis in the original; trans. modified). On Dieter Grimm's position, see Grimm (2001), *Die Verfassung und die Politik*, pp. 215–54. See also Grimm (2004), 'Integration durch Verfassung'. The positions of Grimm and Habermas are compared by Thiel (2008), 'Braucht Europa eine Verfassung? Einige Anmerkungen zur Grimm-Habermas-Debatte'. On the question of a European constitution, see also Frankenberg (2003), *Autorität und Integration*, pp. 73–114.
40 *Die Zeit*, 28 June 2001. Habermas (2006), 'Does Europe Need a Constitution?', p. 101.

41 Looking back, Habermas described the common initiative with the following words:

> After the formal conclusion of the Iraq War, when many people feared a general prostration of the 'unwilling' governments before Bush, I sent a letter to Derrida – as well as to Eco, Muschg, Rorty, Savater, and Vattimo – inviting them to participate in a joint initiative. (Paul Ricoeur was the only one who declined for political reasons; Eric Hobsbawm and Harry Mulisch could not participate for personal reasons.) Derrida, too, was not able to write an article of his own because he had to undergo unpleasant medical tests at the time. However, Derrida very much wanted to be part of the initiative and suggested the procedure which we then followed. I was happy about this. We had last met in New York after September 11. We had already resumed our philosophical conversation some years previously in Evanston, Paris, and Frankfurt. So there was no need for a grand gesture. ('An Interview on War and Peace', in *The Divided West*, pp. 85–112; here: pp. 87f.)

42 Habermas, 'February 15, or: What Binds Europeans', ibid., pp. 39–48; here: p. 40.
43 Ibid., p. 42.
44 Ibid. See also the various statements in the public media, collected in *The Crisis of the European Union* (2012), pp. 101–39.
45 Habermas (2008), 'Europapolitik in der Sackgasse: Nicht die Bevölkerung, die Regierungen sind der Hemmschuh: Plädoyer für eine Politik der abgestuften Integration' [European politics at a dead end: not the populations, but the governments, are the stumbling block: a plea for a politics of integration in stages], in Nida-Rümelin and Thierse, *European Prospects, Europäische Perspektiven*, p. 21. See also *The Crisis of the European Union* (2012), p. 4.
46 Kai Biermann, 'Fern jeder Vision', *Die Zeit*, 22 November 2007. See also Habermas (2007), 'Europa: Vision und Votum'.
47 Habermas (2012), 'The Euro Will Decide the Fate of the European Union', in *The Crisis of the European Union*, pp. 119–27; here: p. 123.
48 'Europa und die neue deutsche Frage: Ein Gespräch mit Jürgen Habermas, Joschka Fischer, Henrik Enderlein und Christian Callies', *Blätter für deutsche und internationale Politik*, no. 5 (2011), pp. 45–63; here: p. 63. Before the discussion, Habermas gave an introductory lecture which was published in the *Süddeutsche Zeitung* (7 April 2011) under the title 'Europapolitik Merkels – von Demoskopie geleiteter Opportunismus' [Merkel's European policies – an opportunism guided by opinion polls].
49 See Habermas (2015), 'Three Reasons for "More Europe"', in *The Lure of Technocracy*, pp. 80–4.
50 Here I refer to the verbatim record of the 'Forum Europa' of 9 November 2012 and to the text 'Stellungnahme für die EZB' of 6 October 2012; emphasis in the original. At another discussion with the parliamentary president Norbert Lammert on 3 February 2012, Habermas steadfastly defended the thesis that only a 'public and far-reaching democratic dispute over a common European future could lead to credible political decisions, which then also impress the financial markets and put speculators who gamble on state bankruptcies in their place.' Habermas praised the fiscal pact, which he said contributed to the establishment of a democratically

organized communal liability. His critical remarks aimed at the refusal to push through transnational economic and social policies with the aim of balancing out the competitiveness of the individual national economies. Against this background, Habermas, like the opposition Social Democrats at the time, demanded economic programmes to stimulate growth. The government, he said, could no longer ignore the fact 'that, within the context of "born" world powers such as the USA, China, Russia, Brazil or India, a demographically shrinking Europe of small states moves into the margins of world history and will soon be unable to exert any influence on problems that can only be solved globally.' I refer to the text of the lecture titled 'Zum Gleichschritt mit der Integration der Staaten' [On keeping pace with the integration of the states]. In an interview with the American political scientist Francis Fukuyama in the *Global Journal* (18 May 2012), Habermas argued that the legitimation crisis of the European Union must be tackled through strengthening the participation of the population. Of the national governments he demands that they should increase the coordination of their national economic policies in order to achieve a common economic government. Habermas took the opportunity to stress once again that a federal state on the model of the United States or the Federal Republic of Germany was not a realistic prospect for Europe.

51 *Der Spiegel*, 12 November 2011, pp. 134–8.
52 Sigmar Gabriel, 'Was wir Europa wirklich schulden', *Frankfurter Allgemeine Zeitung*, 13 December 2011. See *Frankfurter Allgemeine Zeitung*, 15 and 17 February 2012. The former chancellor Helmut Schmidt wrote in *Die Zeit* (5 May 2011) under the heading '. . . aber die Währung ist gut: Wir haben keine Eurokrise, sondern eine Krise der Europäischen Union', that, in current European politics, 'a sovereign disregard for the democratic-parliamentarian principle [is] to be lamented', as Habermas had pointed out. In the *Frankfurter Allgemeine Zeitung* of 23 December 2012, Wolfgang Schäuble said that he would like to see a European government elected by the parliament. In the interview, he also supported the election of a European president. The democratic legitimacy of the European Union, he said, is too weak, and the member states within it too dominant. The speech of the German president, Joachim Gauck, on the future of European unification, given at Bellevue Castle on 7 February 2013, also contained echoes of Habermas's critical analyses and postulates; he emphasized, for example, the necessity of a common European public sphere and demanded the creation of a European agora, a common space for democratic discussion and exchange.
53 Habermas (2012), 'The Crisis of the European Union in Light of a Constitutionalization of International Law – An Essay on the Constitution of Europe', in *The Crisis of the European Union*, p. 6.
54 'Where collectively binding decisions are concerned, the requirement of their deliberative quality must be combined with the inclusion of all potentially affected parties in the processes of negotiation and *decision-making*. For in practical discourses the "yes" and "no" of each potentially affected party is important for epistemic reasons alone.' Habermas, 'Kommunikative Rationalität und grenzüberschreitende Politik', in Niesen and Herborth (2007), *Anarchie der kommunikativen Freiheit*, p. 433.
55 Ibid., p. 436. See Habermas (2012), 'The Crisis of the European Union in Light of a Constitutionalization of International Law', pp. 47ff. The loss of importance suffered by nation-states piqued Habermas's interest

in questions of the theory of international relations. One occasion for pursuing such questions was a debate which began in the *Zeitschrift für Internationale Beziehungen* (ZIB); see Benjamin Herborth, 'Verständigung verstehen: Anmerkungen zur ZIB-Debatte', in Niesen and Herborth (2007), *Anarchie der kommunikativen Freiheit*, pp. 147–74. The climax of this debate was the previously mentioned conference in Frankfurt between 16 and 18 June 2005. At the centre was the question of whether the *Theory of Communicative Action* can usefully be applied to an analysis of international relations. In Habermas's reply to the arguments presented by the participants, most of whom were political scientists, one can sense his satisfaction at the fact that his concept of communicative rationality had apparently had a substantial impact on the discourse in political science. He used the opportunity for a conceptual clarification by drawing a distinction between *arguing* [*Argumentieren*] and *bargaining* [*Aushandeln*] on the basis of this theory of understanding [the German text has the English expressions in parentheses]. In both cases, valid reasons (i.e.. the logic of communicative rationality) are used, but whereas, in the case of arguing, the exclusive aim is to reach a consensus about the subject matter – that is, to bring about the breakthrough of reason, so to speak – in the case of bargaining, reasons are used tactically in order to bring about compromises against the background of existing power relations. With regard to the present situation, Habermas said:

> For the time being the institutions are lacking what would allow for the political control of the vegetative growth of a global society which is characterized by progressive systemic differentiation, violence, increasing disparities and ideological conflicts. And the willingness to cooperate of collective actors, who could promote such institutions, is paralysed by the asymmetric distribution of power and by imperial temptations, by blatant economic inequalities and battles over scarce resources.

Within the sphere of international politics, there is increasing pressure to enter into negotiations. These, however, would need to become more open and transparent for the transnational public sphere, so 'that one day the representatives of internationally negotiating bodies are forced to justify themselves in front of the "forum of global civilization".' Habermas (2007), 'Kommunikative Rationalität und grenzüberschreitende Politik', pp. 429 and 436f. For a critique of Habermas's vision of a global democracy, see Paech and Stuby (2013), *Völkerrecht und Machtpolitik in den internationalen Beziehungen*.

56 Habermas (2007), 'Kommunikative Rationalität und grenzüberschreitende Politik', p. 427. See Habermas, 'Preface', in *The Crisis of the European Union*, pp. vii–xii; here: pp. xf.

57 On the question of democratic constitutionalism, see the study 'Does the Constitutionalization of International Law Still Have a Chance?', in *The Divided West*, pp. 115–93.

58 'Is the Development of a European Identity Necessary, and Is it Possible?', in *The Divided West*, pp. 67–82; here: p. 81.

59 Habermas (1996), 'Citizenship and National Identity (1990)', in *Between Facts and Norms*, p. 500. See Habermas (2012), 'The Concept of Human Dignity and the Realistic Utopia of Human Rights', in *The Crisis of the European Union*, pp. 71–100; here: pp. 85ff.

60 Habermas (2007), 'Europa: Vision und Votum', pp. 518 and 519.

61 While Joschka Fischer has apparently abandoned the idea of a core Europe (see *Der Spiegel*, 28 February 2004), the CDU politicians Norbert Lammert, Angela Merkel and Wolfgang Schäuble sympathize with the idea of a two-speed Europe. In the context of this debate, Habermas pleads for a Europe-wide referendum, an idea he defends against the vice-president of the European Commission, Günter Verheugen (see *Süddeutsche Zeitung*, 21–2 June 2008). According to Habermas, the reason why European integration has begun to falter and is less popular with citizens, especially since the beginning of the financial and economic crisis, is an elitist politics – one he has fiercely criticized on various occasions, for instance in the article 'Entmündigung der europäischen Bürger' [Disenfranchisement of the European citizen] (*Süddeutsche Zeitung*, 7 April 2011), in which he decried the narrow-minded focus on the nation-state, especially in the German government, and predicted that citizens would defend themselves against 'politics without a normative core'.

62 Habermas in *Vorwärts*, January 2012.

63 Habermas ([2004] 2006), 'Does the Constitutionalization of International Law Still Have a Chance?', in *The Divided West*, p. 175.

64 In his analysis of the post-national constellation, Habermas refers to Karl Polanyi ([1944] 2001), *The Great Transformation*. See Habermas ([1998] 2001), 'The Postnational Constellation and the Future of Democracy', in *The Postnational Constellation*, pp. 58–112; here: pp. 84ff.

65 Ibid., p. 71. See also Habermas (1999), 'Der europäische Nationalstaat unter dem Druck der Globalisierung', *Blätter für deutsche und internationale Politik*, 4, pp. 425–36.

66 Habermas ([2005] 2008), 'A Political Constitution for the Pluralist World Society?', in *Between Naturalism and Religion*, pp. 312–52; here: p. 332.

67 Habermas ([1998] 2001), 'The Postnational Constellation and the Future of Democracy', p. 77; emphasis in the original.

68 Habermas (2012), 'The Crisis of the European Union in Light of a Constitutionalization of International Law', p. 10.

69 Ibid., p. 37.

70 Ibid., p. 13; emphasis in the original.

71 Habermas ([2004] 2006), 'Does the Constitutionalization of International Law Still Have a Chance?', p. 175.

72 Ibid., p. 135; see also p. 124.

73 Ibid., p. 140.

74 Ibid., pp. 141f.

75 Ibid., p. 144.

76 Habermas criticizes Kant for preferring the goal of a league of nations over the more distant goal of one nation, against his better judgement. The reason for this, he thinks, was a fear that a world republic might end up levelling out the social and cultural differences between nations. Kant was 'troubled by the tendency toward levelling, and even despotic, violence which seems to be endemic to the structure of a world republic. This is why he falls back on the surrogate of a league of nations.' Habermas ([2004] 2006), 'Does the Constitutionalization of International Law Still Have a Chance?', pp. 143f.; see also pp. 118ff.

77 Ibid., p. 136, and Habermas ([2005] 2008), 'A Political Constitution for the Pluralist World Society?', p. 316.

78 Ibid., p. 333 (trans. modified). See Habermas (2012), 'The Crisis of the

European Union in Light of a Constitutionalization of International Law',
pp. 53ff.

79 Habermas argues that human rights are based on moral convictions that
have been translated into the medium of law. Their moral surplus value
is sustained by the human dignity possessed by every individual. This
'explains the explosive political force of a concrete utopia'. By turning
the indivisible democratic, social and cultural human rights into positive
law, a legal duty is produced. Its purpose is to realize the excess of moral
content – i.e., to meet the historically changing forms of the violation of
human dignity with the means of legally enforceable rights. Habermas
(2012), 'The Concept of Human Dignity and the Concrete Utopia of
Human Rights', p. 75.

80 Habermas (2006 [2004]), 'Does the Constitutionalization of International
Law Still Have a Chance?', p. 118.

81 Habermas (2012), 'The Crisis of the European Union in Light of a
Constitutionalization of International Law', p. 55.

82 Habermas (2006 [2004]), 'Does the Constitutionalization of International
Law Still Have a Chance?', p. 189; see also pp. 100 and 121f.

83 Ibid., p. 174.

84 Ibid., p. 178; see also pp. 186f.

85 See Habermas (2012), 'The Crisis of the European Union in Light of a
Constitutionalization of International Law', pp. 61f.

86 Ibid., p. 63; emphasis in the original.

87 Habermas (2012), 'A Pact for or against Europe?', in *The Crisis of the
European Union*, pp. 127–39; here: p. 138.

Chapter 13 Philosophy in the Age of Postmetaphysical Modernity

1 Habermas (1992), 'The Unity of Reason in the Diversity of its Voices', in
Postmetaphysical Thinking, pp. 115–48; here: p. 139.

2 See Habermas ([1981] 1986), *The Theory of Communicative Action*, vol.
1, p. 138. Habermas provides the detailed justification for the intellectual motif of a postmetaphysical philosophy in relation to various
thematic perspectives in *Postmetaphysical Thinking* ([1988] 1992), *Truth
and Justification* ([1999] 2003), *Between Naturalism and Religion* ([2005]
2008) and *Nachmetaphysisches Denken II* [Postmetaphysical Thinking II],
published in the autumn of 2012.

3 On the critique of the philosophy of consciousness, see Habermas (2009),
Philosophische Texte, vol. 5: *Kritik der Vernunft*, pp. 193ff.

4 Jürgen Habermas (2012), *Nachmetaphysisches Denken II*, p. 32.

5 Dieter Henrich (1987), *Konzepte*, pp. 11–43. See also Henrich (1986),
'Was ist Metaphysik, was Moderne? Thesen gegen Jürgen Habermas'.
Habermas (1985), 'Rückkehr zur Metaphysik – eine Tendenz in der
deutschen Philosophie?'; Habermas (1992), 'Metaphysics after Kant'
and 'Themes in Postmetaphysical Thinking', in *Postmetaphysical
Thinking*, pp. 10–27, 28–53. See also Daniel C. Henrich (2007), *Zwischen
Bewusstseinsphilosophie und Naturalismus*, pp. 29–36.

6 See the informative conversation with Dieter Henrich (2008) 'Was ist
verlässlich im Leben?'.

7 Accordingly, in his second book on postmetaphysical philosophy,
Habermas writes: 'Today, even philosophical arguments can hope to

be accepted as *prima facie* worthy of consideration only within the contexts of the established discourses of the natural and social sciences and the humanities, of the practices of art criticism, of jurisprudence, of politics, and of media-based public communication.' Habermas (2012), *Nachmetaphysisches Denken II*, p. 7.

8 Habermas (1988), 'Eine Rezension', in *Nachmetaphysisches Denken*, pp. 267–79; here: p. 274. [The quotation is from the appendix, which contains Habermas's *Merkur* review article. This is not included in the English edition.]

9 Habermas (1992), 'Individuation through Socialization: On Mead's Theory of Subjectivity', in *Postmetaphysical Thinking*, pp. 149–204; here: p. 177.

10 Habermas, 'Transcendence from within, Transcendence in this World', in Browning and Fiorenza (1992), *Habermas, Modernity and Public Theology*, pp. 226–50.

11 Habermas (2003), 'Norms and Values: On Hilary Putnam's Kantian Pragmatism', in *Truth and Justification*, pp. 213–36; here: pp. 216 and 218 (trans. modified).

12 See Habermas (2012), *Nachmetaphysisches Denken II*, pp. 45f.

13 Ibid., p. 16.

14 Habermas (2003), 'Rightness versus Truth: On the Sense of Normative Validity in Moral Judgments and Norms', in *Truth and Justification*, pp. 237–76; here: p. 273. On the philosophical concept of 'a reason', see Habermas (2012), *Nachmetaphysisches Denken II*, pp. 77–95; esp. pp. 9, 42 and 154.

15 Habermas (1992), 'Themes in Postmetaphysical Thinking', in *Postmetaphysical Thinking*, pp. 28–53; here: p. 35.

16 Habermas (1992), 'The Unity of Reason in the Diversity of its Voices'.

17 'The metaphysical format is characterized by a philosophical thinking which is neither fallibilistic, as the sciences are, nor pluralistic, as interpretations of life in modernity are, which exist only in the plural.' Habermas, 'Eine Rezension', p. 274. See also Habermas ([1985] 1987), 'Excursus on Leveling the Genre Distinction between Philosophy and Literature', in *The Philosophical Discourse of Modernity*, pp. 185–210; here: p. 409 [note to p. 210].

18 Habermas, 'The Unity of Reason in the Diversity of its Voices', p. 140; emphasis in the original.

19 Habermas (2010), '"Bohrungen an der Quelle des objektiven Geistes": Laudatio bei der Verleihung des Hegel-Preises an Michael Tomasello', p. 166. The speech can also be found in Habermas (2013), *Im Sog der Technokratie*, pp. 166–73; here: p. 167. [The text is not part of the English edition.]

20 Habermas (2009), *Philosophische Texte*, vol. 2: *Rationalitäts- und Sprachtheorie*, p. 23.

21 Ibid., p. 11.

22 See Habermas (2009), *Philosophische Texte*, vol. 1: *Sprachtheoretische Grundlegung der Soziologie*, p. 10. Also Habermas, 'Nach dreißig Jahren: Bemerkungen zu *Erkenntnis und Interesse*', in Müller-Doohm (2000), *Das Interesse der Vernunft*, pp. 12–20. See also the afterword by Anke Thyen in the reissue of Habermas (2008), *Erkenntnis und Interesse*, pp. 367–422.

23 On the consensus theory of truth, see Scheit (1987), *Wahrheit, Diskurs, Demokratie*, esp. pp. 86–223. However, this study does not discuss Habermas's revisions to his theory.

24 See Habermas (1984), *Vorstudien und Ergänzungen zur Theorie des kommunikativen Handelns*, pp. 127–83. Also in Habermas (2009), *Philosophische Texte*, vol. 2: *Rationalitäts- und Sprachtheorien*, pp. 208–69.

25 See Lafont (1994), 'Spannungen im Wahrheitsbegriff'; Wellmer (1989), 'Was ist eine pragmatische Bedeutungstheorie'; see also Wellmer (2004), *Sprachphilosophie*, pp. 228–39.

26 Habermas (2009), *Philosophische Texte*, vol. 2: *Rationalitäts- und Sprachtheorien*, p. 27; emphasis in the original.

27 Habermas (2003), 'Introduction: Realism after the Linguistic Turn', in *Truth and Justification*, pp. 1–49; here: p. 39.

28 Ibid., p. 38; emphasis in the original.

29 Habermas (2003), 'Rightness versus Truth: On the Sense of Normative Validity in Moral Judgments and Norms', in *Truth and Justification*, pp. 237–75.

30 Habermas (2003), 'Hermeneutic and Analytic Philosophy: Two Complementary Versions of the Linguistic Turn', in *Truth and Justification*, pp. 51–81; here: p. 68.

31 Habermas (2003), 'Rightness versus Truth', p. 247; emphasis in the original.

32 Ibid., p. 266; emphasis in the original.

33 Ibid., p. 258.

34 Ibid., p. 249. See Habermas (2008), '"I Myself am Part of Nature" – Adorno on the Intrication of Reason in Nature: Reflections on the Relation between Freedom and Unavailability', in *Between Naturalism and Religion*, pp. 181–208; here: pp. 205ff. See also Dews (2001), 'Naturalismus und Anti-Naturalismus bei Habermas'.

35 Habermas (2003), 'Introduction: Realism after the Linguistic Turn', pp. 3f.

36 Habermas (2003), 'Hermeneutic and Analytic Philosophy: Two Complementary Versions of the Linguistic Turn', p. 78.

37 Habermas (1999), 'Rationalität der Verständigung: Sprechakttheoretische Erläuterungen zum Begriff der kommunikativen Rationalität', in *Wahrheit und Rechtfertigung*, pp. 102–37; here: p. 110; emphasis in the original. [This essay is not part of the English edition.]

38 Habermas (2003), 'Introduction: Realism after the Linguistic Turn', p. 8.

39 Ibid., pp. 13 (trans. modified) and 33; emphasis in the original.

40 Ibid., p. 17.

41 Ibid., pp. 9f. See Henrich (2007), *Zwischen Bewusstseinsphilosophie und Naturalismus*.

42 Habermas (2003), 'Introduction: Realism after the Linguistic Turn', pp. 16f. See also Habermas, 'Richard Rorty's Pragmatic Turn', in Brandom (2000), *Rorty and his Critics*, pp. 31–55; here: pp. 34ff. [Also to be found in *On the Pragmatics of Communication* (1999), pp. 343–82; here: pp. 348ff.]

43 Habermas, 'The Language Game of Responsible Agency and the Problem of Free Will: How Can Epistemic Dualism be Reconciled with Ontological Monism?', *Philosophical Explorations*, 10/1 (2007), pp. 13–50; here: p. 36.

44 Habermas (2003), 'Introduction: Realism after the Linguistic Turn', p. 26.

45 Ibid., p. 28. See Habermas (2008), 'Freedom and Determinism', in *Between Naturalism and Religion*, pp. 151–80; here: p. 166:

Epistemic dualism [i.e., the distinction between world and lifeworld, observation and understanding, S. M.-D.] must not be conjured up out of transcendental thin air. It must have *emerged* in the course of an evolutionary learning process and have already proven itself in the cognitive efforts of *Homo sapiens* to come to terms with the challenges of a risky environment. On this assumption, the continuity of natural history that we can conceive at least *on an analogy with* Darwinian evolution, though we cannot form a theoretically satisfying concept of it, can ensure the unity of a universe to which human beings belong as natural creatures. This enables us to bridge the epistemic gap between nature as objectified by the natural sciences and a culture that we always already intuitively understand because it is intersubjectively shared.

46 Habermas (2007), 'The Language Game of Responsible Agency', p. 39 (trans. modified).
47 See Habermas (2012), *Nachmetaphysisches Denken II*, p. 62. Peter Dews correctly emphasizes the 'connection between anti-idealism, anti-scientism, *and* an inclination toward naturalism, which characterizes the specificity of Habermas's oeuvre'. Dews (2001), 'Naturalismus und Anti-Naturalismus bei Habermas', p. 862; emphasis in the original.
48 Habermas (2007), 'Das Sprachspiel verantwortlicher Urheberschaft und das Problem der Willensfreiheit', p. 302; emphasis in the original. [The English text does not contain this passage.]
49 Habermas (1999), '"Reasonable" versus "True", or the Morality of Worldviews', in: *The Inclusion of the Other*, pp. 75–101; here: p. 98.
50 In a recent publication, he writes: 'We observe in European modernity ... an intensification of the awareness of contingency and a growing anticipation of the future, a culmination of egalitarian universalism in law and morality, and a progressive individualization.' Habermas (2010), 'Ein neues Interesse der Philosophie an der Religion?', *Deutsche Zeitschrift für Philosophie*, pp. 3–16; here: p. 10. Also in Habermas (2012), *Nachmetaphysisches Denken II*, p. 109.
51 See Fleischer (1987), *Ethik ohne Imperativ*.
52 Habermas ([1992] 1996), *Between Facts and Norms*, pp. 97 and 24f. See also Habermas (1986), *The Theory of Communicative Action*, vol. 1, pp. 157ff.
53 Habermas ([1988] 1992), 'Metaphysics after Kant', in *Postmetaphysical Thinking*, p. 10–27; here: p. 18; emphasis in the original.
54 Habermas (1991), 'Treffen Hegels Einwände gegen Kant auch auf die Diskursethik zu?', in *Erläuterungen zur Diskursethik*, pp. 9–30; here: p. 30. Also in Habermas (2009) *Philosophische Texte*, vol. 5: *Kritik der Vernunft*, p. 421.
55 Habermas (1997), 'Noch einmal: Zum Verhältnis von Theorie und Praxis', in *Paradigmi: Rivista di Critica Filosofica*, Anno XV, no. 45, pp. 422–42. Habermas (2003), 'The Relationship between Theory and Practice Revisited', in *Truth and Justification*, pp. 277–92; here: p. 279; emphasis in the German original [trans. amended to follow the wording in *Wahrheit und Rechtfertigung*, p. 349].
56 Habermas ([1992] 1996), *Between Facts and Norms*, pp. 320f.; emphasis in the original.
57 Habermas, 'Reply to Symposium Participants, Benjamin N. Cardozo School of Law', *Cardozo Law Review*, 17 (1996), pp. 1477–558; here: p. 1531; emphasis in the original. [The German text quoted deviates from the version in the *Cardozo Law Review*, which does not contain the sentence before the omission.] See Forst (2002), *Contexts of Justice*, pp. 28f. and 193ff.

58 Rainer Forst explains Habermas's notion of a rational justification as one that is based on justified reasons. 'What is considered universal and reasonable [*allgemein-vernünftig*] must be universally justifiable. The business of reason is always a (self-)critical business.' See Forst (2002), *Contexts of Justice*, p. 197.

59 See Habermas ([1991] 1994), 'On the Pragmatic, the Ethical, and the Moral Employments of Practical Reason', in *Justification and Application: Remarks on Discourse Ethics*, pp. 1–18.

60 Habermas ([1983] 1990), 'Discourse Ethics: Notes on a Program of Philosophical Justification', in *Moral Consciousness and Communicative Action*, pp. 43–115; here: p. 104. In another essay, which discusses Rawls's notion of justice, Habermas draws an even clearer line of demarcation between norms and values:

> Norms inform decisions as to what one ought to do, values inform decisions as to what conduct is most desirable. Recognized norms impose equal and exceptionless obligations on their addressees, while values express the preferability of goods that are striven for by particular groups. ... The obligatory force of norms has the absolute meaning of an unconditional and universal duty: what one ought to do is what is equally good for all (that is, for all addressees). The attractiveness of values reflects an evaluation and a transitive ordering of goods that has become established in particular cultures or has been adopted by particular groups: important evaluative decisions or higher order preferences express what is good for us (or for me), all things considered. (Habermas ([1996] 1999), 'Reconciliation through the Public Use of Reason', in *The Inclusion of the Other*, pp. 49–74; here: p. 55)

See also *Die Einbeziehung des Anderen*, pp. 310–36; English: 'Reply to Symposium Participants, Benjamin N. Cardozo School of Law' (see note 57).

61 Habermas differentiates between the pragmatic, the ethical and the moral uses of practical reason:

> Pragmatic questions pose themselves from the perspective of an actor seeking suitable means for realizing goals and preferences that are already given. ... Ethical-political questions pose themselves from the perspective of members who, in the face of important life issues, want to gain clarity about their shared form of life and about ideals they feel should shape their common life. ... In moral questions, the teleological point of view from which we handle problems through goal-oriented cooperation gives way entirely to the normative point of view from which we examine how we can regulate our common life in the equal interest of all. (Habermas ([1992] 1996), *Between Facts and Norms*, pp. 159–61)

See also Habermas ([1991] 1994), 'On the Pragmatic, the Ethical, and the Moral Employments of Practical Reason', pp. 1–18..

62 Habermas ([1996] 1999), 'A Genealogical Analysis of the Cognitive Content of Morality', in *The Inclusion of the Other*, pp. 3–46; here: p. 29.

63 Ibid.

64 See Forst (2002), *Contexts of Justice*, esp. pp. 173–200.

65 Habermas (1990), *Die nachholende Revolution*, p. 119.

66 See Habermas (1996), 'Reply to Symposium Participants, Benjamin N. Cardozo School of Law'.

67 See Finlayson and Freyenhagen (2010), *Habermas and Rawls*. The American and the German philosopher take the fact of a pluralism of values and the principle of tolerance as their starting points and agree that a distinction between morality and ethics must be made. However, Rawls proposes a model of distributive justice on a contractual basis, while Habermas proposes a model of procedural justice. For Rawls, the egalitarian conception of justice entails a redistribution of basic goods in favour of the least well-off.

68 See Habermas ([1996] 1999), 'Reconciliation through the Public Use of Reason', and John Rawls, 'Political Liberalism: Reply to Habermas', *Journal of Philosophy*, 92/3 (1995), pp. 132–80. See also Finlayson and Freyenhagen (2010), *Habermas and Rawls*, and Forst (2014), *The Right to Justification*, pp. 79–123.

69 Habermas ([1996] 1999), 'Reconciliation through the Public Use of Reason', p. 72; emphases in the original.

70 Habermas ([1991] 1994), 'On the Pragmatic, the Ethical, and the Moral Employments of Practical Reason', esp. pp. 8ff. See Wingert (1993), *Gemeinsinn und Moral*, p. 145. Rainer Forst draws attention to the fact 'that the space of ethical justification is three dimensional, that is, that subjective, intersubjective, and objective aspects of evaluation come together here: the question of the good "for me" is interwoven with the question of the "good for us" and always connected with reflection on the good "in itself".' Forst (2014), *The Right to Justification*, p. 65; see also pp. 70ff., 74, and 13–42.

71 Habermas ([1991] 1994), 'On the Pragmatic, the Ethical, and the Moral Employments of Practical Reason', p. 12. On the status of questions concerning justification and application, see Günther (1988), *Der Sinn für Angemessenheit*. For a critical perspective, see Alexy (1994), *Recht, Vernunft, Diskurs*.

72 Habermas ([1991] 1994), 'On the Pragmatic, the Ethical, and the Moral Employments of Practical Reason', p. 12.

73 Anke Thyen is of the opinion that Habermas's discourse ethics is an 'attempt at a rehabilitation of the ethical within morality':

This rehabilitation is plausible within the context of a transformation of purely practical reason into a theory of communicative reason, because the latter rests on a concept of argumentation which cannot ignore the ethical self-understanding of those who engage in the argument. The discourse on moral questions is dependent on the explication of the background of ethical certainties and of pre-understandings. (Thyen (2004), *Moral und Anthropologie*, p. 356)

74 Habermas ([1992] 1996), *Between Facts and Norms*, p. 308; emphasis in the original.

75 Habermas ([1996] 1999), 'The European Nation-State: On the Past and Future of Sovereignty and Citizenship', in *The Inclusion of the Other*, pp. 105–27; here: p. 117 (trans. modified). [The English translation actually speaks, less technically, of a 'guarantor for the social integration . . .'].

76 Habermas, 'Morality, Society, and Ethics: an Interview with Torben Hviid Nielsen', *Acta Sociologica*, 33/2 (1990), pp. 93–114; here: pp. 111f.

77 See ibid.
78 Habermas ([2005] 2008), 'Communicative Action and the Detranscendentalized "Use of Reason"', in *Between Naturalism and Religion*, pp. 24–76; here: p. 49 (trans. modified).
79 Habermas ([1983] 1990), 'Discourse Ethics: Notes on a Program of Philosophical Justification', in *Moral Consciousness and Communicative Action*, pp. 43–115; here: p. 67. See McCarthy (1978), *The Critical Theory of Jürgen Habermas*, p. 330.
80 Habermas has revised his original concept of an 'ideal speech situation'. See Habermas (1984), 'Vorlesungen zu einer sprachtheoretischen Grundlegung der Soziologie (1970/71)', in *Vorstudien und Ergänzungen zur Theorie des kommunikativen Handelns*, pp. 11–126; here: pp. 125f.
81 Habermas (1985), *'A Philosophico-Political Profile'*, p. 86.
82 Habermas ([1992] 1996), *Between Facts and Norms*, p. 323: 'The essentialist misunderstanding is replaced by a methodological fiction in order to obtain a foil against which the substratum of *unavoidable* societal complexity becomes visible. In this harmless sense, the ideal communication community presents itself as a model of "pure" communicative sociation.' (emphasis in the original).
83 Habermas ([1990] 1994), *The Past as Future*, p. 102.
84 Habermas (1985), *'A Philosophico-Political Profile'*, p. 101. Apparently, Habermas has taken to heart Albrecht Wellmer's critical hints. According to Wellmer, 'the formal structures of the ideal speech situation, or of the conditions for an ideal communicative community, when taken as an ideal vanishing point of a linguistic reality, signify not only an ideal condition for rational understanding but, in fact, at the same time a condition of an ideal *being*-understanding [Verständig-*seins*].' Wellmer (1986), *Ethik und Dialog*, p. 101; see also pp. 78ff.; emphasis in the original.
85 Habermas ([1988] 1992), 'Themes in Postmetaphysical Thinking', in *Postmetaphysical Thinking*, pp. 28–53; here: p. 47.
86 The four discursive rules formulated by Habermas are publicness and inclusion; communicative equality; exclusion of deception and self-deception; and the unforced force of the better argument. See Habermas ([2005] 2008), 'Communicative Action and the Detranscendentalized "Use of Reason"', in *Between Naturalism and Religion*, pp. 24–76; here: p. 50.
87 Habermas, 'The New Obscurity', *Philosophy and Social Criticism*, 11/1 (1986), pp. 1–18; here: p. 17; emphases in the original.
88 Habermas, 'Ich bin alt, aber nicht fromm geworden', in Funken (2008), *Über Habermas*, pp. 182 and 185.
89 Jürgen Habermas ([1992] 1996), *Between Naturalism and Religion*, p. 1.
90 Habermas and Eduardo Mendieta (2010), 'Ein neues Interesse der Philosophie an der Religion: Zur philosophischen Bewandtnis von postsäkularem Bewusstsein und multikultureller Weltgesellschaft', *Deutsche Zeitschrift für Philosophie*, 58, pp. 3–16. [An English translation of this interview – 'A Postsecular World Society? On the Philosophical Significance of Postsecular Consciousness and the Multicultural World Society' – is available online at http://mrzine.monthlyreview.org/2010/habermas210310.html.] For Habermas, the sacred has a fascinating authority because, in genealogical terms, he sees morality as having its origin in the symbolically structured sphere of the sacred. He already rendered this idea plausible in *The Theory of Communicative Action*. Under the heading of a 'Linguistification of the Sacred', and following on from

Émile Durkheim, he develops the thesis 'that the concept of a criticizable validity claim derives from an assimilation of the truth of statements to the validity of norms (which was, to begin with, not criticizable).' Habermas (1987), *The Theory of Communicative Action*, vol. 2, p. 70. He assumes that '[t]he normative consensus that is expounded in the semantics of the sacred is present . . . in the form of an idealized agreement *transcending spatio-temporal changes*. This furnishes the model *for all concepts of validity*, especially for the idea of truth.' Ibid., p. 71; emphases in the original [the emphases are omitted in the English translation and have been restored]. See Wellmer's critical comments on this in Wellmer (1986), *Ethik und Dialog*, pp. 151f.

91 Habermas, 'A Postsecular World Society? On the Philosophical Significance of Postsecular Consciousness and the Multicultural World Society', http://mrzine.monthlyreview.org/2010/habermas210310.html.

92 Ibid.

93 Habermas (2008), 'Religion in the Public Sphere: Cognitive Presuppositions for the "Public Use of Reason" by Religious and Secular Citizens', in *Between Naturalism and Religion*, pp. 114–47; here: p. 141.

94 Habermas ([1971] 2012), 'Does Philosophy Still Have a Purpose?', in *Philosophical-Political Profiles*, pp. 1–19; here: p. 12. See Habermas ([1999] 2003), *Truth and Justification*, pp. 159f.

95 See Habermas (2009), *Philosophische Texte*, vol. 5: *Kritik der Vernunft*, p. 32. [Here, at the end of his introduction to the collection of philosophical essays, Habermas writes:

> The attempt at borrowing promising connotations from religious vocabulary in order, allegedly, to gain authenticity is not a question of literary style but of a dissolution of discursive thinking. . . . Religion itself cannot survive without ritual practices. It is this fact, more categorically than the authority of revelation, which separates religion from secular intellectual forms. This should serve as a warning to all philosophy that enthusiastically attempts to cross the methodological threshold between faith and knowledge.]

96 Habermas ([1973] 1988), *Legitimation Crisis*, pp. 118f. See also Habermas ([1971] 2012), *Philosophical-Political Profiles*, p. 11, where Habermas writes: 'But in no case . . . did a philosophy serious about its claim want to replace the certainty of salvation of religious faith. It never offered a promise of redemption.' As early as 4 December 1963, in a letter to Ulrich Schmidhäuser, Habermas wrote: 'I am deeply convinced that an "atheism" that would renounce the possibility of appropriating in its own way the moment of truth in myth, religion, theology and, *a fortiori*, the Christian tradition would necessarily be a pitiful, naked affair.' Bestand Na 60, Vorlass Jürgen Habermas, Archivzentrum der Universitätsbibliothek J. C. Senckenberg, Frankfurt am Main).

97 Bahr (1975), *Religionsgespräche*, p. 15. See Arens (1989), *Habermas und die Theologie: Beiträge zur theologischen Rezeption, Diskussion und Kritik der Theorie des kommunikativen Handelns*. The eleven contributors to this volume pursue the question of which role religion plays as a source of ethical life and human behaviour in Habermas's thinking. They reach the conclusion that, despite his self-confessed 'religious tone-deafness', Habermas ascribes an importance to the world religions analogous to that

of moral philosophy. An overview can be found in Reder and Schmidt, 'Habermas and Religion', in Reder and Schmidt (2010), *An Awareness of What is Missing: Faith and Reason in a Post-Secular Age*, pp. 1–14; Maly (2005), 'Die Rolle der Religion in der postsäkularen Gesellschaft'; Düringer (1999), *Universale Vernunft und partikularer Glaube*.

98 See Andreas Kuhlmann, 'Ohne Trost? Habermas und die Religion', *Frankfurter Allgemeine Zeitung*, 16 February 1988. See Habermas (2002), 'Transcendence from Within, Transcendence in this World', in *Religion and Rationality: Essays on Reason, God, and Modernity*, pp. 67–94; Habermas ([1971] 2012), *Philosophical-Political Profiles*, p. 11.

99 Habermas ([2008] 2010), 'An Awareness of What is Missing', in Reder and Schmidt, *An Awareness of What is Missing*, pp. 15–23; here: p. 15.

100 Habermas (2002), 'Transcendence from Within, Transcendence in this World', p. 75.

101 Habermas ([1988] 1992), 'Themes in Postmetaphysical Thinking', in *Postmetaphysical Thinking*, pp. 28–53; here: p. 51 (trans. modified).

102 Habermas ([2008] 2010), 'An Awareness of What is Missing', p. 16.

103 Ibid., p. 21, and Jürgen Habermas (2008), 'Religion in the Public Sphere: Cognitive Presuppositions for the "Public Use of Reason" by Religious and Secular Citizens', p. 143.

104 Habermas ([2005] 2008), 'Religious Tolerance as Pacemaker for Cultural Rights', in *Between Naturalism and Religion*, pp. 251–70; here: pp. 261f.

105 Joseph Ratzinger was elected as the head of the Roman Catholic Church on 19 April 2005. As Pope Benedict XVI, he promoted the 'de-secularization' [*Entweltlichung*] of the Church, turned against the relativism of values, and spoke out for the freedom of religion as a right beyond mere tolerance. On 28 February 2013, he resigned from office because of his age.

106 See Horster (2006), *Jürgen Habermas und der Papst*.

107 *Zur Debatte*, 1/2004, p. 1.

108 Habermas ([2005] 2008), 'Prepolitical Foundations of the Constitutional State?', in *Between Naturalism and Religion*, pp. 101–13; here: pp. 104f.

109 Ibid., p. 110.

110 Ibid., p. 105.

111 In the conversation with Eduardo Mendieta in 1999, referred to above, Habermas goes so far as to say: 'Adorno bristled against this regressive tendency in postmetaphysical thought when he vowed to keep faith with metaphysics "at the moment of its downfall." . . . In this intention . . . I am in complete agreement with Adorno.' Habermas ([2001] 2006), 'A Conversation about God and the World', in *Time of Transitions*, pp. 149–69; here: p. 161. Religion is capable of keeping alive an awareness of the past and present suffering experienced by an ethically inappropriate life [*eines ethisch verfehlten Lebens*], as well as an 'awareness of what is missing'. At its core, this refers to the deficits resulting from the universal claims of scientism and naturalism, deficits we become aware of on account of the 'normatively imbued description and self-description of "distorted" social relations which violate basic interests'. Habermas ([2008] 2010), 'An Awareness of What is Missing', p. 73.

112 Habermas, with Ratzinger ([2005] 2006), *The Dialectics of Secularization: On Reason and Religion*, pp. 74, 77, 78, and 79.

113 Thomas Assheuer, 'Ruhelos und unbeirrbar', *Die Zeit*, 17 June 2004; Christian Geyer, 'Strukturwandel der Heiligkeit', *Frankfurter Allgemeine*

Zeitung, 21 January 2004; Alexander Kissler, 'Die Entgleisung der Moderne: Wie Habermas und Ratzinger den Glauben rechtfertigen', *Süddeutsche Zeitung*, 21 January 2004.

114 This is the original title of the paper, which was delivered in English.

115 Benedict XVI, Address at the meeting with the authorities and the diplomatic corps, Hofburg, Vienna, Friday, 7 September 2007. The text is available online at http://w2.vatican.va/content/benedict-xvi/en/speeches/2007/september/documents/hf_ben-xvi_spe_20070907_hofburg-wien.html, and in *L'Osservatore Romano: Weekly Edition in English* n. 37 pp. 4f.

116 In the *Neue Züricher Zeitung* (10 February 2007), Habermas wrote:

> Pope Benedict XVI gave the old debate over the Hellenization and de-Hellenization of Christianity an unexpected turn towards a critique of modernity in his recent speech in Regensburg. In so doing, he also answered in the negative the question of whether Christian theology has to engage with the challenges of modern, postmetaphysical reason. The pope refers to the synthesis of Greek metaphysics and biblical faith that is provided by the tradition from Augustine to Aquinas and implicitly denies that there are good reasons for the problematization of faith and knowledge which has, as a matter of fact, arisen within European modernity. Although he rejects the idea of 'putting the clock back to the time before the Enlightenment and rejecting the insights of the modern age', he braces himself against 'the force of arguments which made the synthesis of this worldview burst'. [The Regensburg speech is available online at http://w2.vatican.va/content/benedict-xvi/en/speeches/2006/september/documents/hf_ben-xvi_spe_20060912_university-regensburg.html]

See Habermas ([2008] 2010), 'An Awareness of What is Missing', p. 22. See also Nikolaus Lobkowicz, 'Ein Beitrag, der das Entsetzen erklärt', *Die Tagespost: Katholische Zeitung für Politik, Gesellschaft und Kultur*, 17 February 2007.

117 The passage from the conversation with Eduardo Mendieta in 1999 in its entirety runs:

> Christianity has functioned for the normative self-understanding of modernity as more than a mere precursor or a catalyst. Egalitarian universalism, from which sprang the ideas of freedom and social solidarity, of an autonomous conduct of life and emancipation, of the individual morality of conscience, human rights, and democracy, is the direct heir to the Judaic ethic of justice and the Christian ethic of love. This legacy, substantially unchanged, has been the object of continual critical appropriation and reinterpretation. To this day, there is no alternative to it. (Habermas ([2001] 2006), 'A Conversation about God and the World', in *Time of Transitions*, pp. 149–69; here: pp. 150f.)

118 See Habermas (2008), 'Die Dialektik der Säkularisierung', *Blätter für deutsche und internationale Politik*, 4, pp. 33–46. See also Habermas (2012), 'Religion in der Öffentlichkeit der "postsäkularen" Gesellschaft', in *Nachmetaphysisches Denken II*, pp. 308–28; and Helmut Mayer, 'Was ist mit dem Rest? Jürgen Habermas deutet die Rückkehr der Religion', *Frankfurter Allgemeine Zeitung*, 2 February 2008.

119 See the volume on *Habermas and Religion*, edited by Calhoun et al. in 2013, which contains an extensive reply from Habermas in which he defends his postmetaphysical perspective on post-secular society against objections raised by José Casanova, María Herrera Lima, Maria Pia Lara, Amy Allen, Max Pensky, John Milbank and others. See also Habermas (2009), 'Die Revitalisierung der Weltreligionen – Herausforderung für ein säkulares Selbstverständnis der Moderne?', in *Philosophische Texte*, vol. 5: *Kritik der Vernunft*, pp. 387–416; Habermas (2013), 'Reply to my Critics', in Calhoun et al., *Habermas and Religion*, pp. 347–90.

120 'A Postsecular World Society? On the Philosophical Significance of Postsecular Consciousness and the Multicultural World Society: An Interview with Jürgen Habermas by Eduardo Mendieta', http://blogs.ssrc. org/tif/wp-content/uploads/2010/02/A-Postsecular-World-Society-TIF. pdf, p. 8. [German text: Habermas (2012), 'Ein neues Interesse an der Religion: Ein Interview mit Eduardo Mendieta', in *Nachmetaphysisches Denken II*, pp. 96–119; here: p. 110f.]

121 Ibid., p. 6 (trans. modified). [The existing English translation has 'redemptive memory', which loses the clearly intended allusion to 'Consciousness-Raising or Rescuing Critique?', Habermas's essay on Benjamin; German text: ibid., p. 107].

122 Ibid., p. 12. [German text: ibid. p. 117].

123 Ibid.; emphasis in the original. [German text: ibid., p. 118].

124 I refer to a bundle of manuscripts titled 'Versuch über Glauben und Wissen: Nachmetaphysisches Denken und das säkulare Selbstverständnis der Modern' [Essay on faith and knowledge: postmetaphysical thinking and the secular self-understanding of modernity]. See Habermas (2012), 'Eine Hypothese zum gattungsgeschichtlichen Sinn des Ritus' [A hypothesis on the evolutionary meaning of rites], in *Nachmetaphysisches Denken II*, pp. 77–95.

125 'A Postsecular World Society?' (as in note 120), p. 5. [German text: p. 104].

126 See Habermas (2012), 'Eine Hypothese zum gattungsgeschichtlichen Sinn des Ritus', pp. 87ff.

127 'A Postsecular World Society?' (as in note 120), p. 5. [German text: p. 104].

128 See Tomasello (2008), *Origins of Human Communication*; Habermas (2013), 'Bohrungen an der Quelle des objektiven Geistes: Laudatio bei der Verleihung des Hegel-Preises an Michael Tomasello', in *Im Sog der Technokratie*, pp. 166–73. [The text is not part of the English edition.]

129 Jürgen Habermas (1988), 'Handlungen, Sprechakte, sprachlich vermittelte Interaktionen und Lebenswelt' [Actions, speech acts, linguistically mediated interactions, and the life-world], in *Nachmetaphysisches Denken*, pp. 63–104; here: pp. 100f.; emphasis in the original. ['Personen *sind* symbolische Strukturen, während das symbolisch durchstrukturierte naturhafte Substrat zwar als eigener Leib erfahren wird, aber als Natur den Individuen so äußerlich bleibt wie die materielle Naturbasis der Lebenswelt im Ganzen.' – This text is not part of the English edition.]

130 In an open letter to Plessner, which was originally published in *Merkur* in 1972, Habermas writes:

> Your concept of the *eccentric position* has proven to be extremely fruitful. The ingenious interpretation of laughter and crying confirms the idea of the model according to which the human being is under compulsion repeatedly to re-establish a balance between 'being a body' [*Leib-Sein*] and

'having-a-body' [*Körper-Haben*]; the human being must bridge the distance between the condition of existing as a body [*zuständlicher Leibexistenz*] and objective physical existence [*gegenständlicher Körperexistenz*]. (Habermas (1973), *Kultur und Kritik*, p. 233)

131 I make use of a hitherto unpublished interview of 2008, conducted by Karl-Siegbert Rehberg in written form.

132 Habermas refers to Wilhelm von Humboldt in numerous places of his work, especially to Humboldt's *On Language* (1999). Iso Camartin draws attention to the fact that Humboldt's 'model of understanding based on conversation' is the godfather of the 'concept of society based on the theory of communication'. 'Going beyond Humboldt, Habermas then saw in language not only "the organ which forms thinking" but also the organ of social practice and of experience, of the formation of ego- and group-identities.' Camartin (1991), *Von Sils-Maria aus betrachtet*, p. 46.

133 Habermas (2008), Interview with Karl-Siegbert Rehberg, MS, pp. 1f.

134 Reprinted in Habermas (1973), *Kultur und Kritik*, pp. 89–111.

135 Ibid., p. 108. On this cluster of themes, see Jörke (2005), *Politische Anthropologie*, pp. 73–87 and 127–31.

136 Habermas (1973), *Kultur und Kritik*, p. 107.

137 Ibid., p. 108; emphasis in the original.

138 See Habermas (2012), 'Arnold Gehlen: Imitation Substantiality', in: *Political-Philosophical Profiles*, Polity (Cambridge), pp. 111–28. See also the afterword by Karl-Siegbert Rehberg in Gehlen (2004) *Gesamtausgabe*, vol. 6: *Die Seele im technischen Zeitalter und andere sozial-psychologische, soziologische und kulturanalytische Schriften*, p. 653. On Habermas's critique of Gehlen in *Merkur*, see pp. 160–2 above.

139 Audiotapes of this lecture were transcribed at the time and distributed as pirate copies. In what follows, I refer to personal notes as well as this transcription, although the latter is not authorized by Habermas and contains some mistakes.

140 See Habermas ([1988] 1992) *Postmetaphysical Thinking*, pp. 20 and 45; ([1999] 2003) *Truth and Justification*, pp. 9 and 22ff.; and ([2005] 2008) *Between Naturalism and Religion*, pp. 182f.

141 In the transcript mentioned above, it says: 'ritual forms of behaviour and taboos represent the first institutions which stabilize a precarious consciousness brought about by linguistic interaction and at the same time create the motivational foundation for communicative action through canalization and integration, as well as through regression and compensation.'

142 Habermas (2000), 'Nach dreißig Jahren: Bemerkungen zu *Erkenntnis und Interesse*'.

143 Habermas (1973), *Kultur und Kritik*, pp. 118–94; here: p. 118; emphasis in the original. See also pp. 195–231.

144 Habermas (1973), *Kultur und Kritik*, p. 196; ([1968] 2004) *Knowledge and Human Interests*, 'A Postscript', pp. 351–80; here: p. 365.

145 Habermas (1973), *Kultur und Kritik*, p. 132.

146 Habermas ([1984] 2003), *Vorstudien und Ergänzungen zur Theorie des kommunikativen Handelns*, pp. 192f.

147 See Habermas ([1981] 1987) *The Theory of Communicative Action*, vol. 2, pp. 100ff.

148 Habermas ([1988] 1992), 'Individuation through Socialization: On George

Herbert Mead's Theory of Subjectivity', in *Postmetaphysical Thinking*, pp. 149–204; here: pp. 185 and 190f.

149 Ibid., p. 181; emphasis in the original (trans. modified).

150 In an introductory look at the history of philosophy, Habermas mentions a letter that Rousseau sent to the French statesman Guillaume-Chrétien de Lamoignon de Malesherbes. According to Habermas, the literary genre of the letter reflects a shift in attitude, which he describes as performative. From this, he derives support for the idea of 'explaining the meaning of the expression "individuality" with reference to the self-understanding of a subject who is capable of speech and action, one who in the face of other dialogue participants presents and, if necessary, justifies himself as an irreplaceable and distinctive person'. Ibid., p. 168.

151 In Hegel's early writings, Habermas already sees a move beyond the

> relation of lonely reflection in favour of a complementary relation between individuals who recognize one another [*sich erkennender Individuen*]. The experience of self-consciousness is no longer taken as the original starting point. Rather, for Hegel, it results from the experience of interaction in which I learn to see myself with the eyes of the other subject. The consciousness I have of myself is derivative of an intertwining of perspectives. Only on the basis of mutual recognition [*wechselseitiger Anerkennung*] can self-consciousness form, which must be tied to the reflection of myself in the consciousness of another subject. (Habermas (1968), *Technik und Wissenschaft als 'Ideology'*, p. 13)

152 Habermas ([1981] 1987), *The Theory of Communicative Action*, vol. 2, pp. 4 and 43.

153 See Joas (1980), *Praktische Intersubjektivität: Die Entwicklung des Werks von George Herbert Mead.* See also Créau (1991), *Kommunikative Vernunft als 'entmystifiziertes Schicksal'*, pp. 100–12. Just as Joas points out that Mead's concept of action must be understood in terms of reciprocal relations between subjects and not in terms of linguistic communication, Créau criticizes the 'emphasis placed on the reciprocal recognition of subjects as the fundamental aspect in the constitution of identical meanings'. This, Créau says, is evidence of Habermas's deviations from 'Mead's theory as a result of his Hegelian reading of him'. Ibid., p. 106; see also pp. 166f.

154 Conceptually, Habermas explains, Mead describes the structure of identity as the interaction between the three components of 'I', 'Me' and 'Self'. In accordance with this, the social genesis of the individual can be explained on the basis of a double interaction. As the reactions of partners in interaction to one's own actions are registered, ideas about their point of view are formed, and thus an understanding of one's own person that is represented by the instance of the 'Me'. The 'I' stands for the uniqueness and distinctiveness of the person as a natural being. 'Me' and 'I' interact, thus allowing the individual to form its specific 'Self' as the integrated unity of the subject. See Habermas ([1981] 1987), *The Theory of Communicative Action*, vol. 2, pp. 40ff. and 58ff.

155 Ibid., pp. 98f.; emphases in the original. [Some emphases are omitted in the English translation and have here been restored.]

156 Habermas ([1988] 1992), 'Individuation through Socialization', p. 170.

157 Habermas ([2005] 2008), '"I Myself am Part of Nature" – Adorno on the

Intrication of Reason in Nature: Reflections on the Relation between Freedom and Unavailability', in *Between Naturalism and Religion*, pp. 181–208; here: p. 185.

158 Habermas (2012), *Nachmetaphysisches Denken II*, p. 45.

159 Habermas (2010), 'Bohrungen an der Quelle des objektiven Geistes', in *Im Sog der Technokratie*, in *Between Naturalism and Religion*, pp. 181–208; here: p. 169; emphases in the original. [The text is not part of the English edition.]

160 Habermas (2012), *Nachmetaphysisches Denken II*, p. 12.

161 Habermas ([1981] 1987), *The Theory of Communicative Action*, vol. 2, pp. 77–112. By 'linguistification of the sacred', Habermas here understands 'the transfer of cultural reproduction, social integration, and socialization from sacred foundations over to linguistic communication and action oriented to mutual understanding'. The authority of the holy 'is gradually replaced by the authority of an achieved consensus. . . . The aura of rapture and terror that emanates from the sacred, the *spellbinding* power of the holy, is sublimated into the *binding/bonding* force of criticizable validity claims and at the same time turned into an everyday occurrence.' Ibid., pp. 107, 77; emphases in the original. For a critical assessment, see Joas (1997), *Die Entstehung der Werte*, p. 281.

162 Habermas (2012), *Nachmetaphysisches Denken II*, pp. 14 and 15.

163 This is how Habermas put it in an open letter to Plessner. Habermas (1973), *Kultur und Kritik*, p. 232.

164 Jürgen Habermas (2008), '"I Myself am Part of Nature" – Adorno on the Intrication of Reason in Nature', pp. 187 and p. 202 (trans. modified). [The last quotation reads in German: 'Nun kann sich eine Person ihre Handlungen nur dann selbst zurechnen, wenn sie sich mit dem Körper als ihrem eigenen Leib identifiziert' (*Zwischen Naturalismus und Religion*, p. 208), and is rendered as follows in the English edition: 'A person can regard his actions as accountable only when he identifies with his body as his own lived body.' 'Zurechnen', in this context, vacillates between 'taking responsibility for' and 'identifying as one's own'.]

Chapter 14 Books at an Exhibition

1 See Frank Schirrmacher, 'Thomas Mann: Unterhalter deutscher Ausgewanderter', *Frankfurter Allgemeine Zeitung*, 12 August 2005.

2 The formula 'world power' seems to be taken from a characterization which relates to the international renown of Thomas Mann. See Raddatz (2010), *Tagebücher 1982–2001*, p. 418.

3 Unseld-Berkéwicz (2009), 'Glückwünsche der Verlegerin', p. 52.

4 Richard Sennett, 'Licht im Schattenreich', *Die Zeit*, 10 June 2009. Habermas was very much a practitioner of discourse when he appeared at a conference which took place in his honour at the University of Zurich two weeks before his actual birthday. The central question posed by the organizers, Georg Kohler and Lutz Wingert, was whether democratic governments had been taken hostage by powerful global economic actors. Habermas intervened in the lively discussions over two days, commenting off the cuff on the individual papers.

5 Michael Krüger, 'Menschenrecht und Marillenknödel', *Süddeutsche Zeitung*, 18 June 2009.

6 The title refers to an essay by Habermas from 2007, 'Die Zeit hatte einen doppelten Boden' [Time had two dimensions], in Stefan Müller-Doohm (2007), *Adorno-Portraits*, p. 18.

7 I refer to personal notes from conversations with Habermas, as well as to an unpublished manuscript by Habermas.

8 Habermas, 'Reminiszenzen an Frankfurt' [Reminiscences of Frankfurt], in Müller-Doohm et al. (2009), '*... die Lava des Gedankens im Fluss*', p. 55.

9 Ibid., p. 57; emphasis in the original.

10 I refer to Habermas's manuscript for the speech: 'Ansprache während des Universitätsempfangs', which he kindly put at my disposal.

11 Habermas (2009), *Philosophische Texte*, vol. 1: *Sprachtheoretische Grundlegung der Soziologie*, p. 7; emphasis in the original.

12 Habermas ([2008] 2010), 'A Reply', in *An Awareness of What is Missing*, pp. 72–83; here: p. 73.

13 Habermas also talked about the topic of human rights in his acceptance speech for the Jaime Brunet Prize at the University of Navarra in Spain on 8 May 2008. There, he objected to the fact that the politics of human rights is deteriorating into an instrument used by the competing major powers. A politics 'which pretends to be able to guarantee a self-determined life for its citizens primarily by ensuring economic freedoms' is also problematic, he said. Such a politics destroys 'the balance between the different categories of basic rights. Basic rights can politically redeem the moral promise of respecting the human dignity of every individual only if all categories interact uniformly. Basic rights are indivisible, just as human dignity is the same everywhere and for all individuals.' Habermas (2009), 'Discurso de agradecimiento con motivo de la entrega del Premio Jaime Brunet 2008, Universidad Publica de Navarra, Pamplona', p. 5.

14 See Habermas (2010), 'The Concept of Human Dignity and the Realistic Utopia of Human Rights', *Metaphilosophy*, 41, pp. 464–80; here: p. 467. (Published in German as: 'Das Konzept der Menschenwürde und die realistische Utopie der Menschenrechte', *Blätter für deutsche und internationale Politik*, 8, pp. 43–53.)

15 Audiotapes of the discussion can be accessed at http://blogs.ssrc.org/tif/2009/12/04/rethinking-secularism-the-power-of-religion-in-the-public-sphere/. The title of Habermas's presentation was 'The Political – The Rational Sense of a Questionable Inheritance of Political Theology' and is published in Mendieta and VanAntwerpen (2011), *The Power of Religion in the Public Sphere*, pp. 15–33. (Published in German as '"Das Politische" – Der vernünftige Sinn eines zweifelhaften Erbstücks der Politischen Theologie', in *Nachmetaphysisches Denken II*, pp. 238–56, as well as in Mendieta and VanAntwerpen (2012), *Religion und Öffentlichkeit*, pp. 28–52.)

16 Habermas (2012), 'The Concept of Human Dignity and the Realistic Utopia of Human Rights', in *The Crisis of the European Union*, pp. 71–99; here: pp. 94f.; emphasis in the original. See also 'Das Konzept der Menschenwürde und die realistische Utopie der Menschenrechte', *Deutsche Zeitschrift für Philosophie*, 58/3 (2010), pp. 343–57. The first time Habermas had spoken about human rights and human dignity had been in a lecture at the Center for Human Values at Princeton University in May 2010.

17 Conze et al. (2010), *Das Amt und die Vergangenheit*.

18 See, for example, Hans Mommsen, 'Das ganze Ausmaß der Verstrickung',

Frankfurter Rundschau, 16 November 2010, and 'Vergebene Chancen: "Das Amt" hat methodische Mängel', *Süddeutsche Zeitung*, 27 December 2010; Christopher Browning, 'Historikerstudie "Das Amt"': Das Ende aller Vertuschung', *Frankfurter Allgemeine Zeitung*, 10 December 2010; Ahjrich Meyer, '"Polizeilich näher charakterisierte Juden"': Das deutsche Auswärtige Amt und der Beginn der "Endlösung" in Frankreich', *Neue Züricher Zeitung*, 2 February 2011.

19 Christian Hacke, 'Hitlers willige Diplomaten: Neubeginn trotz personeller Kontinuität: Der Bericht zur Geschichte des Auswärtigen Amtes ist einseitig', *Die Welt*, 26 October 2010; Norbert Frei, 'Das Ende der Weizsäcker Legende: Ein Gespräch mit dem Mitglied der Historikerkommission Norbert Frei über das Selbstverständnis des Amtes, die Beteiligung von Diplomaten am Judenmord und den falschen Eifer der *Zeit* bei der Verteidigung der alten Mythen', *Die Zeit*, 28 October 2010.

20 See Patrick Bahners, 'Wie einmal sogar Habermas überrascht war', *Frankfurter Allgemeine Zeitung*, 14 January 2011.

21 Habermas (2011), 'Großzügige Remigranten: Über jüdische Philosophen in der frühen Bundesrepublik: Eine persönliche Erinnerung', *Neue Züricher Zeitung*, 2 July 2011. See also Habermas (2015), 'Jewish Philosophers and Sociologists as Returnees in the Early Federal Republic of Germany: A Recollection', in *The Lure of Technocracy*, pp. 105–18; esp. p. 105; Habermas (2012), 'Jüdische Stimmen im Diskurs der sechziger Jahre', *Münchner Beiträge zur Jüdischen Geschichte und Kultur*, 6/1.

22 Habermas (2015), 'Martin Buber – a Philosophy of Dialogue in its Historical Context', in *The Lure of Technocracy*, pp. 119–36; here: pp. 120, 122, 130, and 136.

23 Christian Geyer, 'Der gefährlichste mentale Stoff, den man sich denken kann', *Frankfurter Allgemeine Zeitung*, 21 July 2012. Habermas's lecture, titled 'Wieviel Religion verträgt der liberale Staat?' [How much religion can a liberal state tolerate?], was published in a slightly abridged version in *Neue Züricher Zeitung*, 6 August 2012. See also Graf and Meier (2013), *Politik und Religion*.

24 Habermas, 'Wieviel Religion verträgt der liberale Staat?', *Neue Züricher Zeitung*, 6 August 2012.

25 Ibid.

26 Geyer, 'Der gefährlichste mentale Stoff, den man sich denken kann'.

27 Ibid.

28 In an article titled 'Ein Lob den Iren' [A cheer for the Irish] (*Süddeutsche Zeitung*, 17 June 2008), Habermas shows understanding for the Irish 'No' in the referendum on the Lisbon Treaty. The citizens, he writes, had turned against the 'paternalism' of the Eurocrats and did not want to be treated like 'electoral cattle'. Europe would need to become a topic of lively debate in public places. In an interview on 21 May 2010 with Paul Gillespie, a journalist at the *Irish Times*, Habermas repeated his previous criticism (in *Die Zeit*, 12 May 2010) of the fact that there had never been a European election in any member country where the citizens had voted on the basis of anything other than purely national issues. During these years, Habermas gave numerous interviews on the European crisis in almost all of the important European print media outlets. He also signed the appeal by left-wing economists and political scientists of the initiative 'Europa neu begründen!' [A new foundation for Europe!], which was published online in January 2013 under the heading 'Den Marsch in den

Ruin stoppen! Die Krise durch Solidarität und Demokratie bewältigen!'
[Stop the march into ruin! Resolve the crisis through solidarity and
democracy!]. The appeal is available at www.europa-neu-begruenden.de/
sample-page/.

29 Habermas, '"The Political": The Rational Meaning of a Questionable
Inheritance of Political Theology', in Mendieta and VanAntwerpen (2011),
The Power of Religion in the Public Sphere, pp. 15–33; here: p. 20.

30 Ibid., p. 16

31 Habermas, '"Das Politische" – Das vernünftige Sinn eines zweifelhaften
Erbstücks der Politischen Theologie', in Mendieta and VanAntwerpen
(2012), *Religion und Öffentlichkeit*, pp. 28–52; here: pp. 45f. [My translation: the English edition ('"The Political"', p. 28) deviates substantially
from the German text: 'The public use of reason by religious and nonre-
ligious citizens alike may well spur deliberative politics in a pluralist civil
society and lead to the recovery of semantic potentials from religious traditions for the wider political culture.']

32 I quote from the text of the speech given on the occasion of the award ceremony in Vienna on 23 May 2012. The weekly newspaper *Die Furche* used
the opportunity to conduct an extensive interview with Habermas, published on the same day, covering the crisis in Europe. Habermas succinctly
presented his ideas about a 'transnationalization of democracy' without
'invoking the wrong goal of a European federal state'. Habermas (2015),
'The Next Step – an Interview', *The Lure of Technocracy*, pp. 63–72; here:
p. 66.

33 I quote from the text of the speech given upon receiving the Georg August
Zinn Prize on 5 September 2012. Habermas (2015), 'The Dilemma Facing
the Political Parties', ibid., pp. 73–9; here: pp. 73, 74 and 75.

34 Habermas (2015), 'Our Contemporary Heine: There are No Longer
Nations in Europe', ibid., pp. 137-153; here: pp. 146f.

35 Habermas had spoken about Heine at a conference of the Heinrich Heine
Institute in Düsseldorf. The title of his opening lecture was 'Heinrich
Heine und die Rolle des Intellektuellen in Deutschland' [Heinrich Heine
and the role of the intellectual in Germany]. A shortened version was pub-
lished in *Merkur* (June 1986), pp. 453–68, and in Habermas (1987), *Eine
Art Schadensabwicklung*, pp. 25–54. See pp. 234f. and 252f. above.

36 Habermas (2015), 'Our Contemporary Heine', p. 140 (Habermas quotes
from Heinrich Heine (1986), *Religion and Philosophy in Germany*, trans.
John Snodgrass, Albany, NY, p. 96).

37 Ibid., pp. 141, 142, 143 and 145.

38 I quote from the manuscript of the speech, titled 'Aus naher Entfernung:
Bei Gelegenheit der Verleihung des Kulturpreises der Stadt München'
[From a close distance: on the occasion of the award of the Cultural
Prize of Honour of the City of Munich], on 22 January 2013. The text is
published under the title 'Aus naher Entfernung: Ein Dank an die Stadt
München' [From a close distance: a thank-you to the City of Munich] in
Habermas (2013), *Im Sog der Technokratie*, pp. 187–93 [the text is not part
of the English edition]. Habermas had also commented on Starnberg in the
Süddeutsche Zeitung of 12 June 2010:

'Starnberg is, indeed, a Bavarian and unpretentious place' was his
[Habermas's] judgement. He attributes to the county town a 'solid unob-
trusiveness'. Habermas has lived in Starnberg for thirty-eight years now

and makes excursion across the district with his worn-out hiking map. 'I have always considered it an advantage to be allowed to lead an inconspicuous existence. For this, I am grateful to this town', he said a short while ago when he was made an honorary citizen.

39 I quote from the manuscript of the acceptance speech on 29 September 2013.
40 Habermas, *Kleine Politische Schriften I–IV*, p. 9.
41 Habermas (2013), 'Vorwort', in *Im Sog der Technokratie*, pp. 7–10. [Habermas wrote a different preface especially for the English edition; see *The Lure of Technocracy*, pp. vii–xi.]
42 Habermas (2015), 'The Lure of Technocracy: A Plea for European Solidarity', in *The Lure of Technocracy*, pp. 3–28; here: p. 11; emphasis in the original.
43 Ibid., p. 23.
44 Ibid. (trans. modified).
45 Ibid., p. 24 (trans. modified).
46 Ibid., p. 26; emphasis in the original.
47 Cerstin Gammelin, 'Merkel, Kohl und Europa', *Süddeutsche Zeitung*, 29 April 2013.
48 Ibid.; emphasis in the original. See also Bernd Riegert, 'Habermas kritisiert Europas Führung', *Deutsche Welle*, 27 April 2013.
49 I quote from the text 'Jürgen Habermas an der LMU – Eindrücke von einem Meisterdenker, der keiner sein will', published, with Christian Zeller as author, in *Cogito* 11/2012, pp. 17–19.
50 Habermas ([2005] 2008), 'The Boundary between Faith and Knowledge: On the Reception and Contemporary Importance of Kant's Philosophy of Religion', in *Between Naturalism and Religion*, pp. 209–47; here: p. 211 (trans. modified).
51 Habermas ([1997] 2001), 'Israel or Athens: Where does Anamnestic Reason Belong? Johann Baptist Metz on Unity amidst Multicultural Plurality', in *The Liberating Power of Symbols*, pp. 78–89; here: p. 84.
52 Habermas (2013), *Im Sog der Technokratie*, p. 7.
53 Habermas (2015), 'Our Contemporary Heine', p. 143.
54 See Greven (2005), 'Politik als Ursprung theoretischen Denkens', p. 161. This emphasis on the political is both central to all of Habermas's social theory and an important respect in which he diverges from critical theory in the tradition of Karl Marx and Theodor W. Adorno, a point to which Albrecht Wellmer has recently drawn attention in his speech upon receiving the Adorno Prize on 11 September 2006 in the Paulskirche at Frankfurt:

> Adorno in this way, much as Marx had before him, underestimated the emancipatory potential that, concurrent in its emergence with the origins of the capitalist economy, is inherent in the modern, at its core already universalistically understood forms of democracy. Habermas is no doubt correct against both Marx *and* Adorno to insist on a notion of democratic politics, which in Marx fails to find its rightful place because of his 'eschatological' philosophy of history and in Adorno fails to find its place because of his monological construction of the critique of identitarian reason. Adorno's messianism – as well as his mistrust of the possibilities for a genuine change of societal practice – is a pointer to the homelessness

of the political in his theory. Once the problems of capitalism are viewed from within the horizon of a democratic politics, one has not only named the area where possible countervailing forces against the destructive consequences of the capitalist economy are to be localized, but one has also redefined the *problem* that they pose. If there should hence be reasons for holding fast to the more radical impulse of the Marxian and the Adornian critique of capitalism, then this would need to be done in a form that does not fall behind Habermas's democratic 'politicization' of the problem. (Wellmer (2007), 'Adorno and the Problems of a Critical Construction of the Historical Present', pp. 150f.)

55 According to Dirk A. Moses, Habermas's opponent is an ideological community [*Gesinnungsgemeinschaft*] that Moses describes as 'German Germans', which he contrasts with the 'non-German Germans'. Moses sees these non-German Germans, who are sceptically opposed to the idea of the nation-state as the foundation of identity, represented in both the personality and the political philosophy of Habermas. Moses (2007), *German Intellectuals and the Nazi Past*, pp. 105ff.
56 Habermas, *Kleine Politische Schriften I–IV*, pp. 364–7. This is a shortened version of the article as it appeared in *Der Spiegel*.
57 I quote from the manuscript of the speech. Part of it appeared in the left-liberal daily newspaper *La Repubblica* (7 February 2014). Habermas (2014), 'Für ein starkes Europa – aber was heißt das?'.
58 Daniel Sturm, 'Habermas legt der SPD den Finger in die Wunde', *Die Welt*, 2 February 2014.
59 The first edition of the Habermas bibliography compiled by the Italian social scientist Luca Corchia, published in 2010, lists 4,823 books and articles on the philosopher and 764 titles by Habermas himself. In the second edition of 2013, there are 6,700 items on Habermas and 798 items authored by him. It is likely that the bibliographical research undertaken by the Dutch scholar René Görtzen, who is working on a comprehensive multi-volume bibliography, will result in a much higher number of primary and secondary titles overall. Görtzen's bibliography extends over a wider stretch of time, but is not quite up to date. See Corchia (2013), *Jürgen Habermas. A Bibliography: Works and Studies (1952–2013)*. See also Görtzen (1986), 'Habermas's Theorie des kommunikativen Handelns: Eine bibliographische Auswahl'; Görtzen (2000), 'Habermas: Bi(bli)ographische Bausteine. Eine Auswahl'. Then there is the continuously updated internet bibliography of the Habermas forum organized by the Danish scholars Kristian Hansen and Thomas Gregers, which can be accessed at www.habermasforum.dk, as well as the bibliography published by Demetrios Douramanis in 1995 in Australia: *Mapping Habermas: A Bibliography of Primary Literature*. On the occasion of his eightieth birthday, the GESIS – Leibniz Institute for Social Science produced a chronology of literature on Habermas's work compiled by Maria Zens. The selection of 332 titles concentrates on German-language publications. Zens (2009), *Literatur zu Jürgen Habermas aus fünf Jahrzehnten*.
60 See Hacke (2006), *Philosophie der Bürgerlichkeit*, pp. 135f.; Hacke (2009), *Die Bundesrepublik als Idee*, pp. 102–20.
61 Habermas (1982), 'A Reply to my Critics', in Thompson and Held, *Habermas: Critical Debates*, p. 235; emphases in the original [the first emphasis has been omitted in the English translation and has here been restored].

62 Robert Spaemann says: 'Habermas and I always actually handled each
    other with kid gloves. His invectives are directed, rather, against Lübbe.'
    Spaemann (2012), *Über Gott und die Welt*, pp. 207ff. Lübbe, for his part, is
    at least convinced that Habermas will

> become part of the history of philosophy as the theoretician of discourse.
> However: in the . . . controversial discourses, the opponent is by no means
> accepted as a partner in discursive exchange. Rather, he is assumed to
> have morally unacceptable intentions, and thus the discourse as discourse
> already ends at its very beginning. In these cases, the so-called discourse
> is a means for showing that the opponent does not possess the moral and
> social competence which is necessary for an unlimited discursive com-
> petence. Thus, the role of the opponent is at best that of a candidate for
> discourse who is, however, handicapped in his emancipation and in need
> of ideology critique. . . . Any theory of discourse which misjudges the
> indispensable political and general social function of letting be, of remain-
> ing silent, even of forgetting, will have a tendency towards becoming
> illiberal. (Lübbe (2007), *Vom Parteigenossen zum Bundesbürger*, pp. 129f.)

63 Spaemann (2012), *Über Gott und die Welt*, p. 207.
64 See Honneth (2000), *Das andere der Gerechtigkeit*; also Honneth (2009),
    Pathologies of Reason: On the Legacy of Critical Theory. In an article
    congratulating Honneth on his sixtieth birthday, Habermas summed up
    the controversial point from his perspective as follows: 'For Honneth, the
    decisive normative point of reference is not how to make moral freedom
    possible under egalitarian laws, but how to make the ethical freedom of a
    successful relationship with oneself possible in social terms.' Habermas,
    'Arbeit, Liebe, Anerkennung: Von Marx zu Hegel nach Frankfurt und
    wieder zurück: Zum 60. Geburtstag des Philosophen Axel Honneth'
    [Labour, love, recognition: from Marx to Hegel to Frankfurt, and back:
    on the sixtieth birthday of the philosopher Axel Honneth], *Die Zeit*, 16
    July 2009.
65 Boltanski and Honneth (2009), 'Soziologie der Kritik oder Kritische
    Theorie?', p. 88.
66 See Palazzo (2002), *Die Mitte der Demokratie*.
67 Habermas (1999), 'Richard Rorty's Pragmatic Turn', in *On the Pragmatics
    of Communication*, pp. 343–82; here: p. 344.
68 Rorty (1989), *Contingency, Irony, and Solidarity*, pp. 5f.
69 Habermas (1999), 'Richard Rorty's Pragmatic Turn', p. 367. Habermas
    ([1996] 1999), 'A Genealogical Analysis of the Cognitive Content of
    Morality', in *The Inclusion of the Other*, pp. 3–46; here: p. 41. See Rorty
    (2007), *Philosophy as Cultural Politics*, pp. 76ff. According to Rorty, the
    concept of universal validity is superfluous because we should think of
    'rational inquiry as having no higher goal than solving the transitory prob-
    lems of the day'. Ibid., p. 78.
70 Habermas ([1988] 1992), 'The Unity of Reason in the Diversity of its
    Voices', in *Postmetaphysical Thinking*, p. 144. See Habermas (1999),
    'Richard Rorty's Pragmatic Turn', p. 372. At the epistemological level,
    Habermas may 'assume' that Rorty 'contradicts himself within his own
    argumentation. . . . In order to claim universal validity, the claim that
    knowledge depends on a spatio-temporal context would need to be made
    outside of any specific context, which would undermine its own claim, i.e.

the general context-dependence of claims.' At the level of practical action, the assumption of factual truth and moral correctness is a requirement for reliable interaction on the basis of intersubjective understanding. See Auer (2004), *Politisierte Demokratie*, pp. 45–58; here: pp. 55f.

71 Habermas (1999), 'Richard Rorty's Pragmatic Turn', p. 372; emphasis in the original.

72 Frank (1988), *Die Grenzen der Verständigung*, p. 21.

73 Lyotard (1989), *The Differend*.

74 Frank (1988), *Die Grenzen der Verständigung*, pp. 73f. The critique of the political scientist Chantal Mouffe points in a similar direction to that of Lyotard. It focuses on the aim of universalizing the rationalism of a Western model of democracy as well as on the regulative idea of mutual recognition and consensual understanding in the case of political disputes. The latter, according to her, are constitutively antagonistic; they rest on fundamental differences of principle and cannot but be agonistic. See Mouffe (2005), *On the Political*.

75 Luhmann (1990), 'Über systemtheoretische Grundlagen der Gesellschaftstheorie', p. 282.

76 While communication for Habermas is a mutual process of establishing understanding, Luhmann, in his terminology, understands it as the elementary unity of systems. According to Luhmann, all of society, including its sub-systems, organizations and ephemeral interactions, consists of communicative elements. This has two consequences for him: first, it removes the human being from the centre of society, because there cannot be two basic elements of society – communication and human being. The human being, as a 'psychological system', is part of the social environment. Luhmann rejects the model of intersubjectivity developed by Habermas because it reintroduces the human being, as the subject on which society is grounded, through the back door. Second, a new conception of communication emerges. According to Luhmann, communication is not about understanding what a speaker really means. Rather, communication is a process that takes place on three levels (information, message, comprehension) independently of the intentions of the participants. Its aim is coherence [*Anschlussfähigkeit*], the continuation of the social systems which take part in the process. In that sense, it is not understanding [*Verständigung*] that is the goal but, rather, comprehension [*Verstehen*] – i.e., the continuation of communicative processes on the basis of valid rules and structures of expectations. Manfred Füllsack has worked out the similarities and differences in the theoretical architecture of Habermas's and Luhmann's social theories in 'Geltungsansprüche und Beobachtungen zweiter Ordnung: Wie nahe kommen sich Diskurs- und Systemtheorie?'. See also Füllsack (2010), 'Die Habermas-Luhmann-Debatte'.

77 Luhmann (2012), *The Theory of Society*, vol. 1, p. 137.

78 Habermas ([1985] 1987), 'Excursus on Luhmann's Appropriation of the Philosophy of the Subject Through Systems Theory', in *The Philosophical Discourse of Modernity*, pp. 368–85; here: pp. 373 and 384.

79 Ibid., p. 374. Alexander Kluge's *Lernprozesse mit tödlichem Ausgang* contains a fictional scenario, set against the backdrop of a looming major war, in which Habermas engages with Luhmann's systems theory in the 'basement room of Hotel Spitzingsee' during a conference of scholars working in peace studies:

H., the last representative of Critical Theory, and as sensitive as a seismograph, has withdrawn to a basement room of the hotel. Here – blind, because gazing at white-washed basement room walls cannot be called a 'seeing' – he tries to gain an overview. During the afternoon, he has demonstrated the weaknesses of the *conceptual imperialism* of the formation of concepts purely on the basis of systemic steering ('Cutting the foot to size, to make the boot fit'). (Kluge (1973), *Lernprozesse mit tödlichem Ausgang*, p. 199; emphasis in the original [the text is not part of the English edition: *Learning Processes with a Deadly Outcome* (1996), which contains only the title story].

Epilogue

1 'Wer kennt schon seine wirklich spekulativen Motive' – a remark made by Habermas in 2012 at the conference 'Habermas und der Historische Materialismus' [Habermas and Historical Materialism].
2 Habermas ([2005] 2008), 'Public Space and Political Public Sphere', in *Between Naturalism and Religion*, pp. 11–23; here: p. 12 (trans. modified).
3 Habermas (1986), 'The Dialectics of Rationalization', p. 126.
4 Ibid., p. 125 (trans. modified).
5 Habermas ([2001] 2006), 'Symbolic Expression and Ritual Behaviour: Ernst Cassirer and Arnold Gehlen Revisited', in *Time of Transitions*, pp. 53–70; here: p. 64.
6 Habermas ([2005] 2008), 'Public Space and Political Public Sphere', p. 14.
7 Ibid., p. 16.
8 Habermas ([2001] 2006), 'The Finger of Blame: The Germans and Their Memorial', in *Time of Transitions*, pp. 38–50; here: p. 45.
9 Habermas (1986), 'The Dialectics of Rationalization', p. 127. Habermas first comments on the concept of intuitive knowledge in *Knowledge and Human Interests*:

> If we had intuitive access to something immediate, then we would necessarily be able to distinguish with immediate certainty intuitions from discursive certainties.
> But the controversies about the true sources of intuitive knowledge have never led to a satisfactory consensus. This shows that we do not have at our disposal an intuitive faculty for identifying anything immediate . . . The cognitive process is discursive at every stage. (Habermas ([1968] 2004), *Knowledge and Human Interests*, p. 97; trans. modified)

10 Habermas (1986), 'The Dialectics of Rationalization', p. 127.
11 Habermas ([2005] 2008), 'Public Space and Political Public Sphere', p. 12. In an article on Dilthey's theory of understanding others' expressions of life, published in 1984, Habermas writes:

> Life histories are the fundamental elements of the process of life which encompasses the human species. A life history is a self-demarcating system because it is given as a course of life limited by birth and death and is also a context that can be experienced, a context which connects the elements of a course of life, in fact through a 'meaning'. A life history is constituted by life relations. Such life relations consist of an ego, on the one hand, and

objects and human beings, which enter the world of the ego, on the other hand. (Habermas (1984) 'Diltheys Theorie des Ausdrucksverstehens: Ich-Identität und sprachliche Kommunikation', in Rodi and Lessing, *Materialien zur Philosophie Wilhelm Diltheys*, pp. 325f.)

12 Habermas (1986), 'The Dialectics of Rationalization', p. 126.
13 Ibid.
14 Habermas ([2005] 2008), 'Communicative Action and the Detranscendentalized "Use of Reason"', in *Between Naturalism and Religion*, pp. 24–76; here: p. 49. See also Habermas ([1999] 2003), 'Introduction: Realism after the Linguistic Turn', in *Truth and Justification*, pp. 1–49; here: pp. 26ff.
15 See Habermas ([1991] 1994), 'On the Pragmatic, the Ethical, and the Moral Employments of Practical Reason', in *Justification and Application: Remarks on Discourse Ethics*, pp. 10ff.
16 Habermas (1992), 'The Unity of Reason in the Diversity of its Voices', in *Postmetaphysical Thinking*, pp. 115–48; here: p. 144.
17 Theodor W. Adorno (2007), *Negative Dialectics*, New York, p. 408 (trans. modified).
18 Habermas (1992), 'The Unity of Reason in the Diversity of its Voices', p. 144. The Latin quotation taken from Goethe's autobiography, *Poetry and Truth*, translates: 'No one against God but God himself'. The Dutch philosopher Joseph Keulartz is convinced that this saying quoted by Habermas

> can be considered to be the motto of his philosophy as a whole . . . Nothing and no one can turn against God but God himself – that means historical errors can only be corrected historically; only reason is capable of healing the wounds which reason itself has inflicted; only through a radicalization of enlightenment can the dangers of enlightenment be removed. (Keulartz (1995), *Die verkehrte Welt des Jürgen Habermas*, p. 15)

19 Correspondence in Vorlass Habermas.
20 Josef Bierbichler, 'Die Leut' sind im Grunde immer wieder gleich gewesen', *Die Zeit*, 6 October 2011.

Genealogy

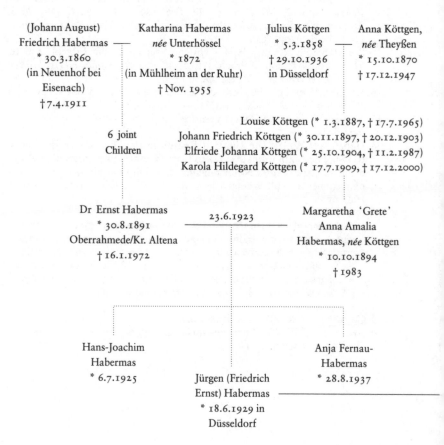

(Johann August)
Friedrich Habermas
* 30.3.1860
(in Neuenhof bei
Eisenach)
†7.4.1911

Katharina Habermas
née Unterhössel
* 1872
(in Mühlheim an der Ruhr)
† Nov. 1955

Julius Köttgen
* 5.3.1858
† 29.10.1936
in Düsseldorf

Anna Köttgen,
née Theyßen
* 15.10.1870
† 17.12.1947

6 joint
Children

Louise Köttgen (* 1.3.1887, † 17.7.1965)
Johann Friedrich Köttgen (* 30.11.1897, † 20.12.1903)
Elfriede Johanna Köttgen (* 25.10.1904, † 11.2.1987)
Karola Hildegard Köttgen (* 17.7.1909, † 17.12.2000)

Dr Ernst Habermas
* 30.8.1891
Oberrahmede/Kr. Altena
† 16.1.1972

23.6.1923

Margaretha 'Grete'
Anna Amalia
Habermas, *née* Köttgen
* 10.10.1894
† 1983

Hans-Joachim
Habermas
* 6.7.1925

Jürgen (Friedrich
Ernst) Habermas
* 18.6.1929 in
Düsseldorf

Anja Fernau-
Habermas
* 28.8.1937

Tilmann Habermas
* 17.5.1956

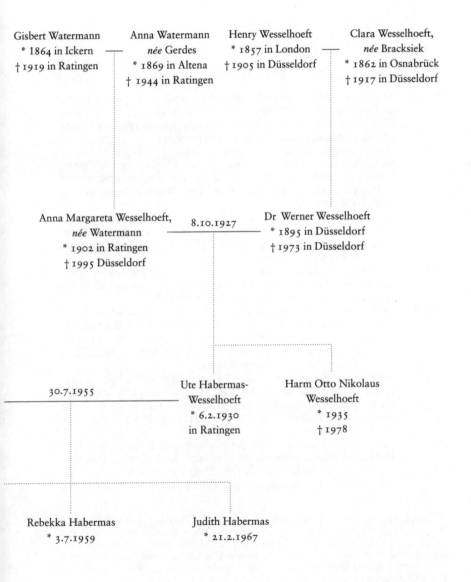

Gisbert Watermann
* 1864 in Ickern
† 1919 in Ratingen

Anna Watermann
née Gerdes
* 1869 in Altena
† 1944 in Ratingen

Henry Wesselhoeft
* 1857 in London
† 1905 in Düsseldorf

Clara Wesselhoeft,
née Bracksiek
* 1862 in Osnabrück
† 1917 in Düsseldorf

Anna Margareta Wesselhoeft,
née Watermann
* 1902 in Ratingen
† 1995 Düsseldorf

8.10.1927

Dr Werner Wesselhoeft
* 1895 in Düsseldorf
† 1973 in Düsseldorf

30.7.1955

Ute Habermas-
Wesselhoeft
* 6.2.1930
in Ratingen

Harm Otto Nikolaus
Wesselhoeft
* 1935
† 1978

Rebekka Habermas
* 3.7.1959

Judith Habermas
* 21.2.1967

Chronology*

1929   Friedrich Ernst Jürgen Habermas, the second of the three children
            of Grete and Ernst Habermas, born in Düsseldorf on 18 June.
            Childhood and youth in Gummersbach (Oberbergisches Land),
            where he attends primary and secondary school.

1949–54   Abitur.† Begins to study philosophy, psychology, German literature,
            history and economics in Göttingen. Studies for one term in Zurich.
            From the winter term 1950–1 continues and completes his studies
            in Bonn. Friendship with Karl-Otto Apel, Wilfried Berghahn and
            Günther Rohrbach.

1954   Completes his doctorate under the supervision of Erich Rothacker
            with a thesis on 'Das Absolute und die Geschichte: Von der
            Zwiespältigkeit in Schellings Denken' [The absolute and history: on
            the ambivalence in Schelling's thought].

1954–6   Works as a freelance journalist for various daily and weekly news-
            papers and cultural journals. Grant from the German Research
            Association. July 1955: Marries Ute Wesselhoeft.

1956–9   Assistant at the Institute for Social Research in Frankfurt am Main.
            First encounter with Theodor W. Adorno and his wife Gretel, as
            well as with Ludwig von Friedeburg. Involvement in various empiri-
            cal research projects, for instance Student und Politik [Students and
            politics]. 1956: Birth of his son Tilmann.

1959–61   Grant from the German Research Foundation for his Habilitation.
            Hands in his notice at the Institute for Social Research and works
            on his Habilitation, The Structural Transformation of the Public
            Sphere, with Wolfgang Abendroth in Marburg. July 1959: Birth of
            his daughter Rebekka.

1961–4   Becomes extraordinary professor of philosophy at the University of
            Heidelberg. Meets Hans-Georg Gadamer, Karl Löwith, and Alex-
            ander and Margarete Mitscherlich. 'Positivist dispute': controversy
            over the logic of the social sciences with Karl Popper and Hans Albert.

---

* English titles are used where English translations exist. The reader should be aware
that, in the case of collections of essays, the English editions are often not identical with
the original German editions, and that sometimes a title essay exists in translation while
the collection of the same name has not been translated. In the latter case, the German
title is given, followed by the English translation of the title essay in square brackets.
† The final examinations at the end of secondary school.

1963	Publication of *Theorie und Praxis: Sozialphilosophische Studien* [Theory and practice: studies in social philosophy].
1964	Succeeds Max Horkheimer as full professor of philosophy and sociology at the University of Frankfurt am Main in the summer term.
1965	First study visit to the USA, where he meets Leo Löwenthal, Siegfried Kracauer and Herbert Marcuse.
1967	Birth of his daughter Judith. Autumn: Visiting professor at the New School for Social Research in New York (Theodor Heuss Chair). After that, numerous visiting professorships at Wesleyan University, University of California (Berkeley and Santa Barbara), Northwestern University, Collège de France (Paris), among others.
1968	In lectures and articles, promotes a fundamental democratization of German universities. Engages in debates with representatives of the student movement. Publication of *Technik und Wissenschaft als 'Ideologie'* [Science and technology as 'ideology'] and *Knowledge and Human Interests*.
1969	Publication of *Protestbewegung und Hochschulreform* [Protest movement and reform of the university].
1970	February–March: Delivers the Christian Gauss Lectures at Princeton University under the title 'Vorlesungen zu einer sprachtheoretischen Grundlegung der Soziologie' [published in English in 2001: 'Reflections on the Linguistic Foundation of Sociology', in *On the Pragmatics of Social Interaction: Preliminary Studies in the Theory of Communicative Action*].
1971	Debates with Niklas Luhmann on systems theory and critical social theory. From October: Director at the Max Planck Institute for the Study of Living Conditions in the Scientific and Technical World.
1972	July: Presents a paper at the symposium in honour of Walter Benjamin: 'Consciousness-Raising or Rescuing Critique – The Actuality of Walter Benjamin'. October: The family moves into their new home in Starnberg.
1973	February: Publication of *Legitimation Crisis*. November: The philosophical faculty of the University of Munich rejects Habermas's application for an honorary professorship.
1974	Receives Hegel Prize of the city of Stuttgart.
1975	Honorary professorship of philosophy at the University of Frankfurt am Main.
1976	Publication of *Zur Rekonstruktion des Historischen Materialismus* [On the reconstruction of historical materialism].
1977	Disputes over terrorism and state of national emergency. December: First visit to Israel, on the occasion of Gershom Sholem's eightieth birthday.
1980	January to April: Visiting professor at Berkeley. 11 September: Receives the Theodor W. Adorno Prize of the city of Frankfurt am Main. Honorary doctorate from the New School for Social Research in New York. Numerous honorary doctorates from German and international universities follow.
1981	Spring: Resigns as director at the Max Planck Institute in Starnberg. Publication of *The Theory of Communicative Action*. From October: Professor of philosophy, in particular social philosophy and philosophy of history, at the Johann Wolfgang Goethe University in Frankfurt am Main.

1983   Takes up his teaching duties at Frankfurt University with a lecture series on 'Theorie der Modernität' [Theory of modernity]. Becomes a member of the German Academy for Language and Literature.

1985   Publication of *Die neue Unübersichtlichkeit* [The new obscurity] and *The Philosophical Discourse of Modernity*. Receives Hans and Sophie Scholl Prize of the city of Munich and the Wilhelm Leuschner medal of the state of Hesse.

1986   'Historians' debate': controversy over the question of the uniqueness of the Holocaust. Leibniz Prize of the German Research Association. Research projects on legal theory with financial support from the Leibniz programme.

1987   Publication of *Eine Art Schadensabwicklung* [A kind of settlement of damages]. Sonning Prize of Copenhagen University.

1988   February: Publication of *Postmetaphysical Thinking*. September: Howison Lectures at the University of California, Berkeley. Paper at the congress 'The Contemporary German Mind' at Johns Hopkins University in Baltimore. Paper at the 18th World Congress of Philosophy in Brighton, England, on 'Individuation through Socialization'.

1989   Honorary doctorate from the Hebrew University of Jerusalem. Festschrift on the occasion of his sixtieth birthday: *Zwischenbetrachtungen im Prozeß der Aufklärung*. Several lectures at the Law School of New York University. Publication of *Die nachholende Revolution* [The belated revolution]. Debate over German unification.

1990   April: Wittgenstein Conference in Frankfurt am Main.

1991   March: Publication of *Justification and Application: Remarks on Discourse Ethics*.

1992   Publication of *Between Facts and Norms*.

1994   22 September: Official retirement. Made 'permanent visiting professor' at Northwestern University, Evanston, Illinois.

1995   Karl Jaspers Prize of the city of Heidelberg. Honorary doctorate from the University of Tel Aviv.

1996   Publication of *The Inclusion of the Other: Studies in Political Theory*. May: Goes on a lecture tour in Hong Kong and South Korea. Lecture at the Korean Society of Philosophy, Seoul, on 'Konzeption der Moderne: Ein Rückblick auf zwei Traditionen' [The conception of modernity: looking back at two traditions].

1998   Debate over cloning, genetic engineering and freedom of the will. Publication of *The Postnational Constellation*. May: Lecture tour in Egypt. June: Paper at the Cultural Forum of the SPD, discussion with Chancellor Gerhard Schröder. September: Paper at the Congress of Sociology in Freiburg, organized jointly by the Swiss, Austrian and German associations. Habermas's contribution titled 'Nach dreißig Jahren: Bemerkungen zu *Erkenntnis und Interesse*' [Thirty years on: remarks on *Knowledge and Human Interests*].

1999   Theodor Heuss Prize in Stuttgart. Publication of *Truth and Justification*. Debates over the war in Kosovo and over genetic engineering. July: Interdisciplinary symposium on 'Die Öffentlichkeit der Vernunft und die Vernunft der Öffentlichkeit' [The public sphere of reason and the reason of the public sphere] at the Goethe University on the occasion of Habermas's seventieth birthday. Receives Hesse's Cultural Prize.

2000   Resident visitor at the Law School of New York University. June: Visits Iran for a week.

2001   April: Visit to China. Lectures at the universities of Beijing and Shanghai and at the Academy of Social Science. Debate over the public use of religion. October: 'Faith and Knowledge', acceptance speech upon receiving the Peace Prize of the German Publishers and Booksellers Association.

2002   June: Visit to Iran, where he delivers a lecture on 'Säkularisierung in der postsäkularen Gesellschaft' [Secularization in a post-secular society] at Tehran University. Lecture at the Europa University Viadrina in Frankfurt an der Oder on 'Religious Tolerance as Pacemaker for Cultural Rights'.

2003   Publicly criticizes the Iraq War and unilateral US hegemony. October: Prince of Asturias Award in Orviedo. September: Paper at the Adorno Conference in Frankfurt am Main: '"I Myself am Part of Nature" – Adorno on the Intrication of Reason in Nature'.

2004   Beginning of the debates over naturalism and freedom. January: Paper and discussion, jointly with Cardinal Ratzinger, at the Catholic Academy in Munich. May: publication of *The Divided West*. November: Kyoto Prize of the Inamori Foundation, where he gives a speech on 'Public Space and Political Sphere – The Biographical Roots of Two Motifs in my Thought'.

2005   Publication of *Between Naturalism and Religion*. November: Awarded the Holberg Prize in Bergen. Acceptance speech on 'Religion in the Public Sphere'.

2006–7 March: Awarded the Bruno Kreisky Prize in Vienna. November: State Prize of North Rhine-Westphalia. December: Speech at the Bielefelder Stadthalle: 'Wer kann wen umarmen: Konsenssuche im Streit: Lobrede auf Ronald Dworkin, den Philosophen, Polemiker und Bürger' [Who can take whom in his arms: speech in honour of Ronald Dworkin, the philosopher, polemicist and citizen].

2008   Publication of *Europe: The Faltering Project*. March: Lectures at the Nexus Institute in Tilburg, Netherlands, and at the University of Aarhus on the theme of 'The Post-Secular Society: What Does it Mean?'. September: Made an honorary member of the German Society for Philosophy and gives an address at the 21st German Congress for Philosophy on the topic of 'Von den Weltbildern zur Lebenswelt' [From world pictures to the lifeworld].

2009   February: *Publication of Philosophische Texte: Studienausgabe in fünf Bänden* [Philosophical texts: collected edition in five volumes]. May: Conference on 'Auslaufmodell Demokratie? Problem und Möglichkeiten demokratischer Selbstbestimmung in der postnationalen Konstellation' [Democracy – a model to be discontinued? Problems and possibilities of democratic self-determination within the postnational constellation] at the University of Zurich on the occasion of Habermas's eightieth birthday. June: '. . . die Lava des Gedankens im Fluss' [The lava of thought in flow . . .], a display of Habermas's work at the German National Library in Frankfurt marking his eightieth birthday. October: Conference on 'Rethinking Socialism' in New York. November: Lecture at the UNESCO conference on 'Philosophy in the Dialogue of Cultures' in Moscow.

2010   Numerous articles on the danger of a failure of the European project. September: Publication of *The Crisis of the European Union: A Response*.

2011   April: Lecture at the European Council on Foreign Relations in Berlin, titled 'Ein Pakt für oder gegen Europa?' [A pact for or against Europe?]. September: Lecture at the 22nd Congress for Philosophy on 'Über die Verkörperung von Gründen' [On the embodiment of reasons]. November: Lecture at the Université Paris Descartes on 'The Crisis of the European Union in the Light of a Constitutionalization of International Law'.

2012   March: Conference at the University of Wuppertal on 'Habermas und der historische Materialismus' [Habermas and historical materialism]. May: Travels to Israel to deliver the first of the annual Buber Memorial Lectures on 'A Philosophy of Dialogue'. June: Publication of *Nachmetaphysisches Denken II* [Postmetaphysical thinking II].

2013   September: Publication of *The Lure of Technocracy*, the twelfth and last volume of the *Kleine Politische Schriften* [Short political writings]. November: Awarded the Erasmus Prize of the Praemium Erasmianum Foundation for services to Europe.

2014   February: Paper at the meeting of the SPD in Potsdam, titled: '"In Favour of a Strong Europe" – What Does This Mean?'

List of Habermas's Lectures and Seminars

The Personal- und Vorlesungsverzeichnis* of the Ruprecht Karls University in Heidelberg lists Jürgen Habermas from the summer term 1962 under 'Extraordinary Professors': 'Jürgen Habermas, Dr phil., Frankfurt a. M., Wolfgangstraße 121 – Philosophy.' From summer term 1964 until 1971, he was listed in the Vorlesungsverzeichnis of the Johann Wolfgang Goethe University as professor of philosophy and sociology and between 1983 and 1994 as professor of philosophy, in particular social philosophy and philosophy of history. From 1980, Habermas announced his lectures and seminars in the 'Kommentiertes Vorlesungsverzeichnis',[†] giving a course outline and a list of relevant literature. In some cases, the title of a course in the Kommentiertes Vorlesungsverzeichnis is not the same as the one given in the general Vorlesungsverzeichnis.

Habermas presented his lectures on the basis of typewritten texts which in some cases run to more than 250 pages. These texts often have handwritten annotations and corrections. Part of the lecture texts are kept in the archive of the Universitätsbibliothek J. C. Senckenberg, Frankfurt am M., Bestand Na 60, Vorlass Jürgen Habermas. They can be located in the Findbuch [inventory] under the rubric 'Typoskripte und Manuskripte' [typescripts and manuscripts], among them: 'Pareto, Durkheim Freud', 'Anthropologie', 'Zur Logik der Sozialwissenschaften', 'Rationalitätskonzepte I und II', 'Schelling', 'Geschichtsphilosophie' and 'Positivismus, Pragmatismus und Historismus'.

The lecture scripts contain extensive bibliographies, listing the literature referred to in the lectures as well as further reading. The language of the lectures indicates that they were clearly written to be performed: 'Thus, you have to prepare yourself for a specialized lecture presenting fairly complicated individual points', or 'Allow me to begin with a prognosis.'

The following list does not contain the titles of the roughly 150 lectures and seminars Habermas gave in the course of eleven years at Northwestern University on topics such as German philosophy in the twentieth century, political philosophy, philosophical anthropology, international law, tolerance and multiculturalism. Nor does it contain the courses taught at New York University (together with Thomas Nagel and Ronald Dworkin) or those at Lucerne University.

---

* Publication listing all teaching staff and courses taught in a particular term.
† Compilation of course descriptions for all courses taught in a particular term.

AG = Arbeitsgemeinschaft [working group]
KO = Kolloquium
ProSE = Proseminar [seminars taken within the first two years of study]
SE = Seminar
Ü = Übung [tutorial]
VL = Vorlesung [lecture]

Rupprecht Karls University

Summer term 1962
VL	Revolution und Tradition: Zur Sozialphilosophie des 18. und 19. Jahrhunderts. [Revolution and tradition: on social philosophy in the 18th and 19th centuries]
SE	Probleme der Wissenschaftstheorie [Problems in the philosophy of science]

Winter term 1962–3
VL	Zur Logik der Geistes- und Gesellschaftswissenschaften [The logic of the humanities and social sciences]
SE	Probleme der Wissenschaftstheorie [Problems in the philosophy of science]

Summer term 1963
VL	Schelling
SE	Schellings Vorlesung zur Methode des akademischen Studiums [Schelling's lecture on methods of academic study]
SE	Probleme der Wissenschaftstheorie [Problems in the philosophy of science]

Winter term 1963–4
VL	Historismus, Positivismus, Pragmatismus [Historicism, positivism, pragmatism]
SE	Zur Wissenschaftstheorie des Neukantianismus [Neo-Kantian philosophy of science]
KO	Propädeutische Fragen der Kybernetik [Propaedeutic questions of cybernetics]

Summer term 1964
VL	Galilei, Descartes, Hobbes
SE	Ursprünge der modernen Erfahrungswissenschaft [Origins of the modern empirical sciences]
Ü	Zu G. H. Mead: *Mind, Self, and Society* [On G. H. Mead's *Mind, Self, and Society*]

Johann Wolfgang Goethe University

Summer term 1964
VL	Geschichte der Soziologie [The history of sociology]

Winter term 1964–5
VL   Wissenschaftstheorie [Philosophy of science]
SE   Hegel, Jenenser Realphilosophie (mit Oskar Negt) [Hegel's Jena Realphilosophie {i.e., his lectures on nature and spirit of 1805–6} (taught jointly with Oskar Negt)]
SE   Ursprünge der modernen Erfahrungswissenschaft (Galilei, Descartes, Hobbes) [Origins of the modern empirical sciences (Galilei, Descartes, Hobbes)]
KO   Doktoranden [Colloquium for PhD candidates]
SE   Für Fortgeschrittene: Analysen gesamtgesellschaftlicher Systeme [For advanced students: comprehensive analysis of social systems]

Summer term 1965
VL   Durkheim, Pareto, Freud
SE   Max Scheler, *Erkenntnis und Arbeit* [Max Scheler's *Erkenntnis und Arbeit* {Knowledge and labour}]
KO   Philosophisches Kolloquium [Philosophical colloquium]
SE   Für Fortgeschrittene: Intrafamiliale Sozialisationsprozesse [For advanced students: processes of socialization within the family]

Winter term 1965–6
VL   Geschichtsphilosophie [Philosophy of history]
SE   Probleme des Naturrechts [Problems in natural law]
KO   Philosophisches Kolloquium [Philosophical colloquium]
SE   Für Fortgeschrittene: Probleme der politischen Soziologie [For advanced students: problems in political sociology]

Summer term 1966
SE   Hegels politische Schriften [Hegel's political writings]
KO   Philosophisches Kolloquium [Philosophical colloquium]
VL   Theoretische Ansätze in der neueren Soziologie [Theoretical approaches in recent sociology]
SE   Für Fortgeschrittene: Abweichende Sozialisationsprozesse [For advanced students: deviations in processes of socialization]

Winter term 1966–7
VL   Probleme einer philosophischen Anthropologie [The problems of a philosophical anthropology]
SE   Hegels Kantkritik [Hegel's critique of Kant]
SE   Für Fortgeschrittene: Theorien der gesellschaftlichen Entwicklung [For advanced students: theories of social development]
KO   Soziologisches Kolloquium [Sociological colloquium]

Summer term 1967
On leave while holding the Theodor Heuss Chair at the New School for Social Research

Winter term 1967–8
VL   Erkenntnis und Interesse [Knowledge and human interests]
SE   Materialistische Dialektik [Materialist dialectics]
ProSE   Max Weber

Summer term 1968
VL   Theorie der Sozialisation [Theory of socialization]
SE   Nietzsches Erkenntnistheorie [Nietzsche's epistemology]
KO   Kolloqium (nur auf Einladung) Colloquium (by invitation only)
SE   Durkheim, Mead, Freud
Ü   Für Fortgeschrittene: Datenanalyse (mit Hansfried Kellner und
      Ulrich Oevermann) [For advanced students: data analysis (taught
      jointly with Hansfried Kellner and Ulrich Oevermann)]

Winter term 1968–9
VL   Sprachphilosophie [Philosophy of language]
SE   Probleme einer materialistischen Erkenntnistheorie [Problems of a
      materialist epistemology]
Ü   Familie als soziales System: Rollenstruktur und Formen der
      Kommunikation (mit Ulrich Oevermann) [The family as a social
      system: role structures and forms of communication (taught jointly
      with Ulrich Oevermann)]
KO   Kolloqium (nur auf Einladung) Colloquium (by invitation only)
Ü   Organisation und Bürokratie (mit Offe) [Organization and
      bureaucracy (taught jointly with Offe)]
Ü   Probleme der statistischen Hypothesenüberprüfung (mit Ulrich
      Oevermann) [Problems in the statistical evaluation of hypothesis
      (taught jointly with Ulrich Oevermann)]
SE   Probleme einer materialistischen Erkenntnistheorie [Problems of a
      materialist epistemology]

Summer term 1969
SE   Probleme einer materialistischen Erkenntnistheorie [Problems of a
      materialist epistemology]
SE   Für Fortgeschrittene: Zur Soziologie totaler Institutionen [For
      advanced students: on the sociology of total institutions]
SE   Probleme der politischen Soziologie [Problems in political sociology]

Winter term 1969–70
SE   Probleme einer materialistischen Erkenntnistheorie [Problems of a
      materialist epistemology]
SE   Für Fortgeschrittene: Probleme des Funktionalismus [For advanced
      students: problems of functionalism]
SE   Für Fortgeschrittene: Probleme der Sprachsoziologie [For advanced
      students: problems in the sociology of language]

Summer term 1970
SE   Zur Logik der Erklärung [On the logic of explanations]
SE   Funktionalistische Analysen gesellschaftlicher Subsysteme
      [Functional analysis of social sub-systems]
SE   Für Fortgeschrittene: Probleme der Sprachsoziologie II [For
      advanced students: problems in the sociology of language II]

Winter term 1970–1

SE   Für Fortgeschrittene: Probleme der Sprachsoziologie III [For
        advanced students: problems in the sociology of language III]
SE   Probleme der Enstehung von Hochkulturen [Problems in the
        emergence of high cultures]
SE   Zur Logik des praktischen Diskurses I und II [On the Logic of
        practical discourses I and II]

Summer term 1971

ProSE   Lektürekurse [Reading class]
SE   Probleme einer Theorie des sozialen Wandels [Problems in the theory
        of social change]

Summer term 1975

SE   Theorie des kommunikativen Handelns [Theory of communicative
        action]

Summer term 1976

SE   Probleme einer Theorie des kommunikativen Handelns [Problems of
        a theory of communicative action]

Summer term 1978

VL   Handlungsrationalität und gesellschaftliche Rationalisierung (mit
        Diskussion) [Rational action and social rationalization (followed by
        discussion)]

Winter term 1978–9

VL   Handlungsrationalität und gesellschaftliche Rationalisierung (mit
        Diskussion) [Rational action and social rationalization (followed by
        discussion)]

Summer term 1980

VL   System und Handlung: zu Parsons' Gesellschaftstheorie [System and
        action: on Parsons's social theory]

Summer term 1981

SE   Theorien der Moderne [Theories of modernity]

Summer term 1983

VL   Theorie der Modernität [Theories of the modern]
KO   Zur Vorlesung [Accompanying the lecture]
SE   Moraltheorie I: Kognitivistische Ethiken der Gegenwart [Moral
        theory I: cognitivist ethics of the present]
SE   Besprechung wissenschaftlicher Arbeiten [Discussion of academic
        work]

Winter term 1983–4

VL	Theorie der Modernität II [Theories of the modern II]
SE	Zum Problem der Sprechhandlungen (mit Karl-Otto Apel) [On the problem of speech acts (taught jointly with Karl-Otto Apel)
SE	Kognitivistische Ethiken II: Moralität und Sittlichkeit [Cognitivist ethics II: morality and ethical life]
KO	Besprechung wissenschaftlicher Arbeiten [Discussion of academic work]

Summer term 1984

KO	Neostrukturalismus (mit Axel Honneth) [Neostructuralism (with Axel Honneth)]
SE	Probleme der Verrechtlichung (mit Spiros Simitis) [Problems of juridification (taught jointly with Spiros Simitis)]
SE	Probleme der Sprachphilosophie (mit Karl-Otto Apel und Charles Taylor) [Problems in the philosophy of language (taught jointly with Karl-Otto Apel and Charles Taylor)]
SE	Moralphilosophie und Entwicklung des moralischen Bewußtseins [Moral philosophy and the development of moral consciousness]
KO	Besprechung wissenschaftlicher Arbeiten [Discussion of academic work]

Winter term 1984–5

Research leave

Summer term 1985

VL	Rechtsphilosophie I [Legal philosophy I]
SE	Individualität, Subjekt, Identität (mit Axel Honneth) [Individuality, subject, identity (taught jointly with Axel Honneth)]
SE	Probleme der Sprechakttheorie (mit John R. Searle) [Problems in speech act theory (taught jointly with John R. Searle]
KO	Besprechung wissenschaftlicher Arbeiten [Discussion of academic work]

Winter term 1985–6

VL	Rechtsphilosophie II Diskussion zur Vorlesung [Legal philosophy II Discussion of the lecture]
ProSE	Logisch-semantische Propädeutik [Logic-semantic propaedeutics]
SE	Individualität, Subjekt, Identität II (mit Axel Honneth) [Individuality, subject, identity II (taught jointly with Axel Honneth)]
KO	Besprechung wissenschaftlicher Arbeiten [Discussion of academic work]

Summer term 1986

SE	Wahrheitstheorien (mit Karl-Otto Apel) [Theories of truth (taught jointly with Karl-Otto Apel)]
SE	Probleme der Verrechtlichung (mit Klaus Günther) [Problems of juridification (taught jointly with Klaus Günther)]
SE	Individualität, Subjekt, Identität III (mit Axel Honneth) [Individuality, subject, identity III (taught jointly with Axel Honneth)]
KO	Besprechung wissenschaftlicher Arbeiten [Discussion of academic work]

Winter term 1986–7

VL Einige Probleme zu einer Theorie des kommunikativen Handelns
[Some problems from a theory of communicative action]
SE Diskussion zur Vorlesung [Discussion of the lecture]
SE Subjektivität und Intersubjektivität bei Sartre (mit Axel Honneth)
[Subjectivity and intersubjectivity in Sartre (taught jointly with Axel
Honneth)]
KO Besprechung wissenschaftlicher Arbeiten [Discussion of academic
work]

Summer term 1987

Research leave

Winter term 1987–8

VL Probleme zu einer Theorie des kommunikativen Handelns
Diskussion zur Vorlesung [Problems from a theory of
communicative action Discussion of the lecture]
SE Zur Sprachphilosophie von Charles Sanders Peirce (mit Axel
Honneth) [On Charles Sanders Peirce's philosophy of language
(taught jointly with Axel Honneth)]
KO Probleme der Rechtsphilosophie (Forschungsgruppe) [Problems in
legal philosophy (research group)]
KO Besprechung wissenschaftlicher Arbeiten [Discussion of academic
work]

Summer term 1988

VL Demokratietheorien [Theories of democracy Diskussion zur
Vorlesung] [Discussion of the lecture]
SE Beyond Objectivism and Relativism (mit Karl-Otto Apel und
Richard J. Bernstein)
SE Ästhetische Theorien im 20. Jahrhundert (mit Axel Honneth)
[Aesthetic theories in the 20th century (taught jointly with Axel
Honneth)]
KO Rechtstheoretische Arbeitsgruppe [Working group on legal theory]
KO Besprechung wissenschaftlicher Arbeiten [Discussion of academic
work]

Winter term 1988–9

SE Ästhetische Theorien im 20. Jahrhundert (mit Axel Honneth)
[Aesthetic theories in the 20th century (taught jointly with Axel
Honneth)]
KO Rechtstheoretische Arbeitsgruppe [Working group on legal theory]
KO Besprechung wissenschaftlicher Arbeiten [Discussion of academic
work]

Summer term 1989
SE　　Zum Pragmatismus von Charles Sanders Peirce [On Charles Sanders
　　　　Peirce's pragmatism]
SE　　Ästhetische Theorien im 20. Jahrhundert (mit Axel Honneth)
　　　　[Aesthetic theories in the 20th century (taught jointly with Axel
　　　　Honneth)]
KO　　Rechtstheoretische Arbeitsgruppe [Working group on legal theory]
KO　　Controversy on Heidegger's Late Philosophy (mit Karl-Otto Apel
　　　　und Hubert Dreyfus)
KO　　Besprechung wissenschaftlicher Arbeiten [Discussion of academic
　　　　work]

Winter term 1989–90
VL　　Einführung in die Philosophie des 20. Jahrhunderts [Introduction to
　　　　20th-century philosophy] Diskussion zur Vorlesung [Discussion of
　　　　the lecture]
ProSE　Grundkurs Philosophie (von Ekkehard Martens und Herbert
　　　　Schnädelbach) [Philosophy: an introductory course (by Ekkehard
　　　　Martens and Herbert Schnädelbach]*
KO　　Rechtstheoretische Arbeitsgruppe [Working group on legal theory]
KO　　Besprechung wissenschaftlicher Arbeiten [Discussion of academic
　　　　work]

Summer term 1990
　　　　Research leave

Winter term 1990–1
VL　　Rechtsphilosophie I [Legal philosophy I] Diskussion zur Vorlesung
　　　　[Discussion of the lecture]
SE　　Neuere Literatur zur Rationalitätsproblematik [Recent literature on
　　　　the problem of rationality]
KO　　Besprechung wissenschaftlicher Arbeiten [Discussion of academic
　　　　work]

Winter term 1991–2
VL　　Zur Philosophie des 20. Jahrhunderts: Cassirer, Lukács, Heidegger,
　　　　Wittgenstein [On 20th-century philosophy: Cassirer, Lukács,
　　　　Heidegger, Wittgenstein [Diskussion zur Vorlesung] Discussion of
　　　　the lecture]
SE　　Ernst Cassirers Philosophie der symbolischen Form [Ernst Cassirer's
　　　　philosophy of symbolic forms]
KO　　Besprechung wissenschaftlicher Arbeiten [Discussion of academic
　　　　work]

Summer term 1992
　　　　Research leave

---

* Ekkehard Martens and Herbert Schnädelbach (eds), *Philosophie: Ein Grundkurs*, 2
vols, Hamburg, 1991.

Winter term 1992–3

VL   Wittgenstein Seminar zur Vorlesung [Seminar accompanying the lecture]

SE   Probleme der Diskurstheorie (mit Karl-Otto Apel) [Problems in discourse theory (taught jointly with Karl-Otto Apel)]

KO   Besprechung wissenschaftlicher Arbeiten [Discussion of academic work]

Summer term 1993

ProSE John Rawls' Politischer Liberalismus [John Rawls's political liberalism]

KO   Probleme der Diskurstheorie (mit Karl-Otto Apel) [Problems in discourse theory (taught jointly with Karl-Otto Apel)]

SE   Die Bedeutungstheorien von Donald Davidson und Michael Dummett (mit Lutz Wingert)] Donald Davidson's and Michael Dummett's theories of meaning (taught jointly with Lutz Wingert)]

KO   Besprechung wissenschaftlicher Arbeiten [Discussion of academic work]

Winter term 1993–4

VL   Rationalitätskonzepte I [Conception of rationality I [Diskussion zur Vorlesung] Discussion of the lecture]

SE   Referenztheorien (mit Lutz Wingert) [Theories of reference (taught jointly with Lutz Wingert)]

KO   Besprechung wissenschaftlicher Arbeiten [Discussion of academic work]

Summer term 1994

VL   Rationalitätskonzepte II [Conception of rationality II [Diskussion zur Vorlesung] Discussion of the lecture]

SE   Probleme der Wahrheitstheorie (mit Lutz Wingert) [Problems in the theory of truth (taught jointly with Lutz Wingert)]

Summer term 1995

KO   Für Doktoranden und Stipendiaten (mit Friedrich Kambartel). Kompakt, nach Ankündigung [For doctoral students and scholarship holders (taught jointly with Friedrich Kambartel). Block seminar, time and date to be announced]

Visiting Professorships

Graduate Faculty, School for Social Research, New York (1967–8)
Institute for the Humanities, Wesleyan University (1972)
University of California, Santa Barbara (1974)
Haverford College, University of Pennsylvania, Philadelphia (1976)
University of California, Berkeley (1980)
Collège de France, Paris (1982)
New York University (joint colloquia with Ronald Dworkin and Thomas Nagel) (1989, 1998 and 2001)
Northwestern University, Evanston (1994–2006, with the exception of 1998, 2001 and 2003)
Stony Brook University (2009)

List of Archives

Archive of the *Frankfurter Rundschau*, Frankfurt am Main
Archive of the Peter Suhrkamp Foundation, Frankfurt am Main (now housed at the German Literature Archive, Marbach am Neckar)
Archive of the Städtisches Gymnasium Moltkestraße, Gummersbach
Archive of the *Süddeutsche Zeitung*, Munich
Archive of the Universitäts- und Landesbibliothek der Universität Bonn, Abteilung Handschriften und Rara
Archive of the Universitäts- und Landesbiblitothek Münster, Historische Bestände
Archive of the Universitätsbibliothek Johann Christian Senckenberg, Frankfurt am Main
Bundesarchiv – Abteilung Militärarchiv [Federal archive – section: military archive] , Freiburg im Breisgau
Deutsche Dienststelle für die Benachrichtigung der nächsten Angehörigen von Gefallenen der ehemaligen deutschen Wehrmacht (WASt) [German office for informing the relatives of those killed in action as members of the former German Wehrmacht], Berlin
German Literature Archive, Marbach am Neckar
International Institute of Social History, Amsterdam
Spiegel Archive, Hamburg
Stadtarchiv Düsseldorf [Archive of the city of Düsseldorf]
Stadtarchiv Gummersbach [Archive of the city of Gummersbach]
Archive of Frankfurt University, Frankfurt am Main
Archive of Philipps University, Marburg
Zeit Archive, Hamburg

The author's own Habermas Archive has five sections:

1 A press archive of about 900 documents from the years 1953 to 2014. This archive contains articles by and about Habermas that appeared in print media, with a focus on national daily and weekly newspapers as well as journals and magazines, such as *Frankfurter Allgemeine Zeitung, Frankfurter Rundschau, Neue Züricher Zeitung, Süddeutsche Zeitung, Die Tageszeitung, Basler Zeitung, Die Woche, Stuttgarter Zeitung, Rheinischer Merkur, Freitag, Der Tagesspiegel, Die Zeit, Der Spiegel* and *Focus*. In addition, there are periodicals such as *Merkur, Neue Rundschau, Frankfurter Hefte, Philosophische Rundschau, Deutsche Zeitschrift für Philosophie, Blätter für*

deutsche und internationale Politik, *Ratio Juris* and *New Left Review*. All original or photocopied items are arranged chronologically, and date, place, author, content and media event [*Kommunikationsereignis*] are registered.

2 An archive of more than sixty published interviews with Habermas, dating from the period between 1969 and 2014. The interviews cover various topics and the interviewers are of various nationalities.

3 Copies of correspondence from Habermas's 'Vorlass'.* Some of them stretch over a long period of time – e.g., the correspondence with Siegfried Unseld, with Helmut Schelsky, with *Merkur* (Hans Paeschke and Joachim Moras), and with the Theorie-Reihe Suhrkamp Verlag.

4 Documentation of all titles and announcements of classes and lectures held at German universities where Habermas taught between 1961 and 1994.

5 Cluster analyses of so-called media events [*Kommunikationsereignisse*] and debates and controversies that stretch over a longer period of time, among them the Heidegger debate (1953); university reforms (1966); student protests (1967); left-wing radicalism (1977); the debate over the educational theses presented by Hermann Lübbe at the congress 'Mut zur Erziehung' [Courage for education] (1978); the debate over armament and 'civil disobedience' (1983); the historians' debate (1986); the debate over reunification (from 1991 to the present); the asylum debate (1992); the debate over the normative implications of genetic engineering (bioethics) (1998); the debate over the memorial to the murdered Jews of Europe (1999); the debate over the Kosovo conflict (1999); the debate at the end of the third Gulf War and the role of America as a normative authority (2003); the debate over the rumour that Habermas swallowed incriminating evidence showing his admiration for Nazism in his youth – the so-called note affair (2006); and the debate over the role of religion in post-secular societies (2003 to the present).

---

* The term is formed in analogy to 'Nachlass' = posthumous papers. Most of the 'Vorlass' is now placed at the Archive of the Universitätsbibliothek Johann Christian Senckenberg, Frankfurt an Main.

Bibliography of Works by Jürgen Habermas*

(German editions followed by English translations)

1 Monographs, collections of essays and articles, edited books

1954: 'Das Absolute und die Geschichte: Von der Zwiespältigkeit in Schellings Denken', unpublished PhD dissertation, Bonn.

1961: *Student und Politik: Eine soziologische Untersuchung zum politischen Bewußtsein Frankfurter Studenten* (co-authored with Ludwig von Friedeburg, Christoph Oehler and Friedrich Weltz), Neuwied and Berlin.

1962: *Strukturwandel der Öffentlichkeit: Untersuchungen zu einer Kategorie der bürgerlichen Gesellschaft*, Neuwied and Berlin.
The Structural Transformation of the Public Sphere, trans. Thomas Burger with Frederick Lawrence, Cambridge, 1989.

1963: *Theorie und Praxis: Sozialphilosophische Studien*, Neuwied and Berlin.
Theory and Practice, trans. John Viertel, London, 1974.

1968: *Technik und Wissenschaft als 'Ideologie'*, Frankfurt am Main.

1968: Part trans. in *Toward a Rational Society*, Cambridge, 1986.
Erkenntnis und Interesse, Frankfurt am Main.
Knowledge and Human Interests, trans. Jeremy J. Shapiro, Cambridge, 2004.

1968 (ed.): *Antworten auf Herbert Marcuse*, Frankfurt am Main.

1969: *Protestbewegung und Hochschulreform*, Frankfurt am Main.

1970: *Arbeit, Erkenntnis, Fortschritt: Aufsätze 1954–1970*, Amsterdam.

---

* The work of Jürgen Habermas can sometimes appear overwhelming, not just in terms of its quantity but also in terms of its 'labyrinthine' quality: collections of essays are named after their title essay (which may be translated, while the collection is not); English editions of collections do not always contain the same material as the German originals; identical material is published in different places, etc. The following resources are useful for finding orientation:
Corchia, Luca, *Jürgen Habermas: A Bibliography, Works and Studies (1952–2013)*, Pisa, 2013 [covers both primary and secondary sources].
Douramanis, Demetrios, *Mapping Habermas: A Biography of Primary Literature*, Sydney, 1995.
www.habermasforum.dk/ [includes regularly updated bibliographies of primary and secondary works since 1992, including information on translations; the bibliographies are maintained by Thomas Gregersen].

1970: *Zur Logik der Sozialwissenschaften*, Frankfurt am Main.
 On the Logic of the Social Sciences, trans. Shierry Weber Nicholson and Jerry A. Stark, Cambridge, 1988.

1971: *Philosophisch-politische Profile*, Frankfurt am Main.
 Philosophical-Political Profiles, trans. Frederick G. Lawrence, Cambridge, 2012.

1971: *Theorie der Gesellschaft oder Sozialtechnologie* (with Niklas Luhmann), Frankfurt am Main.

1971: *Theorie und Praxis: Sozialphilosophische Studien* (rev. edn), Frankfurt am Main.
 Theory and Practice, trans. John Viertel, Cambridge, 1986.

1973: *Kultur und Kritik: Verstreute Aufsätze*, Frankfurt am Main.

1973: *Legitimationsprobleme im Spätkapitalismus*, Frankfurt am Main.
 Legitimation Crisis, trans. Thomas McCarthy, Cambridge, 1988.

1974: *Zwei Reden* (with Dieter Henrich), Frankfurt am Main.

1976: *Zur Rekonstruktion des Historischen Materialismus*, Frankfurt am Main. Part trans. in *Communication and the Evolution of Society*, trans. Thomas McCarthy, Cambridge, 1991.

1977 (ed.): *Entwicklung des Ichs* (with Rainer Döbert and Gertrud Nunner-Winkler), Cologne.

1978: *Politik, Kunst, Religion*, Stuttgart.

1978 (et al.): *Gespräche mit Herbert Marcuse*, Frankfurt am Main.

1979 (ed.): *Stichworte zur 'Geistigen Situation der Zeit'*, 2 vols, Frankfurt am Main.

1979: *Das Erbe Hegels: Zwei Reden aus Anlaß der Verleihung des Hegel-Preises 1979 der Stadt Stuttgart an Hans-Georg Gadamer*, Frankfurt am Main.

1981: *Kleine Politische Schriften I–IV*, Frankfurt am Main.

1981: *Philosophisch-politische Profile* (rev. and extended edn), Frankfurt am Main.

1981: *Theorie des kommunikativen Handelns*, 2 vols, Frankfurt am Main.
 The Theory of Communicative Action, trans. Thomas McCarthy, vol. 1, Cambridge, 1986; vol. 2, Cambridge, 1987.

1982: *Zur Logik der Sozialwissenschaften* (5th rev. and extended edn), Frankfurt am Main.

1983: *Moralbewußtsein und kommunikatives Handeln*, Frankfurt am Main.
 Moral Consciousness and Communicative Action, trans. Christian Lenhardt and Shierry Weber Nicholson, Cambridge, 1990.

1983 (ed.): *Adorno-Konferenz 1983* (with Ludwig von Friedeburg), Frankfurt am Main.

1984: *Vorstudien und Ergänzungen zur Theorie des kommunikativen Handelns*, Frankfurt am Main.
 On the Pragmatics of Social Interaction, trans. Barbara Fultner, Cambridge, 2003.

1984 (ed.): *Soziale Interaktion und soziales Verstehen: Beiträge zur Entwicklung der Interaktionskompetenz* (with Wolfgang Edelstein), Frankfurt am Main.

1985: *Der philosophische Diskurs der Moderne: Zwölf Vorlesungen*, Frankfurt am Main.
 The Philosophical Discourse of Modernity, trans. Thomas McCarthy, Cambridge, MA, 1987.

1985: *Die Neue Unübersichtlichkeit. Kleine Politische Schriften V*, Frankfurt am Main.

Part trans. in *The New Conservatism*, trans. Shierry Weber Nicholson, Cambridge, 1989.

1987: *Eine Art Schadensabwicklung. Kleine Politische Schriften VI*, Frankfurt am Main.
Title essay: 'A Kind of Settlement of Damages (Apologetic Tendencies)', *New German Critique*, no. 44 (1988), pp. 25–39 [special issue on the *Historikerstreit*]; first published in *Die Zeit*, 11 July 1986.

1988: *Nachmetaphysisches Denken: Philosophische Aufsätze*, Frankfurt am Main.
Postmetaphysical Thinking, trans. William Mark Hohengarten, Cambridge, 1992.

1990: *Die nachholende Revolution. Kleine politische Schriften VII*, Frankfurt am Main.

1990: *Vergangenheit als Zukunft*, ed. Michael Haller, Zurich.
The Past as Future, trans. and ed. Max Pensky, Cambridge, 1994.

1990: *Strukturwandel der Öffentlichkeit: Untersuchungen zu einer Kategorie der bürgerlichen Gesellschaft*, with a new preface to the rev. edn, Frankfurt am Main.

1990: *Die Moderne – ein unvollendetes Projekt: Philosophische Aufsätze, 1977– 1990*, Leipzig.
Title essay: 'Modernity: An Unfinished Project', in *Habermas and the Unfinished Project of Modernity*, ed. Maurizio Passerin d'Entrèves and Seyla Benhabib, Cambridge, MA, 1997, pp. 38–55.

1991: *Erläuterungen zur Diskursethik*, Frankfurt am Main.
Justification and Application: Remarks on Discourse Ethics, trans. Ciaran Cronin, Cambridge, MA, 1994.

1991: *Staatsbürgerschaft und nationale Identität: Überlegungen zur europäischen Zukunft*, St Gallen.

1991: *Texte und Kontexte*, Frankfurt am Main.

1992: *Faktizität und Geltung: Beiträge zur Diskurstheorie des Rechts und des demokratischen Rechtsstaats*, Frankfurt am Main.
Between Facts and Norms: Contributions to a Discourse Theory of Law, trans. William Rehg, Cambridge, 1996.

1993: *Vergangenheit als Zukunft: Das alte Deutschland im neuen Europa?*, ed. Michael Haller, Munich.

1995: *Die Normalität einer Berliner Republik. Kleine Politische Schriften VIII*, Frankfurt am Main.
A Berlin Republic: Writings on Germany, trans. Steven Rendall, Cambridge, 1998.

1995: *Theorie des kommunikativen Handelns*, vols 1 and 2, 4th rev. edn 1987, with a preface to the 3rd edition, Frankfurt am Main.

1996: *Die Einbeziehung des Anderen: Studien zur politischen Theorie*, Frankfurt am Main.
The Inclusion of the Other: Studies in Political Theory, ed. Ciaran Cronin and Pablo De Greiff, trans. Ciaran Cronin, Cambridge, 1999.

1997: *Vom sinnlichen Eindruck zum symbolischen Ausdruck: Philosophische Essays*, Frankfurt am Main.
The Liberating Power of Symbols, trans. Peter Dews, Cambridge, 2001.

1998: *Die postnationale Konstellation: Politische Essays*, Frankfurt am Main.
The Postnational Constellation, trans. and ed. Max Pensky, Cambridge, 2001.

1998: *Faktizität und Geltung: Beiträge zur Diskurstheorie des Rechts und des demokratischen Rechtsstaats*, with an afterword to the 4th rev. edn and a bibliography, Frankfurt am Main.
Between Facts and Norms: Contributions to a Discourse Theory of Law, trans. William Rehg, Cambridge, 1996.

1999: *Wahrheit und Rechtfertigung: Philosophische Aufsätze*, Frankfurt am Main.
Truth and Justification, trans. Barbara Fultner, Cambridge, 2003.

1999: *On the Pragmatics of Communication*, ed. and trans. Maeve Cook, Cambridge.

2001: *Die Zukunft der menschlichen Natur: Auf dem Weg zu einer liberalen Eugenik*, Frankfurt am Main.
The Future of Human Nature, Cambridge, 2003.

2001: *Zeit der Übergänge. Kleine Politische Schriften IX*, Frankfurt am Main.
Time of Transitions, ed. and trans. Ciaran Cronin and Max Pensky, Cambridge, 2006.

2002: *Glauben und Wissen: Friedenspreis des Deutschen Buchhandels 2001*, special edn, Frankfurt am Main.

2002: *Religion and Rationality: Essays on Reason, God, and Modernity*, ed. Eduardo Mendieta, Cambridge, 2002 [selection of essays not previously published in this form; the introduction and chapter 8 ('"To Seek to Salvage an Unconditional Meaning without God is a Futile Undertaking": Reflections on a Remark of Max Horkheimer') were written for this collection].

2003: *Zeitdiagnosen: Zwölf Essays*, Frankfurt am Main.

2003: (with Jacques Derrida) *Philosophy in a Time of Terror: Dialogues with Jürgen Habermas and Jacques Derrida*, ed. Giovanna Borradori, Chicago, 2003.
Philosophie in Zeiten des Terrors (with Jacques Derrida), Berlin, 2004.

2004: *Wahrheit und Rechtfertigung: Philosophische Aufsätze*, expanded edn, Frankfurt am Main.
Truth and Justification, trans. Barbara Fultner, Cambridge, 2003.

2004: *Der gespaltene Westen. Kleine Politische Schriften X*, Frankfurt am Main.
The Divided West, ed. and trans. Ciaran Cronin, Cambridge, 2006.

2005: *Zwischen Naturalismus und Religion: Philosophische Aufsätze*, Frankfurt am Main.
Between Naturalism and Religion, trans. Ciaran Cronin, Cambridge, 2008.

2005: *Die Zukunft der menschlichen Natur: Auf dem Weg zu einer liberalen Eugenik?*, expanded edn, Frankfurt am Main.
The Future of Human Nature, trans. Hella Beister and William Rehg, Cambridge, 2003.

2005: *Dialektik der Säkularisierung: Über Vernunft und Religion* (with Joseph Ratzinger), Freiburg, Basle and Vienna, 2005.
The Dialectics of Secularization: On Reason and Religion, trans. Brian McNeill, San Francisco, 2006.

2006: *Politik, Kunst, Religion*, Stuttgart.

2008: *Ach, Europa. Kleine Politische Schriften XI*, Frankfurt am Main.
Europe: The Faltering Project, trans. Ciaran Cronin, Cambridge, 2009.

2008: *Erkenntnis und Interesse*, new edn, Hamburg.

2008: *Protestbewegung und Hochschulreform*, Frankfurt am Main [includes DVD of the documentary *Ruhestörung*].

2009: *Philosophische Texte*, vol. 1: *Sprachtheoretische Grundlegung der Soziologie*; vol. 2: *Rationalitäts- und Sprachtheorie*; vol. 3: *Diskursethik*; vol. 4: *Politische Theorie*; vol. 5: *Kritik der Vernunft*, Frankfurt am Main.
2011: *Zur Verfassung Europas: Ein Essay*, Berlin.
       The Crisis of the European Union, trans. Ciaran Cronin, Cambridge, 2012.
2012: *Nachmetaphysisches Denken II: Aufsätze und Repliken*, Berlin.
2013: *Im Sog der Technokratie. Kleine Politische Schriften XII*, Berlin.
       The Lure of Technocracy, trans. Ciaran Cronin, Cambridge, 2015.

2 Articles, interviews, etc.

1954: 'Die Dialektik der Rationalisierung: Vom Pauperismus in Produktion und Konsum', *Merkur*, 78, pp. 701–23.
1955: 'Jeder Mensch ist unbezahlbar', *Merkur*, 92, pp. 994–8.
1955: 'Review of Leopold Schwarzschild: *Der Rote Preuße*; Auguste Cornu: *Karl Marx und Friedrich Engels*; Ralf Dahrendorf: *Marx in Perspektiven*', *Merkur*, 94, pp. 1180–3.
1956: 'Der Zeitgeist und die Pädagogik: Review of Max Bense: *Das Weltbild unserer Zeit*; Walter Dirks und Max Horkheimer: *Die Verantwortung der Universität*', *Merkur*, 96, pp. 189–93.
1956: 'Notizen zum Mißverhältnis von Kultur und Konsum', *Merkur*, 97, pp. 212–28.
1956: 'Illusionen auf dem Heiratsmarkt', *Merkur*, 104, pp. 996–1004.
1957: 'Das chronische Leiden der Hochschulreform', *Merkur*, 109, pp. 265–84.
1960: 'Verrufener Fortschritt – verkanntes Jahrhundert: zur Kritik der Geschichtsphilosophie: Review of Peter F. Drucker: *Das Fundament für Morgen*; Reinhart Koselleck: *Kritik und Krise*; Hanno Kesting: *Geschichtsphilosophie und Weltbürgertum*', *Merkur*, 147, pp. 468–77.
1960: 'Ein marxistischer Schelling: zu Ernst Blochs spekulativem Materialismus: Review of *Das Prinzip Hoffnung*', *Merkur*, 153, pp. 1078–91.
1963: 'Parteirügen an Schriftsteller – hüben und drüben', *Merkur*, 180, pp. 210–12.
1963: 'Vom sozialen Wandel akademischer Bildung', *Merkur*, 183, pp. 413–27; also in *Arbeit, Erkenntnis, Fortschritt* (1970), pp. 243–57.
1963: 'Karl Löwiths stoischer Rückzug vom historischen Bewußtsein: Review of *Von Hegel zu Nietzsche*; *Der Weltbegriff der neuzeitlichen Philosophie*', *Merkur*, 184, pp. 576–90.
1963: 'Auf- und Abrüstung, moralisch und militärisch', *Merkur*, 185, pp. 714–17.
1963: 'Eine psychoanalytische Konstruktion des Fortschritts: Review of Alexander Mitscherlich: *Auf dem Weg zur vaterlosen Gesellschaft*', *Merkur*, 189, pp. 1105–9.
1964: 'Von der Schwierigkeit Nein zu sagen: Review of Klaus Heinrich: *Versuch über die Schwierigkeit Nein zu sagen*', *Merkur*, 201, pp. 1184–8.
1965: 'Erkenntnis und Interesse', *Merkur*, 213, pp. 1139–53.
1966: 'Die Geschichte von den zwei Revolutionen: Review of Hannah Arendt: *On Revolution*; Hannah Arendt: *Vita activa*', *Merkur*, 218, pp. 479–82.
1966: 'Soziologie', in *Evangelisches Staatslexikon*, ed. Hermann Kunst and Siegfried Grundmann, Stuttgart and Berlin, pp. 2108–13.
1966: 'Nachwort', in G. W. F. Hegel, *Politische Schriften*, Frankfurt am Main, pp. 343–70.

1967: 'Universität in der Demokratie – Demokratisierung der Universität', *Merkur*, 230, pp. 416–33.

1968: 'Technik und Wissenschaft als "Ideologie"? Für Herbert Marcuse zum 70. Geburtstag', *Merkur*, 243, pp. 591–610.

1968: 'Technik und Wissenschaft als "Ideologie"? (II): Klassenkampf und Ideologie heute', *Merkur*, 244, pp. 682–93.

1969: 'Demokratisierung der Hochschule – Politisierung der Wissenschaft?', *Merkur*, 255, pp. 597–604.

1970: 'Nachgeahmte Substanzialität: Eine Auseinandersetzung mit Arnold Gehlens Ethik', *Merkur*, 264, pp. 313–27.

1972: 'Zwischen Kunst und Politik: Eine Auseinandersetzung mit Walter Benjamin', *Merkur*, 293, pp. 856–69.

1972: 'Helmuth Plessner zum 80. Geburtstag', *Merkur*, 293, pp. 944–6.

1972: 'Die Utopie des guten Herrschers: Eine Diskussion zwischen Jürgen Habermas und Robert Spaemann' (with Robert Spaemann), *Merkur*, 296, pp. 1266–78.

1972: 'Bewußtmachende oder rettende Kritik – die Aktualität Walter Benjamins', in Unseld, Siegfried (ed.), *Zur Aktualität Walter Benjamins*, Frankfurt am Main, pp. 173–224.
'Walter Benjamin: Consciousness-Raising or Rescuing Critique', in *Philosophical-Political Profiles*, pp. 129–64.

1973: 'Was heißt heute Krise? Legitimationsprobleme im Spätkapitalismus', *Merkur*, 300, pp. 345–64.

1975: 'Moral Development and Ego Identity', *Telos*, no. 24 (June 1975), pp. 41–55.

1976: 'Legitimationsprobleme im modernen Staat', in Kielmansegg, Peter Graf (ed.), *Legitimationsprobleme politischer Systeme*, Opladen, pp. 39–61.

1976: 'Legitimationsprobleme im modernen Staat', *Merkur*, 332, pp. 37–56.

1976: 'Hannah Arendts Begriff der Macht', *Merkur*, 341, pp. 946–60.

1977: 'Die Bühne des Terrors: Ein Brief an Kurt Sontheimer', *Merkur*, 353, pp. 944–59.

1978: 'Der Ansatz von Habermas', in Oelmüller, Willi (ed.), *Transzendentalphilosophische Normbegründung*, Paderborn, pp. 123–60.

1978: 'Die verkleidete Tora: Rede zum 80. Geburtstag von Gershom Scholem', *Merkur*, 356, pp. 96–104.

1978: 'Umgangssprache, Wissenschaftssprache, Bildungssprache', *Merkur*, 359, pp. 327–42.

1978: 'Gespräch über anthropologische Grundlagen der Gesellschaft' (with Herbert Marcuse), *Merkur*, 361, pp. 579–92.

1980: 'Psychic Thermidor and the Rebirth of Rebellious Subjectivity', *Berkeley Journal of Sociology: A Critical Review*, 24, pp. 1–13 [German version, 'Psychischer Thermidor und die Wiedergeburt der Rebellischen Subjektivität', in *Philosophisch-Politische Profile* (1981), pp. 319–35].

1981: 'Talcott Parsons – Probleme der Theoriekonstruktion', in Matthes, Joachim (ed.), *Lebenswelt und soziale Probleme: Verhandlungen des 20. Deutschen Soziologentages zu Bremen 1980*, Frankfurt am Main, pp. 28–48.

1982: 'In memoriam Alexander Mitscherlich', *Psyche*, 36, pp. 1060–3.

1982: 'Tod in Jerusalem: Am Grabe von Gershom Scholem am Ende einer Ära', *Merkur*, 406, pp. 438–40.

1982: 'Die Kulturkritik der Neokonservativen in den USA und in der Bundesrepublik: Über eine Bewegung von Intellektuellen in zwei politischen Kulturen', *Merkur*, 413, pp. 1047–61.

1982: 'A Reply to my Critics', in John B. Thompson and David Held (eds), *Habermas: Critical Debates*, Cambridge, MA, pp. 219–83.

1983: 'Der Eintritt in die Postmoderne', *Merkur*, 421, pp. 752–61.

1983: 'Sloterdijk zwischen Heine und Heidegger: Ein Renegat der Subjektphilosophie' [Sloterdijk between Heine and Heidegger: A renegade of philosophy of the subject], *Pflasterstrand*, 16 June.

1983: 'Some Conditions for Revolutionizing Late Capitalist Societies [1968]', trans. J. Keane, *Canadian Journal of Political and Social Theory*, 7(1–2), pp. 32–42.

1984: 'Recht und Gewalt – ein deutschesTrauma', *Merkur*, 423, pp. 15–28.

1984: 'Genealogische Geschichtsschreibung: Über einige Aporien im nachtheoretischen Denken Foucaults', *Merkur*, 429, pp. 745–53.

1984: 'Diltheys Theorie des Ausdrucksverstehens: Ich-Identität und sprachliche Kommunikation', in Rodi, Frithjof, and Lessing, Hans-Ulrich (eds), *Materialien zur Philosophie Wilhelm Diltheys*, Frankfurt am Main, pp. 316–38.

1985: 'Die Neue Unübersichtlichkeit: Die Krise des Wohlfahrtstaates und die Erschöpfung utopischer Energien', *Merkur*, 431, pp. 1–14.
'The New Obscurity: The Crisis of the Welfare State and the Exhaustion of Utopian Energies', trans. Phillip Jakobs, *Philosophy and Social Criticism*, 11/1 (1986), pp. 1–18.

1985: 'Rückkehr zur Metaphysik – Eine Tendenz in der deutschen Philosophie? Review of Herbert Schnädelbach: *Philosophie in Deutschland 1831– 1933*', *Merkur*, 439/440, pp. 898–905.

1985: 'Moral und Sittlichkeit: Hegels Kantkritik im Lichte der Diskursethik', *Merkur*, 442, pp. 1041–52.

1985: 'Wolfgang Abendroth in der Bundesrepublik', *Düsseldorfer Debatte*, no. 12, pp. 54–8; also in *Forum Wissenschaft*, vol. 4, pp. 54–5.

1985: 'Rückkehr zur Metaphysik – eine Tendenz in der deutschen Philosophie?', *Merkur*, 439/440, pp. 898–909.

1986: 'Heinrich Heine und die Rolle des Intellektuellen in Deutschland', *Merkur*, 448, pp. 453–68. (Also in *Eine Art Schadensabwicklung*, 1987).

1986: 'Entgegnung', in Honneth, Axel, and Joas, Hans (eds), *Kommunikatives Handeln: Beiträge zu Jürgen Habermas' 'Theorie des kommunikativen Handelns'*, Frankfurt am Main, pp. 327–405.

1987: 'Metaphysik nach Kant', in Cramer, Konrad, Fulda, Hans Friedrich, Horstmann, Rolf Peter, and Pothast, Ulrich (eds), *Theorie der Subjektivität*, Frankfurt am Main, pp. 425–43.

1988: 'Die Einheit der Vernunft in der Vielheit ihrer Stimmen', *Merkur*, 467, pp. 1–14.
'The Unity of Reason in the Diversity of its Voices', in *Postmetaphysical Thinking*, 1992, pp. 115–48.

1988: 'Die neue Intimität zwischen Politik und Kultur: Thesen zur Aufklärung in Deutschland', *Merkur*, 468, pp. 150–5.

1989: 'Ein Brief', in Erd, Rainer, Hoß, Dietrich, Jacobi, Rainer, and Noller, Peter (eds), *Kritische Theorie und Kultur*, Frankfurt am Main, pp. 391–4.

1989: 'Volkssouveränität als Verfahren', *Merkur*, 484, pp. 465–77.

1989: 'Über Titel, Texte und Termine oder wie man über den Zeitgeist reflektiert', in Habermas, Rebekka, and Pehle, Walter H. (eds), *Der Autor, der nicht schreibt*, Frankfurt am Main, pp. 3–6.

1989: 'Grenzen des Neoliberalismus: Gespräche mit Jürgen Habermas', *Frankfurter Hefte*, 4, pp. 370–4.

1991: 'Eine Generation von Adorno getrennt', in Früchtl, Josef, and Calloni, Maria (eds), *Geist gegen den Zeitgeist: Erinnern an Adorno*, Frankfurt am Main, pp. 47–53.

1991: 'A Reply', in *Communicative Action: Essays on Jürgen Habermas's Theory of Communicative Action*, ed. Axel Honneth and Hans Joas, Cambridge, pp. 214–64.

1992: '"Bürgersinn und politische Kultur": Speech on the 125th anniversary of the City of Gummersbach on 18 May 1982', in Böseke, Harry, and Hansen, Klaus (eds), *Herzenswärme und Widerspruchsgeist: Oberbergisches Lesebuch*, Gummersbach, pp. 21–9.

1993: 'Martin Heidegger: On the Publication of the Lectures of 1935', trans. William S. Lewis, in Richard Wolin (ed.), *The Heidegger Controversy: A Critical Reader*, Cambridge, MA, pp. 186–97 [German version, 'Zur Veröffentlichung von Vorlesungen aus dem Jahre 1935 (1953)', in *Philosophisch-Politische Profile* (1981), pp. 65–72].

1993: 'Anerkennungskämpfe im demokratischen Rechtsstaat', in Taylor, Charles (ed.), *Multikulturalismus und die Politik der Anerkennung*, Frankfurt am Main, pp. 147–96.

1993: 'Remarks on the Development of Max Horkheimer's Work', in Seyla Benhabib, Wolfgang Bonss and John McCole (eds), *Max Horkheimer: New Perspectives*, Cambridge, MA, pp. 49–66.

1994: 'Overcoming the Past' (with Adam Michnik), *New Left Review*, 203, pp. 3–16.

1996: 'Heinrich Heine und die Rolle des Intellektuellen in Deutschland', *Merkur*, 573, pp. 1122–37. (Also in *Eine Art Schadensabwicklung*, 1987)

1996: 'Reply to Symposium Participants, Benjamin N. Cardozo School of Law', *Cardozo Law Review*, 17 (1996), pp. 1477–558.

1997: 'Versöhnung durch öffentlichen Vernunftgebrauch', in Hinsch,Wilfried (ed.), *Zur Idee des politischen Liberalismus*, Frankfurt am Main, pp. 169–95.

1997: 'Noch einmal: Zum Verhältnis von Theorie und Praxis', *Paradigmi: Rivista di Critica Filosofica*, 15, no. 45, pp. 422–42 (also in *Kritik der Vernunft*, *Philosophische Texte,* vol. 5, 2009).

1997: 'Regiert das Recht die Politik?' (with Ronald Dworkin and Klaus Günther), in Boehm, Ulrich (ed.), *Philosophie heute*, Frankfurt am Main and New York, pp. 150–76.

1999: 'Der europäische Nationalstaat unter dem Druck der Globalisierung', *Blätter für deutsche und internationale Politik*, 44(4), pp. 425–36.

2000: '50 Jahre Suhrkamp', in Suhrkamp Verlag, *50 Jahre Suhrkamp Verlag: Dokumentation zum 01. 07. 2000*, Frankfurt am Main, pp. 22–6.

2000: 'Der liberale Geist: Eine Reminiszenz an unbeschwerte Heidelberger Anfänge', in Figal, Günter (ed.), *Begegnungen mit Gadamer*, Stuttgart, pp. 51–5.

2000: 'Nach dreißig Jahren: Bemerkungen zu Erkenntnis und Interesse' [Thirty years later: remarks on *Knowledge and Human Interest*], in Müller-Doohm, Stefan (ed.), *Das Interesse der Vernunft: Rückblicke auf das Werk von Jürgen Habermas seit 'Erkenntnis und Interesse'*, Frankfurt am Main, pp. 12–20.

2000: 'Globalization's Valley of Tears', *New Perspectives Quarterly*, 17(4), pp. 51–6.

2000: 'Werte und Normen', *Deutsche Zeitschrift für Philosophie*, 48(4), pp.

547–64; repr. in *Wahrheit und Rechtfertigung*, expanded edn, Frankfurt am Main, 2004, pp. 271–98.

2002: 'Transcendence from Within, Transcendence in this World', in *Religion and Rationality: Essays on Reason, God, and Modernity*, ed. Eduardo Mendieta, Cambridge, 2002, pp. 67–94.

2002: 'Meine gymnasiale Schulzeit: Ausschnitte aus einer geplanten Autobiographie', in *Schwarz auf Weiß: Mitteilungen des Vereins der Förderer und ehemaligen Schüler des Städtischen Gymnasiums Moltkestraße in Gummersbach e. V.*, pp. 51–3.

2005: '"Ich selber bin ja ein Stück Natur" – Adorno über die Naturverflochtenheit der Vernunft: Überlegungen zum Verhältnis von Freiheit und Unverfügbarkeit', in Honneth, Axel (ed.), *Dialektik der Freiheit: Frankfurter Adorno-Konferenz 2003*, Frankfurt am Main, pp. 13–40.

2007: 'Europa: Vision und Votum', *Blätter für deutsche und internationale Politik*, 5, pp. 517–20.

2007: 'Begegnungen mit Gershom Scholem', *Münchner Beiträge zur jüdischen Geschichte und Kultur*, no. 2, pp. 9–18.

2007: 'Die Zeit hatte einen doppelten Boden' [Time had two dimensions], in Müller-Doohm, Stefan (ed.), *Adorno-Portraits: Erinnerungen von Zeitgenossen*, Frankfurt am Main, pp. 15–23.

2007: 'Das Sprachspiel verantwortlicher Urheberschaft und das Problem der Willensfreiheit: Wie lässt sich der epistemische Dualismus mit einem ontologischen Monismus versöhnen?', in Krüger, Hans-Peter (ed.), *Hirn als Subjekt? Philosophische Grenzfragen der Neurobiologie*, Berlin, pp. 263–304 [*Deutsche Zeitschrift für Philosophie*, special volume 15].
'The Language Game of Responsible Agency and the Problem of Free Will: How Can Epistemic Dualism be Reconciled with Ontological Monism?', *Philosophical Explorations*, 10(1), pp. 13–50.

2007: 'Freiheit und Determinismus', in Krüger, Hans-Peter (ed.), *Hirn als Subjekt?*
Philosophische Grenzfragen der Neurobiologie, Berlin, pp. 101–20 [*Deutsche Zeitschrift für Philosophie*, special volume 15].

2007: 'Kommunikative Rationalität und grenzüberschreitende Politik: Eine Replik', in Niessen, Peter, and Herborth, Benjamin (eds), *Anarchie der kommunikativen Freiheit*, Frankfurt am Main, pp. 406–59.

2007: 'Europa: Vision und Votum', *Blätter für deutsche und internationale Politik*, 5, pp. 517–20.

2008: 'Ich bin alt, aber nicht fromm geworden', in Funken, Michael (ed.), *Über Habermas: Gespräche mit Zeitgenossen*, Darmstadt, pp. 181–90.

2008: 'Ein Bewußtsein von dem, was fehlt', in Reder, Michael, and Schmidt, Josef (eds), *Ein Bewußtsein von dem, was fehlt: Eine Diskussion mit Jürgen Habermas*, Frankfurt am Main, pp. 26–36.
'An Awareness of What is Missing', in *An Awareness of What is Missing: Faith and Reason in a Post-Secular Age*, ed. Michael Reder and Josef Schmidt, Cambridge, 2010, pp. 15–23.

2008: 'Eine Replik', in Reder, Michael, and Schmidt, Josef eds), *Ein Bewußtsein von dem, was fehlt: Eine Diskussion mit Jürgen Habermas*, Frankfurt am Main, pp. 94–107.
'A Reply', in Reder, Michael, and Schmidt, Josef (eds), *An Awareness of What is Missing: Faith and Reason in a Post-Secular Age*, Cambridge, 2010, pp. 72–83.

2008: 'Die Dialektik der Säkularisierung', *Blätter für deutsche und internationale Politik*, 4, pp. 33–46.

2008: 'Europapolitik in der Sackgasse: Nicht die Bevölkerung, die Regierungen sind der Hemmschuh – Plädoyer für eine Politik der abgestuften Integration', in Nida-Rümelin, Julian, and Thierse, Wolfgang (eds), *European Prospects, Europäische Perspektiven*, Essen, pp. 15–30.

2008: 'Vorwort', in Sandel, Michael J., *Plädoyer gegen die Perfektion: Ethik im Zeitalter der genetischen Technik*, Berlin, pp. 7–16.

2008: 'Transnationale Verrechtlichung und Entrechtlichung: Nationale Demokratien im Kontext globaler Politik', in Kreide, Regina, and Niederberger, Andreas (eds), *Transnationale Verrechtlichung*, Frankfurt am Main and New York, pp. 9–13.

2009: 'Reminiszenzen an Frankfurt', in Müller-Doohm, Stefan, Schopf, Wolfgang, and Thiele, Franziska (eds), *'. . . die Lava des Gedankens im Fluss': Jürgen Habermas: Eine Werkschau*, Oldenburg, pp. 55–8.

2009: 'Die Revitalisierung der Weltreligionen – Herausforderung für ein säkulares Selbstverständnis der Moderne?' [The resurgence of religion – a challenge for a secular self-interpretation of modernity?], in *Philosophische Texte*, vol. 5: *Kritik der Vernunft*, Frankfurt am Main, pp. 387–416.

2009: 'Discurso de agradecimiento con motivo de la entrega del Premio Jaime Brunet 2008', acceptance speech for the Jaime Brunet Prize 2008 at the Universidad Publica de Navarra, Pamplona, www.unavarra.es/digital-Assets/112/112044_discursoHabermas_09.pdf, pp. 3–5.

2010: 'Das Konzept der Menschenwürde und die realistische Utopie der Menschenrechte', *Blätter für deutsche und internationale Politik*, 8, pp. 43–53.

2010: 'Ein neues Interesse der Philosophie an der Religion: Zur philosophischen Bewandtnis von postsäkularem Bewusstsein und multikultureller Weltgesellschaft', Jürgen Habermas interviewed by Eduardo Mendieta, *Deutsche Zeitschrift für Philosophie*, 58, pp. 3–16.

2010: '"Bohrungen an der Quelle des objektiven Geistes": Laudatio bei der Verleihung des Hegel-Preises an Michael Tomasello' ['Drillings at the source of objective spirit': laudation for Michael Tomasello upon his receipt of the Hegel Prize], *WestEnd*, 7(1), pp. 166–70.

2010: 'Kultur des Gegenwartssinns', *Du: Die Zeitschrift der Kultur*, 803, pp. 36–9.

2011: 'Europa und die neue Deutsche Frage: Ein Gespräch mit Jürgen Habermas' (with Joschka Fischer, Henrik Enderlein and Christian Calliess), *Blätter für deutsche und internationale Politik*, 56, pp. 45–63.

2011: '"The Political": The Rational Meaning of a Questionable Inheritance of Political Theology', in Mendieta, Eduardo, and VanAntwerpen, Jonathan (eds), *The Power of Religion in the Public Sphere*, New York and Chichester, pp. 15–33 [chapter 7 of *Nachmetaphysisches Denken II* (2012)].

2013: 'Demokratie oder Kapitalismus? Vom Elend der nationalstaatlichen Fragmentierung einer kapitalistisch integrierten Weltgesellschaft', *Blätter für deutsche und internationale Politik*, 58, pp. 59–70.

2013: 'Reply to my Critics', in Calhoun, Craig, Mendieta, Eduardo, and VanAntwerpen, Jonathan (eds), *Habermas and Religion*, Cambridge, 2013, pp. 347–90.

2014: '"Für ein starkes Europa" – aber was heißt das?', *Blätter für deutsche und internationale Politik*, 59, pp. 85–94.

3 Interviews

'A Philosophico-Political Profile', *New Left Review*, no. 151 (1985), pp. 75–105.
'Life-forms, Morality and the Task of the Philosopher', in Peter Dews, *Autonomy and Solidarity: Interviews with Jürgen Habermas*, London, 1986, pp. 191–216.
'The Dialectics of Rationalization', in Peter Dews (ed.), *Autonomy and Solidarity*, London, 1986, pp. 95–130.
'Morality, Society, and Ethics: an Interview with Torben Hviid Nielsen', *Acta Sociologica*, 33(2) (1990), pp. 93–114.
'French Views, French Anxieties: An Interview with *Le Monde*', in *A Berlin Republic: Writings on Germany*, trans. Steven Rendall, Cambridge, 1998, pp. 59–67.
'Globalism, Ideology and Traditions', interview with Johann P. Arnason, in *Thesis Eleven*, no. 63 (2000), pp. 1–10.
'An Interview on War and Peace', in *The Divided West*, Cambridge, 2006, pp. 85–112.
'A Conversation about God and the World', in *Time of Transitions*, Cambridge, 2006, pp. 149–69.
'The Next Step – An Interview', in *The Lure of Technocracy*, Cambridge, 2015, pp. 63–72.
'A Postsecular World Society? On the Philosophical Significance of Postsecular Consciousness and the Multicultural World Society', interview with Eduardo Mendieta, http://mrzine.monthlyreview.org/2010/habermas210310.html.

4 Individually referenced chapters from books by Habermas

1974: 'The Classical Doctrine of Politics in Relation to Social Philosophy', in *Theory and Practice*, pp. 41–81.
1974: 'Between Philosophy and Science: Marxism as Critique', in *Theory and Practice*, pp. 195–252.
1976: 'A positivistically bisected rationalism', in *The Positivist Dispute in German Sociology*, pp. 199–225.
1979: 'Toward a Reconstruction of Historical Materialism', in *Communication and the Evolution of Society*, pp. 130–77.
1979: 'Legitimation Problems in the Modern State', in *Communication and the Evolution of Society*, pp. 178–206.
1987: 'Excursus on Luhmann's Appropriation of the Philosophy of the Subject through Systems Theory', in *The Philosophical Discourse of Modernity*, pp. 368–85.
1987: 'Excursus on Leveling the Genre Distinction between Philosophy and Literature', in *The Philosophical Discourse of Modernity*, pp. 185–210.
1989: 'Taking Aim at the Heart of the Present: On Foucault's Lecture on Kant's What is Enlightenment?; in *The New Conservatism*, pp. 173–9.
1990: 'Discourse Ethics: Notes on a Program of Philosophical Justification', in *Moral Consciousness and Communicative Action*, pp. 43–115.
1990: 'Europe's Second Chance', in *The Past as Future*, pp. 73–97.
1991: 'Legitimation Problems in the Modern State; in *Communication and the Evolution of Society*, pp. 178–205.
1991: 'Historical Materialism and the Development of Normative Structives', in *Communication and the Evolution of Society*, pp. 95–129.

556   Works by Jürgen Habermas

1991: 'Toward a Reconstruction of Historical Materialism', in *Communication and the Evolution of Society*, pp. 130–77.
1992: 'Metaphysics after Kant', in *Postmetaphysical Thinking*, pp. 10–27.
1992: 'Themes in Postmetaphysical Thinking', in *Postmetaphysical Thinking*, pp. 28–53.
1992: 'The Unity of Reason in the Diversity of its Voices', in *Postmetaphysical Thinking*, pp. 115–48.
1992: 'Individuation through Socialization: On Mead's Theory of Subjectivity', in *Postmetaphysical Thinking*, pp. 149–204.
1994: 'Overcoming the Past', *New Left Review*, no. 203, 1994, pp. 3–16.
1994: 'On the Pragmatic, the Ethical, and the Moral Employments of Practical Reason', in *Justification and Application: Remarks on Discourse Ethics*, pp. 1–18.
1996: 'Popular Sovereignty as Procedure', appendix I in *Between Facts and Norms: Contributions to a Discourse Theory of Law*, pp. 463–90.
1996: 'Citizenship and National Identity (1990)', in *Between Facts and Norms: Contributions to a Discourse Theory of Law*, pp. 491–515.
1997: 'The Adenauer Restoration's Debts: An Interview with the *Kölner Stadtanzeiger*', in *A Berlin Republic: Writings on Germany*, pp. 83–92.
1997: '1989 in the shadow of 1945: On the normality of a Future Berlin Republic', in *A Berlin Republic: Writings on Germany*, pp. 161–81.
1999: 'A Genealogical Analysis of the Cognitive Content of Morality', in *The Inclusion of the Other*, pp. 3–46.
1999: 'Reconciliation through the Public Use of Reason', in *The Inclusion of the Other*, pp. 49–74.
1999: '"Reasonable" versus "True", or the Morality of Worldviews', in *The Inclusion of the Other*, pp. 75–101.
1999: 'The European Nation-State: On the Past and Future of Sovereignty and Citizenship', in *The Inclusion of the Other*, pp. 105–27.
1999: 'Does Europe Need a Constitution? Response to Dieter Grimm', in *The Inclusion of the Other*, pp. 155–61.
2001: 'On the Public Use of History', in *The Postnational Constellation*, pp. 26–37.
2001: 'Learning from Catastrophe? A Look Back at the Short Twentieth Century', in *The Postnational Constellation*, pp. 38–57.
2001: 'The Postnational Constellation and the Future of Democracy', in *The Postnational Constellation*, pp. 58–112.
2001: 'The Conflict of Beliefs: Karl Jaspers on the Clash of Cultures', in *The Liberating Power of Symbols*, pp. 30–45.
2001: 'Israel or Athens: Where does Anamnestic Reason Belong? Johann Baptist Metz on Unity amidst Multicultural Plurality', in *The Liberating Power of Symbols*, pp. 78–89.
2003: 'Faith and Knowledge', in *The Future of Human Nature*, pp. 101–15.
2003: 'Introduction: Realism after the Linguistic Turn', in *Truth and Justification*, pp. 1–49.
2003: 'Hermeneutic and Analytic Philosophy: Two Complementary Versions of the Linguistic Turn', in *Truth and Justification*, pp. 51–81.
2003: 'Norms and Values: On Hilary Putnam's Kantian Pragmatism', in *Truth and Justification*, pp. 213–36.
2003: 'Rightness versus Truth: On the Sense of Normative Validity in Moral Judgments and Norms', in *Truth and Justification*, pp. 237–76.
2006: 'February 15, or: What Binds Europeans', in *The Divided West*, pp. 39–48.

2006: 'Is the Development of a European Identity Necessary, and Is it Possible?', in *The Divided West*, pp. 67–82.

2006: 'Does Europe Need a Constitution?', in *Time of Transitions*, pp. 89–110.

2006: 'Does the Constitutionalization of International Law Still Have a Chance?', in *The Divided West*, pp. 115–93.

2006: 'The Finger of Blame: The Germans and Their Memorial', in *Time of Transitions*, pp. 38–50.

2006: 'Richard Rorty, *Achieving our Country*', in *Time of Transitions*, pp. 136–41.

2008: 'Public Space and Political Public Sphere – The Biographical Roots of Two Motifs in my Thought', in *Between Naturalism and Religion*, pp. 11–23.

2008: 'Communicative Action and the Detranscendentalized "Use of Reason"', in *Between Naturalism and Religion*, pp. 24–76.

2008: 'Prepolitical Foundations of the Constitutional State?', in *Between Naturalism and Religion*, pp. 101–13.

2008: 'Religion in the Public Sphere: Cognitive Presuppositions for the "Public Use of Reason" by Religious and Secular Citizens', in *Between Naturalism and Religion*, pp. 114–47.

2008: 'Freedom and Determinism', in *Between Naturalism and Religion*, pp. 151–80.

2008: '"I Myself am Part of Nature" – Adorno on the Intrication of Reason in Nature: Reflections on the Relation between Freedom and Unavailability', in *Between Naturalism and Religion*, pp. 181–208.

2008: 'The Boundary between Faith and Knowledge: On the Reception and Contemporary Importance of Kant's Philosophy of Religion', in *Between Naturalism and Religion*, pp. 209–47.

2008: 'Religious Tolerance as a Pacemaker for Cultural Rights', in *Between Naturalism and Religion*, pp. 251–70.

2008: 'A Political Constitution for the Pluralist World Society?', in *Between Naturalism and Religion*, pp. 312–52.

2009: '". . . And to define America, her athletic Democracy": In Memory of Richard Rorty', in *Europe: The Faltering Project*, pp. 3–16.

2009: 'An Avantgardistic Instinct for Relevances: The Role of the Intellectual and the European Cause', in *Europe: The Faltering Project*, pp. 49–58.

2009: 'Media, Markets and Consumers: The Quality Press as the Backbone of the Political Public Sphere', in *Europe: The Faltering Project*, pp. 131–7.

2009: 'Political Communication in Media Society: Does Democracy still have an Epistemic Dimension? The Impact of Normative Theory on Empirical Research', in *Europe: The Faltering Project*, pp. 138–83.

2012: 'Does Philosophy Still Have a Purpose?', in *Philosophical-Political Profiles*, pp. 1–19.

2012: 'Martin Heidegger: The Great Influence (1959)', in *Philosophical-Political Profiles*, pp. 53–60.

2012: 'Karl Löwith: Stoic Retreat from Historical Consciousness', in *Philosophical-Political Profiles*, pp. 79–97.

2012: 'Theodor Adorno: The Primal History of Subjectivity – Self-Affirmation Gone Wild', in *Philosophical-Political Profiles*, pp. 99–109.

2012: 'Arnold Gehlen: Imitation Substantiality (1970)', in *Philosophical-Political Profiles*, pp. 111–28.

2012: 'Walter Benjamin: Consciousness-Raising or Rescuing Critique', in *Philosophical-Political Profiles*, pp. 129–64.

2012: 'Hans-Georg Gadamer: Urbanizing the Heideggerian Province', in *Philosophical-Political Profiles*, pp. 189–97.

2012: 'Gershom Scholem: The Torah in Disguise', in *Philosophical Profiles*, pp. 199–211.

2012: 'The Crisis of the European Union in Light of a Constitutionalization of International Law – An Essay on the Constitution of Europe', in *The Crisis of the European Union*, pp. 1–70.

2012: 'The Concept of Human Dignity and the Realistic Utopia of Human Rights', in *The Crisis of the European Union*, pp. 71–100.

2012: 'After the Bankruptcy: An Interview', in *The Crisis of the European Union*, pp. 102–18.

2012: 'A Pact for or against Europe?', in *The Crisis of the European Union*, pp. 127–39.

2015: 'The Lure of Technocracy: A Plea for European Solidarity', in *The Lure of Technocracy*, pp. 3–28.

2015: 'The Dilemma Facing the Political Parties', in *The Lure of Technocracy*, pp. 73–9.

2015: 'Three Reasons for "More Europe"', in *The Lure of Technocracy*, pp. 80–4.

2015: 'Democracy or Capitalism? The Abject Spectacle of a Capitalistic World Society Fragmented along National Lines', in *The Lure of Technology*, pp. 85–104.

2015: 'Jewish Philosophers and Sociologists as Returnees in the Early Federal Republic of Germany: A Recollection', in *The Lure of Technocracy*, pp. 105–18.

2015: 'Martin Buber – A Philosophy of Dialogue in its Historical Context', in *The Lure of Technocracy*, pp. 119–36.

2015: 'Our Contemporary Heine: There are No Longer Nations in Europe', in *The Lure of Technocracy*, pp. 137–53.

Secondary Literature

Abendroth,Wolfgang, and Negt, Oskar (eds) (1968) *Die Linke antwortet Jürgen Habermas*, Frankfurt am Main.

Adorno, Gretel, and Benjamin, Walter (2005) *Briefwechsel 1930–1940*, ed. Christoph Gödde and Henri Lonitz, Frankfurt am Main.

Adorno, Gretel, and Benjamin, Walter (2007) *Correspondence 1930–1940*, ed. Henri Lonitz and Christoph Gödde, trans. Wieland Hoban, Cambridge.

Adorno, Theodor W. (1981) 'Cultural Criticism and Society', in *Prisms*, trans. Samuel and Shierry Weber, Cambridge, MA, pp. 17–34.

Adorno, Theodor W. (1986) *Kulturkritik und Gesellschaft, Gesammelte Schriften*, vol. 10.2, ed. Rolf Tiedemann, Frankfurt am Main.

Adorno, Theodor W. (1986) 'Was bedeutet Aufarbeitung der Vergangenheit?', in *Kulturkritik und Gesellschaft, Gesammelte Schriften*, vol. 10.2, ed. Rolf Tiedemann, Frankfurt am Main.

Adorno, Theodor W. (1986) 'Die auferstandene Kultur', in *Vermischte Schriften II, Gesammelte Schriften*, vol. 20.2, ed. Rolf Tiedemann, Frankfurt am Main.

Adorno, Theodor W. (1997) 'Offener Brief an Max Horkheimer', in *Vermischte Schriften I, Gesammelte Schriften*, vol. 20.1, ed. Rolf Tiedemann, Frankfurt am Main. pp. 155–64.

Adorno, Theodor W. (1998) 'The Meaning of Working through the Past', in *Critical Models: Interventions and Catchwords*, trans. Henry W. Pickford, New York and Chichester, pp. 89–104.

Adorno, Theodor W. (2003) *The Jargon of Authenticity*, London.

Adorno, Theodor W. (2005) 'Progress', in *Critical Models: Interventions and Catchwords*, New York and Chichester, pp. 143–60.

Adorno, Theodor W. (2007) *Negative Dialectics*, New York.

Adorno, Theodor W., and Horkheimer, Max (2006) *Briefwechsel, 1927–1969*, vol. 4: *1950–1969*, ed. Christoph Gödde and Henri Lonitz, Frankfurt am Main.

Albert, Hans, and Popper, Karl R. (2005) *Briefwechsel 1958–1994*, Frankfurt am Main.

Albrecht, Clemes, Behrmann, Günter C., Bock, Michael, Homann, Harald, and Tenbruck, Friedrich H. (1999) *Die intellektuelle Gründung der Bundesrepublik: Eine Wirkungsgeschichte der Frankfurter Schule*, Frankfurt am Main and New York.

Alexy, Robert (1994) *Recht, Vernunft, Diskurs: Studien zur Rechtsphilosophie*, Frankfurt am Main.

Alsberg, Paul (1970) *In Quest of Man: A Biological Approach to the Problem of Man's Place in Nature*, Oxford.

Alsberg, Paul ([1922] 1985) *Der Ausbruch aus dem Gefängnis – zu den Entstehungsbedingungen des Menschen*, with a preface by Dieter Claessens, Gießen [orig. pubn: *Das Menschheitsrätsel: Versuch einer prinzipiellen Lösung*, Dresden].

Altmann, Rüdiger (1970) 'Brüder im Nichts? Zur Auseinandersetzung von Jürgen Habermas mit Arnold Gehlen', *Merkur*, 24, pp. 577–82.

Apel, Karl-Otto (1971) 'Szientistik, Hermeneutik, Ideologiekritik: Entwurf einer Wissenschaftslehre in erkenntnisanthropologischer Sicht', in Apel, *Hermeneutik und Ideologiekritik*, Frankfurt am Main, pp. 7–44.

Apel, Karl-Otto (1988) *Diskurs und Verantwortung: Das Problem des Übergangs zur postkonventionellen Moral*, Frankfurt am Main.

Apel, Karl-Otto (1998) *Auseinandersetzungen in der Erprobung des transzenden- talpragmatischen Ansatzes*, Frankfurt am Main.

Arendt, Hannah (1993) *Besuch in Deutschland*, Berlin.

Arens, Edmund (ed.) (1989) *Habermas und die Theologie: Beiträge zur theo- logischen Rezeption. Diskussion und Kritik der Theorie des kommunikativen Handelns*, *Theologie und Philosophie* 80, pp. 546–65.

Auer, Dirk (2004) *Politisierte Demokratie: Richard Rortys politischer Antiessentialismus*, Wiesbaden.

Augstein, Rudolf, et al. (1987), *'Historikerstreit': Die Dokumentation der Kontroverse um die Einzigartigkeit der nationalsozialistischen Judenvernichtung*, Munich.

Baecker, Dirk (2012) 'Niklas Luhmann, der Werdegang', in Jahraus, Oliver, and Armin, Nassehi (eds), *Luhmann-Handbuch*, Stuttgart.

Bahr, Hans Eckhard (ed.) (1973) *Religionsgespräche: Zur gesellschaftlichen Rolle der Religion*, Darmstadt and Neuwied.

Barth, Hans (1977) *Truth and Ideology*, trans. Frederic Lilge, Berkeley, Los Angeles and London.

Baumgart, Reinhard (2003) *Ein Leben in Deutschland 1929–2003*, Munich.

Becker, Hartmuth (1994) *Die Parlamentarismuskritik bei Carl Schmitt und Jürgen Habermas*, Berlin.

Becker, Jörg (ed.) (2002) *Medien zwischen Krieg und Frieden*, Baden- Baden.

Becker, Oskar (1963) *Dasein und Dawesen: Gesammelte Philosophische Aufsätze*, Pfullingen.

Beckert, Jens (2009) *Die Anspruchsinflation des Wirtschaftssystems*, Cologne, Max Planck Institut für Gesellschaftsforschung Working Paper, pp. 1–20.

Beier, Katharina (2009) *Zwischen Beharren und Umdenken: Die Herausforderung des politischen Liberalismus durch die moderne Biomedizin*, Frankfurt am Main and New York.

Benhabib, Seyla (1992) *Kritik, Norm und Utopie: Die normativen Grundlagen der Kritischen Theorie*, Frankfurt am Main.

Benjamin, Walter (1999) 'Theses on the Philosophy of History', in *Illuminations*, London, pp. 245–55.

Benn, Gottfried (1996) *The Voice behind the Screen*, trans. Simona Draghici, Washington, DC.

Berger, Thomas, and Müller, Karl-Heinz (1983) *Lebenssituationen 1945– 1948: Materialien zum Alltagsleben in den westlichen Besatzungszonen*, Hannover.

Bering, Dietz (2010) *Die Epoche der Intellektuellen 1898–2001: Geburt, Begriff, Grabmal*, Berlin.

Biebricher,Thomas (2005) *Selbstkritik der Moderne: Foucault und Habermas im Vergleich*, Frankfurt am Main and New York.

Biegi, Mandana, Förster, Jörn, Otten, Henrique Ricardo, and Philipp, Thomas (eds) (2008) *Demokratie, Recht und Legitimität im 21. Jahrhundert*, Wiesbaden.

Blanke,Thomas (2000) 'Theorie und Praxis: Der Philosoph im Handgemenge', in Müller-Doohm, Stefan (ed.), *Das Interesse der Vernunft*, Frankfurt am Main, pp. 486–521.

Blumenberg, Hans, and Taubes, Jacob (2013) *Briefwechsel 1961–1981*, ed. Herbert Kopp-Obestebrink and Martin Treml, Berlin.

Boehlich,Walter, Braun, Karlheinz, Reichert, Klaus, Urban, Peter, and Widmer, Urs (2011) *Chronik der Lektoren: Von Suhrkamp zum Verlag der Autoren*, Frankfurt am Main.

Böhme, Gernot, van den Daele, Wolfgang, Krohn, Wolfgang, et al. (1978) *Die gesellschaftliche Orientierung des wissenschaftlichen Fortschritts*, Frankfurt am Main.

Bohrer, Karl Heinz (2011) 'Ästhetik und Politik: Eine Erinnerung an drei Jahrzehnte des *Merkur*', *Merkur*, 751, pp. 1091–103.

Bohrer, Karl Heinz, and Scheel, Kurt (1996) 'Zum fünfzigsten Jahrgang', *Merkur*, 562.

Boltanski, Luc, and Honneth, Axel (2009) 'Soziologie der Kritik oder Kritische Theorie? Ein Gespräch mit Robin Celikates', in Jaeggi, Rahel and Wesche, Tilo (eds), *Was ist Kritik?*, Frankfurt am Main, pp. 81–114.

Bonacker, Thorsten (2000) *Die normative Kraft der Kontingenz: Nichtessentialistische Gesellschaftskritik nach Weber und Adorno*, Frankfurt am Main and New York.

Bonß,Wolfgang, and Honneth, Axel (eds) (1982) *Sozialforschung als Kritik: Zum sozialwissenschaftlichen Potential der Kritischen Theorie*, Frankfurt am Main.

Bormuth, Matthias, and von Bülow, Ulrich (eds) (2008) *Marburger Hermeneutik zwischen Tradition und Krise*, Göttingen.

Bourdieu, Pierre (1991) *The Political Ontology of Martin Heidegger*, Stanford, CA.

Brandom, Robert (ed.) (2000) *Rorty and his Critics*, Oxford.

Brandt, Willy (1986) *Wir sind nicht zu Helden geboren: Ein Gespräch über Deutschland mit Birgit Kraatz*, Zurich.

Brodkorb, Mathias (ed.) (2011) *Singuläres Auschwitz? Ernst Nolte, Jürgen Habermas und 25 Jahre 'Historikerstreit'*, Banzkow.

Broszat, Martin, et al. (eds) (1983) *Deutschlands Weg in die Diktatur: Internationale Konferenz zur nationalsozialistischen Machtübernahme*, Berlin.

Browning, Don S., and Fiorenza, Francis Schussler (1992), *Habermas, Modernity and Public Theology*, New York.

Brückner, Peter (1977) *Die Mescalero-Affäre: Ein Lehrstück für Aufklärung und politische Kultur*, Hannover.

Brückner, Peter (1978) *Versuch, uns und anderen die Bundesrepublik zu erklären*, Berlin.

Brückner, Peter (1980) *Das Abseits als sicherer Ort*, Berlin.

Brumlik, Micha, Funke, Hajo, and Rensmann, Lars (eds) (2004) *Umkämpftes Vergessen: Walser-Debatte, Holocaust-Mahnmal und neuere deutsche Geschichtspolitik*, Berlin.

Brunkhorst, Hauke (2005) 'Jürgen Habermas: Die rächende Gewalt der kommunikativen Vernunft', in Hennigfeld, Jochem, and Jahnsohn, Heinz (eds), *Philosophen der Gegenwart*, Darmstadt.

Brunkhorst, Hauke (2012) *Legitimationskrisen: Verfassungsprobleme der Weltgesellschaft*, Baden-Baden.

Brunkhorst, Hauke, Kreide, Regina, and Lafont, Cristina (eds) (2009) *Habermas-Handbuch*, Stuttgart.

Buchna, Kristian (2010) *Nationale Sammlung an Rhein und Ruhr: Friedrich Middelhauve und die nordrhein-westfälische FDP 1945–1953*, Munich.

Bude, Heinz (1987) *Deutsche Karrieren*, Frankfurt am Main.

Calhoun, Craig (ed.) (2011) *Rethinking Secularism*, Oxford and New York.

Calhoun, Craig, Mendieta, Eduardo, and VanAntwerpen, Jonathan (eds) (2013) *Habermas and Religion*, Cambridge.

Camartin, Iso (1991) *Von Sils-Maria aus betrachtet: Ausblick vom Dach Europas*, Frankfurt am Main.

Canovan, Margaret (1983), 'A Case of Distorted Communication: A Note on Habermas and Arendt', *Political Theory*, 11(1), pp. 105–16.

Celikates, Robin (2010) 'Habermas: Sprache, Verständigung und sprachliche Gewalt', in Kuch, Hannes, and Hermann, Steffen K. (ed.), *Philosophien sprachlicher Gewalt*, Weilerswist, pp. 275–85.

Cerutti, Furio (1983) 'Habermas und Marx', *Leviathan* 11(3), pp. 352–75.

Conze, Eckhard, Frei, Norbert, Hayes, Peter, and Zimmermann, Moshe (2010) *Das Amt und die Vergangenheit: Deutsche Diplomaten im Dritten Reich und in der Bundesrepublik*, Munich.

Corchia, Luca (2013) *Jürgen Habermas: A Bibliography: Works and Studies (1952–2013)*, Pisa.

Créau, Anna (1991) *Kommunikative Vernunft als 'entmystifiziertes' Schicksal: Denkmotive des frühen Hegel in der Theorie von Jürgen Habermas*, Frankfurt am Main.

Crouch, Colin (2004) *Post-Democracy*, Cambridge.

Dahms, Hans-Joachim (1994) *Positivismusstreit*, Frankfurt am Main.

Dahrendorf, Ralf (1989) 'Zeitgenosse Habermas', *Merkur*, 484, pp. 478–87.

Dahrendorf, Ralf (1990) 'Politik: Eine Kolumne: Eine Mark für Deutschland', *Merkur*, 497, pp. 579–82.

Dahrendorf, Ralf (2002) *Über Grenzen: Lebenserinnerungen*, Munich.

Dahrendorf, Ralf (2006) *Versuchungen der Unfreiheit: Die Intellektuellen in den Zeiten der Prüfung*, Munich.

Dehli, Martin (2007) *Leben als Konflikt: Zur Biographie Alexander Mitscherlichs*, Göttingen.

Demirović, Alex (1999) *Der nonkonformistische Intellektuelle: Die Entwicklung der Kritischen Theorie zur Frankfurter Schule*, Frankfurt am Main.

Demmerling, Christoph, Gabriel, Gottfried, and Rentsch, Thomas (eds) (1995) *Vernunft und Lebenspraxis: Philosophische Studien zu den Bedingungen einer rationalen Kultur*, Frankfurt am Main.

Dews, Peter (ed.) (1986) *Autonomy and Solidarity: Interviews*, London.

Dews, Peter (2001) 'Naturalismus und Anti-Naturalismus bei Habermas', *Deutsche Zeitschrift für Philosophie*, 49(6), pp. 861–71.

Doering-Manteuffel, Anselm (1988) *Die Bundesrepublik Deutschland in der Ära Adenauer*, Darmstadt.

Douramanis, Demetrios (1995) *Mapping Habermas: A Biography of Primary Literature*, Sydney.

Drieschner, Michael (1996) 'Die Verantwortung der Wissenschaft', in Fischer,

Tanja, and Seising, Rudolf (eds), *Wissenschaft und Öffentlichkeit*, Frankfurt am Main and Berlin, pp. 173–98.

Dubiel, Helmut (1999) *Niemand ist frei von der Geschichte: Die nationalsozialistische Herrschaft in den Debatten des Deutschen Bundestags*, Munich.

Düringer, Hermann (1999) *Universale Vernunft und partikularer Glaube: Eine theologische Auswertung des Werkes von Jürgen Habermas*, Leuven.

Dworkin, Ronald (1990) *Bürgerrechte ernstgenommen*, Frankfurt am Main.

Ebbinghaus, Julius (ed.) (1947) *Die große Not: Sammelbroschüre 1946–1947*, Meisenheim am Glan.

Ellwein, Thomas, Liebel, Manfred, and Negt, Inge (1966) *Die Spiegel-Affäre*, vol. 2: *Die Reaktion der Öffentlichkeit*, ed. Jürgen Seifert, Olten and Freiburg im Breisgau.

Enzensberger, Hans Magnus (1973) 'Entrevista 1969', in *Jahrbuch für deutsche Gegenwartsliteratur* 4, ed. Reinhold Grimm and Hermann Jost, Frankfurt am Main, pp. 122–30.

Enzensberger, Hans Magnus (1974) *Politics and Crime*, New York.

Fach, Wolfgang (1974) 'Diskurs und Herrschaft – Überlegungen zu Habermas' Legitimationslogik', *Zeitschrift für Soziologie*, 3(3), pp. 221–8.

Fach, Wolfgang, and Degen, Ulrich (eds) (1978) *Politische Legitimität*, Frankfurt am Main and New York.

Farías, Víctor (1989) *Heidegger and Nazism*, Philadelphia.

Fay, Margaret, Feder, Ernest, and Frank, Andre Gunter (1980) *Strukturveränderungen in der kapitalistischen Weltwirtschaft*, Frankfurt am Main.

Fellinger, Raimund, and Schopf, Wolfgang (eds) (2003) *Kleine Geschichte der Edition Suhrkamp*, Frankfurt am Main.

Fest, Joachim (2010) *Not Me: A German Childhood*, London.

Fichter, Tilman, and Lönnendonker, Siegward (1977) *Kleine Geschichte des SDS: Der Sozialistische Deutsche Studentenbund von 1946 bis zur Selbstauflösung*, Berlin.

Figal, Günter (ed.) (2000) *Begegnungen mit Hans-Georg Gadamer*, Stuttgart.

Finlayson, James Gordon, and Freyenhagen, Fabian (2010) *Habermas and Rawls*, Abingdon and New York.

Fischer, Frank, and Mandell, Alan (2009) 'Die verborgene Politik des impliziten Wissens: Michael Polanyis Republik der Wissenschaft', *Leviathan*, 37, pp. 533–57.

Fischer, Joschka (2008) 'Gründungsfigur des demokratischen Deutschland', in Funken, Michael (ed.), *Über Habermas: Gespräche mit Zeitgenossen*, Darmstadt, pp. 45–57.

Flaig, Egon (2011) 'Die "Habermas-Methode" und die geistige Situation ein Vierteljahrhundert danach: Skizze einer Schadensaufnahme', in Brodkorb, Mathias (ed.), *Singuläres Auschwitz? Ernst Nolte, Jürgen Habermas und 25 Jahre 'Historikerstreit'*, Banzkow, pp. 67–93.

Fleischer, Helmut (1987) *Ethik ohne Imperativ: Zur Kritik des moralischen Bewußtseins*, Frankfurt am Main.

Forner, Sean A. (2007) 'Für eine demokratische Erneuerung Deutschlands: Kommunikationsprozesse und Deutungsmuster engagierter Demokraten nach 1945', *Geschichte und Gesellschaft*, 33, pp. 228–57.

Forner, Sean A. (2014) *German Intellectuals and the Challenge of Democracy: Culture and Politics after 1945*, Cambridge.

Forst, Rainer (2002) *Contexts of Justice*, Berkeley, CA.

Forst, Rainer (2014) *The Right to Justification*, New York and Chichester.

Frank, Manfred (1988) *Die Grenzen der Verständigung: Ein Geistergespräch zwischen Lyotard und Habermas*, Frankfurt am Main.

Frank, Manfred (2009) 'Schelling, Marx und Geschichtsphilosophie', in Brunkhorst, Hauke, Kreide, Regine, and Lafont, Cristina (eds), *Habermas-Handbuch*, Stuttgart, pp. 133–47.

Frankenberg, Günter (2003) *Autorität und Integration*, Frankfurt am Main.

Frankenberg, Günter (2010) *Staatstechnik: Perspektiven auf Rechtsstaat und Ausnahmezustand*, Frankfurt am Main.

Franz, Jürgen H. (2009) *Religion in der Moderne: Die Theorie von Jürgen Habermas und Hermann Lübbe*, Berlin.

Frei, Norbert (1996) *Vergangenheitspolitik: Die Anfänge der Bundesrepublik und die NS-Vergangenheit*, Munich.

Frisch, Max (1986) *Gesammelte Werke in zeitlicher Folge*, vol. 6 and vol. 7, ed. Hans Mayer with Walter Schmitz, Frankfurt am Main.

Frisch, Max (1998) *Gantenbein*, San Diego.

Früchtl, Josef, and Calloni, Maria (eds) (1991) *Geist gegen den Zeitgeist: Erinnern an Adorno*, Frankfurt am Main.

Füllsack, Manfred (1998) 'Geltungsansprüche und Beobachtungen zweiter Ordnung: Wie nahe kommen sich Diskurs- und Systemtheorie?', *Soziale Systeme*, 1, pp. 185–98.

Füllsack, Manfred (2010) 'Die Habermas-Luhmann-Debatte', in Kneer, Georg, and Moebius, Stephan (eds), *Soziologische Kontroversen*, Berlin, pp. 154–81.

Gadamer, Hans-Georg (2001) *Die Lektion des Jahrhunderts: Ein Interview von Riccardo Dottori*, Münster.

Gaus, Daniel (2009) *Der Sinn von Demokratie: Die Diskurstheorie der Demokratie und die Debatte über die Legitimität der EU*, Frankfurt am Main and New York.

Gehlen, Arnold (2004) *Gesamtausgabe*, vol. 6: *Die Seele im technischen Zeitalter und andere sozialpsychologische, soziologische und kulturanalytische Schriften*, ed. Karl-Siegbert Rehberg, Frankfurt am Main.

George, Christian (2010) *Studieren in Ruinen: Die Studenten der Universität Bonn in der Nachkriegszeit 1945–1955*, Frankfurt am Main.

Geuss, Raymond (1987) 'Reviewed Works: *Der philosophische Diskurs der Moderne* by Jürgen Habermas', *Zeitschrift für philosophische Forschung*, 41(4), pp. 682–5.

Gilcher-Holtey, Ingrid (1997) 'Menschenrechte oder Vaterland? Die Formierung der Intellektuellen in der Affäre Dreyfus', *Berliner Journal für Soziologie*, 7, pp. 61–70.

Gilcher-Holtey, Ingrid (ed.) (2008) *1968: Vom Ereignis zum Mythos*, Frankfurt am Main.

Gilcher-Holtey, Ingrid (ed.) (2008) *1968: Eine Zeitreise*, Frankfurt am Main.

Glaser, Hermann (1990) *Kulturgeschichte der Bundesrepublik Deutschland*, vol. 1: *Zwischen Kapitulation und Währungsreform, 1945–1948*; vol. 2: *Zwischen Grundgesetz und Großer Koalition,1949–1967*; vol. 3: *Zwischen Protest und Anpassung, 1968–1989*, Frankfurt am Main.

Glotz, Peter (1989) 'Im weichen Fleisch der Motive und Mentalitäten: Jürgen Habermas als politische Figur: Eine Gratulation', *Die Neue Gesellschaft*, 36(6), pp. 560–3.

Goethe, Johann Wolfgang (2005) *Faust*, Part 1, trans. David Constantine, London.

Görtemaker, Manfred (2005) *Thomas Mann und die Politik*, Frankfurt am Main.

Görtzen, René (1986) 'Habermas' Theorie des kommunikativen Handelns: Eine bibliographische Auswahl', in Honneth, Axel and Joas, Hans (eds), *Kommunikatives Handeln: Beiträge zu Jürgen Habermas' 'Theorie des kommunikativen Handelns'*, Frankfurt am Main, pp. 455–518.

Görtzen, René (2000) 'Habermas, Bi(bli)ographische Bausteine: Eine Auswahl', in Müller-Doohm, Stefan (ed.), *Das Interesse der Vernunft: Rückblicke auf das Werk von Jürgen Habermas seit 'Erkenntnis und Interesse'*, Frankfurt am Main, pp. 543–97.

Graf, Friedrich Wilhelm, and Meier, Heinrich (eds) (2013) *Politik und Religion: Zur Diagnose der Gegenwart*, Munich.

Greven, Michael (2005) 'Politik als Ursprung theoretischen Denkens: Zur intellektuellen Grundintuition von Jürgen Habermas', *Vorgänge: Zeitschrift für Bürgerrechte und Gesellschaftspolitik*, 44(3–4), pp. 152–65.

Grimm, Dieter (2001) *Die Verfassung und die Politik – Einsprüche in Störfällen*, Munich.

Grimm, Dieter (2004) 'Integration durch Verfassung', *Leviathan*, 32(4), pp. 448–63.

Grondin, Jean (1999) *Hans-Georg Gadamer: Eine Biographie*, Tübingen.

Große Kracht, Klaus (2005) *Die zankende Zunft: Historische Kontroversen in Deutschland nach 1945*, Göttingen.

Guldimann, Tim, Rodenstein, Marianne, Rödel, Ulrich, and Stille, Frank (1978) *Sozialpolitik als soziale Kontrolle*, Frankfurt am Main.

Günther, Klaus (1988) *Der Sinn für Angemessenheit: Anwendungsdiskurse in Moral und Recht*, Frankfurt am Main.

Günther, Klaus (2009) 'Im Umkreis von Faktizität und Geltung', *Blätter für deutsche und internationale Politik*, 6, pp. 58–61.

Habermas Arbeitskreis (1972) *Jugendkriminalität und Totale Institutionen: Materialien zu zwei Seminaren*, Frankfurt am Main.

Hacke, Jens (2006) *Philosophie der Bürgerlichkeit: Die liberalkonservative Begründung der Bundesrepublik*, Göttingen.

Hacke, Jens (2009) *Die Bundesrepublik als Idee*, Hamburg.

Halbig, Christoph, and Quante, Michael (eds) (2004) *Axel Honneth: Sozialphilosophie zwischen Kritik und Anerkennung*, Münster.

Hamburger Institut für Sozialforschung (ed.) (1995) *200 Tage und 1 Jahrhundert: Gewalt und Destruktivität im Spiegel des Jahres 1945*, Hamburg.

Hammerstein, Notker (2012) *Die Johann Wolfgang Goethe-Universität Frankfurt am Main*, vol. 2: *Nachkriegszeit 1945–1972*, Göttingen.

Heidegger, Martin (1977) 'The Question Concerning Technology', in *The Question Concerning Technology and Other Essays*, trans. William Lovitt, New York, pp. 3–35.

Heidegger, Martin (2014) *Introduction to Metaphysics*, trans. Gregory Fried and Richard Polt, New Haven, CT, and London.

Heimrod, Ute, Schlusche, Günter, and Seferens, Horst (1999) *Der Denkmalstreit – Das Denkmal? Die Debatte um das 'Denkmal für die ermordeten Juden Europas': Eine Dokumentation*, Berlin.

Heine, Heinrich (1968) *Werke*, vol. 4: *Schriften über Deutschland*, ed. Helmut Schanze, Frankfurt am Main.

Hennis, Wilhelm (1976) 'Legitimität: Zu einer Kategorie der bürgerlichen Gesellschaft', in Kielmansegg, Peter Graf (ed.), *Legitimationsprobleme politischer Systeme: Tagung der Deutschen Vereinigung für Politische Wissenschaft in Duisburg*, Opladen, pp. 9–38.

Hennis, Wilhelm (2000) *Politikwissenschaft und politisches Denken: Politikwissenschaftliche Abhandlungen*, Tübingen.

Henrich, Daniel C. (2007) *Zwischen Bewusstseinsphilosophie und Naturalismus: Zu den metaphysischen Implikationen der Diskursethik von Jürgen Habermas*, Bielefeld.

Henrich, Dieter (1982) *Fluchtlinien: Philosophische Essays*, Frankfurt am Main.

Henrich, Dieter (1986) 'Was ist Metaphysik, was Moderne? Thesen gegen Jürgen Habermas', *Merkur*, 448 (1986), pp. 495–508.

Henrich, Dieter (1987) *Konzepte: Essays zur Philosophie in der Zeit*, Frankfurt am Main.

Henrich, Dieter (2006) *Die Philosophie im Prozeß der Kultur*, Frankfurt am Main.

Henrich, Dieter (2008) 'Was ist verlässlich im Leben? Gespräch mit Dieter Henrich', in Bormuth, Matthias, and von Bülow, Ulrich (eds), *Marburger Hermeneutik zwischen Tradition und Krise*, Göttingen, pp. 13–64.

Herbert, Ulrich (1996) *Best: Biographische Studien über Radikalismus, Weltanschauung und Vernunft 1903–1989*, Munich.

Herbert, Ulrich (1998) 'NS-Eliten in der Bundesrepublik', in Loth, Wilfried, and Rusinek, Bernd-A. (eds), *Verwandlungspolitik: NS-Eliten in der westdeutschen Nachkriegsgesellschaft*, Frankfurt and New York, pp. 93–115.

Herles,Wolfgang (2008) *Neurose D: Eine andere Geschichte Deutschlands*, Munich.

Hilmer, Hans, and Sattler, Christoph (2000) *Bauten und Projekte/Buildings and Projects*, Stuttgart and London.

Hinsch,Wilfried (ed.) (1997) *Zur Idee des politischen Liberalismus: John Rawls in der Diskussion*, Frankfurt am Main.

Hobsbawm, Eric (1994) *The Age of Extremes: The Short Twentieth Century, 1914–1991*, London.

Hogrebe,Wolfgang (2006) 'Von der Hinfälligkeit des Wahren und der Abenteuerlichkeit des Denkens', *Deutsche Zeitschrift für Philosophie*, 54, pp. 221–43.

Holberg Prize Seminar (ed.) (2007) *The Holberg Prize Seminar: Holberg Prize Laureate Professor Jürgen Habermas, 'Religion in the Public Sphere'*, Bergen.

Honneth, Axel (2000) *Das Andere der Gerechtigkeit*, Frankfurt am Main.

Honneth, Axel (ed.) (2005) *Dialektik der Freiheit: Frankfurter Adorno-Konferenz 2003*, Frankfurt am Main.

Honneth, Axel (2008) 'Wie man sich einen Professor vorstellt', in Funken, Michael (ed.), *Über Habermas: Gespräche mit Zeitgenossen*, Darmstadt, pp. 35–44.

Honneth, Axel (2009) *Pathologies of Reason: On the Legacy of Critical Theory*, New York and Chichester.

Honneth, Axel, and Joas, Hans (eds) (1986) *Kommunikatives Handeln: Beiträge zu Jürgen Habermas' 'Theorie des kommunikativen Handelns'*, Frankfurt am Main.

Honneth, Axel, and Joas, Hans (eds) (1991) *Communicative Action: Essays on Jürgen Habermas's 'Theory of Communicative Action'*, trans. Jeremy Gaines and Doris L. Jones, Cambridge.

Honneth, Axel, and Wellmer, Albrecht (eds) (1986) *Die Frankfurter Schule und die Folgen*, Berlin and New York.

Honneth, Axel, McCarthy, Thomas, Offe, Claus, and Wellmer, Albrecht (eds) (1989) *Zwischenbetrachtungen: Im Prozeß der Aufklärung*, Frankfurt am Main.

Horkheimer, Max (1988) *Gesammelte Schriften*, vol. 4: *Schriften 1936–1941*, ed. Alfred Schmidt, Frankfurt am Main.

Horkheimer, Max (1988) *Gesammelte Schriften*, vol. 14: *Nachgelassene Schriften 1949–1972*, ed. Gunzelin Schmid Noerr, Frankfurt am Main.

Horkheimer, Max (1996) *Gesammelte Schriften*, vol. 17: *Briefwechsel 1941–1948*, ed. Gunzelin Schmid Noerr, Frankfurt am Main.

Horkheimer, Max (1996) *Gesammelte Schriften*, vol. 18: *Briefwechsel 1949–1973*, ed. Gunzelin Schmid Noerr, Frankfurt am Main.

Horster, Detlef (2006) *Jürgen Habermas und der Papst: Glauben und Vernunft, Gerechtigkeit und Nächstenliebe im säkularen Staat*, Freiburg, Basel and Vienna.

Humboldt, Wilhelm von (1999) *On Language: On the Diversity of Human Language Construction and its Influence on the Mental Development of the Human Species*, Cambridge.

Ingram, David (2005) 'Foucault and Habermas', in Gutting, Garry (ed.), *The Cambridge Companion to Foucault*, Cambridge, pp. 240–83.

Ingram, David (2010) *Habermas: Introduction and Analysis*, Ithaca, NY.

Iser, Mattias (2008) *Empörung und Fortschritt: Grundlagen einer kritischen Theorie der Gesellschaft*, Frankfurt am Main and New York.

Jaeggi, Rahel, and Wesche, Tilo (eds) (2009) *Was ist Kritik?*, Frankfurt am Main.

Jay, Martin (1987) 'Les extrêmes ne se touchent pas', *Geschichte und Gesellschaft*, 13, pp. 542–58.

Joas, Hans (1980) *Praktische Intersubjektivität: Die Entwicklung des Werks von George Herbert Mead*, Frankfurt am Main.

Joas, Hans (1997) *Die Entstehung der Werte*, Frankfurt am Main.

Jonas, Hans (2008) *Memoirs*, ed. Christian Wiese, trans. Krishna Winston, Lebanon, NH.

Jörke, Dirk (2005) *Politische Anthropologie*, Wiesbaden.

Jung, Thomas (2008), 'Wächter zu sein in finsterer Nacht: Karl Mannheims denksoziologische Bestimmung des Intellektuellen', in Jung, Thomas, and Müller-Doohm, Stefan (eds), *'Fliegende Fische': Eine Soziologie des Intellektuellen in 20 Porträts*, Frankfurt am Main, pp. 43–62.

Jureit, Ulrike (2008) 'Geliehene Väter: Alexander Mitscherlich und das Bedürfnis nach generationeller Selbstverortung im 20. Jahrhundert', in Freimüller, Tobias (ed.), *Psychoanalyse und Protest*, Göttingen, pp. 158–75.

Kailitz, Steffen (2001) *Die politische Deutungskultur im Spiegel des 'Historikerstreits': What's Right? What's Left*, Wiesbaden.

Kailitz, Susanne (2007) *Von den Worten zu den Waffen; Frankfurter Schule, Studentenbewegung, RAF und Gewaltfrage*, Wiesbaden.

Kang, Byoungho (2009) 'Werte und Normen bei Habermas: Zur Eigendynamik des moralischen Diskurses', *Deutsche Zeitschrift für Philosophie*, 57(6), pp. 861–75.

Kant, Immanuel (1970) 'An Answer to the Question: "What is Enlightenment?"', in *Kant: Political Writings*, ed. Hans Reiss, trans. H. B. Nisbet, Cambridge, pp. 54–60.

Kennedy, Ellen (1986) 'Carl Schmitt und die "Frankfurter Schule"', *Geschichte und Gesellschaft*, 12, pp. 380–419.

Keulartz, Josef (1995) *Die verkehrte Welt des Jürgen Habermas*, Hamburg.

Kielmansegg, Peter Graf (ed.) (1976) *Legitimationsprobleme politischer Systeme*, Opladen, pp. 9–38.

Kießling, Friedrich (2012) *Die undeutschen Deutschen*, Paderborn and Munich.

Kleinspehn, Thomas (1999) 'Ein öffentlicher Intellektueller: Der Sozialphilosoph und streitbare Demokrat', Radio Bremen, 9 October.

Klemperer, Victor (1998, 1999, 2003) *Diaries*, vol. 1: *I Shall Bear Witness (1933–1941)*; vol. 2: *To the Bitter End (1942–1945)*; vol. 3: *The Lesser Evil (1945–1959)*, London.

Klimke, Martin, and Scharloth, Joachim (eds) (2007) *Handbuch 1968: Zur Kultur und Mediengeschichte der Studentenbewegung*, Stuttgart.

Klönne, Arno (1958) *Gegen den Strom*, Hannover.

Kluge, Alexander (1973) *Lernprozesse mit tödlichem Ausgang*, Frankfurt am Main.

Kluge, Alexander (1996) *Learning Processes with a Deadly Outcome*, trans. Christopher Pavsek, Durham, NC.

Kluge, Alexander (2000) *Chronik der Gefühle*, vol. 2: *Lebensläufe*, Frankfurt am Main.

Kneer, Georg, and Moebius, Stephan (eds) (2010) *Soziologische Kontroversen: Beiträge zu einer anderen Geschichte der Wissenschaft vom Sozialen*, Frankfurt am Main.

Knowlton, James, and Cates, Truett (eds) (1993) *Forever in the Shadow of Hitler?*, Atlantic Highlands, NJ.

Köller, Wilhelm (1975) *Semiotik und Metapher: Untersuchungen zur grammatischen Struktur und kommunikativen Funktion von Metaphern*, Stuttgart.

Kraushaar, Wolfgang (1998) *Frankfurter Schule und Studentenbewegung*, 3 vols, Hamburg.

Kraushaar, Wolfgang (2006) 'Der nicht erklärte Ausnahmezustand: Staatliches Handeln während des sogenannten Deutschen Herbstepp', in Kraushaar (ed.), *Die RAF und der linke Terrorismus*, vol. 2, Hamburg, pp. 1011–25.

Kraushaar, Wolfgang (2008) 'Ein Seminar im Brennspiegel der Ereignisse', *Mittelweg*, 36, pp. 7–11.

Kroll, Thomas, and Reitz, Tilmann (eds) (2013) *Intellektuelle in der Bundesrepublik Deutschland: Verschiebungen im politischen Feld der 1960er und 1970er Jahre*, Göttingen.

Krovoza, Alfred, Oestmann, Axel, and Ottomeyer, Klaus (eds) (1981) *Zum Beispiel Peter Brückner*, Frankfurt am Main.

Krüger, Hans-Peter (ed.) (2007) *Hirn als Subjekt? Philosophische Grenzfragen der Neurobiologie*, Berlin [*Deutsche Zeitschrift für Philosophie*, Special Volume 15].

Kuby, Erich (1959) *Nur noch rauchende Trümmer: Das Ende der Festung Brest: Tagebuch des Soldaten Erich Kuby*, Hamburg.

Laak, Dirk van (1993) *Gespräche in der Sicherheit des Schweigens: Carl Schmitt in der politischen Geistesgeschichte der frühen Bundesrepublik*, Berlin.

Lafont, Cristina (1994) 'Spannungen im Wahrheitsbegriff', *Deutsche Zeitschrift für Philosophie*, 42(6), pp. 1007–23.

Lafont, Cristina (1999) *The Linguistic Turn in Hermeneutic Philosophy*, Cambridge.

Lampe, Gerhard (2002) 'Medienfiktionen beim NATO-Einsatz im Kosovokrieg', in Albrecht, Ulrich, and Becker, Jörg (eds), *Medien zwischen Krieg und Freiden*, Baden-Baden, pp. 96–102.

Landgrebe, Ludwig (1966) *Major Problems in Contemporary European Philosophy, from Dilthey to Heidegger*, New York.

Langguth, Gerd (2004), 'Alte neue Ressentiments: Habermas, die deutschen Intellektuellen und der Antiamerikanismus', *Internationale Politik*, 59(2), pp. 67–77.

Lau, Jörg (1999) *Hans Magnus Enzensberger: Ein öffentliches Leben*, Frankfurt am Main.

Laugstien,Thomas (1998) *Philosophieverhältnisse im deutschen Faschismus*, Hamburg.

Leendertz, Ariane (2010) *Die pragmatische Wende: Die Max-Planck-Gesellschaft und die Sozialwissenschaften*, Munich.

Lehrstuhl für Jüdische Geschichte und Kultur an der Ludwig-Maximilians-Universität München (ed.) (2012) *Jüdische Stimmen im Diskurs der sechziger Jahre*, Munich.

Lepenies,Wolf, and Nolte, Helmut (1971) *Kritik der Anthropologie: Marx und Freud, Gehlen und Habermas: Über Aggression*, Munich.

Lepsius, M. Rainer (1964) 'Kritik als Beruf: Zur Soziologie des Intellektuellen', *Kölner Zeitschrift für Soziologie und Sozialpsychologie*, 1, pp. 75–91.

Liehr, Dorothe (2002) *Von der Aktion gegen den Spiegel zur Spiegel-Affäre*, Frankfurt am Main.

Loredano, Cassio (1995) *Karikaturen*, Göttingen.

Löwenthal, Leo, and Kracauer, Siegfried (2003) *In steter Freundschaft: Briefwechsel 1921–1966*, ed. Peter-Erwin Jansen and Christian Schmidt, Berlin.

Löwith, Karl (1964) *From Hegel to Nietzsche: The Revolution in Nineteenth-Century Thought*, New York.

Löwith, Karl (1986) *Heidegger – Denker in dürftiger Zeit, Sämtliche Schriften*, vol. 8., ed. Klaus Stichweh, Marc B. de Lannay, Bernd Lutz and Henning Ritter, Stuttgart.

Lübbe, Hermann (1978) *Praxis der Philosophie, Praktische Philosophie, Geschichtstheorie*, Stuttgart.

Lübbe, Hermann (1983) 'Der Nationalsozialismus im politischen Bewußtsein der Gegenwart', in Broszat, Martin, et al. (eds), *Deutschlands Weg in die Diktatur: Internationale Konferenz zur nationalsozialistischen Machtübernahme*, Berlin, pp. 329–49.

Lübbe, Hermann (1989) *Politischer Moralismus: Der Triumph der Gesinnung über die Urteilskraft*, Berlin.

Lübbe, Hermann (2004) *Modernisierungsgewinner: Religion, Geschichtssinn, direkte Demokratie und Moral*, Munich.

Lübbe, Hermann (2007) *Vom Parteigenossen zum Bundesbürger: Über beschwiegene und Historisierte Vergangenheit*, Munich.

Luhmann, Niklas (1990) 'Über systemtheoretische Grundlagen der Gesellschaftstheorie', *Deutsche Zeitschrift für Philosophie*, 38 (1990), pp. 277–84.

Luhmann, Niklas (2012) *The Theory of Society*, trans. Rhodes Barrett, 2 vols, Stanford, CA.

Lukács, Georg ([1920] 1971) *The Theory of the Novel*, Cambridge, MA.

Lyotard, Jean-François (1986) 'Grundlagenkrise', *Neue Hefte für Philosophie*, 26, pp. 1–33.

Lyotard, Jean François (1989) *The Differend: Phrases in Dispute*, Minneapolis.

McCarthy, Thomas (1978) *The Critical Theory of Jürgen Habermas*, Cambridge, MA.

McCarthy, Thomas (1993) *Ideale und Illusionen: Dekonstruktion und Rekonstruktion in der kritischen Theorie*, Frankfurt am Main.

McGuinness, Brian (ed.) (1991) *'Der Löwe spricht. . . und wir können ihn nicht verstehen': Ein Symposium an der Universität Frankfurt anlässlich des hundertsten Geburtstages von Ludwig Wittgenstein*, Frankfurt am Main.

Magenau, Jörg (2005) *Martin Walser: Eine Biographie*, Reinbek bei Hamburg.

Maier, Willfried (1987) 'Stimme oder Körper: Mensch und Natur in Habermas' "Theorie des kommunikativen Handelns"', *Kommune: Forum für Politik, Ökonomie und Kultur*, 3, pp. 41–56.

Maly, Sebastian (2005) 'Die Rolle der Religion in der postsäkularen Gesellschaft: Zur Religionsphilosophie von Jürgen Habermas', *Theologie und Philosophie*, 8, pp. 546–65.

Mannheim, Karl ([1927] 1964) 'Das konservative Denken', in Wolff, Kurt H. (ed.), *Wissenssoziologie*, Berlin and Neuwied, pp. 408–83.

Mannheim, Karl ([1928] 1964) 'Das Problem der Generationen', in Wolff, Kurt H. (ed.), *Wissenssoziologie*, Berlin and Neuwied, pp. 509–65.

Mannheim, Karl (1955) *Ideology and Utopia: An Introduction to the Sociology of Knowledge*, Orlando, FL.

Marcuse, Herbert (1957) *Soviet Marxism: A Critical Analysis*, New York.

Marcuse, Herbert (1965) *Kultur und Gesellschaft*, 2 vols, Frankfurt am Main.

Matuštik, Martin Beck (2001) *Jürgen Habermas: A Philosophical-Political Profile*, Lanham, MD.

Matuštik, Martin Beck (2005) 'Singular Existence and Critical Theory', *Radical Philosophy Review* 8(2), pp. 211–23.

Maurer, Reinhard Klemens (1977) 'Jürgen Habermas' Aufhebung der Philosophie', *Philosophische Rundschau*, 24, suppl. no. 8, pp. 3–70 [special issue].

Mehring, Reinhard (2014) *Carl Schmitt: A Biography*, trans. Daniel Steuer, Cambridge.

Mendieta, Eduardo, and VanAntwerpen, Jonathan (eds) (2011) *The Power of Religion in the Public Sphere*, New York and Chichester.

Merseburger, Peter (2007) *Rudolf Augstein: Biographie*, Munich.

Meyer, Ahlrich (2005) *Täter im Verhör: Die 'Endlösung' der Judenfrage in Frankreich 1940 bis 1944*, Darmstadt.

Michalzik, Peter (2002) *Unseld: Eine Biographie*, Munich.

Mitscherlich, Alexander (1983) *Ein Leben für die Psychoanalyse*, Frankfurt am Main.

Mitscherlich, Alexander (1992) *Society without the Father: A Contribution to Social Psychology*, London.

Mitscherlich, Alexander, and Mitscherlich, Margarete (1975) *The Inability to Mourn: Principles of Collective Behaviour*, New York.

Moses, A. Dirk (2000) 'Eine Generation zwischen Faschismus und Demokratie', *Neue Sammlung*, 40(2), pp. 233–63.

Moses, A. Dirk (2007) *German Intellectuals and the Nazi Past*, Cambridge.

Mouffe, Chantal (2005) *On the Political (Thinking in Action)*, London.

Müller, Harro (1985) 'Habermas im Zentrum', *Merkur*, 438, pp. 720–3.

Müller, Jan-Werner (2010) *Verfassungspatriotismus*, Berlin.

Müller, Jan-Werner (2013) *Das demokratische Zeitalter: Eine politische Ideengeschichte Europas im 20. Jahrhundert*, Berlin.

Müller-Doohm, Stefan (ed.) (1991) *Jenseits der Utopie: Theoriekritik der Gegenwart*, Frankfurt am Main.

Müller-Doohm, Stefan (ed.) (2000) *Das Interesse der Vernunft: Rückblicke auf das Werk von Jürgen Habermas seit 'Erkenntnis und Interesse'*, Frankfurt am Main.

Müller-Doohm, Stefan (2005) *Adorno: A Biography*, trans. Rodney Livingstone, Cambridge.

Müller-Doohm, Stefan (2005) 'Theodor W. Adorno and Jürgen Habermas – Two Ways of Being a Public Intellectual: Sociological Observations Concerning the Transformation of a Social Figure of Modernity', *European Journal of Social Theory*, 8/3, pp. 276–81.

Müller-Doohm, Stefan (2008) *Jürgen Habermas: Leben, Werk, Wirkung*, Frankfurt am Main.

Müller-Doohm, Stefan (2008) 'Jürgen Habermas: Die Aufhebung der Medienphilosophie im öffentlichen Vernunftgebrauch', in Roesler, Alexander, and Stiegler, Bernd (eds), *Philosophie in der Medientheorie*, Munich, pp. 117–32.

Müller-Doohm, Stefan (2008) 'Sagen, was einem aufgeht: Sprache bei Adorno – Adornos Sprache', in Kohler, Georg, and Müller-Doohm, Stefan (eds), *Wozu Adorno? Beiträge zur Kritik und zum Fortbestand einer Schlüsseltheorie des 20. Jahrhunderts*, Göttingen, pp. 28–50.

Müller-Doohm, Stefan (2009) 'Nationalstaat, Kapitalismus, Demokratie: Philosophisch-politische Motive im Denken von Jürgen Habermas', *Leviathan*, 4, pp. 501–17.

Müller-Doohm, Stefan (2010) 'Spätkapitalismus oder Industriegesellschaft?', in Kneer, Georg, and Moebius, Stephan (eds), *Soziologische Kontroversen: Beiträge zu einer anderen Geschichte der Wissenschaft vom Sozialen*, Berlin, pp. 131–53.

Müller-Doohm, Stefan (2012) 'Zukunftsprognose als Zeitdiagnose: Habermas' Weg von der Geschichtsphilosophie bis zum Konzept lebensweltlicher Pathologien', in Tiberius, Victor (ed.), *Zukunftsgenese: Theorien des zukünftigen Wandels*, Wiesbaden, pp. 159–78.

Müller-Doohm, Stefan, and Ziegler, Christian (2008) 'Professionell Heimatloser – Theodor W. Adornos intellektuelle Praxis zwischen Kontemplation und Engagement', in Jung, Thomas, and Müller-Doohm, Stefan (eds), *'Fliegende Fische': Eine Soziologie des Intellektuellen in 20 Porträts*, Frankfurt am Main, pp. 63–84.

Müller-Doohm, Stefan, Schopf, Wolfgang, and Thiele, Franziska (eds) (2009) *'. . . die Lava des Gedankens im Fluss': Jürgen Habermas: Eine Werkschau*, Oldenburg.

Nancy, Jean-Luc (2010) *The Truth of Democracy*, New York.

Nassehi, Armin (2007) *Der soziologische Diskurs der Moderne*, Frankfurt am Main.

Negt, Oskar (1968) 'Studentischer Protest – Liberalismus – "Linksfaschismus"', *Kursbuch*, 13, pp. 179–89.

Negt, Oskar (2009) 'Einheimischer und Welterklärer: Der Philosoph Jürgen Habermas wird 80. Oskar Negt im Gespräch mit Martin Willenbrink', WDR radio broadcast, 30 July.

Nennen, Heinz Ulrich (2003) *Philosophie in Echtzeit: Die Sloterdijk-Debatte: Chronik einer Inszenierung*, Würzburg.

Neumann, Bernd (1996) *Uwe Johnson*, Hamburg.

Nida-Rümelin, Julian, and Thierse, Wolfgang (eds) (1998) *Philosophie und Politik*, vol. 3: *Jürgen Habermas und Gerhard Schröder über die 'Einbeziehung des Anderen'*, Essen.

Niesen, Peter, and Herborth, Benjamin (eds) (2007) *Anarchie der kommunikativen Freiheit: Jürgen Habermas und die Theorie der internationalen Politik*, Frankfurt am Main.

Nolzen, Armin (2010) 'Der Durchbruch der NSDAP zur Massenbewegung seit 1929', in *Hitler und die Deutschen: Volksgemeinschaften und Verbrechen:*

Eine Ausstellung der Stiftung Deutsches Historisches Museum, Berlin, pp. 44–56.

Oevermann, Ulrich (2009) 'Der akademische Lehrer – eine Erinnerung', *Blätter für deutsche und internationale Politik*, 54(6), pp. 44–50.

Oevermann, Ulrich (2010) 'Der Gegenbegriff von Natur ist nicht Gesellschaft, sondern Kultur', in Herrschaft, Felicia, and Lichtblau, Klaus (eds), *Soziologie in Frankfurt – Eine Zwischenbilanz*, Wiesbaden, pp. 369–406.

Offe, Claus (2005) 'Die Bundesrepublik als Schattenriß zweier Lichtquellen', *Ästhetik und Kommunikation*, 36, pp. 149–60.

Ostowoch, Steven T. (1987) 'Der philosophische Diskurs der Moderne', *German Studies*, 10(3), pp. 631–2.

Ott, Hugo (1988) *Martin Heidegger: Unterwegs zu einer Biographie*, Frankfurt am Main and New York.

Padilla, Heberto (1971) *Außerhalb des Spiels*, Frankfurt am Main.

Paech, Norman, and Stuby, Gerhard (2013) *Völkerrecht und Machtpolitik in den internationalen Beziehungen*, Hamburg.

Palazzo, Guido (2002) *Die Mitte der Demokratie: Über die Theorie deliberativer Demokratie von Jürgen Habermas*, Baden-Baden.

Palmier, Jean-Michel (2009) *Walter Benjamin: Lumpensammler, Engel und bucklicht Männlein: Ästhetik und Politik bei Walter Benjamin*, Frankfurt am Main.

Payk, Marcus M. (2008) *Der Geist der Demokratie: Intellektuelle Orientierungsversuche im Feuilleton der frühen Bundesrepublik*, Munich.

Peeters, Benoît (2013) *Derrida: A Biography*, Cambridge.

Pensky, Max (2005) 'Jürgen Habermas, Existential Hero?', *Radical Philosophy Review*, 8(2), pp. 197–209.

Peters, Bernhard (2007) *Der Sinn von Öffentlichkeit*, ed. Hartmut Weßler, Frankfurt am Main.

Piper, Ernst Reinhard (ed.) (1987) *Historikerstreit*, Munich and Zurich.

Polanyi, Karl ([1944] 2001) *The Great Transformation: The Political and Economic Origins of Our Time*, Boston.

Pomykaj, Gerhard (2001) 'Von 1918 bis 1948', in Goebel, Klaus (ed.), *Oberbergische Geschichte*, vol. 3, Gummersbach.

Preuß, Ulrich K. (1987) 'Carl Schmitt und die Frankfurter Schule: Deutsche Liberalismuskritik im 20. Jahrhundert', *Geschichte und Gesellschaft*, 13, pp. 400–18.

Raddatz, Fritz J. (2010) *Tagebücher 1982–2001*, Reinbek bei Hamburg.

Rahm, Claudia (2005) *Recht und Demokratie bei Jürgen Habermas und Ronald Dworkin*, Frankfurt am Main, pp. 400–18.

Rammstedt, Otthein (1986) *Deutsche Soziologie 1933–1945: Die Normalität einer Anpassung*, Frankfurt am Main.

Rapic, Smail (ed.) (2014) *Habermas und der Historische Materialismus*, Stuttgart.

Rawls, John (1997) 'Erwiderung auf Habermas', in Hinsch, Wilfried (ed.), *Zur Idee des politischen Liberalismus*, Frankfurt am Main, pp. 196–262.

Rawls, John (2007) *Lectures on the History of Political Philosophy*, Cambridge, MA.

Reder, Michael, and Schmidt, Josef (eds) (2008) *Ein Bewußtsein von dem, was fehlt: Eine Diskussion mit Jürgen Habermas*, Frankfurt am Main.

Reder, Michael, and Schmidt, Josef (eds) (2010) *An Awareness of What is Missing: Faith and Reason in a Post-Secular Age*, Cambridge.

Reese, Dagmar (2010) 'Zum Stellenwert der Freiwilligkeit: Hitler-Jugend und NSDAP-Mitgliedschaft', *Mittelweg*, 36, pp. 63–83.

Reich-Ranicki, Marcel (2001) *The Author of Himself: The Life of Marcel Reich-Ranicki*, London.

Reichel, Peter (1981) *Politische Kultur in der Bundesrepublik*, Opladen.

Reijen,Willem van, and Schmid Noerr, Gunzelin (eds) (1988) *Grand Hotel Abgrund: Eine Photobiographie der Frankfurter Schule*, Hamburg.

Rensmann, Lars (2004) 'Bausteine der Erinnerungspolitik: Die politische Textur der Bundestagsdebatte über ein zentrales "Holocaust-Mahnmal"', in Brumlik, Micha, Funke, Hajo, and Rensmann, Lars (eds), *Umkämpftes Vergessen: Walser-Debatte, Holocaust-Mahnmal und neuere deutsche Geschichtspolitik*, Berlin, pp. 137–69.

Richter, Pavel A. (2008) 'Die Außerparlamentarische Opposition in der Bundesrepublik Deutschland 1966 bis 1968', in Gilcher-Holtey, Ingrid (ed.), *1968: Vom Ereignis zum Mythos*, Frankfurt am Main, pp. 47–74.

Ridder, Helmut, and Perels, Joachim (2005) 'Stationen im Leben eines Juristen: Helmut Ridder im Gespräch mit Joachim Perels', *Neue politische Literatur*, 50, pp. 365–82.

Riesebrodt, Martin (2010) *The Promise of Salvation: A Theory of Religion*, Chicago.

Ronge,Volker (1979) *Bankenpolitik im Spätkapitalismus*, Frankfurt am Main.

Rorty, Richard (1989) *Contingency, Irony, and Solidarity*, Cambridge.

Rorty, Richard (1998) *Achieving our Country: Leftist Thought in Twentieth-Century America*, Cambridge, MA.

Rorty, Richard (2007) *Philosophy as Cultural Politics*, Cambridge.

Rüsen, Jörn, Lämmert, Eberhard, and Glotz, Peter (eds) (1988) *Die Zukunft der Aufklärung*, Frankfurt am Main.

Safranski, Rüdiger (1994) *Ein Meister aus Deutschland: Heidegger und seine Zeit*, Munich.

Sandel, Michael J. (2008) *Plädoyer gegen die Perfektion: Ethik im Zeitalter der genetischen Technik*, Berlin.

Sandkühler, Hans Jörg (2009) *Philosophie und Nationalsozialismus: Vergessen? Verdrängt? Erinnert?*, Hamburg.

Sartre, Jean-Paul (2004) *Critique of Dialectical Reason*, London.

Schäfer, Gerhard (2000) 'Die nivellierte Mittelstandsgesellschaft – Strategien der Soziologie in den 50er Jahren', in Bollenbeck, Georg, and Kaiser, Gerhard (eds), *Die janusköpfigen 50er Jahre*, Opladen, pp. 115–42.

Scheit, Herbert (1987) *Wahrheit, Diskurs, Demokratie*, Freiburg.

Schelling, Friedrich Wilhelm Josef (1942) *The Ages of the World*, trans. Frederick de Wolfe Bolman, Jr., New York.

Scherf, Wilfried (2009) *Deutsche Diskurse: Die politische Kultur von 1945 bis heute in publizistischen Kontroversen*, Wilhelmshaven.

Schild, Axel (1999) *Zwischen Abendland und Amerika: Studien zur westdeutschen Ideenlandschaft der 50er Jahre*, Munich.

Schlak, Stephan (2008) *Wilhelm Hennis: Szenen einer Ideengeschichte der Bundesrepublik*, Munich.

Schlak, Stephan, and Hacke, Jens (2008) 'Der Staat in Gefahr', in Hacke, Jens, and Geppert, Dominik (eds), *Streit um den Staat: Intellektuelle Debatten in der Bundesrepublik 1960–1980*, Göttingen, pp. 188–206.

Schlich, Jutta (2000) *Intellektuelle im 20. Jahrhundert*, Munich and Tübingen.

Schmidt, Alfred, and Altwicker, Norbert (eds) (1986) *Max Horkheimer heute: Werk und Wirkung*, Frankfurt am Main.

Scholem, Gershom (1992) *Sabbatai Zwi: Der mystische Messias*, Frankfurt am Main.

Schopf, Wolfgang (ed.) (2003) *'So müßte ich ein Engel und kein Autor sein':* *Adorno und seine Frankfurter Verleger: Der Briefwechsel mit Peter Suhrkamp und Siegfried Unseld,* Frankfurt am Main.

Schörken, Rolf (2000) 'Sozialisation inmitten des Zusammenbruchs', in Dahlmann, Dittmar (ed.), *Kinder und Jugendliche in Krieg und Revolution,* Paderborn, pp. 123–43.

Schörken, Rolf (2004) *Die Niederlage als Generationserfahrung: Jugendliche nach dem Zusammenbruch der NS-Herrschaft,* Weinheim and Munich.

Schrader, Lutz (2000) 'Krieg für Menschenrechte? Der Krieg um Kosovo und der kosmopolitische Rechtspazifismus des Jürgen Habermas', in Bilek, Anita, Graf, Wilfried, and Kramer, Helmut (eds), *Welcher Friede? Lehren aus dem Krieg um Kosovo,* Münster, pp. 31–61.

Schülein, Johann August (2000) 'Von der Kritik am "szientistischen Selbstmißverständnis": Zum Verständnis psychoanalytischer Theorieprobleme', in Müller-Doohm, Stefan (ed.), *Das Interesse der Vernunft: Rückblicke auf das Werk von Jürgen Habermas seit 'Erkenntnis und Interesse',* Frankfurt am Main, pp. 376–410.

Schwarz, Hans-Peter (ed.) (2008) *Die Bundesrepublik Deutschland: Eine Bilanz nach 60 Jahren,* Cologne, Weimar and Vienna.

Searle, John R. (2010) *Making the Social World: The Structure of Human Civilisation,* Oxford.

Snyder, Timothy (2010) *Bloodlands: Europe between Hitler and Stalin,* New York.

Söllner, Alfons (1986) 'Jenseits von Carl Schmitt', *Geschichte und Gesellschaft,* 12, pp. 502–29.

Sonnenfeld, Christa (2010) 'Ein Fundstück aus dem IfS-Archiv, Die Freizeitstudie (1957–1958)', *WestEnd,* 2, pp. 156–61.

Spaemann, Robert (1972) 'Die Utopie der Herrschaftsfreiheit', *Merkur,* 291, pp. 735–52.

Spaemann, Robert (1977) *Zur Kritik der politischen Utopie,* Stuttgart.

Spaemann, Robert (2012) *Über Gott und die Welt: Eine Autobiographie in Gesprächen,* Stuttgart.

Specter, Matthew G. (2010) *Habermas: An Intellectual Biography,* Cambridge.

Spiller, Stefan (2006) 'Der Sympathisant als Staatsfeind: Die Mescalero-Affäre', in Kraushaar,Wolfgang (ed.), *Die RAF und der linke Terrorismus,* vol. 2, pp. 1227–59.

Stachorski, Stephan (ed.) (2005) *Fragile Republik: Thomas Mann und Nachkriegsdeutschland,* Frankfurt am Main.

Staudt, Torlaf, and Radke, Johannes (2012) *Neue Nazis: Jenseits der NPD: Populisten, Autonome Nationalisten und der Terror von rechts,* Cologne.

Stöwer, Ralph (2011) *Erich Rothacker: Sein Leben und seine Wissenschaft vom Menschen,* Göttingen.

Suhrkamp Verlag (2000) *50 Jahre Suhrkamp Verlag: Dokumentation zum 1. Juli 2000,* Frankfurt am Main.

Taubes, Jacob (1996) *Vom Kult zur Kultur: Bausteine zu einer Kritik der historischen Vernunft,* Munich.

Taubes, Jacob, and Schmitt, Carl (2012) *Briefwechsel mit Materialien,* ed. Herbert Kopp-Oberstebrink,Thorsten Palzhoff and Martin Treml, Munich.

Taylor, Charles (1992) *Multiculturalism and 'The Politics of Recognition',* Princeton, NJ.

Theunissen, Michael (1981) *Kritische Theorie der Gesellschaft,* Berlin and New York.

Thiel,Thomas (2008) 'Braucht Europa eine Verfassung? Einige Anmerkungen zur Grimm-Habermas-Debatte', in Biegi, Mandana, Förster, Jürgen, Otten, Henrique Ricardo, and Philipp, Thomas (eds), *Demokratie, Recht und Legitimität im 21. Jahrhundert*, Wiesbaden, pp. 163–80.

Thumfart, Alexander (2009) 'Staat, Integration und Solidarität: Dynamische Grundbegriffe im Staatsverständnis von Jürgen Habermas', in Schaal, Gary S. (ed.), *Das Staatsverständnis von Jürgen Habermas*, Baden-Baden, pp. 81–108.

Thünemann, Holger (2003) *Das Denkmal für die ermordeten Juden Europas*, Cologne.

Thyen, Anke (2004) *Moral und Anthropologie*, Habilitationsschrift, Ludwigsburg; published Weilerswist, 2007.

Tiedemann, Rolf (ed.) (1993) *Frankfurter Adorno Blätter II*, Munich.

Tietgens, Hans (1982) 'Studieren in Bonn nach 1945: Versuch einer Skizze des Zeitgeistes', in Kulmann, Wolfgang, and Böhler, Dietrich (eds), *Kommunikation und Reflexion: Zur Diskussion der Transzendentalpragmatik: Antworten auf Karl-Otto Apel*, Frankfurt am Main, pp. 720–44.

Tomasello, Michael (2008) *Origins of Human Communication*, Cambridge, MA.

Traverso, Enzo (2000) *Auschwitz denken – Die Intellektuellen und die Shoa*, Hamburg.

Ueberschär, Gerd R., and Müller, Rolf-Dieter (2005) *1945: Das Ende des Krieges*, Darmstadt.

Unseld, Siegfried (ed.) (1972) *Zur Aktualität Walter Benjamins*, Frankfurt am Main.

Unseld, Siegfried (ed.) (1993) *Politik ohne Projekt? Nachdenken über Deutschland*, Frankfurt am Main.

Unseld, Siegfried (2010) *Reiseberichte*, Frankfurt am Main.

Unseld, Siegfried (2010) *Chronik*, vol. 1: *1970*, ed. Ulrike Anders, Raimund Fellinger, Katharina Karduck, Claus Kröger, Henning Marmulla and Wolfgang Schopf, Frankfurt am Main.

Unseld, Siegfried (2014) *Chronik*, vol. 2: *1971*, ed. Ulrike Anders, Raimund Fellinger and Katharina Karduck, Berlin.

Unseld-Berkéwicz, Ulla (2009) 'Glückwünsche der Verlegerin', in Müller-Doohm, Stefan, Schopf, Wolfgang, and Thiele, Franziska (eds), '. . . die Lava des Gedankens im Fluss': Jürgen Habermas: Eine Werkschau*, Oldenburg, pp. 51–5.

Verheyen, Nina (2007) 'Diskussionsfieber: Diskutieren als kommunikative Praxis in der westdeutschen Studentenbewegung', in Klimke, Martin, and Scharloth, Joachim (eds), *Handbuch 1968*, Stuttgart, pp. 209–21.

Vieth, Andreas (2012) 'Die Sensibilität der Religiösen: Eine kritische Auseinandersetzung mit Habermas' Konzeption religiöser Erfahrung', *Zeitschrift für philosophische Forschung*, 66(1), pp. 49–744.

Walser, Martin (1988) 'Auschwitz und kein Ende', in Walser, *Über Deutschland reden*, Frankfurt am Main.

Walser, Martin (1997) 'Das Prinzip Genauigkeit: Über Victor Klemperer, in Walser, *Werke in 12 Bänden*, vol. 11, ed. Helmuth Kiesel, Frankfurt am Main.

Walser, Martin (1998) *Erfahrungen beim Verfassen einer Sonntagsrede: Mit einer Laudatio von Frank Schirrmacher*, Frankfurt am Main.

Walser, Martin (2002) *Tod eines Kritikers*, Frankfurt am Main.

Walser, Martin (2008) 'Experiences while Composing a Sunday Speech: The Peace Prize Speech (1998)', in *The Burden of the Past: Martin Walser on*

Modern German Identity: Texts, Contexts, Commentary, ed. Thomas A. Kovach, London, pp. 85–95.

Walser, Martin (2010) *Tagebücher 1974–1978*, Frankfurt am Main.

Walser, Martin (2012) *Über Rechtfertigung, eine Versuchung*, Frankfurt am Main.

Walser, Robert (1995) *Sämtliche Werke in zwanzig Bänden*, vol. 8, Frankfurt am Main.

Walzer, Michael (2002) 'Die Tugend des Augenmaßes', in Wenzel, Uwe Justus (ed.), *Der kritische Blick: Über intellektuelle Tätigkeiten und Tugenden*, Frankfurt am Main, pp. 25–38.

Wehler, Hans-Ulrich (1988) *Entsorgung der deutschen Vergangenheit? Ein polemischer Essay zum 'Historikerstreit'*, Munich.

Wehler, Hans-Ulrich (1992) 'Späte Liebeserklärung an meine Schule', in Hansen, Klaus (ed.), *Herzenswärme und Widerspruchsgeist: Oberbergisches Lesebuch*, Gummersbach, pp. 29–35.

Wehler, Hans-Ulrich (2003) *Deutsche Gesellschaftsgeschichte*, vol. 4: *1914–1949*, Munich.

Wehler, Hans-Ulrich (2006) *Eine lebhafte Kampfsituation*, Munich.

Wehler, Hans-Ulrich (2008) *Deutsche Gesellschaftsgeschichte*, vol. 5: *1949–1990*, Munich.

Wehrs, Nicolai (2008) '"Tendenzwende" und Bildungspolitik: Der "Bund Freiheit der Wissenschaft" (BFW) in den 1970er Jahren', *Potsdamer Bulletin für Zeithistorische Studien*, 42, pp. 6–17.

Weidmann, Bernd (2008) 'Karl Jaspers', in Jung, Thomas, and Müller-Doohm, Stefan (eds), *'Fliegende Fische': Eine Soziologie des Intellektuellen in 20 Porträts*, Frankfurt am Main, pp. 200–29.

Weizsäcker, Carl Friedrich von (1981) *Der bedrohte Friede: Politische Aufsätze 1945–1981*, Munich.

Weizsäcker, Carl Friedrich von (2002) *Lieber Freund! Lieber Gegner! Briefe aus fünf Jahrzehnten*, Munich.

Wellershoff, Dieter (2008) *Zwischenreich: Gedichte*, Cologne.

Wellmer, Albrecht (1986) *Ethik und Dialog: Elemente des moralischen Urteils bei Kant und in der Diskursethik*, Frankfurt am Main.

Wellmer, Albrecht (1989) 'Was ist eine pragmatische Bedeutungstheorie? Variationen über den Satz "Wir verstehen einen Sprechakt, wenn wir wissen, was ihn akzeptabel Macht"', in Honneth, Axel, and McCarthy, Thomas (eds), *Zwischenbetrachtungen: Im Prozeß der Aufklärung*, Frankfurt am Main, pp. 318–72.

Wellmer, Albrecht (1992) 'Konsens als Telos der sprachlichen Kommunikation?', in Giegel, Hans-Joachim (ed.), *Kommunikation in modernen Gesellschaften*, Frankfurt am Main, pp. 18–30.

Wellmer, Albrecht (2004) *Sprachphilosophie: Eine Vorlesung*, Frankfurt am Main.

Wellmer, Albrecht (2007) 'Adorno and the Problems of a Critical Construction of the Historical Present', *Critical Horizons*, 8(2), pp. 135–56.

Wellmer, Albrecht (2009) 'Erinnerung an die Anfänge und eine späte Antwort auf einen fastvergessenen Brief', *Blätter für deutsche und internationale Politik*, 6, pp. 48–52.

Weygandt, Wilhelm (1936) *Der jugendliche Schwachsinn: Seine Erkennung, Behandlung und Ausmerzung*, Stuttgart.

Wiehl, Reiner (1996) 'Karl-Jaspers-Preis 1995: Laudatio auf Jürgen Habermas', in Kiesel, Helmuth (ed.), *Heidelberger Jahrbücher*, 40, Heidelberg, pp. 15–23.

Wiese, Benno von (1982) *Ich erzähle mein Leben*, Frankfurt am Main.

Wiggershaus, Rolf (2004) *Jürgen Habermas*, Reinbek bei Hamburg.

Wild, Michael (2002) *Generation des Unbedingten: Das Führungskorps des Reichssicherheitshauptamtes*, Hamburg.

Wingert, Lutz (1993) *Gemeinsinn und Moral*, Frankfurt am Main.

Wingert, Lutz, and Günther, Klaus (eds) (2001) *Die Öffentlichkeit der Vernunft und die Vernunft der Öffentlichkeit: Festschrift für Jürgen Habermas*, Frankfurt am Main.

Woessner, Martin (2011) *Heidegger in America*, Cambridge.

Wolf, Christa (1997), *Parting from Phantoms: Selected Writings, 1990–1994*, Chicago.

Wolin, Richard (2001) *Heidegger's Children: Hannah Arendt, Karl Löwith, Hans Jonas and Herbert Marcuse*, Oxford.

Wolters, Gereon (1999) 'Der "Führer" und seine Denker: Zur Philosophie des "Dritten Reichs"', *Deutsche Zeitschrift für Philosophie*, 47, pp. 223–51.

Wolters, Gereon (2004) *Vertuschung, Anklage, Rechtfertigung: Impromptus zum Rückblick der deutschen Philosophie auf das 'Dritte Reich'*, Bonn.

Young-Bruehl, Elisabeth (1982) *Hannah Arendt: For Love of the World*, New Haven, CT.

Zens, Maria (2009) *Literatur zu Jürgen Habermas aus fünf Jahrzehnten*, Bonn, www.gesis.org/fileadmin/upload/dienstleistung/fachinformationen/recherche_spezial/RS6-09-Habermas.pdf.

Ziegler, Christian (2008) 'Auswahl-Bibliographie zu Theodor W. Adorno ab dem Jahr 2003', in Kohler, Georg, and Müller-Doohm, Stefan (eds), *Wozu Adorno? Beiträge zur Kritik und zum Fortbestand einer Schlüsseltheorie des 20. Jahrhunderts*, Frankfurt am Main, pp. 307–27.

Zimmermann, Rolf (2005) *Philosophie nach Auschwitz*, Frankfurt am Main.

Zoller, Jörg (i.e., Peter Zollinger) (ed.) ([1969]) *Aktiver Streik: Dokumentation zu einem Jahr Hochschulpolitik am Beispiel der Universität Frankfurt am Main*, Darmstadt.

Zöller, Richard (ed.) (1980) *Aufklärung heute: Bedingungen unserer Freiheit*, Zurich.

Index